Handbook of Quality Assurance for University Teaching

This practical and authoritative handbook provides a comprehensive overview of the issues and approaches to assuring quality in university teaching. Including contributions from major international figures, the book contains a wealth of ideas and practical advice to help universities commit to quality in teaching and offers insights into how the topics raised can be directly applied.

The book initially identifies some of the key issues surrounding the topic, such as the evidence-based identification of teaching quality; the training of university lecturers and faculty; external and internal quality assurance; the tension between professional autonomy and governmental regulation; and the involvement of students in developing quality. It then moves on to present ideas and initiatives to address these problems, tackling the subject through four sections:

- Assuring Quality – questioning what quality assurance means and how it might be practised;
- Identifying Quality – examining what knowledge exists at present and how it might be further researched;
- Developing Quality – investigating the development of staff through teacher training and appraisal;
- Case Studies of Quality Assurance – reviewing six case studies of quality assurance in a range of contrasting subjects including the professional subjects of Medicine, Nursing and Teacher Training, which are also addressed systemically in the first section.

Full of practical advice, *Handbook of Quality Assurance for University Teaching* is an invaluable and unique resource for Faculty, Subject Leaders, University Administrators and Quality Assessors.

Roger Ellis is Professor Emeritus in Psychology at both Ulster University and the University of Chester, UK, and editor of *Quality Assurance for University Teaching* published in 1993.

Elaine Hogard is the Director of Assessment and Program Evaluation and a Professor of Program Evaluation at the Northern Ontario School of Medicine, Canada.

The Society for Research into Higher Education (SRHE) is an independent and financially self-supporting international learned Society. It is concerned to advance understanding of higher education, especially through the insights, perspectives and knowledge offered by systematic research and scholarship.

The Society's primary role is to improve the quality of higher education through facilitating knowledge exchange, discourse and publication of research. SRHE members are worldwide and the Society is an NGO in operational relations with UNESCO.

The Society has a wide set of aims and objectives. Amongst its many activities the Society:

• is a specialist publisher of higher education research, journals and books, amongst them Studies in Higher Education, Higher Education Quarterly, Research into Higher Education Abstracts and a long running monograph book series.

The Society also publishes a number of in-house guides and produces a specialist series "Issues in Postgraduate Education".

• funds and supports a large number of special interest networks for researchers and practitioners working in higher education from every discipline. These networks are open to all and offer a range of topical seminars, workshops and other events throughout the year ensuring the Society is in touch with all current research knowledge.

• runs the largest annual UK-based higher education research conference and parallel conference for postgraduate and newer researchers. This is attended by researchers from over 35 countries and showcases current research across every aspect of higher education.

SRHE

Society for Research into Higher Education
Advancing knowledge Informing policy Enhancing practice

73 Collier Street
London N1 9BE
United Kingdom

T   +44 (0)20 7427 2350
F   +44 (0)20 7278 1135
E   srheoffice@srhe.ac.uk

www.srhe.ac.uk

Director: Helen Perkins
Registered Charity No. 313850
Company No. 00868820
Limited by Guarantee
Registered office as above

Handbook of Quality Assurance for University Teaching

**Edited by Roger Ellis
and Elaine Hogard**

Routledge
Taylor & Francis Group

LONDON AND NEW YORK

First published 2019
by Routledge
2 Park Square, Milton Park, Abingdon, Oxon OX14 4RN

and by Routledge
711 Third Avenue, New York, NY 10017

Routledge is an imprint of the Taylor & Francis Group, an informa business

British Library Cataloguing-in-Publication Data
A catalogue record for this book is available from the British Library

Library of Congress Cataloging-in-Publication Data
A catalog record for this book has been requested

ISBN: 978-1-138-73378-7 (hbk)
ISBN: 978-1-138-73380-0 (pbk)
ISBN: 978-1-315-18751-8 (ebk)

Typeset in Galliard
by Apex CoVantage, LLC

Contents

Contributors

Ronald A. Berk is Professor Emeritus, Biostatistics and Measurement, and former Assistant Dean for Teaching at the Johns Hopkins University and a Fellow of the Oxford Society of Scholars. He retired 11.531 years ago to pursue speaking and writing full time. He served 30 years of a life term at Johns Hopkins, where he mentored numerous faculty and hundreds of students. Ron has presented 400+ keynotes in 42 states and 15 countries. He destroyed scores of trees and shrubbery by publishing 14 books (2 on faculty evaluation), 170 journal articles, and 300 blogs. These products reflect his life-long commitment to mediocrity and his professional motto: 'Go for the Bronze!' (For details, see www.ronberk.com or www.iinkedin.com/in/ronberk).

George Brown is a retired professor from the University of Nottingham. In his early career, he developed video-training for student teachers and academics at the University of Ulster and in the 1970s he established Staff Development at the University of Nottingham. As National Co-ordinator of Academic Staff Development for the CVCP in the 1980s he contributed to Staff Development in the UK. He was awarded an honorary doctorate in Odontology for his contributions to Dental Education in Europe. He has published several articles and texts on Higher and Medical Education.

Roni Brown is Deputy Vice-Chancellor, Academic Development and Professor of Visual an Educational Cultures at the University for the Creative Arts. Roni holds a PhD in the History of Architecture and Design from De Montfort University and is published across the disciplines of Design History and Material Culture Studies. Roni's research focuses on user-led content in art and design practice and everyday creativity, extending the field of design history to consider the role of the user in design development and the social value of participatory creative experience. More recently Roni's work focuses on the pedagogical environment of teaching and learning and quality assurance in higher education Art and Design. Roni was an executive member of the Group for Learning in Art and Design (GLAD) 2008–2013, taking forward debates nationally about the student experience in higher education Art and Design. She is Deputy Chair of Trustees for Artswork, the national youth arts agency and Bridge Organisation for Arts Council England South East and Trustee of the Open College of the Arts. Roni is a Principal Fellow of the Higher Education Academy and Fellow of the Royal Society for the Arts.

Karin Crawford is the inaugural Head of the Higher Education Research Institute at the University of Lincoln. Karin has extensive experience, as a teacher, researcher and manager in higher education and has been developing and implementing approaches to student–staff partnerships in higher education for several years. Her interests include exploring practices that support student skill development and engagement both within and beyond the classroom; this has included being active in the development and implementation of 'Student as Producer' at Lincoln and leading on a number of funded research projects exploring different aspects of student learning.

Damian Day is Head of Education at the General Pharmaceutical Council, the regulator for pharmacy in Great Britain. He is responsible for national regulatory education policy development in pharmacy, the quality assurance of pharmacy education and for the pharmacist national examination, the Registration Assessment. He has worked for the Quality Assurance Agency in a number of roles, has worked for the General Medical Council as an accreditor, and in a number of QA roles in Saudi Arabia, Lithuania and elsewhere. A graduate of the University of Durham and Royal College of Music, he is a musicologist by background and worked as an academic for 15 years before moving in to regulation.

Sarah Edmunds is Senior Lecturer in Exercise Psychology in the Department of Sport and Exercise Sciences at the University of Chichester. After completing her PhD at Liverpool John Moores University she worked as a Lecturer in the Department of Sport and Exercise Science at St Mary's University College, and then as a Research Fellow in the Department of Psychology at the University of Westminster, before joining the University of Chichester in 2013. Her research interests are in exercise motivation and behaviour change, and the pedagogy of teaching and learning.

Roger Ellis is Professor Emeritus in Psychology at both the Ulster University and the University of Chester. He edited *Quality Assurance for University Teaching* in 1993 of which this book is the successor. He has taught in five universities and enjoyed a synergy between his teaching and research in promoting student learning and research capability. He has published 11 books and nearly 200 refereed journal articles. His first book was *A Guide to Social Skill Training* and he has maintained an interest in the interpersonal skills of teaching despite falling short of the ideal himself. He is Director of the Social and Health Evaluation Unit which has completed a number of programme evaluations in higher education as well as social and health care. His main current research interests include identity in teaching and learning; curriculum design and learning; and personal development and learning disability.

Lewis Elton is Emeritus Professor of Higher Education, University of Surrey where he had been Professor of Physics (1964–71), Professor of Science Education (1971–85) and Professor of Higher Education (1985–88). He is a higher education adviser to government. His main research interests are in the improvement of teaching and learning and in institutional change in higher education.

Marta B. Erdos is Associate Professor in Mental Health and Community Social Work at the Department of Social and Community Studies, Faculty of Humanities, University of Pécs. Her main area of research interest is programme evaluation. In 2016 she was elected Vice Dean for Education. In 2017 she prepared the Faculty's self-study report for accreditation. She is a member of the Quality Development Advisory Committee of the Faculty. She is leader and founder of the Social Innovation Research Centre, which was established in Hungary in 2008, and then joined Social and Health Evaluation Unit International in 2013.

Cathy Finlay has been a university tutor in the School of Arts, English and Languages at Queen's University Belfast for over 25 years. Her academic background is within

Linguistics, in particular Sociolinguistics and Child Language Acquisition. Although primarily involved with teaching at university level she also at present manages a programme for the introduction of Modern Foreign Languages into the primary-level classroom. She has also contributed to many research projects in Linguistics in previous years.

Liz Fleet has a successful record of teaching and leadership within schools and universities. In 2016, as Deputy Dean at the University of Chester, Liz led the Initial Teacher Education (ITE) Partnership in preparation for and through its OfSTED inspection culminating in 'outstanding' grade. Her current role involves wider university initiatives: QA and curriculum development at University Centre Shrewsbury; and leading developments of ITE Programmes for North Wales in partnership with Bangor University and 'GwE', the Regional Schools' Office. Liz's doctoral studies involved an exploration of teacher educator identity. She is committed to enhancing education and the well-being of children and teachers.

Carol Hall is a nurse and academic whose role includes enabling high-quality international education for nursing and health-care professions. Carol has extensive experience in the design, delivery and quality assurance of nursing education within the UK and more widely, through roles in curriculum development and validation and accreditation. As Education Forum Chair for the UK Royal College of Nursing (2006–15) and Vice President of the Federation of European Nurse Educators (2012–date), Carol has supported influential work developing new nurse education competencies within the European Directive on Mutual Recognition of Professional Qualifications. Carol is Professor of Nursing and currently Director of Undergraduate Education within the School of Health Sciences at the University of Nottingham. She was awarded PFHEA by the Higher Education Academy in November 2014.

Diane Hazlett is Professor of Interprofessional Pedagogy and Practice at Ulster University and currently Director of the Centre for Higher Education Research and Practice. She has previously held leadership roles in health care, as a Speech and Language Therapist and health service manager. At Ulster, as Head of the School of Communication, she taught, researched and managed a range of health, communication and education programmes. She currently supports university academic and learning enhancement for student engagement, professional development and strategic organisational and change initiatives. As a Senior Fellow of the Higher Education Academy, she encourages colleagues to challenge assumptions, collaborate to pursue enhanced practice, share innovations and engage in the pursuit of excellence in higher education learning and teaching.

Lindsay Heywood is an honorary Principal Fellow and Associate Professor at the Melbourne Centre for the Study of Higher Education at the University of Melbourne and director of a specialised educational consultancy service. He is the former Head of the Higher Education Standards Panel Executive where he provided leadership and support to the Panel in revising the Australian Higher Education Standards Framework. He has worked in various academic and executive roles across several faculties in four major Australian universities and as CEO or senior executive in various agencies and professional bodies with standard-setting, quality-assurance and programme accreditation roles. He has a wealth of experience in designing, implementing and monitoring standards and quality systems within and beyond higher education, including as an auditor director with the Australian Universities Quality Agency (AUQA) and the Tertiary Education Quality and Standards Agency (TEQSA). Lindsay has a particular interest in the vocationally orientated aspects of professional education and has worked with many professional bodies in setting professional standards in Australia and overseas. He received an Excellence in Teaching Award from the University of Sydney for outstanding personal contributions to teaching and learning and he is a Fellow of the Australian Institute of Company Directors.

Elaine Hogard is Director of Assessment and Program Evaluation at the Northern Ontario School of Medicine and Professor of Program Evaluation. She has taught in universities in Canada, the USA, the UK and Ireland at all educational levels from undergraduate diploma to PhD supervision. She has published widely in Program Evaluation including theoretical and methodological articles and reports of completed Program Evaluations of education, social and health care. She has worked primarily in professional faculties, where Program Evaluation is key in accreditation processes and she has maintained a longstanding commitment to engaged and effective teaching in higher education. Throughout her career she has particularly enjoyed teaching research methods in applied fields where student learning is quickly apparent via their respective research projects and the topics themselves are highly relevant and beneficial.

Reece Horsley is Student Engagement Co-ordinator at the University of Bath, focusing on utilising student evaluation of their learning and teaching experience to support the development of the student experience. Previously, Reece has coordinated the University of Lincoln's portfolio of academic opportunities, including students recruiting new members of staff, students as members of validation and periodic review panels, as well as Students Consulting on Teaching (SCoTs). Reece has been a Student Reviewer for the Quality Assurance Agency (QAA), carrying out reviews using the Higher Education Review method. During his postgraduate studies, Reece worked as a student researcher on the HEA funded 'Pedagogies of Partnership: What works?' project, aiming to explore the impact of staff–student partnerships across a range of disciplines.

Camille B. Kandiko Howson is Senior Lecturer in Higher Education and Academic Head of Student Engagement at King's College London. She provides leadership in terms of engaging students and staff with areas of educational development policy and student engagement with educational enhancement. In a cross-institutional capacity she works on student engagement and experience enhancement initiatives at KCL, including coordinating student surveys, voice and feedback processes. Her research focuses on international and comparative higher education, with areas of interest in curriculum change, student engagement and learning gain.

Dan Hunt serves as the Founding Associate Dean for Curriculum Innovation at the New York University Long Island School of Medicine. Prior to that he served nine years as Co-Secretary for the Liaison Committee on Medical Education, which is the accreditation agency for medical-degree-granting schools in the United States and Canada. He received his medical degree from Weill Cornell School of Medicine and did his residency in psychiatry at the Hospital of the University of Pennsylvania and while there, earned a master's degree in business administration from the Wharton School of Business.

John A. Hunter is Associate Professor at the University of Otago. His research is concerned with the theoretical and practical implications of group-level behaviour. His research on these issues have focused on intergroup discrimination (e.g. anti-fat attitudes, sectarianism, nationalism and sexism), well-being related outcomes (e.g. alcohol consumption, resilience, self-efficacy), motivation (e.g. control, self-esteem, belonging), socialisation and contact experiences.

Georgina Kirk is a coach and consultant in effective communication, and a motivational speaker, based in Manchester, UK. Originally from London, she discovered the North in 1986, as a BA (Hons) student of Italian and Russian at the University of Manchester. After a few years teaching and training adults in London and Milan, she returned to Manchester and took an MSc in Personnel Management and Industrial Relations at what was then UMIST. Deciding industry was not for her, Georgie opened a language school, which she ran for ten years, becoming increasingly fascinated by the psychology of teaching and learning, and of communication generally. Over four years (part time), she trained as a psychotherapist in Transactional Analysis and now brings practical and psychological techniques together to help her clients to find their voices and put themselves across with clarity and impact.

Joel H. Lanphear's career spans 45 years as a medical educator and administrator in medical schools in the US, Canada and abroad. In addition to developing four new medical schools he was responsible for leading the successful accreditation process in US and Canadian schools. He has served in a broad range of administrative roles in medical schools ranging from Acting Dean, Vice President, Provost, Associate Dean for Medical Education, Senior Associate Campus Dean, and Executive Associate Dean. Dr. Lanphear retired from the Northern Ontario School of Medicine as Professor of Medical Education and was named the school's first Emeritus Professor in 2013. He continues to publish and pursues an active role in medical education activities involving social accountability, curriculum development and quality assurance.

Jerry M. Lewis is an Emeritus Professor of Sociology. He joined the Kent State University Sociology faculty in 1966 receiving the emeritus status in 1996. He continued to teach for several years after becoming an emeritus professor. Lewis received his PhD from the University of Illinois (Urbana). His teaching focused on courses in Collective Behaviour, Sociology of Religion and Introductory Sociology. He received several teaching awards including the Kent State University Alumni Association's Distinguished Teaching Award 1983.

Jessica Lichtenstein is Head of Quality Assurance for Education at the General Medical Council, an organisation that sets and promotes standards for medical education and practice across the United Kingdom. Jessica oversees a quality assurance programme that ensures medical schools and postgraduate medical training programmes meet GMC standards. Having previously worked at the Postgraduate Medical Education and Training Board in the UK, the Joint Committee on Surgical Training at the Royal College of Surgeons, and the Royal College of Nursing, she has 13 years of experience in healthcare education from a regulatory and a professional perspective. Jessica is originally from New York, and graduated with a BA in Psychology and English from Tufts University. She moved to London in 2002 to pursue an MSc in Social Anthropology at the London School of Economics.

Helena Lim is an independent researcher and consultant with over 20 years of experience in UK higher education. Currently Director of HL4 Education Insights and Consultancy Ltd, she has held senior roles at the Higher Education Academy and Southampton Solent University. She previously lectured at the University of Bath and the Open University.

As the founder of the UK and Ireland Higher Education Institutional Research Network (HEIR), she has worked tirelessly to develop this into an internationally respected network. Dr Lim is a Principal Fellow of the HEA as recognition for her contribution to leading innovation in learning and teaching both in the UK and internationally.

Anthony McClaran has been Chief Executive Officer of Australia's Tertiary Education Quality and Standards Agency (TEQSA) since 12 October 2015. Before joining TEQSA, Anthony was Chief Executive of the UK's Quality Assurance Agency (QAA) for six years and prior to that Chief Executive of the UK's national agency for higher education admissions, the Universities and Colleges Admissions Service (UCAS). Anthony is a member of the Board of the International Network for Quality Assurance Agencies in Higher Education (INQAAHE) and the Advisory Council of the US Council for HE Accreditation (CHEA) International Advisory Group. He was Chair of Council and Pro-Chancellor of the University of Gloucestershire from 2007 to 2009.

Saranne Magennis is Director of the Higher Education Policy Unit in Maynooth University, Ireland. She joined Maynooth University from Queen's University Belfast in 1997and worked as Director of Quality, with responsibility for the development of quality assurance, staff and educational development and institutional research, until taking up her current role in 2005. She is a founder member of the All Ireland Society for Higher Education (AISHE) and has edited its online open source journal, *All Ireland Journal for Teaching and Learning in Higher Education (AISHE J)* since 2012. Current areas of interest include supporting new academic writers and researching fully inclusive higher education for people with intellectual disabilities.

Alam Mahbubul is Quality and Enhancement Advisor at London South Bank University and Student Reviewer for the Quality Assurance Agency and HEFCE Teaching Excellence Framework Assessor. He was previously Vice President Student Experience of the London South Bank University Students' Union from 2012–14 and subsequently was Programme Lead for the Students' Union's Student Voice and Engagement initiatives.

Craig Mahoney is Principal and Vice-Chancellor at the University of the West of Scotland (UWS). Mahoney is a passionate believer in the power of higher education to transform lives. Before joining UWS he was CEO of the Higher Education Academy and previously Deputy Vice-Chancellor at Northumbria University. During a distinguished career in academia and sport, he has published widely in the areas of children's fitness, health, sport, exercise, performance and education. A dynamic public advocate of higher education, Professor Mahoney has a keen interest in differentiated student-centred learning, teaching excellence, internationalisation and research-informed teaching. He is an ardent supporter of the use of e-learning technology to support teaching and open educational resources.

Marie C. Matte is the Associate Dean, Compliance, Assessment and Evaluation at Central Michigan University College of Medicine (CMED). Prior to arriving at CMED, she held the position of Associate Dean, Undergraduate Medical Education at Dalhousie University, Interim Accreditation Coordinator, Dalhousie University, Director, Faculty Development at Dalhousie University and Director, Undergraduate Medical Education, Northern Ontario School of Medicine. She has more than 25 years of experience in higher education as an academic administrator. She has extensive and comprehensive experience in health science programme development, curriculum development, student assessment, programme evaluation and programme delivery/implementation.

Internationally, she has been responsible for the design, development, and operationalisation of the Department of Continuing Education at Nachimuthu Polytechnic, Polachi, Tamil Nadu, India. For over 20 years, Dr. Matte has served as an accreditation survey team member, and survey team chair for the Canadian Medical Association (CMA). She is also a member of the Liaison Committee on Medical Education (LCME) accreditation survey team group, where she holds the position identified as educator.

Lynnette Matthews (SFSEDA, PFHEA) is an academic developer at the University of Leicester. She developed the University's Professional Educational Excellence Recognition Scheme (PEERS) and was responsible for it securing Higher Education Academy accreditation. Lynnette has a portfolio of strategic leadership, design and delivery of initial and continuing professional development programmes and awards within the University and nationally. Since 2008, she has been an active member of the Staff and Educational Development Association (SEDA) including chairing the Professional Development Framework (PDF) Committee. She was awarded a Distinguished Teaching Fellowship by the University for her outstanding contribution to the promotion of an effective learning experience for students, and in the support of the development of teaching excellence across the institution.

David Morris is Vice Chancellor's Policy Officer at the University of Greenwich. Prior to that he was Deputy Editor of Wonkhe, the higher education blog and think tank, and before that he worked in the policy team at the National Union of Students. Whilst at NUS he co-authored the NUS *Comprehensive Guide to Learning and Teaching*, which outlined the Union's perspectives on learning and teaching in higher education. At Wonkhe he has written extensively on all areas of higher education policy, including the Higher Education and Research Act, the Teaching Excellence Framework, widening access, university finances and graduate outcomes data. David holds a BA and an MA in History from the University of Durham.

Emily Parkin is the Senior Student Engagement Coordinator at the University of Lincoln. She has worked with students in various roles since being elected as a Sabbatical Officer after graduating from the University of Sunderland in 2011. Emily's role focuses predominantly on changing the perception of how students can contribute to the development and enhancement of learning and teaching – regarding students as key partners in any enhancement activity. This work is specifically targeted at staff members across all areas of the University and empowers students to take leading roles in changing the conversation. Emily is an active member of the RAISE Network and contributes to various national events including QAA and TSEP conferences.

Ruth Pilkington (NTF, SFSEDA, PFHEA) is a freelance educational consultant and currently employed by Liverpool Hope University as Professorial Fellow in Learning and Teaching. Formerly employed by the Higher Education Academy, UK, she contributes to a number of UK institutions' CPD frameworks as reviewer and assessor, and especially with respect to her work on dialogue in the context of fellowship assessment. These roles reflect her profile within academic development nationally in the UK. She has held a number of committee roles in SEDA, and continues to work actively as a member of SEDA PDF Committee. She received National Teaching Fellowship for her work in using dialogic assessment for professional recognition in HE, and supporting lecturers' professional learning from entry through to professional doctoral level. Her publications address professional learning, CPD, dialogic assessment and employability.

Amanda Platt is a Research Associate in Ulster University's Centre for HE Research & Practice (CHERP) and has been involved in the establishment, organisation and promotion of a range of L&T opportunities for staff. She is a fellow of the Higher Education Academy and her main research interests are in the areas of staff engagement and culture in relation to the enhancement of learning and teaching.

Michael Russ has over 40 years' experience of teaching, examining and managing music programmes in higher education. He taught at Ulster University where he became Head of the School of Media and Performing Arts and at the University of Huddersfield where he was Head of the Department of Music and Drama and subsequently Dean of Music, Humanities and Media. He is an Emeritus Professor at Huddersfield. Russ's PhD examined methods of analysing early-twentieth-century post-tonal music and a number of his publications continue that work. He has also published on the Russian composer Mussorgsky including a book on that composer's *Pictures at an Exhibition*. His recent work includes a substantial study of the relationship between Bartók's Sonata for Two Pianos and Percussion and Beethoven's *Waldstein* Sonata, and co-editing three collections of essays on the Catalan composer Roberto Gerhard. He has also published on teaching and learning in higher education. Russ is a past winner of the Westrup Prize for musicology and is a HEA National Teaching Fellow.

Karl Stringer was Lecturer in the School of Computing and Information Engineering, University of Ulster, Coleraine until 2015. He holds a BSc in Biology from the University of Ulster, an MSc in Computer Science from the Queen's University Belfast and a PhD in Physics from the University of Ulster. His research areas are in computing physics and economics, with his recent public-sector work being published in *Education Economics*, *IMA Journal of Management Mathematics* and the *Irish Accounting Review*. He is a Fellow of the Centre for Higher Education Practice, University of Ulster.

Maurice Stringer is Professor of Psychology and Director of the Psychology Research Institute at Ulster University. Following doctoral study at the New University of Ulster, he joined the Northern Ireland Civil Service in 1978 as a Lecturer in Communications. He moved to the Ulster Polytechnic as a Lecturer and Senior Lecturer before being awarded a chair in Psychology at Ulster in 2000. His main research areas are intergroup conflict, health psychology and student feedback. He was Chair of the British Psychological Society's Representative Council, Chair of the Northern Ireland Branch of the Society and served on the Society's Parliamentary and Standing Conference Committees.

Gabor Szollosi is Associate Professor in Social Policy and Social Law. He is Coordinator of Social Policy Master's Programme at the Department of Social and Community Studies, Faculty of Humanities, University of Pécs; and Chair of the Study Programme Development Committee at the Faculty. In 2007 he was honoured by a high level order of the Hungarian Republic.

Marian Traynor has ten years' experience as a Senior Lecturer in the School of Nursing and Midwifery, Queen's University Belfast. She is currently Director of Education in the School and has held this leadership position for the past four years. The role involves not only leading and managing the academic programmes in the School but also working very closely with the professional regulator for nursing (Nursing and Midwifery Council) as well as with the Department of Health. Dr Traynor has experience related to leading on new initiatives and new educational programmes. For example she has recently led on a research initiative to change how applicants to nursing and midwifery are selected and this resulted in the School introducing Multiple Mini Interviews to select candidates. She has teaching and research interest in simulation and interprofessional education (IPE) and was responsible for initiating both uniprofessional and IPE simulation within the School of Nursing and Midwifery at QUB in 2005. Since then IPE simulation has been embedded in both the nursing and medical curricula within the Faculty of Medicine, Health and Life Sciences at Queen's University Belfast. Her research areas include simulation, clinical teaching and assessment, interprofessional education, OSCE, and values-based recruitment.

Eva Vojtek is Assistant Lecturer in Social Policy and Social Services. She is a PhD student in the Interdisciplinary Doctoral School at the University of Pécs. She is responsible for administrative issues of study programmes at the Department of Social and Community Studies, Faculty of Humanities, University of Pécs, Hungary. She has been involved in a number of curriculum development projects and in the internal evaluation of study programmes.

Theanne Walters is Deputy Chief Executive Officer of the Australian Medical Council. She has 25 years' experience in accreditation of medical programmes, and national and international collaborations on standards setting and accreditation. Theanne contributes to international evaluations of medical programmes and accreditation systems via the World Federation for Medical Education and the Western Pacific Association for Medical Education. She is a senior adviser for the World Federation for Medical Education. In Australia, Theanne is deputy chair of the Health Professions Accreditation Collaborative Forum, a coalition of the independent accreditation councils for the regulated health professions.

Shân Wareing is Pro Vice-Chancellor for Education and Student Experience at London South Bank University (LSBU) and a Professor of Teaching in Higher Education. Her previous roles include PVC Learning and Teaching at Buckinghamshire New University, Dean of Learning and Teaching at University of the Arts London, Lecturer in English Language and Linguistics at Roehampton University and Visiting Professor in Linguistics at Michigan State University, USA. She is a past Co-Chair of the Staff and Educational Development Association (SEDA), was a member of the 2014 English Subject Benchmark Review Group, and is a Senior Fellow of SEDA, a Fellow of the Leadership Foundation, a Principal Fellow of the Higher Education Academy, and a National Teaching Fellow.

Jeremy Warren is a chartered psychologist, currently employed as Strategic Research Officer within the Strategic Economic Development Directorate of the University of Chester, UK. He has many years of experience as a public sector performance manager, having held roles within the police service, youth justice and higher education. In these roles he has managed a number of projects that have led to considerable culture change within the relevant organisations. Academically, he has an interest in the formation of personal identity, specifically that aspect of self that pertains to the workplace, and how that sense of professional identity can influence the decisions that we make.

Saranne Weller is Director of Research Informed Teaching in the Centre for Research Informed Teaching at London South Bank University. She has previously been Associate Dean Learning, Teaching and Enhancement at the University of the Arts London and

Senior Lecturer in Higher Education and Assistant Director (Accredited Programmes) of King's Learning Institute at King's College London. She is the author of *Academic Practice: Developing as a Teacher in Higher Education* (Sage, 2015).

Dorothy Whittington has some 30 years' experience of teaching in higher education and is Emeritus Professor of Health Psychology at the University of Ulster. She has taught teachers, psychologists, nurses, doctors, social workers, and many other health professionals and managers. She has led both a large multi-professional school of health sciences, and a health-care research centre. Her research and publication focuses on communication, social skill, and health-care quality, governance and management. She has well over a hundred publications including seven books. Professor Whittington was involved with the Higher Education Academy from 1999. She was Chair of the Advisory Board for Health Sciences 2002–11 and a trustee and member of the full HEA Board 2007–11. For the last four years of her full-time career, Professor Whittington took up a Board-level post as Director of Education and Research in a large NHS Acute Trust in England. Since her retirement she has served for nine years as a non-executive director of the Northern Health and Social Care Trust in Northern Ireland and is currently a non-executive director of the Business Services Organisation, which is an arm's-length body associated with the N. Ireland Department of Health. She has been a member of the General Pharmaceutical Council's education accreditation panel since 2011.

Chris Wilkins is Professor of Education, and has been an Initial Teacher Education tutor at the University of Leicester for the past 20 years, including five years as a programme leader and eight years as Director of Teacher Education. His experience of four Ofsted inspections during this time has contributed to a research interest in the accountability culture of teacher education and in particular the ways in which high-stakes accountability systems impact both on professional development cultures in schools and universities and in the nature of the educational experience they provide. Chris also has significant international experience of supporting teacher education reform, particularly in Eastern Europe and the Middle East and North Africa region.

Ronnie Wilson was awarded his PhD at Sheffield University before his appointment to the University of Ulster, where he was Academic Coordinator for Teaching and Learning in the School of Psychology, then Head of the School 2004–15. He has taught research methods, behavioural statistics, abnormal psychology and comparative psychology for several years. His research interests are in behaviour genetics, the evolution of behaviour and developmental psychology. He is Emeritus Professor of Psychology at the Ulster University.

Roger Woodward started his academic career as Research Officer in Mental Health at Queen's University Belfast, before becoming Lecturer in Psychology at Ulster Polytechnic. When the University of Ulster was founded in 1984, he became its Director of Institutional Research, the first such post in Europe. An active participant in the European Association for Institutional Research, he also helped establish the British and Irish Association for Institutional Research, for which he also served as Chairperson. Latterly, he became Senior Lecturer in Psychology in the University of Ulster, and was President of the Psychological Society of Ireland. He is now retired.

Part I

Assuring Quality

1 Quality Assurance for University Teaching

Issues and Approaches

Roger Ellis

I wrote a chapter of this kind as an introduction to *Quality Assurance for University Teaching* in 1993. On the surface, the landscape has changed considerably since 1993. On the other hand, many of the issues I identified then are still issues and change, or better still development, is not that apparent.

Definitions can make tedious beginnings, but in this case they are still necessary. Quality, quality assurance, and, indeed, teaching itself are still open to a range of interpretations. So, one aim of this chapter will be to look at different ways in which the terms have been used and their implications.

A second aim is to identify some of the key issues in quality assurance for university teaching. These include problems in assuring quality for teaching in the light of two paradoxes. These paradoxes concern scientific knowledge of teaching and learning and its use to evidence practice, and the professional qualification of teachers as teachers. The knowledge paradox is that in universities dedicated to knowledge there is little attention to knowledge about teaching and learning. The qualification paradox is that in universities where much of their work is concerned with professional qualifications, only a minority of lecturers have a professional qualification in teaching. Other issues include outcome measures for teaching and the accreditation of programmes.

A third aim is to make some comparisons between 1993 when *Quality Assurance for University Teaching* was published and the situation in 2018. This will thus be a 25-year progress report. There are four topics on which I want to focus particularly to identify change and perhaps improvement. The first is quality assurance systems, both in universities and applying to universities. The second is the evidence-based identification of quality in teaching and learning and its use to underpin teaching. The third is teacher training for university lecturers. The fourth is the involvement of students in identifying and developing quality.

To conclude the chapter, I will outline the issues and approaches that will be covered in the rest of the chapters in the book and which should, of course, relate to the issues I have raised.

Definitions

In essence quality assurance is about ensuring that standards are specified and met consistently for a product or service. The term is derived partly from manufacturing and service industry, partly from health care. Its adoption for education has been rapid and pervasive. But how appropriate and useful is it for university teaching?

Quality itself is a somewhat ambiguous term since it has connotations of both *standards* and *excellence*. Thus, to talk of 'the quality of teaching' might refer to high or low standards whereas reference to 'quality teaching' implies excellence. The association of quality assurance with excellence may be misleading. It may also be convenient when it masks the assurance of minimum standards only with the appearance of excellence.

Standards of some kind are essential for quality assurance. But standards, like beauty, are usually in the eyes or perceptions of observers. Who are the observers who would identify quality for university teaching? An important idea is that the consumers of a product or service should be the ultimate arbiters of quality. From this stems the idea that quality is that which satisfies a consumer or customer. In its simplest form quality in university teaching would be that which satisfies the primary customer, the student. This notion is expressed more formally by the British Standards Institute: 'Quality is the totality of features and characteristics of a product or service that bear on its ability to satisfy stated or implied needs.' Thus, the needs of students might be stated by them or might be implied on their behalf by the teacher.

Customers or consumers are not always straightforward to identify. Or more usually there are too many of them. For example, who are the consumers of university teaching? In an obvious sense students consume or experience teaching but others who have to be satisfied include colleagues, heads of department, funding bodies, employers, government and society as a whole. All of these may in some sense be identified as customers for the teaching of a university. Teaching is also self-evidently an important element in the identity of the teacher whether it is embraced enthusiastically or not. The producers themselves must be satisfied, too.

A different angle is to conceive quality as fitness for purpose. Hence the quality of a particular machine would be determined by the extent to which it met its stated purpose. Theoretically this kind of quality would exist even if many observers and indeed customers were, at least initially, unable to appreciate it. It is also a more useful definition for situations where there are no obvious customers or where there are multiple customers. Thus, the quality of teaching would be determined by its fitness to achieve stated purposes, presumably with regard to learning and capability.

Learning may be considered in the short term, assessed within the programme, in the medium term as it impacts on employment, and in the long term as it lays the foundations for lifelong learning. University learned may also be positioned on a continuum from instrumental, fulfilling an immediate applied purpose, to liberal, encouraging criticism and dissent. This continuum reflects an abiding tension in university education.

Other definitions include 'conformance to requirement' (Crosby 1984) and 'the predictable degree of uniformity and dependability, at low cost and suited to the market' (Deming 1982). Key concepts here include conformity to standards, and standards that are appropriate for a purpose and satisfy a market. Deming also emphasizes the importance of cost-effectiveness, that is satisfying the market at low or the lowest possible cost.

Of these definitions, the notion of fitness for purpose is perhaps the most straightforward, but soon complicated by the complexity and multiplicity of purposes. However, the idea of a customer or customers who must be satisfied is too important to lose. So, a working definition of quality might be: *Quality refers to the standards that must be met to achieve specified purposes to the satisfaction of customers.*

The purpose of teaching is, of course, learning. So, the quality of teaching is its fitness for the purpose of promoting learning. Unfortunately, there are no laws and precious few theories linking teaching and learning. So, standards would be for teaching, whose effect on learning is largely conjectural. Or quality may be judged by outcomes or performance indicators, whose cause in teaching is unclear.

If quality refers to standards, what is meant by assurance? First, it is important to realize that 'assurance' is transitive: the assuring is done by someone who wishes to assure someone else. Thus, a box of matches carrying the legend 'Quality Assured' is giving a message from the manufacturer to me the customer. It is intended to reassure me that the standards I expect from a match will be met consistently by each match in the box. Thus, *quality assurance* is a process whereby a manufacturer or producer guarantees to a customer or client that the goods or service concerned will meet standards consistently. Who is trying to reassure whom for university teaching? One interpretation is that the university is trying to reassure itself that its teaching is up to standard. Another is that universities, being publicly funded, are trying to reassure society, or at least its representatives, that they are delivering the service they are paid to deliver. At a more basic commercial level universities are trying to assure their customers, whether students, employers or grant-awarding bodies, that their service is up to scratch and worth the money.

While this establishment of confidence is the essence of quality assurance, the term has come to refer to the entire process whereby standards are maintained. It thus subsumes quality control and quality management, both of which will now be considered.

Quality control is the process whereby the product or service, or any part of the process associated with its production or delivery, is checked against a predetermined standard and rejected or recycled if below standard. This is a well-known feature at the end of a production line but it is equally important at all stages from the initial acceptance of raw materials. It is more difficult to apply to a service since once a service has been delivered it cannot be retrieved and recycled. But at least a service can be identified as deficient and steps taken to ensure a better performance next time. This is a more complicated notion of quality control than mere rejection of the substandard and begins to shade into the use of feedback as part of quality management.

The total process whereby a particular organization is managed to achieve and hence be able to assure quality is *quality management*, or, less ambiguously, *the management of quality*. Thus, in order to assure quality a manufacturer will have to manage production to achieve quality consistently. This will involve, at key stages, *quality control*. The management process will be complex and will involve, *inter alia*, specifying standards and procedures; documenting these standards and procedures; regularly checking reality against these standards and remedying any shortfalls; identifying responsibilities; investing in staff training and development and a number of other steps. Central to the whole process will be the identification of a customer's needs and the provision of a product or service to satisfy them. Feedback from customers, whether in detail or, more broadly, through purchase, complaint or rejection, will be crucial. If this management of quality is to be effective it can be argued that all aspects of the organization must be covered and all staff involved: a chain is no stronger than its weakest link. It is this, perhaps self-evident, proposition that has led to the expression *Total Quality Management* (TQM), totality referring to the involvement of all in production and management (not as is sometimes thought the achievement of ultimate and total perfection).

It is doubtful if any university could claim to have a wholly explicit let alone total management system dedicated to ensuring quality in its teaching. Even if there were agreement about standards for teaching and all teachers were involved, the system would also have to cover all support services since each could be demonstrated to have some effect on teaching and learning, however indirectly.

If a firm claims to have a system for the management of quality, *quality management*, then it can be audited to see whether the system does in fact exist and operate as claimed. Thus, there can be a *quality audit*. This is the activity initially carried out by the HEQC Division of Quality Audit (DQA) now by the Quality Assurance Agency. The Agency claims to be auditing the quality assurance mechanisms of universities for teaching. Strictly speaking, if the above definitions are followed, the QAA is auditing the quality management procedures of universities, these being a necessary condition for quality to be assured. These management procedures would be required to specify standards in teaching so that the university can assure customers or anyone else who wants to know that the quality represented in the standards is being achieved.

If the organization aims not only to meet standards but exceed them and perhaps establish new standards, this brings in the idea of *quality improvement* or *quality enhancement*. If such improvement is conceived as a characteristic of an organization built into its processes of monitoring, feedback and change this might be described as *continuous quality improvement (CQI)*.

Audit, then, is checking that someone is doing what he says he is doing. It would require a further step to say whether the organization might be aiming to do the right thing in the first place. Such an evaluation moves into the area of *quality assessment*, which is judging the standards reached by an organization against external criteria. Thus, an external examiner in the present system audits a programme's own assessment procedures to check whether the examining system is operating as planned, but also assesses quality in the sense that the standards reached by the students on the course are compared with those obtaining generally in the higher education system.

We now have a number of terms involving the word quality:

- quality assurance;
- quality management;
- total quality management;
- quality control;
- quality audit;
- quality assessment;
- continuous quality improvement.

The quality of teaching is the standards it must meet. Quality assurance is the process whereby customers, producers or any other interested parties are satisfied that standards will be consistently met. To provide such assurance a system of quality management is necessary. Part of this system will be quality control, whereby conformity with standards is checked and steps are taken if conformity is not achieved. The quality management system may be checked to see if it actually exists and works; this is a quality audit. The products or services may be checked externally to see if standards are being met; this is quality assessment. Finally, there might be a commitment to improvement and development; this entails quality improvement or enhancement.

Issues

These definitions are derived from the literature on quality assurance in manufacturing and service industries, including health. The terms are still relatively new to education generally and higher education in particular. However, while quality assurance has been embraced with almost immoderate enthusiasm by government; this enthusiasm has not always been matched by precision of use or, one suspects, any great understanding of its use elsewhere. For example, both the seminal early White Paper (1991) and the early pronouncements of the then Division of Quality Audit used quality assurance and quality control as if they were interchangeable. It is, therefore, particularly important to be clear at this early stage what is understood by quality assurance and related terms and what kind of activities and procedures might be considered relevant in an educational context. A basic question is whether universities already have procedures that could be described as quality assurance or whether the term implies a radically new approach and practices.

In 1993 I suggested that responses to quality assurance in higher education may be considered as falling into one or more of three categories.

First, there is the view that quality assurance is just a new label for a set of procedures that are well established in higher education. External examination, course validation, professional commitment, peer review and even examination results have all been put forward as aspects of quality assurance for university teaching. Some of these practices are well established and universal; others, while universal, could be improved; others are established in new universities, ex polytechnics, but still relatively novel in more established universities. Quality assurance is thus conceived as more or less *latent* in the university system and just requiring explicit identification to make it manifest.

An opposite view is that quality assurance, as practised elsewhere, represents a novel approach to the establishment and maintenance of standards in universities. Imported from industry or health care, these approaches will give universities a necessary shake-up and, in the process, make them more accountable, student-orientated and cost-effective. Quality assurance will thus involve a *radical* reorientation of universities' approach to their work. From this comes the interest in industry-derived approaches, such as total quality management and BS 9001.

An intermediate view is that universities do indeed have much progress to make to assure quality for their teaching and courses but that they should establish systems and approaches that are distinctive, built on established practices and matching the special characteristics of the academic endeavour. The basis for many of these procedures already exists in university practices but some imports will be desirable for the growth of the system. A system should thus develop which is customized for universities. More ambitiously, it is suggested that the procedures worked out for higher education might, with advantage, be applied in industry.

These three positions I described as the 'latent', the 'radical' and the 'developmental'. They are not mutually exclusive: in clarifying existing procedures opportunity might be taken to effect improvement and there might be some borrowing from practices elsewhere.

These three positions are still valid theoretically but perforce all universities must at least subscribe to the developmental position and the QAA is there to ensure they do. Within that there may be some radical initiatives and the views represented by the latent position probably still exist.

If there is to be an importation of industrial or public service techniques into universities to assure the quality of teaching it is important to separate essence from accidents. Much of the adverse criticism of BS 5750 and then BS 9001 has been based on a concern with its surface features and language rather than its basic approach. Apparently the QAA had considered linking its processes with BS 9001 in part for international currency but had decided against the standard as being overly bureaucratic.

I would suggest that the following are characteristics of quality assurance wherever it occurs.

1 The specification of standards for whatever is conceived as the product or service.
2 The identification of critical functions and procedures that will be necessary to achieve these standards.

3   Constant recourse to the consumer to set and monitor the accomplishment of standards.
4   Documented clarity with regard to both the standards to be achieved and the procedures that must be followed to achieve these standards.
5   A cybernetic approach to standard and procedure setting, which involves monitoring that standards are being met and procedures followed, and taking action to remedy or rectify shortfalls coupled with a regular review of the appropriateness of standards and procedures.
6   The total involvement of all personnel and a commitment to development and training.

All of this preliminary thinking about quality assurance can now be applied to teaching. Do we have clear standards regarding teaching, conceived as a product or service? Are these standards based on evidence of impact on learning? Do we have constant recourse to, say, the student as consumer to validate the standards of teaching? Are the standards for teaching and the procedures that must be followed to achieve these standards set out clearly? Do we follow a cybernetic approach to setting objectives, monitoring performance and acting on feedback? Are all staff in the university committed to quality in teaching and is there a sustained programme of training and staff development to support this? These are all good questions but beg the fundamental question: What do we mean by teaching?

In simple terms teaching is what teachers do. This includes their observable behaviour and the materials they produce and organize. But how observable is the behavior of university teachers? The majority of their work is carried on in private with more or less consenting adults. How common is it for colleagues, including heads of department, actually to observe lectures, seminars, tutorials or any other form of teaching? Even if such observation does occur, is there general agreement about the events observed and their significance? Further, is there agreement about the standards that should be met? Is this agreement underpinned by research on effective teaching?

If teachers produce materials, be they visual aids, handouts or more comprehensive learning packages, then these are more amenable to observation and comment, but to what extent does this take place? Again, what are the standards that distinguish the good from the indifferent? What is their evidential basis?

There is, of course, no point in teaching unless somebody, other than the teacher, learns from it. So, whatever standards are set for teaching would have to relate in some systematic way to the effect of that teaching on desirable learning in students.

There are two crucial complicating factors here. First, and most important, there is no generally accepted science or technology addressing the relationship between teaching and learning. But there is no point in teaching unless someone learns from it. Such knowledge as there is of the effectiveness of various teaching styles is summarized in George Brown and Sarah Edmond's chapter (Chapter 19), but the use of this knowledge it is not widespread among lecturers.

Making a comparison between 1993 and 2018, it cannot be claimed that there have been any dramatic advances in the science and technology of higher education teaching. Brown and Edmond, in their chapter, state that much of the research on learning, assessment and teaching took place in the latter part of the twentieth century and that this research is still relevant until demonstrated otherwise. They point to some interesting studies since this foundation work but nothing that represents a breakthrough empirically or theoretically.

One thing that has certainly changed or emerged since 1993 is developments in IT and the rapid growth of social media. What changes have these brought about? To what extent have they been researched?

Sarah Edmonds in a personal communication suggests the following:

- They have been used to raise the profile of courses, staff and universities. Such behaviour might have been frowned upon in the 1990s.
- They increase accessibility to instruction.
- They encourage more student engagement inside and outside of teaching spaces.
- They develop and encourage collaborative research on teaching between universities.
- They strengthen the connections between alumni and their ex-teachers, which may lead to collaboration on projects and the development of work-based learning.
- Videogames for learning and assessment can be used in situ and online.
- They provide a forum for staff developers in which they can share experiences, knowledge and raise questions about ways to develop teaching, learning and assessment (e.g. the SEDA website).
- They have changed course management and some aspects of assessment and feedback.

This optimistic list provides an agenda for research which remains to be pursued.

Latterly, many research studies have been small scale and qualitative in nature. It is illuminating to locate these in a categorization of research types (Ellis 2006). *Ethnographic* studies are qualitative and carried out on a small sample. Their results are *suggestive* of key variables and relationships. *Survey* studies investigate variables and relationships in a large sample and their results are *indicative* of incidence and relationships. *Experimental studies* manipulate variables in experimental and control groups in a representative sample. Their results are relatively *conclusive*. Within this structure and epistemological hierarchy the majority of higher education research studies are no more than suggestive.

However, the most important issue at this point is not so much whether knowledge exists, but whether it underpins the actions of higher education teachers and is part of a professional debate. Can higher education teaching claim to be research-based? Can higher education teaching be described as 'evidenced practice' to the standards expected, for example, of medicine? I know of no studies that attempt to answer these questions.

The Society for Research in Higher Education has existed for more than 50 years with the broad aim of establishing a research base for higher education. There is no doubt that it can celebrate much valuable activity over that period but dissemination and take-up among university lecturers as a whole remains problematic.

It may be that the developments in teacher training for university lecturers will lead eventually to more appreciation of research findings; more inclination to participate in studies and more commitment to carry out research studies. For that to happen however there will have to be more encouragement and rewards for pedagogic research. As teaching becomes more obviously rewarded within universities and through funding mechanisms, this should be coupled with the encouragement and reward of related research.

A second problem is the ambiguous professional status of university lecturers. While they spend a large, often the largest, proportion of their time teaching, their professional status and credibility derives not from this central activity but from their knowledge of their subject and their capacity to extend that knowledge. Uniquely among so-called professions, there is no formal requirement of training to be a university teacher. In 1993 trained teachers were a minority in universities and while the proportion has increased significantly it is still apparently assumed by a majority that knowledge of the subject and research capability coupled with on-the-job practice and experience are sufficient to ensure professional standards of teaching.

So how many university teachers do hold a teaching qualification? Despite the best efforts of HEFCE, HESA and HEA, the data regarding university teachers with a teacher training qualification in the UK is hedged with reservations. Definition of qualifications have proved problematic and the motivation of lecturers to respond imperfect. Nevertheless, the best figures suggest that 40 per cent of lecturers hold an undefined teaching qualification so the number has moved from a small minority to a significant minority.

More robust data is available from the Higher Education Academy regarding the numbers who have gained Fellowships of the Academy. By 2016–17 this had risen to 72,804 representing 39.2 per cent of the 185,755 academic staff eligible to apply.

While still representing less than half of the population, these figures almost certainly represent substantial progress since 1993 although there is no data available regarding the number of university teachers who were teacher trained in that year. In 1993 the HEA and its Fellowships did not exist. The Institute of Learning and Teaching was established post Dearing in 2000 and merged with the Learning and Teaching Support Network (LTSN) and the TQEF National Co-ordination Team (NCT) to form the Higher Education Academy (HEA) in 2004. The Academy undoubtedly represents the most significant initiative to professionalize university teaching since 1993.

The HEA stands as a beacon of professionalism in higher education teaching and is, so far as I can tell, unique. Its activities, while initially UK based, have a developing international dimension with, for example, fellowship applications from Australia, New Zealand and the USA.

There has certainly been a dramatic growth in the number of training courses available for university teachers. HEA now recognizes 150 programmes. I don't have the figures for 1993 but would estimate they would have been significantly short of that number.

Clearly there are not generally accepted standards for teaching in either its interpersonal or materially based aspects. While there is a substantial literature, teachers as a whole do not concern themselves with it. Despite a significant increase in numbers holding a teaching qualification of some sort, more than half of university teachers do not hold any teaching qualification.

In the absence of standards, a lack of scientific underpinning, and an imperfectly prepared workforce there cannot be procedures to fully guarantee quality in teaching. That is not to say that procedures do not exist in universities nor to set aside the work of the QAA and the HEA. But progress over the next period must be characterized by continued progress in lecturer qualifications and in the discipline of higher education teaching to ensure that their work is evidence-based.

Students, while clearly the recipients of teaching, and indeed its raison d'etre, were rarely conceived as consumers (or customers or clients) in 1993. This has certainly changed to some considerable advantage but with its own dangers. The student voice is now essential in universities' quality assurance procedures and has its place in all national bodies concerned with teaching. In 2017 there are numerous examples of student involvement in evaluating and improving teaching as a number of chapters in this book demonstrate.

One point made strongly by student organizations is that they expect their teachers to be trained. However the majority are still not and there is a pervasive culture which believes that training is, at best, a diversion from more significant activities.

Yet universities do claim that their teaching is of high quality. How is this demonstrated? The answer is in four main ways. First, there are the results that students achieve in their examinations and course work and the consequences of these in degree classifications. Second are indirect indicators such as employment, or value added to capability calculated by relating assessment data to intake characteristics. Third, there is the much-lauded system of external examination. Fourth is the feedback from students on the teaching they receive.

Interestingly, none of these outcome measures are addressing teaching itself.

Two of the outcomes – examination results and external examination – are in the hands of teachers themselves. Teachers are the stock from which examiners are drawn and teachers are responsible for assessing their own students' achievements. This does seem an unduly inbred system for the identification of teaching quality. Furthermore, even if external examiners are objective and genuinely external, they are concerned primarily with assessment, that is with results and the examining scheme. Their comments on teaching as such are at best based on inference.

Since 1993, when course planning and review were essentially the province of polytechnics and certain professional schools, formal procedures for course planning validation and review are now well established in universities even in subjects where they are not required for external accreditation. The QAA reviews UK higher education providers to assess how they maintain their academic standards and in effect quality assures their quality management.

But how close do these procedures actually get to teaching? Typical course documents include statements of aims and objectives bearing upon students' learning, regulations and procedures for admission and assessment of students, and lists of content that will be covered. Teaching methods are usually described briefly and in a routine way. It would be rare if not unique to find a course document that contained detailed, evidence-based standards for the teaching activities of staff and the student experience.

Accreditation is the most significant external element in the quality assurance of university teaching. Broadly defined, accreditation occurs when an action or process officially recognizes an entity, person or organization, having characterisics appropriate for particular functions. More specifically the term is used when a school or course has met the standards set by the accreditors. Thus the QAA accredits universities with regard to their quality management; the HEA accredits individuals for their teaching achievements and programmes as meeting standards for lecturer training. In professional areas, for example medicine, standards are set for the accreditation process itself as discussed in the chapter on medical education.

Accreditation always involves a set of standards against which the university, school, programme or individual is judged. Of particular interest for this book are the standards set for teaching; the evidence regarding teaching that is considered adequate to assure that the standards are being met; and the steps that might be taken to ensure standards are met and shortfalls addressed.

Standard specification and monitoring their achievement is the essence of accreditation. How this operates can be placed along a continuum from tight control to a broad steer with flexibility on how standards are met. This can be described as a dirigiste – laissez-faire continuum and ranges from the complete central control afforded by centrally set examinations to the broad encouragement of creativity in teaching methods which characterizes medical accreditation.

While medical accreditation bodies are not reluctant to specify standards – the LMEC in the USA has 134 of them – they adopt a light touch with regard to teaching methods which are not specified at all. This is justified as encouraging creativity in medical schools but could, equally, reflect the uncertain state of knowledge regarding teaching and learning referred to throughout this chapter.

There are, then, numerous problems surrounding quality assurance for university teaching. We don't know much about teaching, the product, and there is no general agreement on what assuring quality in it might mean for higher education and even how appropriate its techniques might be if imported from other areas. Those ideas and approaches, which are generally accepted as implied by quality assurance, seem difficult or even impossible to apply to teaching.

Yet universities are now required to have some commitment to a quality assurance approach for their teaching. There is now a Quality Assurance Agency whose job it is to audit universities' own quality assurance mechanisms for teaching. It is now necessary, therefore, that all universities should have thought through what quality assurance means to them. They must have at least a working definition of teaching and be able to demonstrate that they have standards for it and methods to ensure that the standards are being met. They must have procedures to monitor standards and put things right when there are deficiencies or shortfalls. At this stage, they must be open to new ideas and experimental in posture, while able to identify their best existing practice and be committed to its development.

One common theme in all approaches to quality assurance is the central importance of staff. Even when an organization is concerned with manufactured goods the quality of these goods depends ultimately on the activities of the people involved. This truism is even more obvious when the organization offers a service, the central nature of which is interpersonal. University teaching is the activities of university teachers that aim to bring about desirable learning in students. Supporting this central teaching venture is a complex structure of administrative and service departments. Managing quality for teaching therefore involves, directly or indirectly, the entire staff of the university. If there is to be progress in quality assurance for teaching then we are faced with a massive exercise in staff development and organizational change.

As a start, it would be important to identify those activities which already exist in universities and which might form part of a quality assurance system. They include both internal and external mechanisms for assuring quality. These are the latent quality assurance functions referred to above. Examples include:

- existing procedures for the planning, approval and review of courses;
- performance indicators for courses, including the intake characteristics of students, wastage rates and final results, and the follow-up of these statistics;
- feedback from students;
- feedback from employers and sponsors;
- external inspection from, for example, professional bodies;
- reviews undertaken by departmental, faculty and university committees;
- staff appraisal and development, including teaching training.

The university should undertake its own quality assurance audit, first to determine those existing procedures that might contribute to quality assurance and then to assess their effectiveness and ways in which they might be improved.

In the light of its overall concept of quality assurance the university might then consider more innovative approaches, including imports from other universities or organizations. This more radical approach might range from the introduction of a fully-fledged total quality management system through the introduction of procedures such as quality circles or local audits to the imitation of best practice from other universities or higher education institutions in the UK or internationally.

A central question should be the extent to which these procedures actually make an impact on teaching, that is the behaviour of teaching staff. It must be recognized that universities in general are relatively distanced in their procedures from this behavior. The most significant development in quality assurance for teaching will be the establishment of teaching itself at the centre of the stage. Thus, course validation and review, student feedback, appraisal, development and promotion will all have to make specific and detailed reference to the behaviour of teachers, including interaction with students, materials produced by teachers to facilitate learning, and the scholarly output of staff concerning teaching.

Twenty-five year report

So at the end of the 25-year period from 1993 to 2018, what kind of report can we give on quality assurance for university teaching?

There is no doubt that university teaching has moved up the agenda in the UK and internationally. At national level there is a Quality Assurance Agency, the Higher Education Academy and the Teaching Excellence Framework (Higher Education Funding Council for England 2016).

The Quality Assurance Agency for Higher Education is an independent body working across all four nations of the UK to raise the standards and quality of higher education. The Agency uses its expertise to support the development of quality assurance systems worldwide. It is in principle centrally concerned with quality assurance for university teaching. The QAA has developed the Quality Code and the Subject Benchmark Statements to offer guidance to universities. Valuable though these are they don't address teaching directly, although it is there by implication as the means to achieve the standards in student experience and achievements specified. A similar body, the Tertiary Education Quality and Standards Agency (TEQSA), operates in Australia.

The Higher Education Academy is a national body that champions excellence in higher education teaching in the UK and throughout the world. It awards fellowships that recognize teaching achievements and accredits continuous professional development (CPD) programmes which are delivered by higher education providers throughout the world. These programmes are accredited against the Professional Standards Framework (HEA, 2011) produced by the Academy which comes closest to a detailed statement for standards in teaching.

The HEA is undoubtedly the major single development for university teaching over the period not only in the UK but worldwide. It fulfils and exceeds the recommendation of the Dearing Report of 1997 that there should be a professional association for university lecturers described as an Institute for Learning and Teaching the functions of which would be to accredit programmes of training for higher education teachers; to commission research and development in learning and teaching practices; and to stimulate innovation.

The Teaching Excellence Framework established by the Higher Education Funding Council for England in 2012 aims to recognize and reward excellence in teaching and learning, and help inform prospective students' choices for higher education. The TEF is analogous to the Research Excellence Framework (REF) in that it aims to relate funding to excellence but in this case in teaching. The longstanding complaint that the Research Excellence Framework skewed the work of lecturers towards research at the expense of teaching can now perhaps be addressed. The TEF can certainly make judgements with participating organizations graded as Gold, Silver or Brass with funding following. It is to be hoped that these judgements are fair but they are not yet transparent in that standards and criteria are still broad with, for example, teaching quality summarized in a brief paragraph. It is to be hoped that these specifications will be developed to reflect best practice and research evidence and to integrate with the work of the HEA.

All universities in the UK, and many elsewhere, will have developed a policy and operational plan to develop and assure quality and excellence in teaching and learning.

The numbers of lecturers who have a teaching qualification and the number of lecturers and support staff who have gained fellowships of the HEA have increased dramatically, although still representing a significant minority, as has the number of lecturer training programmes.

Compared with 1993, students are involved increasingly at programme, school and university levels and nationally through the QAA Student Advisory Board. The QAA's policy is that students should be encouraged to provide feedback on courses, help develop learning and teaching in subject areas, participate in university or college decision-making processes, and represent student views through a students' union or other body. QAA's Quality Code devotes an entire chapter to student engagement. The National Student Survey is the largest survey of its kind in the UK. The Australian Higher Education Standards Framework is structured around the stages of the student experience.

While there has therefore been considerable progress in three of the areas identified at the beginning of the chapter, the development of scientific knowledge regarding HE teaching and learning and its adoption by the profession have lagged behind.

There are at least three shortfalls here. There is not enough scientific knowledge about teaching and learning in HE. There is not enough research being conducted other than small-scale ethnographic studies. Such research as there is is not being adopted as a basis for evidenced practice.

Improving the situation will require action at governmental, university and professional levels and the following are some suggestions for this action.

- The Professional Standards Framework (HEA, 2011) should require an appreciation of and commitment to evidenced practice. This standard should be reflected in other material from HEA and QAA and be a criterion used in the TEF.
- Lecturer training courses should contain material to encourage a commitment to evidenced practice; participation in research, and, eventually, initiation of research. Post-graduate diploma programmes for higher education lecturers should feed into research-based masters programmes.
- The Social Science Research Council should include Higher Education Pedagogical Research in its priorities.
- Universities should encourage pedagogical research internally and link this with programme evaluation and institutional research.

Introduction to the Book

The main purpose of this book is to present ideas and initiatives that are relevant to quality assurance for teaching and the issues discussed above. The chapters are organized in four sections:

1   Assuring quality
2   Identifying quality
3   Developing quality
4   Case studies of quality assurance in six subjects.

Three major issues have led to the main subdivisions of the book. First is the question of what quality assurance might mean and how it might be practised. What kind of national organizations foster quality and by what means? What can universities do internally to foster quality?

Second is the identification of quality in teaching. What knowledge exists at present and how might it be developed?

The third issue is the development of staff through teacher training, appraisal and perhaps personal training.

A fourth idea is to offer insights into how topics raised in the first three sections apply to a sample of individual subjects. Case studies of these subjects are interesting in themselves, and may have resonances in other areas. This section

includes six case studies of quality assurance for teaching in a spectrum of subjects. From the large number possible, there are three professional areas: medicine; nursing and teacher training which link with overview chapters in Part 1; two arts subjects: music, and art and design, and, bridging arts, science and professional training, psychology.

The **Assuring Quality** part consists of four main sections. First there are chapters by leaders from two contrasting but complementary national organizations representing on the one hand external government regulation and on the other collective professional action. *Anthony McClaran* reviews the development of the UK QAA as a national HE agency in the context of the international opportunities, pressures, challenges and responses that have shaped the direction of quality assurance since the Agency was founded in 1997. He identifies key issues, including the tension between peer review and quantitative outcome measures in the context of reduced funding; the relationship between external and internal quality assurance; and the emergence of risk-based approaches to regulation.

Craig Mahony and Helena Lim provide an overview of the changing landscape in learning and teaching across UK higher education (HE) over the past 25 years. They highlight the national initiatives to support and enhance learning and teaching, including the role and impact of national agency bodies, the Higher Education Academy, subject-specific support and the accreditation of higher education teaching.

These two perspectives reviewing on the one hand a central external monitoring agency and on the other professional action including the HEA, are matched by pieces on a British Standard for University Teaching by *Roger Ellis*, which describes an external process with standards for quality management with which universities would have to comply, and a Professional Model for Teaching by *Lewis Elton*. Interest in British Standards has stimulated strong objections, where it is argued that the standard is fundamentally antipathetic to university practices. *Roger Ellis*'s chapter should enable readers to make up their own minds. It is important to grasp that BS 9001 is a content-free standard for the processes of quality assurance and quality management, whatever goods or services are involved. What is missing is a standard for teaching itself, but the BS is not intended to provide that. However, the emphasis on meeting consumers' needs should at least ensure that the university's approach is student-centred.

In his contrasting chapter *Lewis Elton* reflects on the professionalism of university teachers and how this should contribute to quality in teaching. Less than impressed with what he finds, he sets out a unique model for improved practice and comprehensive quality assurance.

In the next part, three chapters look at approaches that might be employed by universities internally to assure quality. *Elaine Hogard*'s chapter considers how the approaches and methods of Program Evaluation might be employed as part of the internal quality assurance procedures of a university. Program Evaluation poses questions about the success and methods of a program and gathers data to answer them. The chapter outlines the approach and techniques of the discipline known as Program Evaluation; and second, it considers their place in the assurance and development of quality in higher education.

Roger Woodward describes Institutional Research which can include studies of teaching and its impact on learning. In his chapter he explores the role of institutional research in gathering data which can inform and improve all aspects of a university's operation.

Jeremy Warren looks at Performance Management and the impact of proxies in indicating quality. The chapter addresses a number of questions related to the impact of performance management policies and processes upon the delivery of good quality teaching and learning. It examines the advantages that can be gained from the analysis of good quality data but also recognizes some of the 'pit-falls and bear-traps' that may be encountered if decision-makers do not take into account the limitations of an over-reliance on metrics.

In the next part there are chapters concerned with professional accreditation where programme providers must meet standards set by professional bodies who will then accredit their compliance with those standards. These include a comparative study of Medical Accreditation by *Elaine Hogard, Dan Hunt, Jessica Lichtenstein* and *Theanne Walters*. The chapter describes issues and approaches in three national bodies: the GMC in the UK; the LMEC in the USA and Canada; and the AMC in Australia. The chapter considers processes for accreditation and standards for accreditation itself. It also looks at the extent to which accreditation standards address teaching and learning.

Carol Hall's chapter on Quality Assurance and Enhancement in Nurse Education addresses key factors in quality assurance and enhancements in nurse education as this applies to those with a responsibility to deliver contemporary nursing education programmes.

Chris Wilkins in his chapter, QA and Accountability in Initial Teacher Education, considers how in recent decades many nation states have increasingly come to see education system reform as central to competing in a global knowledge economy. More broadly, *Damian Day* considers the quality assurance role of Professional Statutory Regulatory Bodies (PSRBs) which form a significant, if sometimes overlooked, part of the quality assurance regime for UK higher education. Currently, 149 PSRBs accredit or otherwise recognize over 14,000 courses. Focusing on the regulation of courses or examinations leading to eligibility to practise they have an influence on the work of most higher education institutions, as they deliver courses leading wholly or in part to practising as a professional. *Damian Day* then considers national examinations which form part of the requirements for practising in a particular profession and represent the strictest form of central control. In some professions, examinations can form the majority of assessment leading to eligibility to practise but in others are part of a more mixed diet. For some professions, national examinations are well established but for others they are a more recent phenomenon. Currently in the UK two major professions – doctors and solicitors – are consulting on the introduction of such examinations.

Students are of course self-evidently at the centre of learning and teaching so the next part considers in three chapters ways in which students might contribute to quality assurance. *Karen Crawford, Emily Parkin* and *Reece Horsley* explore ways in which students can meaningfully participate as partners in different aspects and levels of quality assurance in higher education. *Maurice Stringer, Karl Stringer, Jackie Hunter* and *Cathy Finlay* describe the move from early paper-based assessments of student evaluation to more sophisticated modern approaches using clicker technology, online surveys and cloud-based feedback systems. *Saranne Weller* and *Alam Mahbubul* consider how the role of the student in QA has developed over time from evaluator to partner, at course, institution and national level in the UK, across Europe, the US and Australia.

Finally, there are two comparative perspectives, one from a different professional area and one from a different country. First, *Dorothy Whittington* looks at how ideas and approaches well established in health care might be imported into university quality assurance. Her chapter outlines three phases in the development of health care quality assurance: 'trusting professionals', 'codification and control', and 'engagement and culture'. Initially, quality is assured by guaranteeing the trustworthiness of individual professionals. The next phase involves setting standards that all professionals must meet, and trying to control outcomes. Finally, quality is assured by engaging with professionals to develop an improvement culture across organizations and systems. Comparison is then made with quality assurance in university teaching where elements of each phase are discerned. Health care approaches that could be adapted for higher education are identified.

A different comparative perspective is offered in a chapter on quality assurance for teaching in Hungary where *Marta Erdos Gobor Szellosi* and *Eva Vojtek* explain how changing political, legal and financial factors have contributed to an emergent quality assurance system for universities. Hungary's state socialist legacy still has an impact on contemporary quality assurance practices, though state socialist ideological groundings in academic life were gradually shaped into the more performance-oriented views of knowledge-based societies.

The next section of the book, **Identifying Quality**, looks at different ways in which quality in teaching might be described, conceptualized and researched. A chapter by *George Brown* and *Sara Edmonds* reviews research on effective teaching in higher education. *Ronald Berk's* chapter provides, through a comprehensive literature review, alternative sources of evidence to evaluate teaching, in addition to end-of-programme student reviews. A chapter by *Jerry M. Lewis* looks at the characteristics of those who have received a well-established Distinguished Teaching Award in a State University. Two chapters look at what students consider to be quality in teaching. *Camille Kandiko Howson* reports findings from research on student perceptions and expectations of higher education while *David Morris* assesses the strengths and weaknesses of student feedback as a determinant of quality.

Elaine Hogard describes methods to explicate quality in teaching exemplified through an evaluation of an innovative teaching method in nursing. This evaluation used two methods for identifying, analyzing and categorizing effective teaching, which could have wide utility.

Finally, *Lindsay Heywood's* chapter describes and discusses the design and intent of the Australian National Higher Education Standards Framework which is structured around the student experience.

The third part, **Developing Quality,** includes chapters on approaches to developing quality in teaching. *Saranne Meginnis's* chapter considers how appraisal can contribute to the enhancement of quality in university teaching. It considers the origins of contemporary debate concerning quality and appraisal of quality in higher education. Some practicalities concerning the nature and variety of appraisal schemes and other approaches to quality assurance are considered. The model (or models) of appraisal most likely to make a worthwhile contribution to the enhancement of quality in university teaching is discussed.

In her chapter *Shan Wareing* discusses staff development as a prerequisite for academic quality in the context of the UK Quality Code for Higher Education. In addition she considers the intrinsic value of staff development to enable improvements in the quality of education, and points to multiple other benefits to individuals and to institutions. She considers models and options of staff development in higher education, including postgraduate certificates in learning and teaching, and makes recommendations for effective approaches that support institutional goals and long-term success.

Georgina Kirk provides a novel perspective on staff development from a private sector company that offers personal training to lecturers who feel the need for development. *Lynette Matthews and Ruth Pilkington* in their chapter describe the changes in how academics are being supported and developed within institutions, not just in the UK but globally.

They discuss these developments and then focus on the implementation of the UK Professional Standards Framework (UK PSF) aligned to Fellowship of the Higher Education Academy as a mechanism for shaping professional development, and rewarding and recognizing teaching quality.

The fourth part of the book includes six **case studies** of quality assurance in a range of contrasting subjects including medicine, nursing, teacher training, psychology, music, and art design and media. Three of these, medicine, nursing, and teacher training, are subject to professional accreditation and have matching chapters in the first section of the book. The chapters in Assuring Quality consider accreditation at a systemic level whereas the chapters in this section are written from the programme provider's perspective.

In their chapter, Quality Assurance in North American Medical Schools: Implications of Standards and Processes on Institutional Practices, *Marie Matte* and *Joel H. Lanphear* describe not only the changes in accreditation standards themselves but how institutions have had to respond to them to achieve satisfactory accreditation status. *Marian Traynor* explores the challenges associated with joint accreditation for professional courses using the discipline of nursing as an example. *Liz Fleet* in her chapter describes and reflects on her experience of an OFSTED inspection of an initial teacher education partnership.

Michael Russ in his chapter considers how quality in music provision is evident and examines the issues and challenges that face those designing, teaching, managing and quality-assuring music programmes. *Roni Brown* in her chapter identifies how ideas about quality are practised in teaching and learning in art, design and media and the challenges this poses. In his chapter *Ronnie Wilson* reflects on professional regulation, research training and the development of peer mentorship in UK psychology programmes.

All contributors were invited to conclude their chapter with advice to possible readers. It is hoped that their suggestions will contribute to progress in quality assurance for university teaching.

References

BS 5750 (1987 and 1990) *Quality Systems, Parts 0–4*. London: British Standards Institution.

Crosby, P. (1984) *Quality Without Tears*. New York: McGraw-Hill.

Dearing Report (1997) Higher Education in the Learning Society; www.leeds.ac.uk/educol/ncihe

Deming, W. E. (1982) *Quality, Productivity and Competitive Position*. Cambridge, MA: MIT Press.

Ellis, R. (2006) *Research Methods in Programme Evaluation*. SHEU Occasional Paper 5, University of Chester UK.

Higher Education Academy (2011) *The UK Professional Standards Framework*; https://www.heacademy.ac.uk/system/files/downloads/uk_professional_standards_framework.pdf

Higher Education Funding Council for England (2016) *The Teaching Excellence Framework*; www.hefce.ac.uk/lt/tef

Quality Assurance Agency (2015) *UK Quality Code for Higher Education*; www.qaa.ac.uk/assuring-standards-and-quality/the-quality-code

White Paper (1991) *Higher Education: A New Framework*, Cmnd 1541. London: HMSO.

2 The Quality Assurance Agency

Anthony McClaran

Anthony McClaran reviews the development of the UK QAA as a national HE agency in the context of the international opportunities, pressures, challenges and responses that have shaped the direction of quality assurance since the Agency was founded in 1997. He identifies key issues, including the tension between peer review and quantitative outcome measures in the context of reduced funding; the relationship between external and internal quality assurance; and the emergence of risk-based approaches to regulation. The growing role and significance of international groupings and alliances of agencies, the emergence of international frameworks for standards, and the challenges presented by transnational HE have all played their part in shaping the work of QAA and agencies like it around the world.

Structure

1 Introduction
2 'Quality wars': Agencies and independence
3 Students at the heart of the system
4 Expansion, diversity and risk
5 Quality goes global

1 Introduction

Since its establishment in 1997, the Quality Assurance Agency for Higher Education (QAA), which the author led from 2009 to 2015 as its third Chief Executive, has provided external quality assurance to the higher education sector of the UK. QAA was set up to serve a sector that was significantly smaller and more homogenous than today, and the context in which the Agency now operates has changed enormously. The numbers of students have continued to grow, the sector has been enlarged by HE offered through further education colleges and private ('alternative') providers, and the student interest has emerged, for different and sometimes contradictory reasons, as the central focus of much of the discourse and practice of quality assurance. There have been major challenges to the ways in which quality assurance has been conducted and some questioning of its effectiveness and value.

Yet despite this, quality assurance has, in step with the ever increasing internationalisation of higher education itself, become a global activity, with agencies similar to QAA now present and active in virtually every country with a developed higher education system – and those countries without such an organisation are generally working hard to establish one a rapidly as possible. What are the forces of continuity and disruption that have shaped the direction of QAA over the last twenty years? This chapter will look at some of the most important: who owns quality assurance and what happens when ownership is disputed; what has been the impact of placing students 'at the heart of the system'; how has quality assurance responded to the dramatic increase in the diversity of providers; and what prospects are there for an approach to quality assurance which is genuinely international?

2 'Quality Wars': Agencies and independence

Writing in 2006, the late Professor Sir David Watson described as the 'Quality Wars' the clash between audit and accountability on the one hand, and academic freedom and institutional autonomy on the other, which he claimed had been the site of significant struggle in UK higher education since the 1980s.[1] More specifically, the Quality Wars has become the term used to characterise the battle over the ownership, purpose and remit of the organisations that had emerged in the early 1990s to provide quality assurance and assessment. From 1992, when the Further and Higher Education Act placed a statutory duty on the funding councils 'to secure that provision is made for the assessment of quality of education provided in institutions for whose activities it provides (or is considering providing) financial support' to 1997, when QAA was established, there were in effect two parallel external quality assurance regimes: the institutionally owned Higher Education Quality Council (HEQC), which audited quality at the provider level; and the funding councils' quality assessment divisions, which carried out subject-based inspections intended to be linked to funding.[2]

This dual system survived until 1997, when the creation of QAA brought together the two functions in a single, UK-wide organisation, with the funding councils henceforward contracting with QAA to secure the provision of quality assessment required to fulfil their statutory duties.[3] As Professor Roger Brown, HEQC's Chief Executive throughout its existence, has pointed out, the two regimes drew on quite different origins and philosophies. HEQC's roots were in the Academic Audit Unit,[4] established by the then Committee of Vice-Chancellors and Principles (CVCP) in 1990 in response to a swelling chorus of voices in the late 1980s arguing that universities and their staff, traditionally almost entirely self-regulated, should be subject to some form of external scrutiny.[5] This approach stressed the importance of university autonomy, academic freedom and external scrutiny by peers. In contrast, the quality assessment approach of the funding councils drew on the more inspectorial, regulation-based approach of the Schools' Inspectorate (now Ofsted) and was intended to be linked directly to funding outcomes.

The reason that this division is important, and that the 'Quality Wars' still resonate nearly twenty years on, is that HEQC and the quality assessment divisions of the funding councils embodied the fundamental approaches that are always at play, in differing proportion and shifting balance, in all attempts to establish formal quality assurance arrangements for higher education. Is quality assurance an activity designed to improve and enhance quality, or, through regulation, to ensure that it does not fall below a recognised threshold? Is it essentially an exercise in collective self-regulation by autonomous, independent providers; or one of co-regulation between those providers and an external authority acting on behalf of stakeholders; or external regulation designed to ensure accountability for expenditure, whether by the state or (increasingly) by students themselves? Can quality assurance be about more than one, or all, of these purposes simultaneously? What does it mean for the HE sector to comprise independent entities, particularly when so much public money flows in their direction? Why is it important for a quality assurance agency to be independent, when power to regulate may derive, directly or indirectly, from government statute?

QAA, as it was established in 1997 under its first Chief Executive, John Randall, was an attempt to bring both the assurance and regulatory work together, albeit as separate operational activities. The Agency was (and is) independent, not part of government or even an arm's-length entity, or quango, unlike HEFCE and the other funding councils. Neither is it an agency of Universities UK, like, for example, Universities UK International. QAA is a charity and a company limited by guarantee, with its own board of directors. Its legal owners are UUK, Universities Scotland and Universities Wales, expressing the principle that the quality assurance of a sector comprising legally autonomous entities is a form of co-regulation – but they have only minority representation on the Board, on which, by careful design, the largest single group of directors must be from the independent category – that is, not nominated by or drawn from the universities and colleges quality assured by the Agency. The funding arrangements were established with the same careful attention to balance: drawn partly from institutional subscriptions and partly from contract income for the delivery of assurance services. The Board includes members from the four countries of the UK and, more recently, has been augmented by student and further education college representation.

This structure may seem complex but it brought together the shared interests in, and concepts of, quality assurance in a way that ensured that all had a voice but none could dominate. The statutory and regulatory elements (through the funding councils) were blended with the emphasis on co-regulation and enhancement that had been an important strand of HEQC's (and, behind HEQC, the sector's) approach. The collective interests of the regulated entities were fully represented –but could not outvote the independent members, thus avoiding the danger of regulatory capture.

Thus constituted, QAA could legitimately claim to be independent, notwithstanding some elements that, viewed in isolation, might seem to suggest the contrary. Certainly the European Association for Quality Assurance in Higher Education (ENQA), which subjects all its member agencies to five-yearly external scrutiny, was able to take a very positive view of QAA's independence when it reviewed the Agency in 2013:

> The Panel confirms that QAA is an independent body with autonomous responsibility for its operations . . . QAA acts entirely independently in making its judgements . . . [which] are driven by criteria and methodologies which cannot be influenced by third parties.[6]

The balance thus achieved has been by and large a successful one, leading to the fair claim that the creation of QAA brought the Quality Wars to an end for nearly two decades. But like all careful balances it involved a degree of precariousness which, from time to time, threatened to upset the whole apple cart. Such a threat emerged in the events which brought an end to the parallel systems of institutional review and subject assessment in 2001. Successfully lobbied by the universities, and particularly by those in the Russell Group of research-intensive institutions, the then Secretary of State for Education, David Blunkett, effectively intervened to demand an end to the system of subject review inherited from the funding councils, and by then seen widely as burdensome, bureaucratic and ineffectual in providing a suitably differentiated basis for funding teaching. John Randall fought to defend elements of the system which he believed to be necessary to protect student and public interests and, when it became clear that the battle could not be won, resigned. Subject review was dropped in exchange for a sector commitment to better and more information about teaching quality, and the stabilising hand of Peter Williams, who had been involved in the development of external quality assurance since the early days of the CVCP Academic Audit Unit, was placed on the tiller, to lead QAA through to calmer waters.[7]

More recently, the plans of HEFCE, announced in the autumn of 2014, to put its quality assurance responsibilities out to competitive tender, threatened destabilisation of a more comprehensive sort: the possible break-up of an internationally recognised quality framework which, remarkably, had through careful adaptation survived the full devolution of HE to the parliaments and assemblies of the UK's constituent countries; and its replacement by as many as half a dozen different bundles of contracted-out activity in England alone. Previous adjustments to the quality assurance framework had been the product of careful consultation and discussion between the providers, the funding councils and the QAA itself; now the offer was for a reformed approach so 'light touch' that one former VC likened it to asking 'the regulated whether they would like to continue to be regulated, to which the unsurprising response appears to be "no".'[8] This would be conducted not by the Agency established expressly for the purpose but by successful bidders in a tender exercise – or, as seemed increasingly likely, by the funding council itself.

In the precarious balance between Government, funding council, sector and agency, support for QAA came, perhaps surprisingly, not principally from the sector's representative bodies who, as we have noted, are the Agency's legal owners but from Government itself. Jo Johnson, Minister for Universities and Science from May 2015 after the Conservative victory in that year's general election, was committed to the introduction of a Teaching Excellence Framework (TEF), a purpose for quality assurance which is very far from the bare regulatory minimum approach which was on offer from the Funding Council. In an early speech to UUK,[9] the Minister made it clear that he envisaged an independent external quality body 'from within the existing landscape', as an essential part of the picture as the TEF plans moved forward. As the Government's plans unfolded through Green Paper and consultation (and ultimately through to the passing of the Higher Education and Research Act in April 2017), the contradictions between HEFCE's Quality Assessment Review and the approach of the TEF became increasingly clear, and not just to QAA. HEFCE, traditionally the provider of solutions to some of the sector's knottiest problems, seemed to some to have become instead the source of one which threatened the stability and reputation of the UK's quality assurance system.[10] In the White Paper which set out the Government's final plans for the TEF[11] the threat was explicitly recognised:

> Our higher education system is internationally renowned, something that is reflected by the high number of students who wish to come here to study. Underpinning this reputation is our system of quality assurance, both within providers and externally. The QAA has been at the heart of this, in developing many of the methods, approaches and techniques which have since been adopted across the world.[12]

And yet, the document states:

> whilst we welcome many of the principles adopted by HEFCE's recent reforms, the current legal situation is clearly one that demands reform, as the requirement to procure creates unhelpful uncertainty, and could lead to the operation of the quality system being split up between as many as six different bodies.[13]

In order to reinforce the underpinning of an independent quality agency as an essential part of the future landscape, the White Paper set out plans for the Secretary of State to designate such a body, requiring it to be separate from the Office for Students, the new body that will take over HEFCE's regulatory functions. The fact that HEFCE then went on to award four of its six QA contracts to QAA brought the latest outbreak of the 'Thirty Years' quality wars to a conclusion. Will they reoccur? Almost certainly – quality assurance will always be contested territory and arguably would not be doing its job properly if it were not.

3 Students at the heart of the system

Student engagement and the centrality of the importance of the student experience as a key, and increasingly *the* key context for and purpose of quality assurance was a dominant influence on the development of QAA from 2009 onwards. The criticisms of QAA and its approach which surfaced in the report of the Innovation, Universities, Science and Skills select committee of 2009 (and which were severe enough to lead that committee to call for QAA's immediate reform or abolition within two years),[14] essentially portrayed (unfairly) an activity which had not connected meaningfully with students and their concerns, let alone those of the wider public. Its work, so the MPs argued, was too process-focused, its reports opaque and its impact on actual student experience insufficiently powerful. This was in the context of a report which, said the committee, was unambiguously about 'student engagement and the student experience of university'. It urged a focus on the maintenance of standards, across institutions and over time, to defend the interests of students, together with a shift to serving students and the public rather than the institutions themselves.

Although the Government did not adopt the report's recommendations wholesale, they were influential in setting a new level of expectation around QAA in terms of communication, engagement and renewed relevance. The emphasis on student engagement only intensified over the years that followed. In 2009 the then Labour Government produced its higher education White Paper *Higher Ambitions*[15] which identified the need to ensure that

> students are better informed about what their higher educationn choices will involve . . . that this greater knowledge allows students to lead improvements and change in universities, by demanding better service . . . that rigorous and responsive quality assurance processes are maintained and effectively communicated, to secure student and public confidence in high quality and standards.[16]

Here were key themes which would long outlast the government that had articulated them: the importance of clear information to support student choice; the power of that choice to drive improvements in quality; and the need for quality assurance to reach out beyond the academy, speaking clearly about the quality (and the problems) it finds.

In 2010 the general election resulted in the UK's first Coalition government since the Second World War. Among the many items in its considerable in-tray was the question of the contribution that might be made by students to their tuition in the future, an issue which had been handed to Lord Browne, former CEO of BP, to review prior to the election. The Browne Report recommended the introduction of what were effectively full-cost fees, up to a maximum of GBP 9000 and, in doing so, made this claim:

> We want to put students at the heart of the system. Students are best placed to make the judgment about what they want to get from participating in higher education.[17]

So now the fact that students, at least in England, would be bringing the full tuition fee for their education to the HE institution of their choice added a powerful financial dimension to the notion of choice driving up quality. This would be of lasting significance – far more so than the report's recommendation that QAA be merged with HEFCE, the Office for Fair Access (OFFA) and the Office of the Independent Adjudicator (OIA) to create a single Higher Education Council, a proposal which was immediately dubbed the 'super-quango' and rejected by the Government.

The vision of an information-rich, choice-driven, student-centred, diverse HE market, and the role expected of a quality assurance agency in such a context, was given clearer shape by the Government's subsequent White Paper which, echoing Lord Browne's words, was called *Students at the Heart of the System*. The Government intended, it said, to:

> introduce a risk-based quality regime that focuses regulatory effort where it will have most impact and gives power to students to hold universities to account.[18]

Alongside this development at government level of a student-centric HE system – partly in response to these powerful external drivers and partly drawing on its growing experience (particularly in Scotland) of introducing significant student involvement in many aspects of its work – QAA had embarked upon its own student engagement journey.

Milestones on the journey had included the introduction of the first students on review teams in Scotland in 2003–4 where, in order to support student representatives in colleges and universities, a development body known as SPARQS (Student Participation in Quality Scotland) was created in 2003. More broadly for its work across the UK, in 2007 QAA appointed its first dedicated student engagement officer and from this start went on to develop a student engagement team as a key part of its structure.

Student engagement at QAA was focused on involving and empowering students in the process of shaping their learning experiences, and ensuring that they have the chance to make their voices heard. In its *Strategy 2011–14*, QAA committed the Agency, in the document's very first aim, to listen and respond to the student voice:

Aim 1: To meet students' needs and be valued by them

> We will work to ensure that all students get the best possible educational experience. We will support universities and colleges as they aim to meet and shape students' expectations. We will communicate clearly to students about standards and quality, and will work with them as partners. We will respond to the views and diverse needs of students, and will protect their interests.

The change in tone and priorities from previous strategic plans was striking. The Agency went on to appoint two student members of its Board of Directors and set up a separate Student Advisory Board, which was given a formal role within QAA, and was attended by the Chief Executive and members of the Agency's Board of Directors. The Student Advisory Board ensured that the student voice was heard within QAA and helped to shape its current and future work.

QAA also began the process of selecting and training student reviewers. The response was strong and the Agency soon recruited over 100 students, trained as part of its pool of reviewers. Initial concerns from some of the academics who had worked as reviewers for many years turned to enthusiasm as the quality of the new student reviewers began to make itself felt. Fears that the students might simply pursue a narrow student-focused agenda proved to be misplaced, no doubt partly because QAA had made the decision that the students should be full members of review teams, able to ask about and comment on any aspect of an institutional review. Although some voices continued to argue that the inclusion of students as members of review teams somehow compromised the principle of 'peer review', they were increasingly in the minority.[19] QAA also supported the involvement of students in other aspects of its review processes; for example, through lead student representatives ensuring the coordination of the student voice during reviews and through student submissions which form an integral part of the evidence supplied by providers in advance of a review.

The formal written student submission to the QAA review team provided an opportunity for students to describe the experience of being a student at the provider under review, and to detail how students' views were incorporated into the provider's decision-making and quality assurance processes. The student submission was given equal weighting to the documents produced by the institution during the review process.

QAA also worked hard to expand and improve its communications channels to meet the changing preferences of students, adopting a range of channels and social media networks. In 2013, QAA funded two research grants for research into student engagement across the sector. The first, with King's College Learning Institute in London,[20] focused on student perceptions of quality and standards across around sixteen institutional sites. The second, with the University of Bath,[21] examined student engagement practices at higher providers across the four nations of the UK, using as a benchmark QAA's guidance on student engagement and its indicators of sound practice.

To support higher education providers in their own student engagement, in 2012 the revised *Quality Code* included for the first time a dedicated chapter on this subject, *Chapter B5: Student Engagement*.[22] The chapter focused on the participation of students in quality enhancement and quality assurance, setting out the following expectation about student engagement which higher education providers are required to meet:

> Higher education providers take deliberate steps to engage all students, individually and collectively, as partners in the assurance and enhancement of their educational experience.

4 Expansion, diversity and risk

The 2011 UK Government White Paper, *Students at the Heart of the System* (Department for Business, Innovation & Skills [BIS], 2011), included proposals for a move towards a more risk-based approach to the quality assurance of higher education in England. Although some commentators within the UK viewed this policy direction as radically 'new', it was in reality more evolutionary than the ensuing public debate might have suggested.

In the fifteen years prior to the publication of the White Paper, the UK had already taken a deregulatory path in relation to higher education quality assurance: from the cessation of subject review in 2001 and discipline trails in 2005, to the progressive lengthening of the cycle of review since. Nor were the 2011 proposals for a more risk-based approach entirely new either, such an approach having already been used as the basis for determining the frequency of review in Wales since 2009–10, where a shorter interval between reviews was applied to those institutions with 'limited confidence' or 'no confidence' judgements.

But there was no doubt that certain developments in HE was combining to place the idea of risk-based assurance centre stage. As the sector grew and diversified, the idea of treating all providers in exactly the same way, which had been a dominant design principle of earlier attempts to establish a framework for external quality assurance in what had been, in the late 1980s and early 1990s, still a relatively homogenous sector, seemed less and less credible.

Well-established universities that had now undergone perhaps three full cycles of external review questioned the benefit to them or to stakeholders of simply going through the full process again. Equally, it was clear that in a climate deliberately conducive to sector expansion and new providers, there would be some that would require considerably more scrutiny if the public were to be satisfied that their quality and standards were sufficiently high.

Following the 2011 Government White Paper and a subsequent technical consultation,[23] the steps to implementing a more risk-based approach moved forward with a detailed consultation with the English higher education sector in the summer of 2012, led by HEFCE. QAA acted as expert adviser to HEFCE during the development of the consultation document, entitled *A Risk-Based Approach to Quality Assurance*. The consultation opened in May and closed at the end of July 2012.

The consultation outcomes stated that, for the first time in England, emphasis would be placed on making external review proportionate to the provider's proven track record:

> We are asking the QAA to focus its efforts where they will have the most impact, by tailoring external review to suit the circumstances of individual providers (for instance, by adjusting the frequency, nature and intensity of reviews depending on the provider.[24]

The consultation had proposed new changes to the nature, frequency and intensity of QAA's engagement with providers. Any change, however, would be underpinned by three key principles: first, that a *universal* system of quality assurance would be retained for higher education providers, so that no provider would be exempt from QAA review and that this system would continue to promote enhancement (and not simply regulatory compliance), based on continuous improvement and the effective dissemination of best practice; second, that any new approach to be adopted would be robust and rigorous, enabling HEFCE to fulfil its statutory duty to assess quality in higher education providers that have access to public funding; and third, that students would continue to play a prominent role in assessing their own academic experiences.

The responses[25] showed support from the sector on a range of key issues and, in particular, for the proposal to build on the key principles mentioned above, alongside the then recently revised QAA method of Institutional Review – with its clearer judgments, focus on risk and reduced bureaucratic burden compared with previous methods – as the basis for a more risk-based approach to quality assurance.

At the beginning of 2013, QAA ran a consultation on the details of the new method and in response made some changes. These included adjusting the language used (the term 'risk' needs to be used responsibly if it is not to become a self-fulfilling prophecy) and decoupling the size of provision from the determination of the duration of the review visit. Some additional proposals, such as using international reviewers as part of review teams, were also modified in the light of responses. In making these changes, QAA remained mindful of the need to limit the burden on providers with a strong record in managing quality and standards.

It is worth noting at this point that the debate about the extent to which external quality assurance should be risk-based was, and is, not unique to the UK. Internationally the way was undoubtedly led by Australia which, in a fundamental reform to its HE QA arrangements, swept away state and territory-based regulators and the HE-led Australian Universities Quality Agency (AUQA), and by Act of Parliament[26] established a new federal agency based explicitly on the principle of a risk-based approach to QA. The new agency, the Tertiary Education Quality and Standards Agency (TEQSA) is required under the terms of the TEQSA Act to conduct its work on the basis of three regulatory principles:

regulatory necessity, proportionality and reflecting risk. TEQSA's model, which was not without challenges and difficulties in implementation, has nevertheless been very influential in discussions about the future of quality assurance in other jurisdictions. While some have questioned the possibility of ever successfully implementing a risk-based approach to QA,[27] other voices have been strong advocates of an approach which seeks to focus limited regulatory resources where they are most needed and places the avoidance of harm close to the top of the priorities for external assurance.[28]

The new QAA review method began in 2013–14. It had barely run for a year before there were, yet again, proposals to change the approach to quality assurance in England and, again, it was the language of risk-based assessment that was at the fore.

Various motives have been ascribed to the 'Quality Assessment Review' which HEFCE initiated in 2014. Was it driven by legal advice on the need to put an important service out to tender, by an instinct for organisational preservation at a time when the flow of teaching funding in England was tilting dramatically towards the student and away from HEFCE, or by a desire to push further with the reform of quality assessment in a risk-based direction? As might be expected, it was the latter rationale that featured most prominently in the extensive consultation that stretched through much of 2015. This chapter deals elsewhere with this reform as part of a wider pattern of recurrent struggle and rebalancing between the forces that impinge upon the operation of external quality assurance; here it is sufficient to note that the language of risk-based QA was adopted as a given by HEFCE, QAA itself and the Government in its Green and White Papers on HE regulation – the only debate was about the precise form such an approach should take.

5 Quality goes global

Higher education, from its origins in the city states of medieval Italy, has always been inherently international in outlook and structure. Scholars and students have always sought each other across fluctuating national boundaries, driven by the desire to seek out the best teachers or the most knowledgeable subject specialists and researchers around the globe. But in the modern period, and particularly since the advent of various forms of fee deregulation and the emergence of English as the premier language of academic instruction and dialogue in much of the world beyond the historically Anglophone countries, international higher education has become a vital part, not only of the financial plans of individual institutions, but of the economies of entire countries (education is now, for example, Australia's third largest export industry). So what are the next significant areas for innovation in higher education quality assurance?

Sometimes the structures around HE take time to catch up with the reality on the ground. Sometimes solutions which work well in one place don't readily transfer elsewhere (for example, one can count on the fingers of not much more than one hand the number of countries that have chosen to manage university admissions through a central national agency in the form of the UK's Universities and Colleges Admissions Service). However, quality assurance may be the exception for it is now the case that there are very few countries which do not have, or are not shortly seeking to establish, an external quality assurance agency. Moreover, this development is in some cases well-established now over a number of years and, indeed, decades. And with the widespread emergence of national agencies has come the growth of regional and even global structures, bringing agencies together in representative or peak bodies. INQAAHE (the International Network for Quality Assurance Agencies in Higher Education) is currently celebrating its 25th anniversary. With over

200 member agencies, it complements globally the numerous groupings that have been established at the regional level: ENQA (the European Association for Quality Assurance in Higher Education), APQN (the Asia Pacific Quality Network), ANQAHE (the Arab Network for Quality Assurance in Higher Education), AfriQAN (the African Quality Assurance Network) and, in the US, CHEA (the Council for Higher Education Accreditation).

Of course, these associations often began, as all such groupings do, in order to foster the sharing of information and expertise, the facilitation of networking and, frankly, moral support (regulators can often feel rather misunderstood and unloved!) But as the internationalisation of HE has developed beyond the movement of students or the travels of academics to embrace the transnational delivery of provision in partnerships which span continents, so the structures of quality assurance have sought to provide supporting frameworks of trust, partnership and in some cases mutual recognition.

QAA has been involved in such endeavours since the beginning. Its position as one of the first agencies to be established, its role within the large and internationally successful UK HE system and its contributions at personal and an agency level to the development of the theory and practice of quality assurance have combined to provide QAA with an influential voice in quality assurance's international organisations. QAA was a founder member of ENQA and Peter Williams served as its President. His successor has served on the boards of ENQA, INQAAHE and CHEA's International Quality Group. Over recent years QAA has built up a network of agreements with agencies in China, Singapore, Malaysia, South Africa, Dubai and Australia.

But what is the purpose of all this international activity? It cannot – and must not – be mainly about the agencies themselves, which exist to serve and support students and providers. The real reason is that such cooperation helps to address some of the major challenges presented by transnational HE. Those challenges include the overlap, and occasionally even clash, of different jurisdictions; the burden on providers of having to meet two sets of regulatory expectations; the difficulty of establishing 'equivalence' across what may be very different social and cultural contexts; and the logistical and resource challenges faced by agencies in trying to provide meaningful 'on the ground' assessment in countries across the globe.

For QAA this has meant not only the development of agreements for data, information and even staff sharing referred to above but also approaches such a site review of UK provision in China which it conducted in partnership with the China Academic Degrees and Graduate Education Development Centre (CDGDC) in 2011–2012[29] and the review of provision in Dubai which was completed with the active involvement of the Knowledge and Human Development Authority (KHDA) in 2014.[30]

But the international groupings have a still wider significance, as we see in various parts of the world attempts to draw together statements of principles and quality frameworks which can claim supra-national legitimacy. QAA, for example, has ensured not only that the UK Quality Code meets the needs of its domestic stakeholders but also that it is compliant with the expectations of the European Standards and Guidelines for Quality Assurance (ESG[31]). This in turn enables the UK to meet its obligations under the Bologna Treaty that created the European Higher Education Area.[32]

INQAAHE has established the Guidelines for Good Practice (GGP)[33] and reviews agencies, on a voluntary basis, to see if they meet its expectations. CHEA's International Quality Group has recently promulgated its International Quality Principles, to which it invites agencies around the world to sign up and the intention of which is to 'develop a common understanding of quality by creating a framework that can be used at national, regional and international levels'.[34]

When the next edition of this book is published, will we be describing agencies that are no longer bound to single national jurisdictions, working within frameworks of standards and qualifications that are certainly regional and possibly global?

6 Conclusions

So as we step back and survey the battlefields of the Quality Wars, what conclusions may be drawn by the observer, participant or even the HE administrator tasked with the establishment or improvement of a quality assurance agency? The international perspective with which this chapter concluded is a good vantage point and one which, as the head, successively, of agencies in two countries, I find particularly helpful.

There is no doubt that the international spread of external quality assurance and its strong cross-border structures have supported the exchange of ideas, solutions, strategies and tactics. The development of Australia's TEQSA, as the first national agency to be established explicitly as the expression of a risk-based approach, has been, and continues to be, highly influential. This was certainly the case in the reforms of QAA's approach to assurance described in this chapter and, as quality assurance in England moves to a new phase with the establishment of the Office for Students, a risk-based approach remains central to efforts to manage regulatory resource, concentrate attention where it is most needed and provide assurance that the burden of regulation will be proportionate to need and no greater than necessity demands.

A risk-based approach is by no means the only influential or important strand in the architecture built by the TEQSA Act. The combination of a clear statutory basis for regulation combined with operational independence for the regulatory agency is an effective balance of the various stakeholder interests described earlier in this chapter, and is supported by the scaffolding provided by the Higher Education Standards Framework[35] and the Australian Qualifications Framework (AQF).[36] Risk analysis itself has led to a strong shift in focus from process issues to measurable outcomes, answering one of the recurrent criticisms of 'traditional' quality assurance.

The increasingly strong centrality of the student interest, and indeed the direct involvement of students at every level from institutional quality committees, through review panels, up to agency board, was one of the most significant, encouraging and fruitful developments in the UK's approach to quality assurance during my time at QAA. It is, and deserves to be, influential and indeed inspirational. For all quality assurance agencies, the question of how one integrates such 'student-centricness' at the heart of the theory and practices of external QA is the pressing question of this stage of its development.

Notes

1 Watson, D., *Quality Matters, A QAA Briefing Paper*, Gloucester: Quality Assurance Agency December 2006.
2 The most comprehensive history of the origins and development of HEQC and then QAA is given in Brown, R., *Quality Assurance in Higher Education: the UK Experience since 1992*, RoutledgeFalmer, 2004.
3 Williams, P., QAA Review: Let's avoid another 'quality war', *Times Higher Education*, 16 October 2014.
4 Headed by Peter Williams, who in 2002 became the second Chief Executive of QAA.
5 An account of the work and history of the CVCP AAU may be found in Williams, P., ch 10 of *Quality Assurance in Higher Education*, ed. Alma Craft, pp. 145–164, The Falmer Press, 1992.

 6 *Report of the Panel Appointed to Undertake a Review of the UK QAA for the Purposes of Renewal of Full Membership of ENQA*, 2 July 2013, pp. 48–49, www.enqa.eu/we-content/uploads/2014/01/QAA-review-report-FIN2.pdf
 7 An account of this episode may be found in the article 'Subject to Interference', Donald MacLeod, *The Guardian*, 23 August, 2001.
 8 King, R., HEPI Report No 81, *Response to the Higher Education Green Paper*, January 2016, p. 42.
 9 'Teaching at the Heart of the System', speech by Jo Johnson MP, Minister of State for Universities and Science, to UUK, 1 July 2015.
10 See, for example, 'A tale of two quality systems?', Mark Leach, WonkHE.com, 29 June 2015, in which the author suggested that 'the danger now is that there are two competing quality narratives emerging – one led by the government and the other by HEFCE'. John Morgan, in the *Times Higher Education* of 16 May 2016, wrote a piece headed 'HE White Paper: quality plans back QAA, appear to criticise HEFCE'.
11 White Paper, *Success as a Knowledge Economy*, HMSO, 2016.
12 *Success as a Knowledge Economy*, p. 32.
13 *Success as a Knowledge Economy*, pp. 32–33.
14 Innovation, Universities, Science and Skills Committee, Eleventh Report, Students and Universities, HMSO, 2009, p. 97.
15 White Paper, *Higher Ambitions – The Future of Universities in a Knowledge Economy*, BIS, 2009.
16 *Higher Ambitions*, p. 70.
17 *Securing a Sustainable Future for Higher Education: an Independent Review of Higher Education Funding and Student Finance* ('The Browne Report'), BIS, October 2010, p. 25.
18 White Paper, *Higher Education: Students at the Heart of the System*, BIS, June 2011, p. 10.
19 For an example of this essentially nostalgic view, see C. Raban and D. Cairns in *Perspectives*, vol. 18, no. 4, 2014. In fact, the introduction of student reviewers reinvigorated a system that had been falling into disrepute.
20 Kandiko, C.B. & Mawer, M. (2013) *Student Expectations and Perceptions of Higher Education*, London: King's Learning Institute (available via the QAA website).
21 Van der Velden, G.M., Naidoo, R., Lowe, J.A., Pimentel Botas, P.C. & Pool, A.D., *Student Engagement in Learning and Teaching Quality Management*, University of Bath/QAA, 2012 (available via the QAA website).
22 *UK Quality Code*, ch B5, Student Engagement, is available via the QAA website.
23 See *Government Response to Consultation on a New Fit for Purpose Regulatory Framework for Higher Education*, BIS, June 2012.
24 *A Risk-Based Approach to Quality Assurance: Outcomes of Consultation and Next Steps*, HEFCE, October 2012/27, p. 5.
25 As above; see p. 4 for a summary of key themes in the responses.
26 The TEQSA Act 2011, Compilation No. 9, December 2015.
27 See for example Professor Roger King's article for the Higher Education Policy Institute (HEPI) on 'The risks of risk-based regulation: the regulatory challenges of the higher education White Paper for England', HEPI, 2014/02.
28 The work of Professor Malcom Sparrow at Harvard's Kennedy School of Government has been particularly influential on the thinking and practice of a number of regulatory bodies. See, for example, *The Character of Harms: Operational Challenges in Control* (CUP, 2008).
29 *Review of UK Transnational Education in China 2012*, QAA (via website).
30 *Review of UK Transnational Education in United Arab Emirates*, 2014, QAA (via website).
31 *Standards and Guidelines for Quality Assurance in the European Higher Education Area* (ESG 2015) via enqa.eu.
32 A description of the Bologna Process and the building of the EHEA may be found at ehea.info.
33 INQAAHE's *Guidelines of Good Practice* may be found via inqaahe.org.
34 INQAAHE's *Guidelines of Good Practice* may be found via inqaahe.org.
35 *Higher Education Standards Framework (Threshold Standards) 2015*, Commonwealth of Australia, Federal Register of Legislation, F2015L01639
36 The Australian Qualifications Framework may be found at www.aqf.edu.au.

3 Learning and Teaching Developments Across UK Higher Education

Craig Mahoney and Helena Lim

Introduction

The starting points for this chapter are two paradoxes identified by Ellis (1993) in *Quality Assurance for University Teaching*:

> First, and most important, there is no generally accepted science or technology addressing the relationship between teaching and learning. But there is no point in teaching unless someone learns from it. Such knowledge as there is of the effectiveness of various teaching styles . . . is not widespread among lecturers in universities.
>
> A second problem is the ambiguous professional status of university lecturers. While they spend a large, often the largest, proportion of their time teaching, their professional status and credibility derives not from this central activity but from their knowledge of their subject and their capacity to extend that knowledge. Uniquely among so-called professions, there is no formal requirement of training to be a [university] teacher. Trained teachers are a minority in universities and the recent translation of polytechnics will not affect this proportion dramatically. It is assumed, therefore, that knowledge of the subject and research capability coupled with on-the-job practice and experience are sufficient to ensure professional standards of teaching.

So we begin the story with these paradoxes for HE learning and teaching at the end of the 20th century. It was a point in HE evolution and development that whilst there was an unprecedented rise in the number of individuals accessing higher learning, there were no generally agreed standards for higher teaching. Ellis (1993) identified that in spite of an extensive literature on university teaching, very few teachers actually concerned themselves with it. He goes on to say that 'the teachers themselves are not trained and there is a pervasive culture which believes that training is, at best, a diversion from more significant activities'.

A key moment in time: The Dearing Report

There has been a great expansion in HE in the UK in the last 25 years. This has happened alongside a succession of public policy reviews that have created important structural and funding changes in the HE sector.

One of the most significant of these for the development of learning and teaching was the Dearing Report published in 1997. Formally known as the reports of the National Committee of Inquiry into Higher Education but named after its principal author, Sir Ronald Dearing, then Chancellor at the University of Nottingham, this report was submitted to the Secretaries of State for Education and Employment in England, Northern Ireland, Scotland

and Wales in July 1997. It was commissioned by the UK Government to look into how the 'the purposes, shape, structure, size and funding of higher education, including support for students, should develop to meet the needs of the United Kingdom over the next 20 years, recognising that higher education embraces teaching, learning, scholarship and research' (1997). Dearing's vision was that higher education should contribute to the development of a learning society. The Report made five recommendations that directly related to enhancing learning and teaching in the HE sector:

> Recommendation 8: We recommend that, with immediate effect, all institutions of higher education give high priority to developing and implementing learning and teaching strategies which focus on the promotion of students' learning.
>
> Recommendation 9: We recommend that all institutions should, over the medium term, review the changing role of staff as a result of Communications and Information Technology, and ensure that staff and students receive appropriate training and support to enable them to realise its full potential.
>
> Recommendation 13: We recommend that institutions of higher education begin immediately to develop or seek access to programmes for teacher training of their staff, if they do not have them, and that all institutions seek national accreditation of such programmes from the Institute for Learning and Teaching in Higher Education.
>
> Recommendation 14: We recommend that the representative bodies, in consultation with the Funding Bodies, should immediately establish a professional Institute for Learning and Teaching in Higher Education. The functions of the Institute would be to accredit programmes of training for higher education teachers; to commission research and development in learning and teaching practices; and to stimulate innovation.
>
> Recommendation 15: We recommend that the Institute should:
>
> - develop, over the medium term, a system of kite-marking to identify good computer-based learning materials;
> - co-ordinate the national development, over the medium and long term, of computer-based learning materials, and manage initiatives to develop such materials;
> - facilitate discussion between all relevant interest groups on promoting the development of computer-based materials to provide common units or modules, particularly for the early undergraduate years.

The Dearing Report was a seminal point in UK higher education history. This was the first time the Government had charged higher education institutions (HEIs) with taking a strategic approach to learning and teaching. As Laurillard (2007) succinctly puts it, the 'five recommendations were a strong message to the sector: the quality of learning and teaching must be the focus of individual professionalism, institutional strategy, and national policy'. Hence, the ambitious recommendations in Dearing form the start of this account on learning and teaching developments in UK HE.

Responses to Dearing

In response to Dearing that learning and teaching should have a higher profile in the strategic planning of HEIs, HEFCE launched 'Teaching Quality Enhancement' funding (TQEF) in 1999. It is worth noting that TQEF did not apply in Scotland and Wales. TQEF funding supported learning and teaching development across the English HE sector at three levels: institutional, sector-wide and individual. HEIs would receive TQEF on submitting to HEFCE a

Learning and Teaching Strategy which addressed strategic planning for teaching excellence, research and innovation in learning, teaching and technology. Institution-level TQEF was done by formula, based on student numbers and provided support for the implementation of institutional learning, teaching and assessment strategies. TQEF was used by HEIs to recruit new staff to support developments, for short-term projects, and to establish teaching awards.

Centres for Excellence in Teaching and Learning (CETLs)

There was also selective TQEF investment in 74 Centres for Excellence in Teaching and Learning (CETLs) in 2005. CETLs were based in 73 HEIs – 69 English HEIs and all four HEIs in Northern Ireland. Each Centre was based in a consortium of HEIs and focused on one pedagogic or subject-based theme, for instance, blended learning, assessment, leadership, etc. Funding for CETLs ceased in 2009/10. In the HEFCE and Department of Employment and Learning (DEL)-commissioned summative evaluation of the CETL programme (2011), the authors found:

> The activities and outputs of CETLs were diverse and included: the development of new curriculum content; diagnostic and evaluative tools and toolkits; support materials for staff; new e-Learning and communication systems designed to exploit the potential of Web 2.0; piloting of new approaches to teaching and learning (e.g. use of peer tutoring, active and inter-active learning approaches); research projects and peer-reviewed publications; events, including internal development activities and wider dissemination seminars and conferences.

Institute of Learning and Teaching in Higher Education (ILTHE)

At the sector-wide level, TQEF was used to establish the Institute of Learning and Teaching in Higher Education (ILTHE) in 1999, in response to recommendation 14 in the Dearing Report which called for a national body for learning and teaching. At the time of it establishment, the ILTHE's stated aims were to:

- accredit programmes of learning in higher education,
- commission research and development in learning and teaching practices,
- stimulate innovation (HEFCE, 2003).

The ILTHE was the professional body for all who taught and supported learning in HE. It provided HEIs with the means to help their staff achieve accredited fellowship with its national benchmark for teaching quality. By January 2003, the ILTHE had over 14,000 individual members and had accredited 133 programmes of staff development at 107 HE institutions (HEFCE, 2003).

Learning and Teaching Subject Network (LTSN)

In the same year, the Learning and Teaching Subject Network (LTSN) was also established to provide subject-level support for teaching innovation through 24 Subject Centres based in 21 HEIs and a generic centre which was co-located with the ILTHE in York:

> The centres are setting up networks of practitioners to enable individuals to share and develop their practice. Some will organise demonstration events. The subject centres

are brokers, not centres of excellence. They will provide a comprehensive and coordinated service to departments, course leaders and departmental learning and teaching committees rather than a piecemeal collection of information.

As many learning and teaching issues and practices are common to all subjects, an institution-wide approach is required. This is the remit of the LTSN generic centre, which opens this month.

This, the first of its kind, will offer a national support service. All disciplines will naturally assert that they are different and unique, but the generic centre will try to cross subject boundaries, for example, in approaches to assessment, key skills and problem-based learning. It offers a way to avoid reinventing the wheel.

(Allan, 2000)

National Teaching Fellowship Scheme (NTFS)

At the individual level, the National Teaching Fellowship Scheme (NTFS) was set up in 2000 to recognise and reward academic staff who demonstrated excellence in learning and teaching in HE in England and Northern Ireland, and since 2011, Wales. The NTFS is a competitive process with rigorous criteria for outstanding teaching at departmental level or for institutional and/or cross-institutional contributions with significant impact on student learning. At the outset, individual awards of £50,000 were made to winners. This was reduced to £10,000 in 2006. In the 2016 round, a new Collaborative Awards for Teaching Excellence (CATE) is being piloted. To date, there are nearly 700 NTFs with their own Association for National Teaching Fellows (ANTF), who work closely with the HEA individually and as a collective to further enhance learning and teaching together.

Teaching and Learning Research Programme (TLRP)

In 2000, the research and development in learning and teaching requirement in Dearing received a boost with the Teaching and Learning Research Programme (TLRP). Set up under ESRC, this programme provided substantial research funding for all education sectors, and resulted in 14 projects across HE addressing a wide range of challenges linked to learning and teaching, such as problem-based learning, social diversity and universal access.

The second phase of the Teaching and Learning Research Programme (TLRP) focused on Technology Enhanced Learning (TEL). This TLRP-TEL programme was co-funded by the Economic and Social Research Council (ESRC) and the Engineering and Physical Sciences Research Council (EPSRC). The £12 million programme ran from 2007 to 2012 and supported eight large interdisciplinary projects across the UK focusing on how technology could be used to improve learner outcomes.

At its inception in 2007, Laurilliard stated that TLRP-TEL provided 'a significant opportunity to build research excellence in a field that has received little targeted research funding to help the HE sector'. Richard Noss, Director of TLRP-TEL made the following observations on the potential afforded by TEL, opportunities he felt that UK academics, policymakers and practitioners could afford to ignore:

The potential for learning is clear when we consider the technologies that are present in homes and in people's pockets. But there is little sign that this kind of technology is being adequately exploited for teaching and learning . . .

Education at all levels needs technology that is designed for learning and teaching, not the leftovers of systems designed for quite other purposes. Without it, our schools will languish, locked in an analogue mind-set while the rest of society goes digital. Our economy, our children – indeed all of us – will be the losers.

(TEL, 2012)

The Higher Education Academy (HEA)

In 2003, the English White Paper, *The Future of Higher Education* (DfES), provided substantial public investment to encourage good teaching practice and to reward those who are excellent in teaching. This was reflected in HEFCE's Strategic Plan for the period between 2003 and 2008 which endorses the recognition of excellent teaching and learning as a key element of HE, alongside research:

> Learning and teaching are at the heart of higher education. They are a core activity for all HEIs, and feature strongly in public perceptions of the sector's role and achievements. We welcome the proposals in chapter 4 of the HE White Paper to drive up quality in learning ad teaching, through action to support, promote and reward excellent practice and to inform student choice. We endorse the aim to improve the status and recognition of excellent teaching and learning as a key element in the mission of HE, alongside research. Institutions face the challenge and the opportunity to develop innovative approaches to learning that meet the changing needs of learners and society.
>
> (HEFCE, 2003)

Within the HEFCE Strategic Plan was the target to establish a 'new Academy to support quality enhancement in learning and teaching will be set up by the end of 2004 and its impact reviewed by 2008' (HEFCE, 2003). Earlier in January 2003, the Teaching Quality Enhancement Committee (TQEC) established by the HEFCE, Universities UK (UUK) and the Standing Conference of Principals (SCOP) to review the arrangements for supporting the enhancement of quality in learning and teaching in higher education proposed the creation of a single, central body to support the enhancement of learning and teaching in HE. The new body, provisionally called the Academy for the Advancement of Learning and Teaching in Higher Education at the time of the report, is now known as the Higher Education Academy (HEA). It was formed with the amalgamation of the ILTHE, the LTSN and the National Coordination Team for TQEF into a single organisation consisting of 25 sites distributed throughout the UK: a head office in York and 24 subject centres HEIs. Primarily funded by the four UK funding bodies, with subscriptions from HEIs, the HEA was established in May 2004 to:

- advise on policies and practices that impact on the student experience;
- support curriculum and pedagogic development;
- facilitate development and increase the professional standing of all staff in higher education (HEFCE, 2009).

National Student Survey (NSS)

Another significant development that was to follow was the introduction of the National Student Survey (NSS) in 2005. The NSS is an annual survey of final-year undergraduate students' opinions on the quality of their courses. The survey runs across all publicly funded higher education institutions in England and is available to those in Wales, Northern Ireland and Scotland, as well as further education colleges in England and further education institutions (FEIs) in Wales. Not without its critics, particularly in the early days, it is now generally seen as a useful benchmark to track the success of the sector in responding to the needs of its learners:

> The results are used by senior management teams, academics, students' unions and others to drive improvements in curriculum, teaching and learning quality, learning resources and academic support.
>
> Overall satisfaction levels among students have increased steadily, and satisfaction with assessment and feedback, identified in early surveys as a major concern, has improved markedly.

(HEFCE, 2016)

Joint Information Systems Committee (JISC) and e-learning

The kite-marking of ICT materials in recommendation 15 of Dearing was quickly abandoned as unworkable. Laurillard (2007) observed that while it was a great idea for 'a good solution to the problem of quality', the problem arose when the question of 'who decides' is addressed.

The other proposals in recommendation 15 came to fruition when the Joint Information Systems Committee (JISC) brought aspects of learning and teaching within its remit, and set up its e-learning programme in 2003 to enable 'the development and effective use of digital technologies to support learning and teaching in universities and colleges, so that staff be aided to develop e-learning materials and students could gain benefit and enjoy a more flexible learning experience' (JISC, 2014). Since that date, JISC has supported a number of programmes in the areas including assessment, learner experience, learning and teaching practice, learning environments and mobile learning. However, rather than focusing on research as envisaged by Dearing, the JISC programmes focused on development.

Developments in devolved administrations

HE teaching is a devolved responsibility in Scotland, Wales and Northern Ireland and most decisions are made by each devolved administrations although they also participate on a UK-wide basis, for instance in the NSS or the Research Excellence Framework. The drive to enhance the quality and impact of learning and teaching across all four home nations of the UK has been mainly progressing along similar lines. However, unique to Scotland and Wales is their development of sector-wide Enhancement Themes. The smaller number of HEIs in each of these nations has made this collaborative approach more feasible, something that will be far more challenging to emulate in England.

In Scotland, the Enhancement Themes were started in 2003 and aim to enhance the student learning experience in Scottish HE by identifying specific areas, or themes, for development. Planned and directed by the Scottish Higher Education Enhancement Committee (SHEEC), the Themes encourage staff and students to share good practice and generate ideas and models for innovation in learning and teaching.

Enhancement Themes form part of the wider Scottish Quality Enhancement Framework (QEF) which consists of five inter-related aspects of managing the quality and standards of Scottish HE including Enhancement Themes; enhancement-led institutional review (ELIR); institution-led quality review; the engagement of students in quality management, including the support provided through the national independent development service, student partnerships in quality Scotland (SPARQS); and institutional provision of an agreed set of public information.

The most recent Enhancement Theme is Student Transitions and focuses on transitions into, out of and during university. Themes which have been completed to date include:

- Developing and Supporting the Curriculum (2011–14);
- Graduates for the 21st Century: Integrating the Enhancement Themes (2008–11);
- Research-Teaching Linkages: enhancing graduate attributes (2006–08);
- The First Year: Engagement and Empowerment (2005–08);
- Integrative Assessment (2005–06);
- Flexible Delivery (2004–06);
- Employability (2004–06);
- Responding to Student Needs (2003–04);
- Assessment (2003–04).

In the evaluation of the Themes, Dempsey *et al.* (2015) concluded that 'the influence of the thematic approach to enhancement is profound but mediated'. They go on to explain that national Themes are 'mediated by important key individuals within disciplines and at institutional levels . . . tasked with interpreting, reconstructing and situating nationally relevant resources to the realities and needs of individual HEIs'. In this way, while the learning and teaching agenda has been shaped by Themes, they are 'mediated and translated by organisational priorities' into 'front-line practice'. Their conclusions were similar on student involvement:

> Institutions were clear that student involvement in teaching and learning had been enriched and enhanced by the Themes, although, once again, these processes were mediated by the institutional, school/department and then course or modular interpretations. Our interpretation of this is not that this suggests a deficit but that, this set of translations is inevitable and desirable. What is important is that the processes are transparent, known and effective.
>
> (Dempsey *et al.*, 2015)

In Wales, the Future Directions programme commenced in 2009 as a response to *For Our Future: The 21st Century Higher Education Strategy and Plan for Wales* (Welsh Government, 2009). Like the Scottish Enhancement Themes, Future Directions aimed is to support the enhancement of learning and teaching through partnerships between students and staff, with the sharing of good practice and generation of new ideas and methods. Between 2010 and 2014, there were two Enhancement Themes with three work strands within each:

- Graduates for our Future (2010–13)

  - Students as Partners
  - Learning in Employment
  - Learning for Employment.

- Global Graduates: Enabling Flexible Learning (2013–14)
    - Distinctive Graduates
    - Inspiring Teaching
    - Learner Journeys

The Future Directions programme ended in March 2015 but not before having significant impact on partnership working leading to practical outcomes and a more strategic development of learning and teaching in Wales. It was formally recognised in the Welsh Government's 2013 Policy Statement on Higher Education and included within the Quality Assurance Agency (QAA) Higher Education Review Wales method. In the impact assessment of this programme, Saunders (2014) arrived at the following conclusion:

> Future Directions has achieved considerable impact at individual, institutional and sector levels. There have been beneficial outcomes through developing and disseminating learning and teaching practices for enhancing student experience, with sector bodies and Welsh Government formally recognising Future Directions achievements within policy and strategy statements and guidelines. Future Directions has earned the respect of stakeholders within the higher education sector, extending beyond Welsh borders.

Learning and teaching post-Dearing

It is nearly 20 years since the Dearing Report was published. 'Although some call it "nonsense" and a "political fix", Lord Dearing's landmark report left an enduring legacy in terms of access, quality and, of course, tuition fees . . . [it] fundamentally changed the higher education landscape' (Tysom, 2007). Post-Dearing, public policy and funding across the four home countries of the UK have continued to promote a significant increase in both national and institutional initiatives to develop and enhance the quality and impact of HE learning and teaching. The following sections will consider how these have changed university teaching and student learning.

Professionalising teaching and the leadership of teaching

To date, higher education teaching is one of the few professions left in developed economies that do not have a requirement to have any qualification or licence to practice (Mahoney, 2011). Baume (2006) has noted that university teachers are the last of the 'non-professions'. In stark contrast to elsewhere in education including non-HE areas of post-compulsory education, all teaching staff across the UK are required to be qualified (or qualifying). The UK is not unusual in reflecting this picture, but the situation is changing.

The HEA introduced the UK Professional Standards Framework for Teaching and Supporting Learning (UKPSF) in 2006. THE UKPSF provided a common framework for UK HEIs to benchmark, develop, recognise and reward teaching and learning support roles. Between 2006 and 2011, the sector increasingly engaged with the UKPSF through the accreditation of professional development programmes, and the recognition of individuals as Fellows of the HEA. Fellowships are awarded to staff who have completed accredited programmes or have demonstrable track records of experience that can be mapped to the UKPSF.

In November 2011, the HEA published the revised UK Professional Standards Framework (UKPSF) which recognised the increasing range of teaching and learning support responsibilities undertaken by staff in HE. The revised UKPSF introduced two new categories of Fellowship: Senior Fellow and Principal Fellow. Senior and Principal Fellowships are normally awarded to experienced staff who are able to demonstrate impact and influence in leading and managing learning and teaching contexts. Additionally, Principal Fellows also need to demonstrate sustained and effective records of impact at a strategic level in relation to learning and teaching. According to the HEA website, there are now over 75,000 individuals who are Associate Fellows, Fellows, Senior Fellows and Principal Fellows of the HEA (note there are 181,000 academics teaching in UK higher education according to HESA). In July 2014, there were 134 HEIs with HEA accredited programmes to support the professional development and recognition of staff (HEA, 2014). In an HEA-commissioned investigation, Turner *et al.* (2013) concluded:

> the impact of the UKPSF on the UK HE sector has been significant in most institutions and for many individual teaching staff. Institutions have reported utilising the framework in a myriad of ways including to underpin initial and continuing professional development, to influence learning and teaching strategies, to act as a national benchmark, to provide an aspiration for staff, to underpin promotion and probation policies, and to change the language of learning and teaching.

Concomitant to this development has been the increasing professionalisation of the leadership of learning and teaching in HE. As the late David Watson observed in his reflections of his own teaching journey:

> Academic leadership and management is a necessary (but of course not sufficient) condition of effective learning and teaching, especially in the complex relationships that characterise higher education.
>
> (Watson, quoted in Brown, 2011)

As the momentum for HEIs to strategically manage learning and teaching has picked up pace, so has the increase in professional institutional leadership roles in this area. At the executive level, most, if not all, UK HEIs have a senior colleague, typically, Pro Vice-Chancellors or Deputy Vice-Chancellors, overseeing the learning and teaching portfolio. They will often be responsible for leading strategic thinking around learning and teaching at their institutions including the development and delivery of institutional learning and teaching strategies and meeting associated Key Performance Indicators. At mid-management level, there have also been new positions and roles variously titled Directors or Heads of Learning and Teaching, often based in central learning enhancement units, and Associate or Assistant Deans of Learning and Teaching.

> Within the UK there has been rising activity in promoting and delivering [learning] and teaching development strategies especially since 2003. Gibbs estimates that this area of work, which involved only around 30 active academics, mostly part-time, in the UK in the 1970s, now involves thousands of academic development personnel and substantial institutional investments.
>
> (Parsons *et al.*, 2012)

This growing cadre of staff lead, support and promote the learning and teaching agenda, champion ongoing innovation, all 'while simultaneously endeavouring to enable and support a growing minority of enthusiastic innovators, attempting to persuade the cynical spectators and seeking to neutralise the spoilers/obstructionists' (Kift, 2007). The institutional leadership of learning and teaching requires a 'variety of levels of engagement and influence' and management 'upwards, downwards and sideways'. The HEA and the Leadership Foundation for Higher Education (LFHE) both offer PVC and DVC network groups for senior leaders to discuss and exchange views and insights into current topics. Staff and Educational Development Association (SEDA) and Heads of Educational Development Group (HEDG) provide similar support for middle managers. Networking and support at the disciplinary level is provided for by the HEA and also professional bodies and organisations such as the British Psychological Society (BPS) and the Association for the Study of Medical Education (ASME).

From chalk to mouse: Technology-enhanced learning

Technology has also come a long way since Dearing's vision that all staff and students will be able to optimise the opportunities offered by 'Communications and Information Technology'. Picking up on development post-Dearing, major programmes like the HEFCE-funded e-Benchmarking exercise and related Pathfinder Programme (2005–08) and the Higher Education Funding Council for Wales (HEFCW)-funded Gwella, Welsh Enhancing Learning and Teaching through Technology Programme (2007–11) have built capacity within participating HEIs in terms of understanding processes, practice and provision; increased confidence and maturity in the role of TEL; and enabled the mainstreaming of TEL activities into institutional policy and practices (HEA, 2008, 2011).

In England, the HEFCE-funded project, Changing the Learning Landscape (CLL), ran between 2012 and 2014 to support HEIs in bringing about change in their strategic approaches to technology in learning and teaching. CLL engaged with 145 English HEIs within the first year of the programme through an intensive six-month programme for leaders in learning and teaching; short-term focused consultancy support for institutional teams; and continuing professional development activities and resources for academics and learning technology developers. The main impact of CLL was as an 'enabler of change'. Participating HEIs used CLL as a 'catalyst for change', or 'a starting point for new developments which might not otherwise have happened'. On the outcomes of CLL, the final report states:

> [As a result of CLL] what emerges . . . is a picture of widespread innovation beginning to happen. TEL is proving a way of addressing much broader and deeper changes in pedagogy, curriculum, physical infrastructure and, in some cases, what it actually means to be a student or a teacher in a digital environment.
>
> (LFHE, 2015)

Most HEIs in the UK now make use of technology to support learning, teaching and the student experience. This often includes using virtual learning environments (VLEs) as repositories for course outlines, reading lists and study material and in the case of more progressive HEIs, using VLEs interactively to enable a blended learning experience comprising classroom contact, tutorial support, peer-assisted learning and on-line support.

Student voice/student choice

In the past two decades, increasing emphasis has also been placed on the 'student voice', that is, listening and responding to the values, opinions, perspectives and backgrounds of students. The NSS has been running since 2005; the HEPI-HEA Student Academic Experience Survey since 2006. The QAA has included students as members of institutional audit and review teams since 2009. Student involvement in institutional structures and systems, such as student–staff liaison committees, 'once highlighted as good practice in Subject review and Institutional audit, is now routine' (Kay *et al.*, 2010). National policies such as the Welsh Government's *For Our Future* have also recognised the importance of strengthening the student voice in higher education provision to ensure that students are more than just passive consumers of learning.

The introduction of tuition fees in the UK since 1998 has also had an impact on student expectations, particularly English-domiciled students who were required to pay up to £1,000 a year for tuition in England. From 2006, HEIs in England could charge variable fees up to £3,000 a year. In 2010, following the Independent Review of Higher Education Funding and Student Finance – the Browne Review – this cap was raised to £9,000 a year.

In the 2011, the Higher Education White Paper *Students at the Heart of the System* (BIS, 2011) argued that with prospective students facing higher direct costs than ever before, HEIs were obliged to be more responsive to student choice and demand:

> the increase in tuition fees for English students will mean that the sector will need to focus more than ever on ensuring educational quality. Students, quite rightly, demand value for money, and institutions will have to concentrate on further establishing their effectiveness in order to justify higher fees – the quality of learning and teaching will be key.
>
> (Mahoney, quoted in Parsons *et al.*, 2012)

Different fees arrangements have evolved in the devolved national administrations of Scotland, Wales and Northern Ireland. However, in all three cases, regardless of the funding regime, many of the pressures regarding perceptions of quality and value for money are shared and greater weight has been given to the concepts of student voice and student choice.

Key Information Sets (KIS)

In 2011, HEFCE, Universities UK and GuildHE undertook a consultation on information HEIs are required to publish about their courses. Following the consultation, the Key Information Set (KIS) was developed to give prospective students access to high quality information about different courses and institutions, and thus enabling more informed choices. HEIs were required to gather data for publication from September 2012 and the KIS dataset is updated at least annually. The data is published through the Unistats website where prospective students can search for and compare data and information about HE courses across the UK. The rationale is that better informed students will drive teaching excellence by taking 'their custom to the places offering good value for money . . . We expect our reforms to restore teaching to its proper position, at the centre of every higher education institution's mission' (BIS, 2011).

What is this thing called 'teaching quality'?

As HEIs face more informed choices by prospective students, 'teaching quality emerges as a discriminator for many institutions' (Parsons *et al.*, 2012). The discourse around teaching quality has been at the forefront of UK HE policy. The introduction of fees and subsequent increases in fees in English HE has also focused the attention of prospective students, parents, employers and taxpayers on the quality of the teaching. In the foreword to the Green Paper *Fulfilling Our Potential: Teaching Excellence, Social Mobility and Student Choice* (2015), Jo Johnson, the Minister for Universities and Science made this emphatic point:

> For too long, teaching has been regarded as a poor cousin to academic research. The new Teaching Excellence Framework, which we promised in our manifesto, will hardwire incentives for excellent teaching and give students much more information both about the type of teaching they can expect and their likely career paths after graduation.

Teaching Excellence Framework (TEF)

It is no surprise that in the 2016 White Paper, *Success as a Knowledge Economy: Teaching Excellence, Social Mobility and Student Choice* (BIS, 2016), the Government has announced the introduction of the Teaching Excellence Framework (TEF). It is designed to incentivise excellence and innovation in higher education teaching by introducing a teaching quality assessment mechanism focused on three core metrics: student satisfaction scores (NSS), graduate outcome data (Destination of Leavers from Higher Education – DLHE), and continuation rates and other metrics yet to be developed. It will also draw on qualitative institutional narratives and expert judgements. The TEF will be linked to tuition fees in England. HEIs will need to meet basic standards in 2017/18 and 2018/19 in order to make inflation increases in tuition fees. HEIs taking part in the full TEF will be divided into three tiers after being assessed: meets expectations, excellent, and outstanding. From 2019/20, HEIs who meet expectations will be allowed to increase their fees at a rate equivalent to 50 per cent of inflation; while those in the top two categories will be eligible for a full inflationary rise. If an HEI's TEF level drops, they will be required to lower the fees they charge, including for existing students. At the moment of writing this chapter, HEIs in Scotland, Wales and Northern Ireland can choose to participate in the first year but participation in future years of TEF remains to be decided by the devolved administrations.

The introduction of the TEF is a significant step in the development of learning and teaching in UK HE as the Government is taking on 'the challenge of measuring teaching quality head on so that students can be served better in the future' (BIS, 2016). For the first time, the funding of teaching in HE will be linked to quality and not quantity – a principle that has long been established for research. In terms of the parameters of what constitutes teaching excellence, the 2016 White Paper offers the following:

> We take a broad view of teaching excellence, including the teaching itself, the learning environments in which it takes place, and the outcomes it delivers. We expect higher education to deliver well-designed courses, robust standards, and support for students, career readiness and an environment that develops the 'soft skills' that employers consistently say they need. These include capacity for critical thinking, analysis and teamwork, along with the vital development of a student's ability to learn.
>
> (BIS, 2016)

The Office for Students (OfS)

The 2016 White Paper (England), *Success as a Knowledge Economy*, also set out plans for the creation of the Office for Students (OfS) that will operate 'on behalf of students and tax payers to support a competitive environment and promote choice, quality and value for money. In doing so we will put students at the heart of how higher education is regulated' (BIS, 2016). This new public body will be a new market regulator for the English HE sector and combine some existing functions of HEFCE and the Office for Fair Access (OFFA).

Concluding remarks: Where next?

In 1993, Lewis Elton stated that what the HE sector needed in the few years leading up to the millennium was the following:

> A rapid increase towards the professionalisation of university teaching;
> The establishment of total quality management (TQM) practices at all levels of each university;
> Increasing recognition and resourcing of teaching and rewards for excellence in it.

He recognised that the concept of TQM would need not only total commitment to quality internally within an organisation but also 'some external pressure to ensure the continuation of this commitment':

> In the commercial market, the external pressure . . . is provided by the customers, who may have a choice between different producers who supply goods and services, and who also have means of redress if they are not satisfied.

With the benefit of hindsight, we can speculate if Elton had access to a functioning crystal ball when he was writing. The last 20 or so years have seen the gradual professionalisation of university teaching with an associated increase in the recognition and rewards for excellence. The more strategic management of learning and teaching and its associated KPIs have created more of a TQM culture within HEIs, even if this is at time met with resistance or cynicism. The external pressures have been provided by the introduction of fees and a more marketised HE market, the consequent drive for more and better information for all stakeholders including NSS, KIS and now, the TEF. The HEA has also played a key role as an influencer and driver of change within HEIs. As the champion for teaching excellence, teaching innovation and the professionalisation of teaching, its most notable successes have been the professionalisation of individual teachers; the development of the UKPSF and its associated accreditation and recognition services; and supporting HEIs in developing this within their own organisation. What the UK HE sector has achieved in partnership with the HEA in the professionalisation of teaching has been internationally recognised. The 2013 European Commission report, Improving the Quality of Teaching and Learning in Europe's Higher Education Institutions, recognised that many of the report's recommendations for the European Union have 'already been implemented in the UK and championed by the HEA'. The report goes on to recommend that the European Union should support the establishment of a European Academy for Teaching and Learning (Middlehurst, 2014).

However, the HEA has undergone significant financial challenges in recent years and its future is uncertain. As a result of all the UK funding bodies reducing their core funding by around 30 per cent in 2009, the HEA undertook substantial organisational change, the most significant of these being the replacement of the 24 Subject Centres based in HEIs with Discipline Leads, subject specialists directly employed by or seconded to the HEA. In 2014, the HEA received another blow, when the funding councils decided to withdraw its central funding worth £13.5 million that year. The HEA's funding council grants were cut by £4 million in 2014–15, reduced by another £4 million in 2015–16 and with no further funding from 2016–17. When the funding cuts were announced, the HEA underwent another round of organisational shake-up, reducing its staff base from 180 to around 100. It also accelerated its efforts to be self-sustainable and sought new income streams including offering its services internationally. However the Universities UK review of the agency network in 2016 led to the conclusion that the HEA, LFHE and the Equality Challenge Unit (ECU) should be merged to form a new composite agency with a clarity of purpose yet to be determined and a name still to be decided. A new Board for the merged bodies is to be established from September 2017 with the new agency to be operational by September 2018 (UUK, 2017). Middlehurst (2014) has observed, 'It is both ironic and galling . . . that just at a time when other countries are raising the game and increasing their focus on the quality of teaching and learning, the UK appears to be pulling out from its national-level commitment.'

It is difficult to predict what the next 25, 30 or even 50 years will bring for learning and teaching in UK HE, but current trends would indicate that change will be a constant, particularly in the climate of a reducing public purse. It will be a time of both challenges and opportunities for UK HE. Diversification in the range of providers; the approaches and technologies in the delivery of HE; intensifying global competition; the changing nature of underlying assumptions in the role of universities and its relationship with students and other stakeholder will lead to such profound changes that the very HE system itself will be disrupted.

New technologies and new approaches to learning will provide new opportunities for the way teaching is delivered and how learning occurs, for instance through distance education, online learning, blended learning and open education resources (OER) including Massive Open Online Courses (MOOCs). While traditional, campus-based delivery is still the norm, current pedagogical approaches and models will become outmoded very quickly due to huge advances in technology and a new generation of tech-savvy learners with different expectations. The advent of smartphones, tablets and other forms of technology mean that learners expect more flexible ways of learning, more connected and mobile learning opportunities and for learning that goes beyond the traditional transmission of information. With the explosion of information available online, many HEIs have seen decreasing footfall in their libraries. In a Guardian Higher Education Network discussion on the future of learning and teaching in HE in 2012, one contributor speculated that:

> the traditional university campus could be 'in the minority' as little as 10 years from now. Another predicted a 'Yo Sushi' [conveyor-belt sushi restaurant chain] style approach to HE, where students pick up degree modules from different courses and institutions, combining face-to-face learning with online tutorials and lectures.
>
> (Murray, 2012)

There are already moves, particularly in the private HE sector, to customise the learning experience to suit different individual learning styles. In the coming years and decades, UK HEIs and supporting HE agencies will need to be flexible and re-imagine the HE offer. Gallagher and Garrett (2013) argue that 'the current trajectory of ever bigger campus-based universities relying on large lectures as the core mechanism for teaching students, and increasing tuition fees to cover ever higher fixed costs including research' will be rendered obsolete (quoted in ITaLI, 2015).

Teaching and learning will need to evolve and adapt to new pedagogical models of place, pace and mode of learning. Practitioners will need to think beyond traditional models just to keep apace, and ideally continually refresh their skills. For instance, academics need the knowledge and skills to employ the appropriate pedagogical approaches to effectively support an online learning environment.

As the public funding reduces for HE across all four home nations of the UK, HEIs will need to continue to develop the culture of professionalism in teaching with or without the support of external agencies like the HEA. Commentators such as founding HEA Chief Executive Paul Ramsden (2014) has gone as far as to suggest that the time has passed for the sector to need an HEA:

> Higher education institutions have come a long way since 2004 in improving the quality of their students' experiences and engagement. Australia abolished its equivalent organisation a couple of years ago. The British version provides services, knowledge and expertise that institutions think are important. However, these valued functions could be delivered by opening up the remaining market for specialist support services to a range of providers. A small office attached to the funding councils could support competitive tendering by firms and universities for projects. The day of a central, taxpayer-funded body to support the enhancement of teaching in higher education may well be over.

It is too early to comment on the continuing existence of the HEA, particularly in its new guise in a new, merged body but, hopefully, the momentum for change has been sufficiently successfully embedded within institutional cultures in order to respond to the changing configuration, demands and needs of the HE system. Policy drivers for teaching quality, stakeholder expectations of value for money, the increasingly globalised HE market and the changing needs of learners will continue to drive the transformational journey of learning and teaching. HE is being disrupted and must continually rethink how it delivers learning and teaching if it hopes to thrive in the future. Standing still is not an option.

References

Allan, C. 'How to . . . spread the word on best practice', *Times Higher Education*, 13 October 2000. Accessed on 4 October 2016 at https://www.timeshighereducation.com/news/how-to-spread-the-word-on-best-practice/153788.article

Baume, D. (2006) 'Towards the end of the last non-professions?' International Journal for Academic Development 11(1), May 2006, 57–60.

BIS (2010) *Securing a Sustainable Future for Higher Education: An Independent Review of Higher Education Funding and Student Finance – The Browne Report.* London: HMSO.

BIS (2011) *Students at the Heart of the System.* London: HMSO.

BIS (2015) *Fulfilling our Potential: Teaching Excellence, Social Mobility and Student Choice.* London: HMSO.

BIS (2016) *Success as a Knowledge Economy: Teaching Excellence, Social Mobility and Student Choice.* London: HMSO.

Brown, T., Ed. (2011) *Ten Years of National Teaching Fellowships: Four Stories from Education.* Bristol: Escalate.

Dearing, R. (1997) *Higher Education in the Learning Society. The Report of the National Committee of Inquiry into Higher Education – The Dearing Report.* London: HMSO.

Dempsey, S., Saunders, M. and Daglish, S. (2015) *Evaluation of the Enhancement Themes 2014: Final Report.* Glasgow: QAA.

DfES (2003) *The Future of Higher Education.* Accessed on 31 December 2017 at http://www.educationengland.org.uk/documents/pdfs/2003-white-paper-higher-ed.pdf

Ellis, R., Ed. (1993) *Quality Assurance for University Teaching.* Buckingham: SRHE/Open University Press.

HEA (2008) *Challenges and Realisations from the Higher Education Academy/JISC Benchmarking and Pathfinder Programme: An end of programme review by the Higher Education Academy, Evaluation and Dissemination Support Team.* York: HEA.

HEA (2011) *Enhancing Learning and Teaching through Technology in Wales: Gwella Programme final report.* York: HEA.

HEA (2014) *Institutional Approaches to HEA Accreditation.* York: HEA.

HEFCE (2003) New body proposed to enhance learning and teaching in higher education. Press release issued by the: Higher Education Funding Council for England, Standing Conference of Principals, Universities UK, Higher Education Staff Development Agency, Institute of Learning and Teaching in Higher Education, Learning and Teaching Support Network. Accessed on 4 October at http://webarchive.nationalarchives.gov.uk/20100202100434/http://hefce.ac.uk/news/hefce/2003/tqec.htm

HEFCE (2009) *The Higher Education Academy.* Accessed on 4 October 2016 at http://webarchive.nationalarchives.gov.uk/20100202100434/http://hefce.ac.uk/learning/heacademy/intro.asp

HEFCE (2011) *Summative evaluation of the CETL programme: Final report by SQW to HEFCE and DEL.* Accessed on 31 December 2017 at
https://aces.shu.ac.uk/employability/resources/cetl_evaluation.pdf

HEFCE (2016) *National Student Survey.* Accessed on 4 October 2016 at http://www.hefce.ac.uk/lt/nss/

ITaLI (2015) *Future Trends in Teaching and Learning in Higher Education.* Brisbane: University of Queensland. Accessed on 4 October 2016 at http://itali.uq.edu.au/filething/get/5325/Future_trends_in_teaching_and_learning_in_higher_education_Nov_2015.pdf

JISC (2014) *e-Learning Programme.* Accessed on 4 October 2016 at http://webarchive.nationalarchives.gov.uk/20140702233839/http://www.jisc.ac.uk/whatwedo/programmes/elearning.aspx

Kay, J., Dunne, E. and Hutchison, J. (2010) *Rethinking the Values of Higher Education – Students as Change Agents.* Gloucester: QAA.

Kift, S. (2007) 'An assistant dean, learning and teaching's role in quality assuring assessment' in Frankland, S., Ed. (2007) *Enhancing Teaching and Learning through Assessment.* The Netherlands: Springer.

Laurillard, D. (2007) *The Dearing Report: Ten years on* - Learning and Teaching in Higher Education Paper presented at The Dearing Report: Ten years on conference, Institute of London, London, 25 July 2007.

LFHE (2015) *Changing the Learning Landscape: Connect to the Future.* London: LFHE.

Mahoney, C. (2011) 'How to drive quality teaching'. In *Blues Skies: New Thinking about the Future of Higher Education.* Pearson. Accessed on 11 October 2016 at http://pearsonblueskies.com/2011/how-to-drive-quality-teaching/

Middlehurst, R. (2014) 'Quality enhancement at a crossroads'. WONKHE, 1 July 2014. Accessed on 14 August 2017 at http://wonkhe.com/blogs/quality-enhancement-at-a-crossroads/

Murray, J. 'The future of learning and teaching in higher education.' The Guardian Higher Education Network, 17 April 2012. Accessed on 4 October 2016 at https://www.theguardian.com/higher-education-network/higher-education-network-blog/2012/apr/17/guardian-roundtable-higher-education-academy

Parsons, D., Hill, I., Holland, J. and Willis, D. (2012) *Impact of Teaching Development Programs in Higher Education.* York: HEA.

Ramsden, P. (2014) 'Do we need a Higher Education Academy?' Paul Ramsden Blog, 15 July 2014. Accessed on 14 August 2017 at ps://paulramsden48.wordpress.com/2014/07/25/do-we-need-a-higher-education-academy/

Saunders, D. (2014) *The Future Directions Programme for Higher Education in Wales: Impact assessment report for the Higher Education Academy.* York: HEA.

TEL (2012) *System Upgrade – Realising the Vision for UK Education: A report from the ESRC/EPSRC Technology-Enhanced Learning Research Programme.* Director: Richard Noss, London Knowledge Lab. London: IOE. Accessed on 4 October 2016 at http://tel.ioe.ac.uk/wp-content/uploads/2012/06/TELreport.pdf

Turner, N., Oliver, M., McKenna, C., Hughes, J., Smith, H., Deepwell, F. and Shrives, L. (2013) *Measuring the Impact of the UK Professional Standards Framework for Teaching and Supporting Learning (UKPSF).* York: HEA.

Tysom, T. (2007) 'Dearing still shapes the agenda HE set.' *Times Higher Education*, 27 July 2007. Accessed on 4 October 2016 at https://www.timeshighereducation.com/news/dearing-still-shapes-the-agenda-he-set/209757.article

Universities UK (2017) 'Review recommends changes to higher education sector agencies.' UUK News and Blog, 31 January 2017. Accessed on 14 August 2017 at http://www.universitiesuk.ac.uk/news/Pages/Review-recommends-changes-to-higher-education-sector-agencies.aspx

Welsh Government (2009) *For Our Future: the 21st Century Higher Education Strategy and Plan for Wales.* Accessed on 31 December 2017 at http://gov.wales/docs/dcells/publications/091214hestrategyen.pdf

Welsh Government (2013) *Policy Statement on Higher Education.* Accessed on 10 October 2016 at http://gov.wales/docs/dcells/publications/130611-statement-en.pdf

4 A British Standard for University Teaching?

Roger Ellis

Introduction

I wrote a version of this chapter in 1993 when it seemed distinctly possible that a number of universities would follow the example of Wolverhampton University which used BS 5750 to develop its aspirations for a system of Total Quality Management. In fact this didn't happen for a variety of reasons so this new chapter has no expectations that universities will decide to apply for BS 5750 or its successor BS EN 9001. However I do still believe that the questions raised by a quality management standard can be useful to a university in devising its own systems. In that spirit this chapter still considers how the requirements of such a standard might be applied.

At one time the idea of a British Standard for university teaching would have been dismissed as an extreme case of Jarrett's disease or a reject from the jottings of Laurie Taylor. But now there is a Quality Assurance Agency dedicated to ensuring that universities have quality assurance mechanisms in place. In education generally the rhetoric of equality has yielded to that of quality. So there is some point in looking at quality assurance in general and codifications of best industrial practice in particular. University teachers should get a grip on quality assurance before it gets a grip on them.

I must admit to some responsibility for all this. I suggested (Ellis 1988) that there might be merit in applying quality assurance techniques from manufacturing and service industries to education. I had managed to convince myself and at least five co-authors that there were common issues and problems across service industry, health care, social services and education. In particular there was the central and crucial question of what professionals did and how their behaviour, once we knew what it was, related to outcomes and satisfaction.

My argument in essence was this. It is important to be able to specify standards for products, whether these be material objects or services, and to be able to manage the production process to ensure that these standards are met. In the case of service industries, health care and education, the product and the production line are based largely on the actions of qualified professionals. Yet the behaviour, whether effective or not, of professionals is largely hidden from objective scrutiny. A crucial step in quality assurance would therefore be to make more explicit the actions of professionals and to study their cost-effectiveness in relation to outcomes. Given the importance of professional motivation I commended an approach that would involve them in specifying their standards, in describing and evaluating their actions and in improving the service they offered.

Having advocated this approach I am nevertheless feeling as much apprehension as approbation at the speed with which first the CNAA then the HEQC and now QAA have adopted at least the language of quality assurance. At worst, quality assurance could become

another stick to beat the professional back. We cannot afford another initiative that alien-
ates teachers. I say this not out of any desire to sustain professional power for its own sake
but in simple recognition that there can be no progress in education at any level without
the whole-hearted support of teachers. Education as a product is essentially what teachers
do. One vital lesson we can learn from quality in industry and health care is that assurance
requires a commitment to quality throughout the organization and works best when all play
their part. In the current jargon there must be perceived ownership of quality assurance by
teachers. This is not to say, however, that they should be the sole judges of quality. Their
involvement is in satisfying the consumer and their responsibility is to consumers at several
levels, starting with students but including industry, government and, if this is not too
nebulous, society as a whole. Furthermore, quality assurance does require management and
organization, and ownership includes recognizing responsibilities and divisions of labour
within the system.

In this chapter I want to look at what quality assurance means in industry, with a view to
identifying its essential features. During this review I want to consider how these features
might translate to university teaching if it is conceived as a product or service.

As a preliminary it is important to stress that there is no single set of principles and procedures that constitutes the industrial approach to quality assurance. Rather there are a number of approaches and techniques whose common ground is a commitment to quality and its
assurance. We should therefore select from this patchwork those techniques and procedures
that seem to fit our objectives and mission. There may also be some features of university
teaching and its approach to quality that might with profit transfer to health and industry.

Quality assurance

What does quality assurance mean? Quality is one of those interesting words that has both a
neutral and positive interpretation. In a neutral sense quality refers to the standard achieved.
It is thus acceptable to talk of poor as well as good quality. On the other hand, the label
'quality' is usually associated with high standards and so-called quality goods are assumed
to be the best available. Whether employed neutrally or positively, quality carries with it the
notion of standards that must be met. Assurance then adds the notion that these standards
can be ensured or guaranteed. Thus quality assurance is the process whereby standards are
specified for a product or service and steps are taken to ensure that these standards are consistently met.

In industry, quality effectively means giving satisfaction to a customer. This requires a
partnership between customers and supplier to ensure that the needs of the customer are
adequately defined and that the supplier designs and produces a product or service that can
meet these needs. In this sense the ultimate test of the quality of a product is whether anyone wants to buy it. The market serves to validate fitness for purpose. The object of quality
assurance is thus to ensure that the product consistently achieves customer satisfaction. The
British Standards Institute defines quality as 'the totality of features or characteristics of a
product or service that bear on its ability to satisfy a given need'.

This emphasis on consumer satisfaction is crucial and is a useful touchstone when quality
assurance is complicated and obscured by its application to that elusive service called education. Obviously the producer is the originator of quality but his standards have to be tested
out against a consumer, at least when a market is in operation. Many contracts are set as a
negotiation between supplier and customer to agree standards. Quality assurance is then
concerned with ensuring that these agreed standards are met consistently. But in education,

where a straightforward market is less likely, standards may remain the prerogative of the producer: teachers, like doctors, know best. For much professional activity the producer plays the role of consumer in judging the quality of his actions. The external examiner system is an extension of this.

Of course, consumption is more complicated than a simple individual consumer and his satisfaction. My consumption of a Balkan Sobrani or a Maserati involves secondary consumers of the products of combustion: every individual act has a multiplicity of consequences, many of which may operate to the longer-term disadvantage of the initially satisfied consumer. No doubt the ideal green consumer has a complex view of needs and satisfaction that goes beyond his immediate gratification.

Quality assurance and teaching

Education certainly has a number of consumers beyond the individual student. There is the potential employer of the student, and the society that may benefit from his skills. There are the short-term monitors of the teacher, including her head of department, external examiner and colleagues. There is the critical self-monitoring that characterizes professional action (or so we are told). Without becoming too metaphysical, the student may be conceived as a multiplicity of consumers stretching into the future: the product may not appeal to him today but eventually he will see the point of it. Despite all this there is value in recognizing the student as a consumer here and now, and one who is unlikely to operate in a market with purchasing power and for whom, therefore, special steps must be taken. It is not so much that the student as consumer determines what is of quality in knowledge but that he or she should be the judge of quality in teaching methods.

While quality assurance is not just about consumer satisfaction, meeting the needs of consumers is central and vital. It is therefore worth looking at seven steps followed in manufacturing industry to assure quality. They include:

1   Knowing the customers' needs.
2   Designing a product or service to meet the needs.
3   Guaranteeing the performance of the product.
4   Providing clear instructions for the use of the product.
5   Delivering the product punctually.
6   Providing a back-up service for the product.
7   Using customer feedback to improve the product.

How would a typical university programme, course or unit measure up to these requirements? Remember we are not trying to reinvent the substance of a discipline or field of study, but to determine the best way or ways for a student to learn it as a result of our actions as teachers. Pedagogy is the product.

What do we know of our students' needs? How do we find out? To what extent have the course as a whole and the individual teaching sessions in it been designed to meet these needs? To what extent can we guarantee that doing the things we prescribe, including attending our lectures and undertaking the assignments we set, will guarantee learning? Do we provide clear instructions to help students make the best use of the course? Do we deliver the product, including, for example, not only our direct teaching but feedback on assignments, punctually? Do we provide a back-up service if the planned features of the course are not achieving the learning objectives anticipated? Do we make use of student feedback to improve the course?

So quality is about satisfying the consumer. But assurance implies that quality can be maintained consistently unit after unit. Standards must be met not just in the handmade prototype but also in the everyday production run. At this point it is worth making the distinction between quality control and quality assurance. Quality control means checking a particular product against standards and rejecting any products that do not measure up to these standards. This is, of course, a necessary step but could prove impossibly expensive if most of the products have to be rejected. Quality assurance is about attending to all features of production in such a way as to minimize the number of rejects necessary at the final stage of quality control. Thus quality control is about the product, whereas quality assurance is concerned with the whole process of production. Quality assurance is about managing the entire process of design and production to minimize rejection by quality control.

We now have several key terms. One is product; another is consumer and another satisfaction. Then we have quality; standards; control and assurance. The potential for confusion of these in their application to education is considerable. First the product: is it the actions of the teacher, the actions of the students in response to the teacher, the learning achieved by the students, the students at the end of their course, the course document or the written materials distributed during a course? All of these can properly be considered products with consumers. For the purposes of this exercise I would suggest that we concentrate on the teacher's behaviour and call this the product. This would include: teachers' plans, including course documents, syllabuses, schemes of work and lesson notes; teachers' behaviour, including lecturing, chairing or leading seminars, supervising, tutoring; products generated by the teacher for consumption by students, including blackboard work, transparencies, slides, posters, handouts, workbooks; and materials produced by the teachers for assessment and feedback, including course work and examination questions, and written feedback on performance. This collection of actions and artifacts constitutes the product of which students are consumers. Consumption of these products is intended to produce a result desired by the student, and as consumer he or she will be more or less satisfied with these products.

Quality is the general term for a set of standards for these products. Thus the judgements that are made to differentiate a good example from a bad example would have to be specified as standards. Ideally these should be measurable but at the least they should be amenable to reliable identification by informed judges. Quality control would then be a process whereby products were tested and rejected if they fell below the standards. Quality assurance, on the other hand, would be concerned with controlling the entire process that led to the products. It would be intended to guarantee as far as possible that the products were not rejected at the quality control stage.

A simple example might be a PowerPoint slide produced as a visual aid for a statistics lecture. Standards could be specified regarding the overall dimensions of the slide, the size of numerals, colour contrasts and perhaps the optimum or maximum amount of information that should be included. A slide produced for the lecture could be rejected if it failed to meet these standards and this would be quality control. However, the whole production sequence for the item could be analysed and standards specified for it with a view to ensuring that few, if any, slides would be rejected at the quality control stage. Even such an apparently uncontroversial item might pose problems, first in agreeing standards and subsequently in controlling production. More complex teaching products would be considerably more problematic. But standard setting and quality control are essential elements in the quality assurance approach. In the production of the PowerPoint slide the attitudes and skills of the teacher are crucial. So quality assurance immediately raises questions about the selection, training, monitoring and development of teachers.

In manufacturing industry, the specification of standards for material objects and quality control at the end of the production line are well established and indeed essential. Quality assurance as set out, for example, in BS 5750 and BS EN 9001 is a detailed description of the steps that must be taken to achieve quality assurance. In broad terms this requires an analysis of the production line in terms of input, process, output and outcome. The input is the resources required for the manufacturing process, the process is the transformation of those raw materials into the product, the output is the number of products produced and the outcome is the detailed characteristics of these products and their effects on the consumer. Quality assurance is about identifying and specifying the standards that must obtain for each part of this model and then further specifying procedures that must be followed to ensure that standards are met, problems are identified and solved, and the system maintains quality in the end product. This in its turn requires the establishment of checking procedures, documentation and job descriptions for key operatives. Further along the line it raises questions about the competencies of operatives and the training procedures necessary to ensure, maintain and develop those competencies.

For a manufacturing firm to be certified as meeting a standard a comprehensive audit is undertaken to make sure these various procedures are in place and can be guaranteed to remain in place. There are several key assumptions underpinning this approach. First, and obviously, it is assumed that these various procedures are related to the input and process and that they thus have a direct bearing on the output and outcome. Furthermore, a level of knowledge must exist to allow there to be a confidence regarding the cause and effect relationship between one activity and another. In manufacturing industry, where the primary area of knowledge is derived from the science and technology of materials, this is a reasonable assumption. However, as soon as the human operative is taken into account scientific laws and associated technologies are harder to come by. When the process is primarily interpersonal, albeit mediated through materials, the task is infinitely more complex.

BS 5750

Returning to industry, what was BS 5750? In 1982 a White Paper, *Standards Quality and International Competitiveness*, was issued which identified four broad areas in which the government could help to increase the efficiency of industry and commerce by promoting the importance of quality and encouraging the use of standards. First was the encouragement of independent certification schemes for products, including the development of national accreditation marks and the launching of a quality awareness campaign. BS 5750 was a kind of meta-accreditation against which firms are assessed to determine whether they have an adequate quality assurance scheme in operation and are thus able to manage consistent and consumer-satisfying quality. Second was closer cooperation between government and the British Standards Institution (BSI) to develop relevant and up-to-date standards that could form the basis of public purchasing specifications and be used by British industry to enhance its position in domestic and world markets. Third was a greater commitment by government to adapt these standards into statutory rules and regulations. Fourth was a greater effort by public purchasers to examine how far products built to existing standards could fulfill their requirements as effectively as their own specifications.

There is an important distinction to be made here between standards for a product and standards for the management of design and production. The BSI approach is to specify standards for a whole range of products, from petrol to electric blankets. Coupled with each of these standards, for a particular firm, is the standard for quality management, BS 5750. Thus if I were going into business to produce electric fires and I wished to gain BSI approval, I would have to pass two tests, first that my product met the appropriate standard for electric fires and second that my management of design and production met BS 5750. One problem with applying BS 5750 to education is that there is no product or service standard that covers teaching. Thus institutions are being judged for design and production alone. However, this is not totally inappropriate since BS 5750 requires procedures to be followed to identify consumers' needs and gauge their satisfaction with the product or service in question.

BS 5750 was the most common general quality assurance standard in the United Kingdom and came in booklet form in five parts. Part 0 was concerned with principal concepts and applications and comes in two sections, the first of which is a guide to selection and use, and the second of which is a guide to quality management and quality system elements. Part I was a specification for design and development, including production, installation and servicing. Part 2 was a specification for production and installation. Part 3 was a specification for final inspection and test. Part 4 was described as a guide to the use of BS 5750 and is divided into three parts: first, a specification for design and development; second, a specification for production and installation; third, a specification for final inspection and test. This is not the most user-friendly publication. While Parts 0 and 4 are intended as guides to the central material in Parts 1, 2 and 3, they are not that intelligible in themselves.

BS 5750 has now been replaced by BS EN ISO 9001 which was intended to be more user friendly for service industries. In my view this simplification has lost too much useful detail. For this chapter I am using BS 5750 because I believe it to be more thought-provoking for universities. Since I believe it is highly unlikely that any university would be applying to be registered as having met the standard I feel justified in using the more complex standard.

Further publications that sketch in important background include BS 4R9l, which is a guide to quality assurance, and BS 4778, which covers quality vocabulary (or perhaps more accurately the vocabulary of quality). It is not easy to identify the essence of all this nor for that matter to trace the exact steps that must be followed. It is not surprising that a whole industry of quality consultants and a range of government assistance schemes have grown up to help companies along the path of virtue. However, it is in my view worth the effort since there are key procedures that have demonstrated their effectiveness in industry and could be applied in universities. (Interestingly, the embryonic Academic Audit Unit gave up the struggle and turned instead to the Reynolds report.)

Having been daunted by the sheer opacity of BS 5750 I turned to the British Standards Institute for help. This proved a fascinating inquiry. The apparent irrelevance of BS 5750 for service industry is recognized and attributed to three main factors. First, is its origins in military procurement: the standard was produced as a procurement aid to NATO to ensure that suppliers of expensive military hardware kept to specification. Thus its language is oriented towards large-scale hardware rather than services. Second, the standard was produced by an international committee to satisfy the member nations of NATO and is thus couched in a kind of 'Euroese' which stems from a succession of transliterations. Finally, the standard is concerned primarily with ensuring that a number of management techniques should be in place and can often seem at several removes from specific problems.

I learned that there has been widespread interest in the applicability of BS 5750 to services in two senses. First, there is an interest in extending the approach from material products to services provided to consumers. Second, there is a recognition that in any manufacturing organization many of the activities are services rather than direct manufacture. Within a factory the majority of activity is a series of human services to ensure that the production line is operating. Further, the manufacturer offers not only a product but a service to the purchaser, including delivery and maintenance.

So it was recognized that a new standard may be required to cover service. A draft standard 90/97100 was prepared for public comment and some sections of BS 5750 had been rewritten with a view to making them more intelligible to service industry, health and even education. (Interestingly, there is no record of HEFCE or the CVCP contacting BSI, so maybe they gave up more quickly than I did.) QAA has, I am told, considered joint working with BSI but decided against it as being overly bureaucratic. This, to my mind, in no way reduces the value of applying the standard theoretically to stimulate thought about university processes.

Armed with all this I felt that the most useful thing I could do for this chapter was to concentrate on those parts of BS 5750 which had been revised in a service direction. In particular I concentrated on Part 4, which is described as dealing 'with products and services and attempting to redress some of the unintended residual ambiguities of BS 5750'.

First, it is useful to remind ourselves what BS 5750 is trying to do. It is to help an organization to ensure that the way it is managed will guarantee that its products will consistently be up to standard. It is expected that potential purchasers should make two judgements: first, whether the product is what they want; second, whether the manufacturer can consistently produce to that standard. These are, as any purchaser of a British car in the 1960s would testify, quite different issues. Brilliant design in, for example, the Mini, the Triumph Herald and the Rover 2000 were regularly let down by poor management of consistent quality.

Part 4 identifies, somewhat dauntingly, twenty elements of a quality assurance system:

- Management responsibility;
- Quality system;
- Contract review;
- Design control;
- Document control;
- Purchasing;
- Purchaser-supplied product;
- Product identification and traceability;
- Process control;
- Inspection and testing;
- Inspection, measuring and test equipment;
- Inspection and test status;
- Control of non-conforming product;
- Corrective action;
- Handling, storage, packaging and delivery;
- Quality records;
- Internal quality audits;
- Training;
- Servicing;
- Statistical techniques.

Each of these is given an explanatory paragraph. The provenance of the list in the procurement of machinery is obvious but several of the elements translate to university teaching without any difficulty. Others appear at first sight to be quite inappropriate. There are some that can be applied but more metaphorically than literally, and their vocabulary can be off-putting.

Two preliminary points are worth making before a translation is attempted. First, quality assurance should not be conceived as a disciplinary measure being applied to one part of an organization by another. Specifically it is not 'management' keeping an unruly and incompetent workforce in line. Quality is in everybody's interest since it makes for a successful organization. This applies as much to a university as to a manufacturing company. Second, quality is about the entire organization and thus applies as much to those parts which service the producers as to the direct producers. In university terms this means that quality assurance applies as much to central services as to the faculties and the teachers who are in the front line. Standards and quality assurance are every bit as important for staffing and finance departments as course teams.

The first element, *management responsibility*, includes responsibility for a clearly articulated quality policy, including a mission statement, objectives and a commitment to standards in a recorded statement. This statement should be published throughout the organization and be seen to be supported by management. All employees throughout the organization should be able to understand, or should be trained to be able to understand, these objectives and the commitment required by them to achieve these objectives. Universities have a head-start in this collective understanding of objectives through the collegial system, but efforts must be made to ensure that this embraces all employees. Management is responsible for ensuring that new employees are trained. It is considered important that customers should be aware that the organization has this training policy. In university terms there would be value in our customers, whether they be students consuming our teaching or employers consuming our qualified students, knowing of the university's commitment to quality and training.

Second, management must ensure that there is a clearly understood and effective *structure of responsibility and authority* to achieve the policy objectives. In particular it is stressed that the personnel having the responsibility and authority to control the key elements in the quality system and processes should be identified, and the job requirements should be defined. Of these key elements emphasis is laid on: the prevention of quality deficiencies as defined by explicit standards; the control of corrective action systems to prevent recurrence of quality deficiencies; control to ensure that corrective actions are effective; and, finally, ensuring that the quality system is regularly reviewed to keep it relevant to the organization's objectives. So a key role for responsible individuals is to monitor output against agreed standards, pick up any shortfall, find out why there is this shortfall and do something about it. Whatever system is used to do this should itself be subject to regular review. If our product is, in part at least, face-to-face teaching, how might these ideas apply? There is an assumption, not always made explicit, that lecturers do have standards for their teaching, that they monitor their performance against these standards and take corrective action if they are falling short. But as a university can we be sure of this? Have we actually documented what these standards are? Are there any persons in the organization, other than the teachers themselves, who can claim to fulfill the functions set out in this element? Without this can we claim to ourselves or the QAA that we have a quality assurance system?

This leads on to the next management responsibility, which is for *verification* and the resources and personnel needed to achieve this. Verification is the systematic inspection, checking and testing of products or outputs of all departments to ensure that they are meeting standards, and the testing of the satisfaction of consumers with these products and services. Consumers in this sense include both the customers of the organization and the customers within the organization. It is stressed that reviews and quality audits need to be performed by persons independent of those producing the particular output under review. So management (including the collective if that is the style) must ensure that there are verification or quality control procedures for all identified products and services and that these are conducted by persons other than those who directly produce or provide.

In this section on management responsibilities it is suggested that within the organization there must be a representative who is responsible for the quality system. This might be the sole responsibility of this person or there might be other functions that he or she has to perform. If there are other functions then there must be no conflict of interest.

Finally, management is responsible for a review of the quality system, including two activities: a regular review of documented policies and procedures that define the system, and a review of internal audit results.

This first element addressing the responsibilities of management touches on most of the crucial elements in quality assurance, which are then spelled out in greater detail in the remaining nineteen elements. The notion that quality assurance must be managed is a crucial one for universities but should not be confused with questions of the provenance and tenure of the managers. Whoever assumes these responsibilities will have to address the issue of managing an essentially private and autonomous activity, university teaching, together with support activities that are more obviously amenable to industrial practices, for example estates and purchasing. Whoever performs them and however the control and verification of teaching is tackled, the key elements are the definition of a quality policy, the identification of responsibility and authority for its implementation, the verification of activities against agreed standards and the separation of the reviewers from the reviewed.

The second element is described as the *quality system* and elaborates the detail of the organization required to achieve the objectives set out as management responsibilities. The idea of the system is that it should at every stage ensure that it meets agreed customer requirements. Standards should be arrived at as either an anticipatory or a negotiated response to customer need. This quality system should have two interrelated aspects: (a) the supplier's needs and interests; (b) the customer's needs and expectations. This is a crucial point since it balances the meeting of customers' needs with the necessity to do this in the most economical way. Customers' needs must be met by the planned and efficient utilization of the technological, human and material resources available to the organization. The customer needs assurance and confidence that the supplier has the ability to provide the product or service consistently to the defined quality. As already stated, she makes two judgments: first, does she like the product and, second, does she trust the supplier to produce it?

As part of this quality system it is suggested that a *quality plan*, which identifies the key elements in a product or service and the means by which they are provided and verified, and a quality manual, which brings all documentation together, would be valuable.

The next element is described as *contract review*. This assumes that at some point a contract will be drawn up between the supplier and the customer and that this will be reviewed through the following steps. Requirements should be clearly understood and agreed by both parties and properly recorded. Both parties should go through a defined process to ensure that they have the necessary resources, organization and facilities to fulfill all the requirements of the contract.

This is an interesting way of looking at the student–lecturer relationship and suggests that a more explicit analysis of what both are expected to bring to the teaching–learning relationship might be of value. This is not the same as, but is related to, the contract that the student has with the university. Certainly the contract with the university is cast in the broadest terms and falls far short of the kind of detail anticipated here; at present the contract with the lecturer is likely to be implicit and half understood, with the exception of certain areas of work and no doubt individuals whose disposition is to be more forthright.

The next element, *design control*, emphasizes the importance of taking the customer's needs and translating these in a systematic and controlled way into a specification that defines a product or service. This specification should be such that the product is producible, verifiable and controllable in the operating environment available. The organizational structure, responsibility and authority during the management of design should be clearly defined.

The standard then goes on to spell out in detail the characteristics that should be aimed for in a good design specification and the procedures that should be followed to ensure that it meets customer requirements and that: it is consistent with available resources. While this section is obviously written with the design of a product in mind, it does raise interesting questions about the kind of course plans with which most of us are familiar or becoming familiar. The kind of discipline that must attend a plan which is to be translated into a functioning and economical production line is easily lost in a plan for a series of teaching sessions and subsequent unobservable learning activities. Furthermore, there is rarely an initial contract with a customer to refer to, or the expectation of regular verification of the details of the plan.

Within a university course, documents are one kind of design plan. Departments of the university that serve internal customers also need to design the service they will provide, and in their case the customers are easier to consult. For both groups the key quality activities identified in the standard are:

1   The design specification should comply with the agreed customer requirements and should contain all the necessary information from which a design can be created.
2   The specification should take into account all the problems identified in a full assessment of any hazards associated with the product and include statutory regulations relating to its use, including, for example, safety, environmental issues and liability.
3   During the process of design, acceptance criteria for its required performance should be continually evaluated and means for verification should be provided.
4   Changes in design should be anticipated and carefully evaluated against the original contract, fitness for purpose and amenability to verification.

The next element is *document control*, which emphasizes the importance of a formal and defined system indicating the format of documentation, who produces it, how and by whom it is reviewed and approved and the method of its review and updating. It is stressed that the key to effective quality documentation is to ensure that it is brief while covering the essential points. It is essential that the documented procedures reflect the actual working practices and needs of the organization. The implications of this for course documents are obvious.

The next element covers *purchasing* and the procurement of materials or external services, whether for inclusion in the product or service or to contribute to the quality system. Again, emphasis is placed on ensuring that the materials or services meet an appropriate standard, with the implication that standards will have been specified and verification procedures established. This element also emphasizes the importance of subcontractors being assessed to ensure that they are capable of supplying materials or services of a consistent quality.

The next element, *purchaser-supplied product*, covers those situations where the purchaser provides elements that are then built in to the product supplied. At first, it is difficult to see any direct relevance here to higher education. However, it could be taken as pointing to the key part active involvement by the learner plays in effective teaching. It does point out that the responsibility for non-conforming parts supplied by the customer rests with the customer!

The eighth standard, described as *product identification* and *traceability*, identifies the importance of being able to trace back from a problem to its cause at an earlier point in the production process. This is described as fundamental to the achievement of good quality in a service or product. Product identification refers to the importance of discriminating clearly between products that may appear the same but where there are crucial differences. Specific reference is made to the transfer of responsibility from component parts to personnel when the root cause of a problem is being identified. The basic point here is that when problems arise, presumably in products or services not meeting an agreed standard, it should be possible to trace back to the root cause in order that remedial action might be taken. This root cause is likely to have both human and material elements even in manufacturing industry. In service industry and education, personnel issues will be paramount.

The ninth element is central to quality assurance as opposed to quality control and concerns *process control*. Whether the process is concerned with manufacturing a product or performing a service, it is necessary to specify standards and process limits for each stage leading to the product or service. The features that closely affect the quality of the product or service should be identified from the quality plan where this exists. The standard emphasizes that written procedures or work instructions at each stage of the process should be employed as useful tools for the successful control of the enterprise. It is suggested that inadequate or non-existent work instructions may be a frequent cause of poor quality performance. The standard goes on to detail the precise specifications and control that are necessary for the materials used at each stage of the production process. Traceability and identification apply, of course, throughout the process. The standard refers to special processes where control is particularly important to quality.

Again, this standard has obviously been written with material products in mind. A brief sentence at the end suggests that the performance of services may require planned control during execution and that consideration may have to be given to the levels of skill required and to process checks. University teaching does involve the provision of material products of various kinds to students and here the standard is of direct relevance. Clearly teaching requires skilled performance, whether this is learned on the job, trained for, or, as some seem to assume, innate or a necessary consequence of subject knowledge. What is interesting is the extent to which standards have been specified and verification and control introduced for this service. If shortfalls can be identified, can they then be traced back to their root cause? Can improvements then be implemented and the problem eliminated?

The next element addresses *inspection and testing*. Three phases are identified in which inspection, verification or testing may take place. The first is on receipt of any purchased or subcontracted items or services. The second is during the manufacturing or service preparation stage. The third is prior to final release to the customer. Presumably in the case of a service there could also be checks during the actual service delivery. Records of all checks should be kept in order to aid traceability. Again the message, as in so many of these elements, is that they could be applied exactly as stated to material features of teaching. In the case of the behaviour of the teacher careful, and sensitive, translation would be necessary and the role of the teacher in self-monitoring should be balanced against the need for independent assessment.

The eleventh element covers the *specialist measuring and test equipment* that might be required and the need to control and calibrate that equipment. It is pointed out that the control of measurement consistency must apply to more intangible quality testing measures, such as questionnaires used to gauge customer satisfaction. In effect this element is concerned with the reliability and validity of, and testing procedures used during, the quality assurance process.

Element 12 covers the *inspection and test status* of products and services at all times during the design to delivery stage. The idea is that it should be clearly planned and documented when a product or service is to be inspected and hence there should be no doubt as to its status at particular times in relation to that system. It is not difficult to see the relevance of this consideration to, for example, the status of a syllabus in the validation procedures of a university.

Element 13 deals with what are described as *non-conforming products*, that is, suspect or defective items or aspects of a service. Methods are required to prevent further processing, installation or delivery of such items. This element has been written with clear reference to material objects but in principle applies to any element in a service or the process of production for a service where the element is identified as failing to meet a standard.

It is emphasized that once a non-conforming item is identified this identification should stay in place until some documented action is taken. This action might include scrapping or aborting the item, using it under concession from an appropriate authority, reworking it or repairing it. Repaired or reworked items should be subject to re-inspection. It is important that there should be clearly documented procedures for dealing with a non-conforming item, including the identification of who is responsible for particular actions. The item having been identified and dealt with *per se*, procedures must be initiated to trace the cause of the non-conformity and remedial action taken and checked. The entire process should be documented.

The next element elaborates on the *corrective action* that should be taken when a non-conforming item is identified. The quality system should include a defined method to eliminate the causes of non-conforming products or services by initiating appropriate corrective action designed to remove the root cause of the problem. Corrective action may be immediate or more long term.

It is recognized in this section that a key source of information regarding product non-conformity will be *customer complaint*. All such complaints must be recorded and dealt with and the complaint and subsequent action fully documented. In the longer term there must be regular analyses of customer complaints to identify any trends and to trace these to problems. These problems, if they have not been addressed earlier, should have their causes identified and action taken to eliminate them.

The fifteenth element recognizes the importance of storage packing and delivery in maintaining the quality of a material product. For a service it is suggested that the recording, labelling and identification of its delivery or completion is an important factor in providing evidence that the service has been performed.

The sixteenth element is *quality records*. These records are described as the objective evidence that the quality system is operating. The records should be clearly identified as dealing with a particular product or service, readily retrievable and stored for an agreed period. The type and extent of the records should reflect the nature of the processes or products involved but they should be designed to demonstrate the achievement of the required quality.

The seventeenth element refers to *internal quality audits*. These are planned and documented checks aimed at ensuring that the defined quality system is being operated correctly and effectively. They are designed to ensure:

- that the quality system documentation adequately defines the needs of the business;
- that the documented procedures are practical, understood and followed;
- that training is adequate to ensure that personnel can undertake their allotted tasks.

The timing and frequency of these audits will depend on the importance of a particular part of the system but should be predetermined and recorded. The results of audits should be documented and the records should cover the following:

- the deficiencies found;
- the corrective action required;
- the time agreed for corrective action to be carried out;
- the person responsible for carrying out the corrective action.

The eighteenth element identifies the central importance of *training* to the achievement of quality. This includes specific training to enable personnel to carry out specific tasks and also general training to heighten quality awareness and to develop attitudes. It is suggested that the following steps should be followed. Those tasks and operations which influence quality should be identified. The training needs of individuals who perform these tasks should be identified. Appropriate training should be planned and implemented to cover both specific needs and general awareness. Training and achievement should be recorded so that updating and the filling of gaps can be attended to.

The central issue of teacher training for university lecturers is the most obvious application of this requirement. It is difficult to sustain an argument that quality can be assured for a service that depends primarily on the activities of teachers when there is no formal identification of their necessary skills and the training needed to develop them. There are obviously training implications for all personnel of the university whose functions effect the delivery of teaching.

The nineteenth element is described as *servicing* and is intended to cover what is normally referred to as after-sales service. This is set out entirely with reference to material products and covers such items as special purpose servicing tools, measuring and testing equipment for field installation, instructions for installation and use, the logistics of back-up, and the training of service personnel. As we have found throughout this analysis, the standards apply most obviously to materials and equipment that are provided by the university to its students. For teaching itself servicing would have to be translated into the follow-up that is often necessary to ensure that the first presentation has had its desired effect, and the provision of additional or even remedial help.

The final element covered is described as *statistical techniques*. Statistical methods are advocated as a very powerful tool within the quality process. By statistical methods the standard appears to mean systematic approaches to data collection, analysis and application and covers techniques such as:

- design of experiments or surveys;
- tests of significance, including analysis of variance, regression analysis and factor analysis;
- safety evaluation and risk analysis;

- quality control charts;
- inspection based on statistical sampling.

I have summarized the elements set out in BS 5750 as central to a quality assurance system. As I have stated and the BSI recognizes, these standards were devised to suit manufacturing industry. Specifically they were meant to aid the government purchasing departments to judge whether a supplier managed their affairs well enough to guarantee that standards would be maintained in the goods supplied. The BSI does, however, believe that the system necessary to manage quality in that context can be applied *mutatis mutandis* to the manufacture of any product and, further, to the provision of services. The procedures required by the standard have been distilled from analyses of good managerial practice.

There is thus an essence to the standard which it is important to grasp. It is that effective management of production or delivery requires an explicit approach to the activities of the organization. Standards must be specified in a form that makes it possible to ascertain whether or not they are being met. Critical functions must be identified for all parts of the organization and these must be set out as procedures that describe clearly who does what for or to whom when. These standards must be clearly documented so that everybody knows what they are supposed to do and who is responsible for what. It is then necessary to monitor reality regularly in order to detect any discrepancies from these agreed standards and procedures. If discrepancies are found there must be procedures for remedial action. Furthermore, standards and procedures must be regularly reviewed to ensure that they are still appropriate. There must be procedures to do this.

All this may sound daunting if applied to the elusive process that is face-to-face teaching. But what about learning materials and, more specifically, the support services necessary to produce such materials? Surely BS 5750 could be appropriate for these? At a more general level, what about the entire infrastructure of administrative and service departments in a university, including finance, staffing, estates and the registry. If academic staff are, in large part, their customers, could a BS 5750 approach improve their activities? It is possible to argue that this would be the best focus for new quality assurance procedures. Such as there are at present tend to be concentrated entirely on course and hence academic staff: what about support services?

How intelligible is the standard? Does it simply lack face validity or is it just inappropriate? Some effort has clearly been made to modify the standard to cover services, as well as products, but this is usually in the form of obvious additions to a text that addresses material products and the production line for them. Often this is just a matter of the examples chosen but sometimes, as with test equipment and packaging, the element has no meaning outside the manufacture of products. Apart from these occasional sins of commission there is a conspicuous lack of detailed attention to human factors. These are important in manufacturing, where the production line, if not operated by humans, is certainly served at some stage by them. Furthermore, customers and suppliers will interact at crucial stages and the management function, which is given prior place in the list of twenty elements, is in large part concerned with human resources. It is not that human factors are ignored in the standard but one is left with the feeling that more could have been made in substance and expression of such issues as motivation, attitudes, interpersonal skills and indeed the problems of reliable and valid measurement of human factors, including customer and supplier characteristics.

Nevertheless, there is much to be learned from the direct or modified application of the standard to services generally and education in particular. Certainly the obviously inappropriate aspects of the standard should not be used as an excuse to avoid the central principles.

While I have commented on the standard while setting it out I would now like to summarize what seem to me to be some of the main lessons to be learned from it. First is the idea that there should be standards associated with any product or service and these should be agreed between supplier and customer. Second is the recognition that keeping to these standards will require an *explicit and managed effort* by the supplier, as will delivering the product or service in a cost-effective and profitable fashion.

In order to achieve the successful management of consistent customer satisfaction that is quality assurance, certain steps will be necessary. I have covered the twenty elements specified for BS 5750. Here they are rephrased to suit a university conceived as a firm wishing to assure quality for its teaching service.

---

1   The university must produce a statement of its policy for quality in teaching and learning and ensure that it is understood by all employees of the university, including, but not only, academic staff.

2   The university must identify those responsible for key elements in the assurance of quality in teaching, the range of their authority and their interrelationships.

3   The university must decide how its quality standards will be described and how their accomplishment will be verified and by whom, bearing in mind that there should be some involvement of people independent of the particular output being verified.

4   The university must identify a particular senior person and associated committee responsible for its quality assurance operations.

5   The university must regularly review its management of quality in teaching and learning.

6   The university must set out in detail its system to assure quality in teaching and learning, including its organization and plan for a specified period. The policy, organization, system and plan should be set out in a quality manual or manuals.

7   The university should determine the nature of the contracts that will be established in general and particular with its students. The specific contract at course level should cover the expectations that teacher and students have of each other's contribution to the students' learning.

8   The university must identify the procedure that will be followed for the planning of courses and the validation of these plans against agreed standards. Inter alia, attention should be given to the consumers' contribution to design, the precise responsibilities of individuals and groups in planning and validation, the relation between design and implementation and the status of plans at each stage of the process of planning and validation.

9   The university should specify the documentation required for the assurance of quality with a view to brevity and direct relevance.

10   The university should set and monitor standards for suppliers and subcontractors associated with their teaching service, including both external and internal suppliers.

11   The university should ensure that key elements in teaching and their primary causes are identified in such a way that problems may be traced back to their roots and appropriate action taken.

12 The university should address in detail the process that characterizes teaching and learning and the process that supports teaching in order that those features affecting quality can be controlled, standards can be set and monitored and problems can be identified and solved.

13 The university should devise reliable and valid measures that might be used to test and verify key elements in teaching, planning for teaching, and student response to teaching.

14 The university should identify external inputs that will be necessary to verify the validity of internal quality assurance.

15 The university should devise procedures for identifying teaching that is sub-standard and take steps to remedy sub-standards elements.

16 The university should have established procedures with designated responsibilities to take short-term and long-term corrective action in response to complaints from students.

17 The university should keep such records as will allow objective assessment of the quality assurance system.

18 The university should devise a planned and documented system for internal quality audits of key features of the quality system, including, for example, course validation, staff training and educational services in support of teaching.

19 The university should identify the skills required of teachers to deliver teaching to agreed quality standards and ensure that all staff receive appropriate training.

20 The university should identify the contribution made by its various non-academic staff and associated resources to the meeting of standards in teaching, identify the standards necessary for those services and the skills necessary for personnel involved, and ensure that all staff receive appropriate training.

21 The university should offer training to all staff to encourage positive attitudes towards a comprehensible quality system.

22 The university should ensure that: there is a follow-up to all its teaching to assess its acceptability and effectiveness to students, and that appropriate follow-up action is taken when teaching has not achieved its objectives.

23 The university should systematically gather data relevant to its quality objectives and subject this to appropriate statistical analysis, the results of which then play a part in its review and planning.

This is by no means an exhaustive list but it does represent a direct translation of BS 5750 that is sufficient, I hope, to demonstrate its relevance to our work. When teaching and learning is associated with materials and equipment then the standard is applicable in its present form. It is entirely appropriate to support services in the university that are no different from similar activities in manufacturing and service industries.

There remains the fundamental problem that there is no comprehensive standard for teaching itself and this the universities must produce. That standard should then be combined with an appropriate standard for managing the consistent accomplishment of these standards. BS 5750 provides an option for the latter.

Until a standard exists for teaching itself, management standards such as BS 5750 will be most obviously applicable to the support services of a university. There is no difference in principle or indeed practice between such functions as finance, personnel, estates, accommodation or catering in a university and any other large organization. Such activities would undoubtedly benefit from the customer-oriented, standard setting and monitoring approach of BS 5750 or BS 9001. The same could be said of educational support services, such as the library, computing and audio-visual services, which, while more likely to be found in educational institutions, nevertheless should be amenable to more general approaches.

References

BS 5750 (1987 and 1990) *Quality Systems, Parts 0–4*. London: British Standards Institution.

BS EN ISO 9001 (2015) *Quality Management Systems Requirements*. London: British Standards Institution.

Ellis, R. (ed.) (1988) *Professional Competence and Quality Assurance in the Caring Professions*. London: Chapman and Hall.

5 University Teaching
A Professional Model for Quality

Lewis Elton

Introduction

It is becoming increasingly accepted in the commercial world that the quality of a product or service cannot be maintained either externally from outside an organization or internally from the top of the organization. What is required – and this concept is a principal tenet of total quality management (TQM) – is a total commitment to quality by all members of the organization, although there will always be a need for some external pressure to ensure the continuation of this commitment. In some ways such a commitment may seem a familiar concept to those who carry out a profession, since it is an important feature of any professional work for those who engage in it to accept full responsibility for their work. In practice, in university teaching – and I shall use the term 'universities' throughout this chapter to stand for all types of higher education institutions – this has frequently fallen short of what is required, for three quite separate reasons. First, quality criteria have not been adequately identified and it is indeed neither simple nor uncontroversial to do this. Second, academics have in the past seen their responsibility as pertaining largely to themselves and to their professional associations rather than to their clients and to the organization in which they worked. Finally, we shall see that there must be considerable doubt as to whether those engaged in university teaching can in any real sense be described as professionals.

In universities, we are concerned with two central activities, teaching and research. Academic attitudes and practices are quite different in these two activities and, within the current academic culture, it is much easier to identify quality and professionalism in research than in teaching (Elton and Partington 1991). One difficulty in connection with university teaching, as with any public service, is that, in the case of service industries, health care and education, the product and the production line – taking over these words from manufacturing industry – are based largely on the actions of qualified professionals. Yet the behaviour, whether effective or not, of professionals is largely hidden from objective scrutiny (as pointed out in Chapter 1).

This is demonstrably true of university teaching, which its practitioners often consider to be an activity conducted in private between not always consenting adults. To make professionals publicly accountable for their work and to do so without affecting the work negatively is a crucial issue faced by all the professions, for it is perfectly possible for public accountability to lead to a deterioration of quality (Elton 1991a).

This chapter will, within the context of university teaching, first discuss the concepts of quality and quality assurance and then turn to the question of professionalism. Only then will it be possible to put forward a model for quality assurance in university teaching and to tackle the difficult question of how to provide public accountability and at the same time to maintain or even increase quality.

Quality and quality assurance in university teaching

The word 'quality' is used at present most confusingly in two very different senses. In the first sense it carries with it connotations of excellence (Pirsig 1974). For this I shall use the word 'standard'. The word 'quality' I shall confine to its technical meaning, as defined by the British Standards Institution (BS 5750, 1987 and 1990), i.e. 'the totality of features or characteristics of a product or service that bear on its ability to satisfy a stated or implied need', and I have already used it in this sense in the introduction. I prefer this definition to the similar one of Ellis (1988: 7) as that 'which gives complete customer satisfaction', since the British Standards definition explicitly recognizes that the 'stated or implied need' may in a professional service be in part defined by the professional who supplies the service. Ellis, in explaining his definition, says that 'for much professional activity the producer plays the role of the consumer in judging the quality of his actions'; hence there is no real difference between the two definitions. Incidentally, the professionals perform a dual role, not only do they have an expert understanding of the needs of their customers, they also have needs of their own, related to the maintenance of their professionalism.

Who is the 'customer' in higher education? Is the word even appropriate for a professional relationship or would 'client' be more appropriate? Words carry possibly inappropriate concepts and meanings with them as they are metaphorically transferred to other contexts, and although identifying such contradictions is part of the stock-in-trade of academic discourse, academics have sadly failed to recognize it in the pseudo-business discourse of the past: decade. With this reservation in mind, let us analyze the concept of 'customer' in higher education.

It is common at the moment to say that students are the customers because they pay for the service in fees, but – using the same kind of language – in another sense they are the 'product' for which employers, government, professional associations and society are the customers. In many European countries the very idea of students as customers, let alone as products of higher education, would be totally rejected; they are partners with academics in the pursuit of knowledge. In any case, most of the fees and the other costs of university teaching are borne by the government via the funding councils. So is it the latter who are the customers? What is clear is that there is a multiplicity of customers, not all of whom can be completely satisfied simultaneously.

So on to quality assurance. In the commercial market, the external pressure, which I postulated as needed to fulfill the requirements of TQM, is provided by the customers, who may have a choice between different producers who supply goods or services, and who also have means of redress if they are not satisfied. To provide informed choice, even for such a simple object as a refrigerator, it is necessary to have consumer reports that provide appropriate performance indicators, something that has proved exceedingly difficult, highly contentious and probably very unreliable for, say, a degree course (Johnes and Taylor 1991). To provide redress is even more difficult, since dissatisfied students have lost more than money: they have lost perhaps three years of their lives. For all these reasons, it has in the past been largely the professionals who have been the guardians of quality in a professional service, not the customers. But they should not be the sole arbiters in this matter; they may become negligent or they may be wrong or they may use their power unethically. Following earlier remarks about TQM, I suggest that: they should have the prime responsibility for controlling the quality of their work, but that the external pressure that is always necessary should come through public accountability for their work. Other possibilities, which include external measures of quality, offend against the basic tenet of TQM, stated earlier, that the maintenance of quality cannot be imposed from the outside.

Any scheme for quality control requires three steps:

1   Agreement on the needs that have to be satisfied.
2   Identification of the activities which have to be assessed for their quality.
3   Establishment of procedures that ensures that this quality is maintained.

The documentation of these three steps constitutes a 'quality assurance system' and the availability for public scrutiny of that documentation then provides what is called 'quality assurance'.

Agreement on needs should come out of a negotiated accommodation between the needs of all the relevant 'customers' and of the professionals who provide the service. It relates to the objectives which the service aims to achieve and to the standards of the processes by which they are achieved. In practice, not all concerned have equal access to the resulting negotiations. Thus the objectives of a university degree in, say, engineering, are negotiated between engineering teachers and their professional association, possibly with an input from government, regarding the numbers and kinds of engineers that the course is to produce. The standards at which these objectives are to be achieved are likely to involve the same groups with the addition of an external examiner in the discipline of the degree and colleagues in the university in other disciplines. Neither objectives nor product standards are directly influenced by the students: those who consider taking the course exert an influence through the choice that they can exercise between different courses open to them, while those on the course may have influenced it through their evaluation of it. In the main this influence is often restricted to its process standards what in the here forsworn sense of the word quality is often referred to as the 'quality of the learning experience' – but this need not be so. Society has even less direct influence, although it has not been unknown for its influence to make itself felt through the press. In less directly vocational courses, say in history, students may have a great influence, but the main direct influence on objectives and product standards is likely to come from the teachers of the subject and the external examiner, who between them also represent the interests of their discipline.

The specification of needs separately in terms of objectives, product and process standards is quite essential. An illustration from the hotel trade may make this clearer: the objectives and often the process standards of a hotel are given in its brochure; its product standards are provided by the AA star rating; quality assurance is provided by an assessment of the effectiveness of the control processes that ensure the quality of the service, by, say, the *Good Hotel Guide*. It would appear that the assessment in this case is wholly external, but in practice this is not so – for the best hotels in the Guide it is clear that the assessment essentially consists of a verification of the internal quality control processes, i.e. the quality assurance system, together with a sampling that these processes actually provide quality control. Similarly, in a university, one objective might be to produce a degree course in engineering, with its product an honours degree, while the process standards would relate to the total experience of students on the course.

The idea that the effectiveness of a quality assurance system can be verified selectively in terms of what one or more particular control processes reveal is common in financial audits and is called an 'audit trail'. It was introduced into university quality assurance by Professor

Stewart Sutherland, Chair of the sub-committee of the Committee of Vice Chancellors and Principals (CVCP 1990) that set up the Academic Audit Unit, experience of which in part provides a basis for a practical scheme for quality assurance in university teaching, to be described below. However, before one can formulate such a scheme, it is necessary to ask how far university teachers can in fact claim to be professionals in the sense that this term has been used so far.

University teaching as a profession

What might be the criteria of a profession? The list below has been gathered mainly from Ellis (1988) with some ideas of my own, but it is similar to those provided by others, e.g. Lewis and Maude (1952: 55) and Larson (1977: 208). It is in no sense authoritative and others may add to or subtract from it. I suggest that a list of criteria for a profession ought to include all or most of the following:

- an underlying discipline or cognitive base;
- a body of practitioners;
- a disciplinary organization;
- induction, training and licensing of members;
- communication channels between members;
- rewards and sanctions for members;
- self-reflection, leading to improvement;
- corporate evaluation and feedback;
- a code of ethics and accountability to the profession;
- corporate accountability to society;
- quality assurance of the profession.

The professions of law and medicine would probably satisfy all the above criteria and critics might, not unjustifiably, add another:

- the ability to ensure high standards of remuneration.

This is not, however, a criterion that would apply to the engineering profession, which otherwise also satisfies all the criteria, or to academics as researchers, who otherwise satisfy many of the criteria. Their underlying discipline is not of course 'research', but the discipline in which they research, such as physics or history. However, their claim that they are members of a profession of, say, physicists or historians is not strong, since they cannot apply sanctions to members and do not have a corporate accountability to society. It is also doubtful whether peer review provides quality assurance, although the process of peer-reviewed publications assists in the maintenance of standards.

The situation is much worse when it comes to teaching, as was recognized many years ago by Ashby (1969: 5), who noticed 'a curious gap in the attitude of the profession to that part of its duty which concerns teaching'. In principle, there is an underlying discipline, and the Germans even have a word for it, Hochschuldidaktik, i.e. the pedagogy of university teaching, but few academics are aware of it. There is also a body of practitioners, namely the body of university teachers, but there is no disciplinary organization, induction and training are barely minimal, few know of the journals that should be their communication channels, and neither rewards nor sanctions exist to any significant extent. There is now evaluation and feedback, through appraisal of individuals and increasingly through self-validation corporately, and there is quality assurance through such bodies as the Council for National Academic Awards and the Academic Audit Unit. There is essentially no formal accountability to either the profession or society.

It is apparent that university teachers at present do not constitute a profession. One major obstacle, which could be removed fairly easily, is their lack of training. If this were removed, many of the other criteria for a profession would in due course be fulfilled. No other profession would consider that those who had not been trained and inducted into the profession would be able to maintain quality criteria or even enunciate such criteria. In fact, in the past few years many of our academic leaders have publicly declared that they did not know how to judge quality in university teaching, thereby demonstrating that, as academic teachers, they were less than professional. In contrast, a small band of quite unimportant people who have actually made university pedagogy their discipline have for over a decade published papers (e.g. Elton and Partington 1991) and written books (e.g. Brown and Atkins 1988) that clearly showed that there was no particular difficulty in establishing criteria for quality in university teaching in general, and quite recently (Tysome 1991) the Further Education Unit of the Department of Education and Science has made an attempt to formulate these in terms of competencies. Once proper training has been established, academics may also be expected to engage in the important activity of self-reflection (Schon 1983).

There is a second and more serious difficulty, which stems from a conflict between multiple loyalties. As teachers, academics ought to have a double loyalty, to their discipline, which represents what they teach, and to university pedagogy, which represents whom they teach. The first loyalty, which coincides with their principal research loyalty, is therefore to their discipline association, and this is generally their strongest and often only loyalty. The locus of their second loyalty is more in dispute. It could be the appropriate disciplinary association, i.e. the Society for Research into Higher Education, but for many it is more likely to be their university, for that is where the students are whom they teach. It could be both. Academics as teachers thus potentially have three legitimate and separate loyalties, not an easy position to be in. It is, however, inevitable and has to be allowed for in the professionalization of university teaching. This conflict of loyalties is not actually confined to teaching; there is – or at least ought to be – a similar conflict in research, where 'individual academics and leaders of research entities have a much more direct and active interest in maximizing their operations in a project market of their speciality than in the prosperity of their university' (Ziman 1991). This latter conflict is sometimes avoided by a neglect of the institutional loyalty, but this is neither desirable nor even possible in teaching.

Once academics are professional as teachers, they will have to be aware of one feature of professionalism that was enunciated most brutally by Shaw (1908), namely that a profession is 'a conspiracy to hide its own shortcomings'.

A model for quality assurance in university teaching

We now face a difficulty. In discussing quality assurance for university teaching, we postulated that in line with the tenets of TQM, quality assurance had to arise out of the professionalism of the providers, but we then found that university teachers did not constitute a profession. At the same time, all the evidence of the past decade points to the fact that the strongest pressure for a greater professionalism arises from the public demand for quality assurance. This is a dialectical situation in which, at any one time, demands for better quality assurance lead to greater professionalism, which in turn leads to better quality assurance. Our proposed model includes a feedback process that allows for this. It is described in Figure 5.1.

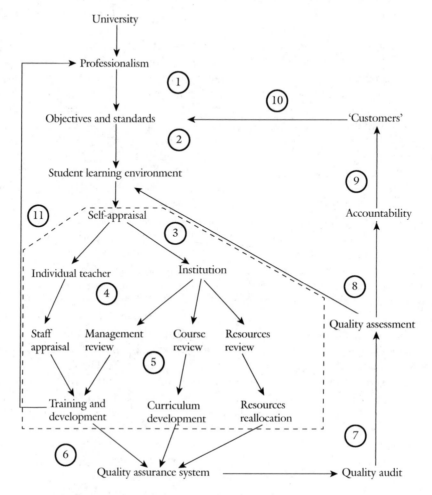

Figure 5.1 A model for quality assurance in university teaching

The stages of the model, with examples of how they might work out in practice, are as follows:

1   The university, through its growing professionalism, defines its objectives and standards in consultation with its customers. (Institutional and departmental plans, in line with the institutional mission, are established in collaboration with representatives from students, employers and the community.)
2   These objectives and standards are interpreted in terms of the totality of the student learning environment. (This is the task of course teams, which, in addition to academics, again might include students, employers and members of the community, as well as those from the central services of the university.)
3   The learning environment is monitored and evaluated through formal procedures of self-appraisal at the levels of the individual teacher and of the institution. (These procedures are preparatory to the similar procedures under procedure 4 below.)

4   The self-appraisal of the teacher is followed by staff appraisal; the self-appraisal of the institution by the appraisal of courses, management and resources. (The current procedures for staff appraisal in some of the universities and those for appraising departments and institutions, which derive in the polytechnics from their CNAA experience, provide examples.)

5   Where appropriate, the outcomes of the appraisals lead to staff training and development, course development and resource reallocations. (Some examples of good practice are beginning to become available across the higher education system.)

6   Procedures 3–5 constitute the quality assurance system.

7   Quality assurance is in the first instance provided through scrutiny by an external quality audit or similar process. (The Academic Audit Unit is developing good procedures, but it at present lacks externality.)

8   A direct quality assessment of the learning environment is provided by regular external peer review and the work of external examiners, which are monitored by the audit process. (At present, such practices exist, but they are mostly inadequate.)

9   Accountability to 'customers' is provided through both audit and assessment, both publicly available. (The Academic Audit Unit issues reports to audited universities, which the Unit expects them to publish. Peer reviews and external examiners' reports are not published at present.)

10   In the light of evidence emerging from the quality assurance process, the university redefines its objectives and standards in consultation with its customers.

11   As a result of training and development, the staff of the university increase their professionalism. Much of this is likely to be in course teams, in connection with curriculum development.

The model follows the general approach to quality assurance in this book:

a)   Setting standards for a good service (1, 2, 10).
b)   Monitoring performance against standards (3, 4).
c)   Remedying shortfalls (5, 11).
d)   Involving consumers in setting and monitoring standards (1, 9, 10).
e)   Managing and evaluating the system for the above (6, 7, 8).

An important feature of the model is that it is developmental. It will fail if the quality assessment is either too weak initially, so that the university does not feel itself under pressure to become more professional, or remains in place too long, so that the university remains inappropriately under tutelage.

The present position, since the abolition of the binary line that divided universities from polytechnics, is that all Higher Education Institutions (HEIs) will be audited by an agency corporately responsible to them, similar to the current Academic Audit Unit. This agency is therefore not independent of the HEIs as a body. The White Paper (DES 1991) and the resulting Further and Higher Education Act of 1992 incorporated such an audit, but added to it an external quality assessment, generated by and directly responsible to the new Funding Councils. After a pilot assessment exercise in both England and Scotland, which was based largely on the traditions and experience of HMI, who conduct assessments wholly externally, Scotland has abandoned this approach and is instead proposing that the assessment should consist of an evaluation of an institution's own quality assessment by assessors recruited for this task by the Funding Council. These assessors would be experts recruited largely from HEIs; what is not clear is whether these would include not only subject experts, but also, as they ought to, educational experts. The use of external experts parallels my proposal of external peer review (see point 8 in Figure 5.1); however, the Scottish proposal is more external to the HEIs than my suggestion, which is that not only the assessment process but also the outcomes should be audited and the results be made publicly available. The English Funding Council has proposed a second pilot exercise, so that its final decisions are not likely to be available for some time. Whatever form the assessment process will eventually take, in both England and Scotland, it is quite definite that it will influence funding decisions. This direct coupling of quality assessment to funding decisions has serious dangers in that it removes any real ownership of the assessment from the HEIs. Past experience has shown that this can result in quality actually decreasing; whether the Scottish approach, which at least starts from self-assessment, can avoid this danger remains to be seen; any approach that is even more external, such as the one that was tried out in the pilot exercises, is most unlikely to avoid it.

Cost-effectiveness through appropriate resourcing mechanisms

Having cast doubt on the wisdom of placing the Quality Assessment Unit with the Funding Councils, I want to draw attention to a way that this placing could be turned to advantage. It is well known that 'throwing money at problems' is rarely a good way to solve them; what is perhaps less well known is that quite small sums, judiciously targeted, can have an effect out of all proportion to their size. An Assessment Unit within the Funding Councils might be well placed to give appropriate financial advice.

The argument depends essentially on the premise that institutions as well as individuals classify their needs in general in a hierarchy originally put forward by Maslow, which is such that a need at a particular level is not perceived as important until those on the levels below are satisfied. The hierarchy has five levels:

5   Self-actualization
4   Self-esteem
3   Love and belonging
2   Safety
1   Physiological

There are, of course, individuals whose personal hierarchies to some extent reorder these levels – one only has to think of the proverbial artist starving in a garret who considers self-actualization more important than the physiological needs for food and shelter – but an institution whose behaviour is governed by the behaviour of its many individual members is unlikely to allow such reordering.

While crumbling buildings may in due course reduce universities as institutions to the physiological level, this has not yet happened. On the other hand, in the present financial climate, where bankruptcy looms, many have clearly found themselves working at the safety level. The result has been what I have called elsewhere (Elton 1989) the Micawber effect in higher education, namely that the difference between being just in the black and just in the red has an effect on institutional attitudes out of all proportion to its size. When resources just exceed basic needs, universities can work at least at level 3, i.e. they tend to cooperate with each other, even if it may be unreasonable to expect that they love each other. If such cooperation is reciprocated, they may move on to develop their own individualities in accordance with their value systems, traditions etc. Broadly speaking, that was the experience of the universities during the expansion of the 1960s and even of the less expansionist 1970s. In the hard 1980s, when resources just failed to match basic needs, universities were reduced to level 2 and started to compete with each other for scarce funds to an extent that is harming the system. A telling example, and by no means the only one, is the effect that the competition for overseas students has had on the standing of British universities abroad. The deleterious effects of competition in a climate of scarcity have been recognized by Sir Graham Hills, the very hard-headed former Principal of Strathclyde University, who has given it as his opinion (Wojtas 1991) that 'cuts must be applied evenly, otherwise you destroy a sense of collegiality, but rewards can be as selective as you like'.

Bearing in mind that 'there is no mechanical relationship between a relative quality judgement and a funding decision, or there shouldn't be' (Ball 1991), what might be funding mechanisms that would ensure both effectiveness and efficiency in line with the principles enunciated above? The UFC policy towards research has been to achieve this competitively through selectivity and hence through concentration of effort in a comparatively small number of universities. Such an approach is clearly inappropriate for teaching, where it is necessary to achieve both effectiveness and efficiency in all universities in an expanding system. Teaching also benefits from cooperation rather than competition, as has been amply demonstrated within the Enterprise in Higher Education (EHE) Initiative (Elton 1991b). The EHE practice of bids for funding, followed by five-year contracts, the achievement of which is assessed annually through institutional visits during the year and an audit of self-assessment at the end of the year, could provide an appropriate funding model. Another possible model is the American model (HMI 1991), in which funding is dependent on accreditation and the adequate quality required for it. The model proposed below uses both the EHE and the US model. In it, the total funding T consists of two parts, T = ST + JT, as follows.

ST This part is adapted from the US model and is much the larger part of the total T. Funding is based on an institutional plan, negotiated between the university and the Funding Council, with funds being essentially allocated on the basis of agreed student numbers in different cost centres. Universities receive their money on the basis of adequate quality, as verified by quality assurance and assessment. If a university falls below that quality, it is given a period in which to improve, during which it might even get increased funds in order to help it to improve, but warned that it risks cutbacks of agreed student numbers if there is no improvement. A financial inducement could come through the Funding Council giving larger numbers of fully funded students to those universities whose missions, plans and curricular objectives are explicitly in line with national needs. This will increase the proportion of students that are fully funded compared to those funded for fees only and thus increase the average funding per student.

JT This part is adapted from the EHE model, regarding funding on the one hand and quality audit and assessment on the other. It selectively supports proposals by universities for teaching excellence through improvements, backed by staff and curriculum development, designed to lead to better teaching at greater efficiency without loss of quality. An important feature of JT would be to encourage developments that are carried out cooperatively in several universities and/or that lead to dissemination of teaching improvements throughout the higher education system. At the same time, the criteria for success would be norm-referenced between universities, thus introducing an element of competition. In contrast to research selectivity, where the reward is for past excellence, the JT factor rewards the promise of future excellence.

Resourcing levels, professionalism and quality

A similar approach, on the basis of the Maslow levels, can be taken to allocating resources within a university. Institutional rewards to academic staff and due recognition of their work are related to 'love and belonging', i.e. level 3, and once universities are at that level they must realize that by differentially 'loving' different contributions from their members, they can strongly influence the latter's behaviour. At present, they are rewarding research for more than teaching, through differences in the recognition and resourcing of these two activities and in the extrinsic rewards to individuals available for them (Elton and Partington 1991). However, quite a small shift in resources towards teaching, combined with a genuine recognition of the value of the work, can have a most significant effect on the quantity and quality of effort put by academic staff into teaching, as the current Enterprise in Higher Education Initiative is demonstrating (Elton 1991b). What has been shown there is that if, in their attitude to teaching, institutions reach Maslow level 3, the effect of rewards and recognition on individual staff is respectively at Maslow levels 3 and 4. Such extrinsic motivational factors are the prerequisite for the all-important intrinsic motivation associated with level 5, which in turn leads to institutional effects at levels 4 and 5. The initiative has also given support to the hypothesis that cooperation is superior to competition in improving the cost-effectiveness of teaching.

The collegiality, which Hills wishes to reinforce, and the shift of resources towards teaching are both positive aspects of a recognition of the increasing professionalism of university teaching. It has to be recognized however, that there is a negative side to this. A university that rewards all its staff for good work and wants to make them feel members of a collegial society may find that some of these members are content to stay at the safety level and do little to contribute to the common weal. Universities have always had a few such people, who took advantage of the system, and they have considered this a small price to pay, since it appeared to be more than balanced by the work and enthusiasm of the majority. However, if in the past dangers of inefficiency may have arisen from academics being too little controlled, the danger now is the opposite. Recent experience has shown that, when universities and their staff are reduced to the level of safety, then they all, or nearly all, play the system. And then both quality and effort deteriorate to the point where, even without any quantified cost-benefit analysis, the results are obviously inferior.

Conclusion

The last remark reinforces earlier conclusions that quality cannot be enforced from outside the university; neither, it may be added, can it be enforced from inside by top management (Pollitt 1990). It can only be achieved through the joint commitment and effort of all those inside it. What this requires over the next few years is:

- a rapid increase towards the professionalization of university teaching;
- the establishment of TQM practices at all levels of each university;
- increasing recognition and resourcing of teaching and rewards for excellence in it.

The achievement of these three objectives amounts to a radical change in culture, ethos and values of universities, which will be resisted by many inside them. Hence external pressures from, say, an independent assessment unit will be needed to 'unfreeze' the present system, in the telling phrase of Kurt Lewin, and to encourage change. But it is equally important that this pressure is, removed, once the change has been institutionalized. If this does not happen, the system will eventually change to one that is even worse than the present one, for permanent tutelage leads first to decline and dependence, and then to revolt. This is one lesson that the West can learn from recent events in Eastern Europe.

References

Ashby, E. (1969) *The Academic Profession*. London: Oxford University Press.

Ball, C. (1991) Quality and qualities: an overview. In Schuller, T. (ed.) *The Future of Higher Education*. Milton Keynes: SRHE/Open University Press.

Brown, G and Atkins, M. (1988) *Effective Teaching in Higher Education*. London: Methuen.

BS 5750 (1987 and 1990) *Quality Systems, Parts 0 to 4*. London: British Standards Institution.

Committee of Vice-Chancellors and Principals (1990) *Letter to Vice-Chancellors and Principals, N/90/1 08*, 15 May. London: CVCP.

DES (1991) *Higher Education: A New Framework, Cmnd 1541*. London: HMSO.

Ellis, R. (ed.) (1988) *Professional Competence and Quality Assurance in the Caring Professions*. London: Croom Helm.

Elton, L. (1989) Higher education in Britain: future uncertain. *Zeitschrift fur Hochschuldidaktik*, 13: 122–36.

Elton, L. (1991a) Teaching excellence and quality assurance. *Zeitschrift fur Hochschuldidahtik*, 15: 102–15.

Elton, L. (1991b) Enterprise in higher education: work in progress. *Education and Training*, 33: 5–9.

Elton, L. and Partington, P. (1991) *Teaching Standards and Excellence in Higher Education: Developing a Culture for Quality*. London: CVCP.

HMI (1991) *Aspects of Education in the USA: Quality and Its Assurance in Higher Education*. London: HMSO.

Johnes, J. and Taylor, J. (1991) *Performance Indicators in Higher Education*. Milton Keynes: SRHE/Open University Press.

Larson, M. S. (1977) *Rise of Professionalism: A Sociological Analysis*. Berkeley: University of California Press.

Lewis, R. and Maude, A. (1952) *Professional People*. London: Phoenix House.

Pirsig, R. M. (1974) *Zen and the Art of Motorcycle Maintenance*. London: Bodley Head.

Pollitt, C. (1990) Doing business in the temple? Managers and quality assurance in the public service. *Public Administration*, 68: 435–52.

Schon, D. A. (1983) *The Reflective Practitioner*. London: Temple Smith.

Shaw, G. B. (1908) *The Doctor's Dilernma*. Reprinted 1946. Harmondsworth: Penguin.

Tysome, T. (1991) Staff face snakes and ladder review. *The Higher*, 15 November.

Wojtas, 0. (1991) Following the gospel according to Groucho. *The Higher*, 20 September.

Ziman, J. (1991) Academic science as a system of markets. *Higher· Education Quarterly*, 45: 41–61.

6 Program Evaluation
A Key to Assuring Quality in Higher Education

Elaine Hogard

The purpose of this chapter is to consider how the approaches and methods of Program Evaluation might be employed as part of the internal quality assurance procedures of a university. The chapter will address four topics. First, it will outline the approach and techniques of the discipline known as Program Evaluation; second, it will consider their place in the assurance and development of quality in Higher Education; third, it will describe a specific method, the Trident, developed for Program Evaluation, and finally, it will consider how the approach might be applied to a program in Higher Education.

Program Evaluation is a systematic method whereby data and information are collected to answer questions about the success and methods of projects, programs and policies. Typically, it focuses on their effectiveness and efficiency since in both the private and public sectors, stakeholders, including funders, managers and practitioners, want to know whether the program they are funding, implementing or promoting is actually achieving its objectives. Funders often insist on some form of Program Evaluation to ensure that they are receiving value for money. Clearly, similar questions can be asked regarding programs and parts of programs in Higher Education.

While Program Evaluation is centrally concerned with these issues of success and value for money, it also has a number of additional benefits. Data gathered in the evaluation can be fed back to practitioners both during the program and at its conclusion to improve delivery in a cycle of continuous quality improvement (McLaughlin *et al.*, 2012). This process of formative and summative evaluation helps providers to learn from their experience and continuously improve their program. Furthermore, Program Evaluation focuses not only on outcomes but on the process whereby the outcomes were achieved. Thus, in Higher Education whilst the success of a program might be judged through its outcomes in terms of student retention or completion, Program Evaluation would also examine the process by which these outcomes had been achieved, that is, the actual teaching and learning methods.

The process of Program Evaluation basically involves posing questions about a program then gathering data to answer them. On the basis of these answers the evaluation concludes with recommendations for future practice and policy. While a Program Evaluation may consider a whole program, the approach can be adopted to evaluate issues or problems arising in parts of the program.

Program Evaluation is now a well-established university subject with professional societies, refereed journals, and chairs in the subject. The subject might be based in Education, Health Care, Social Sciences or Business Studies. The methods used to gather and analyse data involve a range of social science approaches.

In addition to providing a home for the discipline of Program Evaluation many universities have established a Program Evaluation function to evaluate and improve its courses.

This function would address the evaluation of complete programs usually on an agreed cycle or might focus on particular issues or problems that have arisen in the delivery of a program. The results of these evaluations would feed into a cycle of continuous improvement and relate to the requirements of external bodies.

To justify the introduction of a Program Evaluation approach in Higher Education there are several arguments. They are as follows:

- Accountability: the results of an evaluation provide public evidence of the success of a program and lessons learned.
- Quality Assurance: the data gathered through an evaluation feed into the quality improvement cycle of a program.
- Record of Achievement: the formal evidence gathering and reporting of an evaluation places achievements and lessons learned on public record.
- Data for Research: the reliable and valid data gathered in an evaluation can be used in research projects.
- Recommendations for Policy and Practice: evaluations should culminate in recommendations for best practice and policy.
- Dissemination and Publications: the evaluation report is a publication in itself but can also contribute to other publications.

While it cannot be claimed that many of the methods used Program Evaluation – e.g. audits; interviews; questionnaires – are unique to the discipline, the advantages of Program Evaluation are its comprehensive multi-method approach rooted in a substantial literature. The following is a detailed description of a particular approach which we have developed that has proved itself in over 100 evaluations and which can be readily applied to university programs in whole or in part. The method is called 'The Trident' because it focuses a Program Evaluation on three main areas: Outcomes, Process, and Multiple Stakeholder Perspectives (Ellis and Hogard, 2006).

It was first developed to evaluate a category of staff called Clinical Facilitators who were a key part of the Nurse Education program in a university (Ellis and Hogard, 2003). The clinical facilitators were experienced nurses whose job was to supervise the nursing students' clinical placement and to link this practice with the university-based curriculum. They were intended to provide a bridge between theory and practice. The scheme was an innovation and a condition of its funding was there should be an external evaluation of its success. We approached the evaluation through focusing on the outcomes expected for the program and the evidence available for their accomplishment; on the processes of the program, that is the teaching and learning methods employed by the clinical facilitators; and on the views of all those involved in the program including the clinical facilitators themselves, the students, and associated university and hospital staff.

As noted previously, there is a plethora of Program Evaluation designs and approaches available to researchers (see McDavid *et al.*, 2013; Mertens & Wilson, 2012; and Rossi *et al.*, 2004). However, when dealing with an area of Higher Education we have gone back to first principles. We came to the conclusion, after reading widely in the area that evaluations could ask three main questions:

1   Has the program achieved its stated outcomes?
2   What was the process through which the program was delivered?
3   What did everyone involved in the program think of it?

While these questions are obviously related and overlapping they suggested three different data streams and, indeed, social science approaches. The outcomes should ideally be expressed in objective measurable terms amenable to valid and reliable psychometrics. Description and analysis of the process, however, needed some way of reconstructing a complex social process which, ideally, would have involved prolonged participant observation. The multiple stakeholders' perspectives were more phenomenological and depended on the perceptions of individuals and groups including students, nurses, managers and the clinical facilitators themselves.

We identified, in discussion with the providers, that the key outcome for this particular program was the enhanced competence and confidence of the nursing students, which we decided could be measured using Objective Structured Clinical Examinations (Harden *et al.*, 2016) where students had to practise such skills as blood pressure measurement and clinical hand washing in carefully controlled situations where they were assessed by trained examiners.

To capture the process of teaching and learning which made up clinical facilitation it would have been ideal to observe the interaction between student and clinical facilitators over a period. However, this was neither practical nor permissible so we used a version of a social anthropological method called reconstitutive ethnography whereby clinical facilitators were interviewed to tap their recollections of process. These recollections were structured and modeled and the facilitators then validated the constructions (Hogard, 2007). This led to a model of clinical facilitation which has subsequently influenced the nursing curriculum.

Finally, stakeholder perspectives were explored through focus groups and survey questionnaires with common questions.

This Program Evaluation was the test bed for the Trident. The method proved functional in giving a structure to the evaluation and its research questions and data gathering. It was also intelligible to contractors and participants which helped to make the evaluation meaningful and acceptable. It encouraged participation and gave a structure to the final report and recommendations.

The Trident offered a comprehensive systematic Program Evaluation framework. Unlike many educational Program Evaluations, it is not just concerned with consumer (student) views, important though they are, but gathers the perspectives of all stakeholders. It focuses on actual outcomes and impact. It looks separately at the process of delivery and can then link these findings with outcomes and the views of participants.

The Trident offers a framework which permeates the evaluation and structures:

- Evaluation Questions;
- Data Gathering;
- Conclusions;
- Recommendations.

To recapitulate the Trident, poses three main questions and a number of subsidiary questions:

First, is the program meeting its objectives and achieving the intended outcomes? Is there objective, reliable and valid evidence that these outcomes are being achieved? Are all outcomes being addressed, if necessary with new measures? Second, how is the program working; what is the process of delivery? What is actually happening; how can it be described, categorised and analysed? What lessons can be learned from this delivery in relation to outcomes achieved? Third, what do all the people involved: recipients, providers, associates, and managers, think of the program?

You might like to think of a program, however modest, that you would like to evaluate. This could be a part of a whole program or a particular aspect of a program which is posing problems or which represents an innovation.

What were the intended outcomes of the program and how will these be measured? Remember we are not talking about the process of delivery here but the outcomes the process is intended to achieve. What was the process and activities that made up the program? How might these be described and analysed? How might these be linked with outcomes? What did all the participants think of the programme?

We would argue that the Trident can be applied in the evaluation of a whole program or parts of the program or particular problems that have arisen in the program.

The Trident structures evaluation through its focus on three main questions and integrates quantitative and qualitative data. It ensures comprehensive data gathering and facilitates hypothesis testing linking two or three data streams. Perhaps one of its greatest strengths is that it is intelligible to contractors, deliverers and recipients

The outcomes may be described as program objectives or aims but they must be distinguished from the process of delivery. We often find that providers tend to focus on the delivery of their program rather than look at the outcomes that are supposed to be the results of the program. These outcomes must be measurable in some way and not just impressionistic.

For a Higher Education program the most obvious outcome measures are the results of the assessments which make up the program formatively and summatively. It can be helpful to identify any other outcomes the program aims to achieve besides those measured in its assessments. Thus, if a program aims to develop a professional identity in students the evaluation might encourage the use of, for example, innovative identity measures.

Use of so-called Logic Models (Wyatt Knowlton & Phillips, 2013) may be helpful in distinguishing between short-term, medium-term and long-term outcomes. However, the further the outcomes are from the point of delivery, the harder they are to measure. For example, one program that was evaluated was an educational program to encourage student teachers' global awareness. The short-term outcome was an assignment, fairly easily assessed. The medium-term outcome was the use of material on their teaching practice, which was measurable but rather more difficult to access. The long-term outcome was the impact on their future teaching career, which was impossible to measure within the time frame of the evaluation.

Process evaluation is concerned with the actual way the program is delivered. Data for process description may come from program plans and specifications and from records that have to be kept of what has actually happened. Data may depend on interviews with participants to reconstruct what happened. If there is time, structured observation can be helpful as can 'shadowing' of key individuals delivering the program. This is a part of a formal evaluation which can explore the actual teaching and learning which occurs in the program and relate this to outcome measures to try to identify what is causing what.

Multiple Stakeholder Perspectives depend on a thorough analysis to decide who is involved and affected by the program. In management jargon, a 360-degree analysis is required. Typically, stakeholders include:

- Program recipients: students;
- Program deliverers: teachers and support staff;
- Professionals involved in the delivery of the program on, for example, placements;
- Managers.

To give some examples of the Trident in action, here are some Higher Education Program Evaluations where it has been used (see also Hogard and Ellis, 2010; Sines *et al.* (2012); Watt *et al.* (2007).

- Practice Development and Research Units (linking HE with clinical practice);
- Clinical skills labs for multi-professional, pre-service and in-service training;
- Non-medical prescribing postgraduate diploma program;
- Assistant practitioner pre-degree diploma;
- Social work placements for international students;
- Early language development for post-registration speech therapy;
- Personality Disorder Network – post-registration inter-professional training.

Of course, evaluation itself is not without its issues and difficulties. Some of the problems we have faced in our Program Evaluations include outcomes being poorly defined and process being confused with outcomes; process descriptions that are superficial or nonexistent; and stakeholders who are conceived as recipients only. Data gathering can prove difficult in practice although straightforward in principle. Evaluations can lose momentum and have a low priority for those delivering the program. To overcome these difficulties, we have found it helpful to establish, from the start, a Steering Group consisting of those who have contracted the evaluation; those who are delivering or, if possible, receiving, the program, and the evaluators. The Steering Group has to approve the design and methods for the evaluation, facilitate access to data, and receive interim and final reports.

However, the satisfying parts of the job, facilitated, we believe, by the Trident, have included having an impact on Higher Education practice and policy; providing a record of achievement which helps with future funding; and achieving the dissemination of best practice through reports and publications.

When embarking upon a Program Evaluation project the researcher and relevant stakeholders can direct and shape their work by employing a number of guiding questions. The responses to these can then be organized in such a way that the work and its development becomes clear, feasible and much more manageable, especially with regard to varying data sets and data sources. Here are some questions to guide you:.

Expectations and responsibilities

- Why are you undertaking an evaluation of your program?
- How is the program defined: when does it start and finish?
- Is a whole program to be evaluated or simply a part of a program?
- What do you expect to get from the evaluation?
- Who are the group who will be responsible for the evaluation: how will responsibilities for data streams be allocated?
- Who is the leader and champion of the evaluation?
- To whom will the evaluators make recommendations?
- Do you have any concerns regarding the evaluation?

Area 1: Outcomes

- What are the clearest statements of the outcomes which the program aims to achieve?
- By what outcomes would you wish the program to be judged?
- What evidence will be available that these outcomes have been achieved?

- What are the evaluation questions that will be addressed with data?
- What evidence will be available as a baseline to compare the outcomes of a new program with the previous arrangements?
- Who will be responsible for gathering the data?

Area 2: Process

- What are the clearest specifications for the program?
- Would these be sufficiently detailed to allow the program to be replicated?
- What lessons have been learned from the operation of the program so far?
- What are the costs of the program compared with the previous comparable provision (if any)?
- What are the most important innovations in your program?
- How many students will experience your program in the period for the evaluation?
- What methods will be used to gather data regarding the process?
- Who will be responsible for gathering and analyzing the data?

Area 3: Stakeholders

- Who are the stakeholders whose views should be taken into account in evaluating the scheme? Have you included not just recipients but deliverers as well?
- How will the stakeholders' views be gathered?
- Who will be responsible for gathering these views?

Conclusions and recommendations

- What conclusions can be drawn from the answers to the evaluation questions?
- What recommendations can be made regarding practice and policy?
- To whom will these recommendations be made? Are they empowered to implement the recommendations?

References

Ellis R and Hogard E (2006) 'The Trident: A Three-Pronged Method for Evaluating Clinical, Social and Educational Innovations.' *Evaluation* 12(3), p. 372–383.

Harden R M, Lilley P and Patricio M (2016) *The Definitive Guide to the OSCE*. London: Elsevier.

Hogard E (2007) 'Using Consultative Methods to Investigate Professional–Client Interaction as an Aspect of Process Evaluation.' *American Journal of Evaluation* 28(3), pp. 304–317.

Hogard E (2018) 'Identifying Quality in Teaching Using Consultative Methods.' In Ellis R and Hogard E, *Handbook of Quality Assurance for University Teaching*. London: Routledge.

Hogard E and Ellis R (2010) 'An Evaluation of a Managed Clinical Network for Personality Disorder: Breaking New Ground or Top Dressing?' *Evaluation in Clinical Practice* 16(6), pp.1147–1156.

McDavid J, Huse I and Hawthorn L R L (2013) *Program Evaluation and Performance Measurement: An Introduction to Practice* (2nd ed). Newbury Park, CA: Sage.

McLaughlin C C., Johnson J K and Sollecito W A (2012) *Implementing Continuous Quality Improvement in Health Care: A Global Casebook*. Sudbury, MA: Jones & Bartlett Learning.

Mertens D M and Wilson A T (2012) *Program Evaluation Theory and Practice: A Comprehensive Guide*. New York, NY: Guilford Press.

Rossi, P, Lipsey, M and Freeman H (2004) *Evaluation: A Systematic Approach* (7th ed). Newbury Park, CA: Sage.

Sines D, Hogard E and Ellis R (2012) 'Evaluating Quality of Life in Adults with Profound Learning Difficulties Resettled from Hospital to Supported Living in the Community.' *Journal of Intellectual Disabilities* 16(4), pp. 247–263.

Watt V, Hogard E, Ellis R and Erdos M (2007) *Evaluation of Hungarian Social Work and Social Policy Students' Work Placements in Cheshire*. Chester: Chester Academic Press.

Wyatt Knowlton L and Phillips C C (2013) *The Logic Model Guidebook: Better Strategies for Great Results* (2nd ed). Newbury Park, CA: Sage.

7 Institutional Research and Quality Assurance

Roger Woodward

Institutional esearch is defined by Wikipedia as 'a broad category of work done at schools, colleges and universities to inform campus decision making and planning in areas such as admissions, curriculum, enrolment management, staffing student life, finance, facilities, athletics and alumni relations'. This definition reflects the American origins of the discipline. While in Europe, and the U.K. in particular, the growth of the subject has been heavily dependent on its American parenthood, institutional research has developed in a more specific direction on this side of the Atlantic.

For our purposes, I revert to a definition which seems more useful for our present purpose: 'Institutional research may be defined as the activity in which the research effort of an academic institution is directed to the solution of its own problems and to the enhancement of its own performance' (Woodward, 1993, p. 113). This brief is wide, but perhaps not so much so as the former definition. It is useful to consider two distinctions. First, an institutional research unit which a university might establish would have the role of harnessing the research resources of the university to the solution of its own problems: it is the institution that is the client. The problems studied by institutional research are those that arise within the university in its primary functions of teaching, scholarship and research. Other research centres, on the other hand, research the problems of external clients. The second distinction I make is between institutional research and research in higher education. For the latter discipline findings are of interest in their potential to characterise general features of institutions: their students and staff. This question of generalisability is not so crucial to institutional research, where any failure of findings to find applicability beyond the sponsoring institution is not a necessarily a problem.

It follows from this that the concerns of institutional research cannot be established as an autonomous set of professional precepts, developed by likeminded scholars in relative isolation from specific institutional needs. Rather its aims are largely determined by a requirement to be responsive to needs that arise in a particular institution. Generalisation is more likely to apply to methods and approaches than to specific findings.

The need for universities to concern themselves with assuring quality in their teaching provision has been strongly felt for some years now, and is an increasing concern. As argued elsewhere in this book, many reasons can be given for this, and at diverse levels of analysis. From the 1980s it became increasingly recognised that individual recipients of the services of large institutions had the right to expect good service from those institutions. The obvious power of the large bureaucracy, relative to that of the individuals they served, could not be used to evade their responsibilities to those whom they serve. Later, I will return to these matters of justification, but I now turn to some specific contributions of institutional research in this area.

Record keeping

The records that are required for monitoring the quality of university teaching require extensive consideration. They would certainly include objective measures of student performance, which may or may not be adjusted for student intake qualification. They would also include measures of student views on the quality of aspects of university provision. Firstly, however, I will outline the particular role of institutional research in relation to records of objective data. Records are, of course, properly kept by the administrative departments of a university, who have the responsibility to make returns to statutory national bodies. Information returned to such bodies is used, *inter alia,* to provide valuable publication of the nationwide statistics. In the U.K. the Higher Education Statistical Agency (HESA) collect, collate and publish such data.

The records which, I would argue, an institutional research office should keep are subsets of these, or they may not need to be physically distinct. They would be functionally arranged to facilitate the analysis of data for the investigation of likely problems. The data required for quality assurance are mostly present in administrative records, but work needs to be done to make such information apparent and useable. In many cases there is, in common parlance, the problem of not being able to see the wood for the trees. Data protection issues are, of course, highly relevant. The permissible use of personal data needs to be assured in order for investigations to proceed. In the U.K. the Data Protection Act (1998) provides constraints within which such work can be done.

A problem with records kept for administrative purposes is that the level of analysis for returns to national bodies may not be appropriate for the quality monitoring purposes envisaged here. Subject categories, courses, and specific modules provided by university departments do not always have straightforward relationships. Care needs to be taken in drawing conclusions based on data that do not quite fit the unit being assessed. This is why an institutional research unit, anchored in and responsible only to the sponsoring university, is well placed to conduct analyses in such specific contexts.

Before leaving the topic of data records it is worth commenting that, while they are a necessary component for the assurance of quality, data records have quality concerns of their own. Often, only small numbers are available in units of analysis that are required to address the aims of a particular project. York (2017) has offered a useful discussion of this topic and proposes solutions based on collaboration among institutions. Gose (1989) has discussed problems in assuring the accuracy of data deriving from institutional records. There are many standard approaches to checking for errors in data files. However, the approaches used are often checks internal to the system. Checks are seldom made by comparing the data record to some external source of evidence. For example, we may keep a record of applicants who were offered a place at a university but who declined the offer. Do we ever check the data by contacting a sample of those individuals to enquire if the record squares with their own perception of events?

In some cases considerations of the quality of records extends beyond the concept of accuracy. Properly applied, accuracy is a question that only pertains to situations where there is some external referent, of a more definitive nature, with which it is possible to compare the data, at least in principle. If the data agree with the external referent, we call them 'accurate', and if not we call them 'inaccurate'. Frequently, however, such an external referent is lacking, either for want of proper definition or because the arbitrariness of a specified definition is not fully appreciated. In cases like this questions of 'accuracy' may serve only to obfuscate questions of quality, perhaps because they divert attention from considerations about the appropriateness of the definitions with which we work. An example of this is the issue concerning students who voluntarily withdraw from study in a university. Students may be recorded as having withdrawn when they in fact transferred to another course in the university. We may safely call this an error: the record should have shown a transfer code instead of a withdrawal code. Suppose, however, that the student really did withdraw, in the sense that she/he signs a form to that effect, and then perhaps the next week enrolled on another course at the same institution, perhaps because of unawareness of correct procedures or perhaps because a new option was presented. The student will not regard herself has having withdrawn from the institution, but it is misleading to regard the data as inaccurate in this. The issue is one of definition. A further complication arises in cases where students fail examinations badly but, rather than having studies terminated, are offered stringent programmes of resits and sometimes a requirement to repeat a year. This may prove to be too daunting a prospect and the student leaves. The records may, without error, show a voluntary withdrawal: but this is far from the student's perception of events! Sensitivity in considering such issues, going beyond simple statistical analysis, is crucial. Alach (2016) provides an interesting discussion of the conceptual issues surrounding such performance measurement. In order to increase the likelihood of such issues being considered in the context of the decisions they might lead to, an institutional research unit, with a working knowledge of the particular university, has an important role.

Records for the assurance of quality must not only contain objective data, but also the results of subjective ratings. Most immediately we think of student questionnaires. However, the 'clients' of higher education can be construed as categories of individual other than the student. In particular they can include employers and officers of professional bodies who require graduates to perform essential roles in their respective organisations. Questionnaire preparation and analysis are central issues for institutional research. It is important to consider this under the heading of 'record keeping' because of the value of collecting data from questionnaire studies over a period of time. Such longitudinal data can allow results from a class in a given year to be set in the context of those from other years. Employers' perceptions, where these can be continuously monitored, can also provide valuable year by year comparison.

There is, of course, a tension here. Measurement instruments, including questionnaires, always stand in need to continuing development and improvement. But such instruments need to be kept the same or else year by year comparisons cannot be made. At most any revision would have to be kept to a minimum, and interpreters of data would have to be sensitive to any changes made. Grebennikov and Shah (2013) provide interesting discussion of the values of continuous measurement of student perceptions.

The development of measurement instruments

The development of measurement instruments has always been an ongoing concern for institutional research. The importance of this derives from the fact that measurements are seldom neutral. They operationalise the good we seek to attain and the bad we seek to avoid. For universities, how we measure influences strategy. Recent developments in measures of efficiency may have significant implications for university management. Johnes and Tone (2017) discuss how choice of instrument can have marked implication for policy development. Barra and Zotti (2017) discuss how student data can be used in measurement of efficiency in an Italian context.

Research into measurement instruments for student views on teaching has been undertaken for many years and good measurement instruments are available. However, as discussed by Stringer and Finlay (1993), much of the research is undertaken in an American context and its applicability to other cultures of university education in Europe may be questioned. Mathies and Valimaa (2013) develop the idea of specific European needs in matters concerning higher education, in particular the need for a European concept of institutional research. Diversity is an important source of richness of European university education and this diversity extends to individual institutions within countries. There is therefore an important function in developing or adapting measurement instruments to meet the particular circumstances of individual institutions. However, if comparisons are to be made among units, courses or departments within institutions, then there must be a commonality of measurement instruments within the university. The need, therefore, is for research and development of measurement instruments for the individual institution. This, as previously discussed in the present chapter, is the specific function of institutional research.

An issue faced in the development of measurement instruments is whether they should be anonymous or confidential. In the former case instruments are designed in such a way that responses cannot be traced back to any individual respondent. In the latter, they can be so traced but assurance would invariably be given that such responses are confidential to the research team, and no result would be published or otherwise made available, which could be traced to any individual respondent. Anonymity is generally preferred, but confidentiality permits a much richer analysis of results by allowing linkages to objective data. If this course be chosen respondents would need to be fully apprised, and arrangements for confidential storage, analysis and eventual destruction of the data need to be watertight. Data protection implications of such an approach need to be fully considered.

Two classic requirements of measurement instruments are validity and reliability. Validity is the requirement that the instrument really does measure what it purports to measure. Reliability is the requirement that the measurement is consistent. Validity is a hard concept to deal with in our case, where we have no definitive source of student opinion with which to compare results from our questionnaire. Face validity (do the questions appear to address the issues under consideration?) can be established as well as relationships with less formal sources of information. Reliability can be examined in terms of internal consistency by looking at the relationships among responses to particular items.

Research is clearly needed into one particular area of measurement for the recognition of teaching quality: that is, what do we mean by good, and by bad, university teaching? We can, and do, ask students to judge whether the teaching they had experienced was good or bad, but there is little characterisation of what is meant by 'good' or 'bad' teaching in this context. Saunders and Saunders (1993) discussed this issue more fully and attempted such a characterisation through a process of reflective dialogue among expert teachers.

Student views on teaching

The more specific topic of student views on teaching will now be considered. The definition of quality offered by Ellis (1993) – 'that which gives complete customer satisfaction' – raises the immediate question of whom we mean by 'customer' and how we measure 'satisfaction'. Elton (1993) enjoined the use of the term 'client', rather than 'customer' in the context of one who is a recipient of a professional service. As noted earlier, and as discussed by Ellis (1993), there are many interpretations of who should be regarded as the client in university education. For present purposes I take the student as client. This is not to reduce the validity of other nominations, but the case seems strong for four reasons. First, it is students who make their considerable investment of time and experience in the teaching service that the university offers. This is an important investment since, for the majority of students, it is made once in a lifetime. Second, it is students who are the most direct recipients of the service. Third, it is students who make the selection among the alternative suppliers of the service; the different institutions to which admission might be sought. This choice is not unconstrained, of course, since any university may choose to admit or to refuse admission to a student. Lastly (though perhaps not a last reason for a student!), students in the U.K. and many other countries increasingly have to pay the fees for their own tuition. Though often ameliorated by a system of student loans, this financial burden is very considerable for individuals at the stage of life of most students. Interestingly, Vuori (2013) argues persuasively that students should legitimately be regarded as 'customers' even though in Finland, where that study was conducted, fee payment was not involved.

In considering the measurement of student satisfaction with teaching we must immediately address what is perhaps the most fundamental question: why should we be concerned with student satisfaction? Until now, university funding has not depended on such satisfaction although, at the time of writing, introducing such a dependence has been mooted by the U.K. Government as a development in the near future. Students, as noted above, for the most part have only one experience of full-time university education and so the test of satisfaction important to the automobile industry – 'Would you buy the same car again?' – has little relevance.

The fundamental answer to this question is the moral one. The very fact that we invite young people to entrust us with their once in a lifetime experience of university education behoves us to do all we can to ensure the quality of the experience. If this sounds too sententious we should consider Lewis Elton's point that the moral imperative to excellence, irrespective of extrinsic sanction, is the most important characteristic of a profession (Elton, 1993).

A more pragmatic reason for attending to student satisfaction with teaching is that students, although they cannot remake their decisions in the light of experience, can tell others. The potential for such personal recommendation to affect applicants' choice of university will probably depend on the extent to which the university takes its students from a localised geographical area, where it will be more likely that applicants will be personally acquainted with current or former students of the university. Indeed personal acquaintance is not a necessary condition for recommendation to have an effect. University students might well report their experience to the school they formerly attended, where staff might relay this reported experience to existing pupils, who might well be considering choices of university application.

The University of Ulster was such a case, where 76 per cent of its students came from Northern Ireland. In 1987 the Institutional Research Unit asked all students to complete a questionnaire concerning sources of influence on their choice of university. Following piloting, respondents were offered six categories of people who could be expected to have a significant influence on their choice: school principals, school careers officers, other school teachers, university staff, parents, and former students of the University. Former students were by far the largest category of positive influence, ticked by 65 per cent of respondents. It thus appears that there are gains in applications to the University as a consequence of experience of former students. We cannot, of course, be sure that it was satisfaction with teaching that these former students had in mind when they made their recommendation.

Considerations for establishing an institutional research unit

The present author was, to the best of his knowledge, the first Director of Institutional Research in Europe. Some reflections on the establishment of such a unit may therefore be pertinent.

Although the sponsoring institution had some good ideas of what it hoped to achieve by establishing an institutional research unit, it was not thought wise to set particular objectives too early. The role can be clarified as experience emerges. It is also necessary to have the flexibility to respond to important issues and events as they emerge.

Reporting mechanisms require careful consideration. In order to avoid perceptions of sectional interest it should report to the university centrally, rather than to a particular faculty or department. This is a difficult issue since, of course, expertise on pertinent research areas will reside elsewhere in the university. But reporting mechanisms do not preclude good cooperation.

Staffing will always have significant cost implications, and therefore pressures for appointment at relatively junior levels are always present. If the university were to know exactly what it wants to be done, and how to do it, then tasks could probably be done by a supervised research officer. However, this is not usually the case for institutional research. I earlier discussed the issue of student withdrawal and problems in characterising and defining the concept. My experience in the University of Ulster was that it is just this issue of characterisation and definition that was required by the University, before any research analysis could begin. The Director therefore needs to be a person of reasonable depth of experience and understanding, to undertake this.

The matter of expected outputs can and should be considered early. The definition of institutional research given at the beginning of this chapter implies that the primary output should be reports to the relevant committees and senior officers of the university. This is more relevant to the university than papers in academic journals. The latter are, of course, not precluded but inevitably they more often address concerns of research in higher education, rather than institutional research as characterised here. Conference contributions are very valuable, in particular because they provide opportunities for cross-nation discussion and comparison. Indeed, the very institution-specific nature of institutional research accentuates the value of cross-national exchange of ideas The European Association for Institutional Research is very valuable in this context.

Further considerations and conclusions

We have outlined questionnaire approaches, and the use of objective data. Earlier we alluded to an expert systems approach in which characterisation of successful teaching is developed by systematically examining the views and practices of those recognised to be expert and successful in this field (Saunders and Saunders, 1993). A fourth approach would be the systematic and critical appraisal of the behavioural interactions of which commonly occurring teaching situations are comprised. Such an analysis has the potential to go beyond discovering *that* teaching has been successful, to discovering *how* it has been successful. Examples would be the identification of behaviours likely to maintain student concentration, or to identify checks for student comprehension.

It is not clear how we should judge the relative status of results produced from these four approaches. There is some evidence that student and teacher ratings tend to agree, but that both bear rather less relationship to objective criteria. This is a variety of what de Winter Hebron (1984) described as 'a collusion of expectation', in which students and teachers mutually reinforce untested expectations. Consideration of the issue would doubtless be informed by data but it would be wise to consider in advance what judgements might be appropriate in the event of conflicting results. The soundest judgement at this stage is that each source of information is necessary but not sufficient in forming a judgement about teaching quality. Data from experts is insufficient because of the danger of cultures of expertise becoming divorced from requirements of the wider community. This is a danger well encapsulated in the familiar jibe against medical expertise: 'the operation was a success but the patient died'. Data from student feedback, on the other hand, are insufficient because of the risk of identifying good teaching with popular teaching. There is, perhaps, a danger in higher education of teachers courting popularity but avoiding, or oversimplifying, the more difficult topics in the curriculum. It might appear that objective data are sufficient, or at least have a more fundamental status than the others. We must, however, consider it possible that some students get good attainments in spite of, rather than because of, the institution's provision. Students may have a rather poor opinion of the standard of teaching they get and, recognising the need to pass their examinations, seek help from other sources. Objective descriptions of effective teaching have the particular advantage in potentially identifying steps that might be taken to enhance teaching performance.

In all the foregoing accounts, I have argued for the central role of an institutional research unit, with expertise on analysis and detailed awareness of university life. The unit needs to be specially related to its sponsoring institution so that it can entirely focus on that institution's needs. Other conceptions of institutional research can be broader. In America this often means involvement in wider educational communities, other than universities. Often in Europe, institutional research has a considerable overlap with the discipline we call research in higher education: a distinction in which, as I suggested at the beginning of this chapter, is worth keeping for the discipline of institutional research to better serve the role of enhancing quality in university teaching.

References

Alach, Z. (2016) Performance measurement and accountability. *Tertiary Education and Management* 22(1): 36–48.

Barra, C. and Zotti, R. (2017) What we can learn from the use of student data in efficiency analysis within the context of higher education. *Tertiary Education and Management* 23(3): 276–303.

De Winter Hebron, C. (1984) Some problems and pleasures of teaching part-time management students. *Studies in Higher Education* 9(2): 169–181.

Ellis, R. (1993) A British Standard for university teaching? In Ellis, R. (ed.) *Quality Assurance for University Teaching*. Buckingham: Open University Press.

Elton, L. (1993) University teaching: a professional model for quality. In Ellis, R. (ed.) *Quality Assurance for University Teaching*. Buckingham: Open University Press.

Gose, F. J. (1989) Data integrity: why aren't the data accurate? *A.I.R. Professional File* 33.

Grebenikov, L. and Shah, M. (2013) Monitoring trends in student satisfaction. *Tertiary Education and Management* 19(4): 301–322.

Johnes, G. and Tone, K. (2017) The efficiency of higher education institutions in England revisited: comparing alternative methods. *Tertiary Education and Management* 23(3): 191–205.

Mathies, C. and Valimaa, J. (2013) Is there a need for a European institutional research? *Tertiary Education and Management* 19(1): 85–96.

Saunders, C. and Saunders, E. (1993) Expert teachers' perceptions of university teaching: the identification of teaching skills. In Ellis, R. (ed.) *Quality Assurance for University Teaching*. Buckingham: Open University Press.

Stringer, M. and Finlay, C. (1993) Assuring quality through student evaluations. In Ellis, R. (ed.) *Quality Assurance for University Teaching*. Buckingham: Open University Press.

Vuori, J. (2013) Are students customers in Finnish higher education? *Tertiary Education and Management* 19(2): 176–187.

Woodward, R. (1993) Institutional research and quality assurance. In Ellis, R. (ed.) *Quality Assurance for University Teaching*. Buckingham: Open University Press.

York, M. (2017) Tallying the differences between demographic subgroups from multiple institutions: the practical utility of nonparametric analysis. *Tertiary Education and Management* 23(2): 115–124.

8 The Power of Proxies

An Examination of Performance Management Frameworks

Jeremy Warren

This chapter is concerned with a topic which perforce figures in a quality assurance system. The performance which has to be managed includes, of course, the teaching loads and teaching quality of academic staff. To what extent do techniques of performance management actually facilitate or perhaps inhibit the development of quality in teaching and learning?

To address these questions this chapter will provide an overview of the merits and dangers inherent within a performance management culture. Second, it will review the extent to which numerical Key Performance Indicators (KPI) can be used as proxy measures for the estimation of qualitative concepts such as teaching quality or student success. Lastly the chapter will offer some thoughts for the future of HE performance management in the light of the introduction of the Teaching Excellence Framework.

It could be argued that it is not possible to measure something without in some way changing the thing you are trying to measure and this is particularly axiomatic when we consider the case for the introduction of a performance management system (PMS). These systems or frameworks are frequently composed of a number of Key Performance Indicators (KPI), which themselves often distil large amounts of work or practice down to a single measurement figure, which is then intended to act as a proxy for the specific behaviours or work that is of interest. It is this distillation of work to a single value that is both the significant attraction towards and inherent risk contained within KPIs as there is a significant danger of conflating performance measurement into performance management which, as I hope to show in this chapter, is considerably problematic in assuming that the two areas are synonymous.

In order to place the current drive towards performance indicators and metrics, aimed both at Higher Education and the wider public sector, we must consider the historical perspective so that lessons may be learnt from past mistakes and not repeated in the next wave of measures to be introduced. During the thirteen years of Labour government from 1997 to 2010 a substantial performance management 'industry' was created, requiring public agencies to submit vast amounts of data to a number of different departments, with different agencies sometimes being set performance targets which placed them at odds with partner organisations when they were supposed to be working in collaboration with those same agencies. One example of this comes from the criminal justice arena when the Youth Justice Board for England and Wales (YJB) included a reduction target for Youth Offending Teams for the number of young people entering the system who had been given a court-based sanction, either a Referral Order or custodial sentence. In contrast, the Police were to be measured by the Home Office on the number of offences that they brought to justice, with justice in this case being offences that result in a court-imposed penalty. In failing to communicate or coordinate their performance frameworks, the YJB and the Home Office created a degree of tension between YOTs and their local Police force and made it more difficult for both agencies to achieve their expected targets. Whilst it is hoped that such mistakes would not be repeated going forward there is a similar and current issue in UK Higher Education, in what HEIs are being required to manage and address in terms of maintaining income from student fees. The preoccupation of the present Conservative Government with immigration and feeling that they need to be seen to be taking a hard stance on this issue has led to such a significant tightening of the rules in relation to foreign students wanting to study in the UK, such that they are taking their business to other countries in Europe or to the United States.[1] In line with the theme of this chapter, examples such as this demonstrate the dangers that are inherent in actively pursuing a key performance metric without taking sufficient notice of the impacts that such a course will have upon other areas of activity, and the overall performance standards achieved by the organisation.

It should of course be recognised that these issues are not unique to the UK but are part of a wider debate in relation to performance management practices in HEIs worldwide. It is therefore appropriate that we spend some time in reviewing those reported issues and problems from a number of different countries, with different cultural values and approaches to education as well as the different ways in which teaching staff are expected to fulfil their duties. In a review of Performance Based Research Funding (PBRF) systems across a number of countries, with comparison back to the situation in Italy, Abramo *et al.* (2011) found that in non-competitive systems, where top-rated scientists are dispersed amongst all universities rather than concentrating talent in a few institutions, those individuals placed in lower performing institutions may suffer a detriment by association compared to their colleagues who were placed in more highly regarded universities. Issues of employee detriment in addition to other human-resource-related issues were discussed by Decramer *et al.* (2012) in their review of the impact of market pressures upon research units within universities in the Netherlands. In their paper thy suggest that the wide variety of external factors which impact upon research units have led to a wide variety of performance structures being put into place which do not necessarily demonstrate a strong degree of vertical alignment with the institutional priorities of the university. Remaining with the Netherlands for the moment, Hladchenko reviewed the introduction of a PBRF mechanism within Dutch universities, comparing it to the UK experience with this approach to the disbursement of research funds (Hladchenko, 2014, 2015b). Using this methodology, research monies are allocated on the basis of predicted greatest impact, i.e. funds are moved from those universities with poorer research records and numbers of outputs towards those that are perceived to have a greater likelihood of research success with the monies received. Whilst this is good news for those institutions that receive the largest tranche of the research funding available, it is not such good news for those researchers with national or international reputations who happen to work in universities that fall into the second category for funding. Further analysis of university funding was undertaken by Agasisti (2011), who used a series of non-parametric algorithms against publicly available datasets to compare the efficiency of different higher education funding models used by different European countries. The paper concluded that the models used in the UK and Switzerland were more efficient than others in the analysis, whilst recognising the changes to be implemented in the Netherlands which sought to improve the efficient disbursement of the funding available.

Whilst space does not allow for a comprehensive review of performance management frameworks in universities beyond Europe, examples from Pakistan, Canada, the USA and China are considered in order to provide a comparison to the previous discussion. A review of the performance frameworks and quality management systems in use within universities in Pakistan (Asif *et al.*, 2013; Ishaq *et al.*, 2014) used the education criteria for performance excellence from the Baldridge framework,[2] which is used extensively in Pakistan. This framework integrates Leadership, Strategy and Customers, with Workforce, Operations and Results; under the umbrella of Measurement, Analysis and Knowledge Management. However, the authors argue that is little evidence of a theoretical basis for the framework and suggest that performance management frameworks should be based upon organisational mission, operations focus, customer focus, workforce focus, and performance measurement in order to be effective for the individual institution.

These factors are echoed in the work undertaken by Chan (2015) in relation to the performance data that Canadian universities have been required to submit to government since 1988, in the belief that publicly available information will assist student choice in terms of programmes of study at specific institutions. The researchers found, as has already been recognised in the current work, that the imposition of KPIs is not a popular measure for performance or accountability, either for members of teaching staff or individual programmes of study. Instead they note that funding decisions are often taken at a distance that is far removed from the point at which decisions are taken to improve the performance or experience of different academic programmes and that this could result in decisions being made which are ultimately not in the best interest of the students. They also note, as we have recognised, that many of the factors that impact upon student performance in relation to specific programmes of study are often beyond the immediate control of the university, reducing the validity of any performance measures which draw upon data that report such factors.

These findings are echoed in the work undertaken by Nisar (2015) in relation to Higher Education Institutions in the USA. The work reports the changes to the fiscal support provided by the Federal Government to institutions of higher education, with a performance-based framework that is heavily influenced by the principles of improved access, affordability to students, and programme outputs, which represented a substantial change from the previously employed funding model. Using an ecology of games perspective, the researcher suggests that in order to respond to the complexities of the real-world factors which impact upon higher education funding decisions, a number of different policies and funding models should be employed in order to determine the 'best fit' within any given set of circumstances. This is, of course, in contrast to the way that funding decisions are made in the UK, Europe and elsewhere but which may be appropriate for the United States given its own history of such decisions often being made at the level of the State rather than by the Federal Government.

This brief review of HEI performance frameworks in place in countries beyond Europe will conclude with a comparison of UK and China HEI Strategic Alliances (SA), including performance factors, undertaken by Li *et al.* (2014, 2016). The authors found that whilst considerable cultural differences existed between HEIs in China and the UK, the extent to which these became problematic depended upon the nature of the SA entered into, with partners often recognising the cultural differences as sources of mutual interest. They nevertheless note that the impact of such cultural differences are often more serious and significant in non-equity based arrangements, suggesting that the performance frameworks developed to support such arrangements would need to be both focussed and appropriate, which could lead to another set of issues in terms of the engagement of staff with the process.

It could be argued that one of the primary purposes of a performance framework is to estimate the perceived 'quality' of the organisation, whether that is the quality of the members of staff who work for the organisation, the quality of any service provided or the quality of the products or outputs of that organisation. The last few years has therefore seen the development of an increasing literature that seeks to investigate notions of quality and how those ideas may be translated into quality management. Whilst there are many different approaches to the development of a performance management system, two in particular appear to have come to prominence in recent years, at least in the context of measuring performance in HEIs. The first of these, the notion of the Balanced Scorecard, is based upon the principle of comparing measured behaviours against an agreed ideal value, with the difference being used as an indicator for corrective action. The principles underpinning the effective implementation of a Balanced Scorecard approach to performance management in HE settings was reviewed by Hladchenko (2015a), starting with the strategic principles that were suggested by Kaplan and Norton (1996) as being the main reasons for introducing a Balanced Scorecard approach to the measurement of the stated goals of an organisation:

- to clarify and translate vision and strategy;
- to communicate and link strategic objectives and measures;
- to plan, set targets, and align strategic initiatives; and
- to enhance strategic feedback and learning.

These assumptions are predicated on the assumption that an organisation, or HEI in the context of the current work, has a clearly stated set of goals or objectives that can then be fed down to faculties, departments and individual members of staff in a manner such that the performance targets attached to each unit of measurement can be linked back to the whole. Such an organisation is described as being *agency based*, with a significant focus on short-term goals as measures of performance; as compared with a stewardship-based organisation that is based upon organisational and individual values, placing higher degrees of significance upon the preservation, generation of and dissemination of knowledge (Franco-Santos *et al.*, 2013), differences which will be returned to later.

It should be recognised that the landscape within which HEIs operate has undergone a number of seismic shifts in recent years, with the gradual reduction of income from successive governments to be replaced by student fees and a consequent change in the relationships that those students have with their *alma mater*, whilst studying and as *alumni*, increasing expectations of both teaching quality and the wider student experience. These issues were recognised by Eftimov *et al.* (2016) in their discussion of the introduction of a Balanced Scorecard approach to a single faculty, which they suggest could be readily adapted for use by other HEIs, assuming that the institution is moving towards an agency-based style of performance management. It should, of course, be recognised that not all activities undertaken within universities lend themselves to be converted into SMART (Specific, Measurable, Accurate, Realistic and Timely) objectives; for instance, it would make little sense to dictate or mandate the amount of time that academics could spend in support of their students as issues raised vary considerably in their degree of complexity and the resources needed to overcome them; leading to images of Personal Academic Tutors acting like General Practitioners in ushering students out of the door after ten minutes having raised two problems. Whilst that was something of a tongue-in-cheek example, it does nevertheless exemplify the difficulties of reducing academic practice to a series of performance indicators that are then judged to represent the quality of work undertaken by a member of staff (Taylor and Baines, 2012).

The findings of the studies reported above were echoed by those of Elola *et al.* (2016), who reported the results of a survey of all 56 HEIs in Spain which was designed to assess their experiences with the introduction of TQM and BSC approaches to performance management. The researchers found that where lecturers were given the capacity to build positive relationships with their students they would be more likely to exhibit higher levels of job satisfaction but were also more likely to build and maintain long-term relationships with their organisation. – findings that may be of assistance to an HEI that is considering the introduction of a performance framework and has not yet decided upon whether to adopt an agency or stewardship-based model.

The second approach to performance management that has been utilised by higher education institutions in recent years is based on an assessment of 'quality', with a number of tools and models being available, for example, Total Quality Management (TQM), as included within the European Foundation for Quality Management (EFQM) model. It is relatively easy to see how such an approach may have real and significant benefits within a manufacturing industry, where consumers need to be assured that they are receiving good value for money in relation to the goods which they purchase. In such business sectors the idea of quality starts with the production of the raw materials or ingredients and is built into every stage of the production and distribution process before the product reaches the consumer. It is however less easy to see how such an exacting notion of quality may be applied to Higher Education, where so many of the factors in the direct control of a manufacturer are outside of the sphere of influence that may be directly exerted by a university. In contrast José Tarí (2006) suggested in a case-study review of a Spanish university that key factors for the successful delivery of the EFQM approach lay in the degree of 'buy-in' from both management and staff; in addition to the degree and quality of support offered to those taking a role in the self-assessment teams. In an attempt to review the impact of quality on one of those factor areas Rodgers (2008) examined the way in which a quality management approach may be used to improve the services offered by university student's unions, suggesting that quality needs to be seen as a vital element of the management of services which might impact upon different aspects of the student experience, regardless of whether those services are provided by the university directly or by a partner organisation such as the local student's union (Hladchenko, 2015a).

Of course, like a man, no university is an island and therefore needs to understand its own performance and quality management procedures in the context of its sister or competitor institutions.

We therefore come to the notion of benchmarking, the process of comparison that allows an institution to rate its own performance against similar organisations, where those comparisons may be focussed on the UK or take on an international dimension, ideas which were examined by Paliulis and Labanauskis (2015) in order to show how such an approach may complement the performance framework already in place within an HEI. In their conceptual model of how TQM may be applied within an HEI setting, Zakuan *et al.* (2012) identified a number of factors which they propose are essential to the achievement of the identified critical success criteria:

- the commitment demonstrated by management;
- continuous improvement of both staff and processes;
- the recognition of the total customer experience;
- the involvement in and ownership of the TQM process by employees;
- the training received by staff within the organisation;
- the recognition of the importance of communication;
- the engendering of a teamwork-focussed culture.

These, when taken together, form the basis of a performance framework that meets the needs of staff, students and other significant stakeholders. In their assessment of the impact had by the imposition of a TQM approach within an HEI IT department, O'Mahony and Garavan (2012) found that in addition to the factors identified above, post-implementation success required continual and sustained effort on the part of both management and staff as well as the systematic auditing of performance that was built into standard processes as a series of small increments, rather than a large-scale review that is only undertaken periodically. The importance of the role played by senior management in the effective introduction of a TQM approach has already been noted; however, this importance is not reduced once a framework has been implemented, as noted by Osseo-Asare *et al.* (2005) in their paper that identified the explicit factors by which the leadership of an HEI may be classed as 'weak', 'good', 'best and excellent'. Under their classification, practices that were 'best or excellent' were those which were deemed to be both highly important and highly effective; whilst leadership practices defined as 'good' were judged to be highly important but only averagely effective. In contrast to these, those leadership practices defined as being 'weak' were those highly important but less effective issues that will be discussed in the next section in terms of the Teaching Excellence Framework (TEF), to be introduced in the UK in the 2017/18 academic year.

The philosophical position which underpins the TEF was set out by the UK Government in the White Paper 'Success as a Knowledge Economy: Teaching Excellence, Social Mobility and Student Choice' (BIS, 2016). The framework is to be introduced in phased manner, with year one starting in October 2017 where all those institutions that have reached a perceived quality standard will be awarded a 'Meets Expectations' judgement and therefore allowed to maintain their student fee structure in line with inflation.

The three areas to be covered by the metrics of the Teaching Excellence Framework are likely to include student retention, job roles undertaken after university and satisfaction with different aspects of the university provision whilst they were a student. It is assumed by government that these three areas, when taken together, will act as a realistic proxy for teaching quality and indeed there is some basis for that assumption, given that a course which does not retain its students, does not satisfy them whilst at university and which does not lead to a good career path could be said to be unlikely to have good or excellent teaching input. However, there are other reasons why student drop-out of university, are dissatisfied with the student experience or fail to gain a job on their chosen path as soon as they leave, none of which can be laid at the door of the lecturers for failing to deliver good or excellent teaching. However, to return to a point made at the start of this chapter, the Government has stated that the TEF would be based upon data that is already collected as part of the statutory returns made by UK universities to HESA, HEFCE and other statutory bodies and is in danger of confusing performance measurement with performance management, taking data which was configured and collected for one purpose, re-interpreting it in the light of a different set of policy objectives. We therefore find ourselves having come full circle in questioning the ability of a given performance measure to act as a proxy for the work undertaken. Only time will tell if the metrics chosen for the TEF will lead to an increase in teaching quality across the HE sector but specifically within the teaching-focussed post-1992 institutions.

This then begs the question of how individual members of teaching and support staff in HEIs may influence the performance of the institution and help to achieve the required targets. Teelken and Lomas (2009) found that whilst there was a generally high level of support amongst the UK and Dutch academics who took part in their research for the notions of good quality management and the need to improve the student experience overall, there was a level of disagreement as to how the data that supported the requisite performance frameworks should be gathered and analysed. The researchers found that individual academics often resented the very detailed returns that they were required to submit, which eroded their perception of themselves as autonomous professionals with the capacity and responsibility to manage their work effectively. It should however be borne in mind that individual members of an institution's teaching staff each have the capacity to play an influential role in the way that the university is reported as part of the TEF, as their own interactions with students will contribute to the way in which those students respond to the questions in the National Student Survey. The ability of individual lecturers to interact effectively with their students could be said to be highly influenced by the management practices and performance frameworks under which they are required to operate. These management practices were reviewed by McCormack *et al.* (2014) in a comparison of effective and proven management practices used in industry against those in place in over 250 departments in more than 100 institutions. They found that longer established, more research-intensive departments scored higher than teaching-focussed departments in newer universities. Perhaps of greater interest to Heads of Department and other senior managers, the researchers also found that

> scores, particularly with respect to provision of incentives for staff recruitment, retention and promotion are correlated with both teaching and research performance conditional on resources and past performance. Moreover, this relationship holds for all universities, not just research-intensive ones.

It may be that where government and statutory agency pressure is being placed upon universities to adopt a knowledge-based stewardship approach to performance management, that in fact the agentic approach which recognises the professional nature of the academic's role may lead to improved student outcomes overall; actors that were also recognised by Kenny and Fluck (2014) in their assessment of academic staff workloads in Australian universities.

In conclusion, the current drive towards ever more detailed data collection processes, including the re-purposing of that data towards ends that it was not initially designed to meet, has provided universities in the UK and elsewhere with a particular set of challenges which they have always been in a position to influence. As institutions they are therefore left with a choice as to where they focus their activities in order to make the most advantageous return to government that they can, thereby hopefully influencing the amount of grant or other monies that they receive. However, life is rarely that simple and so it is with the application of performance frameworks to HE environments. To clarify then, an institution may decide to follow an agency-based approach, recognising the autonomy and professionalism of its staff and only collecting the minimum amounts of data required to make their statutory returns to government. As a strategy this has much to commend it in the long term, as it has been demonstrated that the likelihood of lecturer job satisfaction and student outcomes improving are high, but the impact upon the institution's reputation will take time to embed itself in the decision making of potential students. In contrast, a university may decide to adopt a more stewardship-based performance framework, where the data collected may provide the evidence for more immediate returns in terms of support from government or the ability of the institution to tell an evidence-based story to potential students. However, the longer-term gains that may be realised under the alternative approach could take longer to achieve; although one thing is certain and that is the need for universities to make themselves more accountable to governments, their own staff and perhaps most important of all, current and future students.

Notes

1 https://www.theguardian.com/education/2015/may/28/study-abroad-uk-students-over seas, accessed 19/11/2016.
2 https://www.nist.gov/baldrige/publications/baldrige-excellence-framework/education, accessed 19/11/2016.

References

Abramo, G., Cicero, T. & D'Angelo, C. A. (2011). The dangers of performance-based research funding in non-competitive higher education systems. *Scientometrics, 87*(3), 641–654. doi:10.1007/s11192-011-0355-4

Agasisti, T. (2011). Performances and spending efficiency in higher education: a European comparison through non-parametric approaches. *Education Economics, 19*(2), 199–224. doi:10.1080/09645290903094174

Asif, M., Awan, M. U., Khan, M. K. & Ahmad, N. (2013). A model for total quality management in higher education. *Quality & Quantity, 47*(4), 1883–1904. doi:10.1007/s11135-011-9632-9

BIS (2016). *Success as a Knowledge Economy: Teaching Excellence, Social Mobility and Student Choice.* London: HMSO.

Chan, V. (2015). Implications of key performance indicator issues in Ontario universities explored. *Journal of Higher Education Policy and Management, 37*(1), 41. doi:10.1080/1360080X.2014.991531

Decramer, A., Smolders, C., Vanderstraeten, A., Christiaens, J. & Desmidt, S. (2012). External pressures affecting the adoption of employee performance management in higher education institutions. *Personnel Review, 41*(6), 686–704. doi:10.1108/00483481211263593

Eftimov, L., Trpeski, P., Gockov, G. & Vasileva, V. (2016). Designing a balanced scorecard as strategic management system for higher education institutions: A case study in Macedonia. *Ekonomika, 62*(2), 29–48. doi:10.5937/ekonomika1602029E

Elola, L. N., Tejedor, J. P. & Ana Clara Pastor, T. (2016). Analysis of the causal relationships in the balanced scorecard in public and private Spanish Universities through structural equation modelling. *The Business & Management Review, 7*(5), 18.

Franco-Santos, M., Bourne, M. & Rivera, P. (2013). *Performance management in UK higher education institutions: the need for a hybrid approach* (Series 3, Publication 8). London: Leadership Foundation for Higher Education.

Hladchenko, M. (2014). Performance agreements in Dutch education. *Euromentor Journal, 5*(3), 34.

Hladchenko, M. (2015a). Balanced Scorecard – a strategic management system of the higher education institution. *International Journal of Educational Management, 29*(2), 167–176. doi:10.1108/IJEM-11-2013-0164

Hladchenko, M. (2015b). Transparency of the managemenr of Higher Education Institutions in the Netherlands. *Euromentor Journal, 6*(4), 30.

Ishaq Bhatti, M., Awan, H. M. & Razaq, Z. (2014). The key performance indicators (KPIs) and their impact on overall organizational performance. *Quality & Quantity, 48*(6), 3127–3143. doi:10.1007/s11135-013-9945-y

José Tarí, J. (2006). An EFQM model self-assessment exercise at a Spanish university. *Journal of Educational Administration, 44*(2), 170–188. doi:10.1108/09578230610652051

Kaplan, R. S. & Norton, D. P. (1996). Linking the Balanced Scorecard to strategy. *California Management Review, 39*(1), 53–79. doi:10.2307/41165876

Kenny, J. D. J. & Fluck, A. E. (2014). The effectiveness of academic workload models in an institution: a staff perspective. *Journal of Higher Education Policy and Management, 36*(6), 585–602. doi:10.1080/1360080X.2014.957889

Li, X., Roberts, J., Yan, Y. & Tan, H. (2014). Knowledge sharing in China–UK higher education alliances. *International Business Review, 23*(2), 343–355. doi:10.1016/j.ibusrev.2013.05.001

Li, X., Roberts, J., Yan, Y. & Tan, H. (2016). Management of cultural differences under various forms of China–UK higher education strategic alliances. *Studies in Higher Education, 41*(4), 774–798. doi:10.1080/03075079.2014.966664

McCormack, J., Propper, C. & Smith, S. (2014). Herding cats? Management and university performance. *The Economic Journal, 124*(578), F534–F564. doi:10.1111/ecoj.12105

Nisar, M. A. (2015). Higher education governance and performance based funding as an ecology of games. *Higher Education, 69*(2), 289–302. doi:10.1007/s10734-014-9775-4

O'Mahony, K. & Garavan, T. N. (2012). Implementing a quality management framework in a higher education organisation. *Quality Assurance in Education, 20*(2), 184–200. doi:10.1108/09684881211219767

Osseo-Asare, A. E., Longbottom, D. & Murphy, W. D. (2005). Leadership best practices for sustaining quality in UK higher education from the perspective of the EFQM Excellence Model. *Quality Assurance in Education, 13*(2), 148–170. doi:10.1108/09684880510594391

Paliulis, N. K. & Labanauskis, R. (2015). Benchmarking as an instrument for improvement of quality management in Higher Education. *Business, Management and Education, 13*(1), 140–157. doi:10.3846/bme.2015.220

Rodgers, T. (2008). Measuring quality in Higher Education: can a performance indicator approach be extended to identifying the quality of students' union provision? *Quality in Higher Education, 14*(1), 79–92. doi:10.1080/13538320802028171

Taylor, J. & Baines, C. (2012). Performance management in UK universities: implementing the Balanced Scorecard. *Journal of Higher Education Policy and Management, 34*(2), 111. doi:10.1080/1360080X.2012.662737

Teelken, C. & Lomas, L. (2009). 'How to strike the right balance between quality assurance and quality control in the perceptions of individual lecturers': a comparison of UK and Dutch higher education institutions. *Tertiary Education and Management, 15*(3), 259–275. doi:10.1080/13583880903073016

Zakuan, N., Muniandy, S., Muhamad Zameri Mat, S., Mohd Shoki Md, A., Sulaiman, S. & Jalil, R. A. (2012). Critical success factors of total quality management implementation in Higher Education Institutions: a review. *International Journal of Academic Research in Business and Social Sciences, 2*(12), 19–32.

9 Quality Assurance in Medical Education

Accreditation and Teaching Standards in Australia, the USA, Canada and the UK

Elaine Hogard, Dan Hunt, Jessica Lichtenstein, Theanne Walters and Roger Ellis

External quality assurance for teaching and learning is a long-standing feature of medical education and is associated with registration as a professional. In many instances, these quality assurance processes result in formal accreditation of programmes. This chapter investigates quality assurance practices in three countries, two of which are formal accreditation processes, building on the survey of accreditation world-wide completed by van Zanten *et al.* (2008).

Van Zanten *et al.* (ibid.) found that there was a significant variation in the structure and quality of undergraduate medical education around the world. They investigated the overseeing of medical education from an international Directory of Organizations that recognize/accredit medical schools (DORA). The Directory includes information on the presence of national accrediting bodies and related data. Medical education accreditation information was pooled by World Health Organization (WHO) regions.

van Zanten *et al.* (ibid.) concluded that although over half of all countries with medical schools indicated that they have a national process for accrediting medical education programmes, the nature of the various authorities and levels of enforcement vary considerably. Despite global trends indicating an increasing focus on the quality of education programmes, data linking accreditation processes to the production of more highly skilled doctors and, ultimately, better patient care are lacking. Investigating current accreditation practices is a necessary step for further research.

This chapter is intended to complement van Zanten's 2008 survey by investigating quality assurance in three countries that have established and developed practices. Three case studies were completed by a senior officer in each body. They were asked to describe their quality assurance or accreditation processes and to identify issues, approaches and problems. In particular, they were asked how their processes set standards for teaching and monitored that these standards were being met. They were asked to identify the evidence they would gather to assess quality in teaching. The three case studies follow.

While the approach of the three bodies to standards in teaching was a primary interest, the case studies also give insights into their processes and their position on the dirigiste–laissez-faire dimension referred to in Chapter 1. Further their procedures highlighted important issues for accreditation world-wide. The term accreditation may be used generally for any process whereby there is some form of official certification that a school or programme has met standards set by external regulators or it may refer to the stricter operationalism adopted by the WHO/WFME. See http://whoeducationguidelines.org/sites/default/files/uploads/whoeduguidelines_PolicyBrief_Accreditation.pdf and WFME.org (the World Federation for Medical Education: Application for Recognition of an Accrediting Agency for Medical Schools).

These require three components in an accreditation: a critical self-study by the school in relation to standards; a visit by a team of peers; and a report indicating the result and any requirements to be met and an agency that requires that improvements related to the standards be made. There is clearly a major issue regarding the extent to which practices world-wide and indeed those in the three case studies in this chapter meet these standards and are properly described as accreditation.

Quality assurance of teaching in medical programmes in Australia

In Australia, medical programmes and the institutions that provide these programmes are covered by a number of quality assurance processes. The system of academic accreditation, managed by the Tertiary Education Quality and Standards Agency (TEQSA) quality assures Australia's higher education providers. A system of professional accreditation for regulated health professions, including medicine, quality assures programmes of study that graduate health practitioners. The Australian Medical Council (AMC) manages the professional accreditation of programmes of study for medicine. Both these external quality assurance systems are ultimately based on the education provider demonstrating that it meets the relevant set of standards.

Quality assurance policies

TEQSA is an independent authority that regulates and assures the quality of Australia's providers of higher education. Its role is to safeguard the interests of current and future students within Australia's higher education system. TEQSA evaluates the performance of higher education providers against the Higher Education Standards Framework (Threshold Standards: http://www.teqsa.gov.au/teqsa-contextual-overview-hes-framework).

The standards are structured under seven domains that align with the student life cycle, from prospective student, through admission to graduation and the award of a qualification. The first domain, Student Participation and Attainment, covers the education-related experiences of students across this life cycle. The remaining domains concern the higher education provider's actions to achieve the educational outcomes expected for students. The Standards for Teaching (domain 3) focus on the provider's activities to guide and facilitate student learning. These standards address: course design, staffing (sufficiency to meet students' educational, academic support and administrative needs), teaching qualifications and skills of academic staff, and quality of and access to learning resources.

The Health Practitioner Regulation National Law Act 2009 (the National Law) regulates the accreditation of programmes of study in 14 health professions, including medicine. Under the National Law, an accreditation authority is authorized to accredit programmes in each profession against approved standards. The AMC is the accreditation authority for medicine.

Rather than the interests of the student, the objectives of the National Law focus on the current and future health care needs of the community. Relevant objectives include:

- to protect the public by ensuring that only health practitioners who are suitably trained and qualified to practise in a competent and ethical manner are registered;
- to facilitate provision of high quality education and training;
- to enable the continuous development of a flexible, responsive and sustainable health workforce and innovation in the education of health practitioners.

The National Law defines accreditation standards as standards used to assess whether a programme of study and its education provider provide graduates with the knowledge, skills and professional attributes necessary to practise the profession in Australia.

The AMC has structured the standards for medical programmes according to key elements of the model for curriculum design and development (articulated for the AMC by Professor David Prideaux, Emeritus Professor of Medical Education at Flinders University):

- situational analysis (context):
- statements of intent (aims, objectives, outcomes);
- content;
- implementation and organizational strategies;
- assessment;
- monitoring and evaluation.

The model shows relationships between these elements based on the emphasis in medical education on outcomes-based education and on the specification of a set of significant and enduring graduate outcomes for a medical programme.

The central features of the model are:

- matching of content and outcomes;
- delivery of the content through the selection of relevant teaching and learning activities;
- driving of student learning towards the outcomes by assessment processes;
- considering the context in which the curriculum operates including management structure, resources, external relations and staffing;
- organization and implementation of the curriculum within available resources, including student characteristics, facilities and educational resources.

Applying this model, the standards developed for medical programmes focus on the specific context and environment in which the medical programme is delivered. The medical programme standards include learning and teaching under the following major headings. Sample standards are provided:

1   Context including recruiting, training and appraising teachers
    1.8.4   The medical education provider follows appropriate recruitment, support, and training processes for patients and community members formally engaged in planned learning and teaching activities.
4   Learning and teaching to support students to become medical practitioners
    4.1   The medical education provider employs a range of learning and teaching methods to meet the outcomes of the medical program.
6   Monitoring and evaluation
    6.1.1   The medical education provider regularly monitors and reviews its medical program including curriculum content, quality of teaching and supervision, assessment and student progress decisions.
8   The learning environment
    8.3.2   The medical education provider has sufficient clinical teaching facilities to provide clinical experiences in a range of models of care and across metropolitan and rural health settings.

Medical education, medical knowledge and medical practice are dynamic, and evolve rapidly. The standards are set at a high level, without specification of detailed approaches, to allow evolution and innovation. For example, under 4.1, a medical programme may use a range of teaching and learning methods from lectures and bedside teaching to problem and case-based learning, flexible delivery and online learning, models and standardized patients for skills teaching, and simulation activities.

These programme-level standards complement the Higher Education Framework Threshold Standards which concern the education provider's institutional processes.

The quality assurance process

Programmes and education providers' continued compliance with the standards is assured through accreditation and quality assurance processes, and transparent reporting of accreditation outcomes. For the AMC and TEQSA these processes include:

- a process for assessing applications for registration or accreditation status, including:
  - the provider submitting an application following a prescribed format, addressing the relevant set of standards; the application being assessed by staff and by experts;
  - visits to the provider's sites to gather evidence through interviews and observations.
- monitoring of accredited/registered programmes and or providers, through regular review of reports and data;
- processes to investigate complaints about accredited programmes or providers.

As well as quality assurance, the AMC focusses on quality improvement by beginning with the education provider critically self-assessing their achievements against the standards. The provider submits its self-assessment with evidence of how the standards are met, and plans for review and development. The AMC then appoints an accreditation team (a team of peers) to assess the programme, and prepare a report on their findings.

Outcomes of these processes

AMC accreditation reports are public, providing transparent assessment outcomes. Reports include:

- a summary of whether each accreditation standard has been met, substantially met or not met;
- commendations of areas of good practice;
- conditions, which indicate that a standard has not been met, and state the timeframe in which the condition must be met;
- recommendations, which are quality improvement suggestions. The provider must advise the AMC on its response to the suggestions.

A review of reports for the last five years shows significant innovation in medical schools' teaching approaches. Over that period, the AMC has commended specific teaching and learning approaches about three times more than it has identified areas where standards are not met. Conditions generally relate to evaluating the effectiveness of new approaches, and formalising interprofessional learning. Innovations commended include the use of scenario-based simulation sessions, a virtual hospital and simulated patient programmes.

In relation to standards on the learning environment, the AMC is twice as likely to set conditions as it is to commend good practice. Areas of concerns relate to support for clinical teachers' professional development, and availability of learning supports across widely distributed programmes. Significantly, reports commend collaboration between medical schools to coordinate medical students' placements to make effective use of clinical sites, to provide students with high quality clinical experience, and to manage clinicians' engagement in teaching.

The AMC learns from its stakeholder interactions as well its accreditation reports. A recent visit to the Northern Territory demonstrated to the AMC how national standards might create barriers to local innovation – what are normal structures or processes in urban Australia or hospital-based teaching may not appropriate for regional or remote Australia, or community-based teaching. Assumptions need to be questioned when standards are written.

Challenges

In 2017, two external reviews of the systems of professional accreditation are underway which raise a number of challenges for the integrity of quality assurance processes:

- A survey of the extent and scope of professional course accreditation practices in Australian higher education (PhillipsKPA Pty Ltd Professional Accreditation Mapping the Territory, Final Report, February 2017; https://docs.education.gov.au/documents/professional-accreditation-mapping-territory)
- A review of the accreditation system for health professions programmes (Australia's Health Workforce: Strengthening the Education Foundation, Independent Review of Accreditation Systems within the National Registration and Accreditation Scheme for Health Professions, Draft Report, September 2017; http://www.coaghealthcouncil.gov.au/Portals/0/Accreditation%20Review%20Draft%20Report.pdf).

Both reviews raise concerns about costs, burden, potential duplication and unclear boundaries between TEQSA's responsibility for academic accreditation and professional accreditation processes. Systems for quality assurance and accreditation of programmes have proliferated, in part based on their success. The report on the survey finds 'Virtually all agree that, if conducted in an appropriate and transparent manner, accreditation is a beneficial process well worth the effort expended.' But education providers now need to respond to a variety of standards and processes and there are calls for greater standardization. For the AMC, this raises the tension between a responsive quality assurance system and the rationale for regulating entry to the medical profession through rigorous accreditation of programmes. The AMC will need to make the case for standards and processes it considers essential while remaining open to opportunities to improve its processes.

Other recommendations in the review of the accreditation system for health professions programmes address the relevance and responsiveness of programmes to future health workforce needs. Interestingly, this review recommends both greater specificity in accreditation standards: for example, to require specific teaching methods (such as simulation-based education and interprofessional education) as well less specificity through outcomes-based accreditation standards, reflecting the tension between using accreditation for top-down change and fostering bottom-up innovation in programmes. This debate is not new, and since workforce reform and innovation in education are objectives of the Australian system of accreditation of health education programmes, it is likely to continue.

The GMC: Quality assurance of teaching in UK medical schools

Introduction

The GMC is the regulator for all stages of doctors' training and professional development in the UK. It aims to ensure that medical education and training reflects the needs of patients, medical students and trainees, and the health service as a whole. It does this by writing guidance and setting/quality assuring against standards in consultation with other health sector organizations, medical schools, students, doctors, patients, and anyone else with an interest in medical education.

While it does not regulate the medical schools directly (this is done through the Quality Assurance Agency for higher education), it determines the skills and behaviours medical students must reach so that they can become doctors, and the standards that schools must meet in teaching and assessing students. This allows it to maintain a list of universities which are able to award medical degrees:

http://www.gmc-uk.org/education/undergraduate/undergraduate_policy.asp
http://www.gmc-uk.org/education/27007.asp

Standards and the Quality Assurance Framework

Promoting Excellence: Standards for medical education and training (http://www.gmc-uk.org/Promoting_excellence_standards_for_medical_education_and_training_0715. pdf_61939165.pdf) set out the requirements for management and delivery of undergraduate and postgraduate medical education and training. The standards are generic and mainly reference quality of teaching in the context of management of medical school programmes and assessment, rather than addressing what is expected around standards of teaching. The GMC quality standards assure the management systems in place in medical schools to assess and improve teaching, and tasks schools with teaching students so that they are able to meet our outcomes for medical graduates (http://www.gmc-uk.org/education/undergraduate/ undergrad_outcomes.asp). The design and delivery of curricula and assessment systems, including approach to teaching, are wholly managed locally by each medical school. This results in a national variation across schools, but the UK system supports this as long as standards and outcomes are demonstrated.

Quality assurance of medical schools is delivered through a quality assurance framework (http://www.gmc-uk.org/education/qaf.asp), consisting of a number of elements which allow the GMC to make a judgement as to whether a school is at risk of not meeting standards, including visiting, evidence collection/analysis, and desk-based monitoring of progress against agreed areas of risk for each school. The UK medical education sector is currently divided into 16 localities, including 13 English regions, Scotland, Wales, and Northern Ireland. The GMC is nearing the end of a seven-year cycle in which it assessed each medical school in the UK against its standards, within each region or country. This regional approach allows the GMC to test each school's management systems by visiting the school and speaking to staff, teachers and students about their experience at the school. This evidence is triangulated with additional evidence gleaned from students and educators in clinical placements at hospitals, general practices, or in the community. Because the regional approach also includes QA of postgraduate training within these providers, the GMC can make judgements about the providers as training environments, and assess the quality of the clinical teaching offered by that organization.

A visit is undertaken only after an extensive assessment of evidence provided by the school and the providers offering placements, as well as consideration of additional data such as QAA reviews of the parent university, and the UK-wide National Student Survey. Although neither of these sources map to GMC standards so their usefulness is limited, there are some relevant generic questions that contribute to GMC visits, e.g. around pastoral support and services.

Visits will largely focus on areas where there is a potential risk of not meeting standards. So, if a pre-visit assessment of the documentary evidence available points to good quality teaching, this may be explored in a more perfunctory way during the visit. Teaching is not directly observed during visits, although students are questioned about their experience of teaching both while in the early years of their courses, and teaching embedded in clinical placements. Medical school staff are questioned about how they approach continuous improvement in teaching, and educators are questioned about the support they receive from the school, and how they obtain feedback about teaching. Detail is collated and calibrated, and a judgement is made as to whether standards are met and whether the teaching produces graduates who meet GMC outcomes.

Reports are produced and published for each medical school and provider visit. Areas of good practice are highlighted, and requirements for improvement are assigned to areas where standards aren't being met. These are monitored periodically.

The processes described above do not put a particular focus on teaching, and the GMC standards are generic. The QAA quality code includes Subject Benchmark Statements, which set out expectations about standards of degrees in a range of subject areas. They describe each academic discipline, and define what can be expected of a graduate in terms of the abilities and skills needed to develop understanding or competence in the subject (http://www.qaa.ac.uk/assuring-standards-and-quality/the-quality-code/subject-bench mark-statements). They work closely with standard-setting organizations in each discipline to produce these. In the case of medicine, QAA has largely delegated this to the GMC. So, although the GMC does not put a clear focus on quality assurance of teaching, we have clear expectations that the medical schools will manage this themselves, with some robustness, continuous improvement and clear demonstration of best practice. The GMC has clear links with a number of national and academic bodies which produce standards and guidance around teaching, particularly in medicine, such as the Medical Schools Council, the Higher Education Academy and the Association for the Study of Medical Education, although these organizations are not directly involved in the GMC's quality assurance processes.

Challenges

Fundamental to delivery and quality assurance of undergraduate medical education is the interface between the medical school and the National Health Service (NHS). Clinical teaching takes place within the NHS, which is controlled by the UK government through the four UK Departments of Health; this brings a political element into oversight of medical education, particularly clinical placements within NHS providers. Health policy decisions can have a major effect on the way medical teaching is delivered in situ. The GMC is an independent regulator, but must respond and adjust policy and practice according to what is being delivered through medical schools and clinical placements.

Another challenge is evidence. Cyclical visiting and monitoring of outcomes of visits provides the most reliable and expansive information. However, more frequent visiting is resource intensive and significantly increases the regulatory burden on medical schools. The GMC's national training survey for postgraduate trainees asks a number of questions about the formative medical school experience, but again this has a limited scope as the focus of this survey is postgraduate training environments. Medical schools vary widely in their curriculum and assessment systems, which exacerbates the lack of comparative data to make determinations on quality.

As noted above, the GMC does not pro-actively quality assure teaching, beyond ensuring standards are met and that local processes are in place to address poor practice, and promote improvement. Again, data here is limited. Although the GMC will interrogate data from partner organizations in relation to teaching to ensure risks can be identified, this is not normally a focus of their QA.

Looking forward

The GMC is developing plans to establish a UK-wide Medical Licensing Assessment (MLA), which would create a single, objective demonstration that those who obtain registration with a licence to practise medicine in the UK can meet a common threshold for safe practice (http://www.gmc-uk.org/education/29000.asp). At the time of writing, how the MLA will contribute to the evidence base that directs QA activity hasn't yet been worked through. However, it is bound to be a valuable data source that will allow some comparison of quality across medical schools. If schools are outliers in terms of outcomes, this would allow the GMC to explore potentially challenged areas, as well as investigate whether the quality of teaching requires improvement.

As the NHS inevitably changes to respond to an aging population, funding cuts and clinical advancements, the way medical schools deliver education and training, and the way the GMC quality assures this, will not remain static for long. This is an additional challenge in delivering a consistent quality assurance programme for medical schools with such variation, within a constantly shifting health care context. This said, the outcomes for all parties involved are clear: to ensure a good experience for students that meets standards, and provide patients with practitioners that meet their needs.

The Liaison Committee on Medical Education: Providing accreditation for medical education programmes in the United States and Canada

Formed in 1942, the Liaison Committee on Medical Education (LCME) is the oldest accreditation agency that solely provides accreditation to medical degree-granting programmes. Operating at the programme level of accreditation, the LCME is comparable to the AMC and is complemented with institutional accreditation agencies as carried out by TEQSA in Australia. The LCME was created in part as a result of manpower shortages as a result of World War II, when the American Medical Association (AMA) and the Association of American Medical Colleges (AAMC) unified their previously independent reviews of medical schools and thus the 'liaison' (AMA and AAMC, 1942). The original mission to ensure the highest quality of learning experience for students and to protect the public remains the focus of the LCME today. The organizational structure retains the history of its creation with the AMA sharing half of the salaried and operational costs with the AAMC, and LCME offices are embedded within each organization, one in Chicago with the AMA and one in Washington, DC with the AAMC (Kassebaum, 1992).

However, the roles of the two associations have changed dramatically. Initially, these two professional associations reviewed school reports and were involved in decisions about accreditation status. Today, these associations continue to have oversight on strategy but have no input on accreditation decisions and do not have access to individual school data. The budgetary relationship and strategic planning is managed by the LCME Council which was formed in 2012 and made up of equal representation from the LCME, the AMA, and the AAMC. The Council, like the associations, has no role in individual school accreditation.

The 17 Canadian medical education programmes are accredited using the same standards and procedures with cooperation of the Committee on Accreditation of Canadian Medical Schools (CACMS).

For over 25 years, the number of medical schools in the United States and Canada was stable at 125 US medical schools and 16 Canadian medical schools. Like most countries around the world, new medical schools began emerging in early 2000. Over a 12-year period and with over 75 initial inquiries exploring starting a new medical school, there are, as of September 2017, 147 US schools and 17 Canadian medical schools.

Like other accreditation agencies, survey visits take place on a regular basis, with eight years being the interval between visits for the LCME. Required annual surveys in the areas of student debt, school finances, admission/curriculum/ and faculty numbers allow ongoing monitoring in between accreditation survey visits. A voluntary, but well subscribed, graduating student questionnaire with over 80 per cent student participation also contributes to the annual monitoring.

The standards in teaching and learning focus on pedagogical approaches that emphasize self-directed learning and a balance of lecture and small group learning sessions as well as a balance between inpatient and outpatient experiences. Mid-course formative feedback is required of all courses and during the clerkships the summative and all-important narrative feedback must be provided to the students within six weeks. Different forms of assessment are required to match the different learning objectives. Social accountability is addressed through requirements for diversity among faculty, staff and students and the requirement that there is coverage of social health care inequities in our society.

The concept of self-directed learning as an accreditation requirement evolved out of the finding that physicians tend to focus their continuing medical education activities in areas that they are already skilled at and don't tend to focus on the gaps in their knowledge and/ or skills. Thus, schools are required to have a sufficient number of self-directed learning activities to teach the skills of lifelong learning. The LCME defines this as follows: 'Self-directed learning involves medical students' self-assessment of learning needs; independent identification, analysis, and synthesis of relevant information; and appraisal of the credibility of information sources' (page 8, *Function and Structure of a Medical School*, March 2017) Identifying gaps in their knowledge, independently finding resources to address that gap, and then getting feedback on the quality of the resource and the synthesis of the information must occur in one learning activity.

This standard like many of the LCME standards is non-prescriptive in that it does not prescribe the specific teaching technique to achieve the outcome of graduating a life-long learner. The pros and cons of non-prescriptive standards are debated in this book. The disadvantage to non-prescriptive standards is the vagueness of the language and the increased attention that must be directed to team training to eliminate personal bias. The advantage of non-prescriptive standards is clearly evident in the self-directed learning approach used by the LCME and many medical education accreditation agencies. By not prescribing exactly how to achieve this, faculty decide how to meet this requirement and how many episodes are sufficient to achieve the required outcome. However, there are innovative examples of schools using research requirements and creative modifications of the classic team-based teaching which have evolved under this accreditation mandate. Had there been a prescriptive direction on how to teach, these innovations might not have come forward. Non-prescriptive standards are at the core of the saying in the United States and Canada that 'if you have seen one medical school, you have seen one medical school'.

The emphasis on narrative feedback, particularly in the pre-clinical part of the curriculum is required for two reasons. First, to identify problems related to professionalism prior to the student entering the clinical setting and also to prepare the student for the future where this more subjective-type feedback will be the dominant form of feedback for the rest of their career.

Finally, many schools have difficulty achieving full accreditation for the diversity standard, particularly when it comes to faculty diversity. This standard is somewhat unique in that it requires the school to address these shortcoming by investing in pipeline programmes and partnerships that are beyond the degree-granting authority of the school. These pipeline programmes must be designed to groom those individuals that the school had determined are missing from their learning environment and/or are likely to address health care inequities. Tracking of the individuals served by these pre-matriculation or pre-employment programmes is essential because the school must show the effectiveness of these efforts.

Beginning around 2010 a notable increase in the number of adverse actions was observed and research was carried out into why schools were being placed on probation or receiving less than full either year terms. While a number of variables might have contributed to this downturn in schools having successful outcomes for the eight-year visit, one variable stood out as a major factor (Hunt *et al.*, 2012). In 2002, the standards were revised from a narrative format to a numbered format to provide clarity to the standards and to enable schools and teams to know more clearly what the LCME wanted as evidence for compliance. These standards were then tied for the first time to the documents that were required for the teams to review prior to the survey visit. In the ensuring years survey team training became better focussed and the LCME itself was better able to determine what was in and what was out of compliance. Unfortunately, with their only eight-year survey intervals schools did not keep track of these changed expectations and were caught less prepared then they had been in previous survey visits, leading to the increase in adverse actions.

The title of the publication describing this phenomenon captures the irony: 'The Unintended Consequences of Clarity'. Further research identified five significant variables that were associated with these adverse outcomes (Hunt *et al.*, 2016). Schools with adverse actions averaged close to 11 of the 134 standards out of compliance compared to the approximately average of four non-compliant standards. Standards that were non-compliant in the previous visit and had resurfaced again as non-compliant was a significant associated factor for a poor outcome. Two specific standards were significantly associated with an adverse action. One was the failure to ensure that students had comparable clinical experiences across different clinical settings and the failure to have a strong central management of the curriculum that ensured integration of content. This latter finding was often associated with strong department control over curricular matters rather than the required central authority.

The final area that was significantly associated with an adverse outcome was a poorly prepared self-study. It is important to appreciate that while having a lot of areas out of compliance was a strong associated factor, it was not just the number of standards that were out that made the difference in outcomes. For example, one school had 14 standards out of compliance and did not have a bad outcome whereas another school had only four and had an adverse outcome just underscoring that the standards directly related to teaching and learning and management of the learning environment were key areas for these decisions. The failure of schools to notice these changes and of the LCME to be more proactive in ensuring that these expectations were known, led to a new standard being introduced in 2014 that requires schools to monitor on an annual basis the accreditation standards and to provide evidence of how they keep in compliance between survey visits.

The increase in new medical schools in the United States and Canada has been mirrored around the world. While most countries have institutional accreditation, which operates at a high level, fewer have the programme level of accreditation that is described in this section of the chapter. This has, among other factors, contributed to an explosion of new schools around the world. Brazil, for example, which is only just now beginning to establish its own medical programme accreditation agency, has seen the number of medical schools jump from 140 to nearly 300 with little known about the quality of the educational experience in these new and often private or for-profit medical schools. With no required licensing examination nor residency requirement, these graduates can move directly into practice with little regulatory oversight into their training or qualifications.

Other countries are experiencing this same phenomenon. In response to the dramatic increase in the number of medical schools with less rigorous or no programme accreditation oversight, the Education Commission for Foreign Medical Graduates (ECFMG), which is the agency in the United States that grants graduates from schools outside of the US and Canada access to the United States Medical Licensing Examination (USMLE), announced in 2010 that by 2023 countries must have accreditation standards and procedures comparable to the LCME or other recognized accreditation agencies such as the World Federation for Medical Education (WFME) or the Australian Medical Council. The WFME carries out the comparability test with a rigorous process that involves an extensive documentation of standards and policies and then sends a team of usually three international experts to observe the country's accreditation team examining a school. The WFME recognition team receive a copy of the team report and then return to the country to observe the accreditation agencies' deliberations about that school. A report is then written and sent to the WFME for their review and decision on recognition. To date, as of 1 May 2017, seven accreditation agencies have achieved this recognition and are located in the United States (LCME), Canada (CACMS), Turkey (TEPAD), the Caribbean (CAAM-HPS), South Korea (KIMEE), Japan (JACME), and for selected Caribbean countries (ACCM). Another US-based recognition process for medical education accreditors is the National Committee for Foreign Medical Colleges which requires documentation of the comparability to LCME standards and policies of non-US accreditation agencies in order to allow US citizens enrolled in these schools to receive US federally subsidized loans. This recognition process does not involve observational teams on site at the host country.

Discussion

Each of the case studies describe a central body in a developed country, which is responsible for setting standards for medical training programmes in that country and assessing programmes against those standards. The General Medical Council (GMC) fulfils that function in the United Kingdom as does the Australian Medical Council (AMC) in Australia. In the USA and Canada there is the Liaison Committee on Medical Education (LCME). While the GMC and the AMC do more than setting standards for primary medical programmes, for example the GMC deals with disciplinary issues for physicians and both assess overseas trained practitioners, the LCME is solely concerned with programme accreditation.

Each of these bodies is responsible for the initial assessment of a medical programme and subsequent review. All three organizations make a judgement about the suitability of the programme to produce licensed medical practitioners and, in principle, their reviews cover all aspects of the programme including its curriculum; teaching and learning methods and resources, including its working relationship with medical services in the community where students undertake their placement/ internship/clerkship. Of particular interest for this book is the approach adopted for the approval of teaching and learning methods in the programme.

There are differences in the cycles followed by the three bodies; LCME accredits for eight years; the GMC approves for seven; and the AMC accredits for six years with possible extension to ten. However, points for improvement can be noted at the assessment and monitored in the period between accreditations.

All accrediting agencies follow a three-fold system involving standards specified by the agency; documentary evidence from the programme provider; and evidence from a visit if it takes place.

Clearly, an accrediting agency has to have standards against which it can judge a provider's programme. These standards can include the kind of practitioner the programme should produce; the student experience during the programme; the teaching provided; the resources necessary to deliver the programme; the relationship between university learning and practice learning; and the resources necessary in the practice learning location.

A medical education programme will be based in a university and participants will be university students, as well as prospective medical practitioners. The AMC and GMC can refer to standard setting agencies for all university students. In Australia, this is the Tertiary Education Quality and Standards Agency (TEQSA), established in 2011. TEQSA is an independent authority that regulates and assures the quality of Australia's providers of higher education. TEQSA's standards for the student experience are described in Lindsay Heywood's chapter (Chapter 25) and employed by the AMC. The GMC can draw on the work of the Quality Assurance Agency referred to in Anthony McClaran's chapter (Chapter 2) and that of the HEA referred to in Craig Mahony and Helena Lim's chapter (Chapter 3). There is no equivalent body to the TEQSA or the QAA in the USA and Canada.

The LCME has 134 standards of which eight are under the heading Teaching and Evaluation. These eight standards are primarily about assessment and make no reference to specific teaching methods. A number of other standards are about objectives for student learning, leaving the faculty to determine the teaching methods to achieve these. One standard specifies that 'a medical school must teach medical ethics and human values' for which students must 'receive instruction'. The phraseology employed might suggest traditional pedagogy but the methods are not elaborated. Similarly, one standard requires 'specific instruction in communication skills'. The term 'instruction' appears again in a standard that requires 'instruction within the basic sciences'.

The AMC has ten broad standards subdivided into 37 subsections. One standard is Teaching and Learning subdivided into Teaching and Learning Approach and Teaching and Learning Methods. The standard for the Approach is that the medical education provider employs a range of learning and teaching methods to meet the outcomes of the medical programme. For the Teaching and Learning Methods there are more focussed standards including:

Standard 4. Learning and Teaching

4.1 The medical education provider employs a range of learning and teaching methods to meet the outcomes of the medical program.

4.2 The medical program encourages students to evaluate and take responsibility for their own learning, and prepares them for lifelong learning.

4.3 The medical program enables students to develop core skills before they use these skills in a clinical setting.

4.4 Students have sufficient supervised involvement with patients to develop their clinical skills to the required level and with an increasing level of participation in clinical care as they proceed through the medical program.

4.5 The medical program promotes role modelling as a learning method, particularly in clinical practice and research.

4.6 Learning and teaching methods in the clinical environment promote the concepts of patient centred care and collaborative engagement.

4.7 The medical program ensures that students work with, and learn from and about other health professionals, including experience working and learning in interprofessional teams

http://www.amc.org.au/files/d0ffcecda9608cf49c66c93a
79a4ad549638bea0_original.pdf

The GMC sets out its standards and requirements in *Promoting Excellence: Standards for medical education and training*. None of the requirements and standards refer specifically to teaching methods, although they are of course implied in the requirement to achieve appropriate learning outcomes for students and to provide suitable support and supervision for learning.

It is clearly not the policy of any of these accrediting agencies to prescribe teaching methods in detail as standards but the AMC goes furthest in that direction. Attention is paid to assessment and feedback, which are, of course, key aspects of teaching and learning, and similarly the curriculum is expected to achieve appropriate outcomes and experiences for students. George Brown and Sarah Edmonds (Chapter 19) identify effective teaching as having three components: learning, assessment and teaching. The less attended elements so far as standard specification for medical education is concerned are the teaching and learning methods employed in the programme, which are implied but not specified. In exemplifying, what isn't covered but could have been readers are again referred to Chapter 19 and the authors' characterization of methods ranging from lectures to private study.

In the work of an accrediting agency there is a balance to be struck between requirements expressed as standards with measurable indicators which must be evidenced and broad standards which allow freedom to the programme provider to devise their own solutions. Earlier we characterized these as poles of a dirigiste to laissez-faire dimension. The three agencies in this chapter follow a relatively laissez-faire approach to teaching methods. This policy may be followed as a matter of principle to allow a measure of academic freedom or because it is seen as a stimulus for creative approaches.

The strict definition of accreditation adopted by the WFME is expressed as five questions in relation to standards for processes if they are to be described as accreditation.

Regarding a **medical school self-study**:

Does the accrediting agency require medical schools seeking accreditation to prepare an in-depth self-study that addresses compliance with the standards? If yes, please provide a blank copy of the self-study document completed by medical schools seeking accreditation.

For a **site visit**:

Does the accrediting agency conduct a site visit (or visits) to a medical school prior to granting accreditation? If yes, which elements (e.g. the school's facilities and resources, students, faculty, curriculum, etc.) are reviewed, and how is the assessment conducted?

For the **report**:

Is a report created by the site visit team based on information provided by the school and/or the on-site review? If yes, please describe the contents of the report and guidelines for generation of the report.

For **accreditation decisions:**

Describe the accrediting agency's process and procedures for making accreditation decisions. Does the process include a decision-making meeting where a report based on an on-site review is adequately discussed and debated?

Finally, for the **activities subsequent to accreditation decisions:**

Describe the accrediting agency's procedures when a currently accredited medical school does not meet accreditation standards on a subsequent review.

Describe the accrediting agency's procedures when a currently accredited medical school does not meet accreditation standards after multiple reviews.

If these are applied to determine whether our three agencies are undertaking accreditation as strictly defined, the LCME undertakes accreditation and the GMC undertakes quality assurance but not accreditation. The AMC appears to undertake accreditation but is in the process of being considered by the WFME to recognize this.

Documentary commentary and evidence provided by the medical school is a key element in the quality assurance process. Obviously, this documentation has to address the standards and will be available to influence the agenda for an accreditation visit. Providers perceive the work involved in providing evidence and preparing for a visit as an additional burden.

Visits and their preparation and follow up are resource intensive for accreditors and providers. Such resource-intensive procedures are often subject to formal evaluation to assess whether objectives are being met in a cost-effective fashion. Two interesting studies are mentioned above, but there appears to be scope for further studies regarding the cost-effectiveness of accreditation procedures.

Our sampling of three organizations from within van Zanten's (2008) initial survey has revealed differences in procedures and their acceptability as accreditation that no doubt reflects the position world-wide. This suggests that a world-wide survey identifying those agencies that do and do not carry out accreditation would be important information for the assurance of quality in medical education and practice.

References

American Medical Association and the Association of American Medical Colleges (1942) *Proceedings of the Conference between the American Medical Association and the Association of American Medical Colleges, February 18, 1942.* Chicago, Illinois. [Association of American Medical Colleges' Archives, Washington, D.C.]

Hunt D, Migdal M, Eaglen R, Barzansky B, & Sabalis R (2012) The Unintended Consequences of Clarity: Reviewing the Actions of the Liaison Committee on Medical Education Before and After the Reorganization of Accreditation Standards. *Academic Medicine* 87(5): 560–555.

Hunt DD, Migdal M, Waechter DM, Barzansky B, & Sabalis RF (2016) The Variables that Lead to Severe Action Decisions by the Liaison Committee on Medical Education. *Academic Medicine* 91: 87–93.

Kassebaum DG (1992) Origin of the LCME, the AAMC-AMA Partnership for Accreditation. *Academic Medicine* 67: 85–87.

van Zanten M, Norcini J, Boulet JR, & Simon F (2008) Overview of Accreditation of Undergraduate Medical Education Programmes Worldwide. *Medical Education* 42: 930–937.

10 Quality Assurance and Enhancement in Nurse Education

Carol Hall

Quality assurance in nurse education is of prime importance to ensure that students are prepared with the knowledge and skills to practise in their professional role upon completion of their studies. Ensuring the safety of patients during the time that learners are prepared is also a key priority. Nurse education programmes strive to integrate high quality academic studies with excellent practice placement experience. Such education ensures that professional learners are able to study the science of nursing integrated with the art of caring and apply their knowledge and skills as professional graduates wherever they may be.

For nurse educators, this creates a complex learning and teaching environment, which has implications for quality assuring and enhancing nursing education. There must be governance in the university setting as may be expected with any academic study course. Indeed, nursing must meet the demands of nationally required benchmarks (Quality Assurance Agency for Higher Education 2001) and meet university and subject-related review processes. However, unlike more traditional and non-vocational study programmes, educational quality assurance and enhancement must also extend across a range of practice environments in order to enable students to gain practical experience, meet legislated hours as a pre-requisite for registration to practise as a nurse and successfully achieve standards of professional competence.

Nurse educators themselves must also be sufficiently prepared to deliver and assess nursing curriculum and to offer the development and enhancement needed to ensure that future nurses meet requirements for practice in a changing world (e.g. American Nurses Association (ANA 2015), World Health Organization (WHO 2009), European Union Directive on the Mutual Recognition of Professional Qualifications 2005/36/EC amendment EU/55/2013). While the finer details of curricula vary globally, regionally and nationally (and may also depend upon whether the education delivery takes place dominantly within the practice or in the academic environment), there is usually a responsibility for nurse educators to demonstrate that they have met minimum training and updating standards to ensure safe and quality assured education (e.g. Nursing and Midwifery Council (NMC 2010, 2017a); National League for Nursing (NLN 2012); Australian Association of Nurse Teachers (ANTS 2010)). This chapter will explore the role of nurse educators in assuring and enhancing quality in nursing education. It will address the preparation they may need to demonstrate fitness to provide nursing education and explore influential factors faced in establishing and monitoring effective practice.

Quality assurance and enhancement mechanisms within nurse education will be explored using examples from the UK at local and national levels and enriched using international perspectives. Assuring and enhancing the quality of the student experience has become increasingly important with the consumerist approach to higher education and within the competitive market for student recruitment. The concluding discussion brings together core elements of academic quality and professional regulatory assurance in a synthesis which outlines key tensions and looks forward to future considerations to be explored further in specific case studies within Chapter 28 of this book.

The role of the nurse educator in assuring the delivery of safe and competent nursing graduates

Nursing is an international profession, defined at the highest levels as a caring activity with accountability to optimise health and provide effective care for those in need. This must be achieved within a context of the individual, and their personal and societal environment. It is therefore critical for nurse educators that they embrace a clear ideology of nursing to deliver an education which enhances the profession and offers an innovative and exciting future. Nursing values relate to a vision of excellence and emanate from the earliest definitions of modern nursing as an international profession. The writings of Nightingale (1859) identify a definition of nursing and this vision has been modified through the World Health Organization (WHO) definition of health (WHO 1948) and the classic work of Henderson (1960) to more modern modifications and adaptations commonplace today, e.g. International Council of Nurses (ICN 2002); American Nurses Association (ANA 2015); Royal College of Nursing (RCN 2014). For nurse educators, this historical background offers context and reason in assisting learners to understand their profession. Contemporary definitions of nursing are also important as they give clear guidance as to the content development which must be developed for the learner and offer messages as to the level of learning expected. A publically acknowledged definition is important for nurse educators in countries that continue to champion the case for nursing. In some cases this is to be properly registered and to ensure study to degree level in order to achieve the required capabilities in decision making and problem solving for today's healthcare situations. Where the case is set within a context of more negative public opinion and national financial restraint, the need for evidence-based argument is critical.

Contemporary definitions offer consensus about the nature of the role of the nurse as an autonomous and decision-making practitioner with a clear accountability for care practice (ICN 2002; EU/55/2013, RCN 2014). Indeed it is notable that best evidence suggests that where education leads to a registerable nursing qualification with a competent authority and where registered nurses are employed together in sufficient numbers, patient outcomes significantly improve. The RN forecast studies across the United States and Europe have examined patient outcomes as related to the level of bachelor's degree as an academic nursing qualification is an important feature (Aiken *et al.* 2014), but also recognise the role of a registerable qualification for nursing (Aiken *et al.* 2016). Indeed, the requirement for registration with a 'competent authority' is an accepted practice standard in many countries and a higher aspiration within global standards for nursing education (WHO 2009).

International differences in the regulation of nursing and nursing education

As practitioners within a globally recognised profession, nurse educators must situate their local practice context within a wider picture. The concept of nursing is at once generic and individual, and it is possible to generate a common understanding and yet be very different. An example of this relates to the role of professional regulation of nurses and nurse educators and those responsible for determining such regulation. The legal term 'competent authority' best defines those undertaking regulation of those permitted to practise in a professional role; this allows differences through enactment and interpretation. It is important to note that professional regulation of nursing and nursing education may be retained or retrieved by governments, giving 'competent authority' to ministerial departments of health or to a generic governmental body such as education, or it may be delegated. Such delegation of authority may be regionally to specific geographies or devolved through a legal order to a professional organisation with a direct accountability for the profession (or both). Further, there may be an historical element to the designation of competent authority. For example in countries where nursing has emerged from a communist authority with the role of medical assistant rather than an identified role of nurse. In these instances the competent authority may be identified within the medical profession (De Raeve *et al.* 2016).

While this is a seemingly high-level example, the implications create different scenarios for nursing across the world which are important for nurse educators' roles in quality assurance of curriculum. In the UK, the 'competent authority' is the Nursing and Midwifery Council (NMC). The NMC is a professional body with power of competent authority delegated by the Department of Health through the enactment of the Nursing and Midwifery Order 2001 (SI/2002/253) which came into force in April 2002 and was amended in 2017 (SI 2017/321).

The NMC is a profession-specific body which is funded by subscription of its registrants and exists to protect the public across the four countries of the United Kingdom. In order to achieve public protection, the NMC sets and monitors standards of education, training, conduct and performance which also include the registration of nurses who meet established requirements for professional practice. In other EU countries such as Germany and Spain and more widely (e.g. including the US and China) quality standards are established nationally, but the role of the competent authority for registration for professional practice, registration/licencing, monitoring and assurance may be delegated to regional authorities, and each region may deliver their responsibilities in slightly different ways. Sub-contracting of programme accreditation and validation processes is also possible. Each of these elements may add different influences into the way in which a nursing programme is to be monitored and for nurses in education these factors add specific consideration in programme preparation.

The relationship between regulation and curriculum development, enhancement and quality assurance

Professional knowledge and competence for nursing practice is ultimately assured through the effectiveness of curriculum delivery and this is significant. Standardised national curriculum or syllabi (originally developed as an historic development in the UK as well as in some other countries) continue in some nations, but have been abolished in others and are a contentious issue. Thompson and Watson (2005) advocated a return to national curriculum within the UK in order to decrease programme variability. While this was not attained, the detailed nature of the NMC standards (2010) reflect opportunities for commonality. At time of writing, new professional proficiency standards and competences and a new framework for nursing education are being proposed for UK nursing education (NMC 2017a, b, c). Once again, these do not prescribe a national curriculum but they are in sufficient detail to require many similar outputs across universities. Some of the proposed changes are challenging and it is critical that nurse educators realise the importance of their voice at this time in ensuring that their future curriculum delivery (and the standards their programmes will be measured against) can be shaped in the best interests of students, nurses and their patients.

In Europe, the idea of standardised/EU curriculum has been also been debated extensively (Keighley 2016) but this has only been achieved to date through offering detailed guidance to existing legislation rather than legislative requirement. Examples include the Tuning Project (Gobbi 2011) competences for nurses graduating within the first cycle of the Bologna Process (1999) and European Federation of Nurses (EFN 2015) interpretation of Article 31 of the EU/55/2013 competencies into learning outcomes. Indeed, even where this legislation does exist there remain considerable challenges in ensuring consistency (Keighley 2016).

The nurse educator's role in assessing and evaluating professional nursing competence

The practical role of educators in the delivery of education for nursing necessarily includes ensuring that the evaluation of competence is completed in a robust and consistent manner which assure that students who complete their studies have achieved all competencies required by the university and the professional regulator. In the UK, this includes a requirement for a nominated nursing education registrant leading the study programme to finally sign off all students in respect of their fitness to practise professionally, including a declaration of the graduand's health, honesty and integrity as well as their completion of all required components of the study programme (NMC 2010). Nurse educators are clearly identified as the gateway to practice within the profession alongside their professional colleagues who assess students in their practice. The practice of signing to identify fitness for practice for a qualifying nurses requires excellent communication with the teaching and practice teams involved in the delivery of the study programme, particularly where study programmes include larger student numbers.

Evaluation of student ability must include a system for student assessment which is determined by nurse educators in their teaching role. Internationally, there have been a range of approaches to assessing nursing student competence and these have changed due to the influences of history and geography. The following illustrations offer two polarised perspectives, one focussed upon endpoint competence which assumes a national 'core' curriculum and a second based upon ongoing assessment of the student and development of competence. These are being shared to offer comparison and to illuminate different approaches to nursing education delivery which may significantly impact upon the nature of quality assurance.

Model 1: Terminal assessment of professional competence

This approach is focussed upon the need for the student to demonstrate an end-point competence to practise as a registered nurse. Although ongoing assessment and achievement of credit may be included for the award of an academic qualification of degree, students of nursing within this model complete their studies with a university approved to a required standard which enables eligibility to undertake a licence examination. The academic qualification and licence to register as a professional practitioner are separate and education may include differing options. There may be a national curriculum or some variation in curricula and with quality assurance achieved through agency accreditation. As an example, China offers a national curriculum where students register for professional practice upon completion of their degree course, through achieving success in the national licencing examination

(NQEQ) within regional centres supported by the state board (Wang *et al.* 2016). A second international example is the US-based National Council Licencing Examination (NCLEX) (National Council of State Boards of Nursing 2017). Depending upon the nature of the core curriculum and the accreditor, students of nursing may learn a range of subjects including sciences, liberal arts or national cultural studies relating to regional or academic legal requirements and applying to all undergraduate students. Competent authorities usually approve professional curricula standards and may also include national textbooks related to the terminal examination which they control, but they may not approve an academic qualification, nor the learners' ongoing progress. Critics of this model identify that although study courses may be approved, process monitoring may be less in focus and this can lead to variability in provision and standard (Spector 2012; Wang *et al.* 2016), while advocates support the opportunity for flexibility for curriculum creativity and identify that a robust terminal assessment should account for public safety (e.g. Thompson and Watson 2005). For nurse educators delivering a quality curriculum within this model, considerable focus will rely upon their development and inclusion of materials and innovations that enhance success rate. The curriculum may be nationally or locally prescribed and may be rigorously monitored for accreditation or may be flexible, but focussed to the final rates of exam completion. Within more liberal curriculum, this model offers opportunities for flexibility in learning provided students meet the endpoint goals successfully and are satisfied with their studies in aiding them to achieve them.

Model 2: Ongoing assessment of professional competence

In this approach, students achieve credit towards both their final academic degree and profession qualification throughout their studies. Upon completion, students have achieved multiple assessments and accumulated sufficient credit for qualification in both professional practice and no further terminal examination is required. This contemporary UK model is also adopted in some EU member states. In principle, the nature of ongoing assessment and the accumulation of credit for work undertaken fits well with the values espoused by the European Higher Education Area's Bologna Process (1999). For nursing across the EU the model must also rely upon stringent governance and monitoring of universities in professional as well as academic settings in order to meet legal requirements. Nonetheless, students of nursing may undertake a range of assessment throughout their study programme which will count towards both their degree and their professional qualification to practice.

These examples are deliberately explained in a dichotomous manner and it is important to note that there are variations. For nurse educators concerned with international quality assurance, it is critical to appreciate that key influences in nursing curriculum depend upon where professional competent authority lies, what historic approach has been taken and who funds education provision.

Accountability and transferability of professional registration

The acceptability of a nursing qualification, with or without additional practice, study or terminal examination is dependent upon individual competent authorities who determine the appropriate assessment of an application from outside of the area. This applies for all nurses who wish to move internationally. It is important for nurse educators to understand that in the EU, professional competence to practise is defined through the EU legal requirement for Nurses Registered in General Care (EU/36/2005 and amendment EU/55/2013). This currently enables automatic sectoral recognition for some nurses across member states. The above act also serves to identify minimum professional requirements for nursing education across all member state in terms of time for practice, theory and access to studies. A nurse applying to an EU nursing study programme must receive a minimum of 4600 hours of study and three years, of which 2300 hours should be in practice and no less than one-third should be in theoretical instruction (EU/55/2013). A nurse studying in the US by comparison has regionally determined clinical practice time and this may not be specified (Spector 2012). For the nurse educators developing curriculum, ensuring these parameters are considered is thus fundamental to delivering an acceptable curriculum

Nurse educator roles in delivering academic and professional standards for nursing education

While it is possible to determine approaches to education delivery and identification of standards using broad examples for comparison as above, when examining the application of quality assurance including both academic and professional standards for nursing it is helpful to focus specifically on one system as an illuminative case.

This section will illuminate how quality assurance for nursing is achieved in England under the devolved academic model currently used by the Quality Assurance Agency combined with the professional quality assurance framework for Nursing and Midwifery (2013, updated NMC 2016) and the Quality Framework imposed by the National Health Service's commissioning body, Health Education England (HEE). It is important to note that although the NMC cover all UK countries, England is being identified rather than the UK as the Scottish, Welsh and NI authorities have slightly different processes resulting from devolvement of education. (A useful table of different authorities and resources can be found on the Mott MacDonald website.) The system outlined in the following section will lay the foundations for further consideration through examining the application of the British system but comparing roles within a different system such as the one currently in place in Portugal.

In England, the role played by the professional 'competent authority' (the NMC) and its subcontracted monitoring team (currently Mott MacDonald) is expansive and subject focussed. This reflects the broad role of the QAA and the universities as generic bodies in establishing academic quality and student satisfaction rather than being specifically professional-subject-focussed with a requirement for patient safety. Indeed, in studies which have no professional accountability, study programmes may undergo no specific subject0related review. (For England, the incoming arrangements for the Teaching Excellence Framework (TEF) do include proposals for a return to subject-level assessment for all subjects but the shape of this remains unconfirmed.) Portugal currently offers an example where subject-level validation and accreditation is still used by the national quality assurance agency for all university study programmes. (At time of writing an experimental parallel institutional review is being implemented: A3ES http://www.a3es.pt/en/). In the case of nursing, professional competence standards are thus determined by the Portuguese nursing regulator but working with the quality assurance agency, who deliver processes for subject-level assurance. Experience of both systems suggests that for nurse educators, the location of scrutiny (within the academic or professional systems) make little difference. However, for British educators, the level and intensity of scrutiny in nursing education is significantly different from that expected of academics within many 'non-professional' study courses. The responsibility and workload requirements in the preparation for such processes cannot be underestimated.

The UK Nursing and Midwifery Council

In respect of the development of nursing programmes, the NMC uses a set of standards for pre-registration nursing education. These are currently under review and a new version is expected for programmes commencing in 2019 (NMC 2017a). The NMC standards (NMC 2010) both require and guide nursing curriculum developers and they also act as a tool for quality monitoring purposes. This is combined with a Quality Assurance Framework (2013, updated NMC 2017) and Handbook for Reviewers which operationalises the process of review (Mott MacDonald and NMC 2017.

The quality assurance review process is undertaken at subject level and is based upon risk management. Evidence is determined through initial validation and cyclical validation visits, and annual monitoring through self-assessment undertaken by nurse educators within approved education institutions. All new providers planning to deliver approved programmes for nursing must be initially approved by the NMC, before submitting proposals for professional programmes for review. A new programme will be required to receive a panel validation, and programmes which require significant (major) modification may also require this. Minor modifications may be undertaken through a desktop exercise. Nurse educators delivering curriculum are expected to prepare for minor and major modifications when they change or adapt curriculum and designated nurse educators will be responsible for leading the self-assessment of nursing programmes. Study programmes are monitored annually by a subcontractor to the NMC operating on their behalf. The subcontracted monitoring process occurs through a self-assessment submission rated by the NMC contractors according to risk and due time. Exceptional reporting and monitoring visits may take place should a university be identified as high risk. All universities are notified approximately six weeks prior to a visit and expected to present all information as required by the monitoring authority. Visits focus on the partnership between the institution delivering the academic programme and their practice partners. This addresses the student journey including systems and processes and support in theory and in practice. Data is collated from practice monitoring and auditing processes undertaken by the school and by other authorities. Student evaluations of practice and of their academic study modules are reviewed alongside other publically available data (e.g. annual National Student Survey (NSS) data, student attrition data and Care Quality Commission (CQC 2017) reviews in respect of placements).

There may be a specific focus upon a particular aspect of preparation (e.g. child nursing or student acquisition of specific skills) and these are determined annually as a focus by the NMC. The NMC identify that it is their role to identify threshold standards to be achieved by all approved education institutions rather than dictate a standardised curriculum.

This position offers flexibility to universities, which can be identified as a difference not always popular with those students and practitioners who believe that a standardised nursing preparation programme serves public safety more transparently. However, flexibility is recognised as beneficial by those who are keen to be able to deliver the best programme possible within their health community.

Quality assurance for nurse educators and those mentoring students within clinical placements

The NMC currently holds the live register for nurses in the UK and is publically accountable for those whose names appear registered. Without registration, practice as a registered nurse is illegal under British law. The role of the NMC includes facilitating revalidation processes for all nurses every three years, initial registration of newly completed graduates and the monitoring and assurance of quality education preparation programmes. Nurse educators employed by the approved institution must be registered on the live register of nurses and periodically revalidate.

Nurses must also currently be registered with the NMC as nurse teachers (RNT) or as Practice Educators or Mentors on a locally held register complying with NMC requirements (NMC 2008), demonstrating achievement of an appropriate qualification to support nursing education. (This is additional to any university requirement for qualification within the area of teaching, although the qualification required can be mutually acceptable.)

In nursing practice, mentors are carefully prepared and stringently regulated in respect of their role, as students spend half of their study programme within a practice setting. Mentors must be in possession of an approved qualification to offer mentorship and they must update annually in accordance with the current Supporting Learning and Assessment in Practice (SLAIP) guidelines (NMC 2008). Those signing off final practice must be identified as sign-off mentors and receive triennial review of their mentorship activity (NMC 2008). Once again at time of writing the role of mentors is being reviewed and the proposed framework for education appears quite different, placing a very different emphasis upon the relationship between nurse educators and those supervising practice learning (NMC 2017b).

The role of Health Education England

The National Health Service Health Education England was established as a Special Health Authority in 2012, but this changed on 1 April 2015, when it became a Non-Departmental Public Body (NDPB), under the provisions of the Care Act (2014). The vision of HEE is to provide the right workforce, with the right skills and values, in the right place at the right time to better meet the needs and wants of patients – now and in the future (HEE 2016a).

In respect of the quality assurance in higher education, the role of Health Education England is currently to commission high quality workforce education for the National Health Service in England, including nursing as well as medical, dental and allied health professions. While this has involved the inclusion of quality monitoring led by HEE regional offices through monitoring local approved education institutions; this remit is an evolving one. Historical funding arrangements for healthcare education are changing, moving course commissioning from the NHS (within the scope of HEE) to students loans distributed via the Higher Education Funding Council for England (HEFCE) in 2017. Although the final ramifications of this move are yet to be fully appreciated, this has meant a shift in focus for HEE from the commissioning of courses to a more focussed role in assuring the learning environment of learners participating within NHS practice environments and expected to enter the NHS workforce. In the recent HEE Strategy and Framework (HEE 2016a, 2016b) the new vision and the mission of the HEE is articulated within six quality domains, which focus upon different aspects of maintaining quality for learners and patients.

The six HEE quality domains are:

1   Learning Environment and Culture
2   Educational Governance and Leadership
3   Supporting and Empowering Learners
4   Supporting and Empowering Educators
5   Developing and Implementing Curricula and Assessments
6   Developing a Sustainable Workforce

(HEE Quality Strategy 2016a, p. 8)

In all of these areas, the HEE Quality Framework which came into force in April 2016, details standards and identifies metrics by which stakeholders are expected to demonstrate quality. Notably most of these metrics co-exist within other assurance mechanisms, making the HEE role one of auditing rather than initiating QA measures. This may however, change as current work has been commissioned to develop a specific survey (NETS) for healthcare students in practice.

Supporting the clinical learning environment

As an internationally defined profession, nursing must ensure the competency of those permitted to practice in order to ensure public safety, whilst often also accounting for differences in public need and expectation within locally defined requirements of health communities. Legally defined and regulated standards and processes facilitate this achievement across the globe, through determination of requirements for threshold competence of graduates who wish to apply for professional registration. (This may be viewed as supporting 'entrustable professional activity' in other disciplines such as medicine.) Professional practice learning for nursing in higher education also has safety implications for public wellbeing and patient safety and thus relevance to many stakeholders including the public (patients' carers and families), employers and those who represent them. Nurse educators have a significant role in establishing, evidencing and evaluating processes to assure the clinical learning environment for students of nursing. Developing and maintaining effective placement learning environments requires robust collaboration between universities operating at a number of levels and a range of health and social care service providers. At the most simple level, nurse educators may work directly with a single placement for student learning and negotiate for the learning opportunities required with the placement manager. This approach works in smaller schools of nursing (e.g. in Portugal, France) and is a commonly observed model for practice. It offers a personal relationship between university tutor and placement staff and enables the development of long-standing quality partnerships which may enhance the student experience and offer a rapid feedback mechanism if there are concerns about the placement for the student. The nurse educator in this situation would be responsible for all aspects of the placement experience, from identifying and booking the placement, to assuring the quality and evaluation of the experience and supporting the students who attend. Agreements tend to be informal and undertake on a good will basis. Where nursing education takes place on a larger scale within a university setting a different approach is required and thus the role of the nurse educator also differs. Arranging quality placements for many thousands of students may include larger-scale national or regional arrangements with specialized teams for the booking and monitoring of placement activities. Nurse educators are still likely to work with placements but may have several placements with which to collaborate and they may participate in specialized audit teams to monitor and evaluate national or regional standards for placement learning environment quality. This more complex model can afford the possibility of greater consensus of expectation across placements but can be influenced heavily by political change. Looking more internationally, nurse educators have played an important role in enhancing the understanding of the clinical learning environment through the development of materials and tools which use innovative educational evaluation. A key project which has been led by nurse educators (Saarikoski *et al.* 2008) is the CLES+ T tool. This uses student and nurse educator evaluation to determine the effectiveness of placement learning. Although this tool cannot be considered predictive in the case of new placements since its main focus is post-event and thus requires students to have the experience in order to report upon their learning, it is a robust and widely accepted model which has been replicated globally to review the effectiveness of placement learning environments for nursing students.

Enhancing learning and assessment of student nurse competence in practice

Case example

In the UK, the parties with stakeholder interest in practice learning environments are currently politically governed as part of arrangements within the National Health Service. Until recently, NHS England commissioned all nursing education through its commissioning arm, Higher Education England, and offered some payment contribution for placement learning. HEE have required academic institutions and placements to subscribe to agreed national placement agreements and minimum audit standards for learning environments. Higher Education England commissioners have also required nurse educators leading programmes to assure that they have met their education quality measures on an annual basis (EQM). This political shift has meant most nursing and healthcare students have become self-funding through HEFCE student loans and are no longer commissioned. Placement tariff funding will still occur, though may be managed differently and universities will be free to negotiate independently of the existing tariff and placement agreements.

While it is expected that the role of the nurse educator in auditing and supporting learning environments will continue, the accountability to stakeholders is currently less clear and more localised agreements look set to return.

The role of the UK Quality Assurance Agency for Higher Education (QAA) and the university in quality assuring professional nursing programmes

The QAA focusses its approach to quality assurance upon the effectiveness of programme delivery within universities in a review process which incorporates all departments systems and processes. Monitoring takes place quinquennially and the review process culminates in an assurance that the university being reviewed is able to manage its responsibilities in assuring all programmes and support systems necessary to meet their threshold outcomes in accordance with the Quality Code (QAA 2015). For nursing and other health professions, the QAA established a set of benchmark standard statements for expectations within nursing in collaboration with healthcare professionals. These are dated (QAAHE 2001) and while they are identified by the QAA as being under review currently it is important to note that they are not identified as a specific requirement for curriculum. Nonetheless, these are considered by universities and must be taken into consideration in developing new programmes or in reviewing student assessment as an external examiner, a role frequently undertaken by nurse educators as part of the wider academic system. They will be evidenced within curriculum specifications held at university level and available for inspection by QAA auditors if required. It is thus important that nurse educators are aware of the existence and details of these benchmarks.

Universities in England have a role in assuring that nursing programmes meet all requirements for QAA assurance as with any other programme within their portfolio. This means that all programmes are subject to annual review by the quality and standards committee and each one must self-assess strengths and weaknesses against core metrics (including recruitment, attrition and completion, success and achievement as well as student satisfaction measured via published evaluation both nationally and locally). For nursing and professional programmes these measures are collated with professional measures in determining programme outputs and currently in determining commissions for funded places for study.

Conclusion

Quality assurance of nursing education globally is complex and in Western countries in particular, this has developed to include stakeholders interested in public and patient safety as well as in education quality.

Using England as an example demonstrates a particularly extensively regulated and politicised provision due to the historically close relationship with the publically funded National Health Service. Nonetheless this is by no means unique, and while one must always consider patient safety first, Spector (2012) made a valid point in questioning the evidence surrounding the paucity of quality evidence for the relationship between education programme quality and patient outcomes in respect of US nursing education. While Aiken *et al.* (2014, 2016) go some way to determining this in respect of level and nature of professional qualification, there is still no large-scale evidence found which specifically correlates professional programme quality metrics with nursing outcomes.

In the UK case example, it can be seen that core stakeholders each have their own accountability and requirements to ensure these are met. Chapter 28 of this text looks in greater detail at how this system is applied practically, but supporting several major stakeholders over an extensive quality agenda is challenging and there are a number of new opportunities which could create a greater efficiency for English HEIs if there is a high-level agreement about what and who should be regulating nursing education. The advent of the subject review component of the Teaching Excellence Framework could lead to a less complicated system if stakeholders worked together to reduce evident overlap where the same metrics are being used. (This is particularly evident in the HEE Quality Framework 2016 where metrics include NSS and QAA measures.)

HEE and the NMC both have a declared focus regarding the maintenance of a quality learning environment. While it is possible to critique the role of HEE in this regard, given that not all clinical placements fall within the NHS and not all students will necessarily work for NHS England, nevertheless HEE's interest in maintaining quality and access to clinical placements in the NHS will operate as a major lever for those supplying nursing programmes. There are still questions however, about the role of HEE in the delivery of funded practice placements. The funding arrangements have not been fully completed at time of publication, leaving the longer-term role of HEE in the quality assurance of universities open to consideration.

References

Aiken LH, Sloane DM, Bruyneel L, Vanden Heede K, Griffiths P, Diomidous M, Kinnunenn J, KozKa M, Lesaffre E, McHugh D, Moreno-Casbas MT, Rafferty AM, Schwendimann R, Scott PA, Tishelman C, Avan Achterberg T, Sermeus W, & RN4CAST Consortium (2014) Nurse staffing and education and hospital mortality in nine European countries: A retrospective observational study. *Lancet* 383(9931),1824–30.
Aiken LH, Sloane D, & Griffiths P (2016) For the RN4CAST Consortium, nursing skill mix in European hospitals: Cross-sectional study of the association with mortality, patient

ratings, and quality of care. *British Medical Journal (BMJ Qual Saf)* Published online first: 15 November 2016.

American Nurses Association (2015) *Nursing Scope and Standards of Practice*, 3rd edition. Silver Spring: American Nurses Association.

Australian Association of Nurse Teachers ANTS (2010) *Australian Nurse Teacher Professional Practice Standards*. New South Wales, Australia. http://www.ants.org.au/ants/

The Bologna Process (1999) Joint Declaration of the European Ministers of Education European Commission, 19 June 1999. http://ec.europa.eu/education/policies/educ/bologna/bologna_en.html

Care Act 2014 (Chapter 23). London: The Stationery Office.

Care Quality Commission (2017) Inspection reports. http://www.cqc.org.uk/what-we-do/how-we-do-our-job/inspection-reports (accessed 29/12/2017).

De Raeve, P, Rafferty AM, & Barriball L (2016) EU accession: A policy window for nursing? *Eurohealth incorporating Euro Observer* 22(1), 10–13.

Directive 2013/55/EU of the European Parliament and of the Council 20 November 2013 amending Directive 2005/36/EC on the recognition of professional qualifications and regulation (EU) No 1024/2012 on administrative cooperation through the Internal Market Information System ('the IMI Regulation'). *Official Journal of the European Union*, 28 December 2013 http://eur-lex.europa.eu/legal-content/EN/TXT/PDF/?uri=CELEX:320 13L0055&from=EN

European Federation for Nurses Associations (2015) *EFN Competency Framework for Mutual Recognition of Professional Qualifications Directive 2005/36/EC, amended by Directive 2013/55/EU EFN Guideline to Implement Article 31 into National Nurse' Education Programmes*. Brussels: European Federation for Nurses Associations. http://www.efnweb.be (accessed 25/08/2017).

Global Advisory Panel on the Future of Nursing and Midwifery Report (2018) *Bridging the Gaps for Health*. Indianapolis: STTI International.

Gobbi M ed. (2011) *Tuning Project – Reference Points for the Design and Delivery of Degree Programmes in Nursing*. Bilbao: University of Deusto Press.

Health Education England (2016a) *HEE Quality Strategy 2016–2020*. https://hee.nhs.uk/sites/default/files/documents/HEE_J000584_QualityStrategy_FINAL_WEB.pdf (accessed 2/1/2017).

Health Education England (2016b) *HEE Quality Framework 2016/2017*. https://hee.nhs.uk/sites/default/files/documents/HEE_J000584_QualityFramework_FINAL_WEB.pdf (accessed 2/1/2017).

Henderson V (1960) *Basic Principles of Nursing Care*. London: ICN.

International Council of Nurses (2002) *The ICN Definition of Nursing*. Geneva: ICN.

Keighley T. (2009) *European Union Standards for Nursing and Midwifery: Information For Accession Countries*. Copenhagen: WHO Regional Office for Europe.

Keighley T (2016) Is there an EU framework for nurse education? *Eurohealth incorporating Euro Observer* 22(1), 14–16.

Mott MacDonald and Nursing and Midwifery Council (2017) *Quality Assurance Handbook*. www.mottmac.ac.com (accessed 29/12/2017).

National Council of State Boards of Nursing (2017) *National Council Licencing Examination (NCLEX) USA*. https://www.ncsbn.org/nclex.htm (accessed 25/08/2017).

National League for Nursing (NLN) (2012) *Nurse Educator Core Competency: Competencies for the Academic Nurse Educator*. http://www.nln.org/professional-development-programs/competencies-for-nursing-education/nurse-educator-core-competency

Nightingale F (1859) *Notes on Nursing: What It Is and What It Is Not*. London: Harrison.

Nursing and Midwifery Council (2008) *Standards to Support Learning and Assessment in Practice (SLAIP)*. London: NMC.

Nursing and Midwifery Council (2010) *Standards for Pre-registration Nursing Education*. London: NMC.

Nursing and Midwifery Council (2016) *Quality Assurance Framework*. London: NMC.

Nursing and Midwifery Council (2017a) *Draft Education Framework: Standards for Education and Training*. London: NMC. https://www.nmc.org.uk/globalassets/sitedocuments/edcons/ec4-draft-education-framework—standards-for-education-and-training.pdf accessed 25/08/2017

Nursing and Midwifery Council (2017b) *Draft Requirements for Pre-registration Nursing Education Programmes*. London: NMC. https://www.nmc.org.uk/globalassets/sitedocuments/edcons/ec5-draft-requirements-for-pre-registration-nursing-and-education-programmes.pdf accessed 25/08/2017

Nursing and Midwifery Council (2017c) *Standards of Proficiency for Registered Nurses*. NMC: London. https://www.nmc.org.uk/globalassets/sitedocuments/edcons/ec7-draftstandards-of-proficiency-for-registered-nurses.pdf (accessed 25/08/2017).

Nurses and Midwives Nursing and Midwifery Order 2001 SI/2002/253

Nursing and Midwifery (Amendment) Order 2017 SI 2017/321. https://www.nmc.org.uk/globalassets/sitedocuments/legislation/nmc-original-legislation-and-amendments.pdf (accessed 25/08/2017).

Quality Assurance Agency (2015) *The Quality Code (2015): A Brief Guide*. London: QAA. https://www.qaa.ac.uk

Quality Assurance Agency for Higher Education (QAAHE) (2001) *Benchmark Statement Health Care Programmes Nursing*. Gloucester: QAAHE. http://www.qaa.ac.uk/en/Publications/Documents/Subject-benchmark-statement-Health-care-programmes—-Nursing.pdf

Royal College of Nursing (RCN) (2014) *Defining Nursing*. London: RCN.

Saarikoski M, Isoaho H, Warne T, & Leino Kilpi H (2008) The nurse teacher in clinical practice: Developing the new sub dimension to clinical learning environment and supervision (CLES) scale. *International Journal of Nursing Studies* 45, 1233–1237.

Spector N (2012) Chapter 3, Transition to practice – An essential element of quality and safety. In Amer K ed., *Quality and Safety For Transformational Nursing: Core Competencies*. New York: Pearson.

Thompson DR & Watson R(2005) All bathwater and no baby: Revisiting a national curriculum and state examination for nursing. *Nurse Education Today* 25, 165–166.

Wang CC, Whitehead L, & Bayes S. (2016) Nursing education in China: Meeting the global demand for quality health care. *International Journal of Nursing Studies* 3(2016), 131–136.

World Health Organization, Department of Human Resources for Health (2009) *Global Standards for the Initial Education of Professional Nurses and Midwives*. Geneva: World Health Organization.

World Health Organization (WHO) (1948) Definition of health. http://www.who.int (accessed 25/08/2017).

Websites

Agencia de availiacaoe accreitaciodo ensino superior A3ES: http://www.a3es.pt/en/

Care Quality Commission (CQC): www.cqc.org.uk/

Mott MacDonald: www.mottmac.ac.com

11 Quality Assurance and Accountability in Initial Teacher Education in England

Chris Wilkins

Introduction

Recent decades have seen a global trend in which nation states have increasingly focused on improving the performance of their education systems in order to enable them to compete in a global knowledge economy (Brown *et al.* 2007). This aligning of educational outcomes with economic development has led to demands for increasingly rigorous scrutiny of system performance, and a growing global consensus that schools and teachers need to be accountable for their effectiveness – and the efficiency with which they utilise state funding.

As a result, policymakers have invested heavily in developing systematic accountability frameworks that harness not just regulatory aspects of the work of schools, but emphasise measuring effectiveness against quantifiable performance indicators relating to student outcomes (Ball 2000). A key driver behind this quantitative focus has been the exponential growth in access to 'big data'; the technological advances in recent decades have allowed policymakers to harness vast and complex data sets to inform performance measurement. The breadth and depth of data generated by education systems now provides the potential for multiple levels of comparison; not just at individual and school level, but inter-school, national and international level. Of the numerous data sets available to policymakers, perhaps the single most significant one is the Organisation for Economic Cooperation and Development's (OECD) Programme for International Student Assessment (PISA), which allows for comparison of outcomes in core skills, knowledge and competences for 15-year-olds in 72 countries.

This 'performative' phenomenon is not unique to education, of course – it is evident in almost all aspects of public service provision. However, the direct linkage of educational outcomes with competitiveness in a global economy has meant that education systems remain the most visible sites of 'high stakes accountability' (Wilkins 2015a).

Accountability in Initial Teacher Education: An international preoccupation

This global focus on 'knowledge competitiveness' has been accompanied by a compelling body of evidence suggesting that the quality of teacher education systems is one of the most significant determinants of the quality of educational outputs (Barber and Mourshed 2007, Ammermüller and Lauer 2009, UNESCO 2011). Across the 'industrialised' nations, key concerns include how to recruit, train and retain high-quality teachers as well as the most effective way of ensuring teachers are adequately prepared for adopting new pedagogical approaches that will in turn prepare students for a rapidly changing world (Wilkins and

Comber 2015; Wilkins 2017). In many, if not all, countries in the 'industrialised' world, policymakers have been increasingly preoccupied with the extent to which their students' outcomes appear to be falling behind those of Asian systems such as Singapore, Korea and Shanghai-China.

Notably, however, although teacher education reforms across the industrialised world frequently cite poor performance in PISA outcomes as justification for what have often been controversial, destabilising – and expensive – initiatives, there are few examples where these appear to be directly inspired by models in place in 'high-performing' Asian systems. Whereas teacher education programmes in the latter prioritise the creation and maintenance of strong cultures of research-informed teacher collaboration and sustained professional development (Jensen *et al.* 2012), politicians in countries playing 'catch-up' have tended to prefer policies that steer teacher education towards a more practically oriented, school-based training model (Maandag *et al.* 2007). The increased enthusiasm for school-based teacher education has been accompanied by strident criticism of supposedly 'over-theoretical' teacher education based in universities (Mutton *et al.* 2017).

This chapter focuses on the evolution of quality assurance and accountability mechanisms operating in Initial Teacher Education (ITE) in England. England has come to be seen by many as in the 'vanguard' of the phenomenon by which the 'performance' of educational institutions (including those involved in teacher education provision) is intensively scrutinised by governments in order to produce improved outcomes and efficiency. This trend towards ever more 'intrusive' accountability models can be witnessed globally, although it is most evident in the so-called 'Anglo-American democracies' (Davies and Guppy 1997), such as the USA (Hirsch 2007), Australia (Connell 2013), New Zealand (Codd 2005) and Canada (Crocker and Dibbon 2008). However, the 'English approach' to regulating in teacher education is notable due to its particularly explicit use of neo-liberal market principles alongside high-stakes accountability mechanisms, and so provides a valuable insight into this global trend.

The English way: High-stakes accountability

In the neoliberal public education system, the prevailing perception of policymakers is that 'consumer choice' can be harnessed to create key instruments for delivering cost-effective, high-quality services; in other words, the outcomes of 'high-stakes' assessment are shared with the 'consumers' of education (students/parents) to inform their choices, alongside a range of incentives for high performers and sanctions for underperformers (Ball 2000). This model has dominated education policy in England since the 1990s, so much so that it has been seen as epitomising the global spread of neoliberal policy reform in public sector governance. Initial Teacher Education (ITE) has been the subject of particular scrutiny during this period, with successive governments pursuing a common agenda designed to reduce the relative autonomy traditionally enjoyed by universities engaged in ITE (Furlong 2013).

One of the key challenges resulting from the intensification of the high-stakes performative accountability model for providers is the tension between a reductionist focus on narrowly defined quantitative outcomes and the notion of effective teacher preparation as being associated with a complex educative process characterised by 'collaboration, reflection and a gradual acculturation into the profession' (Howe 2006, 288).

Those familiar with the English school system will be aware of the significance of the Office for Standards in Education (OfSTED) – and may perceive it as perhaps the most obvious example of 'high-stakes accountability'. The 'OfSTED inspector' has become a character of modern folklore, a ruthless inquisitor striking fear into the heart of teachers everywhere and holding the fate of schools in their hands. It is not surprising, perhaps, that Stephen Ball published his influential research into the impact of OfSTED inspection on teachers under the title 'The teacher's soul and the terrors of performativity' (Ball 2003).

However, OfSTED's remit is wider than schools, encompassing all aspects of services for children and young people. It also includes inspecting the quality of childcare, as well as the focus of this chapter, all provision of education and training leading to Qualified Teacher Status (QTS); usually referred to as Initial Teacher Education (ITE). This chapter provides an overview of the different mechanisms for monitoring the quality of ITE in England, noting along the way the implications of its particular position straddling higher education and the schools sector. Whilst ITE provision is inspected by OfSTED and so bound by the statutory requirements of the Department of Education, around 90 per cent of provision is situated wholly or partly in universities, in most cases leading to postgraduate level academic awards, and so also falling within the higher education quality assurance remit of the Quality Assurance Agency (QAA).

For university Schools of Education, this positioning in the 'liminal space' between two different quality assurance arenas has always presented challenges (Gilroy 1999), and these challenges are likely to become more explicit in the future. In the past, higher education quality assurance of ITE (both internal QA processes and external scrutiny through QAA) has tended to adopt a 'light-touch' approach, implicitly acknowledging the rigour of the OfSTED ITE compliance framework. This chapter traces the evolution of quality assurance and quality assurance of ITE in England over recent decades, and discusses the likely direction of travel in the future (noting that the arrival in higher education of a performative, high-stakes accountability culture to learning and teaching via the Teaching Excellence Framework (TEF) might bring an end to this relative freedom).

The opening of 'the secret garden'

In an era where accountability to demanding OfSTED quality criteria exerts a significant influence on policy and practice in both schools and Initial Teacher Education in England, it is worth noting that this is a relatively recent phenomenon. In the three decades that followed the establishment of universal educational provision, via the 1944 Education Reform Act, schools operated in a landscape of relatively high levels of autonomy in respect of curriculum and pedagogy. This era also saw teaching become a graduate-entry profession, meaning teachers began entering the profession from university-based courses rather than 'Teacher Training Colleges' – a trend noted in other European states at this time (Tatto 2006). The location of ITE in the traditionally self-governing university sector – and the consequential rising social status and political power of the profession – enabled this autonomy from central government control to be maintained well into the 1980s.

The beginning of the shift from professional autonomy to an accountability culture came in 1976, when Prime Minister James Callaghan gave a speech at Ruskin College in which he called for the 'secret garden' of the school to be opened and exposed to public scrutiny (Wilkins 2015a, 229). Although Callaghan's intervention had no immediate practical impact, the Conservative government elected in 1979 was committed to challenging the 'post-war welfare consensus' and replacing this with neoliberal 'free-market anti-statism' (Chitty 2004: 47). This resulted in a raft of policies that have come to exemplify what has been termed New Public Management (Apple 2005), including the devolvement of many aspects of governance and management to school level, 'parental choice' of schools and the establishment of City Technical Colleges. Following the 1988 Education Reform Act, the National Curriculum was introduced in 1990, with OfSTED established two years later (Furlong 2005).

This period of reform also saw an unprecedented incursion into the regulation of university provision, with the establishment of the Council for the Accreditation of Teacher Education (CATE) in 1984, to develop standards by which ITE provision could be judged (and, if necessary, be stripped of accreditation to award Qualified Teacher Status) (Wilkin 1996). Alongside this scrutiny (almost a quarter of a century before the 2010–15 Coalition government's policy of developing a 'school-led' ITE system) came attempts to develop school-led teacher training, through the Licenced Teacher and Articled Teacher Schemes launched in 1988.

During the 1980s and early 1990s, the drive towards a greater accountability in ITE was an ideological one, bringing together neoliberal market principles and a neoconservative campaign to reverse the perceived inadequacies of the progressive egalitarianism of the 1960s and 1970s (Wilkins and Wood 2009). For neoconservative critics, ITE was at the heart of an 'intellectual crisis' caused by 'egalitarian, technicist and romantic ideologies' (O'Keeffe 2006, 198), and so accountability mechanisms focused on input rather than output – on the appropriateness and relevance of ITE course content rather than outcomes for student teachers. Chris Woodhead, Chief Inspector from 1994 to 2000, made it clear that OfSTED's role was to challenge the 'education establishment' and combat a culture of 'complacency and low expectations' (Woodhead 1999). Running parallel to this ideological struggle between progressive egalitarianism and radical conservatism was a fundamental debate about the nature of teaching; essentially, whether the education (or training) of teachers should be positioned as an 'apprenticeship into a craft' or induction into a 'theorised profession/situated judgement' (Wilkins 2015a, 225).

The arrival of a Labour government in 1997 saw a continuance – and intensification – of centralised quality assurance of ITE. However, Tony Blair used the twentieth anniversary of Callaghan's 'Ruskin Speech' to stress that his education reforms would be 'practical not ideological', and to call for teachers to be 'relentlessly . . . held accountable for their performance' (Blair 1996, cited in Wilkins 2015b, 1148–1149). In other words, the emphasis was to shift away from relevance of content, to efficiency and effectiveness. This more instrumental, less ideological approach coincided with the wider trend for public sector accountability systems to be based on a data-driven 'performance auditing'. This increasingly performative culture was allied to the marketisation of many aspects of public sector provision through a 'normalising' rhetoric in which data-driven auditing was portrayed as an inevitable – and incontestable – component of a 'consumer democracy' (Mahony and Hextall 1997). The normalisation of performativity meant that when teachers and teacher educators critique any aspect of accountability mechanisms, they risk being portrayed as obstructionist defenders of professional exclusivity; as both 'barriers to reconstruction' (Barber 1996, cited in Hulme and Menter 2015, 212), and 'the enemies of promise' (Gove 2012).

This has meant that whilst persistent concern has been raised within the teaching profession and the ITE sector regarding the perceived 'coercive instrumentalism' of performative inspection, in wider public and political discourse, high-stakes, data-driven accountability is typically characterised as a 'common-sense necessity' (Torres 2011), echoing Blair's 'post-ideological' positioning.

The New Labour era saw the implementation of Circular 4/98 (DfEE 1998), an exhaustive set of over 100 separate 'Standards for the Award of Qualified Teacher Status' that set out the expectations for student teachers' knowledge and understanding in respect of their planning, teaching and classroom management, and their competence in 'monitoring, assessment, recording, reporting and accountability' (MARRA). In addition, ITE providers were expected to assess their students across an extensive range of subject knowledge (McNamara *et al.* 2008).

The cumbersome 4/98 Standards did not last long, being replaced in 2002 by the more manageable Qualifying to Teach (DfES 2002), with successive revisions in 2007 and 2012, bringing us up to the current Teachers' Standards, comprising a mere eight Standards encompassing expectations, promoting progress, subject knowledge, assessment, behaviour management and wider professional responsibilities (DfES 2012); the Teachers' Standards are replicated in Appendix 1. All ITE programmes are required to demonstrate to OfSTED that they have robust assessment mechanisms in place for judging student teachers' progress against these Standards. For many working in the ITE sector, this led to a period in which at least a degree of autonomy and professional judgement could be brought to bear at the level of programme content and structure (although as discussed later, the recent development of a 'framework for core content' of ITE may signal an end to even this limited autonomy).

Inspection of Initial Teacher Education: The encroachment of performativity

Before OfSTED's remit was extended to include ITE, the sector had enjoyed even more freedom from external scrutiny than schools, and OfSTED's Chief Inspector at the time, Chris Woodhead, explicitly stated that its mission was to challenge the 'education establishment' and combat what he perceived to be a culture of complacency and low expectations (Woodhead 1999).

OfSTED's early inspections of university-based ITE (from 2005) followed a similar format to early school inspections; every aspect of ITE provision, from the content of programme handbooks and seminar/lecture plans to the quality of tutors' teaching was subject to inspectors' scrutiny. These were tense and confrontational experiences on all sides, exposing the cultural differences between what was viewed by higher educationalists as an instrumental, 'technicist' inspection model replacing relationships with Her Majesty's Inspectorate (HMI) characterised by 'informed connoisseurship' (Campbell and Husbands 2000).

From the beginning, the implications of OfSTED's accountability framework has even more 'high stakes' for ITE providers than for schools, as a consequence of the direct coupling of inspection outcomes with funding allocations. In England, the government executive agency responsible for the award of Qualified Teacher Status (formerly the Training and Development Agency (TDA), currently the National College for Teaching and Leadership (NCTL)) also oversees teacher supply and ITE funding. ITE providers are required to submit annual 'bids' for an allocation of places, and OfSTED inspection outcomes are a significant element of the 'performance criteria' set out in this allocations methodology (NCTL 2016). Putting it crudely, a single poor performance in an OfSTED inspection (in fact, at times a less-than-'outstanding' one) can be sufficient to make provision financially unviable and lead to course closure.

The 'maturing' of inspection: Overlaying external scrutiny with self-surveillance

The most significant shift in the work of OfSTED came in 2005, with the introduction of a new inspection framework that required schools to record internal assessments of its own performance and improvement priorities on a 'Self-Evaluation Form' (SEF). The SEF, OfSTED argued, would in effect 'amount to the school's inspection on itself' (OfSTED 2004, 12). This notion of 'intelligent accountability' (Bubb *et al.* 2007, 32) was extended to ITE in 2008, with the introduction of a Self-Evaluation Document (SED). Although both the SEF and the SED were nominally optional, the high-stakes nature of the OfSTED regime meant that they were in effect mandatory; the number of schools and ITE providers who chose not to submit a SEF/SED was thought to be close to zero (Wilkins and Wood 2009).

The 2008–11 ITE Inspection Framework also brought ITE inspection into alignment with school inspections by no longer requiring inspectors to directly examine every single aspect of provision, focusing instead on leadership and management, particularly in relation to course improvement and quality assurance. Previously ITE inspections had observed and made judgements on university teaching sessions and carried out detailed scrutiny of course content, as well as assessing the quality of student teachers' teaching in schools.

The shift towards a self-evaluation model was presented as one in which power was being 'handed back' to the professions, allowing for a more collegial dialogue between providers and inspectors. However, critics argued that the conflation of self-evaluation with a high-stakes accountability framework simply creates a self-inspection culture (Bubb *et al.* 2007; UCET 2011), in which senior and middle managers in schools and ITE effectively become 'the inspector within' (Wilkins and Wood 2009, 294), or as Troman puts it, the 'critical reality definer' (Troman 1997, 362–363).

In this environment, inspection not only becomes 'ever-present', but all-encompassing as well, with every aspect of policy and practice (including performance management, appraisal, induction and mentoring, and professional development) inextricably linked to a perpetual cycle of 'inspection-readiness'. In essence, the rhetoric of 'self-management' and 'handing back power to the professionals' creates an illusion of freedom that masks a 'self-policing' reality that leads to a narrow, normative model of 'good practice' (Ball 2000).

One significant difference between the schools' Self-Evaluation Form and the ITE providers' Self-Evaluation Document was that whilst for schools the SEF was purely for the use of inspectors during 'live' inspection events, ITE providers were required to submit their SED annually to the Teaching Agency (the 'executive agency' responsible for ITE 'funding and quality' during this period). The Teaching Agency then carried out a risk assessment on the provider; this assessment being passed on to OfSTED to enable them to make decisions about the timing, the structure and the 'lines of inquiry' of inspections (OfSTED 2009).

The extent to which political priorities can become embedded in a purportedly independent inspection framework is exemplified by the annual publication during this period of the executive agencies' 'Section 12 priorities', setting out the issues providers were expected to address in the section of their Self-Evaluation Document providing evidence of leaders' capacity to 'secure further improvements and/or to sustain high-quality outcomes' (TDA 2011). By this means the government of the day was able to shape the content and structure of ITE provision to emphasise what came to be seen as 'best practice'; at different times these priorities included the teaching of early reading (then early mathematics), addressing Special Educational Needs and Disability (SEND) and behaviour management.

The dual scrutiny of provision points to a degree of ambiguity about the relationship between the inspectorate and government. Even though OfSTED is intended to operate independently from government (it is formally accountable to parliament rather than the executive), in practice, inspection methodology is heavily influenced by the political agenda of the government of the day. Together with the ability of the executive agency to use providers' quality assurance data to 'steer' inspection processes, this suggests that OfSTED's independence is in reality illusory (Wilkins 2015a).

The additional layer of oversight from the executive agency responsible for funding ITE has not only affected the ways in which senior leaders in ITE providers prepared their Self-Evaluation Documents, but inevitably impacted on strategic improvement priorities. The challenge for providers was both a presentational and a political one, as they needed to satisfy both the strategic priorities of the Teaching Agency (essentially that of the government of the day) and the 'quality agenda' of OfSTED (Wilkins 2015a). Although the Self-Evaluation Document was introduced at a time when the inspection framework was shifting away from detailed quality assurance of programme input, this was a period in which the Teaching Agency, at the behest of government, was attempting to prescribe at a detailed level how providers operated. This included considerable pressure to devolve more control of ITE course content to schools, and intense scrutiny of key areas of pedagogy (most notably, in the teaching of early reading, in the struggle between proponents of systematic synthetic phonics and supporters of a 'whole language' approach) (Wyse and Styles 2007)

Essentially, the environment created was one in which institutions operate in a 'high surveillance, low trust' environment (Mahoney and Hextall 2000, 102), where internal relationships (between senior managers and programme teams) replicate the institutional relationships with OfSTED and the government, and where 'coercive compliance' can prevail at the expense of genuine professional dialogue and collegiality (Wilkins and Wood 2009, 293).

Quality assurance and accountability in the school-led system

The evolution from the Standards set out in Circular 4/98 to the 2012 Teachers' Standards appear to suggest a gradual shift away from a highly prescriptive approach to quality assuring ITE input, towards one which allowed regulators to turn their attention to output, judging the extent to which providers deliver ever-improving outcomes data. Providers are still obliged by statute to comply with accreditation criteria (relating to the selection of candidates, course structure (including balance between school- and university-based elements) and the management and quality assurance arrangements for partnerships with schools) (DfE 2016b). However, OfSTED's judgement about their overall quality is primarily a quantitative one, with the effectiveness and efficiency of provision determined by output measures, the most important of these being recruitment and retention, attainment (against Teachers' Standards) and employability (OfSTED 2015).

Changes in ITE accountability over the past two decades have been accompanied by an explicit drive to create a more diverse market in teacher supply, with a greater emphasis on establishing alternative ITE routes, particularly those either solely led by schools or in more 'balanced' partnerships between schools and universities (Furlong 2005; Hulme and Menter 2015). The election of the 2010–15 Coalition government saw a dramatic escalation in this drive, with Secretary of State Michael Gove declaring his aspiration for a 'school-led system' in his Schools White Paper *The Importance of Teaching* (DfE 2010).

Under the Coalition government, and the Conservative government that was to follow, ITE policies have appeared to return to an ideological agenda, with a discourse dominated by a renewal of the debate about the appropriate balance between skills/competency-focused training and theoretically informed education (Furlong 2013). The government enthusiastically favoured an apprenticeship model of school-based training within a 'school-led system' (ibid.), as Michael Gove consciously resurrected the 1980s neoconservative backlash against progressivism and theory-driven teacher education. Gove's rhetoric, attacking the 'enemies of promise' in a supposed 'education establishment' whom he memorably described as 'the blob' (Gove 2012), is strikingly reminiscent of that of the radical neoconservatives who were so influential in shaping the Thatcher government's education reforms.

As a result of the renewed ideological tension in ITE policy, the post-2010 era has also seen a return to the more adversarial relationship between government and universities in respect of ITE, in which issues of teacher quality and teacher supply are characterised as persistent problems for which radical solutions need to be found.

There is no doubt that there is a significant body of research, from a broad international perspective, that strengthens the case made for developing a school-led model of ITE. In particular, there is a strong consensus drawn from research evidence that extending of the role of schools in supporting the 'clinical practicum' experiences of student teachers, where they are able to develop and model effective teaching, is a critical component of high-quality teacher preparation programmes (Darling-Hammond 2006). However, whilst the school-led reforms in England could be seen to align with this component, Darling-Hammond also argues that teacher preparation programmes also must provide a seamless experience of learning with a coherence and integration of practical teaching experience with more theoretical elements of professional knowledge (of learners and their social/language development, of the curriculum content and goals and of the skills of planning, teaching, assessing learning and managing a productive learning environment) (Darling-Hammond 2006; 303). The move to a school-led system appears to carry a risk of having, over time, an adverse impact on this 'coherence and integration' of professional practice and professional knowledge (Horden 2014).

Where are we now? Where are we heading?

At the time of writing, government policy on quality assurance and accountability in ITE shows every sign of shifting back towards a more input-focused approach. Despite evidence from many sources, notably OfSTED, that the quality of ITE outcomes (whether measured by retention, attainment or employability) have risen steadily over the past decade (OfSTED 2016), the government has commissioned a series of reviews that suggests they continue to be dissatisfied with what providers are offering. The Carter Review (DfE 2015) focused on identifying the core elements of high-quality ITE, leading to the establishment of an 'expert group' charged with developing a 'framework of core content' – in essence a National Curriculum for ITE (DfE 2016a). The make-up of the core content framework group has understandably given rise to considerable anxiety amongst those working in university-based ITE, since it is notable for the lack of representation of the university sector (it is led by the Chief Executive of an Academy Trust and almost entirely comprised of key individuals in school-based ITE, independent sector schools and representatives of 'alternative provision'). Given that the overwhelming majority of ITE provision is 'university-led', it is hard to see this exclusion as being anything other than a conscious and ideologically motivated attempt to marginalise a perceived 'educational establishment'.

The actual proposed 'core content' is unsurprising; in essence it expands on each of the 2012 Teachers' Standards, emphasising aspects that the Carter Review had identified as 'problematic' in current provision. However, this in itself is a fiercely contested issue; Carter's diagnosis of weak or inconsistent aspects of existing provision (such as behaviour management, subject knowledge pedagogy and Special Educational Needs and Disabilities (SEND)) (DfE 2015, 6) appear to be largely based in the flimsy evidence provided by the annual 'Newly-Qualified Teacher Survey', a national survey that was so devalued by low response rates that it was abandoned in 2015. It is certainly contradicted by Michael Wilshaw, Chief Inspector of OfSTED, who in his 2016 Annual Report not only noted a sustained improvement on overall ITE outcomes, but singled out subject knowledge, 'theory-informed practice' and behaviour management as particular strengths (OfSTED 2016, 126). Sceptics may therefore draw attention to the fact that the issues identified in the Carter Review as problematic closely align with the 'revisited neoconservative' priorities of the present government.

Even more worrying for many working in ITE is the recommendations of the Core Content Expert Group that the framework of core content should be used as 'one of the key measures of quality when allocating ITT places' (DfE 2016, 10) and that OfSTED should 'use the framework when making judgements about the quality of training and the leadership and management of an ITE partnership' (ibid., 10). Were this to be enacted by the government, it would signal a return to the situation in the late 2000s when the Training and Development Agency/Teaching Agency 'policed' the content and structure of ITE courses through its annual 'Section 12 priorities' – or perhaps even to the highly prescriptive 'CATE criteria' of the 1980s. In recent years one of the more positive aspects of the ways in which ITE providers are held accountable has been the shift away from a model of prejudging then micromanaging input, to one focused on outcomes.

The 2012 ITE Inspection Framework has also been, for many in the sector, a more positive experience because of the introduction in 2014 of a two-stage inspection process, with inspectors focusing on Leadership and Management, the coherence of the training experience and the standards achieved by students in Phase 1 (between April and June) and in Phase 2 (between October and December) examining the preparedness and competence of Newly Qualified Teachers. The two-stage process is intended to allow inspectors to develop a richer understanding of the context of each provider (with the same Lead Inspectors, and the majority of the wider inspection team, expected to remain the same for both stages), and consequentially lead to a greater degree of collegial dialogue between providers and lead inspectors.

Ultimately, however, the measure of the effectiveness of ITE provision should be the extent to which providers recruit, train and retain student individuals in such a way as to prepare them to become high-quality, resilient teachers and the school leaders of the future, but there are signs that this risks being side-lined by a return to a more politicised attempt to establish a quasi-curriculum for ITE.

Endnote

The evolution of accountability mechanisms in ITE in England over the past 40 years has in many respects exemplified the spread (both geographical and across sectors) of performative policy and practice. The model of data-driven performance management mediated through an institutional leadership culture of 'self-surveillance' and 'incentivised' through market levers is an increasingly familiar one, not just in public sector provision but in the private and 'third space' voluntary/charitable sectors as well. The UK has come to be seen as the world leader in performative governance (Wilkins 2015b), but the model has become increasingly familiar across much of the industrialised world. Furthermore, the growing influence of transnational organisations such as the International Monetary Fund (IMF) and the World Bank has seen performative governance as a key means of 'normalising' neoliberalism across the developing world as well (Olssen and Peters 2005).

A particular characteristic of the 'English model' of holding ITE providers accountable has been its explicit use of market levers to enforce compliance (and conformity). Directly linking inspection outcomes to allocations of funding is an explicit means of politicised control, and one that has frequently been viewed as weakening the capacity of providers to be creative and innovative, promoting instead a 'low-risk' approach that focuses entirely on readily quantifiable and short-term impact (Hulme & Menter 2015; Wilkins 2015a).

Finally, returning to the wider context of higher education in England, it seems unlikely that university-based providers of Initial Teacher Education will be able to continue to dip 'below the radar' in terms of higher education quality assurance mechanisms. As noted earlier, this has been the case for many years with Quality Assurance Agency institutional reviews tending to steer clear of ITE provision on the tacit assumption that that was 'OfSTED territory'; adding to this the fact that the majority of ITE provision in English universities is offered at postgraduate level, and therefore not subject to the tyranny of judgement by National Student Survey (NSS) outcomes, the higher education components of ITE provision has been subject to relatively 'light-touch' scrutiny by both internal and external quality assurance reviewers. However, the introduction of the Teaching Excellence Framework (TEF) may well see this come to an end. It is too early to judge how the TEF might impact upon Initial Teacher Education provision in universities, but those responsible for ITE quality assurance will no doubt be watching warily. Already faced with the demands of working in a sector where the government appears determined to favour school-based providers whilst also under increasing internal pressure to deliver improved research outcomes, the additional demands of contributing to their university's TEF performance (whether in terms of 'metrics' or a narrative about teaching excellence) is unlikely to be greeted with enthusiasm.

As noted earlier in this chapter, the 'duel accountability' for university-based teacher educators of meeting both professional and academic quality assurance standards is a longstanding challenge. This challenge is perhaps greater however as the developing demands of subject-level TEF may intensify the scrutiny ITE providers are subject to from within their own institutions. Given the additional uncertainty about the future of teacher education in universities created by the school-led reforms of recent years, there is a real threat that some university leaders will decide that ITE is too challenging an environment and withdraw completely from the sector (indeed this has happened already in a small number of cases since 2011). ITE providers, therefore, need to ensure that are engaging fully with their institutional leaders and demonstrating clearly the contribution ITE makes to universities.

In the context of the quality assurance of teaching, there is no doubt that teacher educators have a significant contribution to make, but the history of the development of ITE in universities has often led to Schools of Education being somewhat disconnected with wider initiatives associated with quality assurance and developing pedagogic excellence. This is perhaps no longer tenable, and teacher educators need to ensure they are fully engaged in teaching quality assessment at an institutional level and in making senior leaders fully aware of the distinctive contribution they can make to pedagogic innovation. The TEF era can be seen as an opportunity for teacher educators rather than a threat if they can capitalise on the increased attention given to pedagogic quality and the student 'learning journey' by expanding their inter-disciplinary institutional engagement.

The multiple accountability demands on teacher educators also have consequences for their external engagement. Whilst the data-driven environment of performative accountability systems will always bring a danger of a reductionist approach to external quality assurance, the introduction of a two-stage inspection process in 2014 has created an environment in which providers can develop more effective collegial relationships with Lead Inspectors and capitalise on the deeper contextual understanding of inspectors to bring an element of professional dialogue to the process.

Finally, there is a need to accept the political reality that the school-led system is here to stay – and least for the foreseeable future – and this means paying continual attention to sustaining and growing their partnerships with schools. The strength of the school–university partnership has been a significant strength of the English ITE system for many decades now, and whilst the diversification of provision (or fragmentation, depending on your perspective) can create challenges and tensions in these partnerships, it is in the interests of both teacher educators and schools to engage in dialogue to ensure partnership models evolve to not only ensure that teacher supply needs are met, but to share perspectives and good practice in respect of meeting the complex accountability demands of ITE. Ultimately these two are inextricably linked. If the quality – and coherence – of the ITE experience is weakened, this will have a direct influence on recruitment and retention/progression in the teaching profession, creating even more critical supply shortages in the future.

References

Ammermüller, A. & Lauer, C. 2009. School quality and educational outcomes in Europe, in: Dolton, P., R. Asplund, & E. Barth (Eds) *Education and inequality across Europe*. London: Elgar.

Apple, M.W. 2005. Education, markets, and an audit culture. *Critical Quarterly* 47(1–2): 11–29.

Ball, S.J. 2000. Performativities and fabrications in the education economy: towards the performative society. *Australian Educational Researcher* 17(3): 1–24.

Ball, S.J. 2003. The teacher's soul and the terrors of performativity. *Journal of Education Policy* 18(2): 215–228.

Barber, M. 1996. *The learning game. Arguments for an education revolution*. London: Indigo.

Barber, M. & Mourshed, M. 2007. *How the world's best performing school systems come out on top*. London: McKinsey and Company.

Blair, T. 2006. 20 years on. *Guardian*. Accessed online on 23/01/2017 http://education.guardian.co.uk/thegreatdebate/story/0,,586338,00.html

Brown, P., Lauder, H. & Ashton, D. 2007. Education, globalisation and the future of the knowledge economy. *European Educational Research Journal* 7(2): 131–156.

Bubb, S., Earley, P., Ahtaridou, E., Jones, J. & Taylor, C. 2007. The self-evaluation form: is the SEF aiding school improvement? *Management in Education* 21(3): 32–37.

Campbell, J. & Husbands, C. 2000. On the reliability of OfSTED inspection of Initial Teacher Training: A case study. *British Educational Research Journal* 26(1): 39–48.

Chitty, C. 2004. *Education policy in Britain*. Basingstoke: Palgrave MacMillan.

Codd, J. 2005. Teachers as 'managed professionals' in the global education industry: the New Zealand experience. *Educational Review* 57(2): 193–206.

Connell, J. 2013. The neoliberal cascade and education: An essay on the market agenda and its consequences. *Critical Studies in Education* 54(2): 99–112.

Crocker, R. & Dibbon, D. 2008. *Teacher education in Canada: A baseline study*. Society for the Advancement of Excellence in Education. Accessed online on 11/02/2017 at http://www.saee.ca/pdfs/Teacher_Education_in_Canada.pdf.

Darling-Hammond, L. 2006. Constructing 21st-century teacher education. *Journal of Teacher Education* 57(3): 300–314.

Davies, S. & Guppy, N. 1997. Globalisation and educational reforms in Anglo-American democracies. *Comparative Education Review* 41(4): 435–459.

Department for Education. 2010. *The importance of teaching: The schools White Paper 2010*. London: TSO.

Department for Education (DfE). 2012. *Teachers' standards.* London: DfE. https://www.gov.uk/government/uploads/system/uploads/attachment_data/file/283566/Teachers_standard_information.pdf

Department for Education (DfE). 2015. *Carter review of initial teacher training.* London: DfE.

Department for Education (DfE). 2016a. *A framework of core content for initial teacher training (ITT).* London: DfE.

Department for Education (DfE). 2016b. *Initial teacher training criteria and supporting advice: Information for accredited initial teacher training providers (NCTL-00097–2015).* London: DfE.

Department for Education and Employment (DfEE). 1998. *Teaching: High status, high standards, Circular 4/98.* London: DfEE.

Department for Education and Skills (DfES). 2002. *Qualifying to teach: professional standards for Qualified Teacher Status and requirements for Initial Teacher Training, Circular 2/02.* London: DfES.

Furlong, J. 2005. New Labour and teacher education: the end of an era. *Oxford Review of Education* 31(1): 119–134.

Furlong, J. 2013. Globalisation, neoliberalism, and the reform of teacher education in England. *The Educational Forum* 77(1): 28–50.

Gilroy, P. 1999. Inspecting the inspecting of teacher education in England and Wales. *Journal of Education for Teaching: International Research and Pedagogy* 25(3): 215–219.

Gove, M. 2012. Education Secretary's speech on academies, at Haberdashers' Aske's Hatcham College, London, 4 January 2012, accessed online on 12/2/2017 at https://www.gov.uk/government/speeches/michael-gove-speech-on-academies

Hillgate Group. 1986. *Whose schools? A radical manifesto.* London: Hillgate Place.

Hirsch, D. 2007. Assessing No Child Left Behind and the rise of neoliberal polities. *American Educational Research Journal* 44(3): 493–518.

Horden, J. 2014. The logic and implications of school-based teacher formation. *British Journal of Educational Studies* 62(3): 231–248.

Howe, E. 2006. Exemplary teacher induction: An international review. *Educational Philosophy and Theory* 38(3): 287–297.

Hulme, M. & Menter, I. 2015. Performance measurement and accountability: Some reflections on the developments in teacher education in England, 209–223, in: Kuhlee, D., van Buer, J. and Winch, C., *Governance in der Lehrerausbildung: Analysen aus England und Deutschland.* Wiesbaden: Springer

Jensen, B., Hunter, A., Sonneman, J. & Burns, T. 2012. *Catching up: Learning from the best school systems in East Asia.* Melbourne: Grattan Institute.

Maandag, D., Deinum, J., Hofman, A. & Buitink, J. 2007. Teacher education in schools: An international comparison. *European Journal of Teacher Education* 30(2): 151–173.

Mahoney, P. & Hextall, I. 2000. *Reconstructing teaching: Standards, performance and accountability.* London: Routledge Falmer.

McNamara, O., Webb, R. & Brundrett, M. 2008. *Primary teachers: initial teacher education, continuing professional development and school leadership development (Primary Review Research Survey 6/3).* Cambridge: University of Cambridge Faculty of Education.

Mutton, T., Burn, K. & Menter, I. 2017. Deconstructing the Carter Review: competing conceptions of quality in England's 'school-led' system of initial teacher education. *Journal of Education Policy* 21(1): 14–33.

National College for Teaching and Leadership (NCTL) 2016. *ITT allocations methodology 2017–18 (NCTL-20051–2016).* London: NCTL. Accessed online on 23/01/2017: https://www.gov.uk/government/publications/itt-requesting-places-and-allocations-methodology-2017-to-2018

O'Keeffe, D. 2006. Equality and childhood: Education and the myths of teacher training, 197–215, in Hartley, D. and Whitehead, M. (eds) *Teacher education: Professionalism, social justice and teacher education.* Abingdon: Routledge.

OfSTED. 2004. *A new relationship with schools: Improving performance through school self-evaluation.* London: DfES.

OfSTED. 2009. *The inspection of initial teacher education 2008–11: A guide for inspectors on the management and organisation of initial teacher education inspections.* London: OfSTED.

OfSTED. 2015. *Initial teacher education inspection handbook.* September 2015 (No. 150033). London: OfSTED. Accessed online 23/01/2017: https://www.gov.uk/government/publications/initial-teacher-education-inspection-handbook

OfSTED. 2016. *The annual report of Her Majesty's Chief Inspector of Education, Children's Services and Skills 2015/16 HC821.* London: OfSTED.

Olssen, M. & Peters, M, 2005. Neoliberalism, higher education and the knowledge economy: from the free market to knowledge capitalism. *Journal of Education Policy* 20(3): 313–345.

Tatto, M. 2006. Education reform and the global regulation of teachers' education, development and work: A cross-cultural analysis. *International Journal of Education Research* 45, 231–241.

Torres, C. 2011. Public universities and the neoliberal common sense: Seven iconoclastic theses. *International Studies in Sociology of Education* 21(3): 177–197.

Training and Development Agency for Schools (TDA) 2007. *The Revised Standards for Qualified Teacher Status and Requirements for Initial Teacher Training.* London: TDA.

Training and Development Agency for Schools (TDA). 2011. *TDA self-evaluation document (SED) for initial teacher training (ITT) providers.* London: TDA.

Troman, G. 1997. Self-management and school inspection: Complementary forms of surveillance and control in the primary school. *Oxford Review of Education* 23(3): 345–363.

United Nations Educational, Scientific and Cultural Organisation (UNESCO). 2011. *Global Education Digest.* Quebec: UNESCO.

Universities Council for the Education of Teachers (UCET) 2011. *A study of self-evaluation in Initial Teacher Education (ITE) in England: A tool of governmentality?* London: UCET.

Wilkin, M. 1996. *Initial Teacher Training: The dialogue of ideology and culture.* London: Falmer Press.

Wilkins, C. 2015a. The impact of the inspectorate system on Initial Teacher Education in England, 225–244, in Kuhlee, D., van Buer, J. and Winch, C., *Governance in der Lehrerausbildung: Analysen aus England und Deutschland.* Wiesbaden: Springer.

Wilkins, C. 2015b. Education reform in England: Quality and equity in the performative school. *International Journal of Inclusive Education* 19(11): 1143–1160.

Wilkins, C. 2017. Elite career-changers and their experience of initial teacher education. *Journal of Education for Teaching: International Research and Pedagogy* 43(2): 171–190.

Wilkins, C. & Comber, C. 2015. 'Elite' career-changers in the teaching profession. *British Educational Research Journal* 41(6): 1010–1030.

Wilkins, C. & Wood, P. 2009 Initial teacher education in the panopticon. *Journal of Education for Teaching: International Research and Pedagogy* 35(3): 283–297.

Woodhead C. 1999. Platform: why inspections set you free. *Times Educational Supplement*, 14 May 1999.

Wyse, D. and Styles, M. 2007. Synthetic phonics and the teaching of reading: the debate surrounding England's 'Rose Report'. *Literacy* 41(1): 35–42.

Appendix 1
Teachers' Standards

PREAMBLE

Teachers make the education of their pupils their first concern, and are accountable for achieving the highest possible standards in work and conduct. Teachers act with honesty and integrity; have strong subject knowledge, keep their knowledge and skills as teachers up-to-date and are self-critical; forge positive professional relationships; and work with parents in the best interests of their pupils.

PART ONE: TEACHING

A teacher must:

1   Set high expectations which inspire, motivate and challenge pupils

   - establish a safe and stimulating environment for pupils, rooted in mutual respect
   - set goals that stretch and challenge pupils of all backgrounds, abilities and dispositions
   - demonstrate consistently the positive attitudes, values and behaviour which are expected of pupils.

2   Promote good progress and outcomes by pupils

   - be accountable for pupils' attainment, progress and outcomes
   - be aware of pupils' capabilities and their prior knowledge, and plan teaching to build on these
   - guide pupils to reflect on the progress they have made and their emerging needs
   - demonstrate knowledge and understanding of how pupils learn and how this impacts on teaching
   - encourage pupils to take a responsible and conscientious attitude to their own work and study.

3   Demonstrate good subject and curriculum knowledge

   - have a secure knowledge of the relevant subject(s) and curriculum areas, foster and maintain pupils' interest in the subject, and address misunderstandings
   - demonstrate a critical understanding of developments in the subject and curriculum areas, and promote the value of scholarship
   - demonstrate an understanding of and take responsibility for promoting high standards of literacy, articulacy and the correct use of standard English, whatever the teacher's specialist subject

- if teaching early reading, demonstrate a clear understanding of systematic synthetic phonics
- if teaching early mathematics, demonstrate a clear understanding of appropriate teaching strategies.

4   Plan and teach well-structured lessons

- impart knowledge and develop understanding through effective use of lesson time
- promote a love of learning and children's intellectual curiosity
- set homework and plan other out-of-class activities to consolidate and extend the knowledge and understanding pupils have acquired
- reflect systematically on the effectiveness of lessons and approaches to teaching
- contribute to the design and provision of an engaging curriculum within the relevant subject area(s).

5   Adapt teaching to respond to the strengths and needs of all pupils

- know when and how to differentiate appropriately, using approaches which enable pupils to be taught effectively
- have a secure understanding of how a range of factors can inhibit pupils' ability to learn, and how best to overcome these
- demonstrate an awareness of the physical, social and intellectual development of children, and know how to adapt teaching to support pupils' education at different stages of development
- have a clear understanding of the needs of all pupils, including those with special educational needs; those of high ability; those with English as an additional language; those with disabilities; and be able to use and evaluate distinctive teaching approaches to engage and support them.

6   Make accurate and productive use of assessment

- know and understand how to assess the relevant subject and curriculum areas, including statutory assessment requirements
- make use of formative and summative assessment to secure pupils' progress
- use relevant data to monitor progress, set targets, and plan subsequent lessons
- give pupils regular feedback, both orally and through accurate marking, and encourage pupils to respond to the feedback.

7   Manage behaviour effectively to ensure a good and safe learning environment

- have clear rules and routines for behaviour in classrooms, and take responsibility for promoting good and courteous behaviour both in classrooms and around the school, in accordance with the school's behaviour policy
- have high expectations of behaviour, and establish a framework for discipline with a range of strategies, using praise, sanctions and rewards consistently and fairly
- manage classes effectively, using approaches which are appropriate to pupils' needs in order to involve and motivate them
- maintain good relationships with pupils, exercise appropriate authority, and act decisively when necessary.

8   Fulfil wider professional responsibilities

- make a positive contribution to the wider life and ethos of the school
- develop effective professional relationships with colleagues, knowing how and when to draw on advice and specialist support

- deploy support staff effectively
- take responsibility for improving teaching through appropriate professional development, responding to advice and feedback from colleagues
- communicate effectively with parents with regard to pupils' achievements and well-being.

PART TWO: PERSONAL AND PROFESSIONAL CONDUCT

A teacher is expected to demonstrate consistently high standards of personal and professional conduct. The following statements define the behaviour and attitudes which set the required standard for conduct throughout a teacher's career.

- Teachers uphold public trust in the profession and maintain high standards of ethics and behaviour, within and outside school, by:

  - treating pupils with dignity, building relationships rooted in mutual respect, and at all times observing proper boundaries appropriate to a teacher's professional position
  - having regard for the need to safeguard pupils' well-being, in accordance with statutory provisions
  - showing tolerance of and respect for the rights of others
  - not undermining fundamental British values, including democracy, the rule of law, individual liberty and mutual respect, and tolerance of those with different faiths and beliefs
  - ensuring that personal beliefs are not expressed in ways which exploit pupils' vulnerability or might lead them to break the law.

- Teachers must have proper and professional regard for the ethos, policies and practices of the school in which they teach, and maintain high standards in their own attendance and punctuality.
- Teachers must have an understanding of, and always act within, the statutory frameworks which set out their professional duties and responsibilities.

12 The Quality Assurance of Higher Education from the Perspective of Professional, Statutory and Regulatory Bodies (PSRBs)

Damian Day

Introduction

UK higher education is accustomed to being placed under scrutiny: its teaching quality is evaluated by a national student survey, its research quality by a periodic national review and academic peers rank their own institutions in international listings. These kinds of quality measures and ratings are reported routinely and are firmly embedded in the consciousness of higher education. However, there is an additional, well-established but less visible layer of scrutiny and that is the quality assurance work of Professional, Statutory and Regulatory Bodies (PSRBs).

To appreciate the scope of PSRB activity in HEIs we can turn to the Key Information Set (KIS), a uniform set of metrics provided for every university course in the UK maintained by the Higher Education Statistics Agency (HESA). For the 2016–2017 academic year HESA lists 149 PSRBs active in UK HEIs, ranging from bodies accrediting less than a handful of courses (the Church of Scotland and the Association for the Study of Animal Behaviour, for example), through those with a presence in a significant proportion of HEIs (such as the healthcare regulators), to those with a presence in most HEIs: HESA lists the Association of Chartered Certified Accountants (ACCA) as accrediting[1] 437 qualifications and BCS, the Chartered Institute for IT as accrediting 1373. In total in 2016–2017 HESA lists 14,133 courses accredited by PSRBs.

Although PSRB activity in HEIs is not particularly high profile, it is substantial, sustained and growing, for the reasons Michael Eraut suggests:

> Since the war, an increasing number of occupations have taken advantage of higher education for two main reasons. First, getting a degree-entry route established validates the profession's claims to a specialist knowledge base, and hence to professional status. Second, recruitment through the higher education system is critical for sustaining, let alone improving, the relative quality of a profession's intake.
>
> Higher education has also derived considerable benefits from its relationship with the professions. The presence of professionally-focused courses has helped increasingly beleaguered institutions to argue that they do prepare students for employment and also make a more positive contribution to society. They have contributed to the expansion of student numbers, particularly in the public sector; and individual faculties and departments have been able to increase their relative power by incorporating areas of professional training which were previously outside higher education.
>
> (Eraut, 1994, p. 100)

An overview of PSRBs

The PSRBs engaging with HEIs are a diverse group. As the component parts of the acronym would suggest, some bodies regulate professions and professionals; some are established in law and have enforceable statutory functions; and some are voluntary membership bodies. The main groupings are associations, chartered institutes, institutes/institutions, societies and councils. Despite the significant number of PSRBs and the breadth of professional areas they cover, from a public perspective they tend to surface in the public consciousness only when a member of a prominent profession – a doctor, nurse, solicitor or barrister – is struck off for professional malpractice. Turning to Eraut again, he rather pointedly reminds us that the 'reputations of professions in this age of mass media are increasingly dependent on their weakest members' (Eraut, 1994, p117).

Although the focus of this chapter is the education role of PSRBs, a PSRB's role is significantly wider than that. Setting standards is core to the work of most PSRBs –education and training standards being the first set, typically followed by:

1   Practice – the standard that must be met by members/registrants. Commonly these can be standards of 'conduct', 'ethics', 'performance' or 'proficiency' and vary in their detail – with some emphasising the mechanics of the profession and services offered to the public, while others are more general with an emphasis on professionalism and scope of practice;

2   Continuing Professional Development (CPD) or Continuing Education (CE) – the requirement for members/registrants to demonstrate that their practice is current.[2] Again, there is variation, with some standards requiring points accumulation through attendance at accredited CPD/CE events, while others take a less prescriptive approach based on reflective practice; and

3   Fitness to Practise – the standard describing the range of sanctions which can be brought against members/registrants who fail to maintain an appropriate standard of practice. In some cases, fitness to practice mechanisms and sanctions are mandatory in law, in others the PSRB has chosen to implement them voluntarily. Sanctions can range from a case being dismissed, through the issuance of advice and warnings, to restrictions on practice, suspension or erasure/removal.

While education and training standards are used to accredit courses, it is common for there to be a strong link in course curricula to practice standards, sometimes a requirement for students to undertake and record CPD while training and for some students to be subject to university fitness to practise regimes reflecting those for registered professionals (and in addition to normal academic sanctions).

The evolving role of PSRBs

In the last few decades, a changing regulatory landscape has brought about a reappraisal of roles by PSRBs – not just in terms of their functions but also governance and accountability. In some cases, changes have been voluntary but for others change has been prompted by government action. The health regulators are a case in point. Dame Janet Smith's multi-volume report into Harold Shipman, a doctor and serial killer, was a turning point for health-care regulation. Dame Janet was sharply critical of the professionals involved in the case and her criticism extended to the healthcare regulators as well: her principal criticism being that healthcare professionals and regulators were more concerned with external perceptions of professionalism and protecting professionals than they were with public protection.

The pressure for reform of healthcare regulation was kept up after the publication of further reports into other healthcare failings, such as the Kennedy Report into heart surgery at the Bristol Royal Infirmary (2001) and, more recently, the Francis Report into the Mid Staffordshire Foundation Trust (2013). In 2007, government took a broad approach to reforming healthcare regulation with its command paper *Trust, Assurance and Safety: The Regulation of Health Professionals in the 21st Century*, which outlined key underpinning principles for healthcare regulation:

> First, its overriding interest should be the safety and quality of the care that patients receive from health professionals.
>
> Second, professional regulation needs to sustain the confidence of both the public and the professions through demonstrable impartiality. Regulators need to be independent of government, the professionals themselves, employers, educators and all the other interest groups involved in healthcare.
>
> Third, professional regulation should be as much about sustaining, improving and assuring the professional standards of the overwhelming majority of health professionals as it is about identifying and addressing poor practice or bad behaviour.
>
> Fourth, professional regulation should not create unnecessary burdens, but be proportionate to the risk it addresses and the benefit it brings.
>
> Finally, we need a system that ensures the strength and integrity of health professionals within the United Kingdom, but is sufficiently flexible to work effectively for the different health needs and healthcare approaches within and outwith the NHS in England, Scotland, Wales and Northern Ireland and to adapt to future changes.
>
> (*Trust, Assurance and Safety*, 2007)

The paper brought about changes in governance and accountability and also required regulators to focus their work on patient and public need and trust rather than the professionals they regulated. This unambiguous requirement from government affected the work of the healthcare regulators profoundly and has had a clear impact on their education functions, including the ways in which they engage with HEIs. Beyond healthcare, striking a balance between the needs of professionals and the public service they provide has been a feature of PSRB reforms.

Illustrating change – curriculum development

As we have discussed already, a core role for PSRBs is setting education standards for a profession. Here we discuss potential tensions between PSRBs and HEIs in the standards setting process and consider examples of changes over time. The attraction of PSRB accreditation is that it can benefit students wishing to join a profession: those benefits can include access to professional training after graduation, a grade of membership (of a PSRB), exemption from mandatory professional examinations or exemption from the academic component of membership/registration requirements. When developing standards for education and training, even if a PSRB works closely with the subject community as part of the development process, its perspective is a different one: the perspectives are not necessarily mutually exclusive, but tend to have different emphases. A PSRB's stakeholders include academic subject communities and practice communities (its member/registrant base), government and the users of member/registrant services. It is that particular mix of views which drives the development of standards by a PSRB, not just academic considerations.

Taking pharmacy as an example, its origins are in drug discovery and manufacturing, as is clear from early syllabi. Table 12.1 charts the development of syllabi from 1971 to the present day and shows how pharmacy has evolved over 40-plus years from a scientific discipline based on medicine to a profession delivering frontline healthcare. Taking the 1971 and 1981 syllabi together, the emphasis is on drugs and medicine and it is not until the 1990s that 'the practice of pharmacy' is added – when the notion of providing a pharmacy service is explicit. With the emergence of pharmacy practice in the syllabus, comes the need for practitioners to contribute to the delivery of courses and to create spaces for practice-based activity. Moving forward to 2002, patients are mentioned explicitly, shifting courses further towards care delivery and away from unintegrated science and manufacturing – another challenge for laboratory-based practice. In the latest, 2011, iteration of the standards, attitudes and values (that is professionalism) change the nature of the standards again (they were the first set of standards developed in the post-Shipman era). We should not underestimate the challenge for PSRBs and HEIs in managing such significant changes and this has inevitably been the source of lively debate because moving a pharmacy degree from a scientific degree towards a patient-facing professional course has required changes in staffing, including increased collaboration with external practitioners in practice settings and changes to course teaching, learning and assessment. (While UK BPharm/MPharm degrees have changed significantly

Table 12.1 Pharmacy syllabi 1971–2011

Year	Syllabus
1971	1. Chemistry of drugs 2. Pharmaceutical aspects of medicines 3. The action and uses of drugs and medicine
1981	1. Chemistry of rugs 2. Pharmaceutical aspects of medicines 3. The action and uses of drugs and medicine 'There is a fourth element that must be included for a pharmacy degree if it is to be acceptable for the purposes of registration, namely the law, ethics and practice of pharmacy' (Pharmaceutical Society of Great Britain, *Council approval of degrees in pharmacy*)
1991/2	1. Chemistry of drugs, of other constituents of medicines and of biological systems 2. Medicines design and manufacture: materials, methods and quality standards 3. The actions and uses of drugs, medicines and other products 4. The practice of pharmacy
2002	1. The patient 2. Medicines: drug action 3. Medicines: the drug substance 4. Medicines: the medicinal product 5. Healthcare systems and the roles of professionals 6. The wider context
2011	1. How medicines work 2. How people work 3. How systems work 4. Core and transferable skills 5. Attitudes and values

in the period described, a much more radical revision was the move to PharmD degrees from the 1990s in the US.)

Illustrating change – accreditation

In the same way that a consideration of syllabi tells a story about change, so does a similar consideration of approaches to accreditation. Here we will illustrate changes by considering the evolution of pharmacy accreditation teams, often the most significant interface between PSRBs and HEIs.

Returning to the 70s and 80s, the accreditation of pharmacy courses was undertaken by PSRB officer holders and committee members (representatives of the regulatory monopoly) and heads of school (representatives of the oligopoly delivering accredited courses). Moving to the 90s, PSRB office holders (who may or may not have been educationalists) were removed from teams and replaced with representatives from the profession, normally those with an interest in professional education. A decade later, heads of school were replaced with academics of any grade with an interest in pedagogy or course design and pharmacy practitioners, who were required to have expertise in professional education. An external view from elsewhere in education or healthcare was provided by lay members[3] from 2002 and in the current iteration of team membership, recently registered pharmacists have been added – pharmacists with first-hand experience of contemporary education and training.

To summarise the change, a close relationship between the regulator and schools of pharmacy has moved towards a broader approach taking into account a wider range of views – here, views of the users of pharmacy education and pharmacy services. The current teams reflect general themes in regulation – seeking the views of practitioners, users of pharmacy services and students but in doing so they have moved away from the peer review model used traditionally in HEIs for course revalidation.

Limitations of accreditation methodologies

Much PSRB accreditation activity is centred on courses delivered in HEIs and one might think that the focus of accreditation is on course delivery and, perhaps, student feedback, but the reality is different. Where accreditation involves visits, a common pattern of activity is meetings with academics and senior officers of the HEI discussing course philosophy and strategy, teaching, learning and assessment, resources and student views. Often the formal meetings will be supplemented with tours of the facilities. Accreditors will be sent documentation to study in advance but the opportunity to discuss teaching, learning and assessment with academics may be limited to several hours. In some methodologies, the evaluation of a course may not require a visit and even those that do may not actually observe any teaching or review any student work. Interestingly, this approach has not been challenged by HEIs, possibly because it is based on and reflects many of the features of internal course revalidation, where the same proxies are used to judge quality.

The General Pharmaceutical Council has tackled this issue by revising its accreditation methodology to focus on learning outcomes. Meetings about philosophy, strategy, teaching, learning, assessment and resources still take place but the longest and most detailed meetings are devoted to in-depth discussions about learning outcomes. A small number of outcomes are chosen at random and how they are delivered and developed across the years of an MPharm degree is discussed at length with academics – discussing each outcome can take up to 30 minutes. It may not be a perfect substitute for engaging directly with course

Table 12.2 Accreditation team membership 1971–present day

Year	Accreditation team members
1971	1. President/Vice President of Pharmaceutical Society of Great Britain (PSGB) Council 2. Two members of the PSGB Education Committee 3. Two heads of schools (of pharmacy)
1981	1. President/Vice President of PSGB Council 2. Two members of the PSGB Education Committee 3. Two heads of schools (of pharmacy)
1991/2	1. Chair of the Royal PSGB Education Committee 2. Head of school serving on the RPSGB Education Committee 3. Representatives of the main sectors of pharmacy (community/hospital/industry)
2002	1. Team leader (senior pharmacist) 2. Pharmacy academics 3. Pharmacy practitioners (community/hospital/industry) 4. Lay person (patient representative/senior member of other healthcare profession/ expert educationalist)
2011	1. Team leader (senior pharmacist with education experience) 2. Pharmacy academics 3. Pharmacy practitioners (pharmacy education experience expected) 4. Lay member (includes experience of representing the interests of patients or the public/understanding of healthcare regulation, UK healthcare systems and UK higher education/promotes equal treatment. Not a current or previous registrant of a healthcare profession 5. Recently registered pharmacist

delivery but it does provide more substantive assurances about course delivery than other methodologies.[4]

Priorities in setting education and training standards and curriculum design

Taking internal university programme validations as an example of how subjects evolve in an academic context, they tend to emphasise evolution in course design based on the research interests of academics and, from a subject perspective, course change is validated by external, academic subject peers. PSRB education and training standards tend to be developed differently, although HEIs and academics are always key stakeholders. For academics, considerations in curriculum design are the requirements of the regulator, in order to secure accreditation, but also the research interests of staff and the focus of the current course. For PSRBs, the stakeholder group will be different and can include consumers (sometimes mediated through the agency of government or non-governmental bodies), government and the professionals they regulate. From the academic perspective, consumers and government may be arms-length stakeholders but they may be the ultimate consumers of their product – aspiring professionals – and for that reason may drive the development of PSRB education and training standards.

The second difference between academic and PSRB approaches to standards setting and curriculum design centres on the link between education and professional practice standards[5] and the need for courses to deliver novice professionals. Practice standards tend to focus on two areas: the subject matter on which the profession is based and professional behaviour. The recurring tension, which changes over time but is always there, is the extent to which initial education and training should reflect practice – in the case of pharmacy, providing clinical and inter-professional team working experiences alongside the more traditional academic disciplines and the generic attributes of graduates. For PSRBs finding that balance is one of the most difficult aspects of their work.

International perspectives on PSRB work

In common with UK higher education the work of PSRBs is often international. Some PSRBs operate internationally by running training and examinations, others accredit courses delivered overseas by UK HEIs and/or local partners. As an example, on an annual basis the Association of Certified Chartered Accountants (ACCA) examines between 150–200 thousand students in 400 centres in 170+ countries, as well as accrediting the 437 courses in the UK mentioned earlier and another 600 overseas. The UK education brand is strong but its HEIs and PSRBs are working in international markets and face stiff competition from their counterparts in the US, Canada, Australia and New Zealand.

As UK higher education has extended its reach overseas, PSRBs have responded to requests for accreditation outside the UK. In some cases standards and subject matter transfer with relative ease but in other cases they do not. In healthcare, for example, the UK context is particularly difficult to reproduce, given the distinctiveness of the UK's NHS,[6] and because the UK population has its own distinctive health profile. In general, the purpose (real or theoretical) of accrediting healthcare courses overseas is to allow students to practise in the UK, requiring course content to be authentic: this means preparing students for working with an ageing population prone to obesity, hypertension and diabetes managed by a national health service – a profile that simply may not mirror the population or healthcare system of the country in which a course is being delivered.

When accrediting overseas, PSRBs have to consider two key points: 1) risk appetite and 2) equivalence. The principal risk is reputational: accrediting courses overseas that produce graduates unfit to practise in the UK could be damaging to a PSRB and undermining of non-UK professionals in the UK workforce. The secondary risk is how to set a standard that mitigates the risk of overseas delivery: specifically, can non-UK-trained academics and professional practitioners deliver the UK practice context or must there be input from the UK? This brings the principle of equivalence into play. PSRBs have to satisfy themselves that while courses rarely replicate their UK equivalents with 100 per cent accuracy, the degree of equivalence is sufficient to allow overseas delivery to be accredited. If a regulator understands and accepts the risk of accrediting a given course in a given context, and is convinced that that the degree of equivalence in the course is acceptable, then it can be accredited at least with sufficient confidence.

Looking beyond 2017 to new quality regimes

A central theme of this chapter has been the work of PSRBs in higher education as a significant but not especially visible quality assurance activity. So long as there is a demand for PSRB accreditation from students wanting to use higher education study as a stepping stone to working as a professional or while there is a legal requirement for the accreditation of courses, that work will continue. However, the context in which the work is used and its sensitivity may change as a new quality regime is introduced in England.

As is discussed in more detail elsewhere in this volume, a new regulator is being introduced, the Office for Students (OfS), and two of the mechanisms it will use to quality assure higher education will be annual data monitoring and a new system for evaluating teaching, the Teaching Excellence Framework (TEF). Annual monitoring will include the assessment of key indicators, including 'graduate employment (and) progression to professional jobs and postgraduate study' (DfE, 2016), which will certainly include PSRB-accredited courses, and one of the three domains to be evaluated by the TEF will be 'Student Outcomes and Learning Gain'. The criteria for evaluating that domain include 'The extent to which . . . students acquire knowledge, skills and attributes that prepare them for their personal and professional lives' and 'Evidence may include input measures such as employer engagement in the curriculum, course accreditation by professional regulatory or statutory bodies and extracurricular activities designed to enhance employability and transferable skills' (DfE, 2016). In addition to this a 'Provider submission' supporting a case for teaching quality can make reference to 'Recognition of courses by professional, statutory and regulatory bodies (PSRBs)' (DfE, 2016, p. 29). It is too early to tell how this will affect the relationship between HEIs and PSRBs but as fee decisions may depend on the outcome of the TEF, PSRB judgements about the professional suitability of courses may assume an importance beyond subject communities they have not enjoyed before.

Points for further consideration

For joint consideration by PSRBs and HEIs: Although PSRBs and HEIs have a lot to gain from having a positive relationship with each other, the relationship is not always as productive as it could be, mainly because PSRBs and HEIs tend to engage with each other around accreditation cycles rather than on a more frequent basis. Other than submitting annual returns, this can mean engaging perhaps once every three to six years in which time a lot can change. PSRBs and HEIs should consider how best to engage with each other more effectively around areas of common interest.

For consideration by PSRBs: The TEF in England may well change the nature of the relationship between PSRBs and HEIs if TEF outcomes are used to inform accreditation decision. In mid-2017 HEIs have been allocated global teaching gradings, and subject-level gradings may follow. Using either might politicise the relationship between PSRBs and HEIs, which should be borne in mind as the TEF is rolled out. PSRBs are advised to form a firm view on the TEF and how its outcomes might be used by them.

Notes

1 Throughout 'accreditation' will be used to describe the quality assurance activities of PSRBs, but others, such as validation, approval, recognition etc. are used in practice.

2 A more recent feature of healthcare regulation has been the introduction of additional, in-depth periods of checks of practice going beyond CPD, commonly known as revalidation. These schemes tend to be based on scrutiny and discussion of practice, based on CPD submissions, testimonials from peers and feedback from patients or others. As an example, for details of revalidation for medics in the UK go to http://www.gmc-uk.org/doctors/revalidation/9627.asp (retrieved on March 22 2017).

3 Depending on the PSRB, a 'lay' member can mean someone who is not a member of the profession regulated by the PSRB or it can mean not being a member of a wider set of regulated professions.

4 In fairness, it should be noted that some regulators do have methodologies which evaluate practical work.
5 In the Bibliography, GPhC 2015a, 2015b and 2017 document the development of the GPhC's latest practice standards.
6 The universal national health services in England, Scotland, Wales and Northern Ireland.

Bibliography

Baldwin, R., M. Cave & M. Lodge (2012) *Understanding Regulation, Theory, Strategy and Practice*, Second Edition. Oxford: Oxford University Press.

Brown, R. (2004) *Quality Assurance in Higher Education: The UK Experience since 1992*. London and New York: RoutledgeFalmer.

Department for Business, Innovation and Skills (BIS) (2016) *Success as a Knowledge Economy: Teaching Excellence, Social Mobility and Student Choice*. Retrieved on 4 February 2017 from https://www.gov.uk/government/publications/higher-education-success-as-a-knowledge-economy-white-paper

Department for Education (DfE) (2016) *Teaching Excellence Framework: Technical Consultation for Year Two*. Retrieved on 4 February 2017 from https://www.gov.uk/government/uploads/system/uploads/attachment_data/file/523340/bis-16-262-teaching-excellence-framework-techcon.pdf

Department of Health (2007) *Trust, Assurance and Safety: The Regulation of Health Professionals in the 21st Century*. Retrieved from https://www.gov.uk/government/uploads/system/uploads/attachment_data/file/228847/7013.pdf

Eraut, M. (1994) *Developing Professional Knowledge and Competence*. London and New York: Routledge.

General Pharmaceutical Council (GPhC) (2011) *Future Pharmacists, Standards for the Initial Education and Training of Pharmacists*. Retrieved on February 3 2017 from http://www.pharmacyregulation.org/initial-training

General Pharmaceutical Council (GPhC) (2015a) *Patient-Centred Professionalism, a Review of Conduct, Ethics and Performance*. Retrieved on February 3 2017 from http://www.pharmacyregulation.org/standards/development-and-review-our-standards

General Pharmaceutical Council (GPhC) (2015b) *Patient-Centred Professionalism – Response to the Discussion Paper*. Retrieved on February 3 2017 from http://www.pharmacyregulation.org/standards/development-and-review-our-standards

General Pharmaceutical Council (GPhC) (2015c) *Tomorrow's Pharmacy Team*. Retrieved on 3 February 2017 from http://www.pharmacyregulation.org/previous-consultations#2015-no3

General Pharmaceutical Council (GPhC) (2016) *Standards for Pharmacy Professionals*. Retrieved on February 3 2017 from http://www.pharmacyregulation.org/standards

General Pharmaceutical Council (GPhC) (2017) *Standards for Pharmacy Professionals*. Retrieved on 12 July 2017 from https://www.pharmacyregulation.org/standards

Higher Education Statistics Agency (HESA) *KIS record 2016/17 – Professional, Statutory and Regulatory Bodies (PSRBs) and Professional Accreditation of Undergraduate Programmes*. Retrieved February 3 2017 from https://www.hesa.ac.uk/collection/c16061/accreditation_guidance/.html/.html/

Quality Assurance Agency for Higher Education (QAA) (2002) *Pharmacy Subject Benchmark Statement*. Retrieved 3 February 2017 from http://www.qaa.ac.uk/en/Publications/Documents/Subject-benchmark-statement—Pharmacy.pdf

Quality Assurance Agency for Higher Education (QAA) (2014) *The Birth of the Quality Assurance Agencies*. Retrieved 3 February 2017 from http://www.qaa.ac.uk/en/ResearchAndAnalysis/Documents/The-birth-of-the-Quality-Agencies-Griffiths-14.pdf

Smith, J. (2002–2005) *The Shipman Report*. 6 volumes. Retrieved from http://webarchive.nationalarchives.gov.uk/20090808154959/http:/www.the-shipman-inquiry.org.uk/reports.asp

13 Quality Assurance through National Assessments

Damian Day

Introduction

The focus of this chapter is the role of national assessments from the perspective of a national professional regulator. Specifically, it looks at the role of national assessments as independent benchmarks, gateways to a profession and the ways in which they can be used to improve quality. Many people who end up practising in regulated professions are graduates who have been assessed through a variety of means during their degree and in a manner determined by the higher education institution (HEI) at which they studied. HEIs work within a common academic framework and there is a public assumption that this leads to uniformity in standards and outcomes. This chapter tests that assumption from the perspective of a regulator, using performance data from a national examination – the General Pharmaceutical Council's Registration Assessment.

For some regulators and professional bodies, national examinations have been a fact of life for many years: for example, with the exception of a brief hiatus in the 70s, 80s and early 90s, pharmacists have been required to sit national examinations since the mid-nineteenth century. The main gateway to other professions such as accountancy has been by (inter) national examination for many years as well. National examinations, particularly written ones, have their critics, however, a common criticism being that they cannot emulate practice and are, therefore, inauthentic tests of ability. Certainly, one must be clear about what examinations can and cannot test but one of the arguments in this chapter is that properly validated examinations have a part to play in maintaining national standards and address public concerns about competence to the extent that they outweigh their downsides.

In 2017, it is striking that major professions that have not hitherto used national examinations are considering introducing them. In 2016/2017, the regulators for doctors and solicitors in the UK consulted on national examinations and their rationales for doing so are significant in the context of the case being made here. The General Medical Council's rationale for introducing a Medical Licensing Assessment is:

> to create a single, objective demonstration that those applying for registration with a licence to practise medicine in the UK can meet a common threshold for safe practice.
> (General Medical Council, 2016)

For the Solicitors' Regulation Authority and its proposals for a Solicitors' Qualifying Examination:

> It is vital we have a qualification that justifies the high reputation of solicitors of England and Wales around the world. The proposals in this consultation will help maintain and

improve the international standing of solicitors of England and Wales by introducing a consistent, high standard at a time of change . . . At present, there is a range of different ways in which people can become a solicitor and each of them is assessed differently. This means there is no consistent examination at the point of qualification for solicitors, and no mechanism to compare the different pathways . . . At present we cannot be sure that there is a consistent or comparable standard of assessment for qualification across providers who adopt different assessment practices . . . absolute consistency and fairness can only effectively be assured by candidates sitting the same examination.

(Solicitors' Regulation Authority, 2016, pp. 7–10)

To summarise, the regulators cite public confidence, objectivity, comparability and common practice thresholds as key strengths of national assessments.

The evolution of national examinations – linking academia and professional practice

One of the challenges for bodies running national examinations is recognising that they must bridge the gap between university study and professional practice. This is by no means confined to national examining bodies: to an extent it reflects a wider change in professional education at university in which the historic distinctions between propositional knowledge taught in more didactic ways and procedural knowledge acquired in professional practice environments have been removed through the introduction of more integrated curricula with a professional focus. An obvious example of this would be the move from older pre-clinical (science-based)/clinical medical courses at universities towards more integrated curricula, where patient exposure and the application of knowledge are present far earlier in the course than before. This has brought about a change in not only course delivery but especially assessment. This chapter is grounded in healthcare but the change is wider than that: now assessment at university and some national examinations have significant practice-based elements – this can be seen not only in medicine, pharmacy, dentistry and nursing but also in accountancy and law, among others.

Using practice examinations alongside written examinations allows one to broaden what is tested beyond knowledge acquisition and critical reasoning by adding the application of knowledge and demonstrating communication skills in simulated practice settings to the mix. The most tried and tested example of this is the Observed Structured Clinical Examination (OSCE), which has been built in to undergraduate assessment and, increasingly, national examinations. The OSCE is perhaps the classic practical professional examination and while its origins may be in medical education it has been adopted and adapted by many healthcare and non-healthcare educators.

Standardisation is key to such practice-based assessments in order to secure reliability and replicability. The core of OSCEs and similar assessments is the assessed activities undertaken by students/trainees and developing them requires a significant amount of time, money and effort. Activities which are of the right standard, content, focus and free from bias are only achieved if patients/clients are standardised, so that the same scenario is delivered to all students in standardised environments. There is a trade-off to be made when comparing standardising practice-based examinations with live practice but the benefits they bring by being a national standard and by being more realistic than written national examinations is considerable.

Prior to the 1970s, most national examinations were mainly written and based on the recall of propositional knowledge but with the development of practice-based examinations, the normal range of options has expanded to:[1]

- written/multiple choice tests of propositional knowledge;
- written/multiple choice tests of applied knowledge; and
- practice-based tests of applied professional knowledge.

These are explored again later in this chapter in an international context.

National examinations in pharmacy

The next section focuses on the experience of the General Pharmaceutical Council (GPhC) of running a national registration examination, the Registration Assessment. It focuses on (1) performance by certain characteristics and (2) quality improvements resulting from data sharing by the regulator.

The pharmacist pre-registration training year

To contextualise the discussion, the initial education and training for pharmacists in GB takes five years and comprises:

1   a four-year university MPharm degree accredited by the GPhC;
2   a year of professional pharmacy pre-registration training; and
3   a nation registration examination, the Registration Assessment, sat, normally, towards the end of the training year.

The bulk of pre-registration training year takes place in two sectors – community (the 'high street' sector) and hospitals. Emerging trends are an increase in trainees training partly in GP (General Practitioner/US: Family Doctor) practices and internet pharmacies.

In Scotland, there is a single pre-registration training scheme run by a national education and training organisation, NHS Education Scotland (NES),[2] with a compulsory recruitment and selection process. The national health services in England, Scotland and Wales run managed training schemes as do some community pharmacy multiples, mainly the large and medium-sized chains. From 2017, there will be a recruitment scheme in England and Wales run by Health Education England (HEE),[3] which will be compulsory for NHS training places but optional for community ones. In summary, in any given training year there is a mixed training profile, where there are places gained by open competition and others that are not and training schemes which offer packages of support and development for trainees but also trainees who train independently outside those schemes.

The minimum requirement for the training year is that a set of pre-registration performance standards must be signed off by a designated pre-registration pharmacist tutor. In addition to tutor sign-offs, as a minimum all candidates must pass the GPhC's Registration Assessment. It is offered twice a year and candidates are allowed three attempts. Any candidate who fails all three attempts cannot register as a pharmacist. The format of the Registration Assessment is two papers sat on one day: Part 1, a pharmaceutical calculations test and Part 2, a test of applied clinical knowledge, using two types of multiple-choice questions (MCQs): single best answer (where candidates must select the answer that is most clinically appropriate) and extended matching (where a candidate's knowledge of a topic is tested using multiple patient scenarios).

Candidate performance in the GPhC's Registration Assessment

Since 2010, the Registration Assessment has been a source of performance data about candidates. The data sets include performance by:

1　country of pre-registration training (England, Scotland or Wales);
2　university school of pharmacy attended;
3　attempt number (1st, 2nd or 3rd attempt);
4　candidate self-declared ethnicity; and, most recently
5　pre-registration training provider.

The main findings are:

1　Consistently, year on year, hospital trainees outperform their community counterparts: for example, for the June 2015 sitting, the pass rates for 1st sitting candidates were 91 per cent for hospital candidates and 71 per cent for community candidates;
2　Consistently, year on year, Scottish and Welsh candidates outperform their English counterparts: for example, in June 2015 pass rates for 1st sitting candidates were 96 per cent for Scottish candidates, 92 per cent for Welsh candidates and 76 per cent for English candidates;
3　Consistently, year on year, 1st sitting candidates outperform re-sitting candidates: for example, in June 2013, 76 per cent of 1st sitting candidates passed compared to 34 per cent of 2nd sitting candidates and 46 per cent of 3rd sitting candidates.
4　There is consistent, year in year variation in performance by university school of pharmacy attended. Figure 13.1 gives 1st sitting candidate performance by school of pharmacy in June 2015, where the lowest pass rate by school was 48 per cent and the highest 90 per cent – a difference of 42 per cent.

Another significant and consistent variation is the performance of candidates from self-declared ethnic backgrounds (see Figure 13.2). In June 2015, the pass rate for 1st sitting Black African candidates was 55 per cent compared to 89 per cent for Chinese and White British candidates – a pattern that has been replicated consistently year on year. The difference has been so marked that the GPhC commissioned a study into the experience of Black African trainees in pre-registration training (OPM, 2016).[4]

Since 2016 the GPhC has produced performance data by pre-registration training provider (mainly NHS trusts and community pharmacy multiples). It is too early to draw conclusions about trends from the data the GPhC holds currently but there does seem to be variation in candidate performance between providers (see Figure 13.3).

The GPhC has been careful not to draw simplistic cause-and-effect inferences from its analysis of candidate performance but based on the data it holds, the following are likely indicators of success in the Registration Assessment:

1　attending a university school of pharmacy that selects rather than recruits students;
2　entering a professional pharmacist pre-registration training scheme on the basis of competitive selection; and
3　entering a training scheme where one is exposed to a variety of pharmacy professionals and other trainees (the managed training schemes mentioned above).

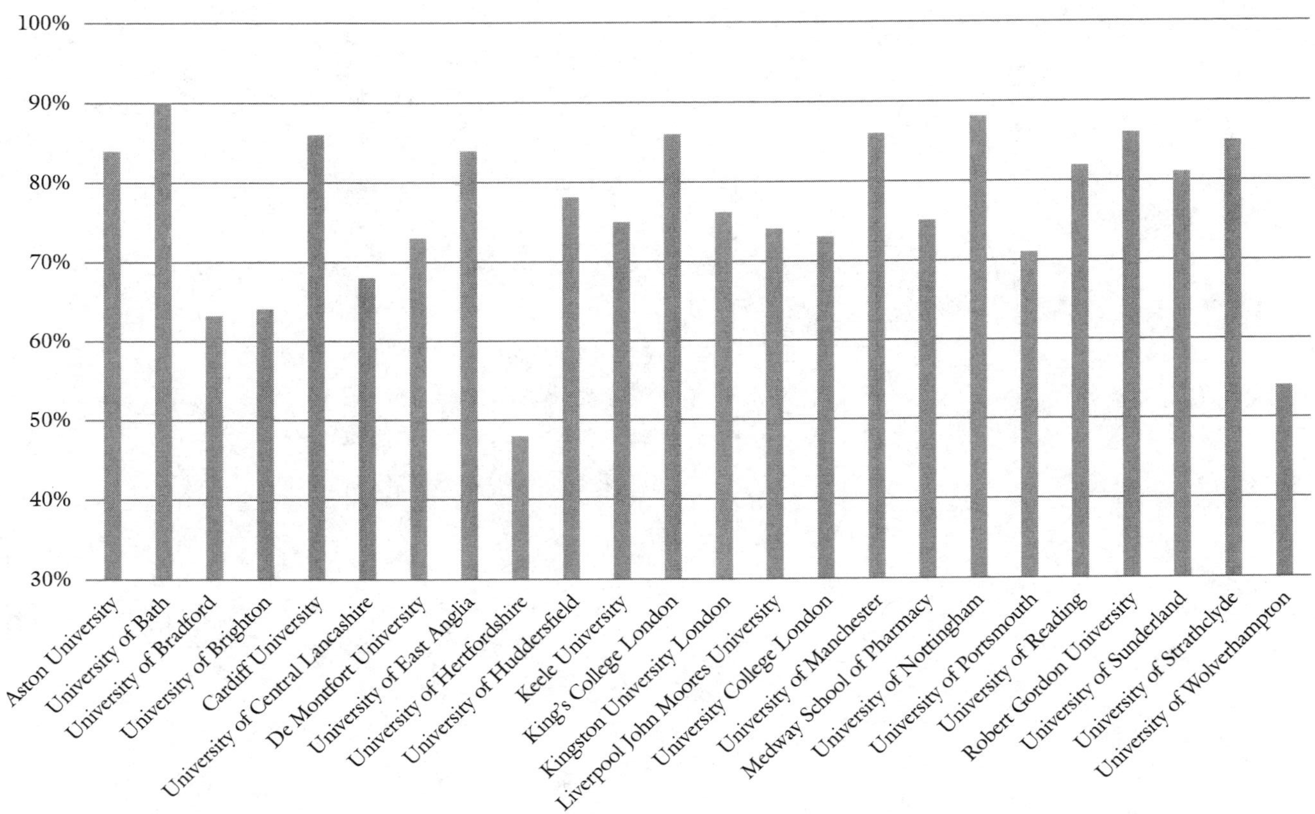

Figure 13.1 June 2015 candidate 1st attempt performance by school of pharmacy

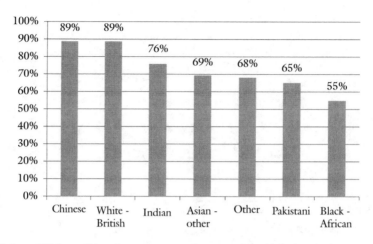

Figure 13.2 June 2015 candidate 1st attempt performance by self-declared ethnicity

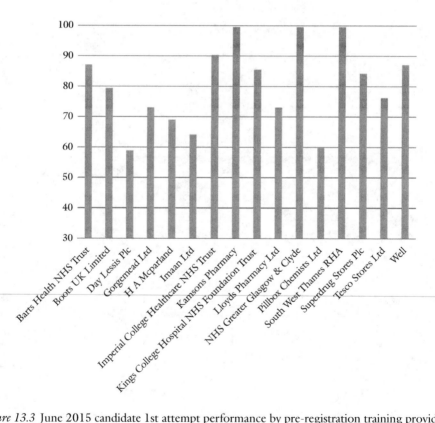

Figure 13.3 June 2015 candidate 1st attempt performance by pre-registration training providers (>13 trainees)

Conversely, attending a school that recruits, securing a non-competitive training place in a pharmacy with limited access to pharmacy professionals and other trainees is likely to lessen one's chances of success in the Registration Assessment.

A logical question is whether performance in the Registration Assessment is reflected in trainee perceptions of their pre-registration training year. Since 2013, the GPhC has commissioned trainee surveys and follow-up analyses of dissatisfied trainees which support the conclusions the GPhC has drawn about variable performance in the Registration Assessment: principally that trainees in non-selective training places who are not supported and are not exposed to best practice do not thrive in training (see Information by Design, 2014 and 2016 and University of Bradford and Information by Design, 2014 and 2015).

Changing practice

The GPhC releases Registration Assessment performance data routinely and, as one might expect, variation in performance has been the subject of some debate in the pharmaceutical press and among education and training providers. What is of most interest to the non-pharmacy reader, perhaps, is whether the data releases have changed practice or not – whether data release has made a difference? This section comprises two lengthy excerpts from interviews with a university head of school of pharmacy and a pharmacy training lead in a major national community pharmacy chain in which they discuss how their organisations have responded to the GPhC's Registration Assessment performance data releases.

First, the view from a university school of pharmacy:[5]

> We're a school of pharmacy that's been recruiting students since 2004, so we've had ten years of graduates . . . The vast majority of our students [are from less advantaged education backgrounds]. [A] challenge [was that] when our students first graduated . . . they then had to find [pharmacist pre-registration training] placements . . . for the year before the pre-registration exam[6] and some of them got excellent placements, some of the struggled a bit to get placements. Many of them ended up in small community pharmacies that had relatively little or no experience of training students for the pre-registration exam. And then we began to see the performance of our students in these exams and it was clear they were performing much less well than almost all schools of pharmacy . . . we looked at that over a couple of years, when our numbers were very poor and put into place some measures . . . to try and improve that. The numbers improved a little bit – we were maybe thinking maybe we'd found many of the issues and ways to resolve [them]. And then I think [when] the fourth or the fifth year of students entered the pre-registration exam and there was a severe dip again . . . it became a problem for us to try and solve. So, the previous head of school [and] the senior team . . . has a series of meetings and put into place a number of measures to address various issues we had identified. [O]ver the last two years our performance has improved considerably so . . . we've been at the average or slightly over the average of how all the schools of pharmacy have performed measured by first time pass rate.
>
> Well, I think one of the issues we felt . . . it's multi-faceted . . . certainly where our students end up being placed [for their pharmacist pre-registration training year] is a bit of an issue and some of them were in places where they were getting a great deal of support with the pre-registration exam and some of them at that time we felt they weren't getting sufficient support and so one of the measures we brought in to place and I think it's been a really important one has been to introduce our own package of

training events throughout the pre-registration year . . . we encourage, we use carrots and sticks to encourage, our students to attend these. We feel if we can get them to engage in that programme around the turn of the calendar year, around January, and then following that . . . over the next few months before the pre-registration exam we think that's made an important difference . . . so that our students are aware of what the pre-registration exam contains . . . so they have an opportunity to practise with mock exams and . . . get feedback on that. [When] they come in in January, we do a weekend with them, we get very high attendance, about 90 per cent of our graduates come. It's partly social, it gets them in as a carrot, but it's partly a stick because they do a mock exam and they get feedback the next day. . . . They don't perform fantastically well, partly because they're not ready to perform at a good level and partly we set it as quite a difficult exam so they know the challenge. And then we follow that up with a series of online events [and] daily questions. We watch them discuss it in [the] form of social media . . . then we have a series of follow-up assessment days where they come together and they prepare for it.

That's a serious investment for us – tens of thousands of pounds that we wouldn't otherwise have expected to invest . . . But we feel it's so important – if the job of the MPharm degree is to train the vast majority of our students to become registered pharmacists, because that's what they go on to do, we need to give them the best opportunity of doing that. And that kind of brings us back to our catchment in terms of the attainment they have coming in. I think . . . on . . . average the grade points are lower than the average you would see around the country and they would come from perhaps at least in many cases grouping that are a problem when it comes to attainment at university. So, if our strategy is to look at students that aren't performing as well as the average and we can take them up to perform at average or better than average that's out selling point as a school. That's what we feel we can bring to these students. We can give them an opportunity to improve and make them competitive with students from elsewhere. It's the opposite to where we were at the beginning but it's now become one of our strengths.

That brings me on to another issue we felt with our students particularly is they're often not fantastically good at performing . . . the first time . . . they see it. Whereas, if they've had a few formative assessments . . . they perform better. So a metric measuring first time pass rate is not a good metric for us, if it genuinely is the first time they've seen an exam whereas if they know what they're going to get, if they've had an experience of mock examinations, of going through the process, then it certainly improves their performance. . . .

Within the course itself we [have brought] in a lot more assessment[s] . . . we set quite high pass marks . . . and at the beginning that's a challenge for students. We make it clear to them we're not here to try and fail them, we're here to help them to get to these levels in the assessments so they're then able to sit the pre-registration exam with some confidence.

(When asked about preparing students for the Registration Assessment – 'teaching to the test')

It's something we do wrestle with. We also wrestle with the argument that we end up over assessing students and we do try and balance that – we have elements of the course that are quite distinct around competencies and passing particular exams and other elements of the course across all the years that are much more about bringing out the rounded nature of what a degree programme is – developing critical thinking skills.

These are the kinds of things that aren't easy to assess but we feel are essential to help our students become lifelong learners.

(When asked about the GPhC releasing Registration Assessment pass rates by school of pharmacy)

. . . it certainly concentrated our minds. It was important that our [new] measures were showing success otherwise it would reflect very badly on us in the public view . . . I think now our position is stronger and we are where we are in terms of the first time pass rate we can use it to our advantage. We can genuinely say to students, with evidence, we can take [them at] a certain [academic] level and we can train [them] into being a pharmacist recognised as being of the quality required. It's obviously a challenge going forward that we have to maintain that, we have to make sure we don't take our eye off the ball . . . We've gone from a place that wasn't very positive to one that was quite positive.

Now the view from a pre-registration training provider:[7]

I'm Head of Pharmacy at Day Lewis, responsible for 300 pharmacies across the group. As part of that role I have Board leadership role for the pre-registration programme and each year we employ between 60 and 80 trainees. If we go back historically Day Lewis used to be a very diverse employer and very much supportive of all pharmacy graduates but particularly those that found it more difficult to get [pre-registration training] places . . . supporting graduates from ethnic minorities but also [those] from different educational backgrounds as well. We used to work with pretty much all the schools of pharmacy across the UK. We used to attend all the careers fairs and we . . . were definitely looking for 'people' people not necessarily students with high academic ability.

Our [pre-registration training programme] was ten monthly sessions . . . and all in house and we pretty much put together the best programme we could at the time and I think you could say it was adequate. With hindsight, adequate wasn't good enough. The training days fitted around the GPhC exam[8] and the topics and . . .we'd make sure the syllabus was covered to ensure that the students were, in our view at that time, ready for the exam.

So, I can remember the day very clearly [when the GPhC first published Registration Assessment results by training provider] . . . there was a C&D [*Chemist and Druggist* magazine] article saying 'Exam results published by company' and I looked down and I saw that our results were close to the bottom if not at the bottom and it really was a shake-up of a moment for us. It was the first time we had looked at the results not just from a student perspective but from a corporate perspective and I think it was at that stage we realised that this could have reputational damage for the Day Lewis Group.

At that stage, before we went in to any planning or action we actually did quite a deep analysis on the results. We looked fairly carefully at that year's results . . . and that correlation was pretty closely matched with the results of the GPhC analysis.[9]

Whilst we recognised there may have been some reputational damage we wanted to make sure we were student focused. We decided to work more closely with some universities as partners . . . We did decide there was a minimum grade of A levels that clearly came through that meant that in future years we would only recruit students that had a minimum of two Bs and a C or above at A level. We decided . . . we would invest heavily with an unlimited budget to make sure the programme gave students [pre-registration trainees] the best possible chance of getting that pass. We set ourselves the goal of a 100 per cent pass rate for our pre-reg students [trainees].

We didn't change the syllabus of our programme but we looked at the content, who was delivering it and our skill set. The first thing we identified was that we didn't have the skill set or in-house expertise in some clinical areas . . . so we worked with UCL [University College London] and put together three additional training days at UCL whereby the lecturers at the university would deliver these gaps in the knowledge where we just didn't have that expertise. The second thing we then did was to recognise that the calculations were absolutely critical for the exam and we worked with an online company, Team Pre Reg, and sent weekly calculations to all of our graduates . . . Towards the end of the programme we identified the students that were then struggling with calculations and we brought in [. . .] who is recognised as one of the industry's leading trainers on calculations to give specific training to those graduates who weren't doing quite so well . . . We also brought in external speakers for all of our content so with our link through the universities we were bringing in university lecturers or leaders in academic training to deliver all the content and the sessions. So, rather doing it in house our programme now has external speakers for all of our training sessions. The final part is that we do a clinical paper at the beginning of all of our sessions along with the calculations. This now means that for every graduate we've now built up quite a big database on clinical and calculations. As we've gone through the year we've ranked all of our students 1 to 70 on the papers that they've done so we know which students are going to clearly move through the exam very easily and those that will struggle and that will then be validated by a half mock we do in April every year and a full mock . . . that we do in May each year.

The outcome in year one of this programme, bearing in mind that the . . . students had already been recruited [was that] we got 98.6 per cent in the exam and this year we have recruited on the two Bs and a C we're confident of getting 100 per cent in the exam.

(When asked about the GPhC releasing Registration Assessment pass rates by training provider.)

No, we wouldn't have made the changes [had the data not been released], we would have continued what we were doing. We believed we were doing the right thing. We thought that it was an adequate programme but the publishing of the results really made us look in the mirror at ourselves, reflecting on how we could move to a much better product and, as a result, did so. This really has helped our whole manpower planning right the way across the business. It also means we've gone on to have very strong relationships with five universities. We have now appointed four teacher-practitioners at those universities with one more to come . . . I think the whole publishing of those results has led to unintended additional activities . . . bringing universities and employers closer together.

International perspectives

National examinations are just as much a part of professional life outside the UK as they are in the UK and many professions rely solely or in part on such examinations as the gateway to registration/membership and practice. In the pharmacy context, there are national examinations in Australia, Canada, New Zealand and the United States but other (non-)healthcare professions have well-established national examinations as well. The need to assess procedural skills as well as propositional knowledge has brought about significant shifts in national examination strategies across the professions, whether in healthcare or elsewhere. We will look at several examples to illustrate the range of options outside the UK.

In the US and Canada, the National Council of State Boards of Nursing oversee the NCLEX-RN (National Council Licensure Examination for Registered Nurses), taken after graduating from an accredited nursing course. It is an online multiple-choice examination and is the final stage (other than health, good character and other checks) before registering and practising as a nurse. Practical skills and communication are tested by schools of nursing.

In Canada, the national pharmacy examination – the Pharmacy Examining Board of Canada's Canadian Pharmacist Qualifying Examination (PQE) – is in two parts: Part 1 – MCQs and Part 2 – OSCEs. The MCQ examination has evolved from a knowledge test to a test of applied knowledge using clinical scenarios and it is supplemented by a practice OSCE. The PEBC's rationale for including OSCEs makes clear that 'Some important professional skills and abilities cannot be measured well with a traditional, multiple-choice question format. As a result, the Board uses both a written, multiple choice assessment and a performance-based assessment.' Testing scientific knowledge is left to schools of pharmacy; practical skills and communication are tested by schools as well but that is supplemented by the national OSCE. The PQE Part 1 is delivered in English, the PQE Part 2 is delivered in English and French and the whole examination is delivered simultaneously across all time zones in Canada.

One of the most well-established and more extensive national examinations is the US Medical Licensing Examination (USLME). Annually its first part is sat by c. 24,000 US medical students and c. 18,000 non-US students. The USMLE is multi-part:

Step 1 is a test of basic science relevant to medicine;
Step 2 CK is a test of applied clinical knowledge and is complemented by;
Step 2 CS, a practical test of clinical skills; and
Step 3, a two-day examining resulting in a license to practise as a physician without supervision.

In healthcare the USMLE is probably the most comprehensive battery of national tests in that it covers basic science, as well as applied clinical knowledge, practical skills and communication. These are all tested in schools of pharmacy on PharmD courses but are then tested for national consistency by the USMLE.

The political dimension

In one important respect, national examinations have a political dimension and that is where immigration and access to labour markets are sensitive issues and national examinations are part of the control mechanisms for entry to a profession. Negotiating access to professions for overseas-trained professionals is not a new issue and for national examining bodies, creating a means of aligning teaching, learning and assessment (and the philosophy of a profession) in the home country through national examinations remains difficult, in that it may not be the knowledge base that is lacking in an overseas-trained person but a different cultural approach to being a professional. National examining bodies have tackled this in a number of ways: (1) requiring overseas practitioners to pass the national examination alongside home students, after verifying qualifications and professional good standing overseas, (2) requiring overseas candidates to reach a higher bar than home students in national examinations, or (3) setting separate qualifying/licensing exams for overseas practitioners.

To return to national examinations in general, stepping back and considering a broad international perspective, they are enduring and widely accepted across professions. As professions develop globally, far from moving away from national examinations they remain trusted ways of setting and testing national standards and, as assessment practices mature and develop, are being used in different and more authentic ways. Apart from remaining up to date and relevant, the challenge for national examining bodies has been to tackle assessing professionalism in its wider sense and we have discussed some of the emerging solutions to this challenging issue in this chapter.

Points for further consideration

For consideration by national examining bodies. National examining bodies are in a unique position in that they hold data which can, if used effectively, be a powerful tool for quality improvement. In this chapter two concrete examples have been given. National examining bodies should consider full data releases, even if doing so may be exposing for some education and training providers: if it leads to change, or at least better informed student choice, it is probably worthwhile doing so.

For consideration by higher education institutions. National examinations do play a role in maintaining objective and uniform standards and it may be challenging for some HEIs to accept that, for a variety of reasons, there are individuals who pass a degree at their institution but cannot pass a national examination. HEIs should consider performance data provided by national examining bodies and its implications for them, in terms of entry requirements, teaching, learning, assessment, curriculum design and student support.

Acknowledgements

My thanks to Tim Rendell, Head of Pharmacy, Day Lewis, and Professor Alistair Mathie, Head, Medway School of Pharmacy, for agreeing to be interviewed for this chapter.

Notes

1 It is now quite common for written/MCQ tests to be delivered online in test centres.
2 *Pre-registration Pharmacist Scheme.* Retrieved on March 30, 2017 from http://www.nes. scot.nhs.uk/education-and-training/by-discipline/pharmacy/pre-registration-pharmacist-scheme.aspx
3 *Recruiting Pre-Registration Pharmacists.* Retrieved on March 30 2017 from https://hee. nhs.uk/our-work/developing-our-workforce/pharmacy-education-training/recruiting-pre-registration-pharmacists
4 For a broader perspective on differential student achievement see also Higher Education Funding Council, 2013, Equality Challenge Unit/Higher Education Academy, 2008 and the National Union of Students, 2010).
5 Taken from an interview with Professor Alistair Mathie, Head, Medway School of Pharmacy, March 23, 2017.
6 The GPhC's Registration Assessment.
7 Taken from an interview with Tim Rendell, Head of Pharmacy, Day Lewis Group on March 21, 2017.
8 The Registration Assessment.
9 Published publicly in GPhC Council papers. See https://www.pharmacyregulation.org/about-us/who-we-are/gphc-council

Bibliography

Australian Pharmacy Council (2017). *Interns.* Accessed 12 April 2017 from https://www. pharmacycouncil.org.au/interns/. NB Information on the APC's Australian Intern Written Examination.

Equality Challenge Unit/Higher Education Academy (2008). *Ethnicity, Gender and Degree Attainment Project, Final Report.* Retrieved on 3 April 2017 from http://www.ecu.ac.uk/wp-content/uploads/external/ethnicity-gender-and-degree-attainment-project-final-report.pdf

General Medical Council (2016). *Securing the Licence to Practise: Introducing a Medical Licensing Assessment, A Public Consultation.* Retrieved 14 April 2017 from https://gmc.e-consultation.net/econsult/uploaddocs/Consult790/MLA%20consultation%20document%20-%20 English%20writeable%20updated%2023.2.17_distributed.pdf

General Pharmaceutical Council (2017a). *The Registration Assessment.* Retrieved 30 March 2017 from http://www.pharmacyregulation.org/the-registration-assessment

General Pharmaceutical Council (2017b). *Registration Assessment Framework.* Retrieved 30 March 2017 from http://www.pharmacyregulation.org/53-registration-assessment-framework

Higher Education Funding Council (2013). *Differences in degree Outcomes: Key Findings.* Retrieved on 3 April 2017 from http://www.hefce.ac.uk/pubs/year/2015/201521/

Information by Design (2014). *GPhC Analysis of Trainee Dissatisfaction – 2012–2013 Pre-Registration Trainees.* Retrieved 30 March 2017, from https://www.pharmacyregulation. org/pre-registration-trainee-survey-2013

Information by Design (2016). *Analysis of Trainee Dissatisfaction – 2013–2014 Pre-Registration Trainee Pharmacists.* Retrieved 30 March 2017 from https://www.pharmacyregulation.org/ pre-registration-surveys-2016

National Union of Students (2010). *Race for Equality: A Report on the Experiences of Black Students in Further and Higher Education.* Retrieved 3 April 2017 from https://www.nus.org. uk/PageFiles/12350/NUS_Race_for_Equality_web.pdf

OPM (2016). *Qualitative Research into Registration Assessment Performance among Black-African Candidates, Report to the General Pharmaceutical Council.* Retrieved 30 March 2017, from https://www.pharmacyregulation.org/sites/default/files/qual-research-into-ra-perfor mance-among-black-african_candidates_final_0.pdf

Pharmacy Examining Board of Canada (PEBC) (2017). *Pharmacist Qualifying Examination.* Accessed 12 April 2017 from http://www.pebc.ca/index.php/ci_id/3147/la_id/1.htm

Solicitors Regulation Authority (2016). *A New Route to Qualification: The Solicitors Qualifying Examination (SQE).* Retrieved 13 April 2017 from http://www.pebc.ca/index.php/ ci_id/3147/la_id/1.htm; https://www.sra.org.uk/sra/consultations/solicitors-qualifying-examination.page#download

United States Medical Licensing Examination accessed 30 July 2017 from http://www.usmle.org/

University of Bradford and Information by Design (2014). *GPhC Survey of 2012/13 Pre-Registration Trainees.* Retrieved 30 March 2017, from https://www.pharmacyregulation. org/pre-registration-trainee-survey-2013

University of Bradford and Information by Design (2015). *GPhC Survey of 2013/14 Pre-Registration Trainees.* Retrieved 30 March 2017, from https://www.pharmacyregulation. org/resources/research/pre-registration-survey-2014

14 How can Students Engage in Assuring the Quality of University Teaching?

Karin Crawford, Reece Horsley and Emily Parkin

Introduction and context

Assuring the quality of university teaching is an activity that requires engagement and commitment from all stakeholders. In this chapter the authors explore the ways in which students can be engaged as partners in different aspects and levels of this work. This introduction to the chapter outlines some issues of context and the authors' stance on these issues, prior to a discussion about levels and forms of student engagement. The remainder of the chapter is structured to consider possible approaches to student engagement in the different levels of quality assurance activity; at school, discipline or programme level; at a university-wide level; and in national and international quality assurance work. The discussion in this chapter relates to students undertaking all forms of higher education study, including part-time, full-time, undergraduate and post-graduate studies. Throughout the chapter, the authors draw on practical examples to illustrate the approaches being examined and, within this, a range of stakeholder colleagues, including students, Students' Union officers, professional services staff and academics have contributed their perspectives on engagement in this work.

The concept of students as partners and the consequent change in relationships between students and staff is a focus of contemporary higher education policy and practice internationally (Healey *et al.* 2014); there is gradual evidence of changes in working practices within institutions. In the UK, the Quality Assurance Agency (QAA) Quality Code Chapter B5 focusses on student engagement as 'the participation of students in quality enhancement and quality assurance processes, which includes but is not restricted to representation of the student view through formal representation mechanisms' (QAA 2012; 4). This has emphasised the growing importance institutions and sector bodies are placing on involving students in not only assessing, but also enhancing the quality of their own and their peers' learning, teaching and wider university experience. Where national quality assurance drivers like this are not in place, the development of this work may be slower, for example in 2013, Bell *et al.* acknowledged that there were 'few examples of active student engagement in curriculum design processes in Australia' (Bell *et al.* 2013; 499). At the same time, higher education across the globe is arguably being increasingly commodified with changes to student fee structures, consumer rights legislation, growing competition and continuing marketisation (Robinson and Hilli 2016); which unsurprisingly impact on the governance and organisational structures that assure the quality of learning and teaching in higher education (Tight 2013; 11). There is potentially 'considerable tension between the ideal of partnership and the effects of consumerist discourse' (Levy *et al.* 2011; 3). Indeed, Popenici (2013; 25) suggests that these 'ideological contradictions' are 'on a collision course', although institutions commonly, through their strategies and literature, aspire to embrace students as partner despite these challenges. In some areas of literature, it is suggested that the challenges and tensions manifest in engaging students in assuring the quality of university teaching result in models of student engagement and quality assurance that are simply not workable or sustainable (Popenici 2013). On the contrary, here the authors contend that it is in part *because* of, and counter to, these tensions that the role and power of students as partners in activities to assure quality and enhance teaching should be proactively embraced. This approach is aligned with aspirations for a more democratic, collaborative, interactive and negotiated form of higher education.

Student engagement and representation

Quality assurance of teaching in higher education can only be considered robust and thorough where students are equal partners in all aspects of the processes at all levels. Before considering the different ways of engaging students in quality assurance activities, it is important to briefly address the problematic nature of the relevant terminology. Many different terms are in use both in the literature and in practice, for example; 'students as partners', 'students as producers', 'students as co-creators', 'student engagement', 'student participation', 'student voice' and 'students as change agents'. Each of these terms will have subtly different meanings to different people, in different contexts and, as such, it is imperative that institutions ensure that the terms they choose to employ are appropriate to the local context and that students and staff have a clear and common understanding about the meanings attached.

At a national level, the expectation that 'higher education providers take deliberate steps to engage all students, individually and collectively, as partners in the assurance and enhancement of their educational experience' (QAA 2012; 6) introduces the necessity to develop a clear understanding of 'students as partners' and what this might look like in practice. Partnership has been defined as a process of student engagement rather than a product (Healey *et al.* 2014) incorporating an emphasis on collective and collaborative work towards a shared goal and challenging 'traditional relationships, power balances and cultures' (Crawford *et al.* 2015). Crucially, therefore, partnership working to assure the quality of university teaching is not a method of consultation, but rather is about working together, sharing power and decision-making.

The concept of power-sharing is important if student engagement in quality assurance is to be truly meaningful. Bovill and Bulley's (2011) ladder of student participation in curriculum design reflects the levels of power that can operate in student–staff partnerships. This model can facilitate dialogue about developing partnerships in institutions, with lower rungs of the ladder reflecting tokenistic approaches and higher rungs of the ladder representing partnerships where students have more control and influence. In practice students and staff will experience changing levels of power and control at different times in the process depending on a range of variables in the context (Bovill 2013). It is important that all staff, administrators and faculty respect students as experts within their own experience and provide the right platform and resources for students to offer their insights. Such practices will facilitate the potential to create unique outcomes which have significant benefits for both the institution and the students (Cook-Sather *et al.* 2014).

The Quality Assurance Agency Quality Code (QAA 2012), referred to earlier, mentions individual and collective student engagement in quality assurance and enhancement. The participation of student representatives, elected through recognised Students' Union processes, in a range of formal university-level committees and structures is part of accepted practice in the UK higher education sector and has been acknowledged in New Zealand as offering 'students the opportunity to engage with and have input into governance, decision making and quality enhancement at all levels' (Ako Aotearoa and NZUSA 2013; 4). However it is evident that to ensure wide engagement and to embrace inclusivity and diversity within such systems is challenging (Ako Aotearoa and NZUSA 2013). Furthermore, the engagement of these representatives in decision-making at discipline, programme and school level, is more likely to be challenged (van der Velden 2013). This situation raises questions about an alternative, or additional route for gauging student insight/expertise at this level, potentially via the engagement of individuals, or the 'non-representative masses', and how this is perceived. These two levels of engagement can be assessed in a number of ways; in particular, effective student representative systems can provide a broad understanding of how, collectively, students perceive particular aspects of the student experience. Understanding the majority perspective is crucial to continuing good practice and enhancing the wider student experience. Students trained to represent the student voice are therefore most appropriate to engage when it is the broad, collective student experience that is of interest, particularly with regard to quality assurance. However, there may be occasions where a deeper understanding of a specific, student experience may be of benefit for quality enhancement purposes, and therefore where non-representative, individual student perspectives can offer meaningful insight.

Representative student engagement

Student representatives are key in the process of ensuring quality assurance and continually enhancing modules, programmes and the institution. Representative engagement in quality processes allows for academics and students to work together in partnership to ensure that the whole student experience is encompassed and included whether it is an Annual Monitoring Report, a programme modification or a new module.

For student representatives, this engagement gives them a greater insight into how their programmes and modules are operated, but also allows them to give a voice on behalf of the students who elected them. Benefits of representative engagement for the student experience can be seen with changes in assessment methods and weighting to the amount of contact hours that take place on a programme. This helps to create a partnership-based environment within quality processes.

John-Paul Dickie, Vice President Academic Affairs,
University of Lincoln Students' Union

Non-representative student engagement

Non-representative engagement in quality assurance not only allows students to impartially reflect on the quality of degrees at their institution, but also educates them in how quality is, and can be assured, within higher education. This provides opportunities for open and informed discussions around the quality of education within an institution, and allows students to objectively reflect on, review and propose solutions to improve quality within a module or course. This contributes to the overall model of student as producer, enabling students to be equal partners in the university community. A strong staff–student partnership within a university community also supports students to get the most out of their university experience by providing student ownership over their academic and wider university experience.

Jennifer Barnes, Student Voice and Impact Manager,
University of Lincoln Students' Union

These two perspectives provide a comparison of the benefits of both representative (collective) and non-representative (individual) student engagement in quality assuring teaching in higher education. They also provide a useful reference point for the remainder of this chapter, where specific examples of both representative and non-representative engagement will be explored.

The role of the student in quality assurance at school and discipline level

There are a number of opportunities for students to have an impact on the quality of their programmes. Student representatives engage regularly in this way by providing their peers' feedback on their experience of learning and teaching on the course. At school level, representatives also contribute to the broader perspective by joining up conversations across closely related disciplines. One method of doing this is course-level student representatives being empowered to offer feedback directly to staff via a formal, committee route, ensuring that the actions are captured and delivered on. This however, is still in the frame of 'consultative' engagement, firmly in the lower rungs of Bovill and Bulley's (2011) ladder model.

To move on from this, providing opportunities for student representatives to collaboratively develop solutions to the issues they are raising, can have significant benefits in enhancing the quality of learning and teaching. An example of this is the idea of student-led working groups with staff invited to attend, 'task-and-finish' style, which feed into the formal committee structure, empowering students to lead on the development of (innovative) solutions contributing meaningfully to theirs, and their peers' student experience. Bell *et al.* (2013) describe a similar approach, which they frame as 'deliberative democracy', working with students in a World Café style, problem-based approach to curriculum development in an Australian university. Another example, from Elon University in North Carolina, USA, involves the development of course design teams (CDT), within which students outnumber staff, working together to develop curricula (Cook-Sather *et al.* 2014; 66–68). This type of working can facilitate true partnership between staff and students by showing a clear respect for, and trust in, the student voice, whilst still enabling staff to share their perspectives equally, offering the chance to bring 'different but comparably valuable forms of expertise to bear on the educational process' (Cook-Sather *et al.* 2014; 8).

In addition to the representative system, individual students have the potential to contribute to enhancing specific elements of teaching and learning in a non-representative way. One example of this is the Students Consulting on Teaching scheme (SCoTs) which offers an objective student perspective on teaching that does not focus on content or relevance, but centres on the pedagogical practices, how they are experienced by students and support their learning (see Crawford 2012, Cook-Sather *et al.* 2014; 70, and similar work by Jensen and Bennett 2016). Student consultants work with academics who are not in their subject area, thereby removing risk of conflicts of interest and, at least in part, addressing concerns about unequal power in the relationship. A similar model is embedded within the Students as Learners and Teachers (SaLT) program at Bryn Mawr and Haverford Colleges in Pennsylvania, USA, where it is acknowledged that students are 'experts about sitting in classes, understanding new concepts, and creating their own learning' (Sorenson 2001 cited in Cook-Sather and Motz-Storey 2016; 168). Such schemes complement the representative system with an 'expert' student perspective on teaching in higher education. It is acknowledged that the concept of 'students as experts' is not universally accepted and embraced (van der Velden 2013), however, at the highest level it is likely that all stakeholders will agree that every student has an opinion on what good teaching is and therefore the authors argue that it is appropriate and important that students are empowered and enabled to share that opinion in a constructive, developmental way.

The following vignettes reflect a student perspective of being a student consultant in the SCoT project and a teacher's perspective of working with a student consultant to enhance the quality of their teaching.

A student's experience of being a student consulting on teaching (SCoT)

Participating as a SCoT has provided an assortment of benefits with networking being the most beneficial. Further to this, an insight into a teacher's perspective is gained whereas in everyday lectures students don't necessarily consider the amount of work which goes into each lecture. For example, teachers include a myriad of multimedia within their lectures to keep students engaged and to aid all forms of learners. Whilst being a SCoT I grew an admiration for teachers who although are not technically minded, wanted to improve their lecturing style to encompass more digital forms of interaction. An example of this is interactive quizzes in which students can participate using their phones and the results can highlight the progress of the students and areas for the lecturer to go over again. Lastly networking through SCoTS has been extremely useful as I've made connections whilst on group observations where you observe a teacher with other students. Furthermore, I've also made connections with teachers who are in a different academic field, which has provided me with an insight into a variety of different degrees. From networking, I've learnt about other projects teachers are involved in at the University, to improve the quality of education for students and I've actively contributed to them; these opportunities were made possible through being a SCoT.

Alex Curtis, 3rd year Computer Science Student

A teacher's perspective of working with students consulting on teaching (SCoTs)

My approach to teaching has developed through a participatory pedagogy where 'teacher and learner work together ethically, critically and inclusively' (Waring and Evans 2015; 104) in the following main ways:

- *Impartiality* of SCoTs prompts critical reflection as they compare what they observe with what they experience in a different discipline. This often produces rich data about the student experience.
- *Focus* of impartial students yields different feedback through observations of teacher–student interactions and teaching delivery issues. Satisfied students engaging well in activities are less likely to share their ideas for improving their academic experience.
- *More open* arrangements are created for me to be more critical and accountable for my teaching practice through self-evaluation. I understand more about barriers faced by particular learner groups and how to overcome them.

I have trained students to become SCoTs over the last three years, which has produced rich data about how students judge quality of teaching. From all my recent conference presentations this area always gets the most delegate attention.

Jasper Shotts, Senior Lecturer in Social Work,
School Director of Teaching and Learning

Thus, whilst it is evident that there are academics who may not always feel comfortable with student engagement in assuring the quality of teaching at programme and discipline level (van der Velden 2013), there is evidence that meaningful, active student involvement in this way can be mutually beneficial, with students 'transform[ing] . . . their own and others' educational experiences' (Cook-Sather *et al.*, 2014; 60).

The role of the student in quality assurance at university level

From a student perspective, quality assurance above discipline level is something that becomes somewhat of an abstract concept to understand. Where programme-level feedback can provide tangible outcomes with language and a context that is familiar, at organisational level those concepts become more plagued with committees and acronyms. This naturally presents more challenges, not only in terms of initial engagement with students, but also in ensuring appropriate support is available to enable students to access a route into joining conversations about teaching.

Students need to be reassured that beneath the guidance, the benchmarks and the standards, at the heart of quality assurance is conversation and discussion about building on positive experiences and developing those that are less beneficial; peer review is the basis for many review systems. This is something that is not novel to their university experience, but something that may get lost in translation. As universities begin to develop the shared language of students as partners and peers within the academic community, this notion of peer review becomes easier to embrace.

Steinhardt *et al.* (2016) suggests that university governance is set out to assure the quality of learning and teaching. For staff, this governance provides the structure and processes by which to work, but for students, this may, in the first instance, be more difficult to identify. The role of Students' Unions therefore becomes of paramount importance in supporting students on this journey.

Core to the Students' Unions, and even more so with the development of the National Student Survey (NSS) block of questions relating to student voice, is the role of academic student representatives. As discussed earlier, representatives have a joint role of collecting and collating the opinions of their peers, but also utilising this feedback to influence and develop changes both locally and institutionally. However, overcoming the challenge of accessibility of the language surrounding quality assurance needs to come first. Identifying opportunities to develop a shared understanding may be a good starting point for engaging students in this way. Embedding quality assurance discussions into representatives' training for example will help to knock down a potential barrier to understanding and, in turn, engagement.

Student evaluation of teaching through module, programme or national surveys, provides a route for engagement, both active and passive, to identify areas of improvement and highlight good practice. Far beyond measuring satisfaction, surveying at all levels of the student population can provide rich data to work from, helping to determine practices for enhancement that students prioritise. One of the challenges therefore, comes from ensuring that, where this feedback is used at institutional level, it addresses the expressed experiences from across the complex makeup of student populations. Working with students to develop action plans to address their evaluations of teaching, enables the student perspective to be more accurately understood and considered more proactively, as opposed to merely hoping to identify impact from subsequent evaluations. This shift from problems being presented to students as partners in creating the solution/solving process is one that requires representative student engagement, working on behalf of a specific demographic; this is where student representatives are particularly valuable. Representing groups of students in university committees can provide 'quick wins' in response to considered debate with staff, allowing appropriate consideration of possible immediate change, long-term solutions or wider developments.

Alongside student insight into the experience that they have, students can contribute to the more traditional quality assurance processes such as validation, re-validation and formal reviews of programmes. For most students, this activity is fundamentally 'behind the scenes', however from a quality assurance perspective this process is integral to the effective running of programmes. Owen (2013), drawing on data from nine UK universities who involved students as full and equal members of academic subject review teams, argues that students have a significant and valuable contribution to these processes, although appropriate guidance and support must be provided. The vignette here describes a student reviewer's perspective of student engagement in these forms of institutional quality assurance processes.

A student's perspective of participating in institutional quality assurance processes

One of the greatest aspects of being a student reviewer was the feeling of really being a valued member of the panel. Sitting along the other panel members, my opinion was greatly valued and I saw the impact of my contributions both in the direction of the review meetings themselves, but also in the final outcome.

Being the student panel member I think allows the students who were contributors to the actual review itself, the course reps and other groups that we interviewed, to actually feel that they could contribute openly and provide their insight into how the course that they study has been constructed.

This, I think, is one of the most important reasons for having a student directly involved in the review meetings. It allows students to talk to students in exactly the same way as staff do; it allows students to actually feel like they are being listened to, but by another student as part of the panel.

Reece Horsley, Student Reviewer during undergraduate
and postgraduate studies

In most circumstances student participation in the process of validating and re-validating programmes comes through student membership on review events (van der Velden *et al.* 2012). Although as part of these events, differing levels of student involvement occur. Cyclical Academic Subject Review examines the quality of programmes and draws on both feedback from students studying the programme taken periodically and insight from current students on that programme alongside other stakeholders. The student membership of this review process therefore requires objectivity to enable effective assurance; students acting as members of the student community rather than of a specific discipline. By doing so, students are independent members of the academic community scrutinising the student experience in a similar way that academics with a strong research profile will look at that element of the validation.

Ultimately however, it remains the university that sets the agenda, at institutional level, with regards to quality assurance processes. This is appropriate as the institution is responsible for evidencing that they meet the quality standards set and have processes in place to ensure that practice is sound. Integral to this and by way of providing this evidence, institutions should ensure that students are active members of the conversation as full and equal members of the academic peer community.

The role of the student nationally and internationally

The notion of students being equal members of the academic community establishes precedent in some institutions, but reaffirms in others that students should be involved in assuring the quality of the teaching that they engage in. This allows students to gain more ownership over their learning experience and see directly the impact that they have as a member of that wider community of learners. However, this idea of community and belonging starts to take a different meaning when it is not just peers within the institution of study, but peers in a much broader sense; at a national or even international level. At this level, a number of organisations, networks and forums now exist to support, inform and develop broader partnership approaches, for example the Student Engagement Partnership (TSEP; http://tsep.org.uk); the RAISE network (Researching, Advancing and Inspiring Student Engagement; http://www.raise-network.com/); and WISEWales (Wales Initiative for Student Engagement; http://www.wisewales.org.uk). SPARQS (Student Participation in Quality Scotland; http://www.sparqs.ac.uk) is an example of an agency that specifically directs it work to student engagement in the quality of the learning experience.

Nationally the idea of representative and non-representative, as well as students as passive and active engagers in quality assurance, remains a key part of the process. Students have had a practical role, through participation in QAA review panels, and a strategic one, through being key members of advisory groups and contributors to the development of quality guidelines themselves. Taking England as an example, the level and form of this involvement can shift with changes in policy and legislation. The impact of the White Paper, *Success as a Knowledge Economy: Teaching Excellence, Social Mobility and Student Choice* (Department for Business, Innovation and Skills 2016) which sets out the introduction of a Teaching Excellence Framework (TEF) and changes to national quality assurance requirements has yet to be fully realised. However, the TEF introduces an emphasis on a range of metrics and a written submission in comparison to separate student and 'institutional' submissions. Thus, although student engagement is still embedded in this work, a potentially changing balance between statutory requirements and quality assurance body roles may result in the passive 'student voice' having more impact than students actively engaging in quality assurance. Through engagement in completing national surveys, it is hoped that students will start to see the repercussions of the merging together of activities that they may not previously have associated with each other: feedback and quality assurance. Therefore, the challenge becomes how to respond to these developments, ensuring ways are found to engage students locally, developing, supporting and enabling them to also engage nationally, by building effective internal mechanisms and feedback loops and empowering all students in internal quality assurance work, beyond those students who are representatives and reviewers. This can, in part, be achieved by building on the sense of community locally to ensure that students feel ownership over their survey responses and therefore engage in the conversations, solution generation and implementation. Additionally, at a national level, students may have opportunities to engage in the work of other networks related to the discipline area of their studies, for example professional, statutory and regulatory bodies (PSRBs) and their processes of approval, recognition or accreditation. This level of engagement enables students to gain a wider understanding of the context of their studies, giving them opportunities to influence professional standards and develop networks with other students and professionals in their discipline.

Across Europe, the creation of a European Higher Education Area and the Bologna Process intergovernmental initiative has led to many changes in higher education systems, with student engagement being central to these developments (Bols 2013). Mirroring some of the national developments outlined above, there are opportunities for students to engage in a range of forums and agencies at this level; for example, the European Association for Quality Assurance (ENQA; www.enqa.eu); and the annual European Quality Assurance Forum (EQAF). However, whilst the Bologna Process may influence developments in higher education globally (Bols 2013), and internationalisation is 'a central force in higher education' (Altbach and Knight 2007; 303) with ensuring quality being 'integral to the international higher education environment' (Altbach and Knight 2007; 209), student involvement in quality initiatives at a global level remains an area for growth and development.

Conclusion

The processes and standards of quality assurance in higher education can be seen to be part of the regulating and controlling mechanisms of a marketised system, furthering notions of 'students as consumers'. However, by re-defining 'the relationship between teachers and students in the production of . . . knowledge' and collaborative practices as discussed in this chapter, it is possible to offer a contrasting and alternative approach to quality assurance in higher education (Neary 2012; 163). In exploring the changing relationship between staff and students in progressing this work, the chapter has provided a range of rich examples of collaborations that demonstrate effective partnership practices at different levels of quality assurance activity. Within this, the chapter has also highlighted the importance of considering engagement of students as a collective, through the representation system and as non-representative individuals.

Whilst it is not possible in this short chapter to address the many challenges that this work undoubtedly raises, it is important to acknowledge that achieving meaningful student engagement is not straightforward. Bovill (2013) highlights the need for changes in values and attitudes to ensure genuine motivation and meaningful commitment from all involved. Furthermore, at the institutional level, the influence and impact of institutional values, context and culture on taking this work forward cannot be understated (Bovill 2013). It is worthy of note that many of the examples of practice in this chapter take place in an institutional culture of embedded, active student engagement in all aspects of university life.

> There is a subtle, but extremely important, difference between an institution that 'listens' to students and responds accordingly, and an institution that gives students the opportunity to explore areas that they believe to be significant, to recommend solutions and to bring about the required changes.
>
> (Dunne and Zandstra 2011; 4)

In closing this chapter, the following practical points support work that will enhance student engagement in assuring the quality of university teaching and provide students with opportunities for wider skill development.

- Administrators, faculty and managers need to value students as experts, actively and explicitly engaging with student perspectives and feedback at all levels; this will benefit the university and its teaching.
- Administrators, faculty, managers and students should work together to consider the most appropriate approach to partnership in the context of the specific activity, in particular whether representative, or non-representative student participation is most appropriate.
- Managers, faculty and students should work together to ensure that students are a full part of the quality processes and have a key role, not only providing comments and feedback, but being integral to developing the solution and making decisions about forward planning.
- Administrators, faculty and managers need to find ways to provide opportunities for students to gain insight into wider university processes and to engage in more depth in their discipline, the development of their discipline and beyond their discipline.
- University staff and students can, through this work, broaden their networks and engage in conversations about learning and teaching that may otherwise not happen.

The final words of this chapter are given over to the National Union of Students (NUS). In their *Manifesto for Partnership*, Wenstone introduces the document stating that

> Students as partners . . . has the potential to help bring about social and educational transformation, as long as we know what we are trying to do and we maintain a critical attitude about the ways the concept is adopted and used.'
>
> (NUS 2012; 1)

References

Ako Aotearoa – The National Centre for Tertiary Teaching Excellence and New Zealand Union of Students' Associations (NZUSA) (2013) *Using the Student Voice to Improve Quality.* www.akoaotearoa.ac.nz/studentvoice

Altbach, P. G. and Knight, J. (2007) 'The Internationalization of Higher Education: Motivations and Realities.' *Journal of Studies in International Education,* 11 (3/4) pp. 290–305.

Bell, A., Carson, L. and Piggott, L. (2013) 'Deliberative Democracy for Curriculum Renewal.' *The Student Engagement Handbook: Practice in Higher Education.* Bingley: Emerald Group Publishing, pp. 499–508.

Bols, A. (2013) 'Harmonisation and the Bologna Process: A Driver for Student Engagement?' in Dunne, E. and Derfel, O. (2013) *The Student Engagement Handbook: Practice in Higher Education.* Bingley: Emerald Group Publishing, pp. 97–110.

Bovill, C. (2013) 'Students and Staff Co-creating Curricula: An Example of Good Practice in Higher Education?' in Dunne, E. and Derfel, O., *The Student Engagement Handbook: Practice in Higher Education.* Bingley: Emerald Group Publishing, pp. 461–476.

Bovill, C. and Bulley, C.J. (2011) 'A Model of Active Student Participation in Curriculum Design: Exploring Desirability and Possibility' in Rust, C. *Improving Student Learning (18) Global Theories and Local Practices: Institutional, Disciplinary and Cultural Variations.* Oxford: The Oxford Centre for Staff and Educational Development, pp. 176–188.

Cook-Sather, A., Bovill, C. and Felten, P. (2014) *Engaging Students as Partners in Learning and Teaching.* San Francisco, CA: Jossey-Bass.

Cook-Sather, A. and Motz-Storey, D. (2016) 'Viewing Teaching and Learning from a New Angle: Student Consultants' Perspectives on Classroom Practice.' *College Teaching* 64 (4) pp. 168–177.

Crawford, K. (2012) 'Rethinking the Student/Teacher Nexus: Students as Observers of Teaching Practice' in M. Neary, H. Stevenson and L. Bell (Eds) *Towards Teaching in Public: Reshaping the Modern University.* London: Continuum, pp. 52–67.

Crawford, K., Horsley, R., Hagyard, H. and Derricott, D. (2015) *Pedagogies of Partnership: What Works?* York: Higher Education Academy.

Department for Business, Innovation and Skills (2016) *Success as a Knowledge Economy: Teaching Excellence, Social Mobility and Student Choice.* Available at https://www.gov.uk/government/uploads/system/uploads/attachment_data/file/523396/bis-16-265-success-as-a-knowledge-economy.pdf (accessed 21.12.17).

Dunne, E. and Zandstra, R. (2011). *Students as Change Agents – New Ways of Engaging with Learning and Teaching in Higher Education.* London: Higher Education Academy.

Healey, M., Flint, A. and Harrington, K. (2014) *Engagement through Partnership: Students as Partners in Learning and Teaching in Higher Education.* York: HEA.

Jensen, K. and Bennett, L. (2016) 'Enhancing Teaching and Learning through Dialogue: A Student and Staff Partnership Model.' *International Journal for Academic Development* 21 (1) pp. 41–53.

Levy, P., Little, S. and Whelan, N. (2011) 'Perspectives on staff–student partnership in learning, research and educational enhancement' in Little, S. (Ed.), *Staff–Student Partnerships in Higher Education.* London: Continuum, pp. 1–15.

National Union of Students (NUS) (2012) *A Manifesto for Partnership.* www.nus.org

Neary, M. (2012) 'Beyond Teaching in Public: The University as a Form of Social Knowing' in Neary, M., Stevenson, H. and Bell, L. (Eds), *Towards Teaching in Public: Reshaping the Modern University.* London: Continuum, pp. 148–164.

Owen, D. (2013) 'Students Engaged in Academic Subject Review' in Dunne, E. and Derfel, O. (2013) *The Student Engagement Handbook: Practice in Higher Education.* Bingley: Emerald Group Publishing, pp. 163–179.

Popenici, S. (2013) 'Towards a New Vision for University Governance, Pedagogies and Student Engagement' in Dunne, E. and Derfel, O. (2013) *The Student Engagement Handbook: Practice in Higher Education.* Bingley: Emerald Group Publishing, pp. 23–41.

Quality Assurance Agency (QAA) (2012) *UK Quality Code for Higher Education: Part B: Assuring and Enhancing Academic Quality: Chapter B5: Student Engagement.* Gloucester: The Quality Assurance Agency for Higher Education.

Robinson, W. and Hilli, A. (2016) 'The English Teaching Excellence Framework and Professionalising Teaching and Learning in Research-Intensive Universities; An Exploration of Opportunities, Challenges, Rewards and Values from a Recent Empirical Study.' *Foro de Educación* 14 (21) pp. 151–165.

Steinhardt, I., Schneijderberg, C., Götze, N., Baumann, J., and Krücken, G. (2016) 'Mapping the Quality Assurance of Teaching and Learning in Higher Education: The Emergence of a Speciality?' *Higher Education* 1 (72) pp. 1–17.

Tight, M. (2013) 'Institutional Churn: Institutional Change in United Kingdom Higher Education.' *Journal of Higher Education Policy and Management* 35 (1) pp. 11–20.

Van der Velden, G. (2013) 'Staff Perceptions of Student Engagement' in Dunne, E. and Derfel, O. (2013) *The Student Engagement Handbook: Practice in Higher Education.* Bingley: Emerald Group Publishing, pp. 77–91.

Van der Velden, G. M., Naidoo, R., Lowe, J. A., Pimentel Bótas, P. C. and Pool, A. D. (2012) *Student Engagement in Learning and Teaching Quality Management, A Study of UK Practices Commissioned by the Quality Assurance Agency.* Bath: University of Bath.

Waring, M. and Evans, C. (2015) *Understanding Pedagogy: Developing a Critical Approach to Teaching and Learning.* London: Routledge.

15 Assuring Quality through Student Evaluation

From Paper to Cloud-Based Approaches

Maurice Stringer, Karl Stringer, John A. Hunter and Cathy Finlay

Introduction

This chapter describes the move from early paper-based assessments of student evaluation to more sophisticated modern approaches using clicker technology, online surveys and cloud-based feedback systems. The authors examine advances that have occurred since the original chapter by Stringer and Finlay (1993) on 'Assuring quality through student evaluation' by examining a range of research-based approaches to student feedback. These include an examination of the factors that underpin student evaluation (Stringer and Irwing 1998) through clicker-based approaches (Stringer and Stringer 2012b) and Google-maps-based approaches (Stringer and Stringer 2012a) to feedback approaches using cloud-based approaches and mobile phones (Stringer *et al.* 2014). The studies highlight both the opportunities provided by new technology in new learning environments but also point out the challenges that need to be addressed as students and staff make increasing use of online devices for both social and educational purposes. The authors have been fortunate in being involved throughout this time in a range of different feedback approaches, which provide a convenient means of tracing feedback development over several decades.

Early questionnaire approaches

Stringer and Finlay (1993) reported the early development of a paper-and-pencil course evaluation feedback system in Ulster that was based on then current questionnaire approaches based largely in the United States. Stringer and Finlay, in their review of feedback approaches, were only able to locate limited work in the United Kingdom (e.g. Adelman and Alexander 1982; Rutherford 1987) and based their approach largely on evaluations carried out in the United States. This paper-based questionnaire approach to feedback became an accepted approach across the University with over 20,000 questionnaires being scanned a year using the FORMIC system, producing both quantitative and limited qualitative feedback to individual staff members. This approach was highly efficient by modern standards and ran for many years within the Social Survey Centre within Psychology. A researcher employed jointly by Psychology and Staff Development was responsible for the data processing and reports of this questionnaire scheme. Questionnaires were produced centrally by Staff Development and given out by staff to students during lecture periods. Staff who lectured on a module were not allowed to administer questionnaires to their own students to avoid bias. Staff Development oversaw this process and the questionnaires were scanned using FORMIC and reports produced on each module for use by academic staff, Heads of School and Deans. The approach adopted was largely summative rather than formative with module evaluations being used in annual staff evaluations with their Heads of School.

This detailed collection of data from both course and later module-based questionnaire approaches provided a useful dataset for research into student views about feedback more generally. Stringer and Irwing (1998) used exploratory and confirmatory factor analyses and structural modelling techniques to examine the utility of Stringer and Finlay's (1993) Teaching Effectiveness Survey (TES). The Factor structure of the TES was supported and found to be similar to both Marsh's (1987) SEEQ and Feldman's (1989) SETE dimensions. The results suggested that a questionnaire based largely on 40 different American instruments could be used effectively with United Kingdom students. Teaching quality was found to be related to course characteristics. Teacher, course and student characteristics were found to explain 88 per cent of the variance in students' overall questionnaire evaluations, allowing the construction of a model of the relationships between teaching quality, feedback and student evaluations (see Figure 15.1).

These large University datasets also allowed researchers to make changes to the University questionnaire over time to improve item reliability. Rae and Stringer carried out several statistical examinations of the University questionnaire dataset leading to item changes to improve reliability of the instrument, which were reported to the University Senate.

The move to online questionnaire approaches

As quality assurance became an integral part of University life, the move to online evaluation was considered by the University questionnaire-working group. Despite the fact that some members of the group argued that return rates would be poor and that students who were questioned about possible online delivery said they would be unlikely to complete these online, the University view about online questionnaire delivery prevailed. While online assessment provides many advantages, for example in freeing up staff time from questionnaire collection and in data collection and analysis, it moves responsibility for feedback into the University administration. Feedback operates best when it is formative, when lecturers can respond quickly to feedback from students. Online approaches, while efficient, arguably

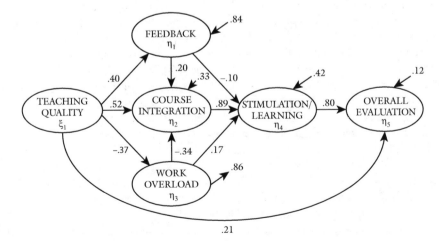

Figure 15.1 Model of the relationships between teaching quality and TES questionnaire factors

lean more toward summative assessment since their primary function tends to be reporting the feedback as part of the University's quality assurance reporting procedures. The centralization of procedures removes feedback flexibility, and in conjunction with students' reluctance to fill in online questionnaires, has led to very poor student return rates, often 15 per cent or less. These poor return rates mean that reliable measures of teaching are not being achieved. Pressure is then placed on staff to encourage students to respond to feedback, which increases perceptions that the main purpose is to provide an institutional return. Feedback to staff from these surveys is also devalued as it is based on low numbers and occurs too late so that changes can only be made for the next cohort of students. Students are being asked to give feedback that will not influence the teaching that they receive on their modules.

Our general disenchantment with traditional feedback approaches, which both students and academic staff perceive to be for summative rather than formative purposes, suggested the need for a new approach. We wanted to adopt a feedback approach that would give both students and academic staff more immediate feedback avoiding the retrospective nature of the clear majority of traditional assessment approaches.

Clicker technology is being used increasingly in universities to help improve classroom interaction and feedback. Its introduction however is controversial, as it poses a challenge to the traditional lecture format. Higher education in the United Kingdom is facing challenging times, with the introduction of fee-paying students and ever-increasing demands on staff to deliver both high-quality teaching and research with limited resources.

Institutions are becoming increasingly corporate in their management approaches and increased class sizes, and changes to the school curriculum leave some staff unsure about the levels of knowledge that modern students bring. It is unsurprising to find that while the research literature suggests that clicker use is largely beneficial (see Kay and LeSage 2009 and Caldwell 2007, for reviews), many staff resent the intrusion of new technology into what has been their own traditional way of delivering material. Similar strains occurred in the introduction of PowerPoint as a delivery method as opposed to chalk and talk or overheads. The increasing proliferation of online courses, distance learning and web resources for programs via Blackboard or other platforms require academics to learn new skills. By contrast, many students use technology with greater ease and can manage multiple contacts via Facebook, Twitter and texting with remarkable ease.

In Northern Ireland, 50 per cent of students go on to university and are geographically dispersed across the province, many with part-time jobs. This places greater emphasis on course material providing a clear foundation for study. The authors' universities are well provided in terms of clicker technology with classrooms supporting the system.

We decided to try to implement a feedback system based on the following principles. Firstly, feedback should be student driven and lecturers should act on it quickly. This is an explicit acknowledgement of the fact that many lecturers feel frustrated by the limited and delayed feedback that our current questionnaire feedback systems provide. In many universities, student feedback questionnaires are completed online and return rates are dropping, making them unrepresentative. Research studies have also cast doubt on the limited use that questionnaire-based feedback has in terms of course change (Kember *et al.* 2002). Our second principle was that the system should allow changes to lecture material, which would be of benefit to students on the course rather than for future groups. Thirdly, we wished to develop a system that was formative, allowing staff to apply a range of techniques to increase comprehension of lecture material. Finally, we wanted a system that would provide structured feedback and link with other university quality assurance practices such as peer assessment, module monitoring and course review.

In devising the system, we wanted a process which would allow students to provide feedback unobtrusively (it would not affect lecture delivery) and anonymously on lecture material which they found difficult. The Turning Point system provided a useful platform but its current use in the university centred on providing a limited number of slides to stimulate discussion or reflection and to monitor attendance. Having tried the system, we felt that while it appeared to be liked by students it was a lot of technology for a few additional slides per lecture. However, the platform provided an opportunity to build in comprehension feedback during lectures. We agreed that the most logical approach was to use a slide-based approach. The idea behind this was twofold. Firstly, we felt that it would be useful to focus students on whether they understood the material being presented to them, and that the end of a slide was an appropriate point at which to reflect on this. Secondly, one of the most difficult problems for staff is adjusting material to accommodate feedback (Abrahamson 2006). We felt that a slide-based approach would greatly help staff to focus on areas of specific difficulty. To help focus attention we decided to add in a countdown in the corner of the slide from 5 to 0, which appeared when the lecturer pressed to change slides. All clicks were captured using the Turning Point data capture system and saved at the end of the lecture. We considered the possibility of making the lecturer immediately aware of comprehension difficulties by revealing the clicker results on the tutor's console however, we decided that this might disrupt the lecture flow and that lecturers needed time to think about the results.We therefore decided that the results would be made available to the lecturer after the lecture. This would enable them to look quickly across the lecture slide profile for slides which revealed comprehension difficulties. The lecturer could then respond to this feedback to the students in the next lecture.

Software was developed to automate the embedding of Turning Point questions into standard slides. The initial approach was to create a PowerPoint template that would allow the easy application of Turning Point components onto any set of slides. This option had to be rejected as some of the components that make up the Turning Point system cannot be embedded in a template document and the slides were not recognized as valid by the system. Since version 2007 of Office the underlying representation of PowerPoint, Word and Excel has changed to an XML-based representation. As an OpenXML SDK (software development kit) was available, which provided programmatic access to these types of files, it was decided to investigate this as a way of adjusting the slides. The XML representation of Office files is governed by an ISO standard (ISO/IEC 29500). PowerPoint files are zipped file containers with an internal directory structure representing the component parts of the presentation (see Figure 15.2).

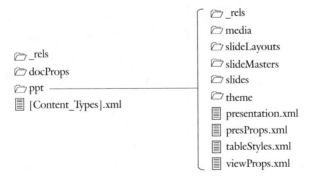

Figure 15.2 The internal PowerPoint representation

The _rels folders contain catalogs of component parts and can occur at the top level, as shown above, and at the level of individual slides. The task was to reverse-engineer what components were being added to the PowerPoint by the Turning Point system. These turned out to be a series of objects representing the text of questions being asked and an OLE (object linking and embedding) chart object to hold the results for each slide. Other changes included the addition of timing components to the slide as well as a number of user-defined XML tables to handle the configuration of Turning Point features.

An early version of the software, as used in the trials, added these features to standard PowerPoint presentations. We decided to revisit some of these design decisions in the light of feedback from these trials. The only visible component was a countdown reminder at the end of each slide to allow students the opportunity to provide feedback (see Figure 15.3).

An introductory slide encouraged students to click their handsets to indicate a point in the lecture at which they were having difficulty understanding. The system captured all such events and although no visible feedback to students was given at the time, the profile of clicks was stored to be examined afterwards by the lecturer to detect 'hot spots' (perhaps better referred to as 'cold spots') in terms of material delivery that was causing comprehension problems. After each lecture, a Turning Point report was generated highlighting 'problem' slides as indicated by total students' clicks.

The multiple-choice flag in the report is how Turning Point views this embedded component, but in practice students either press the '1' key to indicate a problem or don't click at all. Only slides for which there are student responses are presented along with the total number of clicks. Each click represents a separate student as multiple clicks on one handset were only counted once.

Staff who expressed an interest in using the Turning Point system were approached and the feedback system was explained to them. Those who agreed to participate had the system added to their PowerPoint presentations along with an initial slide. This slide explained the countdown system and that students had been asked to give anonymous feedback to the lecturer about their comprehension of lecture material. Participants were informed that the lecturer would use class information to help address comprehension issues and that they were free to decide whether to take part. Once lecturers had completed their feedback session, they presented students with a slide of evaluation questions (see Figure 15.4) and informed them that they were free to respond or not and that the research team would use their responses to evaluate the system.

Quote

- I think there is a world market for maybe five computers.

  Thomas Watson Senior,
      Chairman of IBM, 1943

- There is no reason anyone would want a computer in their home.

  Ken Olsen
      President, Chairman and founder of Digital, 1977

Figure 15.3 Countdown indicator

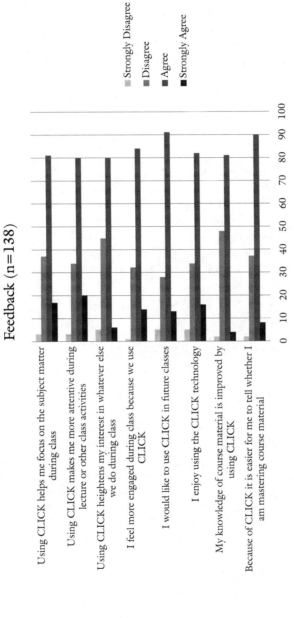

Figure 15.4 Student responses to the feedback

The results suggested that the approach helped students to focus on class material, improving their attention and interest (see Figure 15.4). They also felt engaged in class with the system allowing them to tell whether they were mastering course material. The immediate feedback system was popular with students and allowed staff to appreciate areas of difficulty in course material and make changes to improve general lecture comprehension.

One of the greatest strengths of the approach is its ability to integrate easily and effectively with current university systems. Peer assessment is a common feature of university quality assurance and the current approach provides a more focused role for staff. Sharing feedback with peer assessors on a weekly basis can help the lecturer by providing an additional view on the difficult slides and how these issues could be best tackled. We feel that the system would allow a highly practical side to the peer assessor's role, which would allow an overview of the course and how students were receiving it. It would also be possible to use student groups to help understand these comprehension difficulties. At Ulster, we have a PASS scheme which is a student peer mentoring approach which allows students to help other students with difficult material. Getting student input into areas of difficulties on slides we feel is an important additional element to ensuring changes will increase comprehension.

The system, while formative and lecturer led, could be particularly useful for staff who are having difficulties with course delivery. Heads of School are asked to appraise staff whose modules have been identified as being poorly evaluated by students in terms of the module questionnaire results and/or student performance statistics. The system provides a highly focused way of determining comprehension difficulties and staff can provide a clear outline of what changes they made to address comprehension problems. An agreed introduction of the current approach could provide a more focused and supportive process for both line managers and lecturing staff.

The system also supports course review since clear patterns of comprehension difficulty can be tracked across modules, providing very valuable information about changes to both modules and programmes. If the system was being used across modules, it would help staff to appreciate which areas of the course programme require attention. This helps to provide better progression across modules and indicate how difficulties in one module can be helped by changes in another.

A related approach using Goggle mapping technology to provide students with feedback from a visual progression along a route provides another example of a feedback approach in line with our philosophy of the use of immediate formative feedback for students.

Providing timely feedback to students is an on-going issue at all levels of education. There is much research which highlights the benefits of such formative feedback; see Gikandi *et al.* (2011) for a recent review with particular emphasis on the online and blended learning environments. The feedback issue has been brought into sharper focus in recent years with the increasing class sizes in higher education in the UK alongside an increase in fees and rising student expectations on the quality of course delivery; the student as conscientious consumer (Higgins *et al.* 2002). The use of Virtual Learning Environments (VLEs) is one response to this pressure with their mechanisms for material delivery and feedback. The particular VLE used at Ulster is Blackboard and they have recently introduced a feature, 'Mark Reviewed', that allows course developers to get students to click a button to confirm they have completed a section of the material. Subsequent material can be set via 'adaptive release' to only appear if pre-requisites have been marked as reviewed by the student. A second thread of this work was the efficient way in which the human memory system records and remembers geographic or location-based information. Young people are frequently immersed in online games with huge maps showing pathways and routes available to their character and have little difficulty in remembering all this as it taps into a visual location and mapping facility in humans that dates back to hunting/tracking and finding-your-way-home skills developed very early in history.

We decided to tap into this geographic skill to provide a map representing progress through a series of first-year computing practicals. The expectation was that students would be provided with a 'learning landscape' on which they would get feedback from their sense of progression along a variety of routes as well as creating an association between the easy-to-remember visual map and the less memorable course material. A second aspect was an element of competition created by providing feedback on overall class progression through the tasks.

In the next section, we outline the technical aspects to implementing the system before analyzing how the system operated with a particular cohort and their feedback on using the system. Google mapping technology was chosen to provide the graphical representation since one of the authors had previous experience in programming using the API (application programming interface) provided. The interface allows you to center the map on real geographic coordinates at a particular zoom level with a choice of satellite and terrain views. In our case the map was centred on the Coleraine campus of the University of Ulster and the various trails led outward from this starting point (see Figure 15.5).

This first map is a dynamic one representing each route as the user hovers over an area of the map. Each of the trail destinations is a well-known local town or tourist attraction. On clicking the route the user is shown the Google map with the trail indicated as a series of waypoints (see Figure 15.6).

As students complete the steps in the practical the waypoints change their icon to indicate progression along the route. The route icons also represent hyperlinks to the underlying practical material, allowing students to navigate quickly to any step in the practical. The current system assumes a linear progression – each stage must be completed to progress.

The underpinning Javascript code has to extract from the Blackboard environment the state of the 'Mark Review' buttons associated with each practical step before updating the map.

The state of the 'Mark Reviewed' buttons can be used within Blackboard to conditionally make visible student's subsequent material. This is very flexible in that you can control the release of material based on not only the usual date/time criteria, but also on the basis of the material they have reviewed or quizzes they have attempted; this later facility being used in this study. A multiple-choice quiz was interleaved between stages to test their understanding of the material, but more importantly to prevent a student simply clicking all the review buttons without examining the material.

Adding a Google Fusion layer onto the map allowed an additional icon at each step of the route to change colour dependent on overall class progress. Although students could not see the individual progress of their peers, this feedback was sufficient to allow them to gauge their progress relative to the cohort. This proved difficult to implement as only staff have access to individual student progress details and this required a polling program run on a secure machine to routinely update the Google Fusion tables held in the cloud. The extra information is shown in Figure 15.7.

The Fusion layer provides coloured circles at each waypoint which change colour after a set proportion of the class has completed the stage. The student can also right-click a circle and get the total number of students who have completed that stage.

Students (n=87) were surveyed by questionnaire about the approach. They believed that the quizzes between sections made them concentrate more on the material, although a significant minority felt the questions were too hard. Competition between students was only a

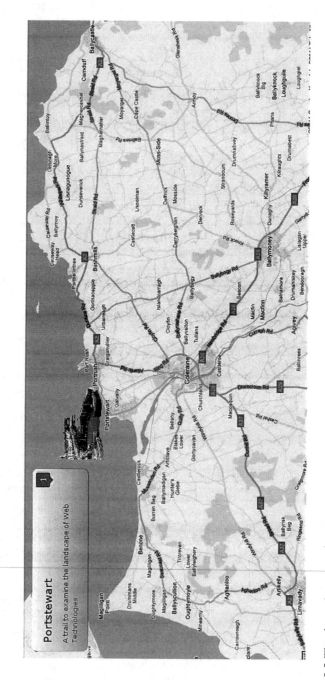

Figure 15.5 The dynamic route selector map

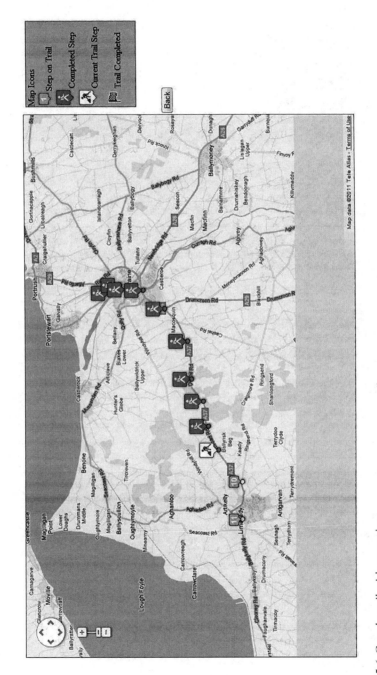

Figure 15.6 Google trail with waypoints

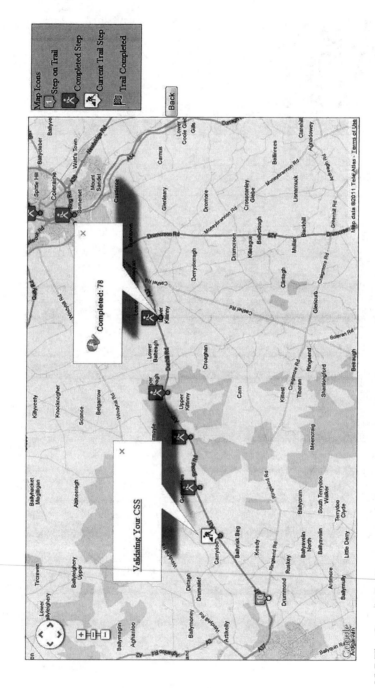

Figure 15.7 The Google Fusion progress layer

significant factor for a minority of students. In general, there was a positive response to using the system, but students were not keen on extending it into formal assessment.

As part of the questionnaire students were also asked to recall the topic associated with each of the nine trails. The results indicate that there was a strong association retained between the geographic trail and the topic covered with up to 66 per cent of students selecting the correct option from nine alternatives for the best remembered down to 47 per cent for the least. A further test to see if student familiarity with the actual driving route was linked with strength of the association between topic and trail did not find a significant effect.

The system provided a map trail analogy to help students to progress through the course material. There is good evidence that students associate the trail with the topic. The system gives a visual indication of how far through the material students have progressed and how they are performing relative to their peers. Some of the problems experienced with the system concerned the linking quiz questions. These currently provide an absolute barrier to progression and it was difficult to pitch these at the correct level. Although these were mostly multiple-choice with unlimited attempts, it is easy to inadvertently set questions with too many alternatives where more than one answer has to be selected. It was also difficult generating sufficient questions for all the stages. This meant that some questions were not tied closely enough to the material covered, which for some students undermined the reason for having questions during the practical.

Non-linear progression would also be possible as a further development with branches to reinforce a topic or supplementary material for students who found the material too challenging. This would allow students to feel that they were in a more exploratory map-like setting where they could choose the low-level detail of the route they followed through the material while still requiring some prerequisite material to progress through key checkpoints. Evidence from the MMORPG (Massively Multiplayer Online Role-Playing Games) community suggests that not only can people remember hugely complex maps in these games, but also enjoy the exploratory nature of the gameplay; see Bian *et al.* (2010) for an application of MMORPG in an educational setting and Goldin *et al.* (2017) for an overview of new approaches in formative feedback in interactive learning environments.

Cloud-based approaches

One of the main drawbacks of clicker-based approaches is that users must commit to a clicker type and they are tied to the lecture delivery platform, e.g. PowerPoint. We have been testing a mobile-phone-based feedback system, which allows students to respond using their own mobile devices. Initial student reaction to the approach was very favorable as it removes the need to hand out clickers in class or for students to purchase them and forget in many cases to bring them to lectures. The majority of students have smartphones, which can be used to provide online responses. We were fortunate to obtain funding from the University of Otago in New Zealand to pilot a phone-based system with students enrolled in lectures at the University. This international perspective gave us the opportunity to examine problems that successful universities face with the influx of fee-paying students from around the world. The number of international students studying at tertiary level in New Zealand has increased by 400 per cent since the late 1990s (Franken 2005). Johnston (2008) outlines well the difficulties faced by international students in the initial years of university study. Despite passing language tests such as IELTS or TOEFL many of these students struggle with the language requirements of higher degree study with some reporting only being able to understand only 20–30 per cent of first-year lecture content. In addition to these initial language difficulties, international students have to contend with an increasingly international staff group. This international staff mix places additional strain on international students as they contend with accents as well as the complexity of a second language.

Lecturers who volunteered to pilot test the approach were talked through the approach and asked to email their lecture slides to the United Kingdom. These slides were then saved as graphic files and uploaded onto Google Drive providing a cloud-based storage system. Once the files were uploaded, they could be accessed via a unique URL for that lecture. This identifier, along with an introductory slide outlining the system, was emailed back to the lecturer in Otago as part of their lecture presentation. Students used their mobile phones to log on at the beginning of the lecture using the link and could move through the lecture slides on their mobiles as the lecture progressed. The layout on students' phones allowed them to use a scale on the top to indicate their comprehension of the slide on a 1–5 scale of clear–unclear and to use a button at the bottom to move back and forward between slides.

Students were able to navigate through the lecture slides on their phones and were encouraged to rate slides if they presented comprehension difficulties. Responses by students were collected via Google and were emailed to the lecturer following class. This method identified quickly slides in the presentation that were causing difficulty to students. As part of the pilot, lecturers agreed to run through the difficult slides in the next session with the students giving immediate feedback.

Getting the right balance between effective feedback and staff workload was a problem we examined carefully. Following Boud and Molloy (2013), we agree 'that teachers need better quality information about student learning difficulties than they have been getting, and that students need to better exercise their skills in eliciting the kinds of information they need' to deal effectively with modern information sources. Staff are prepared to put in extra effort for targeted groups of students who need help, but at the same time do not want to dumb down lectures. To address these competing viewpoints, we developed a three-level feedback approach. Staff routinely provide supporting material online to help students such as extra reading and other material. Slide-based feedback provides a focus for this material and usually only a small number of slides per lecture are identified as posing problems. This allows the lecturer to encourage a group of students to discuss these slides and provide a brief overview of the problems and how students can better overcome these. These discussions form the basis for the first level of online feedback, which helps both the lecturer and students to better understand comprehension issues. The lecturer is encouraged to structure the other two levels by providing reading or materials that provide greater information at level two, building on the first level, and at level three, which more advanced students can explore. We feel this approach allows students to help structure the feedback that lecturers provide while at the same time reinforcing the need for students to work in a structured way through feedback levels to better understand topic areas. Providing feedback at the basic level encourages the use of peer support where it is most useful and gives the lecturer valuable insights into student comprehension difficulties while support at the other two levels ensures that lecture quality is maintained for students who are progressing normally.

The pilot was successful in that it demonstrated that a cloud-based system operated from the United Kingdom could operate with students in New Zealand, although time differences caused delays in feedback via email. In technical terms, the system worked effectively, however lack of WIFI coverage in lecture theatres was an issue in some pilot sessions. Staff found the reports provided by the cloud-based slide feedback system to be very useful in clearly identifying a small number of slides in a lecture presentation reported as difficult to understand. It was reassuring to staff that students only identified a small number of slides across a lecture, allowing them to focus in on areas where students are having most difficulty. The most popular approach adopted by staff was for the staff member to clarify this material in the next lecture so that student feedback was acted upon quickly allowing difficult areas in lectures to be better explained to students.

The system also deals effectively with linked concepts in lectures, which was an issue staff raised during briefing sessions in New Zealand. This is where a concept developed at an early stage in the lecture is elaborated upon in later slides through linked concepts. This can lead to students reporting difficulty at an early stage in the lecture sequence and then reporting no issues later when these concepts are linked. This initially appears like a false positive, however, we argue that it highlights more clearly the process of student understanding. The slide-based approach lets lecturers see this progression more clearly, allowing staff to track understanding over the whole lecture. It also encourages staff to flag linked concepts in the lecture, so that students are reassured that material will become clear later when the concepts are linked. These types of problem areas may be particularly important for weaker students and international students taking courses that are not in their first language. Students report losing motivation following lecture material that they do not understand and have difficulty in paying attention to material in subsequent slides.

Internationally, approaches to student feedback at the formative level are facing difficulties. Darwin (2016) outlines the contesting motives in Australian higher education between student feedback to encourage enhanced quality for students and increasingly metric quality assurance processes, which are driven by universities competing for students internationally. Similarly, Gormally *et al.* (2014) lament the neglected opportunities to promote formative feedback to students in American higher education, with the majority of feedback occurring through institutional student evaluations. In the United Kingdom, the emergence of the Teaching Excellence Framework is placing an increased emphasis on teaching quality and it will be interesting to see whether this leads to more formative feedback approaches or the use of institutional metrics as reported in both Australia and the United States.

The most significant issue in the pilot testing however was the realization that many students use their mobile devices for multiple tasks such as texting and social media usage such as Facebook while in lectures. Studies of students have confirmed that students routinely use their mobile devices during large lectures to text and visit social media sites and that this also negatively affects their performance (see Risko *et al.* 2013; Junco 2012). This usage was demonstrated dramatically in a large lecture taken by the first author at Ulster. A sudden failure of lecture lighting led to students being asked whether they wished to continue in the dark, or with full lighting, as these were the only options left functioning. Students opted to be in the dark since they could see the PowerPoint slides more clearly. This provided an interesting lightshow throughout the remaining lecture period as mobile use became visually apparent in an impressive background glow from beneath their desks. Our cloud-based phone approach highlighted the impact of social media use in lectures and its increasing use in university teaching environments. In the final section, we look at some of the issues and problems increasing social media use amongst students has for higher education.

Challenging #false news

Attempts to reconcile traditional lecture approaches with a new generation of students who make heavy use of social media via smartphones is particularly challenging (see Kuznekoff and Titsworth 2013). There is a growing movement suggesting that lectures should be replaced by flip lecture approaches where new social media approaches can be used to reinforce learning. The difficulty here is that the evidence base for these new approaches is not well researched (see Abeysekera and Dawson 2015). Traditional approaches are being undermined and criticized to fit with this new approach despite the fact that, as Abeysekera and Dawson note, 'there is very little evidence of effectiveness or consistency in understanding what a flipped classroom actually is'. Advocates for change have claimed that the attention span of students beyond ten minutes makes lectures boring for students, despite evidence that this view does not consider individual differences in attention (see Wilson and Korn 2007). The idea that everything needs to be reduced to bite-sized chunks to accommodate a new generation who are continually connected via social media needs to be challenged. Students sit outside lectures on their mobiles rather than talking to the person beside them, many young people prefer online contacts to real contacts, and most cannot sit through a film or a play without using their mobile.

Above all, educators need to be assured that presenting academic material via these new mediums does not dilute science with #false news. It is particularly worrying that many new students cannot distinguish clearly between good evidence sources and poor ones. The worry is that in attempting to accommodate new social media demands into classroom activities we may be encouraging rather than challenging this reliance on unreliable sources of information. Unfortunately, having challenged the traditional lecture, those who support the flipped classroom then move to suggest that final examinations are not required as the curriculum is covered in the classroom activities of the course. This would suit students as they appear to use Google as an external memory (see Sparrow *et al.* 2011), making exams difficult as they are being asked unfairly to do these on one of the very few times they cannot access their internet memory. These changes are being implemented across universities with the creation of new student-led learning approaches in the absence of baseline evidence about their effectiveness.

Perhaps most alarming of all from an educational as well as a broader societal perspective are newly emerging reports of evidence suggesting that multi-tasking associated with the internet may be leading to attention and information selection problems. A quote from Loh and Kanai's (2016) review captures the range and extent of this issue:

> Growing up with Internet technologies, "Digital Natives" gravitate toward "shallow" information processing behaviors characterized by rapid attention shifting and reduced deliberations. They engage in increased multitasking behaviors that are linked to increased distractibility and poor executive control abilities. Digital natives also exhibit higher prevalence of Internet-related addictive behaviors that reflect altered reward-processing and self-control mechanisms. Recent neuroimaging investigations have suggested associations between these Internet-related cognitive impacts and structural changes in the brain.

The suggestion that a new generation of students may be neurologically predisposed to distraction and unable to distinguish between information sources does not augur well for student-led learning approaches. While it is too early to accept the limited evidence for these alarming effects, it should make us think carefully about whether we challenge rather than simply accept these technologies as currently used by students in educational settings.

In a talk to update academics on educational changes, a former secondary headmaster from one of Northern Ireland's leading schools outlined why each of the key skills that universities required of entrants was no longer properly developed in students (such as essay writing etc.) due to exam pressures. Many current students do not come equipped with the skills required to undertake university study. Universities need to address this by challenging students' learning approaches rather than simply trying to incorporate shallow information processing into classroom activities. Student-centred learning rather than student-led learning is required to help them seek out better sources of information to inform their choices and shape their everyday lives. As Canute found, you cannot hold back the waves – the challenge presented by students' over-reliance on social media may prove equally hard to resist in higher education.

Some advice for administrators and faculty using feedback in higher education

- Greater diversity in student intakes, increasing numbers of international students and the need to support students from disadvantaged backgrounds all argue for improved use of feedback to improve lecture comprehension.
- New technologies provide the means to greatly speed up and provide greater formative impact in the use of student feedback.
- Approaches that are immediate allow changes during the lecture programme, aid lecture comprehension, and improve student retention and satisfaction.
- Visual approaches using Google mapping technology provide students with trails to guide them through tasks providing novelty and feedback about their progress.
- Approaches should be careful not to overburden academic staff. Using student groups to focus in on specific areas of difficulty helps lecturers to appreciate these difficulties and in turn encourages them to provide more structured online support.
- Using student feedback to help shape lecturers' support materials allows lecturers to set and maintain standards while at the same time encouraging student input. This partnership approach helps lecturers become more aware of student-identified comprehension difficulties and to order course resources to help students to work through these more effectively.
- The increasing use of mobile technology and social media by students raises issues that needs to be addressed in higher education through evidence-based approaches.
- Higher education institutions and lecturers need to develop more formal systems to help students distinguish more clearly between useful and less useful sources of information.

Acknowledgements

1   The authors are grateful to the University of Otago Internationalization of the Curriculum Committee for a grant to carry out pilot work on the cloud-based phone feedback approach.
2   We would like to thank staff and students in Psychology at Otago for helping us test out this new system and colleagues in Science and Maori support for discussions about applying the system to targeted groups.

3 The authors presented two of the studies reported in this chapter at the Higher Education Authority STEM conference at UCL in London.
4 We would like to thank Ulster University for a grant to fund the development of the clicker feedback system reported in the chapter.

References

Abeysekera, L. & Dawson, P. (2015). Motivation and cognitive load in the flipped classroom: Definition, rationale and a call for research. *Higher Education Research & Development, 34*(1), 1–14.

Abrahamson, L. (2006). A brief history of networked classrooms: Effects, cases, pedagogy, and implications. In *Audience response systems in higher education: Applications and cases* (pp. 1–25). Hershey, PA: IGI Global.

Adelman, C. & Alexander, R. (1982). *The self-evaluating institution*. London: Methuen, 25–28.

Bian, W., Wang, A. I., & Yuanyuan Zhang (2010). Experiences from implementing an educational MMORPG, Games Innovations Conference (ICE-GIC), 2010 International IEEE Consumer Electronics Society, 21–23 Dec, pp. pp.1–8.

Boud, D. & Molloy, E. (2013). Rethinking models of feedback for learning: the challenge of design. *Assessment & Evaluation in Higher Education, 38*(6), 698–712.

Caldwell, J. E. (2007). Clickers in the large classroom: Current research and best-practice tips. *CBE-Life Sciences Education, 6*(1), 9–20.

Darwin, S. (2016). The emergence of contesting motives for student feedback-based evaluation in Australian higher education. *Higher Education Research & Development, 35*(3), 419–432.

Feldman, K. A. (1989). The association between student ratings of specific instructional dimensions and student achievement: Refining and extending the synthesis of data from multisection validity studies. *Research in Higher Education, 30*(6), 583–645.

Franken, M. (2005). Some principles of good pedagogical practice for tertiary international students. *The TESOLANZ Journal, 13*, 43–56.

Gikandi, J. W., Morrow, D. & Davis, N. E. (2011). Online formative assessment in higher education: A review of the literature. *Computers & Education, 57*(4), 2333–2351.

Goldin, I., Narciss, S., Foltz, P. & Bauer, M. (2017). New directions in formative feedback in interactive learning environments. *International Journal of Artificial Intelligence in Education*, 1–8.

Gormally, C., Evans, M. & Brickman, P. (2014). Feedback about teaching in higher education: Neglected opportunities to promote change. *CBE-Life Sciences Education, 13*(2), 187–199.

Higgins, R., Hartley, P. & Skelton, A. (2002). The conscientious consumer: Reconsidering the role of assessment feedback in student learning. *Studies in Higher Education, 27*(1), 53–64.

Johnson, E. M. (2008). An investigation into pedagogical challenges facing international tertiary-level students in New Zealand. *Higher Education Research & Development, 27*(3), 231–243.

Junco, R. (2012). In-class multitasking and academic performance. *Computers in Human Behavior, 28*(6), 2236–2243.

Kay, R. H. & LeSage, A. (2009). Examining the benefits and challenges of using audience response systems: A review of the literature. *Computers & Education, 53*(3), 819–827.

Kember, D., Leung, D. Y. & Kwan, K. (2002). Does the use of student feedback questionnaires improve the overall quality of teaching? *Assessment & Evaluation in Higher Education, 27*(5), 411–425.

Kuznekoff, J. H. & Titsworth, S. (2013). The impact of mobile phone usage on student learning. *Communication Education, 62*(3), 233–252.

Loh, K. K. & Kanai, R. (2016). How has the Internet reshaped human cognition? *The Neuroscientist, 22*(5), 506–520.

Marsh, H. W. (1987). Students' evaluations of university teaching: Research findings, methodological issues, and directions for future research. *International Journal of Educational Research, 11*(3), 253–388.

Marsh, H. W. (2007). Students' evaluations of university teaching: Dimensionality, reliability, validity, potential biases and usefulness. In *The scholarship of teaching and learning in higher education: An evidence-based perspective* (pp. 319–383). Netherlands: Springer.

Risko, E. F., Buchanan, D., Medimorec, S. & Kingstone, A. (2013). Everyday attention: Mind wandering and computer use during lectures. *Computers & Education, 68*, 275–283.

Rutherford, D. (1987). Indicators of performance: Reactions and issues. *Assessment and Evaluation in Higher Education, 12*(2), 94–104.

Sparrow, B., Liu, J. & Wegner, D. M. (2011). Google effects on memory: Cognitive consequences of having information at our fingertips. *Science, 333*(6043), 776–778.

Stringer, K. & Stringer, M. (2012a). A route to success: a google maps feedback system implemented within blackboard. Higher Education Academy Stem Conference presentation, UCL London.

Stringer, M. & Finlay, C. (1993). Assuring quality through student evaluation. *Quality assurance for university teaching*, 92–112.

Stringer, M. & Irwing, P. (1998). Students' evaluations of teaching effectiveness: A structural modelling approach. *British Journal of Educational Psychology, 68*(3), 409–426.

Stringer, M. & Stringer, K. (2012b). Using clicker technology to improve PowerPoint lectures: A student-centred approach to feedback. Higher Education Academy Stem Conference presentation, UCL London.

Stringer M., Stringer, K. & Hunter, J. (2014). Promoting effective communities of practice through student feedback. CHERP Conference, University of Ulster.

Wilson, K. & Korn, J. H. (2007). Attention during lectures: Beyond ten minutes. *Teaching of Psychology, 34*(2), 85–89.

16 The Student Role in Quality

From Data Source to Partner and Back Again

Saranne Weller and Alam Mahbubul

Introduction

When writing about the role of students in the assuring of academic quality in universities in the early 1990s, Stringer and Finlay (1993) acknowledged that, while student course evaluation was well-established in North America, the concept was at that time relatively unfamiliar in the UK. Over two decades later, not only are students central to sector and institutional quality systems but the scope of their role in quality has evolved from evaluator to one of active involvement in institutional quality processes. In 2016, the new Quality Assurance Agency (QAA) *UK Quality Code of Practice for Higher Education* set the expectation that 'Higher education providers take deliberate steps to engage all students, individually and collectively as partners in the assurance and enhancement of their educational experience' (QAA, 2016, p. 6). This commitment to student involvement in UK quality processes reflects wider international trends. For example, both the recent *Standards and Guidelines for Quality Assurance in the European Higher Education Area* (2015), within which the UK *Quality Code* operates, and the Australian Tertiary Education Quality Standards Agency's *Higher Education Standards Framework* (2015) similarly anticipate that universities will involve students in the enhancement of their learning experience as well as the governance and decision-making of their institutions.

The engagement of students in quality processes has the potential to enrich their learning experience and the quality of teaching but can also raise questions and challenges for institutions, staff and students to fully live out the principles of engagement and partnership. This can include how students are supported to fulfil their critical role in quality, how institutions can better respond to the outcomes of student participation in quality processes and how inclusive mechanisms are for involving a diverse student body in quality decisions. These issues apply equally to the assuring of the academic standards of universities as to the emerging role of students in enhancement mechanisms including students as co-creators of curriculum design, as collaborators in the professional development of their teachers, as co-researchers in pedagogic research and as partners in institutional strategic decision-making. This chapter provides an overview of recent approaches to student involvement in assurance and enhancement and addresses some of the assumptions and challenges underpinning the successful engagement of students in quality. It will conclude by making recommendations for the better embedding of students in quality processes in the future.

Different levels of student involvement in quality

In the context of school-level education, Fielding (2001) identified that while involving students in evaluating and shaping their learning experience was gaining ground in educational settings, the definition of what that involvement constituted remained unclear. He proposed a hierarchical model for characterising student participation in institutional review and improvement. This model includes four levels of involvement that are applicable to the different roles of students in higher education quality:

- *Students as a data source*: individuals and institutions collate and make decisions on information about students related to their demographic background, prior learning and performance as well as their attitudes towards learning, attendance and accessing of learning resources with the aim to inform teaching.
- *Students as active respondents*: individuals and institutions engage with students in discussion about their experience to enhance primarily teaching or institutional practice but also influence student learning and engagement with the institution.
- *Students as co-researchers*: individuals, institutions and students work in partnership to deepen their mutual understanding of the student experience and to identify what students can do to contribute to the improvement of the institution.
- *Students as researchers*: students initiate actions to address issues in their learning or institutional experience and the role of the teacher and institution is to learn and respond to the needs of students.

This hierarchy configures student involvement as ranging from a passive feedback role that is teacher-centric to active participation and leadership that is student-centric. It characterises the different modes of engagement in quality for enhancement, assurance and institutional governance. For Fielding, while the 'students as researchers' mode is highly desirable for educational transformation, teachers, students and institutions may choose to adopt different modes of involvement at different times depending on the purpose and context.

Higher education institutions utilise a range of mechanisms to solicit information and student feedback on their experience including module, course or programme evaluations. They can also participate in large-scale sector-level surveys such as the UK National Student Survey (NSS) completed by final-year undergraduates or the Postgraduate Taught Experience Survey (PTES) and Postgraduate Research Experience Survey (PRES) at higher degree level. Targeted surveys such as the global Student Pulse and International Student Barometer go beyond capturing the student retrospective evaluation of their university experience to provide institutions with an understanding of the needs and expectations of students and their decision-making both as learners and selective consumers before, during and after their degree. Despite an increased openness to soliciting student feedback, the introduction of tuition fees in the UK in the late 1990s and the focus of NSS on student satisfaction as an influencer on university practice and driver for university league tables, are seen as indicative of a deliberate marketisation of higher education that is detrimental to the learner identity and academic performance of undergraduate students (Bunce, Baird & Jones, 2017). The development over the last fifteen years of alternative large-scale surveys such as the National Survey of Student Engagement (NSSE) in the US, the Australasian Survey of Student Engagement (AUSSE) and the United Kingdom Engagement Survey (UKES) all aim instead at evaluating the time and effort students invest in meaningful learning and their perceptions of the quality of their learning experience. The engagement orientation of these survey tools potentially restores a conception of the learning and teaching relationship as less transactional and more concerned with a mutual contribution of students, their teachers and their institutions to the academic quality of provision. This aligns with the more active levels of involvement defined in Fielding's model, where students operate as partners, co-creators, experts and drivers for change within the university.

The idea of 'students as partners' and active 'change agents' within universities has been taken up by a range of stakeholders to advocate further for a different type of relationship between institutions and their students. In the UK, the National Union of Students' (NUS) *A Manifesto for Partnership* (2009) upheld partnership as a counter to consumerist rhetoric on the basis that,

> Conceiving of students as consumers is a thoroughly impoverished way of describing the relationship between students and their institutions, which ought to be one of mutual trust, care and respect. The power held by consumers is not the power to intervene and change things, it is the power to 'like' or to 'recommend to a friend', or to make a choice between five identical glossy marketing brochures.
>
> (NUS, 2009, p. 5)

The move towards partnership, they argue, should not be based on small-scale student engagement interventions but represent a whole institution approach because 'partnership is an ethos rather than an activity' (p. 8). This promotion of student engagement in the quality of their educational experience as transformational for students and universities is similarly articulated in a stimulus paper published in 2010 by the UK Quality Assurance Agency on the Students as Change Agents initiative at the University of Exeter. It argues that narrow definitions of the student role in improving the quality of their experience, concerned only with seeking, listening and responding to the student voice, could lead to some benefits through greater institutional awareness of student need but also reinforce the role of students as discriminating customers. They suggest that:

> The Change Agents initiative is about far more than listening to the student voice, with the associated risks of promoting a customer-oriented approach to education. It is a powerful example of the connection between research and education and the way in which this influences changes in practice and provision in students' own learning environments.
>
> (Kay, Dunne & Hutchinson, 2010, p. 7)

Far from simply embedding formal student representational and feedback mechanisms into the traditional governance and decision-making of UK universities, staff–student partnership has become a global agenda that 'might be understood – and embraced – as a movement' (Cook-Sather, Bovill & Felten, 2014, p. xxiii).

'Experts by experience': The scope of the student quality role in higher education

Student involvement in the quality of higher education has been identified not only as performing on different levels but also across a range of areas of activity. This is demonstrated through:

- student engagement in high-impact learning activities that are likely to lead to improved learning outcomes and potentially could include the role of students as not just the recipients but also the active creators of knowledge;
- student engagement in curriculum design including determining the content, teaching, learning and assessment practices as pedagogic consultants and developers;

- student engagement in the building of communities within the university including their role in governance and influencing institutional decision-making (Ashwin & McVitty, 2015; Healey, Flint & Harrington, 2014).

The active student contribution to the achievement of individual quality learning outcomes is first and foremost the basis for quality education. The growth of participatory research and evaluative approaches that recognise the role of service users as 'experts by experience' in sectors including health and social care, however, has informed an enhanced understanding of the potential role and value of the student voice in educational settings (Skilton, 2011; Seale, 2009). As part of the university community, student participation in higher education governance and representation has a long-standing history and status in European higher education (Klemenčič, 2012). Newer roles for students in higher education quality assurance and enhancement beyond advocacy and representational activity now include involvement in curriculum design (Bovill, Cook-Sather & Felten, 2011), programme review and development (Case, Ugwudike, Haines, Harris & Owen, 2014), pedagogic evaluation (Bovill *et al.*, 2010), strategy development (Healey, Mason O'Connor & Broadfoot 2010) and academic development of teaching staff (Dickerson, Jarvis & Stockwell, 2016). In these roles students are seen to 'have access to experiences and information that can improve the quality and accountability of decision-making' (Lizzio & Wilson, 2009, p. 70). Involvement in these enhancement processes also 'catalyzes a revision of students' relationships to their teachers and their responsibilities within their learning' (Cook-Sather & Alter, 2011, p. 37). Yet implementing this step-change in understanding the role of students in assuring and improving the quality of their educational experience is recognised to be challenging for both institutions and individual staff.

Educators may deplore the perceived rise of a consumerist and instrumental approach to university 'where students seek to "have a degree" rather than "be learners"' (Molesworth, Nixon & Scullion, 2009, p. 278) and encourage increased involvement of students in decisions about the student experience as a counter to this rhetoric. Yet changing existing assumptions and expectations about the appropriate roles and responsibilities of teachers and students has been described as a 'threshold concept' in quality enhancement. Increased student responsibility for the quality of their university experience necessarily overturns prior beliefs about the dynamics of staff–student identities and behaviours in ways that can be conceptually 'troublesome' (Cook-Sather & Luz, 2015). Seale (2016) notes that this move from individual to institutional initiatives changes the conception of the role of students and changes the way we evaluate the success of such activities. What this can mean is that while staff, student unions and students might advocate for the transformation of student roles in the assurance and enhancement of academic institutions, Carey (2018) warns that in institutionally endorsed activity 'student engagement is confined to what the institution allows' and that there is also, therefore, 'a need to address what activities the university demands, expects or permits' (p. 13).

Despite an underpinning self-empowerment agenda in the student-as-partners movement, institutions can still retain the power to define the ultimate extent of student influence over institutional mission, strategy and practices. Carey proposes a nested hierarchy of institutional student engagement actions that both foster and limit the different levels of student involvement as defined above:

- *Institution as reactive*: the institution collects and analyses student behaviour and satisfaction to enhance institutional objectives. Student involvement is limited to evaluating their experiences or indicating their preferences.

- *Institution as responsive*: the institution consults with students as experts of their learning experience and invites their participation in university decision-making. While the relationship between students and the institution is based on dialogue and recognition of specific forms of expertise, it is demarcated by institutional needs and priorities.
- *Institution as collaborative*: the institution recognises students as active agents in the functioning of the university and students are encouraged to define and contribute to the evidence that is used and the actions that are taken to effect change in the institution.
- *Institution as progressive*: the institutional role is to respond to student-led calls to action with spaces created within decision-making processes for students to initiate, define and monitor change (Carey, 2018, p. 13).

The mutual responsibility of institutions, students' unions and students to fulfil the principles of student involvement is a fundamental caveat for assumptions about the straightforward implementation of student engagement in quality. For example, a case study of student engagement in the process of programme review and enhancement at Swansea University determined that

> full student 'partnership' in core departmental decisions and actions is perhaps something of a fallacy. Departments have to operate within the boundaries of the institutional mandate. In practical terms, institutional requirements and procedures may assume priority over student requirement.
>
> (Case *et al.*, 2014, p. 14)

This conclusion reflects the difficulties of realising student involvement in quality in a piecemeal way, at individual teacher or department level, without also revisiting, in partnership with students, the wider sector and institutionally defined requirements and quality mechanisms. Van der Velden (2012) suggests that institutional organisational culture is a significant factor in determining the extent to which an institution involves students in quality decision-making. Her analysis draws on a typology of organisational cultures developed by McNay in the mid-1990s. Within this typology, a 'collegium' organisational culture is one founded on academic freedom and autonomy with an emphasis on direct student participation at the department and teacher level. In contrast a 'bureaucracy' organisational culture operates through committee structures with student voice articulated through formal representation and surveys. A 'corporation' organisational culture is led by a strong executive with limited opportunities for methods of consensus-building or input from students. Within this culture, student representation has the role of monitoring and holding the institution accountable for the quality of the student experience. Finally, an 'enterprise' organisational culture is one in which decision-making is strategic and tactical to meet the needs of both students as clients and the higher education market.

Van der Velden suggests that while bureaucratic and corporate institutions can respond rapidly to the demands of external priorities, their

> centralising cultures locate the power of decision-making away from the classroom experience to the committee or senior management level, where detailed or individual student concerns cannot be considered [. . .] it seems much more effective to work with one's Students Union in partnership (collegium), or as a fellow stakeholder (enterprise), either directly or through localised, empowered representation. The collegium and the enterprise culture allow for a more direct involvement with students.
>
> (2012, p. 245)

Implementing student engagement in quality, therefore, is dependent on, or requires a commitment also to whole-institution transformation of organisational culture. The challenge remains that a devolved and agile culture that enables individual students to have direct contact with quality processes also conversely requires a transformation of the external drivers and systemic structures to facilitate genuine collaborative or progressive engagement with student voices at all levels of the institution and sector.

A further challenge to successful involvement of students in the quality of higher education is the way in which student engagement has been largely defined as performative and behavioural. Milburn-Shaw and Walker (2016) note that student engagement, as it is articulated in quality mechanisms such as the NSSE and AUSSE, focuses on measuring the quality of student behaviours such as purposeful engagement, participation and attendance as a means for achieving high-quality learning outcomes. They argue that the 'priority afforded to behavioural engagement has the negative outcome of promoting passive compliance; (p. 5). Macfarlane (2015) goes further, suggesting that universities increasingly require evidence that students are giving

> a *bodily performance* by attending class, or virtually via online forums; a *dispositional performance* through a willingness to participate in learning processes such as group work and class discussion; and an *emotional performance* in respect to social values and practices demanding compliance and confession.
>
> (p. 339, original emphasis)

These performances, he argues are having 'a negative effect on the rights of students as autonomous adults who have entered a voluntary phase of education' (p. 339). While the idea of students-as-partners continues to be extolled, these coexistent expectations about the performative nature of desirable student engagement in learning are increasingly informing the definitions of what constitutes high-quality pedagogy as well as contributing to a reprioritising of the role of students as a data source for measures of quality.

The potential to track students' physical and digital footprint as they enter and exit lecture theatres, libraries and virtual learning environments and combine it with information on their prior qualifications, current assessment grades and demographic data is increasingly promoted as a vital tool in a university's approach to quality assurance and enhancement. For example, it is suggested that these learning analytics can provide individual teachers with information about the progress of their students or the effectiveness of their teaching and learning activities. Institutions can also use the data as a diagnostic tool on a systematic level to identify students at risk of withdrawal or failure for targeted interventions as well as to provide institutional evidence of the quality of the provision to external agencies (Sclater, Peasgood & Mullan, 2016). Similarly the concept of learning gain, or the measure of the difference of student performance at two different points in time, is identified as another way in which large-volume student data can be used to enhance teaching and learning, identify best practice and increase institutional accountability. While learning gain is seen as a potential contributor to the quality of higher education, it is also recognised that it will not be the only measure (McGrath, Guerin, Harte, Frearson & Manville, 2015). Nevertheless, the Higher Education Funding Council for England (HEFCE) has invested in a large-scale ongoing learning gain programme that is piloting a series of thirteen longitudinal projects to test and evaluate the validity of different ways to measure student learning gain (HEFCE, 2016).

This increased focus on big data to evidence quality, while it re-establishes students as a data source within Fielding's typology, is seen as decisive in determining the future shape of higher education internationally at the same time as student partnership is also recognised as an important external and institutional driver. There is a potential for robust measures of learning gain to become part of the metrics alongside NSS data for the new Teaching Excellence Framework in England. The danger is that not only does this underscore the role of students as data sources for quality judgements about higher education but also that, with high-stakes institutional reputation on the line, even opportunities for more active student involvement in quality may be concerned with institutional compliance and competition rather than empowerment of students (Taylor and Robinson, 2009). In the UK, the NUS called for a national boycott of the NSS in 2016 in protest at its use as a key metric in the Teaching Excellence Framework and the proposal to link student feedback to the institutional right to increase tuition fees. This highlights the tensions for students as drivers of quality. On this issue the Vice Provost of University College London, Professor Antony Smith argues that

> There is a risk that it is going to drive a wedge between students and their institutions. They will feel their feedback isn't being used to improve their experience, but as a vehicle to put their fees up.
>
> (Quoted in Fazackerley, 2016)

This tension highlights the sometimes unacknowledged complexities of expertise, authority, legitimacy and how student involvement will be used institutionally and at sector level in ways that complicate the straightforward commitment to involve students in quality assurance and enhancement mechanisms.

Recognising and addressing the challenges of student involvement in quality

As students have been involved progressively as evaluators, discussants, consultants or change agents within their programmes, institutions and national sectors, the difficulties of fostering their successful contribution and ensuring the impact this has on their own and others' experience is increasingly recognised. The challenges include a lack of clarity about the rationale and purpose of student involvement in quality processes, the potentially complicated power relationships between students, staff and institutional structures and the inclusiveness of mechanisms for involving all students in quality. Addressing these challenges remains an imperative to ensure that student involvement in quality is more than tokenistic but leads to confidence in the student experience in higher education especially in the context of the changing quality needs of a massified and diversified sector.

As the claims for the value of student involvement have expanded, Ashwin and McVitty (2015) point to vagueness in defining what engagement constitutes and a problematic lack of criticality about the concept. Students are involved in quality processes at all levels. For example in the UK, at the sector level, external quality assurance processes require the participation of students as peer reviewers as part of QAA Higher Education Review in England and Wales, Enhancement Led Institutional Review in Scotland and the Teaching Excellence Framework. Institutions also need to demonstrate, as part of these reviews, the role that students play in institutional-level quality assurance and enhancement processes. The NUS represents the collective voice of students, campaigns and lobbies on issues relevant to the student experience and supports the representation of students at national and institutional level. Within institutions, local students' unions, representational systems within university committees such as quality and standards committee, academic board, teaching and learning committee as well as course representation and participation of students in course design, validation, annual monitoring and periodic review all embed the student voice in local quality processes. At the individual level, student–staff relationships through teaching and assessment provide information on the quality of the learning experience and identify areas to staff for reflection and improvement. The first challenge therefore is to recognise that the motivations for engagement at the macro, meso and micro levels are informed by different ideologies and can variously function for the purposes of accountability or enhancement and compliance or transformation as well as positioning students as consumers or co-creators (Freeman, 2013). Institutional culture also plays a fundamental role in fostering different levels of student involvement in quality.

A second consideration is that, despite a language of empowerment, student–staff collaborations are based on complex, deep-rooted power relations and that staff and institutions wishing to give more voice to students in quality processes have 'to acknowledge that our roles, expertise, responsibilities, and status are different' from those of students (Cook-Sather *et al.*, 2014, p. 7). Carey (2018) points to the challenges of inviting students into university 'ritualised spaces that discourage involvement' such as committee meetings as well as the expectation that student representatives can 'manage partnership in one context with more submissive relationships elsewhere' in their daily interactions with the university (p. 14). Simply involving students in local enhancement activities does not, in and of itself, lead to transformation of existing power structures, particularly if wider institutional culture is not conducive to collaborative or progressive engagement with student expertise (Kandiko Howson & Weller, 2016).

A third issue for student involvement in quality mechanisms is the question of who actually participates in these processes. The extra-curricular nature of many student engagement activities such as curriculum co-design, student peer review, student pedagogic consultancy and course representation can be a significant barrier. For some initiatives, merit-based selection criteria such as previous academic performance likewise can exclude some of the very students least served by the existing curriculum, pedagogies and representational systems. In different contexts, this can mean students in frequently marginalised demographic groups such as students from ethnic minority or low socio-economic backgrounds, but it could also exclude students who are time-poor such as part-time and commuter students, students with caring or employment commitments, students away from the university on placements or study abroad and students who do not have the confidence or social capital to successfully volunteer for opportunities. Drawing on Fielding's (2004) conceptualisation of the student voice in school settings, Kandiko Howson and Weller (2016) suggest that the sometimes

> pragmatic decision to work in partnership with a few students as representatives of all students means that student pedagogic consultants are potentially co-opted into the normative practice of speaking *for* and *about* others as subjects, rather than as transformative agents that challenge existing beliefs about the learning needs of a diverse student cohort.
>
> (p. 2, original emphasis)

There is a danger that student involvement in quality processes can, therefore, only offer insights from a limited number of perspectives, can deliberately or unintentionally exclude already-silenced voices and potentially reinforce modes of representation that fail to acknowledge difference.

There are a number of ways in which both individuals and institutions can start to address these challenges:

- Define the scope of the role students will have in quality assurance and enhancement activities and provide structured support to enable all students to understand and participate equally within the 'ritualised spaces' of the university (Lizzio and Wilson, 2009).
- Reflect on how student involvement in individual quality processes fits within the wider organisational culture of the university in relation to Carey's (2018) hierarchy of institutional actions. Identify at the outset how to negotiate between the aims and outcomes of student involvement and institutional or external regulation or obligations.
- Discuss questions of power, authenticity and differential expertise openly as part of the process of involving students in quality assurance and enhancement processes and validate the distinctive knowledge and perspective diverse stakeholders bring to understanding complex issues as 'experts by experience'.
- Explore the ways in which macro-, meso- and micro-level opportunities for student involvement in quality processes work together to ensure that individual and local engagement feeds into programme-level and institution-level quality assurance, decision-making and enhancement and vice versa.
- Consider critically the selection criteria and expected modes of participation for student involvement in quality processes, particularly where narrowly-defined, performative measures of engagement or extra-curricular commitments might further exclude unheard voices (Bovill, Cook-Sather, Felten, Millard, & Moore-Cherry, 2016).

Conclusion

While student involvement in quality assurance and enhancement in higher education has the potential to transform the relationship between universities and their students and undermine the student-as-consumer rhetoric of recent policy drivers, there is a danger that student engagement in practice can be tokenistic and reinforce a compliance culture. Failing to acknowledge and address the challenges of implementing effective student involvement at individual, programme, institution and sector level will limit the impact of seeking and responding to the needs of students as 'experts by experience' in higher education. The current direction of international higher education is simultaneously reconfiguring the role of students-as-partners while also conceptualising students as a data source within big data sets. This could offer the opportunity for targeted and personalised learning provision but also an even more sophisticated picture of institutional effectiveness in relation to institutional competitors and benchmarks in the higher education market. How institutions manage the potential tensions between these two agenda is central to the future of student involvement in quality and their relationship to their institutions. Clarifying the role of students and the impact of their involvement within quality processes, making quality processes understandable to students, acknowledging and mitigating the power differentials between students, staff and institutions and paying deliberate attention to making quality assurance and enhancement processes more inclusive are also fundamental to creating a progressive organisational culture of quality.

References

Ashwin, P. & McVitty, D. (2015). The meanings of student engagement: implications for policies and practices, in A. Curaj, L. Matei, R. Pricopie, J. Salmi & P. Scott (Eds.), *The European Higher Education Area: Between Critical Reflections and Future Policies* (pp. 343–359). Cham: Springer International Publishing.

Bovill, C., Aitkin, G., Hutchison, J., Morrison, F., Roseweir, K, Scott, A. & Sotannde, S. (2010). Experiences of learning through collaborative evaluation from a masters programme in professional education. *International Journal for Academic Development, 15(2)*, 143–154. doi:10.1080/13601441003738343

Bovill, C., Cook-Sather, A. & Felten, P. (2011). Students as co-creators of teaching approaches, course design and curricula: implications for academic developers. *International Journal for Academic Development, 16(2)*, 133–145. doi:10.1080/1360144X.2011.568690

Bovill, C., Cook-Sather, A., Felten, P., Millard, L. & Moore-Cherry, N. (2016). Addressing potential challenges in co-creating learning and teaching: overcoming resistance, navigating institutional norms and ensuring inclusivity in student-staff partnerships. *Higher Education, 71*, 195–208. doi:10.1007/s10734-015-9896-4

Bunce, L., Baird, A. & Jones, S. (2017). The student-as-consumer approach in higher education and its effects on academic performance. *Studies in Higher Education, 42(11)*, 1958–1978. doi:10.1080/03075079.2015.1127908

Carey, P. (2018). The impact of institutional culture, policy and process on student engagement in university decision-making. *Perspectives, Policy and Practice in Higher Education, 22(1)*, 11–18. doi:10.1080/13603108.2016.1168754

Case, S., Ugwudike, P., Haines, K., Harris, K. & Owen, J. (2014). The Swansea Student Engagement Project: students and staff as partners in programme review and enhancement. *Enhancing Learning in the Social Sciences*, 1–19. Retrieved from http://www.tandfonline.com/doi/abs/10.11120/elss.2014.00027

Cook-Sather, A. & Alter, Z. (2011). What is and what can be: how a liminal position can change learning and teaching in higher education. *Anthropology & Education Quarterly, 42(1)*, 37–53. doi:10.1111/j.1548-1492.2010.01109.x

Cook-Sather, A. & Luz, A. (2015). Greater engagement in and responsibility for learning: what happens when students cross the threshold of student–faculty partnership. *Higher Education Research & Development, 34(6)*, 1097–1109. doi:10.1080/07294360.2014.911263

Cook-Sather, A., Bovill, C. & Felten, P. (2014). *Engaging Students as Partners in Learning and Teaching: A Guide for Faculty*. San Francisco: Jossey-Bass.

Dickerson, C., Jarvis, J. & Stockwell, L. (2016). Staff–student collaboration: student learning from working together to enhance educational practice in higher education. *Teaching in Higher Education, 21(3)*, 249–265. doi:10.1080/13562517.2015.1136279

Fazackerley, A. (2016, November 22). Universities and NUS plan boycott of flagship teaching rankings. *The Guardian*. Retrieved from https//www.theguardian.com/education/2016/nov/22/universities-nus-boycott-teaching-excellence-framework-tuition-fees

Fielding, M. (2001). Students as radical agents of change. *Journal of Educational Change, 2*, 123–141. doi:10.1023/A:1017949213447

Fielding, M. (2004). Transformative approaches to student voice: theoretical underpinnings, recalcitrant realities. *British Educational Research Journal, 30(2)*, 295–311. doi:10.1080/0141192042000195236

Freeman, R. (2013). Student engagement in practice: ideologies and power in course representation systems. In E. Dunne and D. Owen (Eds.), *The Student Engagement Handbook: Practice in Higher Education* (pp. 146–161). Bingley: Emerald.

Healey, M., Mason O'Connor, K. & Broadfoot, P. (2010). Reflecting on engaging students in the process and product of strategy development for learning, teaching and assessment: an institutional example. *International Journal for Academic Development, 15(1)*, 19–32. doi:10.1080/13601440903529877

Healey, M., Flint, A. & Harrington, K. (2014). *Engagement through Partnership: Students as Partners in Learning and Teaching in Higher Education*. York: Higher Education Academy. Retrieved from https://www.heacademy.ac.uk/system/files/resources/engagement_through_partnership.pdf

HEFCE. (2016). *Learning Gain*. Retrieved 15 December 2016, from http://www.hefce.ac.uk/lt/lg/projects/

Kandiko Howson, C. & Weller, S. (2016). Defining pedagogic expertise: students and new lecturers as co-developers in learning and teaching. *Teaching & Learning Inquiry, 4(2)*. Retrieved from http://tlijournal.com/tli/index.php/TLI/article/view/109

Kay, J., Dunne, E. & Hutchinson, J. (2010). *Rethinking the Values of Higher Education – Students as Change Agents*. Gloucester: Quality Assurance Agency. Retrieved from http://www.qaa.ac.uk/en/Publications/Documents/Rethinking-the-values-of-higher-education—-students-as-change-agents.pdf

Klemenčič, M. (2012). The changing conceptions of student participation in HE governance in the EHEA. In A. Curaj, P. Scott, L. Vlasceanu & L. Wilson (Eds.), *European Higher Education at the Crossroads: Between the Bologna Process and National Reforms* (pp. 631–653). Dordecht: Springer.

Lizzio, A. & Wilson, K. (2009). Student participation in university governance: the role conceptions and sense of efficacy of student representatives on departmental committees. *Studies in Higher Education, 34(1)*, 69–84. doi:10.1080/03075070802602000

Macfarlane, B. (2015). Student performativity in higher education: converting learning as a private space into a public performance. *Higher Education Research & Development, 34(2)*, 338–350. doi:10.1080/07294360.2014.956697

McGrath, C.H., Guerin, B., Harte, E., Frearson, M. & Manville, C. (2015). *Learning Gain in Higher Education*. Santa Monica, C.A.: RAND Corporation. Retrieved from http://www.rand.org/content/dam/rand/pubs/research_reports/RR900/RR996/RAND_RR996.pdf

Milburn-Shaw, H. & Walker, D. (2016). The politics of student engagement. *Politics*, 1–15. doi:10.1177/0263395715626157

Molesworth, M., Nixon, E. & Scullion, R. (2009). Having, being and higher education: the marketisation of the university and the transformation of the student into consumer. *Teaching in Higher Education, 14(3)*, 277–287. doi:10.1080/13562510902898841

NUS (National Union of Students) (2009). *A Manifesto for Partnership*. Retrieved from https://www.nus.org.uk/PageFiles/12238/A%20Manifesto%20for%20Partnership.pdf

QAA (Quality Assurance Agency) (2016). *UK Quality Code for Higher Education: Part B: Assuring and Enhancing Academic Quality*. Chapter B5: Student Engagement. Gloucester: QAA.

Sclater, N., Peasgood, A. & Mullan, J. (2016). *Learning Analytics in Higher Education: A Review of UK and International Practice Full Report*. Bristol: Jisc. Retrieved from https://www.jisc.ac.uk/sites/default/files/learning-analytics-in-he-v3.pdf

Seale, J. (2009). Doing student voice work in higher education: an exploration of the value of participatory methods. *British Educational Research Journal, 36(6)*, 995–1015. doi:10.1080/01411920903342038

Seale, J. (2016). How can we confidently judge the extent to which student voice in higher education has been genuinely amplified? A proposal for a new evaluation framework. *Research Papers in Education, 31(2)*, 212–233. doi: 10.1080/02671522.2015.1027726

Skilton, C. (2011). Involving experts by experience in assessing students' readiness to practise: the value of experiential learning in student reflection and preparation for practice. *Social Work Education, 30(3)*, 299–311. doi:10.1080/02615479.2010.482982

Standards and Guidelines for Quality Assurance in the European Higher Education Area (ESG) (2015). Brussels, Belgium. Retrieved from http://www.enqa.eu/wp-content/uploads/2015/11/ESG_2015.pdf.

Stringer, M. & Finlay, C. (1993). Assuring quality through student evaluation. In R. Ellis (Ed.) *Quality Assurance for University Teaching.* (pp. 92–112). Buckingham: SRHE/Open University Press.

Taylor, C. & Robinson, C. (2009). Student voice: theorising power and participation. *Pedagogy, Culture & Society, 17(2)*, 161–175. doi:10.1080/14681360902934392

Tertiary Education Quality Standards Agency (TEQSA) (2015) *Higher Education Standards Framework.* Retrieved from https://www.teqsa.gov.au/higher-education-standards-framework-2015.

Van der Velden, G. (2012). Institutional level student engagement and organisational cultures. *Higher Education Quarterly, 66(3)*, 227–247. doi:10.1111/j.1468–2273.2012.00521.x

17 Quality Assurance in Health Care
The Implications for University Teaching

Dorothy Whittington

Introduction

Quality assurance in higher education often refers to techniques and procedures first developed in industry and commerce. In fact there is an equally important and separate tradition of quality assurance in health care.

Quality and its assurance are important in health care and in higher education for similar reasons. In each context demographic and technological changes have increased demand for services. Satisfaction of this increased demand requires additional resources but in periods of recession both health and higher education are targets for economic scrutiny and cost cutting. Also both patients and students are increasingly aware of their rights and often more generally knowledgeable. They are therefore less likely to defer to professionals delivering services and more likely to have views on service standards. Professionals in both sectors have responded to these pressures by clarifying and reasserting their claims to special knowledge and competence. Thus funders, consumers and professionals have all declared their entitlement to debate the definition, assurance and improvement of service quality.

This chapter begins by outlining three phases in the historical development of health care quality assurance. They are as follows.

1   Trust in professionals
    Quality is assured by developing institutions through which the trustworthiness of individual professionals can be determined.
2   Codification and control
    Quality is assured by setting standards for practice that all professionals must meet and by assessing outcomes across all relevant areas of practice.
3   Improvement culture
    Quality is assured by engaging with professionals to develop knowledge, skills, and attitudes that engender an improvement culture throughout health care organisations and systems. Practice improvement includes acknowledging and learning from error.

Comparison is then made with quality assurance in university teaching, and health care approaches that could be adapted for higher education are described. The chapter concludes by suggesting that mutual benefit would accrue from regular dialogue between quality specialists in health care and in higher education.

The development of health care quality assurance

Trust in professionals

Concern for health care quality and recognition that practitioners have a duty to uphold standards have a very long history. Hippocrates (c.460–c.370 BCE) not only provided first descriptions of many common ailments but also recommended that practitioners be clean, honest, calm and understanding (Grammaticus & Diamantis, 2008).

By the Middle Ages the merchant and craft guilds were making practical competence and successful completion of apprenticeship a requirement for admission. Membership brought various protections including a degree of monopoly on practice and also permission to advertise high quality goods or services. There is evidence of the existence of a London barbers' guild as early as 1308; and of some of its members carrying out surgical procedures (Jackson, 2008). The 'guild of pepperers' (established in 1180) had members who specialised in the medicinal use of herbs and spices and eventually became the Worshipful Society of Apothecaries of London (Worshipful Society of Apothecaries, 2017). The 'Incorporation of Surgeons and Barbers of Edinburgh' (later the Royal College of Surgeons of Edinburgh) was established in 1505 and required its members to have 'full knowledge of anatomy and surgical procedures' with admission as a 'master' only after 'full testing' of knowledge and competence at the end of the apprenticeship (Royal College of Surgeons of Edinburgh, 2017). In England, Henry VIII gave the College of Physicians its Royal Charter in 1518 so as to licence those qualified to practise medicine and to 'curb the activities' of those who were not (Davenport *et al.*, 2001). Other Royal Colleges emerged as medicine became more specialised but they had a similar focus on education, competence and 'fitness to practice'.

From its inception therefore, professional regulation in health care was both a way of demarcating and protecting professional groups and a way of guiding patients towards good quality. That it was only partly successful is evidenced by the extent of continuing public concern over scandal and quackery. Concern became political agitation in the 18th and 19th centuries and in 1858 the Medical Act was passed. It established the body that became the General Medical Council and gave it powers over the content of medical education. It also required it to maintain and publish an up-to-date register of qualified practitioners and to remove from it practitioners who had engaged in 'infamous conduct in any professional respect' (Rivlin, 1997). The Royal Colleges retained their responsibility for education for specialist practice including 'membership' examinations, success in which would be required for admission to the various specialist parts of the GMC register. They also had responsibility for ensuring that specialist training took place in suitable clinical environments and under the supervision of appropriately experienced practitioners.

Other health care professions began to set up associations and gradually established standards for education and good practice. Legislation for the registration of midwives was passed in 1902 (Stevens, 2002) and for a General Nursing Council in 1920 (Rivett, 1986). A Council for the Professions Supplementary to Medicine was set up in 1960 to maintain registers and regulate training for many other health care groups. Its 2001 successor, the Health and Social Care Professions Council, is now responsible for all registrable health and social care professions other than medicine, nursing, midwifery and pharmacy (which has had its own General Pharmaceutical Council since 2010).

All of these professional bodies promote quality of care through ensuring high standards of practitioner knowledge and competence but there is now a clear distinction between the professional associations, which are independent membership organisations, and the regulatory councils, which are statutory bodies with 'arm's length' accountability to government. Individual professionals are not obliged to join their association, but can only continue to practise by paying a registration fee to their council to maintain their 'state registered' status. The regulatory councils are themselves regulated by the Professional Standards Authority for Health and Social Care. All of this is designed to assure patients and the general public that registered professionals can be trusted to deliver high quality care.

Codification and control

In the early 20th century health care quality assurance began to extend to a wider focus on overall standards of care and on patient and population outcomes. A number of outcome studies appeared in the US and UK in the 1930s, including, for example, regularly published 'enquiries' into preventable maternal deaths, anaesthetic deaths, deaths in people under 50, and perioperative deaths. National and international statistics on mortality and on the incidence and epidemiology of diseases also began to appear. At a less formal level, the long-standing medical tradition of clinical meetings to consider unusual or problematic cases assumed greater importance. Some of these meetings also began to involve nurses, pharmacists and other non-medical clinicians.

By the 1980s quality assurance in health care was a topic of public and professional discussion in many countries, and global organisations like the World Health Organization published guidance and commentary (WHO, 1985). In the UK the Royal College of General Practitioners launched a quality initiative in 1983 (RCGP, 1983, 1985a, 1985b) and by 1990 GPs were involved in quality activities ranging from large-scale patient surveys (Health Care Research Unit, Newcastle Upon Tyne University 1990) to small informal practice meetings (Irvine, 1990).

In hospital medicine, too, many quality schemes were initiated. They were usually referred to as *'medical* audit' (HMSO, 1990; Shaw, 1990) although surveys (Casanova, 1990; Dalley *et al.* 1991) demonstrated that the professions most heavily involved were nursing and physiotherapy. Participation in audit is now a requirement for all postgraduate medical trainees from the Foundation Years through to the higher specialist training grades (General Medical Council, 2016), and applicants for consultant posts are likely to reflect on that experience as a positive feature of their CV. Reporting on audit and other quality improvement activities is also a component of the regular appraisal and revalidation process that all GMC registrants have had to undergo since 2012 (GMC, 2017). Not having participated in quality improvement could thus contribute to adverse appraisal results and, conceivably, to removal of registered status.

Medical audit varies in approach and methodology, as clinical context dictates, but its core features are essentially observation, review and improvement, with a view to the enhancement of clinical outcomes and of patients' experience of care. It is the clinical version of the 'plan, do, study, and improve' quality cycle developed by W. E. Deming for the US army of occupation in Japan (Deming, 1982, 1986). Japan's remarkable economic success in the late 20th century was often attributed to widespread adoption of quality control and improvement techniques and it was assumed that their application to health care would have similar impact.

In the new millennium ever increasing demand for expensive health care coincided with economic recession and global debate on the affordability of publicly funded services of all kinds. This inevitably led to discussion of relationships between health care costs and quality.

In the US both the Medicare/Medicaid system of public health insurance and the profit-driven system of private health insurance were frequently criticised for encouraging the provision of 'unnecessary' care (Ezekiel & Fuchs, 2008; Berwick & Hackbarth, 2012) and the proportion of US GDP devoted to health care was repeatedly shown to be much higher than in other developed countries. OECD statistics for 2015 give 16.9 per cent for the US, 9.9 per cent for the UK and 5.2 percent for Turkey, with a median of 9.5 per cent (OECD, 2017). Despite its substantial history and some notable successes, US health care quality assurance seems to have done little to improve care overall. Community care and public health have been markedly resistant to quality enhancement. Davis *et al.* (2014) compared the US with ten other 'advanced' countries and noted that health care performance was particularly deficient with respect to healthy lives (including infant mortality and life expectancy), access to care, equity and efficiency. Difficulties were compounded by fragmented provision, limited continuity of care and poor communication between providers.

In the UK, concern for quality of care was a primary factor in the genesis of the NHS. Aneurin Bevan, introducing his National Health Service Bill to the House of Commons in July 1948, said that the proposed service was designed to 'universalise the best' and 'to provide the people of Britain, no matter where they may be, with the same level of service'. These statements of intent imply a system for defining 'the best' and establishing standards for 'level of service', i.e. a system of quality assurance. Specific government interest in systems of quality assurance can be detected from as early as the 1950s. The Guillebaud Committee (HMSO, 1956), when given the remit of examining costs in the NHS, commented, 'it is one of the problems of management to find the right indices for efficiency'. They went on to propose comparisons between health authorities in respect of 'average occupancy of beds, length of stay of patients, bed turnover interval, waiting time, etc.'. This was probably the first set of UK 'national targets'.

The Thatcher government's *Working for Patients* White Paper (HMSO, 1989) and the subsequent Health Service Reform Bill established self-governing Trusts and set up the 'internal market' in which 'purchasers' would 'commission' care from 'providers' within centrally controlled budgets. It also confronted the issue of quality assurance directly and proposed participation in what was now called 'clinical' audit for all health professionals. It was the landslide Labour victory of May 1997 however that provided the platform for the most sweeping changes in the UK health care quality systems. Significantly, health care organisations as a whole (not just clinical professionals) would be held accountable for the quality of service they provided and for health care outcomes as well as financial acumen.

The 'New NHS: Modern and Dependable' NHS Reform Act (HMSO, 1997) set out a plan for national service standards, guidance on new drugs and treatments, and public service agreements whereby funding would be tied to quality. It also established a system of 'clinical governance' for every Trust designed to run alongside financial governance and to have parity with it. This was followed in 1998 by a more detailed document *A First Class Service – Quality in the NHS* (Department of Health, 1998) that proposed an overarching national performance framework, bringing together standards for different specialties and areas of activity. A Commission for Health Improvement (CHI) was to be responsible for assessing the extent to which Trusts were achieving standards, and effectively managing clinical governance and quality assurance. Specific targets focusing on mortality figures and cancer referral times were set.

'A First Class Service' was an aspirational document setting out a national vision for high quality care delivered 'through clinical governance underpinned by lifelong learning and professional self-regulation'. Action for quality included recognising the commitment and experience of staff, disseminating and building on good practice, and, for the first time, establishing a national survey of patient views and experience. There was also a commitment to create a 'culture of innovation and improvement' and to improve 'public accountability and openness' while tackling 'unacceptable variations in service quality and equity of access'.

The 1999 Health Act[1] (National Archive, 2017a) formally established both CHI and the National Institute for Clinical Excellence (NICE), which would provide guidance, standards and information on high quality health care. NICE was constituted as an independent body making recommendations 'based on the best available evidence of what works, in terms of both clinical and cost effectiveness'. Each piece of guidance or quality standard is developed by an independent panel of relevant clinicians, scientists and lay representatives. Guidance is disseminated across all NHS organisations and all are expected to have processes in place to take account of it and to implement it expeditiously. NICE has particular responsibility for examining the cost-effectiveness of new treatments, drugs and technologies and has acted as a gatekeeper for their adoption in the NHS. This has led to regular controversy, sometimes strained relations with the pharmaceutical industry, and recurrent political debate over its role in the establishment of NHS resource priorities. NICE was given additional powers to provide similar guidance on social care issues in 2012 when it became the National Institute for Health and Care Excellence but kept the NICE acronym (National Institute for Health and Care Excellence, 2017). In 2014 it was asked for the first time to produce guidance on safe staffing levels.

In 2000 the Blair government published the NHS Plan (Department of Health, 2000) which committed to substantial additional investment and proposed reforms designed to localise service commissioning in new 'Primary Care Trusts'. The aim was to increase patient choice of provider, and provider competition in securing that choice. Provider Trusts were now encouraged to compete for 'Foundation Trust' status by demonstrating to a new regulatory body (now known as Monitor) that they had achieved required standards and, in particular, that they were, and were likely to continue to be, financially viable. Later in 2001 all Trusts providing acute care were allocated 'star ratings' from zero to three which were said to reflect successful standards of performance against targets and overall. Trusts with three stars could apply for Foundation status and the additional autonomy that brought, and those with zero stars were offered 'support in developing an action plan for improvement'. The star rating system was heavily criticised as both unreliable and partial, but performance assessment within a national targets framework became (and remains) a central plank in NHS quality management. By 2002 the framework had expanded and included the now familiar targets for waiting times in Accident and Emergency departments, and for outpatient appointments and inpatient admissions. Responsibility for performance management and assessment also moved from the NHS executive to CHI so that the same body now assessed clinical governance standards and performance standards. CHI became the Commission for Healthcare Audit and Inspection in 2003 and a similar organisation (the Commission for Social Care Inspection) for social care was set up (National Archive, 2017b). The word 'inspection' reflected the manageriality of their new remit. CHAI developed new Trust ratings systems (with increased emphasis on self-assessment), and was given power to recommend 'special measures' where performance was unsatisfactory. It also took on inspection of private and voluntary sector health care providers. The two commissions were eventually merged in 2008 as the Care Quality Commission (CQC) with a remit for 'registration, compliance and enforcement'. Registration with the new commission was compulsory and it had powers to close 'failing' organisations although closure of NHS organisations proved both complex and contentious. Monitor's role in the assessment of financial management and viability remained and the 2012 Health and Social Care Act (National Archive, 2017c) gave it new powers to 'license' all NHS providers whether they had Foundation status or not. It also took over the Trust Development Agency, which had been working to help Trusts working through 'special measures' or otherwise failing to progress to Foundation status. From 2012 therefore all health care providers (NHS and independent, private or voluntary sector) had to register with CQC and all *NHS* providers had to hold a Monitor licence.

The 2002 NHS Plan also outlined new approaches to quality assurance. They included additional powers for the GMC, improving transparency in fitness to practise procedures; and the establishment of the Council for Healthcare Regulatory Excellence (now the Professional Standards Authority) as the regulator of health care regulators. It also proposed annual appraisal for all doctors employed in or contracted to the NHS and a scheme for mandatory recording and reporting of 'adverse healthcare incidents' with an associated national database of such events to be managed by a National Patient Safety Agency. Enhanced patient and public involvement in service decision-making and improvement was also part of the plan and all Trusts were required to set up a patients' 'forum' and to use it and other mechanisms to collect and respond to local feedback on service quality.

In retrospect it is clear that the 2002 NHS Plan included each of the main components of current NHS quality assurance. Thus professional bodies were to have more power but were also to be more publicly accountable; individual clinicians were to undergo annual appraisals and trainees were expected to participate in clinical audit; NICE guidance was to be universally disseminated and implemented; Trusts were to have statutory responsibility for meeting performance standards as well as maintaining financial viability and both were to be externally scrutinised and reviewed; the National Patient Safety Agency was to have responsibility for recording 'adverse incidents' and disseminating information on their occurrence, causes and future prevention; and there was at least a commitment to making better use of patient feedback and opinion at local as well as national levels. Quality assurance was to be 'everybody's business' where it had once been the enthusiasm of a few.

Improvement culture

Actual improvement in service quality however, was less than universal. Contributory factors included economic recession, increasingly expensive drugs and treatments, an older and sicker population, and failure to act on the Wanless Report's (HMSO, 2004) warning that the continuing affordability of universal health care depended on public health and disease prevention including full public engagement with lifestyle change. The years that followed were characterised by a succession of well-publicised health and social care failings and 'scandals', enquiries, expert reports and resulting modifications to quality systems. Each event led to significant change but the most far-reaching changes emanated from the problems encountered at the Mid Staffordshire Hospitals Foundation Trust between 2005 and 2009.

Patients and their relatives had complained to Stafford Hospital about poor care and in some cases about the death of relatives. They were not satisfied with the Trust's response and started to campaign for an independent enquiry. The Healthcare Commission investigated the Trust in 2008 and reported significant concern about mortality rates in patients admitted through A&E. It detailed other substantial inadequacies in care and instances of patients left in 'appalling conditions'. It was clear that Mid Staffs was not delivering the high standards of care notionally required of Foundation Trusts, and an independent enquiry chaired by Robert Francis QC was set up.

Reporting in February 2010 the first Francis enquiry (National Archive, 2017d) was very critical of Trust management, noting that there had been a 'climate of fear' in which targets had to be achieved 'at all costs', and often by ignoring significantly poor care in 'untargeted' areas. The report made eighteen recommendations, one of which was that the Trust should lose its Foundation status. It also suggested that there could be implications for other Trusts and for the processes through which Monitor assessed Trusts for Foundation status. Across the change of government in 2010 both outgoing and incoming Ministers of Health agreed that a broader public enquiry was required and Robert Francis was asked to chair that too.

In similar vein to the first Francis Report, a Health Select Committee report of 2011 noted that both Monitor and the CQC had emphasised their inspectorial 'policeman' role to the detriment of their role in encouraging quality improvement. It also observed that patient feedback was not being properly solicited through patient forums and that there were flaws in how complaints were dealt with. The Health and Social Care Act of 2012 strengthened and clarified the roles of Monitor and the CQC and also set up a new network of patient and client feedback organisations based on localities rather than individual health care organisations. This new 'Healthwatch' system was to facilitate feedback on care received from all relevant organisations and on communication between them. Poor communication with 'partner' organisations had been highlighted in the first enquiry into Mid Staffs hospitals.

The full public enquiry reported in February 2013 (National Archive, 2017e) and focused on system-wide issues as well as local events leading to the substantial failures documented in the earlier reports. It noted that 'warning signs' had been available to the Trust from very many sources including loss of 'star ratings', negative clinical peer reviews, poor reports from Royal College accreditation teams, auditors' warnings on poor risk management systems, aspects of both staff and patient survey results, and internal whistleblowing alleging serious deficiencies in A&E leadership. The Health Care Commission had expressed concern at a relatively early stage but this was not known to other regulatory agencies, including Monitor. The Trust's application for Foundation status was thus allowed to continue and indeed to lead to further staff cuts in an organisation already failing to meet basic care standards. As the report notes 'the quest for Foundation status above all else' led to the prioritisation of financial considerations over staffing levels, service quality and, ultimately, patient safety.

The multiplicity of regulatory and supervisory organisations feeding into the Trust and often failing to communicate with each other was criticised at length but there was also heavy criticism of the Trust's own organisational culture and leadership. It had been 'defensive, secretive, inward looking, and unwilling to accept criticism'. It had also 'accepted poor standards of care' and had 'failed to put the patient first'. The report made almost 300 recommendations for action across the health care system. They included clarification of national quality management and regulation but, more significantly, stronger clinical leadership, patient focus in all contexts, and 'openness, transparency, and candour in all of the system's business'. Specifically, the report proposed a common culture where concerns about poor quality could be raised and discussed without fear; where true information about outcomes could be shared with staff, patients and the public; and where patients who had been harmed by a health care service would be informed of the fact and offered an appropriate remedy whether or not a complaint had been made. These three proposals became known collectively as the 'duty of candour'.

Initial government response to the Francis Report was positive and there were immediate commitments to increase the number of specialist clinicians involved in quality regulation, to improve and speed up professional 'fitness to practice' proceedings, to develop a 'vetting and barring' procedure for managers and to produce more readily accessible performance information. Expert reviews were commissioned examining hospital mortality figures and related methodology (Keogh, 2013) and exploring complaints handling (Clwyd & Hart, 2013).

The Francis emphases on patient safety and promotion of a culture of openness and candour resonated with NHS professionals who had already been involved in pilot quality improvement projects using methods developed by Professor Donald Berwick in the US Institute for Healthcare Improvement (IHI). With the possible exception of the recent 'Obamacare' reforms, US health care has never aspired to universal public funding, and publicly funded health insurance is largely restricted to the very old and the very poor. The '*national* standards' central to NHS quality assurance are generally regarded as unacceptably directive, and the universal NICE guidance on the affordability of new drugs and devices is commonly referred to in the US as NHS 'rationing'. Partly for these reasons US health care quality assurance mostly originates from specific provider groups or from not-for-profit or charitable organisations. The IHI was founded in 1991 as a charitably funded organisation building upon earlier work exploring the applicability of then current quality management ideas, including the Deming cycle and Juran's ideas on Total Quality Management in health care (Deming, 1982; 1986; Juran, 1951). The IHI approach to improvement is based on focus on clear, small-scale, measurable improvements usually worked on by collaborating groups from more than one site or organisation. Success is measured using 'rapid cycle' methods and is then spread out to comparable sites or organisations. The approach has developed over time to include ideas on balancing accountability with 'blame free' reporting of error and is now referred to as 'improvement science' (IHI, 2017a, 2017b). IHI has more recently professed a 'Triple Aim' for improvement of entire health systems by simultaneous focus on population health, patient experience of care and costs of care; but the basic principles remain (Whittington *et al.*, 2015). It has become a worldwide organisation involving large numbers of health professionals in its education programmes, and developing projects with governments, NGOs and health care organisations across the globe.

The Francis Report recommendations did not specifically suggest importation of IHI ideas but it is likely that they led to the commissioning of a review into 'Patient Safety in the NHS' carried out by the founder and President Emeritus of the IHI, Professor Berwick. The review was published in 2013 and among other conclusions it recommended that quantitative targets should be used with caution, that the NHS should abandon blame as a tool, that responsibilities for quality and improvement should be clearer and simpler, and that there was need for much more education in 'improvement science'. Berwick also noted that the NHS system of regulation and accountability was 'complex and bewildering' (Berwick, 2013).

A few months after publication of the Berwick Report, government produced its final response to the Francis enquiry in *Hard Truths: the journey to putting patients first* (Department of Health, 2013). It detailed action already taken, including clarification of the roles of the Care Quality Commission and Monitor, and a new regime for 'failing' Trusts. It also set out commitments to streamline complaints processes; to establish a statutory 'duty of candour' obligation on all registered care providers; to make 'wilful neglect' in care contexts a criminal offence; to make provision of 'false or misleading information regarding care provided' a criminal offence; to raise educational standards for Health Care Assistants and Care Support Workers; and to establish a 'fit and proper person' test for executive and non-executive directors of health care Trusts. Legislation followed in each of these areas.

In addition to these responses, clarification of regulatory roles in 2015 included creation of a new organisation called NHS Improvement, which would bring together Monitor, the Patient Safety Agency (with its responsibility for collating and disseminating information on adverse clinical incidents) and other organisations with responsibility for Trust development and support. Alongside this there would be an independent patient safety investigation group (IPSIS) with a remit to listen objectively to a broad range of patient and stakeholder views. NICE was also allowed to expand its remit to include guidance on safe staffing levels and has since commented on safe registered nurse numbers at ward level. Finally, Robert Francis was commissioned again to undertake a substantial review of 'whistleblowing' policies and the experience of NHS staff whistleblowers (National Archive, 2017f). His recommendations included the appointment of a whistleblowing 'guardian' in every Trust; support for Trusts in setting up clear and consistent whistleblowing procedures and developing 'just' cultures (Boysen, 2013); new approaches to the reduction of bullying; and specific protections for 'vulnerable' groups including students and trainees who might feel reluctant or unable to raise concerns. Government accepted all of these recommendations in April 2016.

The events in Mid Staffs thus led to far-reaching change and development in NHS quality policy and process. Its main components however remain very similar to those referenced in the 2002 NHS Plan. They are as follows.

- The various professional bodies and regulatory councils have responsibility for the competence and fitness to practice of individual clinicians, and for maintaining registers. They accredit initial education in universities and elsewhere; provide and oversee programmes of specialist clinical education, including quality standards and student experience in units taking trainees; and encourage and oversee continuous professional development programmes.
- Individual clinicians (particularly medical practitioners) are required to undergo annual appraisal and to have their registration regularly revalidated (the first four year 'cycle' of revalidation of all GMC registrants concluded in March 2016).
- NICE provides independent evidence-based guidance on the effectiveness and affordability of new treatments and devices. It has recently also provided guidance on staffing. Guidance is regularly disseminated and all NHS organisations are expected to implement it.
- Other more specialist bodies offering guidance and quality assurance include the Human Tissues Authority, the Medicines and Healthcare Products Regulatory Agency (MHRA), and the various organisations involved in quality assurance for pathology services.
- Trusts have statutory responsibility for clinical governance as well as financial governance and there is a system for registration and regular scrutiny through the CQC, and for licensing and regular scrutiny through Monitor. There is a national performance framework and targets are set and reviewed annually. All executive and non-executive members of Trust Boards must be 'fit and proper persons' and there is scrutiny before their appointment.
- NHS Improvement offers support to Trusts in difficulties or undergoing substantial change. It is also responsible for patient safety, which involves collating and responding to Trust reports of adverse incidents (involving actual or potential serious harm to patients) and 'never events' (involving such severe harm that they should never occur). This system is under active review and will be replaced by a new Patient Safety Incident Management System (IPSIS) in 2018.
- There is a 'Healthwatch' network that allows patients or members of the public to offer feedback on local care and experience of services. A national 'Overall Patient Experience

Score' is published annually. It is a composite based on results from surveys carried out in specific areas including inpatient care, outpatient care, A&E and community mental health.

- Trusts have a statutory 'duty of candour' to inform and support patients whose care has been poor or harmful. They are encouraged to develop an open, transparent and 'blame free' culture in which whistleblowers are protected and there are anti-bullying policies and procedures.

- All clinical staff are expected to participate in quality improvement and in many cases career progression or maintenance of registered status depends upon it. All doctors in training must take part in clinical audit and many other student professionals also do so.

Outside of this main framework enthusiasts have embraced other approaches to quality enhancement, often in reflection of their currency in private sector management theory. Thus initiatives have been developed based on Total Quality Management (Juran, 1951), Quality Circles (Ishikawa, 1985), Lean Systems (Hanna, 2007), Kaizen (Graban & Swartz, 2012) and more. There is substantial current activity based on Donald Berwick's IHI principles. There are for example fifteen patient safety 'Collaboratives' located in constellations of NHS organisations and their neighbouring universities. IHI patient safety Collaboratives are short-term learning systems bringing together teams from a number of clinical sites with a clear and relatively small-scale improvement focus. These UK teams have been in place since 2015 and have already reported local achievements including reductions in mortality after emergency laparotomy, reductions in inpatient falls, and increase in percentage of mental health patients returning to clinics on time. Also reflecting IHI, NHS Improvement and the Health Foundation charity have established the 'Q Initiative' which aims to create a UK-wide community of 'Improvement Fellows' working together to implement improvement science and share learning. A foundation community of 231 fellows has been established and the aim is to recruit 5000 participants by 2020.

Elements of current UK health care quality assurance can thus be tracked back to each of its three developmental phases – institutionalisation of trust in professionals; codification and control of quality standards; and finally, the development of a quality improvement culture.

Comparisons with higher education teaching

As noted at the beginning of this chapter, quality and its improvement became important in health care and higher education for similar reasons. In each case, too, they have borrowed and adapted models and methodologies from industry and private sector management theory; but there has been surprisingly little collaboration or cross-reference between them.

Teachers in UK higher education, for example, have never been as clearly 'professionalised' as their health care colleagues. There has been substantial progress in developing the Higher Education Academy (HEA) Professional Standards Framework and in awarding fellowship status through recognition or training, but this is not universal. To date HEA has awarded fellowships to around 75,000 staff, but Higher Education Statistics Agency statistics record a total of around 200,000 academic staff in UK HE. HEA also works with discipline groups and teaching improvement units to encourage CPD but that is some distance from the GMC processes for regular revalidation of competence and registration status. In addition while most universities now have a 'teaching route' to career progression, involvement in teaching quality improvement is not a universal requirement.

Like NHS organisations, university teaching is subject to external scrutiny from diverse sources. In HE they include the various systems of external examination; course accreditation by professional and other bodies; and the interventions of the Quality Assurance Agency (QAA) and the Teaching Excellence Framework (TEF) discussed in other chapters of this book. In both the NHS and HE the standards set and the measures used vary considerably depending on the organisation involved, although there is often common ground. While it can be argued that HEI autonomy has steadily reduced, and that the sector has become more centralised as it has expanded, it would be difficult to identify anything quite like the comprehensive NHS National Performance Framework and its mandatory targets. Likewise it has been difficult but not impossible for regulatory bodies like CQC or Monitor to declare NHS organisations 'failures' but in HE there are no analogue arbiters of poor performance. While (as the Berwick Report implied) that may not be entirely a bad thing, it also means that there are few obvious means of giving HE organisations extra support or putting them in 'special measures'. As discussed in several other chapters the publication of TEF indicators and institutional teaching quality league tables are likely to reflect both the advantages and disadvantages of NHS performance management.

The use to which quality information is likely to be put and who has ownership of it are also likely to have an impact on the procedures developed. As discussed earlier, NHS target setting began as an exercise in raising national standards of care and supporting continuous improvement. But as both the Francis Report and the Berwick Report noted, and as recent government emphases on patient centredness have acknowledged, the pursuit of targets became an end in itself and was in many cases antithetical to care quality improvement. Similarly both Monitor and CQC were set up as bodies that would support NHS organisations to improve quality, but became steadily more concerned with public accountability and league tables. It remains to be seen whether TEF processes will follow a similar trajectory.

HEI susceptibility to media scrutiny and 'scandal' is also rather different in character. In the NHS context 'scandals' are usually generated from poor treatment experienced by specific patients, whereas in HE the media focus is more likely to be on overall student outcomes, or on failures of Board-level governance. There is no 'fit and proper person' test of university Board appointees. The NHS response to public scandal or indeed to internally noted poor or harmful care is altogether more systematic than in HE. In universities high failure or attrition rates, poor NSS results, failure to meet the requirements of professional accreditation or negative external examiner reports will all be internally discussed and remedies sought. They may occasionally also be discussed in the media but there is no equivalent to the central NHS analysis and dissemination of learning and improvement from such 'adverse incidents'. It is also debatable whether reporting of poor teaching at any level is 'transparent and blame free' as Robert Francis and Don Berwick would recommend for health care.

Public involvement and feedback too are differently organised. The 'consumer base' for the NHS is potentially the entire population whereas in HE (even given a 50 per cent cohort participation rate) the size and influence of the student group, or even the wider group of stakeholders including families and employers, will always be more restricted. There is little or no aspiration therefore to a universal 'HE Watch' network like Healthwatch offering information and involvement to every citizen. There are national patient/student surveys in both contexts however and (as discussed in other chapters) similar debates around relationships between apparently positive overall ratings, the incidence of local difficulties, and opportunities for improvement. In both contexts too there are opportunities for patient/ student provision of local feedback and involvement in decision-making at local levels, but again in both contexts the success of such arrangements is variable.

Finally, the success and quality of NHS care is supported by an enormous industry of medical and pharmaceutical research and development, results from which are channelled through specialist groups, Royal Colleges and, in particular, through the evidence sifting and assessment carried out by NICE. The evidence base for university teaching quality is significant but less formidable and HEA can encourage its exploration and implementation but cannot mandate it as NICE can. Voluntary quality improvement activity is widespread in both health care and HE teaching, but again there are more systematic incentives (and sanctions) in the NHS than in HE. The HEA fellowship system however is very like the IHI fellowship system newly established in the NHS, and if IHI principles of widespread education in improvement science, local enthusiasm, and aggregation of small local improvements are sound, then the HEA approach may in the end be just as effective.

Berwick's most recent (Berwick, 2016) IHI commentaries posit three eras in US health care quality assurance. The first is one in which there is substantial reliance on the specialised knowledge, personal probity and beneficence of professionals. In the second (and current) era the emphasis has shifted to accountability, scrutiny, complex measurement and performance management involving sanctions, incentives and lack of trust. Berwick now proposes initiation of a third era in which some of the features of the first and second are preserved. These include professional pride, beneficence and commitment to science from the first era (but not its opacity and protectionism) and transparency and patient engagement from the second (but not its cynicism, 'measurement gone wild', and over-reliance on incentives and transactions rather than relationships). His proposed new era will decrease the focus on finance and reject greed as a core incentive, avoid professional prerogative at the expense of the whole system, embrace transparency, listen properly to patients and to colleagues at all levels, protect civility and recommit to improvement science. While some of Berwick's criticisms are specific to the US system and others may be peculiar to health care it could be suggested that quality assurance in UK university teaching lies somewhere between his first and second eras (or indeed the first and second phases identified in this chapter) and may still need protection from their worst excesses.

In summary, the 'trusting professionals' foundation for quality is less culturally embedded and less institutionalised in higher education than in health care; techniques for 'standard setting and outcome assessment' are less well developed, often contentious, and just as politicised as in health care; and the 'development of an improvement culture' remains a work in progress in both settings.

Health care approaches that could be adapted for higher education

The first premise of this chapter is that scrutiny of health care quality activity offers insights of potential value in the context of university teaching. As is clear from the rest of the chapter there is a substantial literature. There are also many relatively unrecorded initiatives. The few approaches that are discussed here are offered as examples only and the main recommendations to higher education colleagues at all levels are first, to consult the literature but second, to seek out health care colleagues to explore local good practice and even potential collaboration. These approaches are grouped as follows.

- Organisational development for quality improvement;
- Measurement in quality assessment and improvement;
- Learning from error to improve quality;
- Localised quality improvement activity.

Organisational development for quality improvement

The crux of all quality assurance activity is the extent to which it has an impact on the improvement of products or services across systems or organisations. There is, however, a strong vein of criticism in early as well as recent health care literature that suggests that there is not as much impact on care as there might be. Thus the briefing report to the US Bipartisan Commission (US General Accounting Office, 1990) states categorically:

> Quality assurance systems typically concentrate on quality assessment and on the identification of the relatively small number of providers whose care is obviously unacceptable. They do comparatively little to directly improve the overall levels of quality provided by the majority of health professionals.

Twenty-six years later Scoville *et al.* (2016) can still comment:

> Leading health care organisations . . . have spent years building improvement capability and applying it throughout the organisation. But too often hard-won improvements are lost as attention shifts to other priorities and staff revert to the 'old way' of doing things.

This unease about the longer-term impact of health care quality assurance has led to emphasis on the notion that quality action is a form of *organisational development* and that it must be explicitly *managed* as such. Particular themes in the quality management literature include the importance of senior management commitment and involvement; clear delegation and designation of responsibilities; effective communication channels; and staff development and training. Several health care authors (Wilson, 1987; Ovretveit, 1992; Langley *et al.*, 2009; Toussaint, 2015) also comment on the importance of initiating quality assurance schemes gradually and with due recognition of existing quality expertise within the organisation. This is particularly important in professional settings (like health care and education) where reflection on personal practice is an integral part of working life. Suggestions that concern for quality is a complete novelty or that professional judgement is fundamentally worthless are unlikely to encourage acceptance of new quality systems.

A further organisational issue discussed by Juran in his first articulations of Total Quality Management and readdressed in the Scoville *et al.* (2016) exploration of 'drivers' for sustainable health care improvement, is role differentiation at different levels in the organisation. Thus senior and middle management in high-performing organisations have strategic responsibilities for determining improvement priorities and responding to trends in overall quality, emergence of significant instances of poor quality, or unreliability in quality control. Frontline staff however are more than mere passive providers of performance data and escalators of poor-quality problems. For sustainable improvement frontline staff are actively engaged with managers in identifying solutions to problems and suggestions for improvement.

The idea of involving frontline staff directly in identifying quality initiatives goes back to the earliest developments in Japanese quality assurance (Ishikawa, 1985) where staff from all levels were regularly (and frequently) involved together in 'quality circles' discussing potential improvement, even in contexts where quality levels were already very high. In this model the quickest route to quality improvement consisted of simply asking local groups to identify and work on improvement opportunities. In health care a further advantage was that practitioners felt less threatened by the procedure and were motivated to seek out problems rather than to hide them for fear of subsequent sanctions. As Skillicorn (1981) observed:

> Staff physicians are in fact the best equipped to review the problems of their peers. They know their colleagues, they know the institution, and they know the idiosyncrasies of both. And when significant things in patient care go wrong they are tough on their peers, tougher than any external group.

The principle is also central in the improvement 'collaboratives' characteristic of IHI projects where frontline colleagues from different organisations focus on shared areas of practice to explore similarities and differences from which improvement opportunities emerge. Recent analyses of low UK productivity relative to other OECD countries (Ussher, 2016; Allen, 2016) have explored similar territory in suggesting that a significant factor in depressing productivity is that poorly paid or casualised shopfloor workforces are less likely to make suggestions for 'improving efficiency and quality'.

Timmins (2013) also emphasises the significance of frontline engagement in his discussion of the 'aggregation of marginal gains' approach to improvement attributed to the very successful British cycling coach Sir David Brailsford. The approach is characterised by the involvement of all team members in a constant search for minimal improvements, which when aggregated together effect major improvement. As Timmins notes:

> To use the marginal gains approach means genuinely recognising that people are assets. Changes are led by individual goals, not processes. It also requires that you 'think small', allowing incremental improvements to keep people's motivation up and the momentum flowing.

Again this is an idea that chimes with the IHI principle of focusing in the first instance on small-scale change, which is piloted in limited settings and only spread when it is shown to be consistently effective. It would be easily adaptable for higher education.

Measurement in quality assurance and improvement

In health care, measurement of treatment outcomes at population level has proved particularly intractable. As even the earliest authors observed, they are difficult to disentangle from the confounding influences of broader societal variables, such as diet, housing, poverty, and health-related knowledge, attitudes and expectations (Klein, 1980; Donabedian, 1986; Whittington, 1989). In education the assessment of teaching outcomes is similarly confounded by variables such as student ability, motivation, family support and personal organisation.

The problems of outcome measurement have led many health care quality assurance systems to rely heavily on the assessment of input or output variables that could often be expressed in straightforward numerical form. If outcome quality was considered at all it was on a restricted set of short-term indicators specific to the programme of care being assessed. This is directly analogous to higher education. It is relatively easy to measure input in terms of staff and other costs and output in terms of the number of students completing the course or entering employment within a set period after graduation. The difficult parts are the process, when the input is applied through teaching interactions (face to face or otherwise), and the outcome, which is the long-term learning, career achievement, community contribution, and even wellbeing and happiness of graduates. Overall assurance systems designed to demonstrate good use of public money, or for comparison of one organisation with another, is therefore difficult, and surrogates for outcome measurement must be sought.

Service organisations in all sectors are faced with similar problems and at the overall organisational level most have recourse to careful selection of 'key indicators' selected for their apparent validity in reflecting organisational aims and objectives. At Board level NHS organisations make much use of controls assurance documents in which strategic and operational objectives are set out alongside timescales, action required, and ownership and responsibility. Given the scale of most NHS organisations they are always at quite a high level of abstraction from day-to-day activity, and even so they may have to be a sample from a longer list. Those eventually selected for Board attention and scrutiny may for example be associated with areas of critical risk or major change. Sources of assurance are specified and regularly reviewed alongside accounts of achievement or otherwise. Assurance itself can be in the form of explicit measurements or trends analysing the relationships between selected indicators or can be external reviews reflecting the 'expert judgement' of external groups making assessments against explicit or implicit standards. In health care Royal College visitors might comment on numbers of staff qualified to supervise trainee doctors or express views on less measurable factors such as the encouragement of trainees to 'express concern' in line with the 'duty of candour'. In HE, similarly, a PSRB accreditation visit may provide quality relevant information on business plans for the recruitment of suitable staff in precise and explicit terms, but may be somewhat less specific in their discussion of the manner in which the 'spiral curriculum' is or is not achieved.

As Berwick and other IHI colleagues have observed, there is no lack of strategic, high-level measurement in health care. It is often difficult however to point to improvements that have resulted directly from its provision and scrutiny. The 'so what?' question is an important weapon in the intelligently challenging Board member's armoury. D'Avolio and Mate (2016) note that current data systems do an excellent job in supporting the requirements of financial and legal accountability, but that nowhere do their designers 'insert the requirement that we learn from our data or that we should change care to reflect that learning'.

Measurement can however be specifically designed to promote and facilitate improvement. IHI 'science of improvement' principles articulate clear distinctions between measurement for research (or accountability) purposes and measurement in support of improvement. They are as follows.

- Measurement for improvement is not designed to find new knowledge but to apply it in daily practice.
- Measurement for improvement is not based on one large, rigorously controlled and possibly 'blind' test but on a sequence of several small-scale observable measures.
- Measurement for improvement stabilises biases across repeated tests rather than trying to 'control them out'.
- Measurement for improvement does not gather as much data as possible 'just in case' but gathers just enough data to facilitate learning and moving on to the next data gathering and observation cycle.
- Measurement for improvement produces results more quickly than measurement for research and thus accelerates the rate of improvement.

In similar vein Scoville *et al.* (2016) refer back to Joseph Juran's (1999) Total Quality Management model. Juran distinguishes between measurement for 'quality planning' which requires thorough understanding of the evidence base and rigorous scrutiny of data from a wide range of sources, and measurement for quality control, which is tightly related to frequent observation of operational processes as they happen, and is supported by statistical control and analysis, including 'root cause analyses' of error. Measurement for quality assurance (and improvement) in the TQM model makes use of data from quality control to identify potentially beneficial changes which are then tried out and evaluated (in a W.E. Deming PDSA cycle) outside of normal operations, and only embedded into them once their separate data shows them to be useful. It is obviously important to know which is which and when data collection is for one purpose or the other. In higher education, too, application of the 'so what?' question and regular clarification of measurement purpose and validity are of central importance.

Learning from error to improve quality

Health care, like transport, construction and other heavy industry is an activity in which minor error can have catastrophic, life-threatening consequences. There is resulting emphasis in all health care quality systems on analysis of error and its consequences, with a view to prevention of future avoidable harm. NHS Improvement for example is responsible for the National Reporting and Learning System to which all Trusts must report Serious Adverse Incidents (SAIs) (NHS England, 2015). SAIs include acts or omissions in care that result in unexpected or avoidable death; unexpected or avoidable injury resulting in serious harm; abuse; Never Events (e.g. wrong site surgery, retained instruments post-operation); and incidents that have serious impact on an organisation's ability to continue to provide care. There is a systematic framework of guidance for identifying SAIs, and setting up investigations. These can be concise and local; comprehensive and multidisciplinary; or, if partner organisations are involved or if the integrity of the investigation is likely to be challenged, independently convened. All such investigations are likely to use Root Cause Analysis (RCA) as their main tool in establishing what happened and what contributed to its occurrence. They are also required to propose suggestions for prevention of recurrence based on the RCA and to disseminate the results of their investigation appropriately. NHS Improvement is then responsible for collating, prioritising and disseminating results on a UK-wide basis. Principles for management of SAIs include transparency and candour, emphasis on prevention, objectivity, timeliness, scrutiny of whole systems, collaborating with partners, and proportionality. The most recent version of the guidance framework also emphasises that effective learning from SAIs is more likely in a culture that encourages open reporting and is, as appropriate, blame free.

Despite the sophistication of such systems, all 'risk to life' organisations recognise that some level of error is inevitable. This is particularly the case where human skill and response are significant, as in carrying out surgery or piloting an aircraft. In such settings it is clearly better to learn how to prevent an error without ever letting it actually occur. Failure Modes and Effects Analysis (Reason, 2000; Warner, 2015) establishes teams to think about what could go wrong, how it could go wrong and what could be done if it did. In essence, error is simulated rather than being allowed to happen. Simulation techniques based on FMEA are common in pilot training, disaster response training, and a wide range of health and safety contexts. It was first used in health care in pathology and blood transfusion services but has been adopted by the IHI as a useful tool for other settings.

Error and poor quality in higher education are unlikely to have quite such catastrophic consequences but the principle of using failure (or simulated failure) as an opportunity for learning, and disseminating that learning widely, could be equally applicable. Organisations like HEA invest much effort in sharing instances of good practice and innovation but there is limited sharing of learning from poor practice.

Localised quality improvement activity

IHI 'improvement science' (IHI, 2017b) can be characterised as the aggregation of large numbers of localised improvement initiatives as part of a continuously developing improvement culture. Significant innovations that could be adapted for HE include 'Breakthrough Collaboratives', 'Rapid Cycle Testing' and the use of 'Care Bundles'.

Breakthrough Collaboratives are short-term (six to fifteen months) learning systems in which clinicians from groups of organisations (in the UK usually less than ten but more in the US) address apparently intractable problems common to all of them. The basic proposition is that people often know how to resolve an issue but somehow do not do so. The collaborative allows them to share knowledge and experience with new colleagues in a safe environment, to consider relevant evidence and to develop clear and time-limited approaches to problem resolution. IHI mentors (or local mentors with previous IHI experience) attend and facilitate learning sessions. Each organisational team typically sends three of its members to attend three face-to-face meetings over the course of the Collaborative, with additional members working on improvements in the local organisation. Comparable institutional collaborations have been developed in some of the problem-focused activities of the HEA but these have been ad hoc and less systematically developed than in health care.

The initiatives developed in Breakthrough Collaboratives often involve Rapid Cycle Testing. The improvement team begins by clarifying the focus and aim of their initiative. The aim should be clear in its definition and in its scope (e.g. which group of patients, which clinical processes), and time specific (but always relatively short-term). Specific narrowly focused changes with potential for adoption in the local setting are identified through considering the past experience of the teams involved or through considering improvements that have taken place elsewhere. Some are selected for improvement action. The team then establishes how it will know that improvement has occurred and selects appropriate simple, short-term measures (quantitative or qualitative as appropriate). Each selected change is then the focus of a (rapid) Plan Do Study Act cycle. After successful PDSA testing (sometimes in a sequence of tests in similar local units or in the same unit with different patients) the change can be spread throughout the organisation or further (sometimes with additional larger-scale piloting). IHI (or IHI-influenced) Rapid Cycle Testing is now undertaken in health care systems across the world and has been successfully used in a very wide range of clinical specialties. It would not be difficult to adapt for HE settings.

IHI Care Bundles (Resar *et al.*, 2012) were first developed in the context of work with intensive care units across thirteen hospitals aiming to improve the reliability and safety of critical care. The premise of the work was that patient outcomes would benefit from improved multidisciplinary communication and from increased consistency in application of good practice. The focus was to be on aspects of the care process for which there was substantial scientific and clinical evidence and where there was particular risk of great harm and high cost. One of the areas selected was care of patients on ventilator machines. The Care Bundle approach came from the recognition that a small set of care interventions for a defined patient group and setting might lead to greater improvement when implemented together than when implemented separately. Bundles are kept small (three to five is usual) and interventions simple but rooted in evidence. In the ventilator care example the bundle involved:

- elevation of the head of the bed to between 30 and 40 degrees;
- daily sedation 'vacations' and assessment of readiness to come off ventilation;
- prophylaxis for peptic ulcer disease;
- prophylaxis for deep vein thrombosis;
- daily oral care.

Measurement of successful care was a straightforward yes/no check and compliance with the bundle was an all or none measure with no credit being given for some things being done but not others. The standard set was 95 per cent. Most of the clinicians assumed that their units had all of these processes in place but some were shocked to discover compliance rates lower than 20 per cent when baseline measures were made. Checklists were established; PDSA cycles undertaken and substantially improved patient outcomes ensued.

Principles for the design of Care Bundles were developed and the technique spread rapidly. Essentially Bundles are a way of improving consistency in doing things we know we should do but don't do. They are relevant in a wide range of clinical and other team working settings and can be used at any organisational level. They could easily be adapted as 'Teaching Bundles' for improving aspects of HE teaching.

Conclusion

This chapter began by noting that the industrial origins of quality assurance in HE are commonly cited, but parallel developments in health care are much less frequently acknowledged. In fact quality assurance in university teaching may have as much to learn from health care quality assurance as it has from its industrial counterpart.

A number of problems have been shown to be particularly challenging in both settings. These include difficulties associated with the identification and measurement of outcome quality and with teasing out relationships between the processes of care or teaching and desirable outcomes. Measurement of process quality is itself made difficult by the relative centrality of interpersonal behaviour in both teaching and health. While none of these problems has been finally resolved in health care, they have at least been refined and quality innovators in university teaching should find the discussion enlightening.

Health care and university teaching quality assurance have also been shown to share an advantage. In both sectors concern for quality can be taken as axiomatic. Professionals, managers, government and consumers may debate procedures for quality appraisal and improvement but all are fundamentally committed to it. Even where provision is organised through free market systems (as in much US health care) the profit motive is at least theoretically subordinate to the desire to provide a high-quality service. The problem for quality innovators is not so much demonstration of the importance of quality as demonstration of the effectiveness of specific techniques and systems in fostering its improvement.

Finally, the overall trajectory of health care quality assurance (from trusting professionals to codifying standards and assessing outcomes, and on to developing an improvement culture) can be shown to have relevance in university teaching too.

Quality assurance in university teaching and quality assurance in health care have much in common, and quality specialists and innovators in each sector would benefit from the promotion of increased dialogue.

Note

1 The 1998/99 devolution settlements in Scotland, Wales and N. Ireland gave the devolved administrations effective control over health and social care spending. Since then, the four UK systems have become increasingly divergent although some organisations (including almost all professional bodies and also NICE) operate across the UK. For the purposes of this chapter all references to the post-1998 NHS mean NHS England unless otherwise indicated.

References

Allen, K. (2016) Hammond Needs to Look beyond Road Building to Lift the UK's Productivity. *Guardian*, Economics Viewpoint, 27 November 2016.

Berwick, D. (2013) *A Promise to Learn – a Commitment to Act: Improving the safety of patients in England*. London: Department of Health.

Berwick, D. (2016) Era Three for Medicine and Health Care. *Journal of the American Medical Association*, 315(13): 1329–1330.

Berwick D.M. & Hackbarth A.D. (2012) Eliminating Waste in US Health Care. *Journal of the American Medical Association*, 307(14): 1513–1516.

Boysen, P.G. (2013) Just Culture: A foundation for balanced accountability and patient safety. *Ochsner Journal*, 13(3): 400–406.

Casanova, J.E. (1990) Status of Quality Assurance Programmes in American Hospitals. *Medical Care*, 28(11): 1105–1109.

Clwyd, A. & Hart, T. (2013) *Review of the NHS Hospitals Complaints System: Putting patients back in the picture*. London: Department of Health.

Dalley, G., Baldwin, S., Carr-Hill, R., Hennessy, S. & Smedley, E. (1991) *Quality Management Initiatives in the NHS*. No. 3: Strategic Approaches to Improving Quality. York: Centre for Health Economics, University of York.

Davenport, G., McDonald, I. & Moss-Gibbons, C. (2001) *The Royal College of Physicians and Its Collections: An illustrated history*. London: James and James.

Davis, K., Stremikis, K., Squires, D. & Schoen, C. (2014) *How the U.S. Health Care System Compares Internationally*. Mirror, Mirror on the Wall, 2014 Update. New York: The Commonweath Fund.

D'Avolio, L. & Mate, K. (2016) *Making Data Work for Quality Improvement*. Institute for Healthcare Improvement WIHI. <ihi.org/resources/audio and video> Accessed 14/02/2017.

Deming, W.E. (1982) *Quality, Productivity and Competitive Position*. Cambridge, Mass.: MIT Press.

Deming, W.E. (1986) *Out of the Crisis*. Cambridge, Mass.: MIT Centre for Advanced Engineering Study.

Department of Health (1998) *A First Class Service: Quality in the new NHS*. London: HMSO.

Department of Health (2000) *The NHS Plan: A plan for investment, a plan for reform*, Cmnd 4818. London: HMSO.

Department of Health (2013) *Hard Truths: The journey to putting patients first*. London: Department of Health.

Donabedian, A (1986) Criteria and Standards for Quality Assessment and Monitoring. *Quality Review Bulletin*, 14(3): 99–108.

Ezekiel J.E. & Fuchs V.R. (2008). The Perfect Storm. *The Journal of the American Medical Association*, 299(23): 2789–2791.

General Medical Council (2016) *The Gold Guide: A reference guide for postgraduate specialty training in the UK* (6th edn.). London: GMC.

General Medical Council (2017) <gmc-uk.org/home/registration and licensing/revalidation> Accessed 09/02/2017.

Graban, M. & Swartz, J.E. (2012) *Healthcare Kaizen*. Abingdon: Productivity Press, Taylor and Francis Group.

Grammaticus, P.C. & Diamantis, A. (2008) Useful Known and Unknown Views of the Father of Medicine: Hippocrates and his teacher Democritus. *Hellenic Journal of Nuclear Medicine*, 11(1): 2–4.

Hanna, J. (2007) *Bringing Lean Principles to Service Industries*. Harvard Business School Working Papers, 08–001, July. Cambridge, Mass.: Harvard Business School.

Health Care Research Unit, Newcastle upon Tyne University (1990) *North of England Study of Standards and Performance in General Practice*. Newcastle upon Tyne: HCRU, Newcastle upon Tyne University.

HMSO (1956) *Committee of Enquiry into the Cost of National Health Service: The Guillebaud Report*, Cmnd 663. London: HMSO.

HMSO (1989) *Working for Patients*, Cmnd 555. London: HMSO.

HMSO (1990) *Medical Audit*. Working for patients. Working paper no. 6, Department of Health. London: HMSO.

HMSO (1997) *The New NHS: Modern and dependable*, Cmnd 3807. London: HMSO.

HMSO (2004) *Securing Good Health for the Whole Population* (the Wanless Report). London: HMSO.

Institute for Healthcare Improvement (2017a) <ihi.org/home/about us/history> Accessed 13/02/2017.

Institute for Healthcare Improvement (2017b) <ihi.org/home/about us/scienceofimprovement> > Accessed 14/02/2017.

Irvine, D.H. (1990) *Managing for Quality in General Practice*. London: King's Fund.

Ishikawa, K. (1985) *What is Total Quality Control?: The Japanese way*. New Jersey: Prentice Hall.

Jackson, B. (2008) Barber-surgeons. *Journal of Medical Biography*, 16(2): 65 08/02.

Juran, J. M. (1951) *Quality Control Handbook* (6th Edn., 2010). New York: McGraw-Hill.

Juran, J. M. (1999) *Quality Control Handbook* (5th Edition). New York: McGraw-Hill.

Keogh, B. (2013) *Review into the Care and Treatment Provided by 14 Hospital Trusts in England*. London: NHS England.

Klein, R. (1980) *The Politics of the National Health Service*. Harlow: Longman.

Langley, G.J., Moen, R.D., Nolan, K., Nolan, T. & Provost, L. (2009) *The Improvement Guide: A practical approach to enhancing organizational performance*. San Francisco: Jossey-Bass.

National Archive (2017a) *Health Act 1999*. <legislation.gov.uk> Accessed 11/02/2017

National Archive (2017b) *Health and Social Care Act 2003*. <legislation.gov.uk> Accessed 11/02/2017.

National Archive (2017c) *Health and Social Care Act 2012*. <legislation.gov.uk> Accessed 11/02/2017.

National Archive (2017d) *The Mid Staffordshire NHS Trust Inquiry, January 2005 to March 2009*. <webarchive.nationalarchives.gov.uk> Accessed 13/02/2017.

National Archive (2017e) *The Mid Staffordshire NHS Trust Public Inquiry (chaired by Robert Francis QC)*. <webarchive.nationalarchives.gov.uk> Accessed 13/02/2017.

National Archive (2017f) *Freedom to Speak Up: An independent review into creating and open and honest reporting culture in the NHS*. Briefing paper from Sir Robert Francis. <webarchive.nationalarchives.gov.uk> Accessed 13/02/2017.

National Institute for Health and Care Excellence (2017) <nice.org/about/who we are> Accessed 15/02/2017.

NHS England (2015) *Serious Incident Framework: Supporting learning to prevent recurrence*. NHS England Publications Gateway. Accessed 14/02/2017.

OECD (2017) <stats.OECD.org/health/health expenditure and financing> Accessed 09/02/2017.

Ovretveit, J. (1992) *Health Service Quality*. Oxford: Blackwell.

Reason, J. (2000) Human Error: Models and management. *Western Journal of Medicine*, 172(6): 393.

Resar, R., Griffin, F.A. & Nolan, T. (2012) *Using Care Bundles to Improve Health Care Quality*. IHI Innovation Series White Paper. <ihi.org/resources/ihiwhitepapers> Accessed 14/02/2017.

Rivett, G. (1986) *The Development of the London Hospitals System, 1823–1982*. London: The King's Fund.

Rivlin, J.J. (1997) Getting a Medical Qualification in England in the Nineteenth Century. *Medical Historian*, 9: 56–63.

Royal College of General Practitioners (1983) The Quality Initiative. *Journal of the Royal College of General Practitioners*, 33: 523–524.

Royal College of General Practitioners (1985a) *Assessing Quality of Care in General* Practice. London: Royal College of General Practitioners.

Royal College of General Practitioners (1985b) *What Sort of Doctor?* Report from General Practice, 23. London: Royal College of General Practitioners.

Royal College of Surgeons of Edinburgh (2017) <rcsed.ac.uk/the college/about us/history and vision> Accessed 08/02/2017.

Scoville, R., Little, K., Rakover, J. Luther, K. & Mate, K. (2016) *Sustaining Improvement.* Institute for Healthcare Improvement White Paper. <ihi.org/resources/ihi white papers>. Accessed 14/02/2017.

Shaw, C.D. (1990) *Medical Audit: A Hospital Handbook.* London: King's Fund.

Skillicorn, S.A. (1981) A Conversation with Dr. Stanley A. Skillicorn. A leading proponent of integrated problem-oriented quality assurance. *Quality Review Bulletin*, 7(4): 20–23.

Stevens, R. (2002) The Midwives Act 1902: An historical landmark. *The Midwives Magazine*, November 2002.

Timmins, L. (2013) Marginal Gains Can Lead to Big Wins. *Business Value Exchange*, 8 August 2013.

Toussaint, J.S. (2015) A Rapidly Adaptable Management System. *Journal of Healthcare Management*, 60(5): 312–315.

United States General Accounting Office (1990) *Quality Assurance – a Comprehensive National Strategy for Health Care Is Needed.* Briefing report to the Chairman, United States Bipartisan Commission on Comprehensive Health Care, GAO/PEMD-90–14BR. Washington, DC: GAO.

Ussher, K. (2016) *Improving Pay, Progression and Productivity in the Retail Sector.* Joseph Rowntree Foundation Research Reports, November, 2016. York: JRF.

Warner, S. (2015) *Human Error is Inevitable.* <laboratory-manager.advanceweb.com/home/specialties/automation> Accessed 14/02/2017.

Whittington, D. (1989) *Performance Indicators and Quality Assurance in the NHS.* Paper delivered to the European Group for Public Administration Study Group on Quality Assurance and Productivity. Brussels: Institut International des Sciences Administratives.

Whittington, J.W., Nolan, K., Lewis, N. & Torres, T. (2015) Pursuing the Triple Aim: The first seven years. *Milbank Quarterly*, 93(2): 263–300.

Wilson, C.R.M. (1987) *Hospital-Wide Quality Assurance: Models for implementation and development.* Toronto: W.B. Saunders.

World Health Organization (1985) *The Principles of Quality Assurance.* European Reports and Studies, 94. Copenhagen, WHO.

Worshipful Society of Apothecaries of London (2017). <apothecaries.org/home/history/origins> Accessed 08/02/2017.

18 Assuring Teaching Quality in Hungary

Marta B. Erdos, Gabor Szollosi and Eva Vojtek

Introduction

The Hungarian system of higher education, as a context for quality assurance, has been shaped by specific Central and Eastern European traditions as well as recent European developments. The traditions still have an impact on the governing ideas and practices of tertiary education, and largely determine present-day policy debates. The resulting legal and financial conditions are decisive in the development of the domestic system of quality assurance. Budgetary restrictions may hinder quality enhancement and the development of a quality culture. Under such conditions, quality assurance may be recognized as something peripheral or 'bonus' within the institution; in this context, external control and legal regulations may have an increasing role.

Recent internationalization trends, however, may establish a new balance as the domestic academic system is entering the global and highly competitive market of tertiary education. Hungary accessed the European Higher Education Area in 2005. Current improvements in this highly volatile system, namely, the introduction of European Standards and Guidelines 2015 as a basis for internal and external quality assurance, seek to strengthen the existing links to European systems.

1 Social, cultural and historical context of higher education in Hungary

1.1 Pre-transition history of Hungarian tertiary education

The evolution of the Hungarian system of higher education is a path-dependent development with some significant breaking points. The first medieval university with its two faculties, the Faculty of Arts and the Faculty of Law, was established in Pécs in 1367. Hungary's geopolitical position as well as internal conflicts had their destructive impact on early academic life and, after some decades of operation, the medieval institution ceased to exist. The roots of today's institutional system of higher education can be traced back to the 17th century. Slow but stable development following the Humboldtian model of higher education in the 19th century was interrupted by Word War I and the subsequent Trianon Treaty, which resulted in a major loss in territory, population and institutions. Centralization tendencies were very strong at the beginning of the 20th century in the country: 63 per cent of all the students attended the two universities in the capital, and the rate gradually increased to 80 per cent. As a response, decentralizaton began in the 1920s, and four major universities were established in the county seats in the country. In the 1930s the scene of higher education turned into an ideological battlefield. Antisemitism and nationalism – associated with strong revisionist tendencies concerning the Trianon Treaty – corrupted the system. The pre-war era was characterized by re-centralization efforts and budgetary restrictions.

After World War II, the communist regime excluded church and private institutions and radically changed the previous, European-type university structure (Jancsó, 2010). As in the Soviet model, lecturing and research activities were separated, and universities were segmented into individual schools, representing isolated study areas. The system of higher education was under strong and unquestionable political control. The 1950s was an era of open communist dictatorship, in which the elimination of the intelligentsia as autonomous, critical-reflective thinkers was a means of exercising total control over Hungarian society. Professionals were regarded 'non-productive' workers and their income levels did not reach those of the unskilled, 'productive' workers – unless they proved reliable communists and showed definite signs of 'ideological development'. Counter-selection techniques, as forced social mobility of students, served the purposes of strengthening the communist regime: admission to higher education mainly depended on loyalty to the system manifested in Communist Party membership and of working-class origin.[1] Distorted selection and evaluation techniques had their impact on economic performance: announcements on immense growth contradicted people's everyday experiences. The 1956 Revolution changed the ways of exercising power for the ruling regime. Covertly manipulative efforts of the subsequent soft dictatorship were more a menace to the *clarity of thought* than to people's lives (Erdos & Kelemen, 2011). Future generations' main mission was unconditional loyalty to the system:

> The future of the society depends on how we shape youth. It is the utmost interest of the socialist society to bring up young people who can firmly identify with Marxist-Leninist ideas. All their actions should be motivated by these ideas, determining their moral and political behaviour. Our most important task is to equip them with the necessary tools to detect any anti-Marxist-Leninist ideas so that they could fight against them.
>
> (Bakonyi, 1981, in Surányi, 2007)

An overall low performance made the system unsustainable. State socialist ideological groundings in academic life were gradually shaped into more performance-oriented views, supporting early initiations in quality assurance. In 1985, four years before the transition of the social system, reforms were launched with the idea of re-establishing European universities and introducing quality assurance. 'It takes roughly six months to draft a constitution, six years to build a market economy, and sixty years to create a democracy' (Dahrendorf, 1990, in Quigley, 2015, 219). Hungary's state socialist legacy still has an impact on contemporary practices. Accordingly, some of today's quality assurance problems and debates have their origin in these decades.

1.2 Post-transition debates and trends

Tertiary education was a central area of the major social transformations beginning in the 1980s: universities were actively shaping the transformations but were also subjects to these. Frameworks of quality assurance were shaped after the existing European models by governmental efforts and by the institutions themselves. Obligations resulting from Hungary's planned accession to the European Union meant a strong motivation both in the preparatory phase in the 1990s and after the accession in 2004. During the era of rapid transformations, the main areas of debates were the degree of adherence to existing systems or system elements, such as the college/university structure; the degree of autonomy of academic institutions, including processes of integration or federation, rapid expansion manifested in the increasing number of Hungarian students, the status of intermediary organizations between academic institutions and government; and financial issues. (Veres, 2016; Hrubos, 2016; Kováts, 2016).

2 Legal frameworks and structures of quality assurance

Legal guarantees for quality assurance are set out in the law in force in higher education, and in the related implementing regulations. High volatility is a marked feature of the transition: four subsequent laws (Act I. of 1985 on Education, Act LXXX of 1993 on Higher Education, Act CXXXIX of 2005 on Higher Education, and Act CCIV of 2011 on National Higher Education) have been introduced in the past three decades, with 35 amendments and 24 comprehensive policies on tertiary education. These have been complemented by 216 governmental decrees, 88 of which were related to quality assurance and 52 to financing; and by 140 ministerial decrees, 100 of which are on quality assurance and 26 on finances (Derényi, 2016).

The Act I of 1985 and its amendment in 1990 preserved a dual system of 'college' and 'university' education. Colleges offered lower level training, usually in one particular field, and education was prioritized over research. The introduction of doctoral studies, a third element of the previously dual system, followed in 1993: 'The need arose for creating uniform Hungarian tertiary education, and restoring the universitas, and improving the quality of tertiary education' (Eurydice 2004–5, p. 123.) Though Act LXXX of 1993 did not address issues of quality policy and internal quality assurance in detail, it established the Hungarian Accreditation Committee as an authorized intermediary body for external quality assurance. Legal requirements concerning the system of higher education constituted a framework for the activities of the Committee, an advisory organization to support the decisions of the competent authority (Educational Authority). In this reflexive process, legal requirements are translated into quality requirements, which, in turn, influence legislative practices and institutional norms. The Act was a definite move towards institutional autonomy, determining only the frameworks (curricular guidelines) but not the exact content of education.

Internal and external quality assurance standards and guidelines were formulated, and the Hungarian Accreditation Committee (HAC) successfully joined the European Association for Quality Assurance in Higher Education (ENQA) in 2002. In this system, the institutions are obliged to meet certain quality requirements and are free to set additional quality development goals.

The European Credit Transfer System (ECTS)-compatible national system was introduced in 2003. Hungary has accessed the European Higher Education Area and introduced the Bologna system in 2005. The Bologna system is a subject of continual domestic debates: 'The introduction of the Bologna system – an enforced conformity – has not been thought through; consequently, study programmes should be evaluated and reviewed' (Nefmi, 2010). In certain areas, previous (undivided, 'university') forms of training were preserved or reintroduced in the past few years. Though the present-day national system is in accordance with the Bologna model, it is not fully compatible with those of the majority of European countries; rather, it is an amalgamation of the previous and new structures (Derényi, 2016).

The three-pronged structure, encompassing quality policy, external and internal quality assurance was enacted in 2005 (Act CXXXIX). The Act authorized the Minister for

Education to determine quality policies in higher education, and obliged institutions of higher education to implement their own systems of quality assurance. Academic institutions were required to establish and regulate their local systems for quality assurance, to make a detailed programme for quality assurance, and annually evaluate the execution of the programme. Formal requirements of quality assurance were manifested in declarations, regulations, manuals and organizational structures. State, church and private academic institutions are obliged to meet the same quality requirements (Government Decree 19/2012/II. 22/). Though organizational frameworks for quality assurance were established, a national-level culture fostering quality management – including traditions, values, attitudes and commitments to quality development – was not formed (Kerekes, Molnárné Stadler, Orosz & Pintér, 2012).

Presently, a ministerial decree (18/2016 /VIII. 5/) determines what study programmes may be launched; it defines the range of credits representing knowledge areas within the given programmes, and the qualifications to be obtained by completing the programmes. The training and outcome requirements, including the goal of the training, the competencies to be acquired (knowledge, skills, attitude, degree of autonomy and responsibility of the professional); and foreign language requirements (one or two languages, B and/or C levels, depending on the specific study programme) are also determined.

Act CCIV/2011 on National Higher Education classified four different categories of excellence. The institutions which meet the requirements are entitled to extra resources:

1   Priority higher education institutions (between 2013 and 2016, altogether three institutions). Priority institutions serve national strategic goals and should gain international recognition by moving forward in global rankings and by attracting international students.
2   'Research' universities (six universities) are characterized by high-intensity, strategic, basic and applied research activities, national and international research collaborations and innovative R&D networks.
3   'Research' faculties (six faculties) which meet the above requirements on a faculty level.
4   Colleges of applied research (two colleges) provide outstanding, practice-oriented training which is accompanied by applied research related to the priorities of national economy and internationalization.

The 2013 summary by the Educational Authority have identified 20, mostly *quantitative*, indicators of excellence in research capacities, research outcomes, utilization of research, developmental activities and innovations, quality education, international collaborations and labour market relations (Javaslat, 2013; National Reform Programme, 2011).

Parallel to this, the foci and priorities in the original three-actor model were changed. Quality policy issues are not highlighted anymore; and legal requirements of internal quality assurance have been alleviated:

> The maintainer shall evaluate the effectiveness of professional activity and the efficiency of institution operation on the basis of the annual report produced by the higher education institution in compliance with the accounting regulations and the report on the implementation of the institutional quality development scheme, and shall undertake action *by specifying an appropriate deadline where necessary.*
> (Act CCIV of 2011 on National Higher Education Chapter XIX, 43, Section 74 (2), emphasis added)

In the present system, formal quality management regulations have remained part of the organizational and operational rules of the institutions. The implementing regulation, however, does not contain any explicit legal guarantees of internal quality assurance:

> The Government Decree uniformly regulates the preparatory decision-making activities related to the quality evaluation of training, academic research and artistic activities in institutions of higher education and the development of higher education by laying down that the maintenance of high standards in training, academic research and artistic activities in higher education as *the core activities of higher education is primarily the given higher education institution's duty and responsibility.*
>
> (National Reform Programme, 2011, p. 180, emphasis added)

Quality management and outlining a quality policy were not among the strategic goals and activities of the institutions as these were not required by the law. In this context, external evaluation could possibly have balanced out some of the shortcomings in internal quality assurance. However, the competence and autonomy of the Hungarian Accreditation Committee, as an independent body, has become limited. 'The operation of the Hungarian Higher Education Accreditation Committee (HAC) was placed on new foundations' (National Reform Programme, 2011). Certain decisions of the Educational Authority depend on the expert opinion issued by the Committee. With the exception of doctorate schools, however, this is not an obligation but a recommendation. Concerning bachelor and masters programmes, it is the national traditions of academic life that ensure HAC's strong position.

> (3) The Educational Authority shall proceed in matters relating to a) the licensing of the operation of higher education institutions, b) changes to data recorded in the Statutes, c) launch of study programmes, d) the establishment and modification of the maximum number of students admissible, e) the establishment and termination of doctorate schools, f) registration of students' halls maintained by a church, religious legal entity, or foundation. (4) The Educational Authority shall obtain the expert opinion of the Hungarian Accreditation Committee in the procedures set forth in Paragraphs a) and e) of Subsection (3), in Paragraph c) of Subsection (3) in case of launching Bachelor and master programmes, and in Paragraph b) of Subsection (3) in relation to scientific and related educational and research matters. In the course of the procedure specified in Paragraph e) of Subsection (3), the Educational Authority shall be bound by the expert opinion of the Hungarian Accreditation Committee.
>
> (Act CCIV of 2011 on National Higher Education Part 5,
> Chapter XVII, 40, Section 67, 3)

The composition of HAC reflects the role and importance attributed to the different stakeholder groups in quality assurance. Government representation is rather strong:

> The Hungarian Accreditation Committee shall be comprised of 18 members. The minister shall delegate 9 members, the Hungarian Academy of Sciences 2 members, the Hungarian Academy of Arts 1 member, the Hungarian Rectors' Conference 3 members, religious legal entities maintaining higher education institutions 2 members, and the Association of Hungarian PhD. and DLA Students 1 member.
>
> (Section 71 1. (1))

3 Financial issues influencing quality assurance

Adherence to quality requirements also depends on available financial resources. Reliance on state resources is a marked tradition in academic life in Hungary for lack of genuine market relations. Artificial, quasi-market functions have been established by the state; therefore the operation of tertiary education is under strong governmental influence, which is manifested in many areas, such as the streaming of student admissions and R&D activities. The autonomy of the institutions of higher education and striving for quality enhancement are limited by budgetary considerations.

3.1 Number of students: Admissions, graduations and career tracking

The number of students admitted to institutions of higher education doubled between 1990 (76,000) and 1996 (141,000), in an era of rapid expansion (Policity Team, 2011). In addition to newly founded state institutions to respond to the rapidly increasing demand, church, foundation and international institutions appeared. By now, the majority of universities are run by the state though there are some private and church-owned institutions; the rate is inverse for colleges, with the marked dominance of church-run institutions, which also rely significantly on state support. Rapid growth in the 1990s was also motivated by Hungary's planned accession to the European Union. The highest number of students was recorded in 2005/6 and equalled 424,161; from the next year on a marked decline began.

Although policy makers' intention was to establish a 3:1 ratio between bachelor and masters levels, actual numbers reflect a 5:1 ratio. The priority of the Hungarian labour market is to keep the cost of the labour force as low as possible, and employers are often reluctant to pay the price of professionalism. A further problem is poor differentiation between levels (ISCED 2011; levels 5–7) of tertiary education in the Bologna system, which confuses prospective applicants (Derényi, 2016). The 2015 admissions (full-time students) roughly correspond to the 2005 data.

In the first semester of 2015/6, 295,316 students attended the 66 institutions of higher education in Hungary; 210,103 of them were full-time students. Student–lecturer rate was approximately 1:14, with 21,668 lecturers working in the Hungarian system of tertiary education (Central Statistical Office, 2016).

Table 18.1 Number of admissions and applications of full-time students, 2005–2015

Year	Applications	Admissions	Rate of admissions/ applications
2005	91,677	52,957	57.8
2006	84,269	53,990	64.1
2007	74,849	50,941	68.1
2008	66,963	52,081	77.8
2009	90,878	61,262	67.4
2010	100,777	65,503	65.0
2011	101,835	66,810	65.6
2012	84,075	61,350	73.0
2013	75,392	56,927	75.5
2014	79,765	54,688	68.6
2015	79,255	53,069	67.0

Source: Redrawn from Central Statistical Office, 2016

Table 18.2 Number of students in the Hungarian system of higher education

Level/form	Total number of students	Full-time students
Higher education vocational (non-degree)	11,977	8,829
'College' level (previous)	2,186	99
'University' level (previous)	399	246
Bachelor	181,283	138,780
Master	37,182	23,302
Undivided	38,479	32,992
Postgraduate non-degree	16,487	279
PhD, DLA	7,323	5,576
Total	295,316	210,103

Source: Redrawn from Central Statistical Office (2016)

One of the goals of the Europe 2020 Strategy (2010) is to increase the rate of persons with tertiary qualifications to 40 per cent among 30–34-year-olds. Actual target numbers change from country to country. Hungary's goal for 2020 is 30.3 per cent, with 28.1 per cent as a baseline in 2011 (National Reform Programme, 2011). Previous admissions have greatly influenced the 2015 data, which was 34.3 per cent (Eduline, 2016). Strategic requirements for 2020 are met even if the number of admissions will *decrease* in the next few years.

Applications and admissions are an indicator of the perceived societal role of higher education. Equal access is a central theme in the rhetoric of the National Reform Programme (2011). The majority, about two-thirds of students, receive state scholarship for their studies and students may obtain additional stipends to promote equality of opportunity.

Outcomes of the learning process in systems of higher education are an important quality indicator, with components including dropout/slow progress during one's studies, as well as market connections and career development. Dropout is a marked problem at secondary levels (11.5 per cent) and increases to 40–50 per cent in institutions of higher education. The rate of those who were admitted to bachelor-level training in 2010 and successfully obtained a degree in 2015 was only 49.5 per cent. In certain study programmes the rate of dropout is as high as 70 per cent (Stéger, 2015). In the current system, where those who are admitted are expected to graduate, this is a waste of time and finances for the individual and for the entire society. Dropout rates are influenced by:

- the quality of secondary education. For the majority of study programmes, admission is based on secondary school achievements. Previous, competitive entrance examinations were eliminated from the system. Striking evidence of applicants' competence problems is the high rate of formal mistakes in the applications (e.g. the applicant fails to attach documentation of secondary education in due time);
- social factors such as parental support, social network, family commitments and integration into the community of the university;
- psychological factors as attitudes, learning strategies and resilience;
- academic factors such as positive relationship to lecturers, availability of counselling services at the university, student organizations and a wide variety university resources (Bean, 1985, in Molnár, 2012);
- foreign language requirements: 'the lack of the knowledge of foreign languages is often an obstacle to the acquisition of a degree' (National Reform Programme, 2011, 198). Mobility programmes and language courses are planned to improve foreign language

skills. Students often complain that speaking the *language of language exams* (technical skills) is a priority over usable competencies in one or two foreign languages.

Delay in study progress in certain underdeveloped regions within the country has probably been due to relatively high levels of unemployment and low incomes among the young. What used to motivate students to extend their state-financed studies and progress slowly to preserve the stability of their social status, are marked signs of a quarterlife crisis (Tari, 2010). As a response, the government has introduced certain limitations such as loss of state scholarship, an obligation to repay the state scholarship and fewer opportunities to re-take exams etc. The state, the university and the student still have some conflicting interests in the current system of higher education. Extending the length of training equals far more income to the institution. In some study programmes, students are kept in the system as long as possible. In such instances, 'quality education' might be a central element of the accompanying rhetoric, though the delay is more about institutional interests than high-quality requirements.

Complex, central databases for tracking students' and graduates' careers have been introduced in the past decade. Based on a survey involving 85,000 graduates (academic years 2009/10; 2011/12), 70 per cent is employed; 10 per cent has been admitted to a post-graduate programme; another 10 per cent is simultaneously employed and studying in a postgraduate programme; and there is no available information on the remaining 10 per cent (DPR, 2014). The number of young professionals who seek jobs outside Hungary in the European Union – either as 'commuters' or as settlers – is relatively high (Blaskó, 2014). Average monthly income among young professionals is 729 Euros, with the highest incomes in the IT and engineering sectors. Seventy-eight per cent of young graduates are employed in jobs which require their tertiary-level qualifications (DPR, 2014). Connections between tertiary education and the labour market have been strengthened by recent efforts to stream study programmes to serve the demands of the national economy (National Reform Programme, 2011). The high volatility of the global and national economic environment is often a barrier to such striving.

3.2 *Current trends and system of financing*

While the number of graduates has grown as expected, the system has suffered severe budgetary restrictions. Forced expansion after the transition has been accompanied by a 41 per cent cut in finances, which could hardly be balanced by developing a more cost-effective operational response.[2]

The system of financing higher education is rather complicated, as there are different financial allocations within the Budget Law (2015). There are other, mostly European Union, resources which are available for mainstreamed developmental projects to meet strategic goals. Institutions of higher education have some additional sources, such as fees from students who do not receive a scholarship; or incomes from R&D activities. The rate of state support and the expected total income of the institutions was approximately 57 per cent in 2015. Heterogeneity of the resources may explain the existing contradictions in the domestic data.

Today the financial possibilities of an academic institution largely depends on its number of students. Admissions and applications are determined by government policies and resources, by the demographic forces of an ageing society, and by the social problems – such as poverty and unemployment – of the sandwich generation. Altogether, the real value of contributions into systems of higher education has not grown and significant investments

Table 18.3 Budgetary support for higher education, 2010–2016

Year	Support (million EUR)
2010	584.7
2011	612.4
2012	509.7
2013	399.7
2014	422.2
2015	492.7
2016	516.5

Source: Own calculation based on Hungary Government Central Budgets 2009–2016.

have not been made. In this respect, institutions of higher education are not encouraged to make extra efforts in terms of quality assurance. Quality expectations are not proportionate to the available resources.

Since 2014, universities in Hungary have had dual leadership: the rector is the representative of academia and the chancellor represents the government as funder. The chancellor has the ultimate control over all financial issues.

4 Evaluating recent developments in quality assurance

4.1 Two eras of quality initiations

The institutionalized system of quality assurance in higher education has been developed in the past three decades. The process, however, is more about striving and initiative – models, rules and organizations – than about factual descriptions and critical evaluation of the system (Bazsa, 2014; Kováts, 2014; Csekei, Szarkáné & Csirik, 2010; Polonyi, 2008). Two eras of public policies can be distinguished with different impacts on quality issues in higher education. In the first period between 1992 and 2011, a three-actor quality management model was formed. It was the government that determined quality policies, while the Hungarian Accreditation Committee was authorized to conduct external quality assurance, and the academic institutions themselves were responsible for internal quality assurance (Bazsa 2014). Fluctuating balance, as a result of the changing division of power and responsibility among the three main actors, is characteristic of the broad context.

The beginnings of the second era were marked by the enactment of the law of 2011. The Act has introduced a number of significant changes in academic life, among others, in quality issues. From 2012 on, the previous focus on building a quality culture and on determining minimum quality standards were exchanged for excellence initiations (Kováts, 2014). Similar elitist initiations were central to previous German reforms and the lessons learnt there are of key importance in the current context: 'the threat involved is streaming of research based on interests external to science; and the strengthening of political influence over academic life' (Quante, 2010).

As a consequence of legal regulations outlined in part 2, institutions of higher education have published their own quality assurance programmes, but regular updates and evaluations have been missing. Attempts at internal quality assurance might still be driven by partial interest groups and probably represent the 'teething troubles' of domestic evaluation

(Weiss, 1993; Erdos, 2016), such as lack of transparency, inadequate research methodology, biased interpretations and misuse of the results. Recent internationalization of the Hungarian system of tertiary education, however – the search for global markets and connections – is a strong factor promoting constructive changes.

4.2 *The role and autonomy of Hungarian Accreditation Committee*

The Hungarian Accreditation Committee was established as a result of organic development in quality assurance, and of a bargaining process between academia and government. At the beginning, organizational and financial conditions served its high degree of autonomy. After 2012, these conditions have changed; as a result, HAC's full member status within ENQA was suspended and was under review. Two major ENQA criteria had not been met, those of autonomy and adequate financing (MAB 2014). HAC has regained its full member status in 2015 (ENQA News, 16 June 2015).

As a traditionally respected and widely acknowledged advisory board in institutions of higher education, HAC assesses the standard of education and research in each higher education institution. Before the introduction of complex accreditation in 2017, the Hungarian Accreditation Committee evaluated the institutions and their study programmes in two separate processes. They examined the curricula and the qualification requirements as well as the quality of the academic staff and the teaching facilities for programme accreditation. Staffing requirements delimit the maximum number of courses/credits a lecturer may teach; and determine the rate of lecturers with appropriate academic titles (PhD; PhD habil. Associate Professor/Professor; and Doctor of the Hungarian National Academy of Sciences). Institutional accreditation was conducted at least every eight years and was based on a detailed self-assessment as well as on the report of an independent visiting committee. In 2017 the system was changed, and currently accreditation is regarded as one complex process (MAB, 2017).

A peculiar feature of the national quality assurance system is that members of the visiting committee are employed in *competitor* institutions of higher education. Further, setting the requirements was not clearly separated from quality control; HAC had a decisive role in both formulating the standards and controlling the implementation of the same quality standards (Bókay, 2008). Due to recent legal changes, external control is distributed between the Hungarian Accreditation Committee as an advisory board and the Educational Authority as an executive board.

4.3 *European Standards and Guidelines as a new focus*

Hungarian institutions of higher education have gradually become familiar with ENQA standards and guidelines, such as integration of internal and external quality assurance, formulation of explicit intended learning outcomes, focus on programme design and content, modes of delivery, independent programme approval, monitoring students' progress, regular periodic reviews of study programmes, obtaining feedback from the labour market, student participation in quality assurance processes and assessing learning resources. Nevertheless, ESG standards and guidelines were thematized mostly among interested specialists or researchers of the field, HAC members and the Educational Authority. Interpretations in the professional literature concerning standardization and quality assurance have been stemmed in Western, up-to-date conceptualizations and practices (HAC Self-Evaluation Report, 2013). Recently, HAC, as an ENQA member, has basically transformed its previous practices. The new system of quality assurance, complex accreditation introduced in 2017, is based on the European Standards and Guidelines 2015, a set of standards and guidelines on internal and external quality assurance, as well as on the quality assurance agencies themselves (ESG, 2015; MAB, 2017).

Domestic institutions, experiencing the changes of 2017 in the environment of tertiary education, have interpreted this motivating and change-provoking turn, designating the road from the rule of academic authority to student-centred and outcome-focussed approaches as a quantum leap. When interpreting the change they apply two alternative and opposing frameworks, understanding the document more as a standard, representing external control; or as a collection of guiding principles assisting the organizations in building their developmental strategies to provide high-quality tertiary education (Szántó, 2016). The focus of ESG 2015 is teaching outcomes and processes, not academic research and scientific achievements, which are the traditional strengths of the Hungarian university system – with the Hungarian Academy of Sciences in the background as a source of lecturers' reputations. ESG 2015 covers ten different areas for internal quality assurance: policy for quality assurance; design and approval of the study programmes; student-centred learning, teaching and assessment; student admission, progression, recognition, and certification; competencies of the teaching staff; learning resources and student support; information management (in the sense of evidence-based planning and interventions); publicity of academic activities; the continuous monitoring and review of study programmes; and cyclical external quality assurance (ESG, 2015). External quality assurance should be based on internal quality assurance, should employ adequate methodologies, and ensure fairness of the process in terms of professionalism, consistency, transparency, publicity, follow-up, representation of all the concerned parties and the opportunity of appeal. Presently, major areas of marked external control of quality assurance are the establishment and launching of academic programmes; the number of students to be accepted in the individual programmes; and the rate of qualified (i.e. PhD and DSc) lecturers in a programme.

While certain areas are explicitly represented in the legal regulations (e.g. formal requirements of study programmes), and as such, have long been treated as priorities, the Hungarian system as a whole has faced a number of new developmental tasks.

First and foremost, policies for quality assurance are arbitrary. Internal quality assurance is mainly the responsibility of the departments, co-ordinated, assisted and controlled by the educational offices of the universities. The Educational Authority intervenes only in violations of law or in extreme cases of student dropout.

Student-centred approaches and student control is another marked challenge. Students' evaluation of their lecturers' performance is regularly requested, but, as these surveys are less about the course and more about the lecturer, these data can hardly be utilized for evidence-based developmental decisions.

In the domestic tradition, university teachers' competencies are based first and foremost on their scientific achievements (scientometrics, R&D activities) and, to some extent, their previous qualifications. They are not required to enter training to develop teaching skills; in some areas, project funding is available for this purpose but participation in such projects is voluntary and has no positive consequences in one's career. In some instances, practical professional experiences do matter and have been acknowledged since 2016 by the law: a master teacher is not required to obtain a PhD degree but should be a renowned practitioner with substantial experiences.

Controversies between financial conditions and staffing requirements are the main reason of marked delays in the introduction of lecturers' and researchers' complex performance measurements, as an integral part of quality assurance measures at the institutions. Actors' particular interests are another inhibiting factor. Due to centralization tendencies, employer rights, such as differentiation in salaries according to competence and performance (or the termination of employment in some cases), are not exercised by the immediate supervisors (chairs of the departments). Though the Senate as the main decision-making body at institutions of higher education is expected to introduce performance-oriented measures, high power distance between the levels is often a barrier to systematic and effective evaluation of lecturer competence and performance.

In summary, recent introduction of ESG 2015 has introduced new ideas, as concerned parties' – students' and prospective employers' – representation; and transferred the focus from teacher-centred approaches to learning outcomes and teaching methodologies. As a result, new indicators, such as dropout and slow progress during one's studies, are accentuated. Teaching methodologies and actual lecturer competencies, however, are not subject to external control; internal control is most varied and depends on the organizational culture of the given institution.

5 Conclusion

Domestic quality assurance practices are sometimes lagging behind clear-cut guiding principles. Tensions between the guidelines and actual practices are manifested in repeated conflicts among different interest groups, such as government, HAC, students, the labour market and academia. Strategic documents from major universities, especially those with strong connections to the market economy, reflect the formation of a genuine quality culture; whereas in minor institutions internal 'on-paper' rules, and the proliferation of formal organizations, represent their adherence to the minimum requirements determined by the law. Deficiencies are not so much due to shortcomings in knowledge but to lack of financial resources and developmental attitudes and motivations.

Some of the current quality problems and tensions are rooted in Hungarian social and cultural traditions, which are incompatible with the requirements of knowledge-based societies. Continual debates concerning centralization–decentralization strategies, political-ideological influence over academic life, and the idea of direct governmental control, fits and starts modernization efforts, and examples of counter-selection are among the contemporary problems which call for further reforms and underline the importance of internal and external quality assurance.

The question of the autonomy of academic life is perhaps one of the keys to understanding quality assurance problems. Guidelines are sometimes understood as, and transformed into, inhibiting requirements. Universities had been under strict ideological and political control for many decades of the communist era, and in many instances, their activities and main goals since the 1980s were shaped by the idea of the freedom of thought. In the shadow of authoritative traditions, quality assurance frameworks are often interpreted as a means to exercise external control over institutions and lecturers, threatening the brief autonomy of universities. Such interpretations are still dominant over the developmental attitudes that are inherently present in systems of quality assurance.

Government (funder) control is very high at macro levels: in the legal regulations concerning the foundation, integration and organizational structures of an academic institution, including the top leaders' appointment (rector, chancellor). Further, government control is marked in determining the qualifications and the equivalent study programmes (contents and levels), possible study areas and student capacity of a given institution, core content and staffing requirements of the study programmes including lecturers' workload; admission and status of students, the range of fees to be paid by students and in most financial issues. On the other hand, government control and responsibilities are not present at the micro levels. Institutional, internal control at these levels is most varied and may change between the institutions. The idea of systematic and continuous internal quality assurance and thinking in terms of quality cycles concerning the subjects – as proposed in ESG 2015 – is relatively new.

Rigid disciplinary boundaries, lack of inter- and multi-disciplinary approaches and the low prestige of some applied/multidisciplinary areas, denying the *in varietate concordia* European principle, represent a disadvantage and have cultural-historical origins. Forced centralization efforts, distorted competition among academic institutions, requirements that are disproportionate to accessible resources, contradicting regulations in some areas (including those in the labour market), and a relative disregard towards intellectuals in society are among the ills of the Hungarian system of higher education. Collaboration among the concerned parties (stakeholders) is sometimes impeded by the lack of a constructive negotiation culture where the diversity of viewpoints is mutually respected and considered.

The idea that (unevaluated) practice and market relations should govern tertiary education instead of a reflexive relation of practice, research and education has its origin in the simplifications concerning postmodern, functionalist views on academic life. Further, it echoes the 'productive–non-productive' fallacy, though one of the requirements of the Bologna process is organic relations among these areas. Unnecessary parallelisms have their roots in persistent clientalist traditions and individual bargains instead of clear-cut frameworks or constructive competition (Derényi, 2016). In this context, streaming attempts may result in losses in the resiliency and adaptivity of the system.

The recent introduction of new databases and excellence initiations have restarted a discourse on quality issues in which new aspects have emerged. The 2017 turn in quality assurance – the introduction of ESG 2015 – is a definite move from the dominance of external quality control towards building institutions' quality cultures, a major step form Bollaert's (2014) first level to the second, where quality does not depend on individual commitments only but managers think in terms of quality enhancement processes.

If finances, legislation and quality expectations do not harmonize then empty and floating signifiers will dominate the developing quality discourse. Much of the current tensions come from high expectations parallel to budgetary cuts, such as the controversies between HAC staffing requirements and finances. Deficiencies, so natural in such an abundance of reforms, are not improved by introducing more evaluation, but even more reforms. Systematic evaluation before implementing new strategies could significantly improve future results (Ellis & Hogard, 2006; Ellis, 2013).

Strategic planning is a real challenge in a volatile environment, and is often reduced to mere paperwork. Some of the institutions, however, do consider their own institution development plans, a contemporary obligation, as a chance for comprehensive internal evaluation in setting their own direction. Genuine strategic thinking often proves a major factor of institutional success (Derényi, 2016).

Universities as role models, in addition to being objects of external quality assurance activities, are assigned a mission in quality development and value orientation in the society. This tradition is a strong constituent of academic responsibility, irrespective of the rapid changes in the environment. Local-level, voluntary introduction of internal quality assurance systems is a possible direction to meet existing challenges and outline an eligible framework for innovation, resourcefulness and development, and taking responsibilities proportionate to each organizational level.

Notes

1 Soviet-type rationalizations of the practice followed the ideas of communist dictators: 'The intelligentsia – a nanny for the capitalists – was busy patching the philosophical and religious dominance of the bourgeois that had long been worn out and polluted by the blood of working class people' (Gorky, 1950, 289).

2 Today, the entire system is operated on a budget that equals that of a single elite institution in Switzerland or the United Kingdom (Derényi, 2016).

References

Bazsa, Gy. (2014) A minőségügy és az akkreditáció. *Educatio*(1)93–107.

Blaskó, Zs. (2014) *Surveying the absentees – surveying the emigrants. A methodological paper on the SEEMIG pilot study to survey emigrants from Hungary and Serbia.* SEEMIG Working Papers, No. 4, Budapest, Hungarian Demographic Research Institute.http://www.seemig.eu/down loads/outputs/SEEMIGWorkingPapers4.pdf

Bókay, A. (2008) Tanulási eredmények – a felsőoktatás modernizációjának kulcskérdése. in: Krémó, A. (ed.): *Oktatás és képzés 2010 - Műhelybeszélgetések 2007.* Budapest, Oktatási és Kulturális Minisztérium. 123–130.

Bollaert, L. (2014) *A Manual for Internal Quality Assurance in Higher Education with Special Focus on Professional Higher Education.* Brussels: European Association of Institutions in Higher Education.

Central Statistical Office (2016) http://www.ksh.hu.

Csekei, L., Szarkáné Erdélyi T.& Csirik, J. (eds. 2010) *A magyar felsőoktatás az Európai Felsőoktatási Térségben.* Budapest, Oktatási és Kulturális Minisztérium.

Derényi, A. (2016) *A stratégiák szerepe a hazai felsőoktatásban.* Oktatási vonatkozások az egyetem stratégiáiban. Műhelykonferencia. Pécsi Tudományegyetem, Pécs, 2016. június 13.

DPR Zárótanulmány (2014) https://www.felvi.hu/felsooktatasimuhely/dpr/hazai_dpr/friss diplomasok2014_zarotanulmany

Eduline (2016) *Eléggé megugrott a diplomások aránya az EU-ban.* http://eduline.hu/felsooktatas/2016/4/28/Elegge_megugrott_a_diplomasok_aranya_az_EUb_JMTXOF

Ellis, R. (2013) Policy, evaluation and practice. *Szociális Szemle.* (1–2.) 7–9.

Ellis, R. & Hogard, E. (2006) The Trident: A three–pronged method for evaluating clinical, social and educational innovations. *Evaluation* (12) 372–383.

ENQA News (2016) *ENQA welcomes new full member and affiliate agencies. European Association for Quality Assurance in Higher Education.* http://www.enqa.eu/index.php/enqa-welcomes-new-full-member-and-affiliate-agencies/

Erdos, M. B. (2016) *The role of evaluation research in a country in transition.* Buckinghamshire, Buckinghamshire New University - Social and Health Evaluation Unit. Occasional paper no. 14.

Erdos, M. B. & Gabor Kelemen (2011) The finite universe: Discursive double bind and parrhesia in state socialism. *History of Communism in Europe* 2. 281–309

Europe 2020 (2010) http://ec.europa.eu/eu2020/pdf/COMPLET%20EN%20BARROSO%20 %20%20007%20-%20Europe%202020%20-%20EN%20version.pdf

Eurydice (2004–5) *Eurybase. The information database on education systems in Europe. The education system in Hungary.* European Commission. https://slideblast.com/institutions_59cd5f 561723dd55eec302a6.html

HAC Self-Evaluation Report (2013) http://www.mab.hu/web/doc/mabmin/Self_Evaluation_ Report_110313.pdf

Hrubos, I. (2016) A köztes testületek működése és recepciója. In: Derényi, A., Temesi, J. (eds.) *A magyar felsőoktatás 1988 és 2014 között.* Budapest,Oktatáskutató és Fejlesztő Intézet. 81–98.

Jancsó, T. (2010) A magyar felsőoktatás területi szerkezetének és hallgatói létszámának alakulás 1900-tól 1945-ig in: Bottlik, Zs.(ed.) *Önálló lépések a tudomány területén.* Budapest, ELTE TTK. 29–46. http://rtt.elte.hu/sites/default/files/images/eltekotet_2.pdf

Javaslat a nemzeti felsőoktatási kiválóság intézményei minősítésekre (2013) http://ofi.hu/sites/default/files/attachments/a_vezetoi_osszefoglalo_modszertan.pdf

Kerekes, G, Molnárné Stadler, K., Orosz, L.& Pintér, Cs. (2012) *Felsőoktatási Minőségfejlesztési Kézikönyv.* Budapest, Oktatáskutató és Fejlesztő Intézet

Kováts, G. (2014) *A felsőoktatási minőségügy aktuális trendjei.* Budapest, Oktatáskutató és Fejlesztő Intézet

Kováts, G. (2016) Intézményi egyesülések és szétválások: Nemzetközi tapasztalatok és hazai gyakorlat. In: Derényi, A. & Temesi, J. (eds.) *A magyar felsőoktatás 1988 és 2014 között.* Budapest, Oktatáskutató és Fejlesztő Intézet.101–148

MAB (2014) http://www.mab.hu/web/index.php?option=com_content&view=article&id=370&Itemid=882&lang=hu

MAB Önértékelési útmutató (2017) http://www.mab.hu/web/doc/akkreditacio/Intakkr_onert_utmut_ESG_20170526H.pdf

Molnár, B. (2012) *A felsőoktatásban tapasztalható lemorzsolódás lehetséges okai.* https://www.slideshare.net/molnarbea/molnr-beta-lemorzsolds-tanulmny

National Reform Programme of Hungary (2011) http://ec.europa.eu/europe2020/pdf/nd/nrp2013_hungary_en.pdf

Nefmi (2010) *A felsőoktatási törvény koncepciójáról egyeztettek.* http://www.nefmi.gov.hu/miniszterium/2010/felsooktatasi-torveny-egyeztetes

Policity Team (2011) *A magyar felsőoktatás fejlődése a rendszerváltozás óta.* http://www.policity.eu/tanulmany/2011/09/10/a-magyar-felsoktatas-fejldese-a-rendszervaltas-ota/

Polonyi, I. (2008) A felsőoktatás minőségügye. *Educatio*,(1)5–21.

Quante, M. (2010) *A kutatás- és tudománypolitika aktuális kérdései Németországban.* http://www.matud.iif.hu/2010/06/05.htm

Quigley, K.F. (2015) Something old, something new. In Picard, L.A., Groelsema, R. & Buss, T.F. (eds) *Foreign Aid and Foreign Policy: USAID and Eastern Europe.* London, New York: Routledge, 214–236

Standards and Guidelines for Quality Assurance in the European Higher Education Area (ESG) (2015) Brussels, Belgium.

Stéger, Cs. (2015) *Felsőoktatás-pedagógiáról a lemorzsolódás tükrében.* ELTE TTOMC. Tanári Műhely Tanárképzőknek. Budapest, 2015. május 13. http://docplayer.hu/15918365-Felsooktatas-pedagogiarol-a-lemorzsolodas-tukreben.html

Surányi, I. (2007) A szocialista oktatáspolitika Székesfehérvár általános iskolai gyakorlatában. 1948–1990. *Neveléstörténet,* 1–2. http://www.kodolanyi.hu/nevelestortenet/index.php?rovat_mod=archiv&act=menu_tart&cid=35&rid=1&id=263

Szántó, T. (2016) Az ESG kialakulása és megújulása. In: Derényi, A. (ed.), *A felsőoktatás minőségbiztosítási horizontja.* Budapest, Oktatáskutató és Fejlesztő Intézet, 15–24

Tari, A. (2010) *Y-generáció.* Budapest, Jaffa Kiadó

Veres, P (2016) Az 1998–2014 közötti korszak áttekintése a felsőoktatási stratégiai dokumentumok alapján. In: Derényi, A. & Temesi, J. (eds.), *A magyar felsőoktatás 1988 és 2014 között,* 13–34.

Weiss, C. (1993) Where politics and evaluation research meet. *Evaluation Practice,* 14(1), 93–106

Legal sources

Act I. of 1985 on Education

Act LXXX of 1993 on Higher Education

Act CXXXIX of 2005 on Higher Education

Act CCIV of 2011 on National Higher Education http://www.mab.hu/web/doc/hac/regulations/Ftv2012_Eng.pdf

Government Decree 19/2012. (II. 22.) on Specific Issues Regarding Higher Education, Quality Evaluation and Development http://net.jogtar.hu/jr/gen/hjegy_doc.cgi?docid=A1200019.KOR

Act C of 2015 on the 2016 Central Budget of Hungary
Act C of 2014 on the 2015 Central Budget of Hungary
Act CCXXX of 2013 on the 2014 Central Budget of Hungary
Act CCIV of 2012 on the 2013 Central Budget of Hungary
Act CLXXXVIII of 2011 on the 2012 Central Budget of Hungary
Act CLXIX of 2010 on the 2011 Budget of the Republic of Hungary
Act CXXX of 2009 on the 2010 Budget of the Republic of Hungary

Part II
Identifying Quality

19 Effective Teaching?

George Brown and Sarah Edmunds

This chapter is concerned with research on effective teaching in higher education (HE). Inevitably, that concern raises issues of what are the domains of teaching, the nature of effectiveness and the changes in the landscape of higher education (see also Chapters 1, 2, and 3). Before embarking on a discussion of the relevant research, it may be helpful to outline the underlying concepts involved in teaching, then outline the relevant research and explore in the final sections of the chapter some of the influences on teachers and students and the different perspectives on effectiveness. The chapter does not attempt to review comprehensively all the research on effective teaching. Such an undertaking would require a separate handbook. Rather, it provides an outline of the salient features of the research and sets these in the context of the changing nature of HE. Readers interested in detailed reviews of teaching are referred to Brown and Atkins (2002), Devlin and Samarawickrema (2010), Svinicki and McKeachie (2011), Fry *et al.* (2014), and Ashwin (2015).

Learning, assessment and teaching

Exploring effectiveness of teaching involves a consideration of the three closely related domains of learning, assessment and teaching. Figure 19.1 shows their relationship. The degree of overlap may vary from course to course but it can be safely assumed that not all learning is taught, not all teaching leads to learning and, occasionally, what is assessed may not have been taught or learnt.

Learning may be conceived as changes in knowledge, understanding, skills and attitudes brought about by experience and reflections upon that experience. Although it is not often highlighted, it is an intentional activity. Put simply, to learn effectively students need to have the intention to learn. Assessment consists of taking a sample of what students can do, making inferences about their capabilities, estimating and reporting their current worth. It is now commonly used for both assessing directly students' learning or for reviewing programmes or universities at the managerial level as in Quality Assessment and the newly emerging Teaching Excellency Frameworks in the UK (TEF, 2016). Teaching involves both the provision of learning and assessment. It is an intentional activity of providing opportunities for learning and assessment. It operates at the level of face-to-face teaching and the level of course design and course management.

The content of learning may be facts, procedures, skills, ideas and values. The broad goals of learning may be gains in knowledge and skills, deepening of understanding, the development of problem-solving and changes in perception, attitudes, values and behaviour. These changes are brought about through the experience, reflections and intentions of the learner. The experience may be structured as in formal teaching situations or unstructured as in

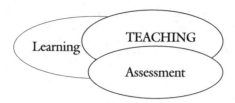

Figure 19.1 Relationship between teaching, learning and assessment

browsing or casual learning from one's peers. Students, of course, may have more immediate goals such as passing or getting a good mark in practicals and written examinations. Last but not least, the major long-term goal of teaching may be the development of capabilities to learn to learn. For it is these capabilities which are the foundations of transferable skills for the preparation for work, continuing professional development, effective lifelong learning and preparation for an unknown future. There is a danger in focussing too closely upon preparing students for their work immediately after graduation rather than for their unknown futures. Even if a person does not change jobs, their job might change.

What counts as effective teaching depends in part on what is conceived as the characteristics of teaching and its major purpose. Stakeholders may differ but there is no doubt that for students, systematic, stimulating and caring teaching are priorities. This was shown by the factor analyses of Ryans (1960), who identified three major factors:

- systematic, business-like versus unsystematic, slipshod;
- stimulating, interesting versus boring, dull;
- warm, friendly versus cold, hostile.

Whilst differences in emphases vary over the years (Marsh, 1987; NSS, 2017), these characteristics have remained remarkably stable and are even found in studies of school students. Similar results were found in 86 per cent of schoolgirls surveyed (n = 11,000) (GDST, 2016).

Entwined in the notions of teaching are effective or 'successful' teaching and the values of 'good' teaching. To illustrate this point, a lecturer may teach a course on statistics based on intended learning outcomes devised by the department. The students take on board the intended learning outcomes and pass the examination with flying colours – and then drop statistics and develop a dislike of statistics which persists into their working lives. The lecturer could be regarded as effective and successful, but was he or she a good teacher? The answers depend, in part, on the valuers and what is valued more: developing long-term attitudes to learning or producing short-term gains. This theme is returned to in the final section of the chapter. Clearly, there is more to estimating or measuring effective teaching than rating face-to-face teaching.

Methods, structures, skills and styles of teaching

Figure 19.2 provides a schematic model of methods, structures, skills and styles which are pertinent to research on teaching and measures of its effectiveness.

At one extreme is the conventional lecture, in which student control and participation is usually minimal. At the other extreme is private study, in which lecturer control and

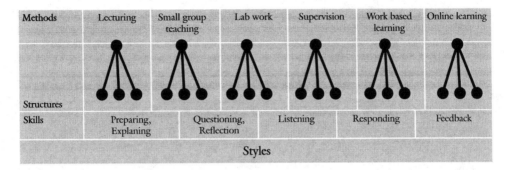

Methods	Lecturing	Small group teaching	Lab work	Supervision	Work based learning	Online learning

Structures

Skills	Preparing, Explaning	Questioning, Reflection	Listening	Responding	Feedback

Styles

Figure 19.2 Methods, structures, skills and styles. The skills underpin the structures and the generic methods of teaching

participation is usually minimal. It should be noted that, even at the ends of the continuum, there is some control on participation by both lecturer and students. In lectures students may choose what notes to take, if any, to look at their laptops to ask questions or even disrupt the class. A student's private study is likely to be influenced by the suggestions of the lecturer, the materials that he or she has provided, the assignments and examinations and the resources that are available online and in the library.

Between the extremes of the continuum one may place, approximately, small group teaching, laboratory work, project, research supervision, work-based learning and online learning. The precise location of these methods of teaching is less easy, for each method of teaching contains a rich variety of structures involving varying proportions of lecturer and student participation. For example, small group teaching may be highly structured and tightly controlled by the lecturer or it may be free-flowing discussion in which the lecturer facilitates occasionally. Laboratory work may be a series of routine experiments specified precisely by the lecturer or a set of guided enquiries in which the student develops hypotheses to test, chooses methods and designs appropriate experiments. A research supervision may be wholly lecturer-directed, another may be wholly student-directed.

These differences within methods of teaching lead to the second level of analysis: structures. Thus within the method of lecturing one may distinguish between a classical structure that divides a topic into segments that are further subdivided, and the problem-centred structure, which focuses upon different solutions to a problem, such as 'What is the relationship between body and mind?' In small group teaching one can distinguish structures such as the mini-lecture, the seminar paper, structured discussions, case studies, question-and-answer sessions and role play (Edmunds and Brown, 2010).

There are two implications of the levels of methods and structures for studies of effective teaching. First, one should be clear what one is comparing. A comparison of the relative effectiveness of two methods may be a comparison of two structures. Second, broad comparisons of methods of teaching can only provide pointers to potentially effective uses of methods. Small group teaching may be the most effective method of encouraging students to talk and think, but in the hands of some lecturers a small group session may be the most effective way of inhibiting discussion and thinking. To ensure that methods are effective one may have to explore the underlying skills used by lecturers and their styles of teaching.

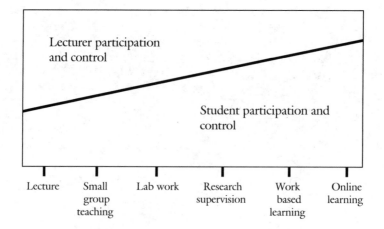

Figure 19.3 A continuum of teaching methods

Skills

In essence, skills, whether of teaching or learning, are constructs used to describe goal-directed sequences of actions that may be learnt and routinised (Hargie, 2011). All skills have cognitive, perceptual, social and motor components but the proportions vary within skills. All types of skills are involved in teaching, although cognitive and social skills are the most important in teaching. One should not, however, undervalue the motor skills involved in some subjects – from fine art to neurosurgery. Nor should one assume that the same label of skill has the same underlying characteristics. Problem-solving skills in Mathematics are not identical with problem-solving skills in English Literature; evaluating evidence in Histopathology is not the same as evaluating evidence in History.

One should also bear in mind that skills are located in contexts and those contexts shape the skills. For transfer to occur, the evidence suggests that:

- transfer is likely to occur when a person understands the underlying principles;
- knowledge and understanding of differences of contexts are necessary;
- training in transfer maximises its possibility.

(Annett and Sparrow, 1989)

These principles have implications for designing and appraising learning situations and for preparing students for different learning situations.

Core skills of teaching

The core skills of teaching are:

- preparing and structuring teaching materials;
- the interactive skills of explaining, listening, questioning, responding to students' comments and answers; providing and giving guidance, assessment and feedback;
- reflecting upon one's own teaching.

These skills do not have a one-to-one relationship with the structures and methods of teaching. Rather they are a personal repertoire that a lecturer may draw upon to shape his or her teaching. The core skills may be subdivided further into subskills and elements or messages. Confusion arises in discussions of the important skills of teaching. Teaching may be regarded as a skill in its own right or a set of skills. Within teaching the use of questioning is a skill, within questioning the use of probing questions is a skill and within probing questions the use of asking for specific examples may be regarded as a skill. Such confusion may be minimized by recognizing that skills necessarily overlap and by deciding upon the level of an analysis that is appropriate for the task.

One should also be wary of over-refined analyses or atomistic approaches to measuring skills or effectiveness. To give an extreme example, it does not follow that because one can analyse teaching interactions or learning outcomes into several bits of information – and one can – that this information is useful for appraising teaching. Rather, one should fit the level of analysis to the task, the method of training to the purpose of training and the background of the trainees and, if practicable, their learning styles. Broadly speaking, analyses based on meaningful wholes and holistic approaches seem preferable to atomistic approaches (Slavin, 1990).

Despite the limitations of the construct of skills, it does provide a basis for analysing teaching, for educating and training teachers in higher education and for assessing effective teaching. It may also be argued that the supra-ordinate skill of knowing when to use a particular skill is as important as the core skills themselves.

Styles

Methods, structures and skills provide a general description of teaching. All these are influenced and modified by the salient personal characteristics of the teacher. Usually these characteristics are brought together in the notions of styles of teaching. A teaching style may be regarded as 'a characteristic response to teaching situations that are perceived as similar'. Such an approach provides a focus for exploring a person's perceptions and actions within a teaching context. It should be noted that how someone teaches in one situation is not necessarily closely related to how he or she teaches in other teaching situations. Hence the danger of generaliising about the effectiveness of a teacher from observations of teaching in one context.

Styles of teaching are also likely to be dependent upon the styles of learning of the lecture and upon the traditions of the subject that is being taught. It is unlikely that one could ever extract an essence of style of teaching that is totally independent of styles of learning and subject, but one can identify and describe broad categories of styles that can then be used to help the lecturer to develop within his or her style and perhaps to change or develop styles. This point is returned to in the section on lecturing.

The framework of teaching and learning described so far has implications for exploring effective teaching. First, as indicated, student learning is only partially dependent upon teaching. The overall quality of the learning environment is likely to have its effects upon the learning styles, strategies and motivations of students. Second, evaluations of teaching that rely solely on observations of teaching methods are likely to neglect the crucial variables of course design, management, preparation and assessment procedures. Third, the wide variations of structures within methods suggest that comparisons across methods in any one study need to be treated cautiously. Cumulative evidence or meta-analyses are likely to yield better guidelines.

Research on learning, assessment and teaching

Much of the research on learning, assessment and teaching took place in the latter part of the 20th century. The research is relevant to discussions of different aspects of effective teaching but one should bear in mind there have been changes in policy, working conditions and probably of some attitudes of teachers and students. However, the research is still relevant until proved otherwise. One should bear in mind that the same concepts may be given new labels or re-emerge after a few decades. Diversity, inclusivity, student engagement and sustainability are continuing issues. The advice of Ausubel remains germane: 'The most important single factor influencing learning is what the learner already knows. Ascertain this and teach him (her) accordingly' (Ausubel, 1968, p. vi).

Research on learning

A knowledge of how students learn (see Brown, 2004) is an important basis for developing one's teaching and estimating the effectiveness of teaching. There are four broad strands of research on learning.

The first strand has been directed towards the effects of personality, motivation and identity on learning (Wittrock, 1986). This was followed by the development of self-directed learning, self-determination theory, sometimes described as heutagogy or self-management of learning (Hase and Kenyon, 2001). Such learning is considered of importance in online learning (see Ten Cate *et al.*, 2011) and postmodernist perspectives on learning (Beijaard *et al.*, 2004). The research shows that the way students perceive themselves and the way they account for their academic successes and failures have a strong bearing on their motivation and their performance. Students are likely to initiate learning, sustain it, direct it and actively involve themselves in it when they believe that success or failure is caused by their own effort or lack of it rather than by factors outside their control. Praise, reward or other positive reinforcements are likely to enhance motivation only if students perceive them to be related to factors over which they have control. Thus building up students' sense of control over their own work, giving them opportunities to exercise responsibility for their own learning, and helping them to develop self-management skills can all help to make them more successful and effective learners. Suggestions of ways of improving a future assignment are likely to be more useful to students than detailed criticisms or praise of the existing assignment These points needs to be borne in mind when considering the effectiveness of feedback to students: an important aspect of a teacher's role.

A second strand is based on studies of cognitive processing. This strand developed partly from the work of Ausubel *et al.* (1978) in the United States and partly from the major domain of experimental cognitive psychology, concerned with information processing (Baddeley, 1999). Ausubel stressed the importance of stimulating prior learning in teaching. He advocated the use of 'advanced organisers', which orient a student towards what is to be learnt, preferably through concrete examples. These organisers are sometimes likened to scaffolds or bridges that link previous knowledge to the new knowledge being acquired. This view is substantiated by reviews of research (Dochy *et al.*, 2003). The strand of cognitive processing has been neglected by writers on research in higher education, but it does provide the core processes of learning and thinking. A model which links its processes is shown in Figure 19.4

A third strand of empirical work has focused on various approaches to learning. The work was initiated by the phenomenographic research of Marton on deep and surface learning.

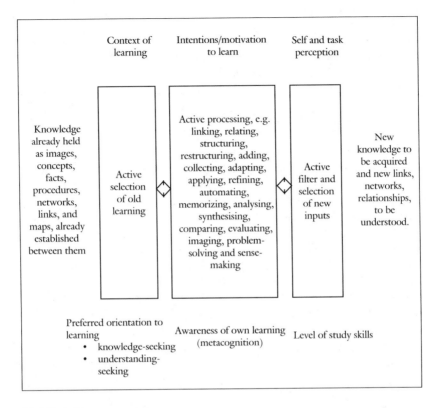

Figure 19.4 Cognitive processing

It was subsequently developed by Entwistle (1997) in the UK and Biggs (Biggs and Tang, 2011) in Australia. The research is summarized in Entwistle *et al.* (2010) and Brown *et al.* (1997, 2014). Three dominant orientations were identified by Entwistle: knowledge-seeking, understanding-seeking and achieving. But it should be borne in mind that people may vary their orientation in different contexts. Those who have a knowledge-seeking orientation search for facts and information. Their learning may be rote; it may be surface learning rather than deep learning. Those with a strong knowledge-seeking orientation are often referred to as 'reproducers'. When oriented towards reproductive learning, learners are not interested in speculating, playing with ideas or searching for deeper meanings. In contrast, those with an understanding orientation are less interested in facts and more interested in searching for understanding and personal meaning. They relate what they learn to their earlier experiences, they explore potential connections, linkages and discrepancies. They tend to be intrinsically motivated. Hence they are likely to be deep problem-solvers, to be creative and independent minded.

Both 'reproducers' and 'understanders' may have varying degrees of achievement motivation. When achievement motivation is high, there is a willingness to switch styles of learning to the one demanded by the system of teaching and assessment. When it is low, they go their own way – sometimes much to the despair of their teachers or supervisors.

These different approaches to learning are not merely learner characteristics. They are associated with a set of characteristics of a learning environment. Ramsden's work (2003) indicates that departments where good teaching was reported were strongly oriented towards personal meaning. Good teaching included such variables as effective lecturing, help with specific difficulties and perceived freedom to learn. Poor teaching included such variables as ineffective lecturing, heavy workload, inappropriate assessment and lack of freedom to learn. In the 'poorer' departments the orientation towards reproductive learning was strong. The use of multiple-choice questions (MCQs) and other forms of tests tended to promote reproductive styles of learning, whereas projects and open-ended assessments promoted independence and deeper strategies of understanding. Similar findings were obtained in a recent study by Cobb *et al.* (2013). They reported that many veterinary students preparing for final examinations based on MCQs used a reproductive orientation. The same students when working on work placements, where assessment was light, used an understanding orientation.

A criticism of findings on contexts of learning is the findings favour courses in some subjects but not in others. There is a tendency to infer that the knowledge-seekers produce superficial learning and the understanding-seekers engage in deep learning. The concomitant implication is that the first orientation is inferior to the second. For some tasks this may be true but not necessarily for all. Knowledge-seeking should not be dismissed out of hand. Knowing that and knowing how to are important in most subjects. For example, a neurologist needs to know the specific neurological function of the optic nerve to make an accurate diagnosis. A linguist needs to learn grammar and vocabulary – perhaps by rote – as part of mastering a language. A historian needs to know the terms of the Treaty of Versailles before attempting an analysis of the causes of World War II. It seems more helpful, therefore, to consider both knowledge orientation and understanding orientation necessary. Effective learning can then be conceived as a continuous process of development, backwards and forwards between the two orientations.

Finally, perhaps the most disquieting findings from this research are that deeper approaches to study and independent learning decline during many undergraduate courses (Biggs, 1987). This is an area which requires more exploration by course designers and researchers.

A fourth strand is provided by Biggs and his associates (see Biggs and Tang, op. cit.) From early work on student learning the SOLO taxonomy (Structure of Observed Learning Outcomes) was developed. With some modifications it may be used for analysing learning tasks and assessing students' work (Bondemark *et al.*, 2004). The five levels of Biggs's schema are:

- pre-structural – the task is not attacked appropriate; the student has not understood the question
- unstructural – one or a few aspects are picked up but understanding is nominal;
- multi-structural – several aspects of the task are provided but not connected;
- relational – the components are integrated;
- extended abstract – the whole is conceptualised at a higher level and set in a wider context.

One hopes the research on student learning will continue. It has illuminated the processes of how we learn. It has implications for course design, assessment, teaching, staff development and the modus operandi of departments and universities.

Research on assessment

The most important finding from research on assessment is if you want change the learning of students, change the assessment. This is perhaps the most powerful change agent in the students' context (Brown *et al.*, 2007, 2014). The common methods of assessment currently are MCQs, essays and other forms of written work and practical work including work-based learning. Various types of MCQs are efficient, but often not an effective way of measuring understanding. Essays are more likely to provide measures of understanding, and direct observation of practical skills can provide useful measures of practical competence. Laboratory notebooks are weak indicators of practical abilities.

A common debate in studies of assessment is course work versus examinations. The advent of course work in the 1960s prompted the debate in terms of testing for learning and testing for grading, formative assessment or summative assessment, assessment for learning or assessment of learning. Marked course work which counted towards a degree classification was relatively sparse and remains so in a few universities. Nowadays most course assignments are multiple sources of summative assessment. Final examinations are sometimes only a part, if any, of the components of the degree awarded. Whether all course work should be assessed remains an open debate. Course work that does not count is likely to be ignored by calculative students. But if all course work counts towards the degree classification then the assessment regime may stultify learning. Final examinations can induce stress and they cannot measure accurately all the important aspects of higher education. The debate continues and, as usual, the controllers of the discourse will shape the future pattern of assessment for learning and assessment for grading.

An important component of the continuing debate is the quality of feedback. Feedback may refer to providing knowledge of current performance or guidance on future performance (sometimes referred to as forward feedback). The general guidelines of effective feedback are that it is meaningful to the recipient, accurate, timely and encourages reflection. The advice is pertinent to students giving feedback to lecturers as well as lecturers giving feedback to students. Anonymity, voluntary feedback and sampling raise issues of the validity of surveys, including the much vaunted National Student Survey (NSS, 2017).

Research on teaching

Most of the research on effective teaching has been based upon the views of students and lecturers. There has been research based on scores on achievement tests or in examinations but such research assumes too close a relationship between teaching and student learning. There has been some research on the views of employers and recent graduates (see Berk, this volume, Chapter 24). As far as we know there is not, as yet, any substantial research on the cognitive processes of lecturers when they are preparing materials for teaching.

The data collection has used quantitative, qualitative and mixed methods of research. It has ranged from in-depth interviews; semi-structured or structured questionnaires; direct observation of teaching; structured observations of teaching using checklist and rating schedules; detailed analyses of video recordings, transcripts of teaching and course documents. Anyone who thinks that teaching in higher education has not been subjected to scrutiny should look closely at the range of research that has already been reported.

The cumulative evidence provides some broad tentative generalisations on the effectiveness of various methods of teaching. Lectures are effective, cheap, efficient methods of presenting information and providing explanations. Practical skills are, obviously, taught more effectively in laboratories but the underlying methodologies and theories may be taught as effectively and perhaps more efficiently in lectures and small group sessions. Small group methods are usually better than other methods at promoting intellectual skills, including problem-solving, and changing attitudes. They are about as effective as other methods of teaching at imparting information. But small group teaching is clearly not an efficient method of imparting information; its particular strength lies in the interplay of views that develop a student's capacity to think. Comparisons of traditional and newer methods of teaching, such as online learning, and simulations often yield results in favour of the newer methods. However, newer methods are often prepared carefully and evaluated systematically, whereas traditional methods of teaching are often not subjected to such rigour. The findings from comparisons of methods assume that each method is a stable phenomenon. But, as indicated earlier, there is a rich variety of structures within each method and within each method there is potential for both competent and incompetent teaching. As well as comparing broad methods of teaching it may be useful to study each method per se, with the intention of identifying the underlying skills involved and their efficacy.

Research on lecturing

Much of the research on lecturing was conducted in the 20th century (Brown and Manogue, 2001). As indicated earlier, various structures of lectures have been identified: the classical that divides the content into sections and subsections; the problem-centred that posits a problem and then provides alternative solutions or perspectives; the sequential that provides a logical progression of reasoning; and the eclectic that uses a mixture of methods. All structures were used in all faculties, although the classical and eclectic were more widespread.

Different styles of lecturing appear to be closely associated with subject content but not with length of experience or status. In one study five styles were identified. These were: the visual information giver; the oral presenter; the exemplary, who used a successful blend of visual and oral approaches; the eclectic, who was less successful at blending visual and oral approaches, who had self-doubts, but a strong commitment to his or her subject; and the amorphous lecturer, whose main characteristics were vagueness and arrogance. Visual information givers were most common in Sciences and Engineering, oral presenters in Arts. Both exemplaries and eclectics were found in all faculties. Amorphous lecturers could be found in all departments but were particularly common in Science, Engineering and Medicine (Brown and Bakhtar, 1987).

Usually, a lecture consists of one person to talking to many. But it does not follow that in a lecture session a lecturer must talk all the time. It has long been known that variations in activities can renew attention (Jones, 1923) but the notion of attention declining only after 20 minutes has been questioned (Bunce *et al.*, 2010). Variations in activities may include mini-discussions, group problem-solving or variations in the activities of the lecturer. But it should also be noted that note-taking requires skill in observing and selecting the key content. This is not a passive activity. For lectures to be an effective mode of teaching students need to take some responsibility for their learning from lectures: intention and active learning by the students is required for lecturing to be effective. This point is often overlooked by those who wish to reject all formal lectures. It is also relevant to other methods of teaching.

The conventional lecture methods are being extended in HE by the introduction of 'flip classrooms'. In essence, they consist of students doing preparation before the class, usually online, and carrying out activities in class. The method will not be unfamiliar to many lecturers but its nomenclature might be. Undergraduates are often required to read a text or consider a problem before attending a lecture or seminar. The flip classroom extends this approach by its use of media and more activity in a teaching session. The reviews by Dodds (2015) and Flaherty and Phillips (2015) suggest flip classrooms can be an effective teaching method and it is liked by students in secondary schools. Several questions about its implementation and effectiveness remain unresolved.

Of the skills of lecturing, explaining has received the most attention. Effective explainers use names and labels rather than pronouns, precise pointing at diagrams and naming of parts, simple definitions, simple sentences, emphases of key points, apt examples, guiding images, metaphors, analogies, repetition and paraphrasing of key points and clear transitions from one subtopic to the next (Land, 1985). As indicated earlier, both lecturers and students value clarity and interest. Evidence from some studies show high correlations between clarity and interest and student achievement (Land, 1985). The characteristics of clarity and interest drawn from the literature are shown in Figure 19.5.

There were differences between lecturers in Arts and Sciences. Logical structure and clarity were valued more highly by Science lecturers and students. Interest, insights and perspectives were valued more highly by Arts lecturers and students. This is not surprising given that the role of lecturer is perceived differently in different subject areas. Arts and Science lecturers also differed in their attitudes towards training. Broadly speaking, science lecturers were more likely to believe that training can improve such skills as logical presentation, use of aids and expressiveness (Brown and Daines, 1981). The scientists' views were borne out by small-scale studies that demonstrated that short courses of training can produce positive changes in lecturing skills. Further details may be found in Brown and Manogue (2001).

As hinted earlier, there has been a neglect of the cognitive processes involved in preparing teaching materials and whilst teaching. It is likely that preparation of teaching materials is a messy non-linear process. Stimulated recall techniques could illuminate some of the differences between ineffective lecturers and effective lecturers in their preparation of teaching materials.

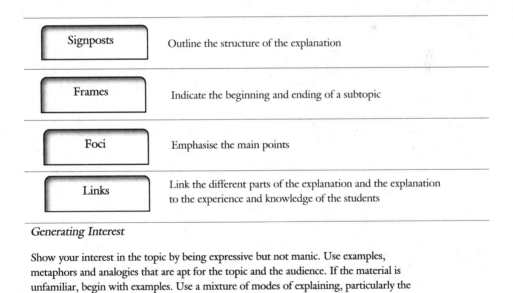

Signposts	Outline the structure of the explanation
Frames	Indicate the beginning and ending of a subtopic
Foci	Emphasise the main points
Links	Link the different parts of the explanation and the explanation to the experience and knowledge of the students

Generating Interest

Show your interest in the topic by being expressive but not manic. Use examples, metaphors and analogies that are apt for the topic and the audience. If the material is unfamiliar, begin with examples. Use a mixture of modes of explaining, particularly the narrative (story telling) mode. Play on the intellectual curiosity of the audience through the use of puzzles and problems.

Figure 19.5 Key characteristics of effective explaining

Research on small group teaching

A major theme of research on small group teaching in the past 50 years has been the efficacy of small group teaching. An early review of over 100 studies used examination results as the sole criteria (Dubin and Taveggia, 1968). They reported that small group teaching was only as effective as other methods of teaching but more costly. Their findings were a gift to financial managers. The reviews by Bligh (2000) and Jaques and Salmon (2007) show that small group teaching is usually better than other methods for promoting intellectual skills and changing attitudes. Edmunds and Brown (2010) provide accounts of the skills of questioning, listening, responding and explaining in small group teaching. They also point to various generic and facilitating methods of small group teaching. Reviews of peer group teaching (usually by older students) show that when used in conjunction with other methods of teaching it increases participation and develops the students' responsibility for their own learning (Falchikov, 2003; Boud *et al.*, 2014)

Small group teaching has the potential for stimulating thinking, sharing reflections and developing discussion skills. But some sessions of small group teaching are dominated by tutor talk and lower levels of thinking. Luker's study (1988) showed that lecturers built on students' ideas less than 2 per cent of the time and the proportion of time devoted to lecturing by tutors in seminars ranged from 7 to 70 per cent.

Baumgart (1976) identified the roles undertaken by tutors in small group teaching. These included instructor, commentator, stage setter, prober and reflexive judge. The reflexive judge appraises a contributor and probes. More thoughtful responses occurred when the tutor appraised and probed. The sessions in which there was more thinking displayed were the sessions that received more favourable student ratings. Jaques and Salmon (2007) add that tutors take other roles: the commentator, who sits at the periphery of the group and only makes occasional comments so the group are aware of the tutor's presence but are not using the tutor as the focus of discussion; the wanderer, who circulates amongst subgroups to help break unproductive discussion and to pick up the issues to use in subsequent whole group discussions; the absent friend, who temporarily leaves the learning space so the group can discuss sensitive issues. All of these modes of working with groups are influenced by the purposes of the group discussion. Small group sessions in the Sciences are usually rather different from small group sessions in the Arts. But both require the skills of questioning, listening and responding. Research reviews of questioning in teaching have consistently found that that teachers and tutors ask many more recall questions than questions that require thought (Dillon, 1997; Hargie, 2017). Other communication skills have been neglected.

Clearly there is still much research required on the structures and methods of small group teaching and its skills and styles. In addition there is a need to explore the feelings and shifts in attitude that occur in different small group structures. Jaques and Salmon (2007) offer suggestions for exploring these issues.

Research on laboratory teaching

The purposes of laboratory teaching are usually considered to be:

- teaching manual and observational skills relevant to the subject;
- improving understanding of methods of scientific enquiry;
- developing problem-solving skills;
- nurturing professional attitudes.

These purposes are now realised through the use of conventional laboratories (labs), remote labs and virtual labs (Gebbins and Perkin, 2013).

If any proof is needed that conventional laboratory teaching can improve technical skills then it may be found in the carefully designed early studies of Yager *et al.* (1969). They demonstrated that technical skills require practice but intellectual skills may be learnt as well in discussion settings as in laboratories. Laboratory teaching fares less well in the development of scientific understanding and methods of enquiry. Boud *et al.* (1986) concluded that cook books are not effective for developing scientific enquiry. Use of the structures concerned with enquiry rather than recipe are also shown to be related to students' interests in laboratory work. When a course stresses solely recipes it promotes reproductive learning. There is a risk that students in such laboratory courses will resort to superficial rote learning and store the knowledge gained as isolated units. Their beliefs and preconceptions are not modified by practical work that is based solely upon recipes (Tisher and White, 1986). It is perhaps these disquieting findings that has led to the development of alternative and augmented methods of laboratory teaching. These are considered in a subsequent paragraph.

The essential skills of demonstrators in laboratories are: explaining and presenting information; questioning, listening and responding; and giving directions. Each of these skills can be subdivided further. For example, the specific skills of a demonstrator are to know how to do and write up the experiment that students are doing; to give brief, clear explanations of processes and procedures; anticipate and recognise difficulties of understanding; ask questions that guide students and clarify difficulties of understanding; offer support and encouragement and know when to help and not help a student.

The training of demonstrators in these skills may go some way towards reducing the uncertainty that demonstrators experience and the wide variations in quality of help that are reported by students. Gebbins and Perkin (2013) report that the most valued characteristics of laboratory work were the hands-on experience, good lab leaders (demonstrators) and linking theory to practice. The least valued were long write-ups and not having sufficient time or practical experience in a lab session. Observational studies of laboratory work show that talk is largely centred upon laboratory procedures and low-level discussion. Lower-level enquiry processes, such as data interpretation or the formulation of conclusions, were detected but uncommon. Even rarer were extended thought questions and discussions of the nature of scientific enquiry (Shymansky *et al.*, 1979).

There do not appear to have been any studies of styles of teaching within laboratory classes, although Bliss and Ogborn (1977) provided clues on students' views of good and bad teaching. Good stories were linked to explicit teaching and demonstration and the provision of freedom to explore within a clear framework. Bad stories centred on the themes of poor laboratory management, chaos and heavily prescriptive regimes. Three styles of learning were identified in a study of students' design of experiments: empiricists, whose methods of scientific enquiry were systematic; borderliners, who got to the heart of the problem but by random methods; and dead reckoners, who only developed recipes (Pickering and Crabtree, 1979). Attitudes of students to practical work in physics was predominantly favourable (Hanif *et al.*, 2009).

Studies of comparisons of hands-on, remote and virtual labs reveal that students had reservations about replacing all hands-on labs with remote labs but they thought remote labs were more effective than simulations (Scanlon *et al.*, 2004). Similar results were found by Nafalski *et al.* (2011) in their carefully designed study of student perceptions of hands-on labs and virtual labs. Students showed greater awareness of experimental design and critical thinking in virtual labs than in hands-on labs and, not surprisingly, greater insight into practical skills in the hands-on laboratories. Lindsay and Good (2007) suggest that learning styles may be useful predictors of achievement in virtual and remote laboratories. Styles are almost certainly products of earlier learning strategies of both demonstrators and under-graduates. It is likely that well-thought-out structures of different forms of laboratories and of course designs can shift students towards a more rigorous approach to learning from laboratory experiences.

Research on project/research supervision

Projects are an extension of enquiry methods in science and engineering, dissertations are extensions of essays in the humanities and some social sciences. Both are preliminaries to postgraduate work. While their purposes, complexity and depth of study required are different, there is sufficient commonality to focus only upon postgraduate supervision.

Supervision consists essentially of a series of meetings with a student or a small group of students to discuss plans, progress and achievements. The supervision may be by a single supervisor, a pair of supervisors or a supervisory committee. There are advantages and disadvantages of each of these approaches but these have been neglected in the literature. Our own preference, and that of many students with whom we have discussed the issue, is a single supervisor is preferable on the grounds that it is difficult to serve two or more masters simultaneously. The proviso being the supervisor is a good one: organised, helpful and caring.

In the UK, the Quality Assurance Agency (QAA, 2012) has issued a comprehensive code of practice which institutions and therefore its supervisors are required to follow. The code includes guidelines on the skills and knowledge expected of supervisors and the support and guidance to be provided to students.

The code provides guidelines but it does not highlight the different modes of supervision in the Arts and Sciences nor consider the pressures upon academic supervisors to publish research. The pressure is felt particularly by science tutors.

Brown and Atkins (2002) listed eleven tasks for effective supervisors in any field:

- Director (determining topic and method, providing ideas);
- Facilitator (providing access to resources or expertise, arranging fieldwork);
- Adviser (helping to resolve technical problems, suggesting alternatives);
- Teacher (of research techniques);
- Guide (suggesting timetable for writing up, giving feedback on progress, identifying critical path for data collection);
- Critic (of design of enquiry, of draft chapters, of interpretations of data);
- Freedom giver (authorises student to make decisions, supports student's decisions);
- Supporter (gives encouragement, shows interest, discusses student's ideas);
- Friend (extends interest and concern to non-academic aspects of student's life);
- Manager (checks progress regularly, monitors study, gives systematic feedback, plans work);
- Examiner (e.g. internal examiner, mock vivas., interim progress reports, supervisory board member).

Subsequently, they developed a simple model for exploring styles of supervision which was used in a European study of student and supervisory preferences (Neerinck *et al.*, 1994) and by Smallwood *et al.* (1996). The model is shown in Figure 19.6.

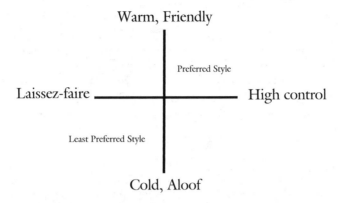

Figure 19.6 Student perceptions of supervisory styles

Generally speaking, Arts supervisors and students prefer more freedom and Science supervisors and students prefer more systematic approaches. Students' preferences change during the course of their research. In the early and final stages, they prefer more direct approaches. In the middle stage they want freedom to explore. However, the overall preferred approach combined professional guidance and personal warmth. The least preferred style was cold and laissez-faire. It was also the least successful in terms of completion rates.

Wright's doctoral work on research supervision (Wright, 1991) showed that effective supervisors, as measured by completion rates, have regular and frequent scheduled meetings with their students, set tasks, review progress regularly, comment on drafts and teach their students time management skills. These approaches were more common in the Sciences than in the Arts. Rudd (1985) reported that many students have problems in areas such as methodological difficulties, time management, writing up and isolation. Many of these are attributed to negligent supervision. Later research is in line with these findings (Taylor and Beasley, 2005; McCullough and Stokes, 2008; Taylor and Kiley, 2014; Phillips and Pugh, 2015).

The first prerequisites of effective supervision are probably to be actively involved in research and to reflect upon one's own experiences as a research student as well as a supervisor. The supervisor needs all the skills required by the research student, including project management and writing skills. In addition, interpersonal and teaching skills come into play from the first meeting to the viva and even beyond, perhaps to the first joint publication. Underpinning these skills are the important skills of planning, structuring and monitoring.

One way of ensuring that supervisions are purposeful working encounters is to consider the structure of an individual supervision. Shaw (1987), after his review of research supervision, concluded that the most useful sequence was:

1 Opening – rapport established.
2 Review – current context established.
3 Definition – scope and purpose of present meeting.
4 Exploration – problem(s), results and so on.
5 Clarification – decisions taken.
6 Goal-setting – decisions taken, next tasks identified.
7 Conclusion – evaluation, summary, disengagement.
8 Recording – notes on supervision made and filed.

Finally, it is worth noting that on the one hand there are those that believe a PhD should be the student's original and independent work in an academic subject. On the other, there are those who believe that a PhD is a training ground in which students acquire a repertoire of skills that may be used within and outwith the academic world. These different orientations lead to different approaches to supervision. In extremis, if the first position is held, then the supervisors are almost superfluous and presumably so too are the bulk of student fees. If the second position is held, then the thesis becomes part of a preparation for a career. Beneath these orientations are questions of value in research supervision that need addressing

Research on work-based learning

Work-based learning has long been part of engineering education (Brennan and Littlle, 1996). The structures of work-based learning (WBL) vary from prior experience before embarking on a course, vacation work, regular weekly commitments during part of a course, one-year placements or an intercalary year, as in modern language courses. Students and employers usually prefer longer placements. The major justifications of WBL are it prepares students for employment, it enriches their university courses and it enables them to make connections between their learning at university and the world of work (Baird, 2005). These aims are laudable but not always fulfilled in practice (Wilton, 2012; Jackson, 2014).

Studies of the benefits of WBL to students, employers and teachers in higher education are reported in Harvey *et al.* (1997, 1998) and Sheridan and Linehan (2011). They include:

- For students:

    - working in a setting which puts theories into practice;
    - developing an awareness of workplace culture;
    - appreciation of the rapidly changing world of work;
    - opportunity to develop a range of personal attributes (e.g. time management, self-confidence);
    - development of key interactive skills (e.g. team working, interpersonal and communication skills);
    - short-term financial benefits – some students get paid while on work placement;
    - enhanced employment prospects;

- in some cases, living and working in another culture.
- For employers:

    - setting up of a new research project;
    - completion of specific tasks;
    - opportunity to give a potential recruit a trial without obligation;
    - extra workers at low cost.

- For staff in higher education

    - opportunity, in some subjects, to see their subject area in practice;
    - enhancement of student learning skills;
    - satisfaction of seeing students developing and maturing;
    - using employer contacts to ensure that their teaching is up to date;
    - to encourage employers to participate on course validation panels.

Sheridan and Linehan (op. cit.) report student concerns about work placements. These included anxieties about the work required, lack of guidance by work tutors and, for some students, the costs incurred in travel and accommodation. Many considered that the award of pass/fail was not sufficient for a year of work experience, others that portfolios were a waste of time. The effective assessment of work-based learning remains a thorny issue.

Widely used methods of learning and assessment are personal learning plans and reflective portfolios (Lemanski *et al.*, 2011). The latter may be tightly structured so they almost become 'tick box' exercises or they may require deep personal reflections by the students on their learning and the opportunities provided by the workplace. Personal reflection does develop student learning (Moon, 2004) but care must be taken over the design of the portfolio and the guidance provided to students so that it is a useful instrument for both learning and assessment. Other forms of assessment are reports by work-placement tutors or visiting tutors, but these, too, have potential weaknesses. Not surprisingly, the quality of the learning experience and the amount of supervision across these structures may vary from a laissez-faire approach to a tight formal structure (Duignan, 2003). The Code of Practice (QAA, 2012) may have moved work-based learning towards more formal structures but the question remains: how does one measure the quality or effectiveness of work-based learning?

One common measure of the effectiveness of work-based learning is the degree classification awarded to students who have done one-year work placements and those who have not. Those who have done one-year work placements tend to obtain better degrees (Mayo and Jones, 1985; Davies, 1990; Gomez *et al.*, 2004). But the results prompt several questions. Amongst these are:

- Will the results hold if all students on a programme do work placements?
- Do better students choose to do placements?
- Are companies choosing the better students?
- Do placements increase motivation to study?
- Do placements provide preparation for the long-term future of companies and students?

These questions are at the heart of the value and effectiveness of work-based learning.

The generic learning skills for students to develop on work placements are generally agreed to be use of information technology (IT); numeracy; communication; group working; time management; learning to learn (Overton *et al.*, 2009). To these we would add learning how organisations and communities function. These skills are an important prerequisite of workplace tutors and to these should be added the skills required to tutor the work placement students. The latter are similar to those of an effective research supervisor, which were discussed earlier.

Research on online learning

Online learning refers to any learning which is undertaken through digital technology, usually outside the classroom. The learning may also occur in classrooms when required by the teacher. (Sometimes in classrooms students also use their laptops or tablets ostensibly for online learning purposes.) Online learning may be part of a blended learning system (a combination of face-to-face teaching and computer-based learning) (Vaughan, 2007) or a form of private study. Its forerunner in the UK was probably the distance learning courses of the Open University (OU). The OU provides a useful online introduction to online learning (Open University, 2017). The advent of computers has certainly enriched learning experiences, but it also has the potential for overwhelming students with information which may be neither useful nor accurate. Hence the importance of designing good courses which develop critical thinking and use appropriate tools of assessment. Nowadays MCQs and many other forms of assessment are provided and marked online. Essays are often marked by the assessors (not the computer, as yet) online.

The ascending hierarchy of structures of online learning, are 'drill and practice' programmes such as Duolingo (www.duolingo.com); hypertext and hypermedia, which are in essence miniature linked libraries of information but are not interactive; simulations of practical tasks that are interactive; and tutorial systems that are interactive and responsive (Laurillard, 2002). The latter provide different pathways and give explicit feedback. Within the structures of online learning are different methods. For online learning these are dependent upon the computer literacy of the designers as well as their knowledge and expertise in teaching, learning and assessment. Automated feedback, except in the most sophisticated tutorial systems, may not address the particular strength or weakness of a student or be couched in unfamiliar terms. 'You need to develop your critical thinking' may not be meaningful to some students. Online learning packages are only as good as the designers who have made them (McCabe and Gonzales-Llores, 2017). For the development of online courses, comparison of methods is not as important as comparisons of structures within methods.

There are plenty of writings on online learning. A quick search of Google Scholar revealed over a million articles and texts have been published since 2000 but there is little empirical evidence that they are more effective than traditional methods: they are certainly cheaper. MOOCs (massive open online courses) have become a burgeoning interest to universities and private providers (Daniel, 2012; Universities UK, 2013; Li Yuan and Powell, 2014; Bonk *et al.*, 2015). The US Office of Education claim that MOOCs are at least as effective as other forms of teaching but not as costly. Their findings were based on an analysis of 51 studies. Blended forms based on MOOCS and face-to-face teaching fared better than MOOCS alone (US Department of Education, 2010). An Australian study of student completion and performance in a MOOC was dependent on the frequency of use by students and their personal motivation (De Barba *et al.*, 2016). A systematic review of early developments of MOOCs is provided by Liyanagunawardena *et al.* (2013).

There are two broad types of MOOCS: eMOOCS and cMOOCS. eMOOCS are closely related to transmission models of teaching and learning supported by computer-based assignments and feedback but little, if any, personal contact between student and lecturer. cMOOCS are more closely related to models of participative learning and are still developing (Bates, 2014). There are more eMOOCS than cMOOCS currently available. Often their selling point is the lectures are provided by knowledgeable experts from prestigious universities. But there is more to effective teaching than knowledge of a subject. The interest in eMOOCS seem to be driven more by business models of universities and private providers than concerns for educational effectiveness.

Appraising the effectiveness of courses

The initial work of Biggs led him to develop a model of constructive alignment (Biggs, 2015). The model is a powerful tool for examining the effectiveness of a programme or module. Figure 19.7 is based on his model.

The model is based on the argument that all the components of a course should be closely aligned. Thus the aims of the programme shape its modules, which in their turn shape

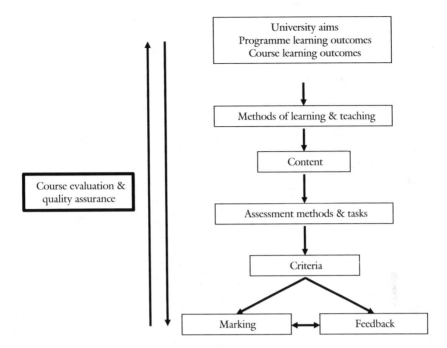

Figure 19.7 Course alignment

the aims and intended learning outcomes of its modules. These determine the methods of teaching and the intended learning outcomes of the teaching sessions. The assessment and feedback are aligned with the teaching. Course evaluations are based on the components. The model has a strong appeal to course designers, administrators and external quality scrutineers. Biggs claims that constructive alignment is not a rigid system since the course designers can build into the course a high level of aims and learning outcomes. However the intended learning outcomes are devised by the teachers and their managers. They are not necessarily the intended learning outcomes of the students. There are the issues of freedom versus control in constructive alignment.

Spheres of influence on teachers and student

Figure 19.8 outlines the sources of influence upon the individual student and teacher. The model is the obverse of a nuclear model. The stronger influences are from the outer shells, not the centre. The global economy is changing and this has consequential effects upon the international scene and government policies. It influences a government's attitudes to financing higher education and the ideological question of whether HE should be financed by the individual or the community (Troschitz, 2017). As higher education systems became more internationalised, there is a national concern that there is less freedom and more control of what teachers and students are expected to do and consequently what counts as effective teaching. To complicate matters further, there appears to be conflicts within as well as between each sphere of influence. At the govermental level, there are conflicts between those who prefer a light touch and those who prefer tight control; between those who adopt

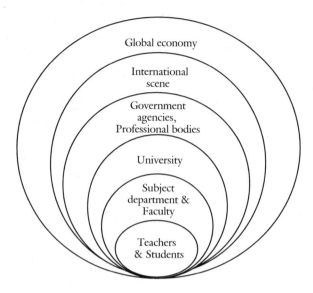

Figure 19.8 Spheres of influence on teachers and students

a neo-liberal stance of a 'free' market and those who insist on greater governmental regula-tion. Examples of these are the requirements specified by the current QAA and the emerging Teaching Excellency Framework (TEF; Ramsden, 2016). Professional organisations such as HEA, SEDA, and others are influenced by government policy, and these may be promot-ing approaches which some of their members regard as of doubtful value rather than useful or effective. On the basis of the requirements of government agencies, the universities are required to develop codes of practice for departments and faculties. Teachers may have inner conflicts about the plethora of course work assessments, the absence of weekly tutorials, the detailed intended learning outcomes and the advocacy of some methods of teaching. Other teachers may also question the rigidity of the system. Students' control of what they learn and how they learn is restricted. All of these influences limit the freedom of teachers and students and shape the discourse of what counts as effective teaching. In short, effectiveness is determined by values and the stance of the stakeholders. The questions 'Effectiveness for whom?' and 'Effectiveness for what purpose?' are salient. The brief article by Hinchcliffe (2017) on Max Weber is relevant to this debate – as are the questions raised 25 years ago by Atkins *et al.* (1993).

Effective teaching?

It should be clear from the discussion so far that shot through the whole of the research on learning and teaching are questions concerning the nature of effectiveness and its relation-ship to quality assurance. Notions of effectiveness are dependent upon the values, status, purposes and context of the observer. Measures of effectiveness may be based upon publicly expressed values or upon the values in operation in the context of learning. The two are not necessarily identical and they are related to the distinctions often made between rhetoric and reality, espoused theories and theories in use. To complicate matters further, reports of other people's approaches to effectiveness are themselves inevitably value-laden. Hence what follows may seem polemical to some readers and too bland to others.

Our core suggestion to all stakeholders is: 'Be careful what you wish for.' Governments who want more private providers of higher education should look carefully at the quality and financial structures of many private universities in the United States and Australia (Fielden and Middlehurst, 2017). If effectiveness measures, in practice, are concerned primarily with cheapness and efficiency, then we run the risk of not providing a well-informed, future-oriented skilled workforce. The concern to drive down unit costs runs the risk of moving institutions towards lectures and computer-based assessments. Yet the research shows that undue emphasis upon lectures and such assessments are likely to yield passive, compliant, surface learners. For students, effectiveness is likely to be related to systematic, stimulating and caring teaching that leads to success in their studies and beyond. Certainly this view is borne out by the research on teaching and learning reviewed in this chapter. It also appears to be the underlying philosophy of the recently instituted Teaching Excellence Framework (TEF) in the UK, although its criteria and metrics are curiously neglectful of teaching in the conventional sense of providing opportunities to learn by a tutor or team of tutors (PSA, 2017).

Obviously, emphases on these factors will vary across students and subject and each of these factors is, in practice, complex and challenging.

Government agencies and professional bodies may need to consider whether their concern for standardisation might stifle creativity and the initiative of students and teachers. Employers might consider whether preparation for employment should be focused primarily on first jobs or the uncertain futures of their organisations. Universities and their human resource departments may need to recognise that there are differences between subject groupings and subjects. One size does not always fit all. There is a need for departments to identify their values, establish their measures of effectiveness and act upon their findings. Within the departments themselves there may be divisions of opinion on whether the primary aim is education in the subject or education through the subject. Again, different measures of effectiveness may be necessary. All of this in the context of the university's policy and current government regulations and 'guidelines'.

Some universities have a further challenge: demonstrating high research activity. Effectiveness in teaching and undergraduate learning in such institutions may be as much concerned with efficiency as with quality or effectiveness. Some departments value the use of small group methods and project supervision whereas others prefer large lectures and formal examinations. The espoused values and values in use in a department may not align. Departments and teachers may need to consider whether there is sufficient deep and critical thinking in their approaches to learning and assessment. Students are being encouraged, by such devices as frequent requests for feedback on teaching and modules, to see themselves as consumers. This may affect their views of effectiveness. Yet the notion of student as consumer may fit uncomfortably with the notion of student as deep, active processor and generator of learning.

Clearly, questions of values are at the heart of the debate on effectiveness and quality of teaching. Effectiveness and quality, however, are not necessarily synonymous or even stable concepts. Their precise relationships are outside the domains of empirical research. Empirical research can inform and illuminate issues of effectiveness and quality. We hope this chapter has made a useful contribution to that debate.

Bibliography

Annett, J. & Sparrow, J. (1989) Transfer of training: A review of research and practical implications. *APLET Journal* 22: 116–124.

Ashwin, P. (2015) *Reflective Teaching in Higher Education*. London: Bloomsbury.

Atkins, M.J., Beattie, J. & Dockrell, W.B. (1993) *Assessment Issues in Higher Education*. Employment Department, Further and Higher Education Branch.

Ausubel, D. (1968) *Educational Psychology: A Cognitive View*. New York: Holt, Rinehart & Winston.

Ausubel, D., Novak, J. & Hanesian, H. (1978) *Educational Psychology: A Cognitive View* (2nd Ed.). New York: Holt, Rinehart & Winston.

Baddeley, A.D. (1999) *Essentials of Human Memory*. Hove: Psychology Press.

Baird, D. (2005) Work: Getting the most from work experience. *New Law Journal*, 155: 360–361.

Bates, T. (2014) Comparing xMOOCs and cMOOCs: Philosophy and practice. Available at http://www.tonybates.ca/2014/10/13/comparing-xmoocs-and-cmoocs-philosophy-and-practice/. Accessed 25 Feb 2017.

Baumgart, C.P. (1976) Verbal interaction in university tutorials. *Higher Education* 5: 301–317.

Beijaard, D., Meijer, P.C. & Verloop, N. (2004) Reconsidering research on teachers' professional identity. *Teaching and Education* 20: 107–128.

Biggs, J. (1987) *Student Approaches in Learning and Studying*. Melbourne: Australian Council for Educational Research.

Biggs, J. (2015) Constructive alignment in university teaching. *HERDSA Review of Education* 1. Available at: https://www.tru.ca/__shared/assets/Constructive_Alignment36087.pdf. Accessed 22 Feb 2017.

Biggs, J. & Tang, C. (2011) *Teaching for Quality Learning at University*. London: SRHE.

Bligh, D.A. (2000) *What is the Point in Discussion?* Oregon: Intellect Books.

Bliss, J. & Ogborn, J. (eds) (1977) *Students' Reactions to Undergraduate Science*. London Heinemann.

Bondemark, L., Knuttsen, K. & Brown, G. (2004) A self-directed summative examination in problem-based learning in dentistry: A new approach. *Medical Teacher*, 26, 46–51.

Boud, D., Cohen, R. & Sampson, J. (2014) (eds) *Peer Learning in Higher Education: Learning from and with each other*. London: Routledge.

Boud, D., Dunn, J. & Hegarty Hazel, E. (eds) (1986) *Teaching in Laboratories*. London: SRHE.

Bonk, C.J., Lee, M.M., Reeves, C.T. & Reynolds, T.H (eds) (2015) *MOOCs and Open Education Around the World*. New York: Routledge.

Boulton-Lewis, G.M. (1995) The SOLO taxonomy as a means of shaping and assessing learning in higher education. *Higher Education Research and Development* 14(2): 143–154.

Brennan, J. & Little, B. (1996) *A Review of Work Based Learning*. London: Quality Support Centre, Open University.

Brown, G. (2004) *Helping Students Learn: A supplement to the Routledge Falmer Key Guides for Effective Teaching in Higher Education series*. London: Routledge.

Brown, G.A. & Atkins, M.J. (2002) *Effective Teaching in Higher Education*. London: Routledge.

Brown, G.A. & Bakhtar, M. (1987) Styles of lecturing: A study and its implications. *Research Papers in Education*, 3: 131–153.

Brown, G.A. & Daines, J.M. (1981) Learning from lectures. In Oxtoby, E. (ed.) *Higher Education at the Crossroads*. London: Society for Research in Higher Education.

Brown, G. & Edmunds, S. (2009) Learning from lectures. In Dent, J.A. and Harden, R.M. (eds) *A Practical Guide for Medical Teachers*. Elsevier.

Brown, G.A. & Manogue, M. (2001) Refreshing lecturing: a guide for lecturers. AMEE medical education guide No 22. *Medical Teacher* 24: 231–244.

Brown, G., Bull, J. & Pendlebury, M. (1997, 2014) *Assessing Student Learning in Higher Education*. London: Routledge. Reprinted 2014.

Bunce, D.M., Fiens, E.A. & Niels, K.Y. (2010) How long can students pay attention in class? A study of student attention decline using clickers. *J. Chem. Educ.*, 87(12), 1438–1443.

Cobb, K.A., Brown, G.A., Jaarsma, A.D.C. & Hammond, R.A. (2013) The educational impact of assessment: A comparison of DOPS and MCQs. *Medical Teacher* 35: e1598–e1607.

Daniel, J. (2012) Making sense of MOOCs: Musings in a maze of myth, paradox and possibility. *Journal of Interactive Media in Education*. Available at http://jime.open.ac.uk/articles/10.5334/2012-18/. Accessed 25 Feb 2017.

Davies, L. (1990) *Experience-Based Learning within the Curriculum – A Synthesis Study*. London: Association for Sandwich Education & Training and Council for National Academic Awards (CNAA).

De Barba, P.G., Kennedy, G.E. & Ainley, M.D. (2016) The role of students' motivation and participation in predicting performance in a MOOC. *Journal of Computer Assisted Learning* 32(3): 218–231.

Devlin, M. & Samarawickrema, G. (2010) Effective teaching in a changing higher education context. *Higher Education Research and Development* 29(2): 111–124.

Dillon, J.T. (1997) Questioning. In O. Hargie (ed.) *The Handbook of Communication Skills*, 2nd Edn. London: Routledge.

Dochy, F., De Rijdt, C. & Dyck, W. (2003) Cognitive prerequisites of active learning. *Higher Education* 3: 265–284.

Dodds, M. (2015) Evidence for the flipped classroom in STEM. Available at https://www-users.cs.york.ac.uk/~miked/publications/flipped_classroom.dodds.pdf. Accessed 19 Feb 2017.

Dubin, R. & Taveggia, T.C. (1968) *The Teaching-Learning Paradox: A Comparative Analysis of College Teaching Methods*. Eugene, OR: Center for the Advanced Study of Educational Administration, University of Oregon.

Duignan, J. (2003) Placement and adding value to the academic performance of undergraduates: reconfiguring the architecture – an empirical investigation. *Journal of Vocational Education and Training* 55(3), 335–350.

Duolingo (Official site: www.duolingo.com)

Edmunds, S. & Brown, G. (2010) Effective Small Group Learning. AMEE Guide no. 48. *Medical Teacher* 32(9): 715–726.

Entwistle, N. (1997) Contrasting perspectives on learning. In F. Marton, D.J. Hounsell & N. Entwistle (eds) *The Experience of Learning*, 2nd Edn. Edinburgh: Academic Press.

Entwistle, N., Christensen Hughes, J. & Mighty, J. (2010) Taking stock: An overview of research findings. *Research on Teaching and Learning in Higher Education*, pp. 15–51.

Falchikov, N. (2003) *Learning Together: Peer Tutoring in Higher Education*. London: Routledge.

Fielden, J. & Middlehurst, R. (2017) *Alternative Providers of Higher Education*. Higher Education Policy Institute Report 90. Available at HEPI The-alternative –providers-of-higher-education – Report-90–04_01_17. Accessed 6 March 2017.

Flaherty, J. and Phillips, J. (2015) The use of flipped classrooms in higher education: A scoping review. *The Internet and Higher Education* 25(2): 85–95.

Fry, H., Ketteridge, S. & Marshall, S.A. (eds) (2014) *Handbook for Teaching and Learning in Higher Education*, 4th Edn. London: Routledge.

GDST (2016) First GDST Survey. Available at https://www.gdst.net/article/gcses-contribute-bottleneck-mindset-among-teenagers. Accessed 19 Feb 2017.

Gebbins, L. & Perkin, G. (2013) *Laboratories for the 21st Century in STEM Higher Education*. Centre for Engineering and Design Education, Loughborough University. Available at http://oro.open.ac.uk/38849/1/Labs_for_21st_century.pdf. Accessed 19 Feb 2017.

Gomez, S., Lush, D. & Clements, M. (2004) Work placements enhance the academic performance of bioscience undergraduates. *Journal of Vocational Education and Training* 56(3): 373–385.

Hanif, M., Sneddon, P.H., Al-Ahmadi, F.M. & Reid, N. (2009) The perceptions, views and opinions of university students about physics learning during undergraduate laboratory work. *Eur. J. Phys.* 30: 85–96.

Hargie, O.F.W. (2011) *Skilled Interpersonal Communication*, 5th Edn. London: Routledge.

Hargie, O.F.W. (2017) (ed.) *Handbook of Communication Skills*, 5th Edn. London: Routledge.

Harvey, L., Moon, S., Geall, V. & Bower, R. (1997) *Graduates' Work: Organisational Change and Students' Attributes*. Birmingham: Centre for Research into Quality (CRQ) and Association of Graduate Recruiters (AGR).

Harvey, L., Geall, V. & Moon, S. (1998) *Work Experience: Expanding Opportunities for Undergraduates*. Birmingham: Centre for Research into Quality, University of Central England.

Hase, H. & Kenyon, C. (2001) *From Andragogy to Heutagogy*. Available at: file://localhost/at http/::www.psy.gla.ac.uk:~steve:pr:Heutagogy.html. Accessed 26 Feb 2017.

Hegarty-Hazel, E. (1986) Research on laboratory work. In Boud, D., Dunn, J. & Hegarty-Hazel, E. (eds) (1986) *Teaching in Laboratories*. London: SRHE.

Hinchcliffe, G. (2017) Max Weber and the rationalisation of education. *SRHE News* 27: 23–24.

Jackson, D. (2014) Employment skill development in work-integrated learning: Barriers and best practice. *Studies in Higher Education*, 40(2): 350–367.

Jackson, N. (2006) *Work Placements and Placement Learning: Views of work placement tutors and colleagues involved in placement management*. Surrey: Surrey Centre for Excellence in Professional Training and Education.

Jaques, D. & Salmon, G. (2007) *Learning in Groups: A handbook for face-to-face and online environments*, 4th Edn. London: Routledge.

Jones, H.E. (1923) Experimental studies of college teaching. *Archives of Psychology* 68(45), 101–104.

Land, M.L. (1985) Vagueness and clarity in the classroom. In Husen, T. & Postlethwaite, T.N. (eds) *International Encyclopledia of Educational Research Studies*. Oxford: Pergamon.

Laurillard, D. (2002) *Rethinking University Teaching*. London: Routledge.

Lea, J. (2015) *Enhancing Learning and Teaching in Higher Education*. Buckingham: Open University Press.

Lemanski, T., Mewis, R. & Overton, T. (2011) *An Introduction to Work-Based Learning*. Higher Education Academy, Physical Sciences Centre, University of Hull.

Lindsay, E. & Good, M. (2007) *Learning Styles as Potential Predictor of Student Achievement in Remote and Virtual Laboratory Classes*. https://www.researchgate.net/publication/2513 94345_Learning_Styles_a_Potential_Predictor_of_Student_Achievement_in_Remote_and_Virtual_Laboratory_Classes. Accessed 21 Feb 2017.

Liyanagunawardena R.L, Adams, A.A. & Williams, S.A. (2013) *MOOCs: A systematic study of the published literature 2008–2012*. Available at http://www.irrodl.org/index.php/irrodl/article/view/1455/2531. Accessed 24 Feb 2017.

Li Yuan & Powell, R. (2014) *MOOCS and Open Education: A White Paper JISC 2014*. Available at http://www.thepdfportal.com/moocs-and-open-education_101588.pdf. Accessed 26 Feb 2017.

Luker, P.A. (1988) Some case studies of small group teaching. Unpublished PhD, University of Nottingham.

Marsh, H.W. (1987) Students' evaluations of university teaching: Research findings, methodological issues, and directions for future research. *International Journal of Educational Research* 11(3): 253–388.

Mayo, R.H. & Jones, L.L. (1985) The effect of a sandwich year on degree classification. *Proceedings of the Fourth World Conference on Co-Operative Education*, pp. 428–431, Napier College, Edinburgh.

McCabe, M. & Gonzales-Llores, P. (2017) *Essentials of Online Teaching: A Standards-Based Guide*. London: Routledge.

McCullough, A. & Stokes, P. (2008) *The Silent Majority: Meeting the needs of part-time students*. London: SRHE.

Moon, J.A. (2004) *A Handbook of Reflective and Experiential Learning*. London: Routledge.

Nafalski, A., Nedic, Z. & Machotka, J. (2011) Remote Engineering Laboratories for Collaborative Experiments, 2nd World Conference on Technology and Engineering Education, Ljubliana, 8 Sept 2011.

Neerinck D., Brown, G. & Lapiere, D. (1994) *Supervision of Science Research: An International Study.* Brussels: Ministry of Education and Science.

NSS (2017) National Student Survey Questionnaire. Available at https://www.ipsos-mori.com/Assets/Docs/Publications/nss-questionnaire.pdf. See also http://thestudentsurvey.com/students.php and http://www.hefce.ac.uk/lt/nss/http://www.hefce.ac.uk/lt/nss/. Accessed 20 Feb 2017.

Open University (2017) Living with the internet: learning online. Available at https://www.amazon.co.uk/dp/B01D8X6UJU/ref=rdr_kindle_ext_tm. Accessed 25 Feb 2017.

Overton, T., Wallace, R. & Murray, B. (2009) *Effective Practice in Industrial Work Placement.* Higher Education Academy Physical Sciences Centre University of Hull. Available at https://www.heacademy.ac.uk/system/files/effective_practice_in_industrial_work_placement.pdf. Accessed 24 Feb 2017

Phillips, E.M. & Pugh, D.S. (2015) *How to Get a PhD: A handbook for students and their supervisors,* 6th Edn. Maidenhead: Open University Press.

Pickering, M. & Crabtree, R.H. (1979) How students cope with lab. procedures. *Journal of Chemical Education* 56: 587–588.

PSA (Political Studies Association) (2017) *TEF (Teaching Excellence Framework) Bulletin.* Accessed 20 June 2017.

QAA (2012) *UK Quality Code for Higher Education.* Available at http://www.qaa.ac.uk/assuring-standards-and-quality/the-quality-code/quality-code-part-b. Accessed 22 Feb 2017.

Ramsden, P. (2003) *Learning to Teach in Higher Education,* 2nd Edn. Abingdon: Routledge.

Ramsden, P. (2016) The TEF is a waste of time and money. https://paulramsden48.wordpress.com/2016/06/22/the-tef-is-a-waste-of-time-and-money/. Accessed 8 Feb 2017.

Reeve, J., Deci, E.L. & Ryan, R.M. (2002) Self-determination theory applied to educational settings. In Deci, E.L. & Ryan, R.M. (eds) *Handbook of Self-Determination Research.* New York: University of Rochester Press, pp. 183–204.

Rudd, E. (1985) *A New Look at Post-Graduate Failure.* London: NFER-Nelson.

Ryans, D.G. (1960) *Characteristics of Teachers.* Washington, DC: American Council of Education.

Scanlon, E., Colwell, C., Cooper, M. & Di Paulo, I. (2004) Remote experiments, re-versioning and re-thinking science learning. *Computers in Education* 43: 153–163.

Shaw, M. (1987) The tutorial: an analysis of skills. Unpublished PhD, University of Nottingham.

Sheridan, I. & Linehan, M. (2011) *Work Placements in Third Level Programmes.* Dublin: REAP CIT Press. Available at https://scholar.google.co.uk/scholar?hl=en&q=Lineham+and+Sheridan&btnG=&as_sdt=1,5&as_sdtd=. Accessed 23 Feb 2017.

Shymansky, J.A., Kyle, W.C. & Pennick, J.E. (1979) How do science laboratory assistants teach? *Journal of College Science Teaching* 9: 24–27.

Slavin, R.E. (1990) Mastery learning reconsidered. *Educational Research* 60: 300–302

Smallwood, A., Bragan Turner, D. & Brown, G. (1996) *Helping Arts Students to Do Research: A guide and a programme.* Sheffield: UCoSDA.

Svinicki, M.D. & McKeachie, W.J. (2011) *McKeachie's Teaching Tips: Strategies, research and theory for college and university teachers,* 14th Edn. Belmont, CA: CENGAGE Learning.

Taylor, S. & Beasley, N. (2005) *A Handbook for Research Supervisors.* London: Routledge.

Taylor, S. & Kiley, M. (2014) Supervising research students. In Fry, H., Ketteridge, S. and Marshall, S.A. (eds) (2014) *Handbook for Teaching and Learning in Higher Education,* 4th Edn. London: Routledge.

TEF (2016) Teaching Excellency Framework. Available at http://www.hefce.ac.uk/lt/tef/. Accessed 20 Feb 2017.

Ten Cate, O., Kusurkar, R. & Williams, G. (2011) How self-determination theory can assist our understanding of the teaching and learning processes in medical education, AMEE Guide no. 59. *Medical Teacher* 33: 961–973.

Tisher, R.P. & White, R.T. (1986) Research on natural science. In Wittrock, M. (ed.) *Handbook of Research on Teaching,* 3rd Edn. New York: Macmillan.

Troschitz, R. (2017) *Higher Education and the Student.* London: Routledge.

Universities UK (2013) *Massive Open Online Course: Higher Education's digital moment?* http://www.universitiesuk.ac.uk/highereducation/Documents/2013/. Accessed 26 Feb 2017.

US Department of Education (2010) *Evaluation of Evidence-Based Practices in Online Learning: A meta-analysis and review of online learning studies.* Available at https://www2.ed.gov/rschstat/eval/tech/evidence-based-practices/finalreport.pdf. Accessed 5 March 2017.

Vaughan, N. (2007) Perspectives on blended learning in Higher Education. *International Journal of ELearning* 6(1): 81–94. Available at http://search.proquest.com/openview/46e2267895697c7a4c98e8b842881443/1?pq-origsite=gscholar&cbl=27101. Accessed 26 Feb 2017.

Wilton, N. (2012) The impact of work placements on skills development and career outcomes for business and management graduates. *Studies in Higher Education*, 37(5): 603–620. Available from: http://eprints.uwe.ac.uk/1449

Wittrock, M.C. (1986) Students' thought processes. In Wittrock, M.C. (ed.) *Handbook of Research on Teaching*, 3rd Edn. New York: Macmillan.

Wright, J. (1991) Studies of research supervision. Unpublished PhD thesis, University of Nottingham.

Yager, R., Engen, H.B. & Snider, B.C F. (1969) Effects of the laboratory and demonstration methods upon the outcomes of instruction. *Journal of Research in Science Teaching* 6: 76–86.

20 Teaching Styles of Award-Winning Professors

Jerry M. Lewis

Introduction

This chapter looks at the teaching styles of award-winning professors. (Professor is used in this chapter in the American style of occupation, not the British style of rank: it is equivalent to teacher.) The data are primarily drawn from in-depth interviews with professors at Kent State University in Kent, Ohio, USA. The analysis is supported by popular writings about successful teachers as well as the limited literature on the subject. The chapter concludes with policy discussions in areas including the value of teaching awards, student evaluations, peer evaluations and the hiring of staff.

John Henry Newman (1912) wrote that a professor displays 'science in its most complete and winning form, pouring it forth with the zeal of enthusiasm, and lighting up his own love of it in the breast of his hearers'. There are many ways this 'lighting up' can be achieved in the educational enterprise. It is the perspective of this chapter that award-winning professors represent a rich fount of resources of knowledge and expertise in lighting up undergraduates. Both the neophyte teacher and the experienced professional can learn from outstanding teachers. However, it is difficult to get at the knowledge and expertise of these teachers in a systematic way.

The quest for knowledge about award-winning teachers is often complicated by stereotypes that shape perceptions of outstanding teaching. When one tries to study teaching, even excellent teaching, one is confronted with two problems. First, there is the 'bad day' stereotype. The argument is that most university professors are, because of training and intellect, good teachers but are prone to off or bad days on occasion. Hence, when studying teaching, the researcher must be careful in assuring that he or she has not caught the teacher being studied on a 'bad day'. Second, there is the 'pornography' problem. Paraphrasing a well-known American Supreme Court Judge (Potter Stewart), 'I can't define pornography but I know it when I see it', this stereotype says that it is difficult to define (and study) outstanding teaching, but easy to recognize it.

My solution to these stereotypes was to study award-winning professors. First, these teachers were clearly not having 'bad days' when I studied them at least in terms of teaching. Second, they had been defined by both students and peers as distinguished in their profession. Many of these had been so recognized on a number of occasions.

Kent State University

Before I discuss the results of my research, it seems appropriate to look at the cultural context and environment of these excellent teachers, that is the city of Kent and Kent State

University. The University was founded in 1910 as a college and became a university in 1935 when it expanded beyond its original teacher-training goals. It is located in northeastern Ohio. It is roughly 470 miles (about 760 kilometers) west of New York City and about 40 miles southeast of Cleveland, Ohio. Kent State University (KSU) consists of the main campus plus eight regional campuses. The main campus in Kent is a large, wooded site on about 1,200 acres of slightly rolling land with 100 buildings and a golf course and airport nearby that are affiliated with KSU. The library has over a million volumes in its open stacks.

The University is so large that it operates a bus system, which is also available to residents of the city of Kent ('Tree City') as its main routes reach various points in Kent. The city has a population of 30,000 and that rises to around 54,000 when the students are attending KSU. The university employs 1,000 faculty members and 3,000 other employees. The dormitories house 7,000 students, mostly freshmen. Many students commute each day or evening and also work. The city of Kent has numerous houses and apartments that are rented to students.

The Distinguished Teaching Award (DTA)

The DTA is given every autumn to three teachers at Kent State University. About 60 to 80 teachers are nominated. The award carries a prize of $1,000. Professors are nominated using ballots that are distributed to students, staff and alumni (see Appendix 9.1). Early in the autumn of each year, the Alumni Association appoints a committee of students, staff and alumni to choose the award-winners. Generally ten professors are selected as finalists. They will receive the Outstanding Teaching Award (OTA). Then the committee picks three staff members as Distinguished Teachers. The awards are presented on homecoming weekend, with both the DTA and OTA winners receiving considerable public recognition. In general, both DTA and OTA winners treat the award as a significant item for their curricula vitae.

Each autumn the ten outstanding teacher awards (OTA) are announced. From these ten, the Distinguished Teacher Award (DTA) winners are selected. The ten are acknowledged at a banquet and given plaques, and the three that receive the $1,000 prizes are announced at that time. All are given a write-up in the local newspaper. There is also a wall with photographs of each year's DTAs just outside a special dining room open to the public and the university community in the student centre. This constitutes a hall of fame.

There are three assumptions about the award process. First, because each committee begins *de novo* every autumn, they generally work out procedures following the guidelines of the Alumni Association for standards of teaching excellence. Second, no particular subject is inherently more teachable. Thus, from the point of view of *subject matter*, every professor has a chance to be nominated for the award. Third, every professor has a chance of being nominated for the award in terms of student exposure. If a professor is a strong teacher, this will become known and consequently he or she will be nominated by a colleague, a student or a former student for the award competition.

Teaching styles of Distinguished Teaching Award-Winners

I begin by discussing the research procedure and then turn to the examination of types of teaching styles.

Research procedure

I tape recorded in-depth interviews with the winners of the Alumni Association's Distinguished Teaching Award (DTA). I completed interviews with 50 of the 65 eligible candidates. The interviews were transcribed, and I did a qualitative analysis for this chapter. The interviewing focused on several aspects of undergraduate teaching. First, the professor's social and academic background was described. Second, various aspects of the teaching enterprise were explored, including: philosophies of teaching and learning; styles of lecturing; lecture support materials, such as handouts, overhead projections or films; and outside-the-classroom projects. Third, techniques of testing and grading used by the professor were investigated. Fourth, the perceptions that the award-winning professor had of the joys (and sorrows) of undergraduate teaching were examined. These interviews generated a wealth of material about the craft of teaching represented in the three divisions of the university (sciences, social sciences and humanities) as well as many of its departments.

Styles of teaching

I was able to identify five styles of teaching used by the professors interviewed. They are presented in order of importance and are labeled goal-setting, preparation, enthusiasm, humour and (last but not least) performance.

Goal setting

Award-winning professors clearly have goals in mind when they organize and present their undergraduate courses. These goals are a mixture of the philosophical and pragmatic. They want to communicate the excitement of their discipline as well as the core knowledge of the subject, particularly in its most up-to-date form. To illustrate, I draw on the comments of three teachers, from English, Geology and Psychology.

> [My goals] are to teach a sense of order . . . within the enjoyment of what one is reading and the questions that one asks there is an inner order. In addition I want to communicate why I am an English major.
>
> (English professor)

> I try to make the student feel that what I was teaching them at that moment was the most important possible thing that they could learn in their entire four years of undergraduate studies.
>
> (Geology professor)

> One major goal that I think of myself trying to accomplish is to challenge everyday misconceptions . . . I view that as perhaps one function of the course and maybe one function of liberal arts.
>
> (Psychology professor)

In their comparative study of award- and non-award-winning professors, Tollefson and Tracy (1983) found this to be the second most important variable for both groups. That is, goal setting was second ranked by them. (The first ranked characteristic was enthusiasm, which is discussed here separately.)

Preparation

Award-winning teachers spend considerable effort and time on preparation. Tollefson and Tracy (1983) report this to be the third most important variable. Indeed, during my interviews, I became concerned about my own preparation when I learned through the research how much time professors spend getting ready for lectures.

> [Preparing a lecture on a Shakespeare play] I'll go over it three or four times and I will write. Then, I'll look at the notes from the critics and see how they fit into my own ideas.
>
> (English professor)

> The day before I was going to lecture on a particular subject, I would go through my file of overhead projection displays . . . So, I would go through my mental gymnastic of my lecture the second time. In a sense, I went through my lecture three times before I gave it to the class.
>
> (Geology professor)

Another professor in the sample, a sociologist, said he prepared three times as well: at the start of the semester, at the beginning of the week of the particular class and on the day of the lecture.

Enthusiasm

This is probably the best-known variable associated with good teaching. Both of the groups in the Tollefson and Tracy study ranked it as the most important factor in outstanding teaching. However, my interviews indicate that enthusiasm is not as one-dimensional as it might seem. I found a difference between enthusiasm for the subject and enthusiasm for students be they quick to learn or less than quick. Students, in some instances, can get in the way of the professor. I had expected the kindly 'Mr Chips'. That was clearly not the case.

> I want to share my enthusiasm. So I take off a mile a minute in the classroom and feel free to digress.
>
> (English professor)

> I try to make the student aware of the fact that . . . regardless of what they are going to do in subsequent life, geology is going to impact on them.
>
> (Geology professor)

Humour

The factor of humour was important to the teachers. I found that they used it in a variety of ways, which can be summarized in the following typology. One dimension concerns the extent to which the humour is spontaneous or planned, the other the degree to which the humour relates to the subject matter of the course. These two dimensions interact to produce four prototypes:

- type I, planned related;
- type II, spontaneous related;
- type III, planned unrelated;
- type IV, spontaneous unrelated.

Thus the situational variable ranges from planned to spontaneous humour. A planned act of humour is one that the teacher anticipates using at a specific time in the course. It can range from a cartoon on an overhead projection to a long joke. In contrast, a spontaneous act of humour occurs at any time in the class and can range from a witty remark based on a student comment to a messed-up experiment in chemistry class.

The contextual variable relates to the subject of the course. The acts of humour are directly related to the subject of the class or not directly related. For example, a professor might want to illustrate a point in the lecture with a joke or cartoon. Many American textbooks also do this in both the social and natural sciences. In contact, some professors like to use humour that is not necessarily related to the topic of the course.

The vast majority of humour falls into type I, although instances of types II and III were reported in my interviews with outstanding teachers. Here are examples of type I:

> I will pun. That's the limit of my intellectual ability to create humour is the pun. And they are usually very terrible. I will frequently lighten a situation.
>
> (English professor)

> I think the most humorous thing I did was tell stories, often on myself, about a geological situation. [I slipped] off the edge of the cliff and fell 40 feet.
>
> (Geology professor)

The psychology professor is often a type III in his use of humour: 'One liners. I guess if I could be Johnny Carson sometimes. I would like to be one of those stand-up comedians.' Another professor, a sociologist, begins almost every lecture with a joke that may be type I, but often is not related to the course subject matter (type III).

Performance

Many award-winning professors enjoy the performance aspect of teaching. Some actually report some sort of a high from the lecturing experience. When one hears 'I would really miss teaching', I think this refers to the entertaining aspects to a large extent. An administrator from another university said it bluntly: 'All good teachers are hams.'

When I presented this variable at the University of Ulster, it caused a reaction, most of it negative. One member of the audience went so far as to ask if teachers should join the Royal Shakespeare Company. While I do not want professors to go that far, I think they should be sensitive to the performance dimensions of effective lecturing.

In my own teaching, I have been influenced by the analytical theory of Erving Goffman as developed in his book, *The Presentation of Self in Everyday Life* (1959). His theory of social interaction, called dramaturgy, uses theatrical images to explain impression management. Impression management is exactly what professors do in the classroom. They affect students in more ways than simple words. The entire performance counts. Goffman notes that in any social situation there is a 'front' region where social acts are carried out and a 'back' region where these acts are prepared. Further, social action in front regions is generally contradicted in the back region. For Goffman, both these regions are socially determined. For example, a professor can struggle with a point in the back region of his or her office. Further, he or she can express this struggle on the face or through body language. However, when the professor enters the stage (front region) of the classroom, this struggle must disappear, and an aura of confidence in one's ideas should be presented. In other words, walking into a classroom is much more than just 'walking into a classroom'. *The teacher is going on stage.*

Walter Dyer reported the teaching of Charles Edward Garman, a famous philosopher at Amherst College in Massachusetts. When he illustrated a point, it was theatre. Dyer wrote (Peterson 1946):

> Garman's illustrations were famous and wide in scope. He drew from sociology, economics, business, politics, literature, domestic relations, and law, as well as from religion and philosophy. In making his academic points he dealt with living issues. He displayed a positive genius for apt illustration and example. A large part of the value of the course was the imparting of general knowledge as well as the stimulation of thinking.
>
> One of Garman's illustrative anecdotes was so characteristic and succinct that some of us learned it verbatim and were accustomed to recite it in unison on frivolous occasions. It was first presented, I believe, in connection with a discussion of the doctrine of the atonement or vicarious punishment. It ran as follows:
>
> 'In a shire town in England a man was sentenced for stealing sheep, and the judge said, "I convict you not for stealing sheep but that sheep may not be stolen in the future." Then the culprit arose in open court and said, "What is that to me?" And sure enough,' concluded Garman, leaning over his desk and fixing us with his piercing gaze, 'what was it to him?'
>
> It is impossible to describe the impressive manner in which Garman presented his illustrations, or their effectiveness in driving home his point. It was largely in the way he did it. I shall never forget the day he recited Tennyson's *Flower in the Crannied Wall*. It was like listening to the voice of an oracle.

Clearly Garman saw the value in performance.

The humour and performance variables were not found by Tollefson and Tracy (1983) to be important by the faculty in their samples, although earlier research by others did report that presentation skills were important. However, the prevalence of these two factors in my interviews justifies more research into the questions raised by these variables.

In summary, my interviews with award-winning teachers identified five factors that shaped these outstanding teachers' perceptions of the teaching enterprise. They were: goal-setting, preparation, enthusiasm, humour and performance. I do not wish to claim that all professors have to use the approaches I have identified in this sample of successful teachers. But I do suggest we can learn from them.

I think there are several things that both the beginning teacher and the veteran would gain from examining the reflections of award-winning professors. First, at the lowest level, new techniques can be learned. Second, and more importantly, the teacher adds to insight of his or her own joys and tribulations about teaching by learning of the experiences of award-winning professors. They do learn that they are not alone. Finally, and most importantly, these teachers generate a sense of pride in their craft. There are many good men and women who continually struggle with questions about what is good undergraduate teaching and learning. In concluding my chapter I want to raise some policy questions that stem from my research.

Policy issues

There are three policy issues relevant to my research. They are: the value of teaching awards, student evaluations and the hiring of staff.

Teaching awards

As the reader can clearly see, I am in favour of teaching awards for university lecturers. Indeed, at my own university it is possible to win an award at the departmental, collegiate and university levels as well as from professional societies and associations. Perhaps we Americans overdo awards, but they do have value. The psychological value of positive rewards, such as awards and public recognition, is well documented, as is the basic value of compliments and encouragement. What are the basic values for teaching awards?

First, *awards recognize the teaching accomplishments of men and women who have put considerable thought into their craft.* I found that the money and honour of the awards were deeply appreciated by the teachers I interviewed.

Second, it created a cadre of people who are *willing to share their teaching expertise* with others. For my research, only one professor refused to be interviewed and he, ironically, was from the College of Education. It is possible that this cadre can, as role models, become a source of innovation for the teaching process – although it would be 'Pollyannish' or overly optimistic of me to claim that this happened at Kent State.

Third, teaching awards *squarely commit universities to the proposition that teaching is important.* (Knowledge alone does not mean one can communicate it to others automatically.) This commitment to the importance of teaching often waxes and wanes with academic fashion or administrative leadership. However, a 'baseline' teaching award does serve as a friendly reminder to the university leadership that the staff and students value teaching.

The giving of teaching awards may carry with it some social costs. As Tollefson and Tracy (1983) note, 'non-award-winning faculties frequently argue that teaching awards are won capriciously'. In a 1975 study that I replicated in 1990, I looked at one aspect of the fairness question to see if the OTA and DTA winners reflected the demographic of the faculty. The data for 1975 are reported in Table 20.1. For data sources, I have used current faculty records, general catalogues, graduate catalogues, Kent State University archives and a few interviews with nominating committee members.

It would be expected that the distribution of staff in the two award categories would parallel that of the general faculty. That is, if we assume that good teaching is possible in any subject and nomination and election procedures are fair, then the award categories should reflect the demographic characteristics of the general faculty population.

In evaluating the evidence in this report, I treated any percentage difference of 10 per cent or more as a real difference. Thus, with regard to sex, the data show the DTA and OTA award-winners reflecting the sex ratio of the 1974–5 faculty distribution, while the DTA category is over-represented by holders of the doctorate. Academic rank in the OTA is close to the general faculty distribution, but the associate professor rank is over-represented in the DTA category because of the three-year rule (see below). The variables of college award-winners and time at KSU seem to be clearly out of phase with the 1974–5 staff distribution. The latter variable, time, is easy to understand since the rules of the award programme specify that a professor must have been at KSU for at least three years before he or she is eligible to be nominated. (I found only two cases where the three-year rule was not followed.) However, the college of the winners is a puzzle. Arts and sciences are greatly over-represented in both DTA and OTA categories, although more so in the DTA group.

The data suggest two things. First, the OTA category is more representative than the DTA category. This fact, combined with an examination of the total distribution of award-winners compared to the faculty of 1974–5, suggests that the top twelve really reflects

Table 20.1 Selected demographic characteristics of distinguished and outstanding teaching award-winners

Demographic characteristics	DTA (n = 23)		OTA (n = 39)		1974–5 faculty (n = 836)	
	f	%	f	%	f	%
Sex						
Male	18	78	33	85	644	77
Female	5	22	6	15	192	23
Highest degree						
Doctorate	16	70	25	64	492	59
Masters	6	26	8	20	289	35
Bachelors	1	4	1	3	45	5
Other	0	0	5	13	10	1
Academic rank						
Professor	6	26	12	31	252	30
Associate prof.	10	44	13	33	241	29
Assistant prof.	4	17	12	31	263	31
Instructor	1	4	1	2.5	80	10
Unknown	2	9	1	2.5	0	0
College/school						
Arts and Sciences	16	69	20	51	322	39
Business Admin.	2	9	3	8	72	9
Education	1	4	4	10	157	19
Fine and Prof. Art	2	9	6	15	186	22
HPE and R	2	9	5	13	46	5
Library Science	0	0	0	0	8	1
Nursing	0	0	1	3	45	5
Time at KSU (mean years)	12.8		9.1		9.1	

quality teaching. On the other hand, there are some biases in the selection of the DTA, most notably in the area of the college of the winner, with an over-representation of arts and sciences staff. I replicated this study in 1990 and found a slight decline in the percentage of arts and science teachers who had won the award. There was a corresponding increase in the percentage of professors from other disciplines.

In summary, every effort should be made to ensure that the reality and the perception of reality are very close to each other. Every effort needs to be made to guarantee that all staff have a fair chance of winning the awards.

Student evaluations

The United States probably does more student and peer evaluations than Britain or Europe. Nevertheless, the accountability trends will probably increase as the student consumer movement in academia increases.

The teachers in my sample generally approved of student evaluations and used them to study their own teaching. This was particularly true of any qualitative material. What they objected to was the use of teaching evaluations for tenure and promotion, particularly when administrators gave much attention to small quantitative differences.

My interviews indicate that the questions on teaching evaluation forms are too narrow in focusing primarily on student–teacher interaction and levels of learning. While these variables are certainly important, my interviews indicate that evaluation should be broader, looking at issues of goals as well as the presentation aspects of college teaching.

Hiring of staff

In the United States, it was estimated that there would be at least a 50 per cent turnover in staff in the 1990s. Consequently, considerable numbers of staff would have to be hired for replacements. I think this fact has two major implications for hiring. My research indicates that newly minted PhDs should be evaluated in broader terms than just knowledge of subject and research abilities. Good teaching is a fairly complicated process, and we must decide if new staff are going to make the commitment to quality. In the interview process for selecting new staff, some schools do include a requirement of a presentation by a prospective teacher to get some idea of the quality of the ability to teach – to communicate to a class and with a class.

Second, and clearly related to the first point, is the notion of teacher training. Those of us in the business of training PhDs must ensure that our students are willing and prepared to think about the complexities of quality teaching. We must think of our PhDs as more than researchers and ask them to be, even in training, total faculty members. This suggestion may call for considerable reorganization in the way PhDs are trained in the United Kingdom and Europe. There are various ways some graduate programmes meet this need for exposure to the ideas of excellent teaching, including some credit given for a short course (with lots of individual practice time and evaluation) in teaching, seminars, schedules of guest lectures by graduate students with peer and faculty evaluation and constructive discussion of the presentations before and after any additional class-leading time by the advanced graduate student.

Conclusions

This chapter has described Kent State University's Distinguished Teaching Award and the sociological context in which it has developed. It has presented results of in-depth interviews with winners of the award. Five teaching factors were identified as used by these professors. The chapter concluded with some policy suggestions derived from the research.

References

Goffman, E. (1959) *The Presentation of Self in Everyday Life*. New York: Doubleday.

Newman, J. H. (Cardinal) (1912) *The Idea of a University*. Notre Dame, IN: University of Notre Dame Press.

Peterson, H. (ed.) (1946) *Great Teachers*. New York: Vintage Books.

Tollefson, N. and Tracy, D. B. (1983) Comparison of self-reported teaching behavior of award-winning and non-award-winning university faculty. *Perceptual and Motor Behavior*, 56: 39–44.

Appendix 1

The Kent Alumni Association's 1990 Distinguished Teaching Awards

You are invited to submit your nomination for the 1990 Distinguished Teaching Awards, Kent State University's most prestigious faculty honors. Sponsored by the Kent Alumni Association and funded through the KSU Foundation, the Distinguished Teaching Awards competition is in its 24th year. To date, cash grants amounting to $68,000 have been presented to 65 top faculty members. This indicates the importance which the Alumni Association places on superior classroom teaching.

On Homecoming Weekend, October 5 and 6, 1990, a minimum of three KSU faculty members will be honored with cash awards of $1,000 each for their outstanding achievements in collegiate teaching. But first they MUST BE NOMINATED, and that is up to you.

All Kent students, alumni, faculty, and staff members are eligible to submit nominations for the awards. We ask that before completing a nomination form, you review completely the eligibility requirements listed in this brochure. There are a great many ideas concerning what constitutes effective teaching which, in part, may arise from variations in subject matter, grade level of the students, and class size. It is hoped that the general criteria will aid you in making an effective nomination.

Make your nomination as complete as possible. Of necessity, the judging must be somewhat subjective and the committee which selects the finalists and winners generally tends to place emphasis on the quality rather than the quantity of nominations. A new selection committee is named each year and is composed of nine students, six faculty members, a representative of the office of the Vice President for Academic and Student Affairs, and three alumni.

Return your ballot in person or by mail to the Kent Alumni Association, Alumni Center. All nominations must contain your signature and the contents will be available only to the selection committee and to members of the Kent Alumni Association's Awards Committee. Deadline for nominations is July 2, 1990.

Eligibility

1 A faculty member, to be nominated, must have been on a full-time teaching contract at the Kent or any regional campus of the University for a minimum of five years, including the current academic year.
2 A faculty member must have taught at least one course in two of the three semesters during each of those five academic years. (For purpose of these awards, Summer Sessions are considered one semester and the academic year extends from the beginning of Fall Semester through Summer Sessions of the following calendar year.)

3   Those receiving the awards must be on a current University contract during the semester in which the awards are presented.

4   Those who have won a Distinguished Teaching Award in previous years are no longer eligible. A complete list of previous winners is printed here.

Honored

Photos of all winners, engraved in metal, are enshrined in the DTA Hall of Fame across from the Schwebel Garden Room on the third floor of the Kent Student Center.

Winners

These previous winners are no longer eligible for Distinguished Teaching Awards:

Rudy Bachna
Joseph Baird
Kathleen Bayless
Normand Bernier
Carol Bersani
George Betts
Mary Kay Biagini
Fay Biles
Richard Brown
Ottavio Casale
Stanley Christensen
Robert Clawson
Barbara Cline
Richard B. Craig
Kenneth Cummins
Thomas Davis
Norman Duffy
Donald Dykes
Halim El-Dabh
Keith Ewing
Raymond Fort
Glenn Frank
Doris Franklin
Alfred Friedl
Nenos Georgopoulos
Raymond Gesinski
Hugh Glauser
George Harrison
Virginia Harvey
William Hildebrand
Herbert Hochhauser
Emily Hoover
John Hubbell
Lawrence Kaplan

Marvin Koller
Bebe Lavin
Jerry Lewis
Sanford Marovitz
John Mattingly
John Mitchell
Vernon Neff
Gerald Newman
Lowell Orr
John Parks
Vivian Pemberton
Paul Pfeiffer
L. Brian Price
Thomas Pynadath
Thomas Reuschling
Jeanette Reuter
David Riccio
James Rinier
Michael Rogers
Carl Rosen
Gwen Scott
Paul Sites
Mel Someroski
Nathan Spielberg
Robert Stadulis
Robert Tener
Martha Walker
Evert Wallenfeldt
Kathleen Whitmer
Harold Williams
Donald Wonderly

Official Nomination Form: Distinguished Teaching Awards

Please check your status: 0 student; 0 alumnus/a; 0 faculty/staff.

Name of nominee ——————————
Nominee's department ——————————
Your full name ——————————
Your address and phone (students- Kent address; faculty/staffdepartment) ——————

For Students
Your college, year, major ——————————

For Alumni
Kent degree(s), date(s) granted
List courses taken under nominee (number or title)
Approximate date(s) course(s) taken

CAUTION

This is not a popularity contest. Simply submitting a faculty member's name is not enough. Only those nominations which include complete information are forwarded to the selection committee.

Rate your nominee on a scale of 1 to 5 (top score is 5) in each of the following categories and use space provided to explain the teacher's performance in each area. Give examples.

Ability to communicate subject matter effectively.

Demonstrates a comprehensive knowledge of subject matter.

Communicates an enthusiastic interest in the field of study.

Stimulates thinking and develops understanding.

The student's intellect is challenged.

Methods of evaluation genuinely reflect the student's understanding of relevant course material.

Takes a personal interest in students and is willing to help.

(LIMIT COMMENTS TO ADDITIONAL SHEET PROVIDED ON REVERSE SIDE)

21 Identifying Quality in Teaching Using Consultative Methods

Elaine Hogard

Introduction

This chapter describes an evaluation of a form of university teaching known as Clinical Facilitation. Clinical Facilitation takes place at the interface of higher education and clinical practice in nursing and involves the supervision of student nurses on their clinical placement. The evaluation is relevant to the identification of quality in teaching in two ways. First, the evaluation model employed uses a three-pronged approach to investigate the process of teaching in relation to learning outcomes and the views of the various stakeholders involved. Second, the teaching itself was investigated and categorized using an innovative form of reconstitutive ethnography. Both the trident evaluation method and reconstitutive ethnography have potential for the identification of quality in teaching.

A number of problems and issues led to the establishment of the Pilot Clinical Facilitation Project. These included concerns about:

- the clinical placements available for student nurses;
- the supervision available on these placements (Jacka & Lewin 1986; Polifroni *et al.* 1995);
- the competencies and skills that students were developing as a consequence of the placements (UKCC 1999); and
- the collaboration and communication – or lack of it – between service and higher education (Department of Health 1999).

Although student nurses in the UK now spend half of their time on placements in hospitals and the community, supervisory support for them has weakened as a result of the abolition of the 'clinical tutor' role and the increased load on practitioners (Jowett *et al.* 1994; Twinn & Davies 1996; May *et al.* 1997). Ward staff are so busy caring for patients that they do not have time to supervise students (Bligh 1995; Wilson & Jennet 1997), and research evidence suggests that students are not learning all the skills they need (Luker *et al.* 1996; Macleod Clark *et al.* 1996).

In addition, or perhaps because of, many students and newly qualified staff are leaving nursing. The 18-month pilot scheme, an evaluation of which is presented in this chapter, introduced a category of staff called Clinical Facilitators (CFs) into the acute medical and surgical wards of the hospital trusts of an education and training consortium to work with pre-registration nursing students. The CFs were experienced, skilled and up-to-date nurses who were able to work directly with students and with ward and education staff to improve supervision and placement learning (Rowan & Barber 2000). Twelve CFs were appointed to the medical and surgical wards of six NHS Trust sites. The term Clinical Facilitator appears to be of recent origin (Rowan & Barber 2000). However, the job of supervising the learning of nursing students on placement is as old as nurse training itself, and has been (and is) undertaken by various persons, including clinical tutors, mentors, assessors/mentors, university link tutors, as well as staff nurses, ward sisters and ward managers (Campbell *et al.* 1994). Nevertheless, the use of a new title for this project encouraged an innovative approach to practice and also allowed for the evaluation that is described here.

The CFs were intended primarily to enhance the competence of pre-registration nursing students on clinical placement. On appointment, they were asked to review their objectives and they proposed five key objectives, which were accepted by the education and training consortium. These objectives were:

- to work alongside staff to enhance the pre-registration students' experience within the clinical settings of acute medicine and surgery, complementing the clinical setting by use of workshops and group settings;
- to improve the clinical competence of pre-registration student nurses within the clinical settings of acute medicine and surgery;
- to facilitate broader external/internal communication links;
- to maintain their own clinical professional credibility as a clinical practitioner;
- to monitor the effectiveness of the role.

These problems have been characterized (Ellis & Hogard 2001) as two deficits: a deficit in placements and their supervision and a deficit in competence on qualification. The CFs were intended to address these deficits through enhanced supervision of placements.

The evaluation strategy

Following an earlier attempt to evaluate the pilot scheme internally with a single but complex questionnaire, the evaluation proper commenced in Year Two (a year after the pilot began) and ended when the pilot ended in Year Three. Thus, no pre-testing of competence was possible. A novel multi-method approach was developed with three main components: 1) outcomes measurement; 2) process analysis; and 3) multiple stakeholder perspectives. The methods used and findings from each component are discussed in separate sections, following details of the 12 CFs involved in the pilot scheme.

A general profile of the CFs shows that there were 14 women and 2 men participating in the scheme (including returning and maternity posts), but no more than 12 in post at any one time. The CFs were all first-level nurses registered on parts 1 and 2 of the United Kingdom Central Council (UKCC) register – that is, the adult branch. They all had at least five years of post-registration experience and most had reached senior staff nurse levels of grade F and G, with some coming from ward management positions. The CFs had varying educational qualifications. Most had completed the English National Board (ENB) 998 course, 'Teaching and assessing in clinical practice'. Some were enrolled on or had completed the City and Guilds 7307: Further and Adult Teaching Certificate or its higher education equivalent, the Postgraduate Certificate in Education. A few CFs already held Bachelor's degrees, while some were studying for that level of qualification. One CF had completed their Master's degree while working as a CF. All were participating in staff development of some kind, for which support had been provided by the Consortium.

The project director took a positive and proactive position regarding staff development from the start of the project. Ten per cent of the overall budget was set aside for this purpose. The CFs were encouraged to produce personal development objectives, and they were supported to attend courses and study days consistent with those objectives.

Outcomes measurement

The major objective of the pilot scheme was to enhance the clinical competence of pre-registration nurses. This principal objective would be the main outcome against which the success of the scheme would be judged. It was anticipated that there would be university assessments of the students that could be compared for those who did and did not receive Clinical Facilitation. These assessments were intended to provide feedback to students and, crucially, to determine progress on the course and the final academic award and licence to practise. It was hoped that it would be possible to compare the results of students who had and had not received Clinical Facilitation in otherwise broadly comparable circumstances, and that this would be sensitive to the effects, if any, of Clinical Facilitation. Unfortunately, the assessment schedules, while based on judgements in a number of areas of work, did not record these but culminated in a single binary judgement of safe or not safe to practise. In effect, this amounted to a simple pass/fail judgement. The overwhelming majority of students passed (97 per cent). This emphasis insufficiently differentiated for evaluation purposes. It may also reflect different value systems regarding assessment and differentiated results and uncertainty regarding competencies and assessment.

Frustrated in these two directions, the evaluators decided to model an approach that could have been employed had the evaluation been planned from the start. This was to devise Objective Structured Clinical Examinations (OSCEs) for a selection of basic nursing competencies (Roberts & Brown 1990) and to compare the scores on these OSCEs for groups of students who had or had not received Clinical Facilitation. OSCEs were devised by groups of university and ward staff for three basic skills: temperature taking (TT), blood pressure measurement (BPM), and social hand washing (SHW). Ten-minute practical examinations were organized with simulated patients and two assessors, and assessment schedules were devised and piloted. Representative groups of students who had and had not received Clinical Facilitation but whose experience was otherwise comparable were identified, and 57 students with group sizes 30 CF and 27 non-CF were examined. It is important to note that the OSCEs themselves would have to address more advanced skills to provide a valid exit measurement, and they would need inter-rater reliability to be of any use in making comparisons. In addition, with such numbers, statistical power was obviously weak but the intention was to pilot and demonstrate an approach rather than to generate significant data. In fact, at a non-significant level, students who had received clinical facilitation performed slightly better at TT and BPM but slightly worse at SHW than those who had not received clinical facilitation. In the absence of objective outcome measures, the evaluation had to rely on the perspectives of stakeholders as indicators of the success of the scheme. These are described later in this chapter.

Process analysis

The second major aspect of the evaluation was the process analysis of what the CFs actually did in practice. Thus the identification of the teaching approaches adopted by the CFs was a key objective. This was approached through consultation with the CFs themselves, involving in-depth interviews, focus groups and questionnaires. The objective was to produce a comprehensive description and modelling of clinical facilitation that would come from consultation with the participants and would be verified by them as authentic.

It was here that the evaluation was most innovative technically and substantively. There is a dearth of studies that actually describe and analyse the practice of nursing and nurse education. Insufficient use has been made of consultation with professionals themselves. In principle, three approaches could be adopted to elucidate professional practice. One would be based on detailed observation of practice. A second, used extensively, would be determining and codifying practice and procedures from first principles. A third approach would be to arrive at descriptions through consultation with the professionals themselves. These three approaches could be termed the empirical, the analytical and the consultative (Ellis 1988).

The first approach, involving naturalistic observation of the CFs at work, was impractical in the time scale and circumstances of the research; the second would also have been too time consuming, and raised fundamental questions of validity. Hence, it was decided to follow a consultative approach based on in-depth individual interviews and focus groups with the 12 CFs themselves. Models of Clinical Facilitation emerging from the first interviews would then be verified by the CFs themselves in a second round of individual interviews, thus following the iterative approach described by Mehan (1979) as a 'constitutive ethnography'.

During the first round of interviews, the CFs were asked, 'what motivated you to become a Clinical Facilitator?' The CFs' responses fell into four broad categories, which tended to overlap. First, there were statements about their commitment to nursing as a profession, to the practice of nursing, to nurse education and to the nursing students. They indicated the ways in which the post would allow them to put this commitment into practice. Second, there were statements about their own competence and suitability for the post, including reference to their practical nursing skills, teaching skills, capacity to motivate and ability to meet challenges. They also saw the post as a logical development of their career from practitioner to educator of novice practitioners. Third, there were references to the potential of the post to improve the learning experience of students and hence the quality of nursing. Finally, there were references to the post bridging the gap between theory and practice, and between higher education and service.

The CFs were then asked, 'what skills should a Clinical Facilitator possess to be successful in the post?' The CFs described an individual who would need to be extremely deft in communication skills, diplomacy and tact in order to work productively between stakeholders in education and service. Not surprisingly, comprehensive nursing experience and clinical credibility were also considered imperative for work as a CF.

In the main part of the interview, the CFs were then encouraged to describe their activities through a form of critical incident analysis (Flanagan 1954). This was approached in several ways. The CFs were asked to describe a typical day's or part day's activities: to recall incidents when their practice was successful and, conversely, when it was less successful. In describing their work, CFs were encouraged to relate accounts of their own activities to those of their students, to students' learning and to aspects of the competent nurse's role. Generally, CFs were able to describe their own activities but found it difficult to relate those activities to specific student learning outcomes.

A detailed list of activities was distilled from the transcripts of the first interviews; these provided the starting point for the second set of interviews, in which CFs were asked to verify, expand or modify the list and, again, to relate their activities to student learning outcomes. They were also invited to comment on a four-level model of Clinical Facilitation and, at the first level, the six aspects of supervision and/or teaching that had emerged from analysing the transcripts of the first interview. Whilst CFs were able to provide more examples of instances, these did not affect the model, which was verified by the CFs as appropriate. They were keen to emphasize that they supported students in their learning, but felt that this commitment to support informed each supervisory behaviour rather than being a category itself.

Following these second interviews with the CFs, the four-level model of Clinical Facilitation was confirmed. This model was based primarily on the material from the interviews, but also took account of descriptions of possible roles given by managers in higher education in their individual interviews. Whilst recognizing the value of face-to-face supervision and the management of student learning, education managers stressed the potential value of a single coordinator of placement learning for a ward or group of wards who could also contribute to securing and quality-assuring placements in the following ways: direct face-to-face supervision of students; the management of student learning through arranging learning experiences and supervision/instruction of students by others; maintaining an overview of student placement and learning at an organizational level, for example a group of wards in a hospital; and undertaking a strategic planning role for a higher education institution in securing and quality-assuring clinical placements. The work of these CFs, based on their descriptions, appeared to be primarily at the supervisory and managerial levels, with some contributions at the organizational level. They had no opportunity to fulfil a strategic role.

The responses given by the CFs mainly concerned their work at the supervisory level of direct face-to-face teaching of students, and that is the focus of this chapter. On the basis of the detailed list of activities generated by their responses, the supervisory role was categorized provisionally into six main types of activity or teaching methods:

- demonstrating a skill to a student;
- pointing out good practice to a student (denotation);
- giving the student a chance to practise a skill;
- discussing the student's work with them;
- giving the student a chance to practise in a skills laboratory or workshop; and
- giving the student a lecture about a skill.

Following the second round of interviews, the models were circulated to the CFs, who discussed them at their regular meeting and finally confirmed them as appropriate at a focus group with the researchers.

This process analysis is a good example of the reconstitutive ethnography method that can be a useful tool for the investigation and elucidation of professional client interaction (Hogard 2007) and specifically of teacher–student interaction. It is grounded in the perceptions and reflections of the teachers. It is iterative and progressively focused. It is captured and categorized in a form that can be verified by the teachers. The results of the process analysis can also be considered and validated by the students and other stakeholders. Critically, it can be related to the concurrent or subsequent outcomes of the process.

Multiple stakeholder perspectives

The third aim of the evaluation was to solicit the views on clinical facilitation of the key stakeholders. These stakeholders included the students, the ward staff, the university staff, the educational and health service managers involved and the CFs themselves. Finding out what all the different stakeholders think of a particular scheme or innovation is of obvious value and significance, but should not be mistaken for an outcome measure unless stakeholder satisfaction had been specified as a key objective. In this scheme, the key objective was the increased competence of students and the difficulty in measuring that was described earlier. Student views on the extent to which their competence had been enhanced are important but are logically and operationally discrete from an objective assessment of whether they are competent or not. Indeed, the views of ward staff and university staff may also fall short of the desirable standards of objectivity, validity and reliability.

Stakeholder views were solicited through three main methods: individual interviews; focus groups, and a questionnaire. The participants in this part of the study were the 12 CFs, 16 university staff who were link tutors, 150 ward staff who worked with the CFs, 7 education managers, 2 consortium managers and 600 students who received clinical facilitation. (All university nursing staff act as link tutors, so these link tutors can be considered as representative of the university nursing staff.) The CFs contributed data through interviews, focus groups and a questionnaire; the university staff through focus groups and a questionnaire; the ward staff through focus groups and a questionnaire; the managers through interviews and a questionnaire; and the students through one focus group and a questionnaire. The method chosen reflected the number of participants in relation to the time available.

The questionnaire was piloted to ensure intelligibility and was structured to include similar questions for each group to allow for comparison and contrast. As a part of the questionnaire, respondents were asked to complete two rank-ordering questions. The first asked respondents to place six key roles involved in the supervision of students in rank order in relation to their contribution to student learning. These roles were those of CF, assessor/mentor (the ward nurse trained to support and assess student learning), link tutor (the member of university staff responsible for the student), staff nurse, ward sister and health care assistant. The second question asked respondents to rank the six aspects of CF activity identified earlier according to their value for student learning. Other sections of the questionnaire invited respondents to evaluate the extent to which the CFs had met each of their five objectives and, in more open-ended questions, to identify the strengths and weaknesses of the scheme and to evaluate various ways in which it might be developed.

The use of common elements in the questionnaires completed by students, ward staff, university staff and the CFs themselves allowed for interesting comparison and contrast.

The first comparison concerns the rank ordering of key roles with regard to their usefulness to students' learning on placement. There is a strong consensus here, with all agreeing that the assessor/mentor is the most useful person. This was reassuring, since the assessor/mentor was the designated person responsible for supervision and assessment and was trained for that purpose. Most place the CF next except for the university staff, who placed the staff nurse higher. Most place the staff nurse third, with the exception of the university staff. The ward sister is placed next by most, the exception being the students, who rate the health care assistant higher. The university link tutor is considered least useful by all except the university staff who are, of course, link tutors.

The most striking feature was the strong consensus between judges, but with some minor differences of view from the university staff and the students. The university staff seem somewhat more wedded, not unexpectedly, to the official system of placement supervision, with assessor/mentor and staff nurse being the top two and the CF coming in at three. The students rate the health care assistant higher than the others, which may indicate a feature of the informal as opposed to the formal system. The CFs' view of themselves is reflected in the views of the students and ward staff. There is general agreement that the university link tutor is not as useful to students as the other persons, but the university staff rate this post one place higher than the others.

The second ranking question concerned the teaching methods that CFs identify themselves as using. Respondents were asked to rank the methods with regard to their utility for student learning on placement. The most striking feature was the total consensus between CFs, students and ward staff and the significantly different view that the university staff appear to take on four items. With regard to consensus, there is strong agreement that demonstrating a skill comes first and practising a skill second. The next most useful item is pointing out good practice, then practice in a skills lab or workshop, discussing the student's work and giving a lecture. The university staff, on the other hand, attributed higher utility to discussion than to practice, and preferred lectures to skill labs and workshops.

In the second section of the questionnaires, respondents were invited to strongly agree, agree, be neutral, disagree or strongly disagree or express uncertainty in response to eight positive statements about the CFs and their work. Amongst these eight statements were five that addressed specifically the five key objectives that the CFs set for themselves and three others – one concerning the impact of the CFs on students' work with patients and two concerning the contribution of the CFs to the university programme.

In evaluating the accomplishment of objectives by the CFs, most respondents, students and CFs, either strongly agreed or agreed with every item with the exception of one. University link tutors were more undecided. Overall, most stakeholders felt the CFs had met their five primary objectives, and this is a strong affirmation of the value of the scheme. One objective where agreement was less evident was that concerning the facilitation of broader external and internal communication links.

The university staff were less in agreement with the statements than the other two groups, with mean scores in the 3 band, but nevertheless were in agreement overall.

Following the results of this three-pronged evaluation the research report concluded with a number of recommendations to service and education. These recommendations aimed to affect policy and practice with regard to learning, supervision and assessment of student nurses on clinical placement.

Discussion and recommendations

This chapter has described an evaluation of a pilot scheme to introduce CFs into the medical and surgical wards of six general hospitals to facilitate the placement learning of student nurses. These facilitators, a new category of staff, were introduced to address two problems: the shortage of adequately supervised placements and the deficit in clinical skills of newly qualified nurses. The context for these problems was national difficulties in recruiting and retaining nurses. The facilitators were distinctive in that, unlike other ward staff and university staff, they were dedicated full time to the supervision and facilitation of student learning in the wards. Clearly, they made a quantitative contribution to supervision and increased the amount that students received. Students, ward staff and university staff were unanimous in agreeing that the CFs had met four of the key objectives, including the central one regarding the enhancement of clinical competence in students. The only doubts were expressed regarding the communication objective, and this might well reflect the imprecise but potentially wide-ranging nature of the objective itself. While this implies that their contribution was qualitatively appropriate, no comparison was made with the qualitative aspects of the work of assessor/mentors or others to ascertain if the CFs had made a distinctive contribution rather than providing more of the same. The fact that the assessor/mentors were rated ahead of the CFs might suggest that qualitatively their contribution was comparable. This area would merit further research, and the model of clinical supervision would provide a comparative benchmark.

It was straightforward to identify the desired outcomes of the scheme in terms of the enhanced clinical competence of the students in a range of key competencies. Finding reliable and valid measures of the accomplishment of these outcomes proved problematic. The assessment schedules used by the university were insufficiently differentiated to allow for comparison between those students who had received clinical facilitation and those who had not. OSCEs, which would have provided appropriate outcome measures, were not employed by this university. Whilst assessment of clinical practice is a problematic area in nursing and indeed in other caring professions, there has been significant progress in the assessment of nursing, including the further development of OSCEs (Harden *et al.* 2016). The use of such approaches would have facilitated this part of the evaluation had they been employed in this university. However, it was beyond the scope of the evaluation to introduce them. Further research linking facilitation and facilitators to measurable outcomes is required and would need to be a coordinated national project.

The CFs in this pilot were given a broad brief to enhance the clinical competence of students. How they should work was left largely to the CFs themselves. It was therefore important to capture the details of their working methods. The investigation of the process of Clinical Facilitation used a consultative method involving in-depth interviews with the CFs themselves. This produced a model of Clinical Facilitation that included four possible levels of operation and a six-fold characterization of direct face-to-face supervision. Whilst these six aspects of supervision, including observation of good practice, practice and receiving feedback on practice, are predictable, they are authentic reflections of the views of the facilitators and are indicative of the kind of information that can be adduced regarding professional practice through the use of consultative methods as distinct from direct observation. The six activities were subsequently rated for utility by students, ward staff and university staff. There was a consensus that the most useful methods involved demonstration and observation of good practice, practice and receiving feedback on practice. University staff placed a relatively higher value on lectures and discussion than the other stakeholders, which probably reflects their different perspective on the curriculum as a whole. Further research would be necessary to authenticate these methods and to study their relationship with outcomes. It would also be necessary to identify and evaluate the extent to which others involved in practice education employ such methods and to identify the optimal skills mix between, for example, assessor/mentors, other ward staff, university staff and CFs.

The CFs are an expensive resource in that they are additional to both clinical and university staff and are paid at the same grade as ward managers. This chapter has highlighted different levels of role that they might undertake beyond the direct supervision that is the focus of this research. These include: a managerial role, coordinating and supporting all those who contribute to student learning; an organizational role, where they coordinate placements in a hospital or group of wards; and a strategic role, where they work as agents of the university to secure and quality assure placements. Further studies would be required to compare and contrast the cost-effectiveness of these roles. Consideration must also be given to the introduction of facilitators into other settings than the medical and surgical wards of this pilot.

The evaluation of a particular form of teaching described in this chapter used two relatively novel approaches which can make a contribution to the elucidation of quality in teaching. First, was the three-pronged approach to the evaluation of teaching focusing on outcomes, process and multiple stakeholder perspectives (Ellis and Hogard 2006). This proved its utility by highlighting the lacuna in outcome measures for the key objective of the teaching and by giving the process of teaching in the form of Clinical Facilitation more attention than is often the case. Second, was the use of reconstitutive ethnography, a form of consultation, as an approach to data-gathering regarding the practice of Clinical Facilitation itself (Hogard 2007).

At the beginning of the chapter, two deficits were identified in nurse education, concerning placements and their supervision and clinical competence on qualification. By their very existence, the Clinical Facilitators improved the quantity of supervision available – but at a cost. The quality of their supervision was perceived as good by the students and other stakeholders. The lack of valid and reliable outcome measures in this particular setting precluded any definitive statement on their effect on clinical competence, although certainly the stakeholders believed their teaching had met this key objective. Of great interest to this book is the progress made in elucidating the processes of teaching and learning that made up Clinical Facilitation.

As a model for the elucidation of any particular form of teaching this study is exemplary in two ways. First the trident approach places teaching in relation to its outcomes in learning and the views of all stakeholders. Each of these three elements requires its own research questions and appropriate data streams to answer them.

Of particular importance is the investigation of the process of teaching itself and the method which constructs the description and categorization of teaching through the recollections and reflections of teachers themselves. This method – reconstitutive ethnography – can provide a substantial body of data describing teaching itself and allow for a verified categorization of that teaching.

References

Bligh J. (1995) The clinical skills unit. *Postgraduate Medical Journal* 71, 730–732.

Campbell I.E., Larrivee L., Field P.A., Day R.A. & Reutter L. (1994) Learning to nurse in the clinical setting. *Journal of Advanced Nursing* 20, 1125–1131.

Department of Health (1999) *Making a Difference.* HMSO, London.

Ellis R. (1988) *Professional Competence and Quality Assurance in the Caring Professions.* Chapman & Hall, London.

Ellis R. & Hogard E. (2001) *An Evaluation of the Pilot Project for Clinical Placement Facilitation.* Chester Academic Press, Chester.

Ellis R. & Hogard E. (2006) The trident: a three-pronged method for evaluating clinical, social and educational innovations. *Evaluation* 12, 372–383.

Flanagan J. (1954) The critical incident technique. *Psychological Bulletin* 51, 327–359.

Harden R.M, Lilley P. and Patricio M. (2016) *The Definitive Guide to the OSCE.* Elsevier, London.

Hogard E. (2007) Using consultative methods to investigate professional-client interaction as an aspect of process evaluation. *American Journal of Evaluation* 28, 304–317.

Jacka K. & Lewin D. (1986) Elucidation and measurement of clinical learning opportunity available to student nurses. *Journal of Advanced Nursing* 11, 573–582.

Jowett S., Walton I. & Payne S. (1994) *Challenges and Changes in Nurse Education: A Study of the Implementation of Project 2000.* National Foundation for Educational Research (NFER), Slough.

Luker K., Carlisle C., Riley E., Stilwell J. & Davies C. (1996) *Project 2000: Fitness for Purpose.* Department of Health, London.

Macleod Clark J., Maben J. & Jones K. (1996) *Project 2000: Perceptions of the Philosophy and Practice of Nursing. Report to the English National Board.* The Nightingale Institute, King's University, London.

May N., Veitch L., McIntosh J. & Alexander M. (1997) *Preparation for Practice: Evaluation of Nurse and Midwife Education in Scotland 1992 Programmes. Final Report to the National Board of Scotland.* Glasgow Caledonian University, Glasgow.

Mehan H. (1979) *Learning Lessons.* Harvard University Press, Cambridge, MA.

Polifroni E.C., Packard S.A., Shah H.S. & MacAvoy S. (1995) Activities and interactions of baccalaureate nursing students in clinical practice. *Journal of Professional Nursing* 11, 161–169.

Roberts J. & Brown B. (1990) Testing the OSCE: a reliable measurement of clinical nursing skills. *Canadian Journal of Nursing Research* 22, 51–59.

Rowan P. & Barber P. (2000) Clinical Facilitators: a new way of working. *Nursing Standard* 14, 35–38.

Twinn S. & Davies S. (1996) The supervision of Project 2000 students in the clinical setting: issues and implications for practitioners. *Journal of Clinical Nursing* 5, 177–183.

United Kingdom Central Council (UKCC) (1999) *Fitness for Practice.* UKCC, London.

Wilson D.B. & Jennett P.A. (1997) The medical skills centre at the University of Calgary medical school. *Medical Education* 31, 45–48.

22 Student Engagement with and Perceptions of Quality and Standards

Camille B. Kandiko Howson

Introduction

This chapter draws on primary data from a UK-based study of student expectations and perceptions of higher education. It offers recommendations for quality assurance, enhancement and institutional practices to focus on what matters to students, and also to raise the profile of the student voice in policy. A fundamental question about quality in higher education explored is the relationship of student engagement discourse and what matters to students.

Student engagement

Student learning can be predicted by the quality of effort that is put into their educational experience (Astin, 1985). Student involvement, or engagement, provides an instructive focus for researching the student experience. Quality assurance determinations need to take into account how students engage, and how institutions can encourage and support educationally purposeful activities (Coates, 2005).

The concept of student engagement represents two key components (Kuh, 2003). The first is the amount of time and effort students put into academic pursuits and other activities that decades of research show are associated with high levels of learning and development (Chickering & Gamson, 1987; Ewell & Jones, 1996; Pascarella & Terenzini, 2005). The second is how institutions allocate their resources and organise their curriculum, other learning opportunities and support services (Kuh, 2003). These areas measure how institutions provide the environment for students that lead to the experiences and outcomes that constitute student success, broadly defined as persistence, learning and degree attainment (Kuh, 2001). Essential to student engagement are students' expectations, and subsequent perceptions, of the student experience (Lowe & Cook, 2003).

Student involvement, or engagement, provides an instructive focus for researching the student experience. Quality assurance determinations need to take into account how students engage, and how institutions can encourage and support educationally purposeful activities (Coates, 2005). These good educational practices have been translated into Student Engagement surveys, starting in the US and profligating around the world.

The individual student approach of North-American-style student engagement is contrasted with much of the collective and representational student engagement work in the UK, which has been defined by the national quality assurance body, the Quality Assurance Agency (QAA) as the participation of students in quality enhancement and quality assurance processes, resulting in the improvement of their educational experience (QAA Quality Code, Chapter B5, 2012). This has led to a more individualistic basis to student engagement in North America and Australia, contrasted with a more collective, or representative, approach in the UK.

Student experience

This chapter goes beyond looking at how students viewed their role in quality assurance and enhancement processes, to focus on students' perspectives of their student experience and the issues that affected the quality and standards of their experience. This provides a student perspective on higher education, which covers a broad range of issues not always considered in context with one another by higher education sector bodies, research reports or even institutions, with often rigid divides between academic and professional services.

In many ways, 'the student experience' is fused with the commodification of education, arguably occluding more diverse perspectives on both 'students' and 'experience' (Sabri, 2011). The research reported on in this chapter aims to understand the student experience from students' perspectives, highlighting the individual nature of each student's own experience and raising awareness of what matters to students in higher education. Further, this work provides examples of issues affecting quality and standards of higher education from students, in context of their experience and from the voice of individual students.

Student expectations

This chapter explores data on findings from a QAA-funded study involving focus groups at 16 institutions, across institutional types, in the UK. Concept map-mediated interviews (Kandiko & Kinchin, 2013) with undergraduate students were used to elicit students' expectations and perceptions of quality, standards and the student learning experience. This provides comparative information on how students in a variety of fee regimes across the UK (and across year groups) conceptualise their student experience.

Data collected from students on their expectations and perceptions of quality, standards and the student learning experience is a key part of bringing the student voice into quality assurance structures and institutional decision-making. This is relevant as the position of students in relation to higher education is dramatically changing in some countries, such as student-as-customer in England, compared to no-fees for Scottish home students. This empirically based study provides a framework for how the student voice can feed into quality assurance decisions, and highlights what matters to students. This works complements and goes beyond literature-based reports (Gibbs, 2010; Trowler, 2010) and quantitative studies (Bekhradnia, 2013) and captures a more holistic view of the student experience than student feedback surveys of teaching and learning (Griffin *et al.*, 2003).

Methodology

This research took a mixed methods approach, combining a critical analysis of the literature and primary data collection through qualitative concept map-mediated interviews (Kandiko & Kinchin, 2013), which were triangulated with secondary data from institutional and sector policy analysis to explore student perceptions of higher education quality and standards. The project approach was grounded in capturing and providing a vehicle for student voices, and was supported throughout by undergraduate student input and reflection.

Interviews were conducted with over 150 students in 16 higher education institutions, representing four general institutional types (research-intensive, teaching-intensive, regional-focused and special interest) across the countries and regions of the UK. Data was analysed from institutional documents and focus groups with students (primarily Years 1 and 2) from a wide range of departments and disciplines, reflecting academic subjects, pre-professional courses and joint honours degrees. The selection of participants aimed to represent the diversity within UK higher education, including part-time, mature, international and European Union students.

In the interviews and focus groups, students were asked to make concept maps of their higher education experience. Concept map use within qualitative research can facilitate the eliciting of perceived importance of concepts and the visualising of the relationships between concepts (Wheeldon & Ahlberg, 2012). The concept map generated was then used as a point of departure for a series of questions about how students' experiences mapped against their expectations of higher education, and follow-up questions about a number of questions related to quality and standards.

Analysis

Data were analysed using a multifaceted approach designed to incorporate the interview and focus group and concept map data. An initial phase of analysis consisted of informal coding of interview transcripts as data was collected to inform further interviews. Following the data collection phase, concept maps of students' higher education experience were collected along with transcripts of interviews and focus groups. Open coding was conducted using grounded theory on selected transcripts, allowing themes to emerge from the data itself. These were compared with emergent themes from the concept maps and the codes were then refined into more abstract focused codes. The concept maps were analysed visually initially. Major thematic areas were identified and categorised. This iterative process between the data sources produced the six themes, with supporting concept maps, discussed below. Selected maps were chosen to illustrate key themes identified in the interview data.

Consumerist ethos: Student perceptions of value

There was no noticeable trend in changes to students' expectations and perceptions of higher education from first-year (higher fee-paying) and second-year (lower fee-paying) students. What did emerge was a 'consumerist ethos' across all student years and across countries in the UK with different fee regimes, with four main components. The first was contact time, and whether students were getting sufficient contact time for the amount they were paying (regardless of what that was). The second theme was about what resources the institution offered and what additional costs students faced. Next, there was a sense of 'symbolic value', in both a tangible sense (such as contact hours) but also more ephemeral, such as the institutional investment in students and student life, buildings and spaces. Lastly, students noted the reputational value of a degree (and their subject) and of the institution.

Student expectations of the learning environment: Minimum standards

Most students had minimum standards in mind in relation to the learning environment. If these were met, they often had little to say. If they were not met, students were often quite vocal about their discontent. Instrumentally, students expect a reasonable number of (available) computers, regular wi-fi access and sufficient (available) library books. They also expect functional and adequate learning spaces. Organisationally, students expect coherent timetabling and course structures. Interpersonally, students had expectations of lecturers with a sound knowledge of the course material and ability to deliver it.

Beyond the course: Student expectations for employability

Students had expectations about their institution's responsibility for employability. This included formal services such as internships, careers guidance and networking, and informal aspects such as skills that could be gained through volunteering, social activities and sports. If this was done outside the course, some students asked if it should be part of the formal timetabled activities.

Feedback: For me, for others or where did it go?

Feedback to and from the institution (although this usually referred to the course from the students' perspective) was a significant concern. Students rarely heard whether or how their feedback was acted upon. Students did not distinguish between feedback from the course, institution, course representatives or the Students' Union or guild. A concern emerged as to whether the feedback was to help students' own experience or help other students' experience, with students much more interested in the former.

Lecturers: Good, bad and apathetic

Students' perceptions about 'good' lecturers were that they were passionate and knowledgeable about the subject, approachable, willing to invest time in students and offered close tutorial support. 'Bad' teaching included notes being read off PowerPoint, reading direct off lecture notes, not knowing the material and being unwilling to engage with students. Students praised good teaching but had a minimum standard of at least apathetic teaching, acknowledging that every course would have good and bad lecturers. Several students made comments about 'wanting to fire bad teachers' given what they were, or could be, paying.

Individuality of student experiences: Trajectories in and out of higher education

An important note is the individuality of each student's own experience, including their reasons for attending university, where they chose to study, what they want to get out of their degrees. Students' incoming expectations stemmed from family and friends; secondary schooling and FE; and the general media/political discourse. Students' expectations after university included employment; improved quality of life; and knowledge of their subject/profession, both for employment and an expanded worldview. Students were concerned about fair processes and regulations but also a degree of personalisation and tailoring, as seen in Figure 22.1.

Discussion

Being part of a community and having a sense of belonging were the most important environmental aspects of quality for students. This related each individual's engagement with the institution, and the institution with them, for the enhancement of the student's overall learning experience. This resonates with the North-American-style student engagement

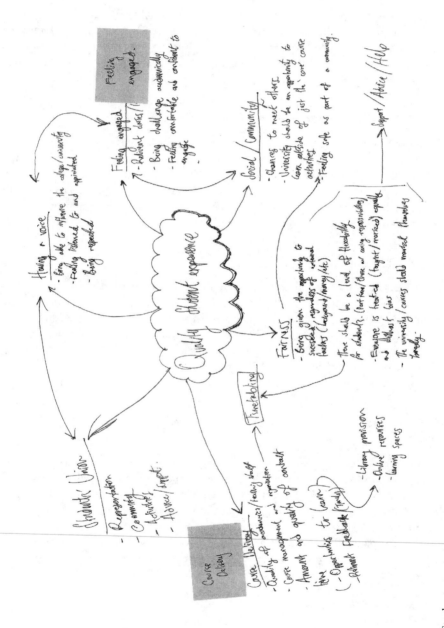

Figure 22.1 Student concept map

approach widely disseminated through national Student Engagement surveys. Students wanted opportunities to interact with other students through Students' Union societies and clubs, institutional activities and other social opportunities; students from a variety of institutions spoke of wanting activities less centred on drinking, particularly with respect to Students' Union events.

The importance of community and a sense of belonging was a frequently mentioned aspect of students' higher education experience. Community was generally seen as developing from face-to-face experiences and involved students being known, being welcomed and having opportunities to participate in the institutional community. For some students this was largely limited to the students and staff on their course, particularly for mature and part-time students. Students' views of their role in the institution took on more of a sense of collegiality and friendliness than a strong partnership approach – most students did not mention wanting to be more involved in decision-making, they focused on wanting individual problems they had resolved.

Engagement was conceptualised in the context of each individual's engagement with the institution, and the institution with them, for the enhancement of the overall learning experience rather than in a 'representational' context. Students related to the academic community at the course level. This indicates the importance of local-based partnership work for engaging students and suggests institutions should avoid overreliance on representational forms of student engagement. Students' views suggest more of 'a partnership of aims' with staff on their course rather than 'a partnership of means', indicating more of a sense of collegiality with staff, rather than large-scale, high-level partnership work.

Overall, students wanted more opportunities for engagement. To students, engagement meant all students having opportunities to engage with course and institutional-based activities. Students wanted more interaction with staff, both within the classroom experience and beyond. Students wanted opportunities to meet and interact with other students, engage with their course and participate in extra-curricular activities, both social and academic-related.

Impact

This research offers a better understanding of student perceptions of quality and standards, leading to the possibility of more effective partnerships within (and across) institutions. It also provides a more developed understanding of how perceptions vary across institutional types and regional settings. This aims to facilitate academic and student groups that are better equipped to understand issues relating to quality and standards and thus to facilitate change.

The research methodology presented offers a design for an analytical activity for institutions and others to explore students' expectations and perceptions of quality, standards and the student learning experience in local contexts. Students developing concepts maps of their experiences and participating in focus groups can be embedded in quality assurance frameworks, institutional decision-making and developed to support students-as-partners within and beyond institutions.

There is also relevance to policy, particularly about how students are experiencing higher education under a variety of different fee regimes – including within single institutions (such as with English students in Welsh universities) and across different national systems. As notions of quality increasingly focus on students, it is important to 'get to know' students and their expectations at course, institutional, national, regional and global levels. Student voices should be part of the quality conversation, but as noted from the research, representative structures alone are not sufficient. Each student is concerned about her own experience as well as those of other students.

Conclusion

Students have positive perceptions of higher education, but also clear expectations in mind of what institutions should provide to support and enable their learning and enhance their career prospects. Students wanted to be challenged in their learning, but also supported by the institution. Students almost exclusively spoke of their educational learning experience in terms of their course. This raises the need for strong course-level management of the curriculum, quality and standards, with a clear structure of academic management mirroring undergraduate student-facing aspects, including local feedback and evaluation, module and course review. There needs to be institutional-level support and management of quality enhancement and quality assurance of student engagement, individually and collectively, which can be coordinated through dedicated offices or senior appointments. Together this would allow for evaluation and feedback processes to be managed at the course level and coordinated at the institutional level, keeping in mind to seek, ask and report on feedback to and from students.

The trajectories of students into higher education and out of higher education are highly influential in shaping their perspectives. The question of what is 'quality' or 'good' about a particular institution should thus be framed within the contingent question of what a student is looking for in an institution, which may or may not be academic reputation. Whatever the institutional type, institutions need to develop a community and help students transition into it. Staff need to be supported by their institutions to provide the interaction and guidance that is important to students.

Across institutions there needs to be a focus on how students can enhance their employability within, related to and beyond their course. Students are investing significant amounts of time and money in their education, and expect institutions to do the same. At the same time, students need to be held responsible for their role in the institution, and further opportunities for students to engage should be encouraged. There is much work to be done across the higher education sector to support students, staff and institutions in this endeavour, working *with* not *for* students.

Moving forward

Reflecting internationally, students in this UK-based study were more interested in the North-American individual-based approach to student engagement. However, many students reflected on the important social and representative function of representative Students' Unions. This offers an interesting perspective to other countries, which have different traditions of student governance and approaches to democratic representative structures. It is important to reflect on student engagement in approaches to quality at a variety of levels, including for students' courses of study, institutionally and nationally as well as balancing individual and collective approaches.

The methodology of this study can easily be replicated in specific institutions or across countries to reveal how students' themselves conceptualise quality and standards. Students' expectations and perceptions of their higher education experiences can then inform institutional and national policy. This is not always a direct activity, for example more contact hours may not always be a pedagogically sound approach to enhancement, but knowing what matters to students can shape minimum thresholds, provide insight into explaining the nature of higher-level study to students, and direct institutional policies.

References

Astin, A. W. (1985). Involvement: The cornerstone of excellence. *Change, 17*(4), 35–39.

Bekhradnia, B. (2013). *The academic experience of students in English universities 2013 report.* London: Higher Education Policy Institute (HEPI).

Chickering, A. W., & Gamson, Z. F. (1987). Seven principles for good practice in undergraduate education. *AAHE Bulletin, 39*(7), 3–7.

Coates, H. (2005). The value of student engagement for higher education quality assurance. *Quality in Higher Education, 11*(1), 25–36.

Ewell, P. T., & Jones, D. P. (1996). *Indicators of "good practice" in undergraduate education: A handbook for development and implementation.* Boulder, CO: National Center for Higher Education Management Systems.

Gibbs, G. (2010). *Dimensions of quality.* York: Higher Education Academy.

Griffin, P., Coates, H., McInnis, C. & James, R. (2003). The development of an extended course experience questionnaire. *Quality in Higher Education, 9*(3), 259–266.

Kandiko, C. B. & Kinchin, I. M. (2013). Developing discourses of knowledge and understanding: Longitudinal studies of PhD supervision. *London Review of Education, 11*(1), 46–58.

Kuh, G. D. (2001). Assessing what really matters to student learning: Inside the National Survey of Student Engagement. *Change, 33*(3), 10–17, 66.

Kuh, G. D. (2003). What we're learning about student engagement from NSSE: Benchmarks for effective educational practices. *Change, 35*(2), 24–32.

Lowe, H., & Cook, A. (2003). Mind the Gap: Are students prepared for higher education? *Journal of Further and Higher Education 27*(1), 53–76.

Pascarella, E. T. & Terenzini, P. T. (2005). *How college affects students: A third decade of research.* San Francisco: Jossey-Bass.

Quality Assurance Agency (2012). *UK Quality Code for Higher Education. Part B: Ensuring and Enhancing Academy. Chapter B5: Student Engagement.* Gloucester: QAA.

Sabri, D. (2011). What's wrong with 'the student experience'? *Discourse: Studies in the Cultural Politics of Education 32*(5), 657–667.

Trowler, V. (2010). *Student engagement literature review.* York: The Higher Education Academy.

Wheeldon, J., & Ahlberg, M. K. (2012). *Visualizing social science research: Maps, methods and meaning.* Thousand Oaks, CA: Sage.

23 Beyond Satisfaction
Student Voice, Student Engagement, and Quality Learning

David Morris

If you're a university teacher, particularly in an arts, humanities, or social sciences discipline, it is very likely that you have had a conversation with a student or a parent about the scarcity of 'contact hours' on many university courses. Such complaints are intimately linked to debates about threshold standards and quality, and popular and media perceptions about the 'quality' of university teaching.[1] University leaders have had to defend the sector from similar criticisms by politicians, such as in a remarkable Commons Select Committee report in 2009 which found that 'it appears that different levels of effort are required in different universities to obtain degrees in similar subjects, which may suggest that different standards may be being applied'.[2]

Universities have continually protested about how they aim to facilitate independent study and effort, and have pointed to research that clearly shows that higher numbers of contact hours do not necessarily improve learning outcomes. The eminent Graham Gibbs's *Dimensions of Quality*, published in 2010, was in some ways a response to this aforementioned select committee report.[3] Yet seven years later, the debate over contact hours has not gone away. If anything, the matter has been intensified by the tripling of tuition fees in England in 2012. Like it or loathe it, contact time is intrinsically tied up in conceptions of 'value for money', quality, and whether degrees are 'worth it', and continued government pressure on the sector has eventually led to the imposition of the controversial Teaching Excellence Framework.

Yet to some teaching practitioners, this is even greater justification for dismissing the misguided hysteria over contact hours. Students, so the argument goes, have been encouraged by fees to see their education as something they purchase, but they don't understand that education is more about the work that the student puts in. Marketisation is believed to have encouraged students' laziness and a sense of entitlement. Students, it is argued, do not have the necessary experience or professional knowledge to know what is best for their education; that is the very purpose of academic professionalism and independence.[4]

Yet however one looks at it, it is clear that there is a wide gap in understanding between teachers and students who are debating the merits of more or fewer contact hours. Such a divide is damaging for teaching and learning, and needs to be bridged if students' engagement with their studies is to be improved.

Debates about the merits of different methods of or approaches to education often tend towards disagreements about one or another party's right to express an informed an opinion about 'what is best'. In schools policy often revolves around the tussle between teachers, parents, and government officials, with each claiming a particular legitimacy for education policy being bent to their will. Research suggests that service 'users' (parents, pupils, students) in education typically have a less positive view of the effectiveness of education systems than service 'providers' (managers and teachers).[5] In recent years, higher education has seen a similar debate emerge over the legitimacy of students' views on the quality of their education, and arguments over contact hours are just one such example.

A great deal of time and effort is now devoted to hearing and understanding student opinions on the state of their teaching. The National Student Survey is one of the largest surveys of any kind in the UK, and is a key performance indicator in almost all universities. Its importance, underlined by its use in major league tables, has only grown as it provides three of the six core metrics in the 2017 TEF. QAA's Quality Code devotes an entire chapter to student engagement, and almost all university departments will facilitate some form of student representation system. On top of the NSS, students are surveyed extensively on their modules, experience of campus life, and general wellbeing. We perhaps have more data about what students are thinking and feeling than any other section of the UK population through instruments such as module evaluation questionnaires, student accommodation surveys, the Times Higher Education Student Experience Survey, the HEA-HEPI Student Academic Experience Survey, the HEA's Postgraduate Taught and Postgraduate Research Experience Surveys, the iGraduate International Student Barometer, and more.

Despite – or perhaps because of – this effort to understanding what students think, there is a great deal of unease in the academy about the power which the student voice now appears to exercise. Responding uncritically to students' wishes is considered to be contrary to the authority and wisdom of the academy, and students are often criticised for not knowing what is in their best interests. The 'tyranny of the consumer' is thought to be a stick to beat universities with, and a sign of the degeneration created by a market ethos.[6]

Yet as I will argue here, there is remarkable synergy between what students frequently highlight as important to their education and what established pedagogical research has shown to be effective for learning, particularly when it comes to educational outcomes. Universities and teachers should be open to critical engagement with student feedback on their learning experiences, and by doing so can improve those students' learning and their institution's educational success.

Far from being an incentive to 'dumb down' or abandon standards, there is plenty of available evidence to suggest that students as a collective have a very real interest in making the most of their university experience. There is a great deal of alignment between teachers' aspirations for their students and students' aspirations for themselves. But there is also a communications gap between the two parties.[7] This challenge of communication and mutual understanding is one which universities must address when utilising student surveys, student representatives, and student voice, in order to achieve real improvements to the student learning experience.

Misinterpreted – why student voice gets a bad reputation

Almost any policy or research paper on 'student engagement' begins with a definition of terms.[8] In modern UK higher education parlance, 'student engagement' can refer to any number of the following activities:

- Student engagement with their *studies* – the conventional and pedagogical definition of the term, and that which is more commonly used in North America and Australia. This can be measured in surveys such as the National Survey of Student Engagement.
- Student engagement with their *university environment* – typically utilised by extra-curricular functions of universities including students' unions, and often related to student wellbeing and employability.

- Student engagement with *quality assurance and enhancement* – the definition employed by QAA, referring typically to student representation, and sometimes a byword for student surveys such as the NSS.
- Student engagement with *institutional management and governance* – also primarily concerned with student representation, this use of the term by students' unions implies an assertion of students' collective interests within the university.

This is by no means an exclusive list. 'Student engagement' has become so ubiquitous that it is at risk of becoming a cliché, and attempts to parse out its various and often confused meanings suggest a frustration at the lack of precision with which it is deployed.[9] This lack of precision is just as common in the criticism often levelled at student engagement activities. Fears about students asserting power over the academy appear to reflect a profound anxiety about the respect for academic and educated wisdom, particularly within an increasingly market-driven sector.[10]

Student engagement's multiple meanings represent a high aspiration for the active and motivated learner, fully immersed in their studies and university community. The ethos of the 'engaged student' is consistent across any of the above activities: they study hard, but they also take a critical view of their learning environment and work to be an active citizen within it.[11] On the flipside, institutions that encourage and listen to student voices will create more engaging environments for student learning and development; listening to the student voice becomes a means of reflective practice for teachers and course designers. As Gibbs suggests:

> those institutions that are serious about student engagement are probably serious about all kind of other quality enhancement mechanisms, and care about their students, at the same time.[12]

This point has been consistently argued by the National Union of Students in recent years. The NUS argues that student engagement is not merely a virtuous activity or an assertion of students' interests over those of academics, but a means to improving students' learning and development, and thus integral to any university's mission.[13] Furthermore, the NUS frames engagement and partnerships as a fundamental challenge to marketisation and the forces of consumerism:

> The consumer model could create a dangerous imbalance – the role of educators is reduced; students' power appears great, but is in fact limited to commenting only on what has been sold to them, and student satisfaction is substituted for learning . . .
> . . . students as partners offers a valuable alternative to the rhetoric of consumerism. Regardless of whether students agree with the values and characteristics of the funding model in which they sit, they may adopt behaviours we associate with consumerism unless we offer a new and compelling way of thinking about learning."[14]

In particular, the NUS argues that respect and concern for student voice is an effective way of addressing particular challenges that universities face in ensuring an equitable learning environment for students traditionally underrepresented in higher education, in order to tackle pernicious issues such as the black and ethnic minority attainment gap.[15]

Yet aside from these arguments, there is some very clear evidence that making an effort to understand students' experiences can be a useful measure of effective teaching and learning, particularly if done through robust and well-designed survey instruments. The most thorough research into student surveys that evaluate teaching is reliable and stable and much less affected by hypothesised biases than is commonly assumed. Indeed, teachers and students tend to rate teaching very similarly.[16]

That is not to say that surveys don't deserve some of their criticism. The wide range of survey instruments used in higher education across the English-speaking world means that not all student surveys are equally effective, and not all student surveys are utilised in effective ways. The NSS, though a reliable survey, is most commonly used to compare universities, despite not being robust enough to do so.[17] The NSS lacks a clear unit of analysis: students are asked to rate their 'course' which consists of many multifaceted elements – modules, teachers, assessments etc. – that might vary significantly in quality. This variety and sometimes disjuncture caused by modular-based programmes is a theme we shall revisit.

There are also continued concerns that students' responses can be biased towards their teachers, particularly on the grounds of gender or race. Students have been shown to have differing expectations of men and women teachers, which in turn can influence their evaluations of them.[18] One analysis of NSS results did not find a link between gender and student satisfaction, but did find a link between student satisfaction and a higher percentage of white teachers. Such links clearly need to be investigated further, and are further reasons for caution, particularly when using student feedback as a 'hard' measure for performance management.[19]

Yet used properly, student survey data is a useful feedback tool for teachers and universities and should not be rejected out of hand. Like all data and statistics, it should be handled with care and deftness. A lot of the resentment directed at the use of student surveys is their role in performance management and target setting for staff, but such criticisms tend to throw the baby out with the bathwater; criticism of how data is used should be distinguished from questioning the validity of the data itself, and perhaps more importantly, should not negate the student voices that such data represents.[20] HEFCE's own review of the strengths and weaknesses of the NSS has emphasised the need for such triangulation with other sources of data, as has the Higher Education Academy.[21]

Data will also always be an approximation of students' complex experiences. Students' learning cannot be condensed into a few agree/disagree questions.[22] This is all the more reason for teachers, departments and universities to be in a constant dialogue with their student body – usually though chosen representatives – about what students are doing, what they are thinking, and how they are learning.

What do students care about?

Aside from the NSS, new research is being regularly released and informing policy on university students' expectations, experiences and behaviours in learning and teaching. Each piece of research, along with what we know from the NSS, is beginning to give a fairly consistent picture of students' views on the quality of university education.

The NSS itself has been notable for consistently showing relative student dissatisfaction with the quality of assessment and feedback. This 'bank' of five questions on the NSS is actually two fairly distinct mini-sections: two questions on the quality of assessment, and three on the quality of feedback. Despite lower scores overall, the bank's overall average is generally brought up by responses to the questions on assessment, and students' evaluation of feedback on assessment is even lower than the averages suggest. Along with assessment and feedback, course organisation management now scores much lower than the other sections of the NSS. Both are themes that come up regularly in other research.

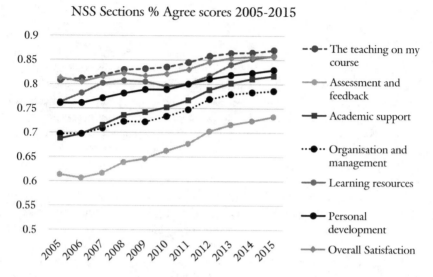

NSS Sections % Agree scores 2005-2015

- --●-- The teaching on my course
- Assessment and feedback
- Academic support
- ...●.. Organisation and management
- Learning resources
- Personal development
- Overall Satisfaction

Figure 23.1 National NSS scores by section, 2005–2015

Table 23.1 Common outcomes of research into students' experiences in higher education

NUS and QAA 2012[23]	QAA 2015[24]	HEA-HEPI 2016[25]
Students desire more interactive and small group teaching sessions.	Students value 'face-to-face' interaction with teaching staff.	Students equate contact time and levels of workload with 'value for money'.
Students desire more individual contact time with their personal tutors.	Students desire a 'personalised' teaching experience in small groups or individual settings.	Feedback on assessment and supportive teaching staff are highly correlated with satisfaction.
Students want contact time to better support and align with independent learning.	Students want their views on course quality to be responded to quickly and dynamically.	Students receive feedback on assessment more slowly than they would prefer.
Students get less verbal feedback than they would prefer.	Students value being part of an academic and pastoral community.	The most common reason for students' expectations not being met was not putting in enough effort themselves.
Students are motivated to study by wanting to do the best they can and the love of their subject.		

The above grid summarises the main themes in three significant pieces of research into students' attitudes towards UK undergraduate education in recent years. The NUS and HEA-HEPI research are primarily quantitative surveys, whilst the QAA research is qualitative.

The matter of feedback once again crops up in each of these reports, with a clear gap emerging between students' expectations and experiences. Students' concerns about feedback, contact time, and interaction are now part of most institutions' background noise, cropping up year upon year. Primarily as a result of the NSS, universities have been

Table 23.2 Common principles of effective teaching and learning in higher education

Chickering and Gamson, *Seven Principles of Good Practice in Undergraduate Higher Education*[27]	John Biggs, *Seven Characteristics of Effective Teaching Contexts*[28]	Wabash National Study, *High Impact Practice Areas in Higher Education*[29]
Student–teacher contact	Metacognitive control	Good teaching and high-quality interactions with teachers, which includes:
Cooperation among students	Relevant learner activity	
Active learning	Formative feedback	
Prompt feedback	Student motivation	• faculty interest in teaching and student development;
High student 'time-on-task' and effort	Interconnected knowledge base	• prompt feedback;
High expectations	Social learning	• quality of non-classroom interactions with teachers;
Respects diverse ways of learning	Teacher quality	• teaching clarity and organisation.
		Challenge and high expectations
		Interactional diversity
		Deep learning

particularly exercised in trying to amend feedback on assessment to make it more responsive to students' wishes. Feedback policies, often with fixed turnaround times, appear to have only part-succeeded. Whilst feedback scores have improved in line with the rest of the NSS, they still lag far behind other parts of the survey.

Feedback is only one of what Gibbs calls a 'small range of fairly well-understood pedagogical practices that engender student engagement'.[26] This range of practices that Gibbs alludes to has cropped up in the conclusions to multiple studies of effective pedagogy. There are interesting parallels between the findings of research into pedagogical effectiveness and the above research into students' attitudes towards their teachers and their learning.

Students' desire for feedback, engaging contact with their teachers, motivation to study, and being a part of a community, can all be linked to the findings of the below studies. Feedback on assessment, effective academic support, and well-designed courses are the prerequisites for metacognition, student motivation, cooperation and high student 'time-on-task'. By distinguishing these effective pedagogical outcomes from the processes needed to enable them, students and teachers can have much deeper and more meaningful conversations about the quality of education being provided and better identify aspects of teaching that might be failing to engender student learning.

Translating the student voice – reading between the lines

Utilising the student voice and student engagement for improving the quality of teaching and learning is nonetheless a challenging and iterative process; a means of reflective practice and metacognition by teachers as well as students, where the answers and insights are not always obvious. In any democratic or customer environment the challenge for decision makers (in this case, teachers) is to interpret and understand the experiences of the collective populace or service user (in this case, students). This is the balance between outright paternalism and consumer-tyranny that universities need to find, in order to create the most effective (and dare I say it, satisfactory) learning environments.

Many pieces of student research often see students suggesting solutions to problems that haven't been identified specifically enough. We might be reminded of the classic scene from the film *Moneyball*, where Brad Pitt's character chastises his team of baseball scouts for not being clear enough about what they want to fix:

Ken Medlock: We're trying to solve the problem here, Billy.
Brad Pitt: Not like this you're not. You're not even looking at the problem.
Medlock: We're very aware of the problem. I mean . . .
Pitt: Okay, good. What's the problem?
Medlock: Look, Billy. We all understand what the problem is. We have to replace . . .
Pitt: Okay, good. What's the problem?
Medlock: The problem is we have to replace three key players in our lineup.
Pitt: No. What's the problem?

Discussions about the common areas of tension between students and their teachers – contact hours, feedback on assessment, class sizes, and academic support – could perhaps do with an injection of the wisdom above. Having an honest conversation between teachers and students about teaching quality requires being specific and clear about the problems that are trying to be solved. To paraphrase Walter Lippmann, students and teachers 'live in the same world, but they think and feel in different ones', and both create subjective, abridged impressions of the quality of learning and teaching either being delivered or received.[30]

Let's go back to the matter of contact time. When students complain about this, it's worth questioning the real source of the dissatisfaction. Perhaps complaints about contact hours are actually complaints about the lack of a holistically engaging learning experience? There is a heuristic at play in students' criticism, a shortcut which assumes that more contact hours will lead to the real outcome that they desire: an engaging, challenging, growth-provoking education, as described by the above models of effective undergraduate instruction. Contact hours aren't the problem; instead it is the lack of an engaging learning environment. More contact hours might be the solution, but it is also possible they are not. Nonetheless, complaints about contact hours could be a 'warning light' for reflection and dialogue about the effectiveness of the course in question.

This 'translation' of student feedback builds upon what we know about heuristics and cognitive biases from behavioural science.[31] Solving the complex problems provided by student feedback requires probing around these heuristics, identifying what they might tell us about barriers to students' learning, and deciding on corrective actions to improve such learning.

The lessons on behavioural science also apply the other way around, to instructions given by teachers to their students. Complaints about contact hours have led to academic departments and the wider sector embarking on public relations campaigns about the importance of independent study.[32] Universities are at risk of a 'do as we say, not as we do' failure if the solution is constantly trumpeted as merely 'explaining' to students why independent study is important.

The same goes for learning outcomes. As Gibbs argues, learning outcomes have never been more clearly stated, and yet this seems to have had little benefit for student learning:

My experience is that nearly all courses nowadays have stated learning outcomes and they are still often incoherent in terms of the educational processes involved. The theorists might reply that this is because the outcomes have not been stated properly. But I believe that you need a sense of what students are supposed to be doing, not just where they are heading.[33]

Whilst studying, students are having information thrown at them every single day. They are learning their course content, learning metacognitive skills from their teachers, hearing about social and extra-curricular activities from their wider institutions, and are perhaps also subject to more targeted commercial advertising than any other social group. This information overload means that merely stating learning outcomes on course handbooks will simply not cut it. Such outcomes have to become self-evidently obvious from the activities that students engage with on their course.

This is the very metacognition referred to in the above models – the point where students become self-aware of their behaviours and are thus able to maximise their learning. Listening to and constructively engaging with student feedback is another way for teachers to facilitate such metacognition, exploring the process of learning itself and searching together for the optimal way of obtaining the desired learning outcomes. For teachers, this might mean going beyond accepting what students are saying at face value (e.g. 'we want more contact time'), and asking themselves what students' feedback *really* means.

Alignment and success

As Gibbs has argued, a great deal of teaching practice in higher education is determined by habit and convention rather than developing learning, and universities are frequently criticised by even their own leaders for being fundamentally conservative institutions that shirk at innovation.[34] Course leaders should evaluate the extent to which their courses are best structured to actively incentivise student effort, time on task, and learning. Student engagement and feedback on their courses can be a catalyst for such evaluation and reflection.

John Biggs suggests that three common assumptions about education quality need to be questioned in universities: that lectures and tutorials are the default teaching methods, that the focus of quality reviewers should be on teacher activity, and that relevant learning only happens within the classroom. It is significant that the available research into students' attitudes towards the education suggests they think similarly: students recognise the importance of their own effort, they find extra-classroom learning valuable, and they desire the kind of small group and individual interaction with their peers and teachers that lectures simply cannot provide.

Biggs has also criticised the modular system of course design that fails to develop student learning in a linear way and prevents 'constructive alignment'; students' struggle to see how the disjointed elements of their course piece together. As Biggs puts it, 'teaching and learning take place in a whole system, which embraces classroom, departmental and institutional levels. A poor system is one in which the components are not integrated, and are not tuned to support high-level learning'.[35]

A typical course structure of weekly or bi-weekly lectures, augmented by fortnightly seminars or tutorials, and assessed by an end-of-term summative essay, may have slowly developed out of habit, but it is necessarily a particularly well-integrated system. Innovative use of regular formative assessment, feedback, and small group class time will make students more actively engaged in their studies.

The obvious challenge here for course designers is that regular feedback on assessment and small-group or individual instruction are labour- and time-intensive activities. The removal of student number controls, the pressures on universities' finances, and the pressure to rapidly expand courses has presented particular challenges for efficient use of academics' teaching time. Oxford and Cambridge's renowned tutorial system is an excellent example of engaging, personalised, feedback-intensive teaching at work, but it is only possible because of the ancient institutions' exceptionally strong financial position.[36] However, Gibbs' 'TESTA' framework for more effective assessment is a starting point that could vastly improve students' perspectives on the usefulness of assessment and assessment feedback.

Constructive alignment of higher-end learning activities, particularly deep interaction with teachers and fellow students, and feedback and reflection on assessed work, is not easy to achieve. It is not something that would be easy to evidence directly through a student survey. Yet students do have an intuitive sense of how well the constituent parts of their course fit together, and we can certainly infer it from the available evidence of students' perspectives on feedback, assessment, course organisation, and academic support.

The crucial point is that students are more likely to feel 'satisfied' and fulfilled by their courses if they are incentivised – rather than merely instructed – to undergo effective learning behaviours. Just being told that 'independent study is important' is not enough – courses have to be designed well so that it feels important to students. Similarly, students cannot merely be told that their high expectations for quick feedback on assessment are unrealistic; dissatisfaction with this is a very real indication that slow feedback is damaging students' learning.

In contrast to some critics of student surveys and feedback, there is no conclusive evidence that students simply desire the best qualification for the least effort, and that this in turn determines their levels of satisfaction in surveys.[37] In fact, the evidence we do have shows the very opposite. Students care very much about the depth and breadth of their learning, and recognise that they need to work hard to get the most out of a university education.[38] Learning and effort, rather than being the inverse of satisfaction, are actually aligned with it.

Rather than defensiveness, course leaders should respond to their students' critical feedback openly, yet they should always seek to infer the subtext of students' criticism. In particular, teachers should look for indications from students' feedback – particularly if it concerns feedback on assessment, academic support, course organisation, or contact hours – that might indicate a shortfall in students' engagement with their studies and the effectiveness of their learning.

Recommendations for practice

- Teachers should use student survey data as a 'warning light', particularly on topics such as contact hours, assessment and feedback, and course design. But they should not be slaves to it.
- Qualitative student engagement with representatives can help 'translate' the student voice provided in data and instant feedback into better understanding where there may be gaps in quality provision.
- Practitioners should regularly evaluate whether certain 'habits' of higher education delivery, such as modular courses, reliance on summative assessment, and heavy use of lectures are actually encouraging effective student learning behaviours.

Notes

1 Scandal of the university students who get fewer than 100 hours' teaching a year, *Mail on Sunday* (27 April 2013), http://www.dailymail.co.uk/news/article-2315920/Scandal-university-students-fewer-100-hours-teaching-year.html

2 House of Commons Innovation, Universities, Science and Skills Committee (2009), *Students and Universities, Eleventh Report of Session 2008–09, Volume I*, p. 98.

3 Gibbs, G. (2010), *Dimensions of Quality*, (Higher Education Academy).

4 Should students be partners in curriculum design?, *Times Higher Education* (17 December 2015), https://www.timeshighereducation.com/features/should-students-be-partners-in-curriculum-design#survey-answer. Williams, J., 'Should we silence the student voice?', *Spiked Online* (24 September 2013), http://www.spiked-online.com/newsite/article/should_we_silence_the_student_voice/14073#.WVUozRPyuLI

5 Katiliute, E. (2005), *Issues of Education Policy Implementation: Differences in Education Stakeholders' Attitudes*, Paper presented at the European Conference on Educational Research, University College Dublin, 7–10 September 2005.

6 Anonymous Academic (2015), My students have paid £9,000 and now they think they own me, *Guardian*, 18 December 2015, https://www.theguardian.com/higher-education-network/2015/dec/18/my-students-have-paid-9000-and-now-they-think-they-own-me

7 Jones, S., Who gains from the grumbles?, *Wonkhe* (11 January 2016), http://wonkhe.com/blogs/who-gains-from-the-grumbles-2/

8 See, for instance, Trowler, V. (2010), *Student Engagement Literature Review*, (Higher Education Academy).

9 Gibbs, G. (2014), Student engagement, the latest buzzword, *Times Higher Education* (1 May 2014), https://www.timeshighereducation.com/news/student-engagement-the-latest-buzzword/2012947.article

10 Hardy, C. and Bryson, C. (2010), Student engagement: paradigm change or political expediency? *Networks* (9), pp. 19–23. Anonymous Academic (2015). Naidoo, R. and Williams, J. (2014), The neoliberal regime in English higher education: charters, consumers and the erosion of the public good, *Critical Studies in Education*, pp. 1–18.

11 Trowler, *Student Engagement Literature Review*, p. 5.

12 Gibbs, G. (Jan 2016), Student engagement is a slippery concept, (SEDA) https://thesedablog.wordpress.com/2016/01/27/53ideas-42/.

13 National Union of Students (2012), *A Manifesto for Partnership*.

14 Ibid.

15 National Union of Students (2014), *Radical Interventions in Teaching and Learning*.

16 Marsh, H. and Roche, L. A. (1997), Making students' evaluations of teaching effectiveness effective: The critical issues of validity, bias, and utility, *American Psychologist*, Volume 52, Issue 11, pp. 1187–1197.

17 Cheng, J. and Marsh, H. (2010), National Student Survey: Are differences between universities and courses reliable and meaningful?, *Oxford Review of Education*, Volume 36, Issue 6, pp. 693–712.

18 Andersen, K. and Miller, E. (1997), Gender and student evaluations of teaching, *Political Science and Politics*, Volume 30, Number 2 (1997), pp. 216–219.

19 Bell, A. and Brooks, C. (2016), Is there a magic link between research activity, professional teaching qualifications and student satisfaction? Available at SSRN: https://ssrn.com/abstract=2712412 or http://dx.doi.org/10.2139/ssrn.2712412

20 Copeland, R. (2014), *Beyond the consumerist agenda: Teaching quality and the 'student experience' in higher education*, (University and College Union).

21 Callender, C., Ramsden, P. and Griggs, J. (2014), *Review of the National Student Survey*. Buckley, A. (2012), *Making it count: Reflecting on the National Student Survey in the process of enhancement* (Higher Education Academy).

22 Copeland, *Beyond the consumerist agenda*.

23 National Union of Students and Quality Assurance Agency (2012), *Student Experience Research*.

24 Kandiko, C. and Mawer, M. (2015), *Student Expectations and Perceptions of Higher Education*, (Quality Assurance Agency).

25 Neeves, J. and Hillman, N. (2016), *The 2016 Student Academic Experience Survey*, (Higher Education Academy and Higher Education Policy Institute).

26 Gibbs, *Dimensions of Quality*, p. 5.

27 Chickering, A. W. and Gamson, Z. F. (1987), Seven Principles for good practice in undergraduate education, *American Association for Higher Education Bulletin*, March 1987, pp. 3–7.

28 Biggs, J. and Tang, C. (2011), *Teaching for Quality Learning at University*.
29 Wabash National Study of Liberal Arts Education, *High Impact Practices and Experiences from the Wabash National Study*, https://www.beloit.edu/academicaffairs/assets/Wabash_High_Impact_Practices_Summary_2013.pdf
30 Lippmann, W. (1922), *Public Opinion*.
31 Fox, C. (2006), The availability heuristic in the classroom: How soliciting more criticism can boost your course ratings, *Judgment and Decision Making*, Volume 1, Number 1, pp. 86–90.
32 For example, Russell Group (2014), A passion for learning: the student experience at Russell Group universities. Gil., N, Sixth form students: get ready for an education without spoon-feeding, *Guardian* (23 January 2014), https://www.theguardian.com/education/2014/jan/23/sixth-form-students-university-spoonfeeding.
33 Gibbs, G. (Nov 2015), Courses work as integrated systems (SEDA), https://thesedablog.wordpress.com/2015/11/04/53ideas-34-courses-work-as-integrated-systems/.
34 Gibbs, G. (June 2014), Many patterns of teaching in HE simply follow conventions (SEDA), https://www.seda.ac.uk/resources/files/publications_154_9%20Many%20patterns%20of%20teaching%20in%20HE%20simply%20follow%20convention.pdf. PA Consulting (2015), *Lagging Behind: are UK universities falling behind in the global innovation race?*
35 Biggs, J., *Aligning Teaching for Constructing Learning*, (Higher Education Academy), https://www.heacademy.ac.uk/system/files/resources/id477_aligning_teaching_for_constructing_learning.pdf. Ramsden, P. (1992). *Learning to Teach in Higher Education*, p. 107.
36 Gibbs, G. and Simpson, C., *Does Your Assessment Support Your Students' Learning?*, http://artsonline2.tki.org.nz/documents/GrahamGibbAssessmentLearning.pdf
37 Budd, R. (2017), Undergraduate orientations towards higher education in Germany and England: problematising the notion of 'student as customer', *Higher Education*, Volume 73, Issue 1, pp. 23–37.
38 Neeves, and Hillman, *2016 Student Academic Experience Survey*.

Bibliography

Andersen, K. and Miller, E. D. (1997), Gender and student evaluations of teaching, *Political Science and Politics*, Vol. 30, No. 2 (Jun., 1997), pp. 216–219.

AnonymousAcademic(2015),Mystudentshavepaid£9,000andnowtheythinktheyownme,*Guardian*, 18 December 2015, https://www.theguardian.com/higher-education-network/2015/dec/18/my-students-have-paid-9000-and-now-they-think-they-own-me

Arum, R. and Roska, J. (2011), *Academically Adrift: Limited learning on college campuses*. Chicago: University of Chicago Press.

Bell, A. and Brooks, C. (2016), *Is there a Magic Link between Research Activity, Professional Teaching Qualifications and Student Satisfaction?* Available at SSRN: https://ssrn.com/abstract=2712412 or http://dx.doi.org/10.2139/ssrn.2712412

Biggs, J. (2003), *Aligning Teaching for Constructing Learning* (Higher Education Academy), https://www.heacademy.ac.uk/system/files/resources/id477_aligning_teaching_for_constructing_learning.pdf

Biggs, J. and Tang, C. (2011), *Teaching for Quality Learning at University*. London: Higher Education Academy.

Budd, R. (2017), Undergraduate orientations towards higher education in Germany and England: Problematizing the notion of 'student as customer, *Higher Education*, Volume 73, Issue 1, pp. 23–37.

Brown, S. (2004), Assessment for learning. *Learning and Teaching in Higher Education*, Issue 1.

Buckley, A. (2012), *Making it Count: Reflecting on the National Student Survey in the process of enhancement*. London: Higher Education Academy.

Callender, C., Ramsden, P. and Griggs, J. (2014), *Review of the National Student Survey*.

Cheng, J. and Marsh, H. (2010), National Student Survey: Are differences between universities and courses reliable and meaningful?, *Oxford Review of Education*, Volume 36, Issue 6, pp. 693–712.

Chickering, A. W. and Gamson, Z. F. (1987), Seven principles for good practice in undergraduate education. *AAHE Bulletin*, Volume 39, Issue 7, pp. 3–7.

Copeland, R. (2014), *Teaching Quality and the 'Student Experience' in Higher Education*. London: UCU.

Fox, C. (2006), The availability heuristic in the classroom: How soliciting more criticism can boost your course ratings, *Judgment and Decision Making*, Volume 1, Number 1, pp. 86–90.

Gibbs, G. (2010), *Dimensions of Quality*. London: Higher Education Academy.

Gibbs, G. (2012), *Implications of 'Dimensions of Quality' in a Market Environment*. London: Higher Education Academy.

Gibbs, G. (2014), Student engagement, the latest buzzword, *Times Higher Education* (1 May 2014), https://www.timeshighereducation.com/news/student-engagement-the-latest-buzz word/2012947.article

Gibbs, G. (June 2014), Many patterns of teaching in HE simply follow conventions (SEDA), https://www.seda.ac.uk/resources/files/publications_154_9%20Many%20patterns%20 of%20teaching%20in%20HE%20simply%20follow%20convention.pdf.

Gibbs, G. (Nov 2015), Courses work as integrated systems (SEDA), https://thesedablog.word press.com/2015/11/04/53ideas-34-courses-work-as-integrated-systems/.

Gibbs, G. (Jan 2016), Student engagement is a slippery concept, (SEDA) https://thesedablog. wordpress.com/2016/01/27/53ideas-42/.

Gibbs, G. and Simpson, C., Does your assessment support your students' learning?, http:// artsonline2.tki.org.nz/documents/GrahamGibbAssessmentLearning.pdf

Gil., N. (2014), Sixth form students: get ready for an education without spoonfeeding, *Guardian* (23 January 2014), https://www.theguardian.com/education/2014/jan/23/sixth-form-students-university-spoonfeeding.

Hardy, C. and Bryson, C. (2010), Student engagement: paradigm change or political expediency? *Networks* (9), pp. 19–23.

Higher Education Academy (2012), *A Marked Improvement: Transforming assessment in higher education*. London: Higher Education Academy.

Higher Education Academy (2014), *The Role of HEFCE in Teaching and Learning Enhancement*. London: Higher Education Academy.

House of Commons Innovation, Universities, Science and Skills Committee (2009), *Students and Universities, Eleventh Report of Session 2008–09*, Volume I, p. 98.

Jones, S., Who gains from the grumbles?, Wonkhe (11 January 2016), http://wonkhe.com/ blogs/who-gains-from-the-grumbles-2/

Kandiko, C. and Mawer, M. (2015), *Student Expectations and Perceptions of Higher Education*. London: Quality Assurance Agency.

Kaplan et al. (2013) *Using Reflection and Metacognition to Improve Student Learning*. Virginia: Stylus.

Katiliute, E. (2005), Issues of Education Policy Implementation: Differences in Education Stakeholders' Attitudes, Paper presented at the European Conference on Educational Research, University College Dublin, 7–10 September 2005.

Lippmann, W. (1922), *Public Opinion*. New York: Free Press Paperbacks.

Mail on Sunday (2013), Scandal of the university students who get fewer than 100 hours' teaching a year, *Mail on Sunday* (27 April 2013), http://www.dailymail.co.uk/news/article-2315920/ Scandal-university-students-fewer-100-hours-teaching-year.html

Marsh, H. and Roche, L. A., (1997), Making students' evaluations of teaching effectiveness effective: The critical issues of validity, bias, and utility, *American Psychologist*, Volume 52, Issue 11, pp. 1187–1197.

Naidoo, R. and Williams, J. (2014), The neoliberal regime in English higher education: charters, consumers and the erosion of the public good, *Critical Studies in Education*, pp. 1–18.

National Union of Students (2012), *A Manifesto for Partnership*. London: NUS.

National Union of Students (2014), *Radical Interventions in Teaching and Learning*. London: NUS.

National Union of Students (2015), *Comprehensive Guide to Teaching and Learning: A resource for students' unions*. London: NUS.

National Union of Students and Quality Assurance Agency (2012), *Student Experience Research*. London: NUS.

Neeves, J. and Hillman, N. (2016), *The 2016 Student Academic Experience Survey*, London: Higher Education Academy and Higher Education Policy Institute.

PA Consulting (2015), *Lagging Behind: Are UK universities falling behind in the global innovation race?* London: PA Consulting.

Price et al (2012). *Assessment Literacy: The foundation for improving student learning*. Oxford: Oxford Brookes University.

Ramsden, P. (1992). *Learning to Teach in Higher Education*, 2nd edn. Oxford: Routledge, p. 107.

Russell Group (2014), *A Passion for Learning: The student experience at Russell Group universities*. London: Russell Group.

Thomas, L. (2012), *Building Student Engagement and Belonging in Higher Education at a Time of Change: Final report from the What works? student retention & success programme*. London: Higher Education Academy.

Times Higher Education (2015), Should students be partners in curriculum design?', *Times Higher Education* (17 December 2015), https://www.timeshighereducation.com/features/should-students-be-partners-in-curriculum-design#survey-answer

Trowler, V. (2010), *Student Engagement Literature Review*. London: Higher Education Academy.

Wabash National Study of Liberal Arts Education (2013), *High Impact Practices and Experiences from the Wabash National Study*, https://www.beloit.edu/academicaffairs/assets/Wabash_High_Impact_Practices_Summary_2013.pdf

Wingate, U. (2007) A framework for transition: supporting "learning to learn" in higher education. *Higher Education Quarterly*, Volume 61, No. 3, July 2007, pp 391–405.

Williams, J. (2013), Should we silence the student voice?, Spiked Online (24 September 2013), http://www.spiked-online.com/newsite/article/should_we_silence_the_student_voice/14073#.WVUozRPyuLI

24 Beyond Student Ratings

Fourteen Other Sources of Evidence to Evaluate Teaching

Ronald A. Berk

Introduction

Start spreading the news: Student ratings are not leaving today or anytime soon. However, as the title of this chapter indicates, student ratings are not the only option to provide evidence in the evaluation of teaching. There is a broad range of alternatives to consider beyond student ratings in the delicate decision-making processes to improve teaching and determine the promotion and tenure of faculty.

Yet, despite the constant barrage of attacks on the integrity, reliability, and validity of student ratings (Barre, 2015; Berrett, 2015; Gooblar, 2017; Kamenetz, 2014; Quintana, 2017), their use in higher education is at an all-time high. So what do student ratings actually contribute to decisions about teaching and faculty? Should they be abandoned? Should you focus on the other options? Let's start with a brief review of . . .

1. Student end-of-course ratings

The student rating scale has been the primary measure of teaching effectiveness for more than three-quarters of a century. Currently, student ratings are 'always used' as a major source of information to evaluate teaching performance by 94.2 percent of four-year liberal arts colleges in the U.S. (Miller & Seldin, 2014). In fact, the evaluation of teaching has been in a metaphorical cul-de-sac with student ratings as the universal performance barometer in universities worldwide. Perceptible barometric changes occur as students exercise their critical role in the teaching–learning feedback system. Their input in formative and summative decision-making has been recommended on an international level (Griffin & Cook, 2009; Strategy Group, 2011; Surgenor, 2011).

More has been written on this topic in higher education than any other. To date, there are nearly 3,000 references to student ratings (Benton & Cashin, 2014), with the first journal article published over 95 years ago (Freyd, 1923). There is more research on and experience with student ratings than all of the other measures of teaching effectiveness combined (Berk, 2006, 2013d). That's tankers of research. If you need to be brought up to speed quickly with the research on student ratings, check out these readily available reviews (Benton & Cashin, 2012, 2014; Gravestock & Gregor-Greenleaf, 2008; Hativa, 2014a, 2014b; Kite, 2012). (NOTE: For a parody of the history of student ratings, see Berk, 2013d.)

With student ratings at the top of the leaderboard accompanied by an incredible volume of scholarly products and practices in academia, you would think that they would be the ideal solution to evaluate teaching. So . . .

What's the problem with student ratings?

There are four major limitations to using ONLY student ratings for decision-making: (1) students' limited qualifications as raters, (2) technical inadequacy and bias, (3) misuse of scales and misinterpretation of ratings, and (4) inadequate source of evidence for decision-making. Let's examine the significance of these limitations.

Students' limited qualifications as raters. As informative as student ratings can be, there are numerous behaviors and skills that define teaching that students are not qualified to rate, such as a professor's knowledge and content expertise, teaching methods, course design and organization, use of technology, quality of course materials, assessment instruments, and grading practices (Ali & Sell, 1998; Calderon, Gabbin, & Green, 1996; Cashin, 1989; Cohen & McKeachie,1980; Coren, 2001; d'Apollonia & Abrami, 1997a; Green, Calderon, & Reider, 1998; Hoyt & Pallett, 1999; Keig & Waggoner, 1994; Marsh, 2007; Ory & Ryan, 2001; Svinicki & McKeachie, 2014; Theall & Franklin, 2001).

What's left that students can legitimately rate? They can provide feedback at a certain level in most of those areas, but it will take peers and other qualified professionals to rate those skills in depth. There are so many teaching behaviors to measure. Students should answer only those items that are directly within their purview of expertise and behaviors they have observed or experienced throughout the course. The validity standard (or criterion) is as follows: Each measure should be completed by those individuals (students, instructor, other faculty, administrators, or employers) who are in the best position to provide the most accurate information; otherwise, that information may be invalid or biased.

Technical inadequacy of ratings and bias. Student rating scales are constantly being attacked on technical grounds, especially home-grown forms compared to those developed commercially (Berrett, 2015; Uttl, White, & Gonzalez, 2017; Wieman, 2015). The validity of the ratings has been challenged by Nilson (2012) and Uttl *et al.* (2017) in three areas: (1) relationship between student ratings and learning (see Ryalls, Benton, & Li, 2016), (2) sources of bias in the ratings, including professor's charisma, physical attractiveness, personality, gender, age, race/ethnicity, rank, and class length (also see Addison & Stowell, 2012; Basow & Martin, 2012; Benton & Ryalls, 2016; Boring, 2017; Boring, Ottoboni, & Stark, 2016; Li & Benton, 2017; Macnell, Driscoll, & Hunt, 2014; Marsh, 2007; Spooren, Brockx, & Mortelmans, 2013), and (3) accuracy and veracity of the ratings, especially in the context of online administrations.

In reviewing the validity studies of the 1970s and 1980s compared to the more recent wave of research findings, Nilson (2012) concluded that evidence substantiating the validity of student ratings had diminished significantly, and their usefulness in decisions about faculty should be reexamined. Uttl *et al.*'s. (2017) meta-analysis of those multisection validity studies led the researchers to recommend that institutions should abandon student ratings as a measure of teaching effectiveness. This study was the most compelling indictment of student ratings to date.

However, the latest scrutiny of Uttl *et al.*'s. (2017) analyses by Ryalls *et al.* (2016) repudiated most of their conclusions. At present, a consensus of experts on student ratings agrees that properly constructed scales, used and interpreted appropriately, are far superior technically in their reliability and validity to all proposed alternative measures based on the vast psychometric research that has accumulated over several decades (Arreola, 2007; Benton & Cashin, 2012, 2014; Benton & Ryalls, 2016; Berk, 2006, 2013c, 2013d; Hativa, 2014a, 2014b).

Misuse of scales and misinterpretation of ratings. Despite the guidelines, instructions, and manuals that accompany student rating scales, they are still administered at many institutions under uncontrolled, unstandardized, and/or inappropriate conditions which can significantly decrease the response rate and render the answers invalid (Berk, 2006, 2013d). The numerous procedures available to maximize response rate for both face-to-face (f2f) and online administrations are often ignored (Berk, 2006, 2012, 2013a, 2013d). Even worse are the misinterpretation of the ratings for instructional changes and administrators' decisions about faculty based on meaningless, trivial ranked differences (Berk, 2006, 2013d) and misuse of global ratings (2013b). Both administrators and faculty need to be Mirandized on the proper use and interpretation of ratings for the decisions being made in their institution.

Inadequate source of evidence for decision-making. Based on these reported limitations and weaknesses, student ratings can provide only one portion of the information needed to infer teaching effectiveness. Unfortunately, that is pretty much all that is available at most colleges and universities. When those ratings alone are used for decision-making, the decisions will usually be based on incomplete and biased evidence.

Without additional evidence of teaching effectiveness, student ratings can lead to incorrect, unfair, and evil career decisions about faculty that can affect their contract renewal, annual salary increase, merit pay, professional development, and promotion and tenure (Wines & Lau, 2006). Administrators pushing to use only student ratings for these decisions continues unabated. Even discriminatory practices based on age, gender, race, ethnicity, sexual orientation, religion, and other protected classes may occur, knowingly or unknowingly, because of how these scales are used (U.S. EEOC, 2010).

BOTTOM LINE: Student ratings from well-constructed scales are a necessary, but not sufficient, source of evidence to evaluate teaching comprehensively.

Multiple sources of evidence

Since the 1990s, the practice of augmenting student ratings with other data sources of teaching effectiveness has been gaining traction in community colleges, liberal arts colleges, universities, medical schools/colleges (Berk, 2005, 2006), and other institutions. Such sources can serve to broaden and deepen the evidence base used to evaluate courses and the quality of teaching (Arreola, 2007; Benton & Cashin, 2012; Berk, 2005, 2006, 2013d, 2018; Braskamp & Ory, 1994; Cashin, 2003; Gravestock & Gregor-Greenleaf, 2008; Hoyt & Pallett, 1999; Knapper & Cranton, 2001; Ory, 2001; Seldin, 2006; Theall & Feldman, 2007; Theall & Franklin, 1990).

In fact, several comprehensive models of "faculty evaluation" that include multiple sources of evidence have been proposed (Arreola, 2007; Berk, 2006, 2009b, 2013d; Braskamp & Ory, 1994; Centra, 1993; Gravestock & Gregor-Greenleaf, 2008). Some models attach greater weight to student and peer ratings and less weight to self, administrator, alumni ratings, and other sources. All of these models can be used to arrive at formative and summative decisions.

Fourteen other sources of evidence

What are the options? There are 15 potential sources of evidence of teaching effectiveness (Berk, 2018). Student end-of-course ratings were already examined. There are 14 other sources. The major categories of sources include students, instructor, other faculty, administrator, and employer. All of the sources apply to f2f, online, and blended/ hybrid courses. Here is a list of those sources:

STUDENTS

1   Student end-of-course ratings
2   Student midterm feedback
3   Student exit and alumni ratings
4   s = Student outcome measures

INSTRUCTOR

5   Self-ratings
6   Teaching scholarship
7   Teaching awards

OTHER FACULTY

8   Peer classroom observations
9   Peer review of course materials
10   External expert ratings
11   Mentor's advice
12   Video classroom review
13   Teaching/course portfolio review

ADMINISTRATOR

14   Administrator ratings

EMPLOYER

15   Employer ratings

Berk (2005, 2006) critically examined the value and contribution of most of these sources for measuring teaching effectiveness. This chapter is an update and extension of those reviews based on the current state of research and practice. A 'Bottom Line' recommendation for each source will also be proffered to guide future practice. Beyond student ratings, let's consider the other 14 sources.

2. Student midterm feedback

Instead of waiting until the end of the semester to obtain student feedback on your teaching, you can collect information during the semester with student interviews or an anonymous survey. Here are three options:

1   Quality control circles (QCC) (Shariff, 1999; Tiberius, 1997; Weimer, 1990) – involves assembling a group of student volunteers to meet regularly (bi-weekly) to critique teaching and testing strategies and pinpoint problem areas. Suggestions for improvement can be solicited from these students. The instructor can also report the results of the meetings to the entire class to elicit their responses. The information to accrue from the unstructured "circle" and class interviews with students on teaching activities can

be extremely useful for making changes in instruction. This technique permits student feedback and instructional change systematically throughout a course.

2 Small-group interviews (Small Group Instructional Diagnosis: SGID) (Bennett, 1987; Clark, & Redmond, 1982; Hancock, Nickson, Chaudhury, & Ismail, 2014) – class is divided into small groups with a peer or graduate student probing strengths and weaknesses to make midterm adjustments. The group interviews involve the entire class, but are conducted by someone other than the instructor. This may be a colleague in the same department, a graduate teaching assistant (TA), or a faculty development or student services professional. The interviews, which typically occur at the end of class, require about 15–30 minutes. The facilitator can use an unstructured discussion format with leading questions to stimulate students' responses or a structured rating scale to probe strengths and weaknesses of the course and teaching activities (Wentzell, Blue, & Evins, 2016). Some of the questions should be broad enough to elicit a wide range of student perspectives from the groups. An electronic version of SGID in real-time or chat-room mode can also be used.

3 Five-minute feedback paper (FMFP) – 20, 30, or 50 percent into the course students are asked to evaluate your teaching by answering two questions: What teaching methods are most effective in your learning?, and What specific suggestions do you have to improve my teaching? This survey can serve as a proxy for the previous interviews. The anecdotal input can be solicited anonymously via paper and pencil or electronically in class or online outside of class (also see Sathy, 2017). You can then compile the results (listing all comments) and post them for your students. Address every comment in the next class or online module. Your feedback will hold you accountable to your students for your commitment to specific changes.

The information collected from these strategies should be used by the instructor to make midterm adjustments for teaching improvement. The instructor should reply to the students' responses at the beginning of the next class or online and should attempt to implement as many of the students' suggestions as possible during the remainder of the course. (NOTE: There is evidence that instructors who conduct these midterm assessments tend to receive higher end-of-course student ratings than instructors who do not [Marsh, Fleiner, & Thomas, 1975; Overall & Marsh, 1979]). Why wait? Get bashed by your students early in the semester and get better ratings at the end.)

BOTTOM LINE: All three methods can provide valuable feedback for teaching improvement during the course. The QCC is an excellent technique to provide constant student feedback. The SGID group interview as an independent measurement at midterm can be very informative to make 'half-time' adjustments. The FMFP is a very efficient and effective method to obtain anonymous comments from the entire class and establish accountability with your students.

3. Student exit and alumni ratings

Another strategy to tap students' opinions about the teaching, courses, and the program is to survey them with a rating scale as graduates. What do students really remember about their instructors' teaching and course experiences? The research indicates: A lot! However, only 7.2–10.1 percent of liberal arts colleges are using long-term follow-up data or alumni opinions as a factor to evaluate teaching (Miller & Seldin, 2014).

A longitudinal study by Overall and Marsh (1980) compared 'current-student' end-of-term ratings with 1- to-4-year-alumni after-course ratings in 100 courses. The correlation was .83, and median ratings were nearly identical. Feldman (1989b) found an average correlation of .69 between current student and alumni ratings across six cross-sectional studies. Alumni seem to retain a high level of detail about their course-taking experiences for up to five years (Centra, 1974; Kulik, 2001). The correlations decrease as students' memories fade over time (Drucker & Remmers, 1951).

Exit and alumni ratings of the same faculty and courses will essentially corroborate the ratings given previously when the alumni were students. So what should alumni be asked? E-mailing or snail mailing a rating scale one, five and ten years later can provide new information. That scale should address the quality of teaching, the usefulness of course requirements, attainment of program outcomes, the effectiveness of admissions procedures, preparation for graduate work, preparation for the real world, and a variety of other topics not measured on the standard student rating scale.

This retrospective measurement can elicit valuable feedback on teaching methods, course requirements, assessment techniques, integration of technology, exposure to diversity, and other topics across courses or for the program as a whole. The unstructured responses may highlight specific strengths of faculty as well as furnish directions for improvement.

BOTTOM LINE: Although exit and alumni ratings are similar to original student ratings on the same scale, different scale items about the quality of teaching, courses, curriculum, admissions, and other topics can provide new information. Alumni ratings should be considered as another important source of evidence on teaching effectiveness for formative and program decisions.

4. Student outcome measures

Most of the sources of evidence in this review are direct ratings of teaching behaviors. Student learning outcome measures are a sticky source because they are indirect. Teaching performance is being inferred from students' performance—what they learned in the course. That relationship seems reasonable. After all, if you're an effective teacher, your students should perform well on measures of achievement and exhibit growth during the course in their knowledge of the subject. Despite the logic of using this source, a paltry 2.2 percent of liberal arts colleges 'always use' student exam performance for summative decisions related to teaching evaluation (Miller & Seldin, 2014).

More than 80 correlational studies have examined the relationship between student ratings and achievement based on common examinations given in courses with several sections. Meta-analyses of this research by Cohen (1981), d'Apollonia and Abrami (1996, 1997b, 1997c), and Feldman (1989a) aggregated the results to produce significant mean correlations only in the .40s. In more recent studies, the coefficients were even lower (Clayson, 2009; Weinberg, Hashimoto, & Fleisher, 2009). There was considerable variation in the coefficients reported, not just in size, but in direction as well (Carrell & West, 2010; Clayson, 2009; Marks, Fairris, & Beleche, 2010).

Uttl *et al.*'s (2017) meta-analysis of all of these multisection studies revealed no significant correlations between the student ratings and learning. The researchers recommended that institutions give minimal or no weight to student ratings as a measure of teaching effectiveness. The correlations in these studies temper the conclusion that students give high ratings to instructors from whom they learn the most and low ratings to instructors from whom they learn the least. To the contrary, students tend to assign higher ratings to teachers who have higher achievement standards (Benton, Guo, Li, & Gross, 2013).

Proponents of learning outcomes as a source of evidence argue that pre- and post-testing to gauge students' learning can be used to measure faculty effectiveness and improve instruction (Crouch & Mazur, 2001; Dori & Belcher, 2005). Using gain scores to infer teaching effectiveness is a shakier methodology than the previous multisection correlational designs. There is an extensive list of 40 factors that can explain the change between a pre-test and post-test other than what the instructor does in the classroom (Berk, 1988, 1990, 2014, 2016). The American Statistical Association (2014) reported that in the K–12 sector 'most studies find that teachers account for about 1% to 14% of the variability in test scores' (p. 2). That means that the majority of variation in students' scores is attributable to the numerous factors outside of the teacher's control.

The crux of the problem is this: How does one isolate teaching as the sole explanation for student learning? Performance throughout a course on tests, projects, reports, and other indicators may be influenced by the characteristics of the students, the institution, and the outcome measures themselves, over which faculty have no control (Berk, 1988, 2014; Everson, 2017). The list of intractable problems in isolating teaching performance, even within a single course, in students' gain or success on any outcome measures may not be attributable solely, or, in some cases, even mostly, to the effectiveness of the teaching—student performance ≠ teaching performance (Berk, 2014, 2016).

Fenwick (2001) recommended that the results of standard outcome measures, such as tests, problem-solving exercises, projects, and simulations, be aggregated across groups of students for program assessment decisions about teaching methods and program improvement. This is a nontrivial feat since course content, students, and measures naturally vary from course to course. Even if you could design a standardized outcome measure that could be administered in different courses, all of the other student, class, and content differences would remain. What would the outcome measure results tell you about teaching in each course? Not a lot. Teaching performance differences would be inextricably mixed with all of the other differences among courses (Berk, 2014, 2016; Everson, 2017).

BOTTOM LINE: Student learning outcome measures should not be employed as a source of evidence of teaching performance for summative decisions. They may be used tentatively for formative decisions; however, even then, the results should be interpreted with caution in conjunction with the direct data sources described in this chapter for individual teaching improvement.

5. Self-ratings

How can we ask faculty to rate their own teaching? Is it possible for instructors to be impartial about their own performance? Probably not. It is natural for anybody to portray themselves in the best light possible. Unfortunately, the research on this issue is skimpy and inconclusive. The few studies found that faculty rate themselves higher than (Centra, 1973a; Feldman, 1989b), equal to (Bo-Linn, Gentry, Lowman, Pratt, & Zhu, 2004; Feldman, 1989b), or lower than (Bo-Linn *et al.*, 2004) their students rate them. Highly rated instructors give themselves higher ratings than less highly rated instructors (Doyle & Crichton, 1978; Marsh, Overall, & Kessler, 1979). Superior teachers provide more accurate self-ratings than mediocre or putrid teachers (Barber, 1990; Centra, 1973b; Sorey, 1968).

Despite this possibly biased estimate of our own teaching effectiveness, this estimate provides support for what we do in the classroom AND can present a picture of our teaching unobtainable from any other source. Most administrators agree. Among liberal arts college academic deans, 67.6 percent always include self-ratings for summative decisions (Miller & Seldin, 2014). The Carnegie Foundation for the Advancement of Teaching (1994) found that 82 percent of four-year colleges and universities reported using self-ratings to measure teaching performance. The American Association of University Professors (1974) concluded that self-ratings would improve the faculty review process. Further, it seems reasonable that our assessment of our own teaching should count for something in the teaching effectiveness equation.

So what form should the self-ratings take? The faculty activity report (a.k.a. 'brag sheet') is the most common type of self-ratings. It describes teaching, scholarship, service, and practice (for the professions) activities for the previous year. This information is used by administrators for decisions about contract renewal and merit pay. This annual report, however, is not a true self-rating of teaching effectiveness.

When self-ratings' evidence is used in conjunction with other sources for personnel decisions, Seldin (1999) recommended a structured form to display an instructor's teaching objectives, activities, accomplishments, and failures. Guiding questions should be asked in the areas of classroom approach, instructor–student rapport, knowledge of discipline, course organization and planning, and teaching. Wergin (1992) and Braskamp and Ory (1994) offered additional types of evidence that can be collected.

The instructor can also complete the student rating scale from two perspectives: as a direct measure of their teaching performance and then as the anticipated ratings the students should give. Discrepancies among the three sources in this triad—students' ratings, instructor's self-ratings, and instructor's perceptions of students' ratings—can provide valuable insights on teaching effectiveness. The results may be very helpful for targeting specific areas for improvement. Students' ratings and self-ratings tend to yield low positive correlations (Braskamp, Caulley, & Costin, 1979; Feldman, 1989b). Further, any differences between those ratings do not appear to be explained by instructor or course characteristics, such as years of experience, gender, tenure status, teaching load, preference for subject, and class size (Centra, 1973b; 1993).

Overall, an instructor's self-ratings demonstrate their knowledge about teaching and perceived effectiveness in the classroom (Cranton, 2001). This information should be critically reviewed and compared with the other sources of evidence for personnel decisions. The diagnostic profile of those ratings should be used to guide teaching improvement.

BOTTOM LINE: Self-ratings are a major source of evidence to consider in formative and summative decisions. Faculty input on their teaching completes the triangulation of the three direct-observation sources of teaching performance: students, peers, and self.

6. Teaching scholarship

The scholarship of teaching and learning according to the Carnegie Academy for the Scholarship of Teaching and Learning (CASTL), is 'a public account of some or all of the full act of teaching—vision, design, enactment, outcomes, and analysis—in a manner susceptible to critical review by the teacher's professional peers and amenable to productive employment in future work by members of the same community' (Shulman, 1998, p. 6). (TRANSLATION: Contribute to a growing body of knowledge about teaching and learning (T & L) in higher education by presenting at T & L conferences and publishing in T & L journals.) This scholarship is analogous to the research scholarship in various disciplines.

Presentations and publications in T & L on innovative teaching techniques and related issues are indicators of teaching expertise. Research on important questions in T & L can not only improve a faculty member's effectiveness in their classroom but also advance practice beyond it (Hutchings & Shulman, 1999). Evidence of teaching scholarship may consist of presentations on new teaching methods, such as research, workshops, and keynotes at teaching institutes and conferences.

There are more than 400 state, regional, national, and international conferences (see http://cetl.kennesaw.edu/teaching-conferences-directory). A few of the best interdisciplinary conferences include the Lilly Conference on College Teaching (plus regional conferences), International Conference on the Scholarship of Teaching and Learning, International Conference on College Teaching and Learning, International Society for Exploring Teaching and Learning Conference, Society for Teaching and Learning in Higher Education Conference (Canadian), and Improving University Teaching Conference. All have websites for further information. There are also discipline-specific conferences that focus exclusively on teaching and educational issues, such as the National League for Nursing (NLN) and Association for Medical Education in Europe (AMEE) Conference.

Publication-wise, there are opportunities to publish in peer-reviewed 'teaching' journals. There are more than 500 teaching journals (see http://cetl.kennesaw.edu/teaching-journals-directory). Examples are the *Journal on Excellence in College Teaching, College Teaching, Journal of Scholarship of Teaching and Learning, Canadian Journal for the Scholarship of Teaching and Learning, International Journal of Teaching and Learning in Higher Education, Research in Higher Education,* and *Assessment and Evaluation in Higher Education.*

For faculty who are already conducting research and publishing in their disciplines, this source of evidence for faculty assessment provides an opportunity to shift gears and redirect research efforts to the teaching and learning domain. Contributions to scholarship in a discipline and T & L can appreciate an instructor's net worth in two categories rather than in just one.

BOTTOM LINE: Teaching scholarship is an important source of evidence to supplement the other sources. It can easily distinguish the 'teacher-scholar' and very creative faculty from all others for summative decisions.

7. Teaching awards

What does this topic have to do with teaching effectiveness? Well, the concept is somewhat narrower than the other sources of evidence. The link is the process by which the award is determined. A faculty nominee for any award must go through a student vote and/or a grueling assessment by a panel of faculty judges according to criteria for exemplary teaching. The evidence of teaching effectiveness is limited by the award criteria and review and the pool of nominees.

The most recent estimates in the 1990s indicate that nearly 70 percent of two-year colleges and liberal arts institutions and 96 percent of research universities surveyed have awards or programs honoring exemplary teaching (Jenrette & Hayes, 1996; Zahorski, 1996). There is a scarcity of studies on the value of teaching awards as an incentive for teaching improvement (Carusetta, 2001). The judgments range from YES (Seldin & Associates, 1999; Wright & Associates, 1995) to NO (McNaught & Anwyl, 1993; Ruedrich, Cavey, Katz, & Grush, 1992; Zahorski, 1996). There has been considerable criticism of the selection process in particular, which tends to be erratic, vague, suspicious, and subjective (Knapper, 1997; Menges, 1996; Weimer, 1990).

BOTTOM LINE: As a source of evidence of teaching effectiveness, at best, teaching awards provide worthwhile information only on the nominees, and, at worst, they supply inaccurate and unreliable feedback on questionable nominees. The merits of teaching awards should be evaluated in the context of an institution's network of incentives and rewards for teaching.

8. Peer classroom observations

In the early 1990s, Boyer (1990) and Rice (1991) redefined scholarship to include teaching. After all, it is the means by which discovered, integrated, and applied knowledge is transmitted to the next generation of scholars and students. Teaching is a scholarly activity. Webb and McEnerney (1995) argued that teaching can be as creative and scholarly as original research.

If teaching performance is to be recognized and rewarded as scholarship, it should be subjected to the same rigorous peer review process to which a research manuscript is subjected in a refereed journal and then whacked by the editor. In other words, teaching should be judged by the same high standard applied to other forms of scholarship: peer review. Peer review as an alternative source of evidence seems to be climbing up the assessment ladder, such that more than 60 percent of liberal arts colleges use peer observation for summative decisions about faculty (Miller & Seldin, 2014)

Peer review of teaching involves peer observation of in-class teaching performance. It requires a rating scale that covers those aspects of teaching that peers are better qualified to assess than students. The scale items typically address the instructor's content knowledge, delivery, teaching methods, learning activities, assessment methods, and the like (see Berk, Naumann, & Appling, 2004; Chism, 2007; Roberson, 2006). After adequate training on observation procedures with the scale, the peer and instructor schedule the class(es) to be observed (Center for Teaching Effectiveness, 1996; Sullivan, Buckle, Nicky, & Atkinson, 2012; Webb & McEnerney,1997). The ratings may be recorded live with one or more peers on one or multiple occasions (van der Lans, van de Grift, van Veen, & Fokkens-Bruinsma, 2016) or from video-recorded classes.

Despite the intended complementary relationship between student ratings and peer observation, Murray (1983) found a striking comparability. Among the results, trained observers reported that highly rated instructors were more likely to repeat difficult ideas, speak emphatically or expressively, and be sensitive to student needs.

Unfortunately, there is considerable resistance by faculty to peer observation as a complement to student ratings (Berk, 2006). Most of the reasons or perceptions are legitimate based on how different institutions execute a peer review system. A few can be corrected to minimize bias and unfairness and improve the representativeness of observations.

However, there is consensus among experts that peer observation data should be used for formative rather than for summative decisions (Aleamoni, 1982; Arreola, 2007; Cohen & McKeachie, 1980; Keig & Waggoner, 1994, 1995; Millis & Kaplan, 1995). In fact, 60 years of experience with peer assessment in the military and private industry led to the same conclusion (Muchinsky, 1995). Employees tend to accept peer observations when the results are used for constructive diagnostic feedback instead of as the basis for administrative decisions (Cederblom & Lounsbury, 1980; Love, 1981).

BOTTOM LINE: Peer ratings of teaching performance provide the most complementary source of evidence to student ratings (Berk, 2006). They cover many of those aspects of teaching that students are not in a position to rate. Student and peer ratings, viewed together, furnish a very comprehensive picture of teaching effectiveness for teaching improvement. Peer ratings should not be used for personnel decisions unless an instructor consents.

9. Peer review of course materials

Peer review of teaching materials requires a different type of scale to rate the quality of the course syllabus, instructional plans, texts, reading assignments, handouts, homework, tests/projects, and other elements of the course. Nearly 43 percent of liberal arts colleges always use ratings of syllabi and exams for summative decisions about teaching performance (Miller & Seldin, 2014). Sometimes teaching behaviors associated with fairness, grading practices, ethics, and professionalism are included.

BOTTOM LINE: This review is less subjective and more cost-effective, efficient, and reliable than peer observations. However, peer observations are the more common choice because they provide direct measures of the act of teaching. Use both forms of peer review in a comprehensive system, where possible.

10. External expert ratings

Instead of one or more peers rating teaching performance, suppose one or two strangers observed the teaching. Imagine teaching a course on 'Film Directing,' and Steven Spielberg is your rater. Hiring 'teaching' and/or 'content' experts who are thoroughly trained and armed with an observational rating scale has been recommended as another source of evidence (Arreola, 2007). As outsiders, they have not been contaminated with the politics, issues, gossip, and biases of the institution, yet. They know no one. What they see is what they will rate, maybe.

This approach does not eliminate the reasons faculty object to in-class observations. Although external observers will still be subjective to some degree in their ratings because of biases and baggage brought into the institution, they will not be infected by personal bias, unless the instructor, upon immediate contact, is totally repulsive or a knucklehead. It is preferable that multiple observers over multiple occasions be used to estimate interrater reliability.

There has been no research comparing peer and external ratings of the same instructors. However, Feldman (1989b) did review the findings of several studies that correlated student ratings with external observer ratings. The average correlation was a modest .50. That means about 25 percent overlap between the ratings but, in general, very different perceptions of teaching performance.

Although observations by outsiders are plagued by most of the same limitations as observations by peers, they seem worthy of consideration. Aside from the cost of recruiting a team of experts to conduct multiple reviews of every instructor in a department, it is a viable alternative to peer ratings. Faculty can learn a lot from these teaching experts. They may be especially valuable for junior faculty or a young department in need of teaching expertise.

BOTTOM LINE: External expert ratings of teaching performance can serve as a proxy for peer ratings or as a separate legitimate source of evidence on its own. Using an institution's rating scale, outside teaching experts, properly trained, can provide fresh insights for teaching improvement. As with peer ratings, the evidence gathered by these experts should not be used for personnel decisions without the instructor's consent.

11. Mentor's advice

A trusted colleague, master teacher, faculty developer, graduate student, or another knowledgeable confidante can advise on call, answer questions, provide feedback on teaching ideas, serve as a sounding board, and troubleshoot teaching problems in confidence for an individual instructor (Braskamp & Ory, 1994). Teaching mentors can be just as valuable as research mentors to guide and encourage faculty toward constant improvement. In fact, research on 'consultative feedback' by a trusted mentor can lead to changes in teaching effectiveness (Marincovich, 1999; Penny & Coe, 2004).

BOTTOM LINE: A mentor can furnish valuable ongoing formative feedback on teaching for sustained growth over time. That feedback can supplement the more formal peer observation. A teaching 'growth paper' can be prepared by the mentor for both formative and summative evidence.

12. Video classroom review

Everyone is doing videos. Make an effort to produce a simple video of your teaching, and, if you sing or dance, it might go viral. We simply do what we do best: talk. I mean teach.

To assure a good quality product, solicit the resident videographer, IT expert, or a colleague who wants to be a director like Martin Scorsese. Schedule a recording of one typical class or a best and worst class to sample a variety of teaching. Don't perform. Be yourself to provide an authentic picture of how you teach. The product is a DVD. It is hard evidence of your teaching.

Who should evaluate the video?

A   Self, privately in office, but with access to medications
B   Self completes peer observation scale of behaviors while viewing, then weeps
C   One peer completes scale and provides feedback
D   Two or three peers complete scale on the same video and provide feedback

These options are listed in order of increasing complexity, intrusiveness, and the amount of information produced. All options can provide valuable insights into teaching to guide specific improvements. The choice of option may boil down to what an instructor is willing to do and how much information he or she can handle.

Braskamp and Ory (1994) and Seldin (1999) argued the virtues of the video for teaching improvement. However, there's only a tad of evidence on its effectiveness (Fuller & Manning, 1973). If the purpose of the video is to diagnose strengths and weaknesses on one or more teaching occasions, faculty should be encouraged to systematically evaluate the behaviors observed using a rating scale or checklist. Behavioral checklists have been developed by Brinko (1993) and Perlberg (1983). The results from these instruments can identify aspects of teaching that need to be changed.

Whatever option is selected, the result of the video should be a profile of positive and negative teaching behaviors followed by a list of specific objectives to address the deficiencies. This direct evidence of teaching effectiveness can be included in an instructor's self-ratings and teaching portfolio. The video is a powerful documentary of teaching performance.

BOTTOM LINE: If faculties are really committed to improving their teaching, a video is one of the best sources of evidence for formative decisions, interpreted either alone or, preferably, with a peer's or mentor's input. If the video is used in confidence for this purpose, faculty members should decide whether it should also be included in their self-ratings or portfolio as a 'work sample' for summative decisions.

13. Teaching/course portfolio review

The teaching portfolio is not a single source of evidence; rather, it is a shopping mall of most of the 14 sources described in this chapter, assembled systematically for the purpose of promotion and tenure decisions. In fact, portfolio is derived from two Latin root words: port, meaning 'carry,' and folio, meaning 'a wheelbarrow load of my best work to the appointments and promotions (A & P) committee with the hope of being promoted.'

The term portfolio has been associated with the visual arts, architecture, modeling, and financial investments. It is a humongous, thin, flat, zippered leather case containing photographs, sketches, drawings, blueprints, securities, and stock tips, which represent a person's 'best work'" This package is presented to an employer with the prospect of being hired.

Teaching portfolio is 'a coherent set of materials, including work samples and reflective commentary on them, compiled by a faculty member to represent their teaching practice as related to student learning and development' (Cerbin & Hutchings, 1993, p. 1). Now we have two elements to consider: work samples and reflective commentary. If you think this stuff is new and innovative, you're wrong. Work samples have been used in management and industry to measure the performance of employees for more than 60 years.

Knapper (1995) traced the most recent origins of the teaching portfolio to the work of a committee of the Canadian Association of University Teachers (CAUT). The chair, Shore (1975), argued that faculty should prepare their evidence for teaching effectiveness—a 'portfolio of evidence' (p. 8). What emerged was *The Teaching Dossier: A Guide to Its Preparation and Use* (Shore & Associates, 1986). In the 1980s, this Guide became the portfolio bible, and the idea spread like the flu: in Canada as the 'dossier,' in the United States as the 'portfolio' (Seldin, 1980; Seldin, Miller, & Seldin, 2010), and in Australia (Roe, 1987) and the United Kingdom as the 'profile' (Gibbs, 1988).

So what should we stick in the portfolio-dossier-profile to provide evidence of teaching effectiveness? The Guide recommends 49 categories grouped under three headings: 'Products of Good Teaching,' 'Material from Oneself,' and 'Information from Others.' Knapper and Wright (2001) offer a list of the ten most frequently used items from a faculty survey of North American colleges and universities (O'Neil & Wright, 1995):

1 Student course and teaching evaluation data which suggest improvements or produce an overall rating of effectiveness or satisfaction;
2 List of course titles and numbers, unit values or credits, enrollments with brief elaboration;
3 List of course materials prepared for students;
4 Participation in seminars, workshops, and professional meetings intended to improve teaching;
5 Statements from colleagues who have observed teaching either as members of a teaching team or as independent observers of a particular course, or who teach other sections of the same course;
6 Attempts at instructional innovations and evaluations of their effectiveness;
7 Unstructured (and possibly unsolicited) written evaluations by students, including written comments on exams and letters received after a course has been completed;
8 Participating in course or curriculum development;

330 Ronald A. Berk

9   Evidence of effective supervision on Honors, Master's, or Ph.D. thesis;
10   Student essays, creative work, and projects or fieldwork reports.

(pp. 22–23)

They suggest three categories of items: (1) a statement of teaching responsibilities, (2) a statement of teaching approach or philosophy, and (3) data from students. This is considered a bare-bones portfolio.

There is a critical underlying notion that is often overlooked in the submission of the portfolio: The portfolio headings and the extensive list of sources of evidence of teaching effectiveness are designed to impress the most cynical, imperceptive, biased, and/or ignorant faculty on an A & P committee. That impression is that teaching IS a scholarly activity comparable to the list of publications and presentations presented as evidence of research scholarship. Teaching practice is not just a list of courses and student rating summaries. Research and publications remain major factors in evaluating faculty performance in 40–52 percent of liberal arts colleges (Miller & Seldin, 2014).

Based on a synthesis of components appearing in teaching portfolios cited in the literature and used at several institutions (Berk, 2005, 2006), here is a fairly comprehensive list of elements sorted into three mutually exclusive categories:

1   Description of Teaching Responsibilities

   a   Courses taught
   b   Guest presentations
   c   One-on-one teaching (e.g., independent studies, scholarly projects, thesis/dissertation committees)
   d   Development of new courses or programs
   e   Service on curriculum committees
   f   Training grants

2   Reflective Analysis (5–10 pages)

   a   Philosophy of teaching
   b   Innovative and creative teaching techniques
   c   Mentorship of students and faculty
   d   Participation in faculty development activities
   e   Scholarship of teaching
   f   Recognition of effective teaching

3   Artifacts (appendices—evidence to support above claims)

   a   Syllabi
   b   Handouts
   c   Exams/projects
   d   Student work samples
   e   Use of technology
   f   Student ratings
   g   Peer ratings
   h   Alumni ratings
   i   DVDs of teaching
   j   Teaching scholarship
   k   Consultations on teaching

Since this portfolio requires considerable time in preparation, its primary use is for career decisions—promotion and tenure (Berk, 2002; Diamond, 2004; Seldin *et al.*, 2010). It is an important factor and always used in these decisions at nearly 70 percent of liberal arts colleges (Miller & Seldin, 2014). However, a variation on this theme called the 'Socratic portfolio' has been recommended to provide direction and to kick-start a graduate student's teaching career (Border, 2002). The name refers to the dialogue and collaboration between the apprentice student and multiple mentors that occur during the program.

The teaching portfolio is a self-rating on steroids. It is performance enhanced. One is required to take major responsibility for documenting all teaching accomplishments and practices. Completing the reflective component alone would benefit all graduate students and faculties if they would just take the time to prepare it.

Estimates of the reliability of promotions committee judgments by 'colleagues' based on portfolios are impressive (Anderson, 1993; Centra, 1993; Root, 1987). These judgments should be based on a rating scale to ensure a systematic evaluation of teaching. A variety of forms have been reported in the literature that may be useful as prototypes from which you can build one tailored to your definition of teaching effectiveness (Braskamp & Ory, 1994; Centra, 1975, 1993; Centra, Froh, Gray, & Lambert, 1987; French-Lazovik, 1981; Murray, 1995).

BOTTOM LINE: As a collection of many of the sources of evidence described herein, the teaching portfolio should be used by graduate students during their program to provide focus for their faculty careers. For faculty, it should be reserved primarily to present a comprehensive picture of teaching effectiveness to complement the list of research publications for promotion and tenure decisions.

14. Administrator ratings

Deans, associate deans, program directors, and department heads can evaluate faculty for annual merit review according to criteria for teaching, scholarship, service, and/or practice (Diamond, 2004). After all, administrators were or still are faculty with expertise on teaching methods, classroom assessment techniques, and content in some field. The administrators may observe teaching performance and examine documentation in the other three areas, prepared by each faculty member. They can also rate faculty on contributions to the instructional program, such as learning environment, curricular development, and mentoring other faculty on teaching improvement (Hoyt & Palett, 1999) and professionalism related to teaching. However, administrators' ratings may rely heavily on secondary sources.

The department chair (79.1 percent) and dean (67.6 percent) remain the dominant sources of information on teaching performance other than student ratings (94.2 percent) in liberal arts colleges (Miller & Seldin, 2014) for summative decisions. These percentages have increased nearly 10 percent over the past decade. Committee evaluation and colleagues' opinions still play a pivotal role (41–52 percent) in those decisions (Miller & Seldin, 2014). Administrator ratings of teaching performance require a more generic scale than the type completed by students.

Typically, for annual review, administrators distribute a structured activity report to faculty to furnish a comprehensive picture of achievement in all areas over the previous year. The more explicit the categories requested in the report, the easier it is for faculty to complete and for administrators to assess. The administrators can then rate the overall quality of performance in each category. A separate rating scale may be created just for this purpose. The total 'summed' rating across categories can then be used to determine retention or dismissal or merit pay increases.

BOTTOM LINE: Administrator ratings are typically based on secondary sources, not direct observation of teaching or any other areas of performance. This source furnishes a perspective different from all other sources for annual review, merit pay decisions, and recommendations for promotion.

15. Employer ratings

What real-world approach to evaluating teaching effectiveness could tap employers' assessment of graduates? Did they learn anything from their program of study? Are they successful? Are they making more money than the faculty?

Although few colleges are gathering this information, it is worth considering as a source of evidence. After time has passed, at least a year, an evaluation (a.k.a. performance appraisal) of the graduate's on-the-job performance can furnish feedback on overall teaching quality, curricular relevance, and program design. Depending on the specificity of the outcomes, inferences may be drawn about individual teaching effectiveness. However, this measure is limited because it is indirect and based on program outcomes. There is no research on its utility.

The first step is to track down the graduates. The effort involved is often the greatest deterrent to surveying employers. The admissions office usually maintains records of employment for a few years after graduation. When graduates change jobs or escape to developing countries, private investigators and bounty hunters will be needed to find them. Seppanen (1995) suggests using unemployment insurance databases to track graduates' employment history, which can be linked directly to the institution's information systems.

Next, decide what behaviors to measure. Program outcomes can be used when the school is preparing a graduate for a specific profession, such as teaching, nursing, medicine, law, accounting, engineering, or cybersecurity.

These outcomes along with questions about satisfaction with employee performance can be assembled into a rating scale to determine the quality of their KSAs (knowledge, skills, and abilities) based on performance (see Berk, 2006). The ratings across graduates can pinpoint faculty, course, and program strengths and weaknesses about job performance.

BOTTOM LINE: Employer ratings provide an indirect source of evidence for program evaluation decisions about teaching effectiveness and attainment of program outcomes, especially for professional schools. Job performance data may be linked to individual teaching performance but on a very limited basis.

How do you select the right sources of evidence?

Triangulation

So far, what one simple conclusion can be drawn? 'This is really boring! Get to the point.' Wait! There must be some legitimate conclusion. 'Oh. There is no perfect source of evidence.' Bingo! Every source is different in form and substance from all of the other sources and can supply unique information. However, all sources are also fallible, usually in ways distinct from each other. For example, the unreliability and biases of peer observation ratings are not the same as those of student ratings; student ratings have other weaknesses (Marsh, 2007; Nilson, 2012).

So, what should you do? Since no single source can get the job done, draw from three or more different sources of evidence. The strengths of each source can compensate for weaknesses of the other sources, thereby converging on a decision about teaching effectiveness that is more accurate and reliable than one based on any single source (Appling, Naumann, & Berk, 2001). This notion of triangulation is derived from a compensatory model of decision-making.

Nuhfer (2010) argued that the evaluation of teaching is a fractal form with extensive neural networks and, therefore, far too complicated to be measured with any single source. Given the complexity of measuring the act of teaching in a real-time classroom environment, online virtual class, or hybrid-time class, it is reasonable to expect that multiple sources can provide a more accurate, reliable, and comprehensive picture of teaching effectiveness than just one source. However, the decision maker should integrate the information from only those sources for which validity evidence is available. The quality of the sources chosen should be beyond reproach.

Complementary multiple sources

At present, there is a paucity of empirical evidence to support the use of any particular combination of sources (e.g., Barnett, Matthews, & Jackson, 2003; Stalmeijer, Dolmans, Wolfhagen, Peters, van Coppenolle, & Scherpbier, 2010; Stehle, Spinath, & Kadmon, 2012). However, there is evidence on the relationships between student ratings and several other measures that supports their complementarity. Benton and Cashin's (2012) research review reported the relationships between student ratings and ratings from observers, self, alumni, and administrators, which were low to moderate. Here are the actual validity coefficients with student ratings: trained external observers (.50 with global ratings), self (.30–.45), alumni (.54–.80), administrators (.47–.62; .39 with global ratings). Those correlations indicate there are a lot of new information and insights on teaching to be gained by tapping those additional sources of evidence.

Beyond student ratings, is it worth the extra effort, time, cost, and aggravation to develop the additional measures mentioned previously? Are you squirming, queasy, or shuddering at the prospect of undertaking that initiative? Hurling is normal. This is not for the faint of heart. Consider what you have to gain in the decisions you make.

As you build your instruments, it should become clear that they are intended to measure different teaching behaviors that contribute to teaching effectiveness. Each measure should cover a separate chunk of behaviors that are complementary, not redundant; however, some overlap of behaviors may be justified for corroboration. Each tool should contribute significant, new information not measured by existing instruments.

Matching sources of evidence to the decision

Consider all 15 sources of evidence currently available based on my preceding review and bottom-line recommendations according to the research and experiences of others (Berk, 2005, 2006, 2009b, 2013d, 2018). The decision should drive the choices of evidence. Think carefully about the decision regarding the timeframe, conditions, information needed, and the faculty about whom the decision will be made. Which sources seem to be most appropriate for your decisions? Pick the highest quality sources for the specific decision. Prioritize the sources before you begin the task of collecting the evidence, which may involve the design and construction of new measures.

Currently, in addition to chair and dean ratings (68–79 percent), the most widely used sources for summative decisions in liberal arts colleges are student end-of-course ratings

(94.2 percent), self-ratings (67.6 percent), peer classroom observation (60.4 percent), and peer review of course materials (52.5 percenet) (Miller & Seldin, 2014). To jump-start your selection of sources, here are my top picks, based on the literature, for formative, summative, and program decisions:

Formative decisions (instructor improves and shapes the quality of teaching)

- Student end-of-course ratings;
- Student midterm feedback;
- Peer classroom observation;
- Peer review of course materials;
- Self-ratings;
- Video classroom review;
- Mentor's advice;
- External expert ratings.

Summative decisions (administrator's annual review for contract renewal and merit pay)

- Student end-of-course ratings;
- Self-ratings;
- Teaching scholarship;
- Peer classroom observation (report written expressly for summative decision);
- Peer review of course materials (report written expressly for summative decision);
- Mentor's review (progress report written expressly for summative decision).

Summative decisions (committee's review for promotion and tenure)

- Teaching/course portfolio review (across several years' courses).

Program decisions (faculty review of curriculum, admissions and graduation requirements, and program effectiveness)

- Student end-of-course ratings;
- Student exit and alumni ratings;
- Student outcome measures;
- Employer ratings.

You probably noticed one particular source among the potential 15 that was conspicuously omitted from most of my recommended sources: learning outcome measures. Suffice it to say for now, isolating students' course achievement at one point in time or their gains over time that are attributable directly to teaching is nearly impossible (Berk, 2014, 2016; Everson, 2017). The complexity increases considerably when attempting to compare faculty who teach different courses with different measures. It would be extremely difficult to defend student performance as a valid source of evidence of teaching effectiveness for any individual decision.

The multiple sources that were recommended previously for each decision can be configured into the 360-degree multisource feedback (MSF) model of assessment (Berk, 2009a, 2009b) or another model for accreditation documentation of teaching evaluation. The sources for each decision may be added gradually to the model. Building the model is an ongoing process custom-tailored for each institution.

Final recommendations for practice

So now that you've seen my picks, which sources are you going to choose? So many sources, so little time! Which sources do you already have? What is the quality of your measures used to provide evidence of teaching effectiveness? Are all faculty stakeholders involved in the current process?

You have some decisions to make, starting with 'Where do I begin?' Here are a few suggestions:

1   Assemble a small faculty ad hoc committee. Handpick appropriate 'teachers' for your committee members, including at least one professor with expertise in measurement and evaluation and one or two students. Work will be involved.
2   Map the outcomes for the semester (or quarter) and year. Discuss a plan of attack. What are the highest priorities? Consider whether accreditation review is on the horizon or somewhere else. That could change the priorities.
3   Start with student ratings. Consider the content and quality of your current scale and determine whether it needs a minor or major tune-up for the decisions being made (Berk, 2010; Boysen, 2016). Decide what has to be done and who will do it.
4   Review the other sources of evidence with your faculty to decide the next steps. All stakeholders must be involved in these decisions. Don't be disheartened by the inevitable pushback. Just take this one step at a time. Which sources will your faculty embrace as reflecting best practices in teaching? Weigh the pluses and minuses of the different sources. Prepare options for your faculty.
5   Decide which combination of sources is best for your faculty. Identify which sources should be used—although prepared differently—for both formative and summative decisions, such as self and peer ratings, and which sources should be used for one type of decision but not the other, such as administrator ratings and teaching portfolio.
6   Design a detailed plan to build those sources, one at a time gradually, to create an evaluation model for each decision (see Berk, 2009b). Delegate responsibility for and ownership of the various tasks involved. Faculty must make a professional commitment to 'put it on the line'. (REMEMBER: Administrators do not have time for these steps. They just need the data that faculty has agreed to use for decision-making.)

Whatever combination of sources you choose to use, take the time and make an effort to design the scales, administer the scales, and report the results appropriately. The accuracy of faculty evaluation decisions depends on the integrity of the process and the validity and reliability of the multiple sources of evidence you collect.

This endeavor may seem rather formidable and you will probably receive pushback from some faculty, but keep in mind that you are not alone in this process. Your faculty and administrators are all vested. Their careers depend on the outcomes. Solicit their input at every decision step of this journey. Your colleagues at other institutions are also probably struggling with the same issues. Maybe you could pool resources to get through it.

References

Addison, W. E., & Stowell, J. R. (2012). Conducting research on student evaluations of teaching. In M. E. Kite (Ed.), *Effective evaluation of teaching: A guide for faculty and administrators* (pp. 1–12). E-book retrieved on June 6, 2012, from the Society for the Teaching of Psychology website http://teachpsych.org/ebooks/evals2012/index.php

Aleamoni, L. M. (1982). Components of the instructional setting. *Instructional Evaluation*, 7, 11–16.

Ali, D. L., & Sell, Y. (1998). *Issues regarding the reliability, validity and utility of student ratings of instruction: A survey of research findings*. Calgary: University of Calgary APC Implementation Task Force on Student Ratings of Instruction.

American Association of University Professors. (1974). Committee C. Statement on teaching evaluation. *AAUP Bulletin*, 60(2), 166–170.

American Statistical Association. (2014). *ASA statement on using value-added models for educational assessment*. Retrieved on May 1, 2016, from http://www.amstat.org/policy/pdfs/ASA_VAM_ Statement.pdf

Anderson, E. (Ed.). (1993). *Campus use of the teaching portfolio: Twenty-five profiles*. Washington, DC: American Association for Higher Education.

Appling, S. E., Naumann, P. L., & Berk, R. A. (2001). Using a faculty evaluation triad to achieve evidenced-based teaching. *Nursing and Health Care Perspectives*, 22, 247–251.

Arreola, R. A. (2007). *Developing a comprehensive faculty evaluation system: A handbook for college faculty and administrators on designing and operating a comprehensive faculty evaluation system* (3rd ed.). Bolton, MA: Anker.

Barber, L. W. (1990). Self-assessment. In J. Millman & L. Darling-Hammond (Eds.), *The new handbook of teacher evaluation* (pp. 216–228). Newbury Park, CA: Sage.

Barnett, C. W., Matthews, H. W., & Jackson, R. A. (2003). A comparison between student ratings and faculty self-ratings of instructional effectiveness. *Journal of Pharmaceutical Education*, 67(4), Article 117.

Barre, E. (2015, July 9). *Do student evaluations of teaching really get an "F"?* Houston, TX: Center for Teaching Excellence, Rice University. Retrieved on June 8, 2017, from http://cte.rice.edu/blogarchive/2015/07/09/studentevaluations

Basow, S. A., & Martin, J. L. (2012). Bias in student evaluations. In M. E. Kite (Ed.), *Effective evaluation of teaching: A guide for faculty and administrators* (pp. 40–49). E-book retrieved on June 6, 2012, from the Society for the Teaching of Psychology website http://teachpsych.org/ebooks/evals2012/index.php

Bennett, W. E. (1987). Small group instructional diagnosis: A dialogic approach of instructional improvement for tenured faculty. *Journal of Staff, Program, and Organizational Development*, 5(3), 100–104.

Benton, S. L., & Cashin, W. E. (2012). *Student ratings of teaching: A summary of research and literature* (IDEA Paper No. 50). Manhattan, KS: The IDEA Center. Retrieved on April 8, 2012, from http://www.theideacenter.org/sites/default/files/idea-paper_50.pdf

Benton, S. L., & Cashin, W. E. (2014). Student ratings of instruction in college and university courses. In M. B. Paulsen (Ed.), *Higher education: Handbook of theory & research* (Vol. 29, pp. 279–326). Dordrecht, The Netherlands: Springer.

Benton, S. L., Guo, M., Li, D., & Gross, A. (2013). Student ratings, teacher standards, and critical thinking skills. Paper presented at the annual meeting of the American Educational Research Association, San Francisco, CA.

Benton, S. L., & Ryalls, K. R. (2016). *Challenging misconceptions about student ratings of instruction* (IDEA Paper #58). Manhattan, KS: The IDEA Center.

Berk, R. A. (1988). Fifty reasons why student achievement gain does not mean teacher effectiveness. *Journal of Personnel Evaluation in Education*, 1, 345–363.

Berk, R. A. (1990). Limitations of using student achievement data for career ladder promotions and merit pay decisions. In J. V. Mitchell, Jr., S. L. Wise, & B. S. Plake (Eds.), *Assessment of teaching: Purposes, practices, and implications for the profession* (pp. 261–306). Hillsdale, NJ: Erlbaum. Retrieved on February 2, 2014, from http://digitalcommons.unl.edu/burosassessteaching/10/

Berk, R. A. (2002). Teaching portfolios used for high-stakes decisions: You have technical issues! In *National Evaluation Systems, How to find and support tomorrow's teachers* (pp. 45–56). Amherst, MA: Author.

Berk, R. A. (2005). Survey of 12 strategies to measure teaching effectiveness. *International Journal of Teaching and Learning in Higher Education*, 17(1), 48–62. Retrieved on January 28, 2014, from http://www.isetl.org/ijtlhe/pdf/IJTLHE8.pdf

Berk, R. A. (2006). *Thirteen strategies to measure college teaching: A consumer's guide to rating scale construction, assessment, and decision making for faculty, administrators, and clinicians.* Sterling, VA: Stylus.

Berk, R. A. (2009a). Beyond student ratings: "A whole new world, a new fantastic point of view." *Essays on Teaching Excellence*, 20(1). (http://www.podnetwork.org/publications/teaching excellence/05-06/V17,%20N2%20Berk.pdf)

Berk, R. A. (2009b). Using the 360° multisource feedback model to evaluate teaching and professionalism. *Medical Teacher*, 31(12), 1073–1080. (DOI:10.3109/014215908025 72775)

Berk, R. A. (2010). The secret to the "best" ratings from any evaluation scale. *Journal of Faculty Development*, 24(1), 37–39.

Berk, R. A. (2012). Top 20 strategies to increase the online response rates of student rating scales. *International Journal of Technology in Teaching and Learning*, 8(2), 98–107.

Berk, R. A. (2013a). Face-to-face versus online course evaluations: A "consumer's guide" to seven strategies. (MERLOT) *Journal of Online Learning and Teaching*, 9(1), 140–148.

Berk, R. A. (2013b). Should global items on student rating scales be used for summative decisions? *Journal of Faculty Development*, 27(1), 57–61.

Berk, R. A. (2013c). Top 5 flashpoints in the assessment of teaching effectiveness. *Medical Teacher*, 35(1), 15–26. (DOI: 10.3109/0142159X.2012.732247) (http://informahealth care.com/doi/abs/10.3109/0142159X.2012.732247)

Berk, R. A. (2013d). *Top 10 flashpoints in student ratings and the evaluation of teaching: What faculty and administrators must know to protect themselves in employment decisions.* Sterling, VA: Stylus Publishing.

Berk, R. A. (2014). Should student outcomes be used to evaluate teaching? *Journal of Faculty Development*, 28(2), 87–96.

Berk, R. A. (2016). Value of value-added models based on student outcomes to evaluate teaching. *Journal of Faculty Development*, 30(3), 73–81.

Berk, R. A. (2018). Start spreading the news: Use multiple sources of evidence to evaluate teaching. *Journal of Faculty Development*, 32(1).

Berk, R. A., Naumann, P. L., & Appling, S. E. (2004). Beyond student ratings: Peer observation of classroom and clinical teaching. *International Journal of Nursing Education Scholarship*, 1(1), 1–26.

Berrett, D. (2015, November 29). Can the student course evaluation be redeemed? *The Chronicle of Higher Education*. Retrieved on February 20, 2016, from http://www.chronicle.com/article/Can-the-Student-Course/234369

Bo-Linn, C., Gentry, J., Lowman, J., Pratt, R. W., & Zhu, R. (2004, November). Learning from exemplary teachers. Paper presented at the annual Lilly Conference on College Teaching, Miami University, Oxford, OH.

Border, L. L. B. (2002). The Socratic portfolio: A guide for future faculty. *PS: Political Science & Politics*, 25(4), 739–743. (http://www.apsanet.org/section_223.cfm.)

Boring, A. (2017). Gender biases in student evaluations of teaching. *Journal of Public Economics*, 145, 27–41. (DOI:10.1016/j.jpubeco.2016.11.006)

Boring, A., Ottoboni, K., & Stark, P. B. (2016). Student evaluations of teaching (mostly) do not measure teaching effectiveness. *ScienceOpen Research*. (DOI:10.14293/s2199–1006.1.sor-edu.aetbzc.v1)

Boyer, E. (1990). *Scholarship reconsidered: New priorities for the professoriate.* Princeton, NJ: The Carnegie Foundation for the Advancement of Teaching.

Boysen, G. A. (2016). Using student evaluations to improve teaching: Evidence-based recommendations. *Scholarship of Teaching and Learning in Psychology*, 2(4), 273–284. (http://dx.doi.org/10.1037/stl0000069)

Braskamp, L. A., Caulley, D. N., & Costin, F. (1979). Student ratings and instructor self-ratings and their relationship to student achievement. *American Educational Research Journal, 16*, 295–306.

Braskamp, L. A., & Ory, J. C. (1994). *Assessing faculty work: Enhancing individual and institutional performance*. San Francisco: Jossey-Bass.

Brinko, K. T. (1993). The practice of giving feedback to improve teaching: What is effective? *Journal of Higher Education, 64*(5), 54–68.

Calderon, T. G., Gabbin, A. L., & Green, B. P. (1996). *Report of the committee on promoting evaluating effective teaching*. Harrisonburg, VA: James Madison University.

Carnegie Foundation for the Advancement of Teaching. (1994). *National survey on the reexamination of faculty roles and rewards*. Princeton, NJ: Carnegie Foundation for the Advancement of Teaching.

Carrell, S. E., & West, J. E. (2010). Does professor quality matter? Evidence from random assignment of students to professors. *Journal of Political Economy, 118*(3), 409–432.

Carusetta, E. (2001). Evaluating teaching through teaching awards. In C. Knapper & P. Cranton (Eds.), *Fresh approaches to the evaluation of teaching* (New Directions for Teaching and Learning, No. 88, pp. 31–46). San Francisco: Jossey-Bass.

Cashin, W. E. (1989). *Defining and evaluating college teaching* (IDEA Paper No. 21). Manhattan, KS: The IDEA Center.

Cashin, W. E. (2003). Evaluating college and university teaching: Reflections of a practitioner. In J. C. Smart (Ed.), *Higher education: Handbook of theory and research* (pp. 531–593). Dordrecht, The Netherlands: Kluwer Academic Publishers.

Cederblom, D., & Lounsbury, J. W. (1980). An investigation of user acceptance of peer evaluations. *Personnel Psychology, 33*, 567–580.

Center for Teaching Effectiveness. (1996). *Preparing for peer observation: A guidebook*. Austin, TX: The Center for Teaching Effectiveness, University of Texas.

Centra, J. A. (1973a). Effectiveness of student feedback in modifying college instruction. *Journal of Educational Psychology, 65*(3), 395–410.

Centra, J. A. (1973b). Self-ratings of college teachers: A comparison with student ratings. *Journal of Educational Measurement, 10*, 287–295.

Centra, J. A. (1974). The relationship between student and alumni ratings of teachers. *Educational and Psychological Measurement, 32*(2), 321–326.

Centra, J. A. (1975). Colleagues as raters of classroom instruction. *Journal of Higher Education, 46*, 327–337.

Centra, J. A. (1993). *Reflective faculty evaluation: Enhancing teaching and determining faculty effectiveness*. San Francisco: Jossey-Bass.

Centra, J. A., Froh, R. C., Gray, P. J., & Lambert, L. M. (1987). *A guide to evaluating teaching for promotion and tenure*. Acton, MA: Copley.

Cerbin, W., & Hutchings, P. (1993, June). The teaching portfolio. Paper presented at the Bush Summer Institute, Minneapolis, MN.

Chism, N. V. N. (2007). *Peer review of teaching: A sourcebook* (2nd ed.). Bolton, MA: Anker.

Clark, D. J., & Redmond, M. V. (1982). *Small group instructional diagnosis: Final report*. Washington, DC: Fund for the Improvement of Postsecondary Education.

Clayson, D. E. (2009). Student evaluations of teaching: Are they related to what students learn? A meta-analysis and review of the literature. *Journal of Marketing Education, 31*(1), 16–30. Retrieved on February 16, 2017, from http://jmd.sagepub.com/content/31/1/16.full.pdf+html

Cohen, P. A. (1981). Student ratings of instruction and student achievement: A meta-analysis of multisection validity studies. *Review of Educational Research, 51*, 281–309.

Cohen P. A., & McKeachie, W. J. (1980). The role of colleagues in the evaluation of teaching. *Improving College and University Teaching, 28*, 147–154.

Coren, S. (2001). Are course evaluations a threat to academic freedom? In S. E. Kahn & D. Pavlich (Eds.), *Academic freedom and the inclusive university* (pp. 104–117). Vancouver: University of British Columbia Press.

Cranton, P. (2001). Interpretive and critical evaluation. In C. Knapper & P. Cranton (Eds.), *Fresh approaches to the evaluation of teaching* (New Directions for Teaching and Learning, No. 88, pp. 11–18). San Francisco: Jossey-Bass.

Crouch, C. H., & Mazur, E. (2001). Peer instruction: Ten years of experience and results. *American Journal of Physics*, 69, 970–977.

d'Apollonia, S., & Abrami, P. C. (1996, April). Variables moderating the validity of student ratings of instruction: A meta-analysis. Paper presented at the annual meeting of the American Educational Research Association, New York.

d'Apollonia, S., & Abrami, P. C. (1997a). Navigating student ratings of instruction. *American Psychologist*, 52, 1198–1208.

d'Apollonia, S., & Abrami, P. C. (1997b). Scaling the ivory tower, Part 1: Collecting evidence of instructor effectiveness. *Psychology Teaching Review*, 6, 46–59.

d'Apollonia, S., & Abrami, P. C. (1997c). Scaling the ivory tower, Part 2: Student ratings of instruction in North America. *Psychology Teaching Review*, 6, 60–76.

Diamond, R. M. (2004). *Preparing for promotion, tenure, and annual review: A faculty guide* (2nd ed.). Bolton, MA: Anker.

Dori, Y. J., & Belcher, J. (2005). How does technology-enabled active learning affect undergraduate students' understanding of electromagnetism concepts? *Journal of the Learning Sciences*, 14(2), 243–279. (http://dx.doi.org/10.1207/s15327809jls1402_3)

Doyle, K. O., & Crichton, L. A. (1978). Student, peer, and self-evaluations of college instruction. *Journal of Educational Psychology*, 70, 815–826.

Drucker, A. J., & Remmers, H. H. (1951). Do alumni and students differ in their attitudes toward instructors? *Journal of Educational Psychology*, 42(3), 129–143.

Everson, K. C. (2017). Value-added modeling and educational accountability: are we answering the real questions? *Review of Educational Research*, 87(1), 35–70. (http://journals.sagepub.com/doi/full/10.3102/0034654316637199)

Feldman, K. A. (1989a). The association between student ratings of specific instructional dimensions and student achievement: Refining and extending the synthesis of data from multisection validity studies. *Research in Higher Education*, 30, 583–645.

Feldman, K. A. (1989b). Instructional effectiveness of college teachers as judged by teachers themselves, current and former students, colleagues, administrators, and external (neutral) observers. *Research in Higher Education*, 30, 137–189.

Fenwick, T. J. (2001). Using student outcomes to evaluate teaching. A cautious exploration. In C. Knapper & P. Cranton (Eds.), *Fresh approaches to the evaluation of teaching* (New Directions for Teaching and Learning, No. 88, pp. 63–74). San Francisco: Jossey-Bass.

French-Lazovik, G. (1981). Peer review: Documentary evidence in the evaluation of teaching. In J. Millman (Ed.), *Handbook of teacher evaluation* (pp. 73–89). Newbury Park, CA: Sage.

Fuller, F. F., & Manning, B. A. (1973). Self-confrontation reviewed: A conceptualization for video playback in teacher education. *Review of Educational Research*, 43(4), 469–528.

Freyd, M. (1923). A graphic rating scale for teachers. *Journal of Educational Research*, 8(5), 433–439.

Gibbs, G. (1988). *Creating a teaching profile*. Bristol, England: Teaching and Educational Services.

Gooblar, D. (2017, May 31). No, student evaluations aren't "worthless." *Chronicle Vitae*. Retrieved on June 6, 2017, from https://chroniclevitae.com/news/1814-no-student-evaluations-aren-t-worthless?cid=at&utm_source=at&utm_medium=en&elqTrackId=82121c92a9514c93bc15c5b7601dc6f9&elq=7e78f00e5df94d5280e706170379a9c5&elqaid=14140&elqat=1&elqCampaignId=5932

Gravestock, P., & Gregor-Greenleaf, E. (2008). *Student course evaluations: Research, models and trends.* Toronto, Canada: Higher Education Quality Council of Ontario. E-book retrieved on May 6, 2012, from http://www.heqco.ca/en-A/Research/Research%20Publications/Pages/Home.aspx

Green, B. P., Calderon, T. G., & Reider, B. P. (1998). A content analysis of teaching evaluation instruments used in accounting departments. *Issues in Accounting Education,* 13(1), 15–30.

Griffin, A., & Cook, V. (2009). Acting on evaluation: Twelve tips from a national conference on student evaluations. *Medical Teacher,* 31, 101–104.

Hancock, E., Nickson, S., Chaudhury, S. R., & Ismail, E. (2014, November). What students want: Examining small group instructional feedback results. Paper presented at the 39th annual Professional and Organizational Development (POD) Network in Higher Education Conference, Dallas, TX.

Hativa, N. (2014a). *Student ratings of instruction: A practical approach to designing, operating, and reporting.* Oron Publications. nhativa@gmail.com

Hativa, N. (2014b). *Student ratings of instruction: Recognizing effective teaching.* Oron Publications. nhativa@gmail.com

Hoyt, D. P., & Pallett, W. H. (1999). *Appraising teaching effectiveness: Beyond student ratings* (IDEA Paper No. 36). Manhattan, KS: Kansas State University Center for Faculty Evaluation and Development.

Hutchings, P., & Shulman, L. S. (1999). The scholarship of teaching: New elaborations, new developments. *Change,* 31(5), 11–15.

Jenrette, M., & Hayes, K. (1996). Honoring exemplary teaching: The two-year college setting. In M. D. Svinicki & R. J. Menges (Eds.), *Honoring exemplary teaching* (New Directions for Teaching and Learning, No. 65). San Francisco: Jossey-Bass.

Kamenetz, A. (2014, September 26). Student course evaluations get an 'F'. *NPR Ed: How Learning Happens.* Retrieved on June 10, 2017, from http://www.npr.org/sections/ed/2014/09/26/345515451/student-course-evaluations-get-an-f

Keig, L. W., & Waggoner, M. D. (1994). *Collaborative peer review: The role of faculty in improving college teaching* (ASHE/ERIC Higher Education Report, No. 2). Washington, DC: Association for the Study of Higher Education.

Keig, L. W., & Waggoner, M. D. (1995). Peer review of teaching: Improving college instruction through formative assessment. *Journal on Excellence in College Teaching,* 6(3), 51–83.

Kite, M. E. (Ed.). (2012). *Effective evaluation of teaching: A guide for faculty and administrators.* E-book retrieved on June 6, 2012, from the Society for the Teaching of Psychology website http://teachpsych.org/ebooks/evals2012/index.php

Knapper, C. (1995). The origins of teaching portfolios. *Journal on Excellence in College Teaching,* 6(1), 45–56.

Knapper, C. (1997). Rewards for teaching. In P. Cranton (Ed.), *University challenges in faculty work: Fresh perspectives from around the world* (New Directions for Teaching and Learning, No. 65). San Francisco: Jossey-Bass.

Knapper, C., & Cranton, P. (Eds.). (2001). *Fresh approaches to the evaluation of teaching* (New Directions for Teaching and Learning, No. 88). San Francisco: Jossey-Bass.

Knapper, C., & Wright, W. A. (2001). Using portfolios to document good teaching: Premises, purposes, practices. In C. Knapper & P. Cranton (Eds.), *Fresh approaches to the evaluation of teaching* (New Directions for Teaching and Learning, No. 88, pp. 19–29). San Francisco: Jossey-Bass.

Kulik, J. A. (2001). Student ratings: Validity, utility, and controversy. In M. Theall, P.C. Abrami, & L. A. Mets (Eds.), *The student ratings debate: Are they valid? How can we best use them?* (New Directions for Institutional Research, No. 109, pp. 9–25). San Francisco: Jossey-Bass.

Li, D., & Benton, S. L. (2017). *The effects of instructor gender and discipline group on student ratings of instruction* (IDEA Research Report No. 10). Manhattan, KS: The IDEA Center.

Love, K. G. (1981). Comparison of peer assessment methods: Reliability, validity, friendship bias, and user reaction. *Journal of Applied Psychology,* 66, 451–457.

Macnell, L., Driscoll, A., & Hunt, A. N. (2014). What's in a name: Exposing gender bias in student ratings of teaching. *Innovative Higher Education*, 40(4), 291–303. (DOI:10.1007/s10755-014-9313-4)

Marincovich, M. (1999). Using student feedback to improve teaching. In P. Seldin & Associates (Eds.), *Changing practices in evaluating teaching: A practical guide to improved faculty performance and promotion/tenure decisions* (pp. 45–69). Bolton, MA: Anker.

Marks, M., Fairris, D. & Beleche, T. (2010, June 3). *Do course evaluations reflect student learning? Evidence from a pre-test/post-test setting*. University of California, Riverside. Retrieved on June 10, 2017, from http://faculty.ucr.edu/~mmarks/Papers/marks2010course.pdf

Marsh, H. W. (2007). Students' evaluations of university teaching: Dimensionality, reliability, validity, potential biases and usefulness. In R. P. Perry & J. C. Smart (Eds.), *The scholarship of teaching and learning in higher education: An evidence-based perspective* (pp. 319–383). Dordrecht, The Netherlands: Springer.

Marsh, H. W., Fleiner, H., & Thomas, C. S. (1975). Validity and usefulness of student evaluations of instructional quality. *Journal of Educational Psychology*, 67, 833–839.

Marsh, H.W., Overall, J. U., & Kessler, S. P. (1979). The validity of students' evaluations of instructional effectiveness: A comparison of faculty self-evaluations and evaluations by their students. *Journal of Educational Psychology*, 71, 149–160.

McNaught, C., & Anwyl, J. (1993). *Awards for teaching excellence at Australian Universities* (Research Working Paper No. 93.1). Melbourne, Australia: University of Melbourne Centre for the Study of Higher Education. (ED 368–291)

Menges, R. J. (1996). Awards to individuals. In M. D. Svinicki & R. J. Menges (Eds.), *Honoring exemplary teaching* (New Directions for Teaching and Learning, No. 65). San Francisco: Jossey-Bass.

Miller, J. E., & Seldin, P. (2014, May-June). Changing practices in faculty evaluation: Can better evaluation make a difference? *Bulletin of the AAUP*, 100(3). Retrieved on March 25, 2017, from www.aaup.org/article/changing-practices-faculty-evaluation#.WNawXW_yvIV

Millis, B. J., & Kaplan, B. B. (1995). Enhance teaching through peer classroom observations. In P. Seldin & Associates (Eds.), *Improving college teaching* (pp. 137–152). Bolton, MA: Anker.

Muchinsky, P. M. (1995). Peer review of teaching: Lessons learned from military and industrial research on peer assessment. *Journal on Excellence in College Teaching*, 6(3), 17–30.

Murray, H. G. (1983). Low inference classroom teaching behaviors and student ratings of college teaching effectiveness. *Journal of Educational Psychology*, 71, 856–865.

Murray, J. P. (1995). The teaching portfolio: A tool for department chairperson to create a climate for teaching excellence. *Innovative Higher Education*, 19(3), 163–175.

Nilson, L. B. (2012). Time to raise questions about student ratings. In J. E. Groccia & L. Cruz (Eds.), *To improve the academy: Resources for faculty, instructional, and organizational development* (Vol. 31) (pp. 213–228). San Francisco: Jossey-Bass.

Nuhfer, E. B. (2010). *A fractal thinker looks at student ratings*. Retrieved on August 11, 2012, from http://profcamp.tripod.com/fractalevals10.pdf

O'Neil, C., & Wright, W. A. (1995). *Recording teaching accomplishment: A Dalhousie guide to the teaching dossier* (5th ed.). Halifax, Canada: Dalhousie University Office of Instructional Development and Technology.

Ory, J. C. (2001). Faculty thoughts and concerns about student ratings. In K. G. Lewis (Ed.), *Techniques and strategies for interpreting student evaluations* (Special issue) (New Directions for Teaching and Learning, No. 87) (pp. 3–15). San Francisco: Jossey-Bass.

Ory, J. C., & Ryan, K. (2001). How do student ratings measure up to a new validity framework? In M. Theall, P. C. Abrami, & L. A. Mets (Eds.), *The student ratings debate: Are they valid? How can we best use them?* (Special issue) (New Directions for Institutional Research, No. 109) (pp. 27–44). San Francisco: Jossey-Bass.

Overall, J. U., & Marsh, H. W. (1979). Midterm feedback from students: Its relationship to instructional improvement and students' cognitive and affective outcomes. *Journal of Educational Psychology*, 71, 856–865.

Overall, J. U., & Marsh, H. W. (1980). Students' evaluations of instruction: A longitudinal study of their stability. *Journal of Educational Psychology, 72,* 321–325.

Penny, A. R., & Coe, R. (2004). Effectiveness of consultation on student ratings feedback: A meta-analysis. *Review of Educational Research, 74,* 215–253.

Perlberg, A. E. (1983). When professors confront themselves: Towards a theoretical conceptualization of video self-confrontation in higher education. *Higher Education, 12,* 633–663.

Quintana, C. (2017, May 30). As summer sets in, a chance to regard the good, bad, and ugly of student evaluations. *The Chronicle of Higher Education.* Retrieved on June 10, 2017, from http://www.chronicle.com/article/As-Summer-Sets-In-a-Chance-to/240203?cid=db&elqTrackId=f40f875f469340448ee2b8647b354cc5&elq=32c4887aa10d4d4885390a178bb44c01&elqaid=14197&elqat=1&elqCampaignId=5962

Rice, R. E. (1991). The new American scholar: Scholarship and the purposes of the university. *Metropolitan Universities,* 1(4), 7–18.

Roberson, W. (Ed.). (2006). *Peer observation and assessment of teaching.* El Paso, TX: The Center for Effective Teaching and Learning & Instructional Support Services, University of Texas.

Roe, E. (1987). *How to compile a teaching portfolio.* Kensington, Australia: Federation of Australian University Staff Associations.

Root, L. S. (1987). Faculty evaluation: Reliability of peer assessments of research, teaching, and service. *Research in Higher Education, 26,* 71–84.

Ruedrich, S. L., Cavey, C., Katz, K., & Grush, L. (1992). Recognition of teaching excellence through the use of teaching awards: A faculty perspective. *Academic Psychiatry,* 16(1), 10–13.

Ryalls, K., Benton, S., & Li, D. (2016, November). *Response to "Zero correlation between evaluations and learning."* IDEA Editorial Note #3. Manhattan, KS: Kansas State University, Center for Faculty Evaluation and Development. Retrieved on March 16, 2017, from http://www.ideaedu.org/Portals/0/Uploads/Documents/Response_to_Zero_Correlation_Between_Evaluations_Teaching.pdf

Sathy, V. (2017, March 28). The sweet spot of midsemester feedback (blog). ACUE Community. Retrieved on March 30, 2017, from https://community.acue.org/blog/viji-sathy-sweet-spot-midsemester-feedback/

Seldin, P. (1980). *Successful faculty evaluation programs.* Crugers, NY: Coventry.

Seldin, P. (1999). Self-evaluation: What works? What doesn't? In P. Seldin & Associates (Eds.), *Changing practices in evaluating teaching: A practical guide to improved faculty performance and promotion/tenure decisions* (pp. 97–115). Bolton, MA: Anker.

Seldin, P. (2006). Building a successful evaluation program. In P. Seldin & Associates (Eds.), *Evaluating faculty performance: A practical guide to assessing teaching, research, and service* (pp. 1–19). Bolton, MA: Anker.

Seldin, P., & Associates. (Eds.). (1999). *Changing practices in evaluating teaching: A practical guide to improve faculty performance and promotion/tenure decisions.* Bolton, MA: Anker.

Seldin, P., Miller, E., & Seldin, C. A. (Eds.). (2010). *The teaching portfolio: A practical guide to improved performance and promotion/tenure decisions* (4th ed.). San Francisco: Jossey-Bass.

Seppanen, L. J. (1995). Linkages to the world of employment. In P. T. Ewell (Ed.), *Student tracking: New techniques, new demands.* San Francisco: Jossey-Bass.

Shariff, S. H. (1999). Students' quality control circle: A case study on students' participation in the quality of control circles at the faculty of business and management. *Assessment & Evaluation in Higher Education, 24,* 141–146.

Shore, B. M. (1975). Moving beyond the course evaluation questionnaire in evaluating university teaching. *CAUT Bulletin,* 23(4), 7–10.

Shore, B. M., & Associates. (1986). *The teaching dossier: A guide to its preparation and use* (rev. ed.). Ottawa, Canada: Canadian Association of University Teachers.

Shulman, L. S. (1998). Course anatomy: The dissection and analysis of knowledge through teaching. In P. Hutchings (Ed.), *The course portfolio: How faculty can examine their teaching to advance practice and improve student learning*. Washington, DC: American Association for Higher Education.

Sorey, K. E. (1968). A study of the distinguishing characteristics of college faculty who are superior in regard to the teaching function. *Dissertation Abstracts*, 28(12-A), 4916.

Spooren, P., Brockx, B., & Mortelmans, D. (2013). On the validity of student evaluation of teaching: The state of the art. *Review of Educational Research* 83(3), 1–45.

Stalmeijer, R. E., Dolmans, D. H., Wolfhagen, I. H., Peters, W. G., van Coppenolle, L., & Scherpbier, A. J. (2010). Combined student ratings and self-assessment provide useful feedback for clinical teachers. *Advances in Health Science Education, Theory, and Practice*, 15(3), 315–328.

Stehle, S., Spinath, B., & Kadmon, M. (2012). Measuring teaching effectiveness: Correspondence between students' evaluations of teaching and different measures of student learning. *Research in Higher Education*, 53(8), 888–904. (DOI: 10.1007/s11162-012-9260-9)

Strategy Group. (2011). *National strategy for higher education to 2030 (Report of the Strategy Group)*. Dublin, Ireland: Department of Education and Skills, Government Publications Office. Retrieved on July 17, 2012, from http://www.hea.ie/files/files/DES_Higher_Ed_Main_Report.pdf.

Sullivan, P. B., Buckle, A., Nicky, G., & Atkinson, S. H. (2012). Peer observation of teaching as a faculty development tool. *BMC Medical Education*, 12, 12–26. (DOI: 10.1186/1472-6920-12-26)

Surgenor, P. W. G. (2011). Obstacles and opportunities: Addressing the growing pains of summative student evaluation of teaching. *Assessment & Evaluation in Higher Education*, 1–14, iFirst Article. (DOI: 10.1080/02602938.2011.635247)

Svinicki, M., & McKeachie, W. J. (2014). *McKeachie's teaching tips: Strategies, research, and theory for college and university teachers* (14th ed.). Belmont, CA: Wadsworth.

Theall, M., & Feldman, K. A. (2007). Commentary and update on Feldman's (1997). "Identifying exemplary teachers and teaching: Evidence from student ratings." In R. P. Perry & J. C. Smart (Eds.), *The teaching and learning in higher education: An evidence-based perspective* (pp. 130–143). Dordrecht, The Netherlands: Springer.

Theall, M., & Franklin, J. L. (1990). Student ratings in the context of complex evaluation systems. In M. Theall & J. L. Franklin (Eds.), *Student ratings of instruction: Issues for improving practice* (New Directions for Teaching and Learning, No. 43) (pp. 17–34). San Francisco: Jossey-Bass.

Theall, M., & Franklin, J. L. (2001). Looking for bias in all the wrong places: A search for truth or a witch hunt in student ratings of instruction? In M. Theall, P. C., Abrami, & L. A. Mets (Eds.), *The student ratings debate: Are they valid? How can we best use them?* (New Directions for Institutional Research, No. 109) (pp. 45–56). San Francisco: Jossey-Bass.

Tiberius, R. (1997). Small group methods for collecting information from students. In K. T. Brinko & R. J. Menges (Eds.), *Practically speaking: A sourcebook for instructional consultants in higher education*. Stillwater, OK: New Forums Press.

U.S. EEOC (United States Equal Employment Opportunity Commission). (2010, September). *Employment tests and selection procedures*. Retrieved on August 20, 2012, from http://www.eeoc.gov/policy/docs/factemployment_procedures.html.

Uttl, B., White, C. A., & Gonzalez, D. W. (2017). Meta-analysis of faculty's teaching effectiveness: Student evaluation of teaching ratings and student learning are not related. *Studies in Educational Evaluation*, 54, 22–42. (DOI:10.1016/j.stueduc.2016.08.007). Retrieved on April 5, 2017, from https://www.chrisstucchio.com/blog_media/2016/assorted_links_nov_3_2016/Meta_analysis_of_faculty's_teaching_effectiveness_Student_evaluation_of_teaching_ratings_and_student_learning_are_not_related__student_evaluations_meta_analysis.pdf

van der Lans, R. M., van de Grift, W. J. C. M., van Veen, K., & Fokkens-Bruinsma, M. (2016). Once is not enough: Establishing reliability criteria for feedback and evaluation decisions based on classroom observations. *Studies in Educational Evaluation*, 50, 88–95. (https://doi.org/10.1016/j.stueduc.2016.08.001)

Webb, J., & McEnerney, K. (1995). The view from the back of the classroom: A faculty-based peer observation program. *Journal on Excellence in College Teaching*, 6(3), 145–160.

Webb, J., & McEnerney, K. (1997). Implementing peer review programs: A twelve step model. In D. DeZure (Ed.), *To improve the academy* (Vol. 16, pp. 295–316). Stillwater, OK: New Forums Press and the Professional and Organizational Development Network in Higher Education.

Weimer, M. E. (1990). *Improving college teaching: Strategies for developing instructional effectiveness*. San Francisco: Jossey-Bass.

Weinberg, B. A., Hashimoto, M., & Fleisher, B. M. (2009). Evaluating teaching in higher education. *Journal of Economic Education*, 40(3), 227–261. Retrieved on February 16, 2017, from http://dx.doi.org/10.3200/JECE.40.3.227-261

Wentzell, G., Blue, J., & Evins M. (2016, November). Responding effectively to students' feedback from small-group instructional diagnosis. Paper presented at the 36th annual meeting of the Lilly Conference on College Teaching, Miami University, Oxford, OH.

Wergin, J. E. (1992, September). Developing and using performance criteria. Paper presented at the Virginia Commonwealth University Conference on Faculty Rewards, Richmond, VA.

Wieman, C. (2015, February 6). A better way to evaluate undergraduate teaching. *Change: The Magazine of Higher Learning*, 47(1). Retrieved on December 14, 2016, from http://www.tandfonline.com/doi/full/10.1080/00091383.2015.996077   (DOI.org/10.1080/00091383.2015.996077)

Wines, W. A., & Lau, T. J. (2006). Observations on the folly of using student evaluations of college teaching for faculty evaluation, pay, and retention decisions and its implications for academic freedom. *William & Mary Journal of Women and the Law*, 13(1), 167–202.

Wright, A. W., & Associates (1995). *Teaching improvement practices: Successful strategies for higher education*. Bolton, MA: Anker.

Zahorski, K. J. (1996). Honoring exemplary teaching in the liberal arts institution. In M. D. Svinicki & R. J. Menges (Eds.), *Honoring exemplary teaching*. (New Directions for Teaching and Learning, No. 65). San Francisco: Jossey-Bass.

25 Developing a Higher Education Standards Framework

Lindsay Heywood

1. Introduction

This chapter describes and discusses the development of a higher education standards framework (HES Framework 2015[1]) for Australia. The HES Framework 2015 is central to the recently established (2011) national standards-based system for regulation of higher education in Australia by the Tertiary Education Quality and Standards Agency (TEQSA). Development of the HES Framework 2015 broke new ground in educational quality assurance. Lessons from developing the Framework will be of interest to others who may be contemplating a standards-based approach.

2. Historical background

External quality assurance and regulation of higher education in Australia have evolved over three decades. This has been partly in response to concerns about sustaining the quality of education in an environment of markedly increased education of international students in Australia and offshore, significant growth in participation in higher education overall and the advent of an increasing number of private providers of higher education.

External quality assurance of higher education began with peer reviews of universities in the 1990s, ultimately leading to the establishment of the Australian Universities Quality Agency (AUQA) in 2000. AUQA conducted 'fit-for-purpose' audits of higher education providers and audited the state/territory regulatory authorities that were regulating private providers of higher education at that time. While this system was intended to improve higher education, it was not standards-based and AUQA did not have legislative authority.

The growth in international education saw the advent of national legislation (1) including a national code of practice (the National Code), since amended (2), to protect the interests of international students studying in Australia on a student visa. All providers and programs involving international students must comply with the legislation and the National Code (now also regulated by TEQSA).

3. Move to national regulation of higher education

The new national regulatory system commenced in 2011. A pivotal driver was the Bradley Review of Higher Education 2008 (3), which recommended the establishment of a national regulator to replace the multi-jurisdictional system of regulation by the Commonwealth and the states/territories. A period of extensive debate and consultation preceded the change, culminating in the advent of the Tertiary Education Quality and Standards Act 2011 (TEQSA Act) (4), which established:

- TEQSA as a national regulator;
- an inaugural HES Framework (HES Framework 2011) for TEQSA to regulate against initially; and
- a Higher Education Standards Panel to advise the Minister for Education on making and varying (future) standards in the HES Framework.

By way of background, similar moves from a multijurisdictional regulatory system to a single national system were occurring around the same time in vocational education, healthcare (registration of practitioners and accreditation of programs of study) and childcare (regulation of childcare agencies and related matters).

In the context of standard setting, it is instructive to note the multifaceted objectives of the TEQSA Act:

(a) to provide for national consistency in the regulation of higher education; and
(b) to regulate higher education using:

   (i) a standards-based quality framework; and
   (ii) principles relating to regulatory necessity, risk and proportionality; and

(c) to protect and enhance:

   (i) Australia's reputation for quality higher education and training services; and
   (ii) Australia's international competitiveness in the higher education sector; and
   (iii) excellence, diversity and innovation in higher education in Australia; and

(d) to encourage and promote a higher education system that is appropriate to meet Australia's social and economic needs for a highly educated and skilled population; and
(e) to protect students undertaking, or proposing to undertake, higher education in Australia by requiring the provision of quality higher education; and
(f) to ensure students undertaking, or proposing to undertake, higher education, have access to information relating to higher education in Australia.

4. The Inaugural Higher Education Standards Framework (2011)

The TEQSA Act established an inaugural standards framework (HES Framework 2011) and enabled the Commonwealth Minister to make standards within the HES Framework (as a legislative instrument). The transitional legislation provided for an early review of the inaugural Framework. That Framework represented, in large part, a translation[2] of the former (non-legislative) National Protocols for Higher Education Approval Processes that were intended to guide the regulation of higher education that was undertaken by states and territories prior to the advent of the new national higher education regulator (TEQSA). The HES Framework 2011 (5) is now superseded.

5. Interactions in the existing legislative environment

The advent of the TEQSA Act added to an already crowded legislative environment. The inaugural HES Framework 2011, and regulation against it, overlapped in part the requirements of international student legislation and the National Code and some of the requirements of the Australian Qualifications Framework (AQF) (6). The sector had also been exposed to many other significant legislative changes and a series of significant reviews (7).

6. The inaugural Higher Education Standards Panel

The TEQSA Act established the Higher Education Standards Panel (the Panel) to provide independent advice directly to the Commonwealth Minister for Education on making and varying standards for higher education within the HES Framework and related matters. This arrangement enshrined an important separation between the making of standards and their application by TEQSA for regulatory purposes. The Act also required that the Minister must not make or vary standards without seeking advice from the Panel. The independent nature of the Panel and the requirement for the Minister to seek the Panel's advice were seen by the sector as welcome safeguards in moving to the new regulatory environment.

7. Methods

The Panel chose an iterative consultative mode of operation based on the concepts of action research, in which it developed proposals based on its own expertise and research and then took those proposals to the sector and other stakeholders (over 80 groups and individuals) to explain the proposals and to obtain feedback that led to refinements of the Panel's original proposals.

The inaugural members of the Panel appointed by the Minister were technical experts with senior level expertise encompassing higher education, research, executive management, quality assurance and regulation of higher education.[3] Some stakeholders expressed a preference for a representative model for the Panel but the Minister maintained a preference for a small expert Panel. The Panel responded to this sensitivity with a commitment to widespread consultation with its stakeholders (8) and a communication strategy that culminated in fourteen communiques with the sector, three formal calls for comment, over 100 formal consultations with the sector and other stakeholders and over 20,000 visits to a dedicated (now de-commissioned) website. Most of the artefacts from the inaugural Panel's consultations can be found on the current Higher Education Panel website (9).

8. Goals in revising the HES Framework 2011

After an analysis of the prevailing context and taking soundings from key stakeholders, the Panel set itself some initial working goals for revision of the HES Framework 2011. These included:

- have regard to the current standards but nonetheless take a fresh view informed by other types of standards;
- anchor the new HES Framework to the objectives of the TEQSA Act;
- obviate any known difficulties with the style, format, content or utility of the current standards;
- try to ground the revised standards in the usual language and activities of higher education;
- minimise the number of standards consistent with achieving their purpose;

- ensure the new standards continue to be effective for a regulatory purpose;
- foster a decrease in regulatory burden wherever practicable.

Further goals emerged as the Panel's work progressed and feedback was obtained from the sector:

- enhance focus on student experiences, learning outcomes and access to information;
- emphasise outcomes rather than inputs and processes and adopt a non-prescriptive approach wherever practicable;
- design the standards to be suitable for internal quality assurance as well as external regulation;
- foster gathering of evidence of meeting the standards in the course of the ordinary business of higher education providers;
- streamline and harmonise requirements of the HES Framework with related requirements, particularly the National Code and the AQF;
- provide an integrated standards document that includes explanations, elaborations and guidance, such as reference points;
- promote ownership of the new HES Framework by the sector.

9. Standards comparators

In contemplating the form a revised HES Framework might take, the Panel reviewed many styles and types of standards. These included the existing standards of the HES Framework 2011, examples from the International Organization for Standardization (ISO), standards developed by professional bodies and discipline communities, standards for accreditation of professional programs, approaches taken by AQUA and international frameworks for business improvement. The Panel noted in particular the value of a conceptual framework to underpin the organisation of quality frameworks, such as found in the Baldrige Business Model (10), the European Foundation for Quality Management (EFQM) Excellence Model (11) and the Australian Business Excellence Framework (12). The Panel also informed itself about TEQSA's regulatory experiences with the existing standards, including perceived strengths and opportunities for improvement.

10. Conceptual basis for Framework development

As noted above, the Panel was attracted to the concept of an underlying model to provide an organising framework for the HES Framework and to ground the Framework in the ordinary business of higher education provision. This represented a departure from the inaugural Framework, which was developed solely for regulation. The Panel could not locate a precedent for such a model in higher education and set about developing its own, drawing on various approaches from other sectors.

After exploring a number of iterations, the Panel settled on a conceptual model as an initial working tool, as shown in Figure 25.1. The model places the student experience as the centrepiece, surrounded by the actions taken by the provider to deliver the student experience, to achieve its mission and to assure itself of quality outcomes. The broken outline used for the provider acted as a reminder that providers may take various forms and have varying reach, including arrangements with other parties who may or may not be registered providers.

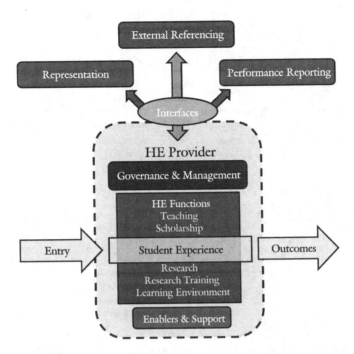

Figure 25.1 Initial conceptual model underpinning development of a revised HES Framework, showing the particular characteristics of higher education that the Panel chose to focus on in standards development

The primary purpose of this model was to provide a systematic framework for the Panel to decide on which elements of the model would be likely to require standards and, if so, what might be the focus of those standards. Through its subsequent iterations, this model ultimately led to the seven 'domains' of the finished framework, which proved widely acceptable in the sector.

11. Impact of an institutional and program focus

An early step for the Panel was to consider the 'unit of analysis', or level of detail, that would be the focus of the HES Framework and its standards. The TEQSA Act requires TEQSA to register providers and to accredit courses (programs) of study proposed by providers that do not have self-accrediting authority. The fundamental focus of regulation is thus at institutional and program level, rather than at the level of individual units of study (subjects) or particular disciplines within courses. Further, the Panel hoped to focus on outcomes rather than processes wherever practicable, i.e. the 'what' vs the 'how'. The upshot of these contextual factors was that many characteristics of the institution would be covered at some level of aggregation (i.e. above disciplines/subjects) and some inputs and processes would receive little attention in favour of the outcomes sought.

A noteworthy exemplar is teaching. This is considered in the aggregate and by outcomes, including learning outcomes, rather than by individual disciplines. The Panel did not see its role as developing a detailed set of technical standards on good teaching and how to teach, particularly at a discipline level. Instead, the HES Framework would apply to all disciplines, but not in specific detail. The Panel saw this as a sound approach. First, it felt that choosing detailed pedagogy lies at the heart of the professional responsibilities of teachers and should not be prescribed by national standards. Second, it was unlikely that a set of national standards could usefully specify the diversity of particular approaches that might be seen across many different disciplines. Nonetheless, the standards can still set boundaries around the aggregate outcomes of teaching, towards which teaching effort can be directed, irrespective of the disciplines involved. In effect, the HES Framework is clear about the outcomes to be achieved for all courses, while leaving teachers and teaching teams free to choose how best to achieve those outcomes for their discipline.

In taking this 'higher level', non-disciplinary, outcome-orientated and non-prescriptive approach, the Panel did not wish to devalue teaching technique for particular subjects, but acknowledged that different levels of analysis are appropriate for different regulatory purposes. By way of a parallel development, the Panel noted significant contemporary activity in developing discipline-specific learning outcomes for several disciplines (13), which it saw as a helpful adjunct to the HES Framework at discipline level.

12. Form and style of proposed standards

The Panel also considered the preferred form of standards statements, noting among the comparators it reviewed that a common form of presentation is one of an 'overarching' standard statement, which is accompanied by subsidiary standards statements, such as this example from the original HES Framework 2011:

> 1.0 The higher education provider is reputable and accountable for the higher education it offers.
>
> 1.1 The higher education provider has education as a principal purpose, with governance and management of its Australian higher education operations located in Australia.
>
> 1.2 Members of the higher education provider's corporate governing body and the higher education provider's key personnel demonstrate that they are 'fit and proper' persons . . .

The Panel considered that this form of standards statements is prone to difficulties such as inconsistencies or incoherencies between the stem and the subsidiary elements (as in this example) and difficulties in interpreting and assigning regulatory priorities among the stem and elements. The HES Framework 2011 contained a mix of standards, some of this form and others where the heading is simply taxonomic, rather than a standard statement. In the light of potential for confusion in the form shown above, the Panel decided that it would propose a model where 'headings' are taxonomic only. This, too, obtained strong acceptance in the sector.

In considering the style for standards statements. The Panel noted a mix of styles among the examples it reviewed including prescriptions, rules, directives, statements and imperatives. The Panel decided to propose standards in 'statement' form, written in the passive voice such as:

> The expected learning outcomes for each course of study are specified, consistent with the level and field of education of the qualification awarded, and informed by national and international comparators.

The Panel saw this as a description of a proposed 'state of affairs' that invites an observer, whether internal or external, to determine whether such a state of affairs exists. The Panel saw this as useful for both internal quality assurance and external regulation. This particular example also illustrates the Panel's preference for an outcome focus and a non-prescriptive approach (i.e. focussing on the outcome required, but not on how the outcome is achieved). This was also supported strongly by the sector.

13. Reflecting the TEQSA Act

The Panel formed an early view that its work should reflect the objectives of the Act (see above), in so far as they seemed directly relevant to standard setting or the use of the standards by TEQSA.

In relation to a risk-based approach, the TEQSA Act (Section 13) enshrines three basic principles of regulation:

- the principle of regulatory necessity;
- the principle of reflecting risk; and
- the principle of proportionate regulation.

These principles typify contemporary approaches to regulation. For example, the Australian Health Practitioner Regulation Agency (AHPRA) (another national regulator, which was established about the same time as TEQSA for different purposes) articulates similar guiding principles (14).

In all areas of our work we:

- identify the risks that we are obliged to respond to
- assess the likelihood and possible consequences of the risks, and
- respond in ways that are proportionate and manage risks so we can adequately protect the public.

Similar principles underlie the so-called 'right-touch' approach to regulation advocated by the Professional Standards Authority for its regulatory roles in the United Kingdom (15).

While these risk-based principles are primarily intended to apply to regulatory interventions by the regulator, the Panel took the view that a risk-based approach would be fostered if it was an integral characteristic of the new standards as well. For each proposed standard, the Panel questioned whether such a standard was necessary, whether it encompassed a risk to the quality of education or another objective of the TEQSA Act and whether it could impose an unreasonable burden on a provider.

14. Standards development process

The Panel adopted a two-step process for standards development (16). First, the Panel selected and defined the characteristics of a provider using both the model outlined in the previous section and the collective judgement of the Panel members to agree on whether standard statements should be developed. Second, the Panel assessed proposed standards against its review criteria, including their linkage to the objects of the TEQSA Act. In other words, the Panel's decision making was guided initially by the question of whether or not a standard should be developed and, if so, whether the proposed standards seemed fit for their intended purpose.

In so doing, the Panel identified existing and proposed standards that it felt were unnecessary because, for example, a standard sought to regulate an aspect of educational provision that was already regulated effectively in another way (e.g. by other legislation or another proposed standard). The Panel favoured standards that focussed on an outcome rather than an input or process leading to the same outcome. The Panel acknowledged that selection of measurable or demonstrable 'outcome' characteristics rather than process characteristics may not always be possible, or practicable, or even desirable in some cases. In assessing whether a standard reflected an underlying risk(s), the Panel formed a view on whether failure to manage such risks could have a material impact on quality. In determining the potential burden of meeting a standard, the Panel drew on its collective experience of delivering higher education and implementing internal quality assurance mechanisms.

The upshot of these analyses was that many proposed standards were discarded (around 30 per cent) on the basis of one or more regulatory principles. An indirect effect of considering necessity was that the proposed standards became more outcome focussed. For example, the Panel chose to place little emphasis on internal management processes in favour of an emphasis on the outcomes such processes aim to achieve. As a result of its assessments the Panel felt that the standards it would propose to the sector were consistent with the basic principles of regulation incorporated in the Act and, in so far as the standards would guide regulation, they would be consistent with and potentially facilitate a risk-based approach to regulation.

Once proposed standards had been considered from a risk-based standpoint, further consideration was given to the other objectives of the TEQSA Act. This tended to expose gaps in coverage of existing and proposed standards, such as the scope and nature of information provided to current and prospective students (see e.g. TEQSA Act Objective (f) above).

The proposed draft standards were also reviewed in relation to their applicability to all providers of higher education, their suitability for any accepted or reasonably anticipated modes of participation or models of delivery, and whether or not the draft standards would be likely to inhibit the diversity of educational offerings in Australian higher education. In addition, the proposed standards were assessed in relation to their departure from the current standards, and the potential impact this may have on the sector.

The Panel also considered whether evidence of compliance is likely to be available, or could be obtained reasonably readily. Such evidence should ideally be available from the provider's normal business operations and internal quality assurance processes. Finally, the Panel considered whether the proposed standards were proportional to the intrinsic level of risk of not delivering quality outcomes and that any revisions to the existing standards were not likely to lead to an unreasonable increase in regulatory burden (noting that revisions could, in some cases, potentially lead to a decrease in regulatory burden).

15. Revised HES Framework 2015

The revised HES Framework 2015 was formally made by the Minister on 7 October 2015 (17). The Framework is arranged in two major Parts:

> Part A: Standards for Higher Education (applicable to all providers of higher education, irrespective of their classification as a provider)

Part B: Criteria for Classification of Higher Education Provider Categories (B1)[4]

Criteria for Seeking Authority for Self-Accreditation of Courses of Study (B2)

Part A is divided into the following seven 'Domains', each of which contains individual standards statements aggregated in taxonomically related 'sections', e.g. Course Design, Staffing (see Appendix for Section headings).

1   Student Participation and Attainment
2   Learning Environment
3   Teaching
4   Research and Research Training
5   Institutional Quality Assurance
6   Governance and Accountability
7   Representation, Information and Information Management.

Part A applies to all providers at all times, irrespective of category of provider (which is determined by the Standards in Part B).

16. Significant changes to the HES Framework 2015

The new HES Framework 2015 includes many changes from its predecessor in the form, style and structure of the Framework including, for example, having the student experience as a specifically identified and prominent section of the Framework. Nonetheless, about 50 per cent of the new standards statements represent a similar intent to that of their predecessors, despite a change of form.

About 25 per cent of the new standards encompass new aspects and about 25 per cent reflect the requirements of the National Code for international students, with a view to harmonising the requirements of the National Code and the TEQSA Act. Substantive changes include:

- increased specific reference to learning outcomes (both coursework and research training);
- inclusion of specific standards for research and research training;
- reduced emphasis on structures and management processes in favour of outcomes;
- increased public information requirements;
- clear accountabilities for internal quality assurance;
- more specific governance accountabilities;
- prescribed accreditation of courses of study by professional bodies, where such accreditation is required for graduates to be able to practise.

17. Dealing with unresolved issues

Notwithstanding the widespread support for the proposed HES Framework, some aspects aroused markedly divergent views. For example, many respondents felt that the Standards should require that all teachers hold a formal teaching qualification, while many others were equally adamant that this was neither necessary nor realistic in the current environment. In the small number of cases of such dichotomous responses, the Panel exercised its collective judgement and explained its actions to the sector (18).

18. Impact of standards on educational outcomes

The Panel saw the new HES 2015 Framework as enshrining good practice in managing risks to the quality of educational experiences and outcomes. Some academically significant examples are highlighted here.

Credit and Recognition of Prior Learning [1.2]: While these standards foster recognition of prior learning, the key tests are that the award of credit is not simply a matter of convenience; it must neither disadvantage students nor affect the integrity of the course of study or the qualification awarded.

Orientation and Progression [1.3]: Mechanisms to detect students at risk of unsatisfactory progress are required in all courses of study, as are mechanisms for assessing the preparedness and needs of student cohorts, to provide early formative feedback and to offer learning support if needed.

Learning Outcomes and Assessment [1.4]: Learning outcomes must be specified, demonstrably consistent with the level of education (e.g. Master's degree) and compared nationally and internationally. All outcomes must be assessed (by valid mechanisms) and grades benchmarked. Learning outcomes must include specific and generic knowledge and skills consistent with the field of education as well as for employment (including for registration for professional practice), further study and life-long learning. Learning outcomes and assessments for research training are seen to be comprehensive and go beyond the traditional prescription of 'contribute to knowledge' or the like.

Course Design [3.1]: Course design must demonstrably engage with advanced current knowledge and emerging theories and concepts and, like learning outcomes, must be consistent with the level of study involved.

Staffing [3.2]: There are rigorous requirements for academic staffing, encompassing both individual teachers and the collective overall staff profile, that ensure academic leadership appropriate to the level of study involved. Staff who do not fully meet the staffing requirements (e.g. experienced practitioners who do not have a higher degree) may teach specialised components of a course, but only when overseen by staff who meet the requirements.

Course Approval and Accreditation [5.1]: All courses must be approved through rigorous academic scrutiny that is competent to assess the design, delivery and assessment of the course independently of the staff involved with the course. All courses must meet and continue to meet all of the relevant requirements of the HES Framework 2015.

Academic and Research Integrity [5.2]: There are rigorous requirements for maintaining integrity for both staff and students.

Monitoring, Review and Improvement [5.3]: Systemic quality assurance and performance monitoring mechanisms are required at an institutional level. These must inform the corporate governing body and should be readily visible to the regulator when needed. This is a key mechanism to reduce regulatory burden.

Delivery with Other Parties [5.4]: Where a provider makes an arrangement with another party for delivery of a course, the primary provider remains fully accountable for quality assurance and ensuring the requirements of the HES Framework are met by the other party.

Academic Governance [6.3]: Rigorous outcomes for academic governance are specified (although without specifying structures for doing so, such as an academic board) and these must inform the corporate governing body's governance and accountability roles.

Information for Prospective and Current Students [7.2]: Providers must give access to information to allow students to be informed participants in their educational experience and to make informed decisions without untoward surprises.

19. Use of the HES Framework 2015 by TEQSA

The new HES Framework 2015 came into operation on 1 January 2017, after being available to the sector for over a year to assist both the sector and TEQSA in preparing to meet the new requirements by 2017. TEQSA has developed extensive guidance material for the sector (19) and continues to develop further material as required.

20. Potential lessons for others

The Panel had many opportunities to reflect on the directions it had proposed throughout its iterative process, informed by extensive constructive feedback from the sector and other stakeholders. Some salient matters are highlighted below.

- Starting afresh: While the Panel used the existing standards as a reference point and a point of departure, it became increasingly clear that the form, utility and adoption of the new Framework all benefited from a fresh conceptual approach to standards development.
- Anchoring to the TEQSA Act: Constant reference to the objects of the TEQSA Act including the basic principles of risk-based regulation (necessity, risk, proportionality) continued to reinforce the relevance and utility of the standards, while potentially reducing regulatory burden for providers and TEQSA.
- Conceptual framework: Formulating the new Framework around the characteristics of educational provision grounded the standards in a coherent framework and avoided duplication and redundancy. Locating the student experience as the centrepiece of the framework was not only well-received by all stakeholders including student bodies, it provided a coherency for student attainment that was absent hitherto.
- Language: The use of language and forms that are familiar to the sector was welcomed by the sector.
- Dual purpose standards: The Panel was constantly encouraged by sector feedback in its decision to write the standards for internal quality assurance and monitoring purposes for providers as well as for external regulatory purposes. This represented a departure from the inaugural standards, which were written primarily for regulatory purposes. An important additional perceived benefit of this approach is that the evidence required for regulatory purposes is intended to be obtained largely in the course of ordinary business rather than being created for regulatory purposes, with consequent reductions in regulatory burden.
- Outcomes focus: An increased emphasis on outcomes rather than inputs and processes not only streamlined and reduced the number of standards, but also invited flexibility for the provider in how those outcomes can be achieved. The Panel (and the sector) regarded the increased emphasis on learning outcomes, including specific learning outcomes for research training, as important areas of focus for the new standards.
- Hierarchy of standards: The presence of overarching standards (Corporate governance & Accountability, Institutional Quality Assurance) that require a provider to demonstrate internally that it is meeting the requirements of the HES Framework provides a basis for TEQSA to satisfy itself that a provider is meeting the requirements of the standards with minimal initial external regulatory intrusion.
- Harmonisation of legislative requirements: As far as practicable the new HES Framework 2015 was harmonised with the National Code for international students with a view that TEQSA may be able to make regulatory decisions in relation to both the requirements

of the National Code and the HES Framework with a single regulatory intervention, a potential reduction in regulatory burden valued by providers and TEQSA alike.

- Information: The new standards require more information to be accessible in the public domain than hitherto, with attendant benefits for students and potentially reduced regulatory burden for TEQSA. For many providers the new requirements will not pose any additional effort, although for some it will mean improving access to information.
- Consultation: Continuing broad consultation was not only crucial to refinement of the new standards but also appeared to enhance 'ownership' of the standards in the sector, resulting in a smooth passage of the proposals through ministerial consultation with the sector.
- Diversity of provision: The Panel was conscious of and agreed with the sector's view that standards should not lead to 'standardisation'. Throughout its work the Panel continued to confirm that proposed standards would be applicable to any provider and that they neither stifled, nor were inconsistent with, any reasonably expected mode of delivery or participation in higher education.
- Working with TEQSA: While the new HES Framework 2015 was developed independently of TEQSA (although TEQSA was kept abreast of developments at all times), in the latter stages of its work the Panel worked closely with TEQSA to ascertain that the proposed Framework would indeed be workable for the regulator. This revealed a number of aspects of the standards that were refined to ensure regulatory effectiveness without changing the intent of the standards.

21. Future developments

The Australian Government has heralded coming reviews of the Provider Category Standards (outside the scope of the original review) and the Australian Qualifications Framework. The international student legislation has been reviewed recently (20), (21). Like its predecessor, the new HES Framework 2015 is intentionally based on the fundamental unit of a course (program) of study, which ordinarily leads to the award of higher education qualification or part thereof. The Panel noted the growing emergence of disaggregated models of participation and delivery in higher education and commissioned (in collaboration with the then Commonwealth Office for Learning and Teaching) a study of the potential impact of these models on future standards development (22). The coming and recent reviews of the regulatory system, together with feedback from TEQSA and the sector on the application of the HES Framework 2015 for regulatory purposes, can be expected to be part of the current Panel's agenda in helping to shape future developments of the HES Framework.

Acknowledgements

The author acknowledges that the work described here reflects the expertise and dedication of the Chair and the Members of the Higher Education Standards Panel and the skilled support provided by the other members of the Executive to the Panel, which was led by the author. It was a privilege to be part of this important development in higher education.

Notes

1 Formally known as the Higher Educations Standards Framework (Threshold Standards) 2015.
2 This was carried out through a consultative process established by the Commonwealth Department of Education and predated the establishment of the inaugural Higher Education Standards Panel.

3 The inaugural membership of the Panel, and the members' affiliations at the time of their appointment, was:

- Emeritus Professor Alan Robson AM CitWA (Chair), former Vice-Chancellor of the University of Western Australia;
- Professor Richard James, Pro Vice-Chancellor (Participation and Engagement) and Director of the Centre for the Study of Higher Education, University of Melbourne;
- Ms Adrienne Nieuwenhuis, Director – Quality, Tertiary Education, Science and Research, South Australian Department of Further Education, Employment, Science and Technology and Member, National Skills Standards Council;
- Emeritus Professor David Siddle, former Deputy Vice-Chancellor (Research), University of Queensland;
- Professor Joanne Wright, Deputy Vice-Chancellor and Vice President: Academic, University of South Australia.

4 Essentially unchanged from HES Framework 2011, aside from minor editorial changes for consistency with the revised standards. The Provider Category Standards of HES Framework 2011 were beyond the scope of this initial review of the Framework.

References

1. Educational Services for Overseas Students Act 2000 (2000). Retrieved from https://www.legislation.gov.au/Details/C2004A00757
2. *National Code of Practice for Providers of Education and Training to Overseas Students 2017* (2017). Retrieved from https://www.legislation.gov.au/Details/F2017L00403
3. *Review of Australian Higher Education (Bradley Review)* (2008). Retrieved from https://docs.education.gov.au/node/38481
4. Tertiary Education Quality and Standards Act 2011 (2011). Retrieved from https://www.legislation.gov.au/Details/C2011A00073
5. *Higher Education Standards Framework (Threshold Standards) 2011* (2011). Retrieved from https://www.legislation.gov.au/Series/F2012L00003
6. *Australian Qualifications Framework (2nd edition)* (2013) Retrieved from https://www.aqf.edu.au/
7. *Higher Education Funding in Australia, Department of Education and Training, Canberra* (2015). Retrieved from https://docs.education.gov.au/node/38481
8. *Higher Education Standards Panel Communique 1: Introduction to the Higher Education Standards Panel and its Operation* (2012). Retrieved from https://docs.education.gov.au/node/37763
9. *New Higher Education Standards – Stakeholder Consultation* (2012–2014). Retrieved from https://www.education.gov.au/stakeholder-consultation-0
10. *The Baldrige Business Model* (1992). Retrieved from http://www.baldrige21.com/Baldrige%20Model.html
11. *Overview of the EFQM Excellence Model* (2013). Retrieved from http://www.efqm.org/sites/default/files/overview_efqm_2013_v2_new_logo.pdf
12. *The Australian Business Excellence Framework* (2004). Retrieved from https://www.saiglobal.com/improve/excellencemodels/businessexcellenceframework/
13. *Discipline Scholars Network – Final Report 2013* (2013). Retrieved from https://vtasnetwork.files.wordpress.com/2014/07/discipline-scholars-network-final-report-2013.pdf
14. *Australian Health Practitioner Regulation Agency Regulatory Principles for the National Scheme* (2017). Retrieved from http://www.ahpra.gov.au/About-AHPRA/Regulatory-principles.aspx
15. *Professional Standards Authority Policy Report: Right Touch Regulation* (2015). Retrieved from http://www.professionalstandards.org.uk/publications/detail/right-touch-regulation
16. *Higher Education Standards Panel Communique 5 – Decision Criteria and Standards Development Process* (2012). Retrieved from https://docs.education.gov.au/node/37771

17. *Higher Education Standards Framework (Threshold Standards) 2015* (2015). Retrieved from https://www.legislation.gov.au/Details/F2015L01639
18. *Higher Education Standards Panel Communique 14: Final Proposed Higher Education Standards Framework* (2014). Retrieved from https://docs.education.gov.au/node/37789
19. *TEQSA Contextual Overview of the New HES Framework* (2017). Retrieved from http://www.teqsa.gov.au/teqsa-contextual-overview-hes-framework
20. Education Services for Overseas Students Amendment (Streamlining Regulation) Act 2015 (2015). Retrieved from https://www.legislation.gov.au/Details/C2015A00171/Download
21. *National Code of Practice for Providers of Education and Training to Overseas Students 2017* (2017). Retrieved from https://www.legislation.gov.au/Details/F2017L00403
22. Ewan, C. (2016). *Higher Education Standards in a Disaggregated Learning Environment Final Report 2016*. Retrieved from http://www.olt.gov.au/resources/good-practice?text=ewan

Appendix

Higher Education Standards Framework (Threshold Standards) 2015

The Higher Education Standards Framework

PART A: Standards for Higher Education

1 Student Participation and Attainment

    1.1 Admission
    1.2 Credit and Recognition of Prior Learning
    1.3 Orientation and Progression
    1.4 Learning Outcomes and Assessment
    1.5 Qualifications and Certification

2 Learning Environment

    2.1 Facilities and Infrastructure
    2.2 Diversity and Equity
    2.3 Wellbeing and Safety
    2.4 Student Grievances and Complaints

3 Teaching

    3.1 Course Design
    3.2 Staffing
    3.3 Learning Resources and Educational Support

4 Research and Research Training

    4.1 Research
    4.2 Research Training

5 Institutional Quality Assurance

    5.1 Course Approval and Accreditation
    5.2 Academic and Research Integrity
    5.3 Monitoring, Review and Improvement
    5.4 Delivery with Other Parties

6 Governance and Accountability

    6.1 Corporate Governance
    6.2 Corporate Monitoring and Accountability
    6.3 Academic Governance

Part III
Developing Quality

26 Staff Development and Quality Assurance

Shân Wareing

Why does staff development matter?

Staff development is a necessity in higher education, and the benefits which accrue from it are multiple and powerful. The need for staff development is amplified by changes in the national and global environment.

In a profession which exists to increase knowledge and skills, and improve career and life opportunities through a commitment to learning and individual development, the organisational and personal benefits of staff development might be expected to need little explanation. Staff development is required for navigating an academic role. It improves teaching by locating practice in theories of learning and best practice, and introducing examples of innovation, including innovations using technology. It results in improved experiences and achievements for students. It helps staff feel confident and successful at their jobs and can fire ambition in staff to improve the effectiveness of teaching, and supports academic career progression. It enables individual staff and academic communities to adapt to and thrive in a changing environment.

This chapter identifies and discusses how staff development is a prerequisite for academic quality, and how it enables improvements in the quality of education. It considers models and options of staff development in higher education and makes recommendations for effective approaches that support institutional goals and long-term success.

Terminology

As the language around staff development varies considerably, it is worth a comment on the terminology, and some of the causes for variation.

In North America, the Professional and Organizational Development Network in Higher Education (POD) includes 'faculty and organizational development' in its mission; the Higher Education Research and Development Society of Australasia (HERDSA) refers to 'professional development'; the Society for Teaching and Learning in Higher Education (SOTL) states it provides 'opportunities for professional development', amongst other activities. The Australian Higher Education Standards Framework Domain 3 refers to 'continuing scholarly activity' and the acquisition of 'skills in teaching, learning and assessment relevant to the needs of the student cohorts involved'. The UK QAA Quality Code talks about 'qualifications', 'development', 'professional development', and 'support for staff'. Another UK national body, the Higher Education Academy, use varied terms including 'support for career development', 'training and events', 'improving learning and teaching', 'professional development', and 'helping institutions achieve their objectives'.

Many higher education providers have organisational development departments, probably within or affiliated to human resources, which may be responsible for staff development across a very wide range of activities, for example including manual handling, health and safety, team working, leadership, equality and diversity, recruitment, probation, as well learning and teaching or educational use of digital technologies. These can all fairly be described as staff development, which is one reason terms such as educational, academic and curriculum development are deployed, to distinguish learning and teaching-related professional development from other staff development activity. However, 'educational development' and 'academic development' can seem aimed at academic staff and therefore to exclude professional services staff who also support and educate students directly, as in the case of library staff, for example. From an HR perspective, 'staff development' may have been replaced by concepts such as 'staff engagement', 'organisational development' or the more ambitious 'organisational transformation'. It is important in developing and deploying these concepts and terms that the specific requirements of academics and their professional development needs are not lost.

In my view, staff development is a transparent, unpretentious and inclusive term which covers academic and professional services, allows itself to be narrowed down (as QAA has done), to include qualifications or other support, and to focus on specific areas of activity. It is therefore used throughout this chapter.

Quality assurance and enhancement

There are many aspects of quality assurance and enhancement in which academics must participate with professional expertise. For example, academic staff are responsible for ensuring equity of academic standards between HE providers and between markers. This requires skills and understanding of national reference points with regard to how to design suitable learning outcomes, how to structure learning to enable students to achieve those learning outcomes, and how to assess whether the learning outcomes have been achieved. This fundamental aspect of the academic role is complex and challenging, requires study, practice and support, often initially supported through postgraduate certificates of higher education.

Staff may find themselves with areas of responsibility relating to the safeguarding of academic standards within a short time of taking up post: participating in evaluations and penalties for suspected academic misconduct, considering academic appeals, or reviewing extenuating circumstances. These are complex areas of students' life at university where errors can result in litigation and reputational damage. In the UK, comparability of standards with other providers and with national expectations is ensured through the external examiner system. Involvement in external examining of courses has become more complex and more significant in recent years, and as a result institutional support and training for external examiners has increased.

Ultimately, staff development is necessary for providers to meet national and international expectations of higher education. The Australian Higher Education Standards Framework (Threshold Standards) 2015 section 3.2 states:

> Staff who have leadership/oversight roles or teach significant components of a course of study must meet certain specified capabilities and qualifications as outlined in the Standards, including requirements for continuing scholarship that informs their teaching.
>
> These requirements include knowledge of contemporary developments in the field they are teaching (which is informed by continuing scholarly activity), skills in teaching,

learning and assessment relevant to the needs of the student cohorts involved, and a qualification at least one level higher than is awarded for the course of study, or equivalent experience.

(Tertiary Education Quality and Standards Agency 2015)

In the UK, higher education operates in the context of a national *Quality Code for Higher Education* (2014). The UK Quality Code 'sets out the Expectations that all providers of UK higher education are required to meet' (QAA 2014) to remain in good standing. The Quality Code regards staff development as fundamentally necessary to academic quality:

Higher education providers assure themselves that everyone involved in teaching or supporting student learning is appropriately qualified, supported and developed.

Quality Code for Higher Education (2014),
Chapter B3, Indicator 4

Higher education providers determine what is necessary to demonstrate that a member of staff is qualified to fulfil their role in teaching or supporting learning; whether this means the individual holds a relevant formal qualification will depend on the circumstances. . . . Staff are encouraged to value their own and others' skills, to recognise that they have a responsibility to identify their own development needs, and to engage in initial and continuing professional development activities.

Quality Code for Higher Education (2014),
Chapter B3 p. 15

Why else does staff development matter?

The extrinsic compliance factor for quality assurance is important, but there are also multiple intrinsic reasons to value and invest in staff development, importantly including the ability of organisations to respond effectively to change in higher education. Higher education must operate successfully in new fields and activities. This cannot be achieved if staff operate only in accordance with previously established practices. Some priorities in these new expectations include:

- teaching for diversity and inclusivity;
- optimised outcomes for students in terms of employment;
- improved quality of life and career opportunities for staff;
- support for a diverse talent pipe-line for future requirements within the organisation;
- institutional ability to respond effectively and efficiently to new demands.

These areas are discussed individually below.

Teaching for diversity and inclusivity

There is an internationally recognised and persistent gap in attainment associated with students' ethnicity, irrespective of entry qualifications and socioeconomic background. In 2013 in the UK (at the time of writing the most recent data), a student from an ethnic minority background entering higher education would have a 16 per cent lower chance of leaving with a first class degree or 2.1 than a White British student (Equality Challenge Unit 2017).

The gap is much wider for Black British students compared to White British students, at 29 per cent. There is a body of research into the causes of this phenomenon and actions to improve the situation (e.g. Berry and Loke 2011; Australian Government Department of Education and Training 2017b).

Institutional actions to address and reduce the ethnicity-based attainment gap may include staff development such as equality and unconscious bias training for staff; reviewing the curriculum for ethnocentricity (bias towards the culture of the dominant ethnic group); a focus on good pedagogic practice such as explicit assessment criteria and latitude about assignment topics and formats; knowing and using the names of all students including those from other cultures whose names may be unfamiliar. These developments are not intuitive else the attainment gap would not be so profound or so persistent. Institutions have to take an active decisions to reduce the attainment gap, and this can only be achieved by educating staff about unconscious bias and inclusive pedagogies.

Another challenge for staff, to be very warmly welcomed from an inclusivity point of view but nevertheless demanding in terms of curriculum design and delivery, is teaching that does not disadvantage students with disabilities. There is an expectation in UK and Australian HE that curriculum is designed and delivered to be inclusive of students with disabilities. There are many straightforward ways in which universal design can be the default approach to teaching (e.g. Burgstahler 2015) but unless you have been taught that way yourself, it is not automatic and staff development is essential to ensuring all students can participate fully in activities and learning. Teachers are usually happy to work towards what is required but they often do not know what to do; central staff development units do not necessarily have the specialist knowledge necessarily either.

There is considerable variation in the chances of a student completing their award successfully and in a timely way, linked significantly to students' socioeconomic background. Scholarship into factors which improve student perseverance and success is extensive (e.g. Tinto 1994, James 2008, Thomas *et al.* 2017). The role of academic staff in supporting student perseverance, success and timely completion is complex, and staff being adequately prepared for their teaching and pastoral roles as academics makes a significant difference to individual students and institutional outcomes. The Australian Higher Education Participation and Partnerships Fund has been established specifically to help address this (Australian Government Department of Education and Training 2017a).

Student employability

The responsibilities of educators have shifted and expanded considerably in recent years, driven by numerous factors including government policies, the costs and funding models of an expanded higher education system, and changing employment patterns. While Stefan Collini and others make the case for the value of education solely for its own sake (Collini 2012), there are many, including many students and their families, who expect a direct link between a higher education award and a well-paying and reliable job. Employability is a scholarly area in its own right (e.g. Dacre-Pool and Qualter 2013); employers are stakeholders who are consulted in the development of UK subject benchmarks (e.g. QAA 2015) and ensuring the curriculum aligns with the needs of employers, industry and practice requires developing a set of skills and approaches supported and accelerated through staff development. In England this has become a success measure for higher education providers (e.g. HEFCE 2016).

Institutional ability to respond effectively and efficiently to new demands

As already mentioned, staff development is partly about responding to changes in the environment. Technology increases the options to learn at a distance, at a time of your suiting, to access different forms of information, to keep different forms of records, to collaborate differently, and to use simulations and models. Changes in employment and demographics create a need for different kinds of education and training. New providers using different models of provision exert commercial pressure on existing providers who need to adapt to retain market share, let alone grow. To respond to all these requirements for change, academic staff need to be well prepared in terms of pedagogy, and other specifics such as the application of technology to teaching. This can only be achieved by high-quality, continuous staff development.

Staff development benefits to individuals

One of the most important and most affective aspects of staff development is that it makes people feel better about their jobs and their lives. It helps people undertake work quicker, better, more effectively, and enjoy it more. It makes it easier to complete tasks and go home at the end of the day. It allows staff to deploy their skills more effectively, and to have the satisfaction of personal growth. It helps staff manage stress and become better at coping effectively and constructively with complex situations.

Staff development is a very important aspect of individual career development, and the ability to succeed in a role and then to progress into position with more challenge and responsibility. It is important to staff feeling positive that they have options, at a micro level for example, when faced with the attainment gap between their students on the basis of ethnicity, or students who persistently flout academic integrity principles however often referencing is explained. It is also important to the wellbeing of staff that if for personal reasons or career reasons they want to work somewhere different, they are appointable and have opportunities elsewhere. For this to be possible, staff need to develop and grow professionally. A lack of investment in professional development for academic staff will result over time in a moribund depressed and negative staff, unable and unwilling to adapt or lead change.

Leadership of the future

Another imperative for investing in staff development is to ensure the future success of higher education. We need strong and ambitious staff at every level of the university, keen to learn and grow and progress professionally, and take on the challenges of leading education. Minority groups are much less represented in senior posts in universities around the world, and there is a salary pay gap based on ethnicity as well as a gender pay gap. Actively ensuring that underrepresented staff have opportunities for development, and that all staff have equalities and unconscious bias training is a requirement for changing this, for a fairer higher education sector, one which offers more appropriate role models for diverse students, and one which fully uses the talent and passion of all staff working in higher education (Equality Challenge Unit 2016).

Staff development makes a very important contribution to a sense of institutional community. It is often said that higher education is very 'siloed', that people tend to work in their own specialist area, possibly unaware of the needs, activities and contributions of other areas. Staff development is an excellent opportunity to bring people together to build a shared understanding of the organisation's strategy, mission and focus. It enables people from different roles and parts of the university to develop productive cross-department working relationships and build a shared language around professional topics. These are vital to an organisation's ability to get its day-to-day business done and to respond effectively to a crisis.

Staff development is also an essential factor in increasing the diversity of senior university staff. Minority groups are very underrepresented in leadership positions. Skilled and able people from minority groups are not progressing up the university career structure in proportion to their representation in wider society and in less senior roles. The consequences of this are multiple. Talent is lost, ultimately damaging the quality of university leadership. It reduces the ability of universities to provide role models for diverse students and junior staff, and the homogeneity of senior management can reduce the organisation's ability to review and amend its processes and structures to be more inclusive. Homogeneity has also been shown to be a risk in terms of optimum decision making (Rock and Grant 2016).

What should staff development look like?

Higher education prepares many students for careers in professions through credit-bearing awards accredited by national bodies. Teaching in higher education is likewise a profession with professional knowledge, skills and values, and like other professions, it develops over time. This is made explicit by Vorster and Quin (2015) considering the future of staff development in South African universities.

Universities in some countries link the achievement of a suitable teaching qualification to successful completion of probation for academic staff. The UK professional standards framework provides a structure for staff at different stages of their careers to map their skills, values and experience, and apply for recognition either directly from the national body (the Higher Education Academy) or their own employer via an accredited institutional scheme. The most frequent offer is a 60-credit postgraduate certificate. Most Australian universities have Graduate Certificates in Higher Education, and the Australian framework has the expectation of an appropriate teaching qualification as mentioned above. A summary of some of the considerations in this area is provided by Southwell 2012.

An initial qualification is preparation for teaching, but it will be obvious even from this brief chapter how multi-faceted and complex teaching in higher education is. Therefore continuing professional development is necessary, as in other professions, to deepen skills and enrich understanding, to keep pace with new developments, and to network with colleagues who can help benchmark current achievements and standards and collaborate for new projects.

In terms of options for continuing professional development, there is a wide range of possibilities, depending on funding and time available. While some are expensive there are also very low-cost options. In Canada and the USA, the concept of the Scholarship of Teaching and Learning (SoTL) is used as a continuum from taking scholarly and evidence-informed approaches to practice, to investigating your own practices and their outcomes to sharing these outcomes locally and beyond. Conference attendance, and presenting papers and posters to peers, is a means to get an overview of current developments in a field. A cheaper option is attending internal or external networks, seminars and events. Higher education providers usually offer a programme of staff development and training. A chance to participate in a funded or major research project is an excellent form of staff development, but requiring less resource and time, action research is another way to explore changes in giving feedback or activities in class (broadly speaking, action research is the process of systematically trying a different way of doing something and seeing if it works). Scholarship and reading are very flexible, personal and cheap ways of staff development, with university libraries stocking educational development texts, and an enormous range of articles and blogs are available online. A versatile and low-cost form of continuing professional development is to ask colleagues, internal and external, for permission to shadow them and interview them about their practice and approach.

What is necessary for effective staff development?

In order for staff development to be effective and successful, it needs to be understood and valued by organisations, managers and individuals. It needs to be integrated into organisational quality assurance, to be aligned and practical for example in supporting processes like extenuating circumstances, academic integrity, use of the institution's online learning systems or activities like online marking. It needs to be in the culture, recognised and rewarded in meaningful ways within the institution, consistent with role requirements and opportunities for development and promotion. It needs to be invested in, strategic, communicated and delivered professionally, evaluated and developed in partnership with participants. It should be driven by the institutionally required and driven by individual interests and career plans. It must be for all career stages.

The significance, and complexity, of staff development is regularly underestimated. Institutional staff development has a cost, which may be direct in terms of funding courses, accreditation or conference attendance, and or indirect, in the time staff give to their own development, and in structuring the organisational environment to value and reward staff development (e.g. ensuring appraisal and progression opportunities identify and incentivise staff development). When budgets are tight, it is an easy area to cut, as the impact on students' experience and students' outcomes probably will not be felt within a year, or even within the term of office of the current executive team. However, failure to invest in staff development is short-sighted – for individuals, for departments and for higher education providers. This chapter has made a case for staff development being the cornerstone of quality assurances and essential for long-term institutional success.

Acknowledgements

With grateful acknowledgments and thanks to Nancy Turner, Director of Teaching and Learning Enhancement, University of Saskatchewan, and Professor Belinda Tynan, Deputy Vice-Chancellor Education and Vice-President, RMIT University. Australia for their contributions to this chapter.

References

Australian Government Department of Education and Training (2017a) Higher Education Participation and Partnerships Program. https://www.education.gov.au/higher-education-participation-and-partnerships-programme-heppp (accessed 15/11/17).
Australian Government Department of Education and Training (2017b) *National Priorities Pool 2015 Projects.* https://www.education.gov.au/national-priorities-pool-2015-projects (accessed 15/11/17).

Berry, J & Loke, G (2011) *Improving the degree attainment of Black and minority ethnic students.* Equality Challenge Unit and the Higher Education Academy. https://www.ecu.ac.uk/wp-content/uploads/external/improving-degree-attainment-bme.pdf (accessed 14/11/2017).

Burgstahler, S (2nd ed. 2015) *Universal Design in Higher Education: From Principles to Practice,* Boston: Harvard Education Press.

Collini, S (2012) *What are Universities For?* London: Penguin.

Dacre-Pool, L and Qualter, P (2013) 'Emotional Self-Efficacy, Graduate Employability and Career Satisfaction: Testing the Associations'. *Australian Journal of Psychology* (online), http://clok.uclan.ac.uk/8529/ (accessed 15/11/17).

Equality Challenge Unit (2016) *Equality and Diversity in Learning and Teaching in Higher Education: Summary of Papers.* Equality Challenge Unit and Higher Education Academy joint conferences: https://www.ecu.ac.uk/publications/ecu-hea-compendium/ (accessed 14/11/2017).

Equality Challenge Unit (2017) *Degree attainment gaps.* Published at https://www.ecu.ac.uk/guidance-resources/student-recruitment-retention-attainment/student-attainment/degree-attainment-gaps/ (accessed 14/11/2017).

Higher Education Funding Council for England (2016) *Teaching Excellence Framework.* http://www.hefce.ac.uk/lt/tef/ (accessed 14/11/17).

James, R, Bexley, E, Anderson, A, Devlin, M, Garnett, R, Marginson, S and Maxwell, L (2008) *Participation and Equity: A Review of the Participation in Higher Education of People from Low Socioeconomic Backgrounds and Indigenous People.* Centre for Research in Higher Education, Deakin Research Online, http://dro.deakin.edu.au/eserv/DU:30006777/devlin-participationandequity-2008.pdf (accessed 14/11/2017).

QAA (2014) *The Quality Code.* http://www.qaa.ac.uk/home (accessed 08/08/17).

QAA (2015) *English Subject Benchmark.* http://www.qaa.ac.uk/en/Publications/Documents/SBS-English-15.pdf (accessed 14/11/17).

Rock, D and Grant, H (2016) 'Why Diverse Teams are Smarter.' *Harvard Business Review.* https://hbr.org/2016/11/why-diverse-teams-are-smarter (accessed 15/11/17).

Southwell, D (2012) *Good Practice Report: Revitalising the Academic Workforce.* Australian Learning and Teaching Council. file:///C:/Users/wareings/Downloads/Revitalising_Academic_Workforce.pdf (accessed 14/11/17)

Tertiary Education Quality and Standards Agency (2015) *Higher Education Standards Framework (Threshold Standards.* http://www.teqsa.gov.au/teqsa-contextual-overview-hes-framework (accessed 15/11/17).

Thomas, L, Hill, M, O' Mahony, J, and Yorke, M (2017) *What Works: Student Retention and Success Programme.* https://www.heacademy.ac.uk/knowledge-hub/supporting-student-success-strategies-institutional-change. Paul Hamlyn Foundation and the Higher Education Academy (accessed 14/11/17).

Tinto, V (1994) *Leaving College.* Chicago: University of Chicago Press.

Vorster, J-A, and Quinn, L (2015) *How Academic Staff Development Can Contribute to Changing Universities.* http://theconversation.com/how-academic-staff-development-can-contribute-to-changing-universities-51163 (accessed 14/11/17).

27 Reflections from a Centre for Academic Development in a Shifting Context

A Case Study

Diane Hazlett and Amanda Platt

Introduction

The major focus of this chapter is to present a case study of our experiences in a centre for academic development, charged with offering and engaging staff in L&T-related professional development and enhancement opportunities. The Centre for Higher Education Research & Practice (CHERP) was established in 2009, within the Staff Development Unit, with its primary role to implement and progress the L&T strategy in collaboration with other stakeholders. This department was initiated by the PVC Learning and Teaching who identified the need for specific academic development, contextually focussed professional leadership and strategic profiling of quality teaching and learning to enhance the student experience. The institutional narrative is situated within an increasingly challenging external and internal metrics-driven context where teaching excellence, recognition and the student experience are the key areas of focus across the sector. Drawing on illustrative evidence from institutional research, our discussion reflects upon six years of enhancement activities and presents our Centre's strategy for the future, underpinned by a more holistic quality model to achieve institutional objectives.

In respect of the importance of engaging staff to enhance the learning environment, CHERP has regularly sought to elicit staff views, expectations and behaviours in relation to CHERP activities and the impact it has had on their practice. Online staff surveys, feedback from events and reflective narratives from members of our community of practice have been utilised to gather this invaluable intelligence. The need for such information became increasingly important following the setting of targets for recognition, when it became apparent during informal conversations with staff that some were engaging with enhancement opportunities mechanistically to fulfil institutional requirements for recognition and/or promotion. We were also aware of differences in the levels of staff engagement within and across schools and that best practice events had a tendency to attract staff with a historic record of engagement with L&T. It was apparent that these issues would challenge the achievement of institutional aims and objectives around L&T, which requires the engagement of a critical mass of staff (Gibbs, 2013). This also signified a need to reflect on the role of the Centre and the efficacy of existing approaches to academic development (Debowski, 2014) to guide the direction of future tactics for enhancement.

First, however, we begin with an overview of the discipline of academic development that considers the field's key challenges and shifting approaches, the importance of institutional research for evaluation of change, impact and the evolving role and approaches of academic developers in encouraging institutional and individual change.

Contemporary academic development

The field of academic development emerged over 40 years ago; its overall goal to is to enhance L&T by supporting and facilitating the development of academic teaching practices (Gibbs, 2013; Roxå & Mårtensson, 2017). It is argued that 'embedding and sustaining change in teaching practices requires academic developers to find ways to engage the vast majority of staff' (Gibbs 2013:11). However, garnering academics' commitment to teaching development activities is an unrelenting challenge that has been ascribed to a general lack of interest in L&T (Martensson *et al.*, 2012), a lack of available time and the perceived importance of research over teaching (Cannell and Gilmour (2013).

The nature of academic development activities has shifted dramatically, with diversity in its position in university settings, structures, roles and activities. Gibbs (2013) provides a useful summary of the plethora of endeavours and the ways that institutional academic development and its tactics for enhancement have grown, changed and progressed. For example, he notes that the focus has shifted from: teaching to learning; classroom to learning environment; and from individual teachers to course teams, departments and leadership.

Internationally, Academic Development Units (ADUs) have moved from a peripheral role to a strategic position within universities. This shift has expanded their role beyond the initial mission of supporting professional development for teaching. In a longitudinal study based on data provided by ADU directors in the United Kingdom, Gosling (2009) acknowledges that while there is diversity in activities, structures and approaches, there are two predominant areas with regard to their role: (1) the professional development of staff in learning and teaching and other academic duties, and (2) a shared strategic responsibility for implementing strategies for learning, teaching and assessment, for encouraging innovation, and for enhancing teaching quality.

Fernández and Márquez (2017) noted the same trend in Norway (Havnes & Stensaker, 2006), Sweden (Roxå & Mårtensson, 2008), Switzerland (Rege Colet, 2010), and Denmark (Kolmos, 2010), where these units have shifted from being technical units dedicated to helping individuals become good teachers to more broadly conceived units that target the organisations, frameworks and infrastructure that connect teaching and learning. This new role for ADUs has also been an object of study in Australia (Holt *et al.*, 2011), where ADUs are being rebranded as Learning and Teaching Centres, and follow this trend in broad terms in various countries around the world (Land, 2004).

Nonetheless, despite the attempts of academic developers and other stakeholders to enhance HE teaching, for the most part, it is proposed that teaching practices have been impervious to change (Mårtensson *et al.*, 2011). Indeed, several studies have highlighted the influential power of culture and context in the development of L&T, whereby academics' behaviours and attitudes towards teaching are influenced by the socio-cultural environment within which it takes place. Knight and Trowler (2000) contend that institutional demands to improve teaching will have little impact in departmental environments that do not support and encourage staff to develop their teaching. Moreover, departmental leadership has been shown to play a pivotal role in creating a context that is favourable to the enhancement of learning and teaching (Gibbs *et al.*, 2008; Billot *et al.*, 2013; Platt & Floyd, 2015).

Gibbs (2013) suggests that the acknowledgement of the significance of culture and environment has shifted the focus of academic development from individual academics to programme teams and departmental leadership.

Case study evaluation

Within the UK, national drivers have been introduced to promote and raise standards in teaching practice and ultimately the student experience – for example, the UK Professional Standards Framework (UKPSF), a nationally recognised framework for benchmarking success within HE teaching and learning support (HEA, 2011), and the introduction of the Teaching Excellence Framework (TEF) in 2016 'to help inform student choice and recognise and reward excellent teaching . . . to raise the profile of teaching globally and promote and reinforce our diverse sector's reputation for teaching excellence' (HEA, 2016). Vardi (2011) observes that these national devices for enhancement have had an important impact on institutions in the way they have been assimilated into institutional strategies and have infiltrated all levels of the organisational context as performance indicators. Academic developers have a pivotal role in interpreting these developments and then encouraging their adoption in their own universities (Debowski, 2014:50).

Griffiths (1993) evaluated her role as an academic staff development officer in establishing the Staff Development Unit at the University of Ulster. Through strategic positioning, this unit shaped a quality assurance culture through a programme of activities, including the Postgraduate Certificate in Teaching in Higher Education and 'Directory of Innovations in Teaching and Learning'. The approach was inclusive, supporting academic and non-academic staff in a more systematic way, by raising the profile of teaching and learning and highlighting the importance of a workforce who are supported by sustained development and training for all staff.

As Director of CHERP from 2014, I was tasked with strategic developments to generate opportunities for staff to engage with enhancement activities around teaching practice, supporting scholarship and pedagogic research. Indeed, as presented in Table 27.1, CHERP has created a range of professional development opportunities for staff to share and learn from each other's practice, such as funded projects, conference and best practice events, development of an internal pedagogic journal and a Peer Supported Review (PSR) process which provides staff with an opportunity to develop and evidence practice innovations with the support of colleagues.

With over 800 academic staff, at the end of academic year 2013–14, it was established that Ulster's overall baseline of academic staff holding HEA recognition was 43 per cent. Senate, Senior Executive Team and Council agreed a target for Ulster for 75 per cent of academic staff to achieve HEA Fellowship or equivalent teaching qualifications by the end of 2015–16. As senior managers, line managers and staff became more aware of UKPSF targets, there has been an increased understanding of the value of professional development, recognition and the benefits to the student learning experience. At the previous reporting point in July 2016, Ulster University held 72 per cent (an increase from 60 per cent in July 2015) of academic staff holding a category of HEA Fellowship. In 2017, there is an overall institutional level of 81.5 per cent of staff holding a category of fellowship, with over 100 Senior and Principle Fellows recognised for their leadership in Learning and Teaching.

Mirroring Vardi's (2011) observation about the integration of national drivers into institutional strategies, since 2013 the UKPSF has been explicitly incorporated into Ulster's L&T strategy along with the setting of challenging targets, in 2014, for staff to gain UKPSF recognition. More recently, senior management has begun to consider the institutional implications of the forthcoming TEF and has since anchored the concepts of 'teaching excellence' and 'student experience' in the new strategic plan as priority areas of focus.

Table 27.1 Examples of CHERP activities that align with Gibbs' (2013) Areas of Activity for educational development

---

Area of Activity (Gibbs): Example CHERP Activity

Developing individual teachers

- Postgraduate Certificate of Higher Education Practice (PGCHEP)
- Peer-Supported Review Scheme (PSR)
- Internal L&T Distinguished Teaching Awards
- ENHANCE internal UKPSF recognition scheme
- National Teaching Fellowship Scheme (NTFS)

Developing groups of teachers

- Community of Practice – membership of CHERP
- L&T champions
- UKPSF mentors
- Collaborative Awards for Teaching Excellence (CATE)
- HEA 'What Works' team enhancements

Developing 'learning environments'

- Learning Landscapes strategic change project
- Active Learning pedagogies
- Active Learning classrooms
- Student-led evaluation of spaces

Developing the institution

- Internal scheme for UKPSF recognition
- Alignment of Promotion Pathways to UKPSF
- Revision of promotion criteria for L&T pathways

Influencing the external environment

- Engagement with HEA, SEDA, LIHE, HEDG
- Expert reference group of international Visiting Professors

Identifying emergent change and spreading 'best practice'

- L&T Development Funding and dissemination through internal best practice events
- Annual L&T conference

Developing students

- Student-led projects
- Collaboration with UUSU
- Students as partners in HEA 'What Works'

Developing quality assurance systems

- Annual Subject Monitoring
- National Student Survey (NSS)
- Teaching Excellence Framework (TEF)
- Academic Development Needs Analysis

Developing the credibility of teaching improvement efforts

- Internal L&T Awards
- Promoting external (NTFS & CATE) awards
- UKPSF ENHANCE scheme for recognition
- Postgraduate Certificate of Higher Education Practice (PGCHEP)

Undertaking educational development research/evaluation

- Institutional research: local level leadership of L&T, and staff engagement with L&T
- International research on impact of UKPSF Fellowship
- Student Engagement research

Supporting the scholarship of teaching across the institution

- Peer-Supported Review
- Internal pedagogic journal
- Dissemination of scholarship opportunities through best practice events
- Online learning and teaching repository called SupporTaL

Adapted from Gibbs (2013)

However, there is a view that managerial targets to enhance teaching can foster compliance among staff (Knight & Trowler, 2000; Mårtensson *et al.*, 2014; Gibbs *et al.*, 2008) that does not necessarily lead to enhancement. The setting of UKPSF targets signalled a significant shift in the learning and teaching context whereby engagement with enhancement opportunities moved from being optional for staff to necessitous in the way that the dimensions of the UKPSF require staff to evidence effective practice through engagement with appropriate enhancement activities, such as those provided by CHERP. In the former 'discretionary' context, staff engagement with enhancement activities grew slowly whereas the target-driven environment resulted in a dramatic increase in the level of staff engagement across the range of learning and teaching activities.

Institutional research

In planning academic development, institutional research was undertaken to delve into and more fully appreciate the key issues that shape and characterise staff engagement at Ulster. Evidence suggests that such tactics have a greater prospect of being effective if they are founded upon and enlightened by 'institutional intelligence' (Zepke *et al.*, 2012:331) about the nuances and undercurrents that exist in their particular institutional setting (Field, 2015). The study began in 2015, a year after the introduction of UKPSF targets and a few months in advance of a significant period of organisational change that has resulted in changes to leadership and management structures, a reduction in the numbers of staff, students, courses and schools, and the revision of the strategic plan and objectives.

Drawing on our own awareness of issues and informed by previous studies, the research sought to investigate three key issues in relation to staff engagement with L&T opportunities, namely: patterns of staff engagement, motivations and obstacles to engagement, and staff perceptions of the school-level situational context around the importance of and support for learning and teaching. The study adopted a mixed methods approach that included analysis of internal staff engagement data for patterns of engagement (2010–16), an electronic survey of the 250 academic members of our internal learning community (66 responded) and 13 interviews with academics who responded to the survey; the latter were transcribed and examined to uncover the key themes, differences and similarities in staff perceptions and behaviours around L&T opportunities.

Gibbs' (2013) reflective article on the shifting character of educational development identifies overarching approaches that can be utilised to develop an institution's learning and teaching. Adapting Gibbs' Areas of Activity for the purpose of this discussion, Table 27.1 illustrates how CHERP's range of endeavours align with these broad approaches. Drawing on interview extracts, the discussion then considers staff perceptions and responses to a selection of key strategies and activities.

The interviews revealed that the stimulus to engage with academic development activities was either an inherent enthusiasm for teaching or a specific extrinsic incitement such as attendance at a CHERP best practice event, a professional body obligation, the PGCHEP course, an inspiring colleague or fears around future employment. However, in all instances these types of extrinsic variables were instrumental in supporting and sustaining engagement irrespective of the original source of motivation.

All accounts alluded to the widespread view that research is held with a much greater esteem and worth than enhancement activities. Several interviewees spoke of how this standpoint is firmly anchored in the mind-sets of some colleagues. Relatedly, what emerges from the accounts is a disparity of opinions and behaviours among staff around the value of

CHERP activities and L&T more generally. The following discussion attempts to illustrate how these differences in staff responses to key CHERP activities offer a valuable insight into how such divergent viewpoints have a bearing on the engagement of staff which is so critical to the achievement of enhancement objectives.

Postgraduate Certificate in HE Practice (PGCHEP)

A lecturer with ten years of experience recalled how as a new member of staff with very little teaching experience he was enthused by the PGCHEP, its assessments and colleagues he met on the course. He spoke of how his teacher-centred and naive approach to teaching was transformed by his experiences on the course and put him on a path that encourages him to continually reflect on his teaching activities so that the 'the learners can learn better and be better'.

In contrast, another experienced member of staff who did not become engaged with L&T until several years in post spoke of undertaking the PGCHEP at the start of her academic career and recollected how she 'was maybe only doing it to tick a box'. Another respondent noted how his opinion of the course conflicted with that of his colleagues: 'The PGCHEP is seen very much as a hurdle . . . I enjoyed it, but the perception of others is that it is a waste of my time.'

Internal best practice events

CHERP offers a series of best practice events throughout the year and these are promoted as an opportunity to disseminate teaching practices and experiences and also to learn from colleagues from other disciplines across the institution. One academic described how she dramatically altered her 'to the point and without any gloss' approach to teaching following an inspirational talk by a colleague from another school:

> It was just the way [the presenter] did that, I just wouldn't have thought of it that way . . . So that sort of changed the way that I present to my students . . . I set them tasks and they do more in class and there's more discussion and we work on case studies and role play. And I think myself and the students have got a lot more out of that.

Another interviewee spoke of how, in order to conform with professional body obligations, she attended these enhancement events with a view to making her teaching practice more effective:

> So I had to find out a bit more about the theory behind teaching. I felt that I had to make it a bit more robust and that what I had prepared was backed up by evidence . . . I think attending the CHERP conference and events has made me a bit more aware.

Negatively, another very engaged individual revealed how colleagues have sought out CHERP events, not for enhancement but rather for the perfunctory purpose of building up a track record of engagement in support of an application for UKPSF recognition and/or promotion. The respondent suggests that such individuals have 'no desire to bring anything to the table or enhance their own practice' but concedes that their mechanistic approach is simply the 'downside of a target' set by the institution.

UKPSF recognition

Attention was drawn during some interviews to constructive developments within the institution, such as UKPSF recognition, changes to promotion criteria and CHERP activities, that interviewees felt had promoted the importance and value of L&T.

> So now I hope that there is a spot lamp on L&T because it's been quite good recently, over the last few years . . . CHERP has a good positive vibe, people like being associated with it.
>
> T&L recently . . . it now has, certainly on paper, a more equal standing with research and that has been a massive cultural shift within the university. And has certainly served the cause to raise the profile of T&L.

The consistent view that research and its outputs continue to be held in higher esteem and worth than enhancement activities is reported as colleagues have been publicly criticised by co-workers for wasting their time on 'worthless' L&T activities. The following extract offers an important insight into how the perceived importance and value of research can influence staff engagement:

> So staff who are not intrinsically motivated will weight it up . . . So if it's making a decision, 'am I spending this week doing x or y?' they are going to do what is going to be valued.

Scholarship of Teaching and Learning

Similarly, diverging views on the value of SoTL and pedagogic research were also exposed. For example, a member of staff asserts that his engagement with pedagogic research has benefited his teaching practice and career:

> I have to admit I have done very well in just engaging in research activity that is pedagogical . . . So that to me is complete validation that this is useful, purposeful and has impact.

However, others spoke of how their peers actively sought to dissuade them from it, with one respondent indicating that he would redirect his efforts towards discipline research if told to do so by someone in a position of power:

> they just think that the [pedagogic] research stuff is 'don't be bothering with that, you are wasting your time'. And it is like 'water off a duck's back', I genuinely believe that what we are doing is good stuff so I just crack on. Unless I am told to stop doing it, in which case I will.

In a variety of forums, it has also become apparent that some staff who would like to engage in SoTL/ pedagogic research have difficulty with writing for this genre, with some expressing that a lack of confidence or fear around writing for this genre being a hindrance to their engagement. This is echoed in the account of a mentor who noted the recurrence of mentees with a 'lack of self-belief, lack of confidence'.

Just as research and L&T are viewed as competing priorities, the interviews exposed a recurring perception among staff that quality assurance and quality enhancement are

separate and conflicting parts of their job role, with the intensification of the former typically considered to have added to staff workloads thereby reducing the time available for the
latter. This issue is evident in the following extracts:

> There is very much a culture change . . . I think Ulster is just very different now and
> the targets on staff are different and there is more pressure . . . And then if you are not
> meeting it, there are reports and action plans. That's what we spend our time doing,
> writing reports.
>
> As academics, we need to have time to think and ruminate and that doesn't necessar-
> ily mean you will produce an outcome there and then. But if you take away the thinking
> time where are the new ideas/concepts going to come from? You are just doing things
> and ticking boxes.

Learning Landscape and Active Learning Projects

As we focus more on the student learning experience, our new campus developments will
offer the opportunity for using a greater range of flexible learning environments, with more
interactive, informal and social types of learning. The institution-wide Learning Landscape
transition project aims to address the wider strategic goal for learning, teaching and student
experience that learning spaces should be 'student-centred' rather than 'teacher-centred';
have the necessary technology to meet student and subject needs; support pedagogic,
multidisciplinary, multimedia formats that engage students and are flexible, ergonomically
comfortable, functional and multi-usable. Cross-faculty Active-Learning projects were completed and evaluated in 2016–17 to determine how these different kinds of learning spaces
and technologies might support collaborative learning pedagogies creatively and productively in practice.

The concept of Learning Landscapes (Dugdale, 2009; Neary & Saunders, 2011) or
Learning Ecologies (Siemens, 2007; Ellis *et al.*, 2008) capture the interrelatedness of learning in the many kinds of physical and virtual spaces in which it can take place.

> The Learning Landscape is the total context for students' learning experiences and the
> diverse landscape of learning settings available today – from specialized to multipur-
> pose, from formal to informal and from physical to virtual. The goal of the Learning
> Landscape approach is to acknowledge this richness and maximize encounters among
> people, places and ideas, defined by envisioning overlapping networks of compelling
> places and hubs which can offer choices to users and generate synergies through adja-
> cencies and the clustering of facilities.
>
> (Dugdale, 2009:52)

There has been ongoing dialogue and developments towards more interactive pedagogic
approaches (e.g. constructivist, problem-based, experiential, Active Learning) demanding
more small-group teaching in flexible spaces, such as SCALE-UP (student-centred active
learning environments, particularly for UG programmes; Oblinger, 2006) and TEAL
(technology-enabled active learning; Dori & Belcher, 2005). With greater mobility, students have a choice where they can work, so new space models need to focus on enhancing
quality of life as well as supporting the learning experience. The main strategic aim of this
approach has been to encourage teams to design learning, pre-empting new environments,
space and technologies which would support more collaborative, enquiry-based learning.

So collaborative learning for us is about moving away from the idea of the teacher as the facilitator . . . it's more about collaboration, learning from members of the class and breaking down the power barriers.

I was interested in the first year curriculum because I think it had been quite some time since it was visited in terms of really trying to amend and alter what we do because of more current understanding of the transitional issues that students face.

I think I learnt so much from them and what they were doing that what I found in my feedback this semester from those students, who've now moved on to the next year, is 'I couldn't have done the essay now, this year, if I hadn't done what you did with us last year.'

Conclusions and recommendations

There is a belief that strategies for enhancement are more likely to be fruitful if they are grounded upon an appreciation of the situational context around teaching and learning (Bamber *et al.*, 2009; Knight & Trowler, 2000; Gibbs, 2013; Zepke *et al.*, 2012). Bamber *et al.* (2009:2) suggests that this institutional information provides an opportunity to refine strategies for enhancement in keeping with the environment in which they are being implemented. They argue that the implementation of policies for change without a grasp of the contextual setting is unlikely to propagate authentic and lasting change. Similarly, Field (2015) contends that academic developers, charged with promoting and supporting enhancement activities, need to be sensitive to the nuances in their institutional setting.

This institutional research indicates that the increasing focus on quality-assurance-related metrics and targets could engender superficial engagement that conceals the true extent of enhancement activity. At Ulster, although 80 per cent have achieved HEA UKPSF Fellowship, a subset of the academic population engage in enhancement activities and levels of engagement are inconsistent across schools. In the past, our role as academic developers has been more coordinative but with new structures, increased staffing and resources to achieve new institutional KPIs, our provision will need to be strategically integral to implementation in practice. Staff engagement is more challenging in a period of organisational change and while goals across new faculty and school structures are changing, the current context encourages compliance. While there are issues around sustainability and changing priorities, local levels of staff engagement are greater in schools with a culture that explicitly encourages and supports staff commitment to learning and teaching. Moreover, the stance of local leadership regarding the importance of learning and teaching will have a pivotal role in influencing staff perceptions of the performance culture at school level.

Given that the embedding of change in teaching practices requires the commitment of almost every teacher (Gibbs, 2013), it is uncertain whether current strategies and levels of engagement are sufficient to achieve Ulster's objectives and aspirations around teaching excellence. Given the diversity in scale and levels of engagement with quality enhancement activities, findings indicate a need to review existing structures, resources, activities and approaches to academic development. We are currently developing and extending future strategic programmes in Curriculum Design, Professional Reward and Recognition and opportunities to innovate in new blended learning environments.

In conclusion, Debowski (2011:21) indicates that 'this responsive approach has the potential to be most influential in shifting cultures, community practice and leadership capabilities'. While this case reflects the trend towards a more strategic alignment to the wider institutional and national change agenda, we must not forget that it takes time to embed rationale, relationships and partnership working to share and implement changes in values, behaviour and practices. While an understanding that collaborative endeavours are more likely to achieve sustained and transformative change, this partnership, community approach has involved the identification and 'problematising' of strategic priorities, with a dialogic approach to engaging academic teachers in conversations about teaching and student learning. 'The result is a trace of learning and knowledge-production linked to genuine experiences made by academic teachers . . . inspired by the scholarship of teaching and learning' (Roxå, & Mårtensson, 2017:103).

References

Bamber, V., Trowler, P., Saunders, M. & Knight, P. (2009) *Enhancing learning, teaching, assessment and curriculum in higher education*. McGraw-Hill Education (UK).

Billot, J., West, D., Khong, L., Skorobohacz, C., Roxå, T., Murray, S. & Gayle, B. (2013) Followership in higher education: academic teachers and their formal leaders, *Teaching and Learning Inquiry: The ISSOTL Journal* 1:2, 91–103.

Cannell, P., & Gilmour, A. (2013) *Staff: enhancing teaching, Final project report*. The Open University in Scotland.

Debowski, S. (2011) The quality agenda: where does academic development sit? In L. Stefani (Ed.), *Evaluating the effectiveness of academic development principles and practice*, 17–30. New York, NY: Routledge.

Debowski, S. (2014) From agents of change to partners in arms: the emerging academic developer role, *International Journal for Academic Development*, 19:1.

Dori, Y. J., & Belcher, J. (2005) How does technology-enabled active learning affect undergraduate students' understanding of electromagnetism concepts? *The Journal of the Learning Sciences*, 14, 243–279.

Dugdale, S. (2009) Space strategies for the new learning landscape, *Educause Review*, 44:2, 51–63.

Ellis, R. A., Goodyear, P., Prosser, M., & Calvo, R. (2008) Engineering students' conceptions of and approaches to learning through discussions in face-to-face and online contexts, *Learning and Instruction*, 18, 267–282.

Fernández, I., & Márquez, M. D. (2017) Educational development units in Spain: current status and emerging trends, *International Journal for Academic Development*, 1–17.

Field, L. (2015) Whither teaching? Academics' informal learning about teaching in the 'tiger mother' university, *International Journal for Academic Development*, 20:2, 113–125.

Gibbs, G. (2013) Reflections on the changing nature of educational development, *International Journal for Academic Development*, 18:1, 4–14.

Gibbs G., Knapper, C. & Piccinin, S. (2008) Disciplinary and contextually appropriate approaches to leadership of teaching in research-intensive academic departments in higher education, *Higher Education Quarterly*, 62:4, 416–443.

Gosling, D. (2009) Educational development in the UK: a complex and contradictory reality, *International Journal for Academic Development*, 14:1, 5–18.

Gosling, D., & D'Andrea, V.-M. (2001) Quality development: a new concept for higher education, *Quality in Higher Education*, 7:1, 7–17.

Griffiths, S. (1993) Staff development and quality assurance. In Ellis, R. (Ed.), *Quality Assurance for University Teaching* (pp. 248–269). SRHE & OUP.

Havnes, A., & Stensaker, B. (2006) Educational development centres: From educational to organisational development? *Quality Assurance in Education*, 14:1, 7–20.

Higher Education Academy (HEA). (2011) *The UK Professional Standards Framework for teaching and supporting learning in higher education*. [ONLINE] Available at: https://www.heacademy.ac.uk/system/files/downloads/ukpsf_2011_english.pdf [Accessed 3 January 2017].

Higher Education Academy (HEA). (2016) *Are you TEF ready? The Teaching Excellence Framework*. [ONLINE] Available at: https://www.heacademy.ac.uk/institutions/consultancy/TEF [Accessed 3 January 2017].

Holt, D., Palmer, S., & Challis, D. (2011) Changing perspectives: Teaching and learning centres' strategic contributions to academic development in Australian higher education, *International Journal for Academic Development*, 16:1, 5–17.

Knight, P., & Trowler, P. (2000) Department-level cultures and the improvement of learning and teaching, *Studies in Higher Education* 25:1, 69–83.

Kolmos, A. (2010) Danish faculty development strategies. In A. Saroyan & M. Frenay (Eds), *Building teaching capacities in higher education: a comprehensive international model* (pp. 61–81). Sterling, VA: Stylus.

Land, R. (2004) *Educational development: discourse, identity and practice*. Maidenhead: McGrawHill Education.

Mårtensson, K., Roxå, T., & Olsson, T. (2011) Developing a quality culture through the scholarship of teaching and learning. *Higher Education Research & Development*, 30:1, 51–62.

Mårtensson, K., Roxå, T., & Stensaker, B. (2014) From quality assurance to quality practices: an investigation of strong microcultures in teaching and learning, *Studies in Higher Education*, 39:4, 534–545.

Neary, M., & Saunders, G. (2011) Leadership and Learning Landscapes: the struggle for the idea of the university, *Higher Education Quarterly*, 65:4, 333–352.

Oblinger, D. (2006) *Learning spaces*. Louisville, CO: Educause.

Platt, A., & Floyd, S. (2015) Preparing for the UKPSF at Ulster: an exploration of the role the academic manager plays in engaging and supporting staff preparedness for professional recognition, *SEDA Educational Developments*, 16:1, 5–10.

Rege Colet, N. (2010) Faculty development in Switzerland. In A. Saroyan & M. Frenay (Eds), *Building teaching capacities in higher education: a comprehensive international model* (pp. 43–60). Sterling, VA: Stylus.

Roxå, T., & Mårtensson, K. (2008) Strategic educational development: A national Swedish initiative to support change in higher education. *Higher Education Research and Development*, 27:2, 155–168.

Roxå, T., & Mårtensson, K. (2017) Agency and structure in academic development practices: are we liberating academic teachers or are we part of a machinery supressing them? *International Journal for Academic Development*, 22:2, 95–105.

Siemens, G. (2007) Connectivism: Creating a learning ecology in distributed environments. In T. Hug (Ed.), *Didactics of microlearning: concepts, discourses and examples* (pp. 53–68). Munster; Waxman.

Vardi, I. (2011) The changing relationship between the scholarship of teaching (and learning) and universities, *Higher Education Research & Development*, 30:1, 1–7.

Zepke, N., Butler, P., & Leach, L. (2012) Institutional research and improving the quality of student engagement, *Quality in Higher Education*, 18:3, 329–347.

28 Appraisal Schemes and Their Contribution to Quality in Teaching

Saranne Magennis

Introduction

It is both with a sense of privilege and of trepidation that any author may accept the opportunity to revisit views expressed in a paper that is now approaching a quarter of a century old.[1] Working at a distance of so many years and from the perspective of a career that has mainly been based outside the UK higher education and quality assurance system, it has nonetheless proved an irresistible opportunity. The task presents a number of challenges: in the first instance, the world of higher education has altered greatly in terms of the relativities of power and relationships of trust and autonomy in the intervening years. The stated territory of the paper – to address the issue of appraisal schemes, their characteristics and their role, in the enhancement of teaching quality, maintains its validity, though the details of approaches in use have changed through the years. The more dramatic changes, however, have probably been in terms of the context in which they operate. Consequently, the approach adopted is to pose a series of questions around what has changed and what remains the same, addressing both the theoretical frameworks at play and the practical solutions in operation. Simultaneously how my own views have changed in the light of that quarter of a century of experience has been indicated.

At the time of writing the original article, the centrality of the purpose of higher education was noted as a context for making judgments concerning quality. In that context I commented on the fact that despite the significant changes in the range and characteristics of the student population, John Henry Newman remained among the standard reference points in relation to the nature and purpose of a university. Whether it provokes laughter or tears, it should probably be noted that the Cardinal is still in the mix.

In the original chapter, the approach taken was to look at the theoretical first and then consider the practical question under discussion – the value of appraisal schemes in the enhancement of teaching in higher education. In reflecting on the paper at a distance of a quarter of a century, I prefer on this occasion to start with the practical solutions, the implementation of some of which have been part of my own work during that intervening time.

Drawing together the threads at the conclusion of the chapter, seeking an appropriate model for the appraisal of teaching in that time and place, the chapter concluded that teachers in higher education were generally in favour of appraisal if it was 'developmental in style and fair in its design and implementation'. The evaluation, in order to have impact on the quality of teaching in practice, needed teacher involvement at every level of its design and implementation, drawing on professional expertise and solving the problem of non-utilization that had been discussed. At the time many approaches to the quality of teaching were under consideration. Identified as essential were institutional commitment to quality in teaching and a variety of approaches to suit a variety of circumstances.

Fundamental to the endeavor was judged to be the establishment of a higher profile for teaching quality within institutions. Indicators of that profile included support for research into teaching in higher education and provision of training, both initial and in-service, signalling that teaching was taken seriously in the institution.

In relation to the final suggestion that 'ongoing monitoring of the teaching performance of each mernber of staff in an institution' offered among the strongest indications of institutions taking teaching seriously, this now seems less clear. While identifying good practice and pin-pointing areas for improvement are valuable, and while reliable information on actual practice provides a basis for building on strengths and remedying weaknesses, there are questions that might be raised about how that information might best be collected and the impact collecting it might have on relationships within an institution.

Looking then in practical terms at what has worked and what has not in the enhancement of teaching in higher education, based on my experience in quality assurance and staff and educational development, and this is unapologetically experiential, my conclusions include that:

- Quality assurance exercises work, in so far as they do work, by creating, even compelling, a space for collective reflection and dialogue among members of the departments and institutions under review, through which matters of concern to that department or institution can be improved. When the time is ring-fenced for that specific purpose, enhancement is possible, and almost guaranteed.
- Appraisal at an individual level, offers similar benefits: time is created for personal reflection and documentation of practice, and for discussion. It is timetabled as an entitlement, with the head of department. An agenda typically covers current achievements and future plans with self-assessment at its heart and with an opening provided for training and support.
- Again, based on experience, if required to identify the most effective development in the enhancement of teaching in higher education, the widespread adoption, both in the UK and in Ireland, of accredited teacher training in higher education would come top of the list.

From practice to theory

In reverse order when compared to the original paper, a small foray into the theoretical is now proposed. At the time of writing the original article, the centrality of the purpose of higher education was noted as a key contextual issue for making judgements concerning quality. Against that background, I commented that despite the significant changes in the range and characteristics of the student population, John Henry Newman remained among the standard reference points in relation to the nature and purpose of a university. Writing today, and through the intervening years, the long shadow of the Cardinal is still present. There is little argument that change has dominated much of the discourse in higher education since the latter years of the 20th century and that the domination continues in this early part of the current century. Despite changes in the language in which higher education is described and the multiplicity of changes broadly based in governmental policy, Newman's idea still inhabits the imagination, although it contrasts with the contemporary reality.

Deem has argued that:

> Until quite recently, the notion that the activities and cultures of universities either required managing or were, in any meaningful sense, 'managed', would have been regarded as heretical. Universities were perceived as communities of scholars researching and teaching together in collegial ways; those running universities were regarded as academic leaders rather than as managers or chief executives.[2]

The new managerialism in question is generally used as a shorthand for the adoption by public sector organizations of organizational forms, technologies, management practices and values more commonly found in the private business sector.[3]

In some ways it unsurprising that the university should have absorbed such activities and practices, especially in the light of government pressures to become more competitive and efficient. Smith and Webster remark that 'the university has tended to absorb and accumulate the changing aspirations – and perhaps also the presumptions – of successive generations'.[4] Adaptation is widely recognized as an effective survival strategy. However, the model has also come to disappoint.

> The community of scholars was once seen as a model of rational and disinterested discourse and thus has come to be regularly pilloried for the proclivity of academic factionalism and internecine dispute.[5]

Any understanding of the university as it exists today must take cognisance of numerous accretions and challenges from the society in which we now live, precursors of which were already present at time of writing the original. Warner and Plafreyman, writing in 1997, offered a list of no less than 41 key issues facing UK higher education, remarking that:

> the contributors have managed to flag up the essential themes of UK HE over the past 25 years, and to identify the likely key issues with which the system will need to grapple over the next 25.[6]

Although the list was compiled nearly 20 years ago, many of the issues seem as relevant today as they were at the time of its writing, and likewise it seems as relevant to Irish higher education as to the UK system in which their initial commentary was made.

Questions and issues that higher education is facing, often for reasons of government policy, regulation or financial constraint, led these authors to an inquiry about the nature and role of higher education and the institutions in which it takes place in contemporary society. Broadly speaking, their list encompassed:

1   the social, political and economic context in which contemporary higher education operates;
2   key dichotomies that impact on the sector;
3   changing perceptions of the student experience;
4   altered understandings of academic work and responsibilities.

The title of Richard Pring's paper 'The Changing Nature of Universities: economic relevance, social inclusion or personal excellence?'[7] offers a useful categorization of the parameters within which contemporary higher education defines itself or is defined. It focusses attention on some of the key debates: the entrepreneurial or corporate institution, serving national economic growth, the engine of societal equality and social inclusion or the locus of personal academic excellence and success. Bearing in mind that higher education comes with a long history, but also acknowledging the reality of change in society and its institutions, Pring's view that there is 'a constant need to find a new synthesis of that which one wants to preserve and that which requires change and development' offers a useful summary of the operation of the adaptative strategy of higher education.[8]

John Henry Newman, already mentioned in passing above, and in the original chapter, remains a reference point in discussions of what a university is. Today, coming from a post-modern commitment and recognizing the social and political elitism of the age in which Newman wrote, it is important to lay the ghost of Cardinal to rest.

Newman wrote *The Idea of a University* in a very different time for a very different society. Based on lectures given by Newman in 1852 in the context of a proposal to establish a Catholic university in Dublin, the book has become something of a canonical work and despite its archaic prose, its sectarian intent, cultural imperialism and its strongly gendered approach it remains a constant reference point in considerations of the nature of higher education up to the present day.

Opinions differ and applications of Newman's work to contemporary higher education vary. In *The Idea of the University: A Reexamination*,[9] Jaroslav Pelikan noted that there is a 'crisis of self-confidence' in the university sector, and uses Newman's *Idea of a University* as a gateway to a consideration of the assumptions underlying university practices today. He declares that Newman's *The Idea of a University* is 'the most important treatise on the idea of the university ever written in any language' (cited by Collini, 2012).[10] Pelikan discusses the relevance of Newman's conception of knowledge for the university today in relation to his perception of a tension between the aims of liberal and professional education. Economic factors tend to encourage students to opt for professionally relevant courses and to seek value for money, as costs of a university education rise. The liberal ideal is easily lost. Newman considered that:

> Th[e] process of training, by which the intellect, instead of being formed or sacrificed to some particular or accidental purpose, some specific trade or profession, or study or science, is disciplined for its own sake, for the perception of its own proper object, and for its own highest culture, is called Liberal Education . . . And to set forth the right standard, and to train according to it, and to help forward all students towards it according to their various capacities, this I conceive to be the business of a University.[11]

From a contemporary perspective, Newman's notion of objective knowledge is problematic for many. Social, political, cultural and personal subjectivities are often seen as embedded in knowledge. Even in the 'hard' sciences, the presence of the observer is acknowledged. Nonetheless, Newman's starkly idealistic statement of the mission of a university is useful precisely because of its definitive quality. There is no fudging. In an age when the language of higher education has become imbued with the corporate language of the business world, this draws us back into one of the major dichotomies about the role and purpose of higher education – a liberal education or a training for the world of work.

However, it must be remembered that the world in question was male and privileged and at least in the case of Newman himself, ultimately religious in perspective and intent. Nonetheless, it is useful to reflect on the dichotomy: should higher education follow the liberal education model or the more practically focussed and professional model? The question itself, in the form that Newman states it, is long answered and courses with a utilitarian leaning seem to have won the day. But the contemporary restatement of the question might well be whether current government policy towards higher education, with its emphasis on the economic contribution that institutions are expected to make, undermines something fundamental in the nature of higher education. Views differ on what that nature might be.

Newman was, however, aware that the practicalities of life and society were important too. Though committed to liberal education, rather than the utilitarian view that studies should have a practical end, he says:

> If then a practical end must be assigned to a University course, I say it is that of train-ing good members of society. Its art is the art of social life, and its end is fitness for the world.[12]

Jaroslav Pelikan is a great admirer of Newman's idea of a university but he differs on a number of points and it is arguable that Newman might not reciprocate the admiration. As Zimmerman notes in her review of Pelikan's book:

> unlike Newman, Pelikan is an exponent of the modern research university, and this leads him to revise Newman's definition in several ways. First, he excises the theological component of Newman's argument, stating, "it is of course not mandatory to share his theological stance if one wants to engage him in dialogue about the idea of the univer-sity" (Pelikan, 1992, p.9). Indeed, there are few nowadays who would share Newman's stance. The Roman Catholic doctrine of God was central to his idea of the university. It was a science and as such a necessary prerequisite to the "teaching of universal knowl-edge" which was the university's sole mission.[13]

Pelikan also disagrees with Newman's conviction that the role of the university is teaching and not research and so his dialogue with Newman's idea is based on an edited version of the idea:

> Teaching is subordinated to research in Pelikan's model, which is based on the nation's top research institutions with their undergraduate colleges, graduate and professional schools, research libraries, and academic presses.[14]

Pelikan's discussion, is thus limited in its application. The elite research universities to which he refers enrol a small percentage of the total student population in contemporary higher education.

Frank M. Turner's edited collection consists of a series of articles on different aspects of Newman's work. Sara Castro-Klarén points to many of the issues that arise from Newman's boundedness within the Victorian attitudes of his time. She notes that Newman was deeply ethnocentric and that civilization in his view meant western civilization, tracing its heritage to Greece and Rome. His views on other cultures, as illustrated by his remarks on Chinese culture, are quoted by Castro-Klarén:

> I am not denying of course the civilization of the Chinese, for instance, though it be not our civilization; but it is a huge, stationary, unattractive, morose civilization. Nor do I deny a civilization to the Hindoos, nor to the ancient Mexicans . . . [but] none

of them will bear a comparison with the Society and the Civilization which I have described as alone having a claim to those names.[15]

Castro-Klarén also identifies a key ideological issue in Newman's work which causes difficulties to the modern reader. She suggests that 'writing is for Newman a creative, autonomous activity and stands in marked contrast to the passive, receptive nature of reading'. This understanding of reading which denies the reader a role in the creation of meaning in the text was unquestioned in Newman's day, but to the contemporary mind the act of reading is interpretive, tentative and undertaken from an individual perspective that brings with it its own history and values. Castro-Klarén is of the view that Newman, and indeed many of his contemporaries, lacked the:

> reciprocity of cultural and intellectual respect within the study of literature, which arises from a mutual recognition of subjectivities of persons from different backgrounds and experiences.[16]

The contrast between Newman's world of objective truth grounded in the divine, in which the role of the academic was to bring students towards a grasp of the true and the civilized, and Ronald Barnett's contemporary explorations of higher education, could hardly be more marked. Barnett has written that:

> A genuine higher learning is subversive in the sense of subverting the student's taken-for-granted world, including the world of endeavour, scholarship, calculation or creativity, into which he or she has been initiated. A genuine higher education is unsettling; it is not meant to be a cosy experience. It is disturbing because, ultimately, the student comes to see that things could always be other than they are. A higher education experience is not complete unless the student realizes that, no matter how much effort is put in, or how much library research, there are no final answers.[17]

Stefan Collini makes a similar point, commenting that in a university setting:

> Undergraduates are being introduced to the modes of enquiry appropriate to various disciplines; what they develop, ideally, is not simply mastery of a body of information, but the capacity to challenge or extend the received understanding of a particular topic.[18]

Theodor Adorno has stated it eloquently:

> Thinking is not the intellectual reproduction of what already exists anyway. As long as it doesn't break off, thinking has a secure hold on possibility. Its insatiable aspect, its aversion to being quickly and easily satisfied, refuses the foolish wisdom of resignation . . . Open thinking points beyond itself.[19]

Richard Pring, in an address to the Institute for the Advancement of Learning, has also reflected on the pervasive sense of change, this time at an institutional level, rather than at the level of the individual student journey, stating:

> There is no 'essence' of university – some fixed and unchanging core of values and activities which are picked out by this word. Universities (or institutions of higher

education) are part of a wider network of social and educational institutions, and this network will constantly be changing in recognition of or in response to changing economic and social factors.[20]

This is chosen as a starting point because of an epistemological and ontological stance, committed to change as fundamental in reality. This stance takes as a delineating metaphor for the realities in which we reside Heraclitus' great image of the river, which maintains the integrity of its reality only through the constant changing of its waters. The second reason is related though distinct – it is a leaning towards the postmodern, as a useful approach to understanding what universities are and what they do in contemporary societies. Understanding what they do is the framework for judging how these activities may be enhanced.

These statements are, of course, made with two provisos. Firstly, neither statement is to be interpreted as implying the concepts of constant change and the orientation towards the postmodern are my 'grand narratives'. Secondly, neither statement is intended to imply that there is nothing of value in previous understandings of higher education. In the context of the continuous change in mission and core values that characterizes contemporary higher education, Richard Pring's view is apposite:

> it is useful to analyse what those core values and activities are at any one time, lest something of value might be lost in the changing understanding of those institutions. There are, perhaps, certain values and commitments which ought to be preserved and yet are being endangered. On the other hand, one should not, in preserving those values and commitments, turn a blind eye to the wider social and economic forces which inevitably impinge on universities, affecting their financial basis or their status within the wider community or the expectation people have of them in terms of their usefulness to the wider society.[21]

Ronald Barnett has devoted the better part of a career to the subject of higher education. In a recent article in *The Times Higher Education Supplement* he stated:

> For 40 years, I have been fascinated by one question: "What is a university?" After all, the idea of the university conjures hopes of human understanding, wise action and communication in and across the world. And yet these ideas have been in difficulty for more than a century. My own experience in working across the sector has both fuelled these interests and testified to the challenges of realising the university's large ideals. To this end, I have written a series of books on the matter, which – doubtless immodestly – have sought to suggest some ideas and principles as a way of answering my abiding question.[22]

Barnett acknowledges that the question is being asked in numerous ways and in various locations across the worlds, he finds that:

> [T]he public debate remains depressingly thin and is marked by a poverty of imagination. For the most part it sidesteps the fundamentals and instead concerns itself with technical issues as to the financing of the system. . . . Where the purposes of the university are seriously engaged, a dominant view quickly becomes apparent: the idea of the "entrepreneurial university" that should not just understand it is part of the global economy but vigorously play out that part.[23]

A market analysis is applied in which the university is portrayed as the producer and seller of knowledge products and services that can give it financial independence, releasing it from financial dependence on the state and, though this is less explicitly stated, freeing the state from its responsibility to fund universities. All of this fits well with the neoliberal drive to impose market mechanisms in public services. The discourse register used in understanding higher education evolves to include terms such as 'global economy', 'competition', 'success', 'customers', 'surplus income', 'multiple income streams' and 'knowledge transfer'.[24]

Barnett characterizes this entrepreneurial university as 'an endorsing philosophy'. By this he means that: 'It notes that the university is caught up in the burgeoning knowledge economy and sets out a mission that further encourages movement that is already under way.'[25] Rather than challenging the *status quo* it, promotes the entrepreneurial university as the only valid model.

This might lead to the view that the debate around the idea of higher education is already over and yet ideas of the university multiply. In a turbulent age, characterized by a rapid circulation of ideas, Barnett offers us the challenge of identifying a structure into which these numerous ideas might fit, a structure that reveals a pattern to the multiplying ideas. He suggests that new concepts can be imagined that might come to have some weight and durability of their own, critical concepts that are also 'feasible utopias' that may support us in finding a way to believe again in the university.

Collini recounts the story of Mark Pattison, whom he says is often taken to represent the opposite conception of the university being a supporter of the research university as an ideal, but who kept a framed photograph of Newman on his mantelpiece to the end of his life.

> British universities have kept a framed photograph of Newman on their mantelpieces for 150 years now, partly, as with most mantelpieces, to show off the classiness of their social connections; partly as a memento of more idealistic days, rather like an invitation to a college reunion; partly to avoid the protests that would follow from removing it; partly just to hide the cracks in the wall they cannot afford to have repaired.[26]

It is interesting to consider whether the cracks are now so pervasive that it is better to remove the photograph and examine the cracks openly as they would seem to be characteristics of the institution rather than blemishes. Higher education is undoubtedly fragmented when compared to the unitary ideal Newman espoused, but that fragmentation may be a positive reflection of a diverse society, a new ideal rather than a failure.

Collini approaches the question of what a university is from a different angle, asking, 'What are universities for?' This is a useful change in perspective, from definition in the abstract to a more practical focus: what we ask of a university and expect of it. He points to a paradox in university self-identity:

> Universities across the world in the early twenty-first century find themselves in a paradoxical position. Never before in human history have they been so numerous or so important, yet never before have they suffered from such a disabling lack of confidence and loss of identity.[27]

Rather than a close analysis of the activities of the university from an insider perspective, Collini aims:

> while being realistic and reasonably well-informed about the contemporary state of universities, to start from further away in order to revitalize ways of understanding the

nature and importance of universities that are in danger of being lost sight of in the present.[28]

In his examination of what universities are for, he states that he is:

> looking for something more than mere statistical or taxonomic summary, something which captures their quiddity as institutions, the distinctiveness of teaching or studying in them, by contrast to a range of other social institutions.[29]

He suggests that, at a minimum, at least four characteristics might apply:

- That it provides some form of post-secondary-school education, where 'education' signals something more than professional training.
- That it furthers some form of advanced scholarship or research whose character is not wholly dictated by the need to solve immediate practical problems.
- That these activities are pursued in more than just one single discipline or very tightly defined cluster of disciplines.
- That it enjoys some form of institutional autonomy as far as its intellectual activities are concerned.[30]

Collini acknowledges that this is a fairly minimal approach or 'a pretty spare characterization'[31] but it establishes a basic framework.

Kavanagh examines the contemporary through the metaphor of the fool from medieval courts. He sketches the history of the university from medieval times as a fool who has given allegiance to a series of sovereigns – the Church, the State, professions, the military and the corporate world. In his view, the contemporary multiversity has a paradox at its heart:

> The multiversity is paradoxical in that it presents itself as a radical institution, when often its conduct is quite conservative. Likewise, it happily depicts itself as a cloister, an ivory tower aloof from the world and yet it readily embraces the desires and wishes of external groups, such as the Church, State, Professions, and Military.[32]

According to Kavanagh's analysis, the university can be understood through a postmodern lens:

> One way of capturing the confused nature of the University is to leverage tropes favoured by the "postmoderns" that seem especially applicable to the contemporary institution. It is at once virtual, reflexive, fragmented, ambiguous, decentred, contradictory, devoid of fundamentals, inconsistent, and multi-faceted.[33]

At the same time, today's university 'is also a corporate conglomerate that is embedded in, dependent on, and constituted by information and communication technologies'.[34]

According to Kavanagh:

> The postmoderns have burrowed away at the institution's foundations and traditions, raising profound questions about ideas such as the canon as "self-evident repositories of enlightenment" (Aronowitz & Giroux, 1991: 15), and the notion that intellectual

knowledge, as interpreted by the academy, should be privileged over other types of knowledge (such as practical knowledge, gossip and folk wisdom).[35]

Kavanagh uses a sequence of metaphors to describe the nature of the postmodern university and to highlight how it diverges from previous visions. He uses the term 'multiversity' introduced by the then Chancellor of the California university system, Clark Kerr, to capture the diversity of activities in major research universities:

> If the liberal university espoused by Newman was akin to a village with its priests, and Flexner's vision of a modern university was analogous to a one-industry town with an intellectual oligarchy, the multiversity is a city of infinite variety, in which there is a lower sense of community but also less sense of confinement. And if there is a diminished sense of purpose, there are also more ways to excel.[36]

It probably does not need a strictly postmodern sensibility to recognize aspects of the contemporary university described as:

> a maze of major fault lines: student v. faculty, professors v. non-professorial teaching staff, academics v. administration, full-time v. part-time, humanists v. scientists, research v. teaching, production v. consumption of knowledge, liberal education v. vocational training, radical thought v. conservative practice.[37]

In such a world it is not surprising that 'some might pine for Kant's university of reason, or the University of Culture', but in Kavanagh's view:

> the contemporary university is perhaps better understood as the institutional manifestation of modernity's ontological uncertainty, insecurity and ambiguity.[38]

Indeed, it seems to exist in a state of ongoing crisis, and at once yearns for an unchanging ideal and a fruitful relationship with wider society, so long as it does not impinge on its freedom to do exactly as it pleased.

Even in the crisis literature, reasonable and rational ideas abound. The context of uncertainty has been discussed by Ronald Barnett in a number of his publications. In his paper 'University Knowledge in an age of supercomplexity',[39] Barnett (2000) considers the meaning of knowledge in the context of the contemporary university. In the contexts of many other social institutions such a consideration might be viewed as esoteric or even self-indulgent. In the context of the university, however, it is fundamental. Historically, the university has defined itself, and been defined, in terms of its relationship to knowledge. It has been a key source of knowledge, as well as a central hub of the dissemination of knowledge across society, albeit defined according to the varied dominant discourse and definitions of society at different times in its history. In the contemporary age this relationship faces numerous challenges and many acknowledge:

> That the university is no longer the sole or even the main source of production of knowledge in society. By definition, the 'knowledge society' (Stehr 1994) is a society in which knowledge is produced in and across society as such.[40]

Barnett suggests that there is a feeling that the knowledge function of the university is being destabilized. At its extreme, Barnett remarks, 'Some, indeed, have come to suggest that we are witnessing "the end of knowledge" in higher education'.[41] This 'end of knowledge' thesis takes, according to Barnett, three particular forms.

> *Substantively*, it is felt that the knowledge sustained by the university has no particular status: it simply takes its place and its chances amid the proliferating knowledges that society has now to offer. *Ideologically*, it is felt that the knowledge for which the university stands lacks legitimacy: it can simply be understood as a set of language games of a rather privileged set of occupational groups ('academics') that reflects their interests and marginal standing to the rest of society. *Procedurally*, it is implied that the university can now secure its future only by marketing its knowledge wares; in the process, its knowledge becomes performative in character and loses its power to enlighten[42].

Barnett agrees that much of this analysis is correct but he disagrees with the conclusion. He acknowledges the need for changes in the knowledge functions of the university though he does not see this as an end to the more traditional approach. This traditional approach, which was in large measure definitive of the university as such, was characterized by three important elements, each of which is challenged in the contemporary world:

> Historically, the term 'university' has come to stand for a *universal* sense of knowledge. 'Universal' has three senses: firstly, that there can be no bounds to an inquiry: in principle, any inquiry is a universal enquiry since it might lead anywhere across different domains of knowing. Boundaries cannot be set *a priori*. Secondly, that knowledge is potentially criticizable by anyone. No one can be excluded from commentating on knowledge claims. Knowledge claims should therefore be open, fully in the public domain. In this sense, a knowledge claim is a universal claim. Thirdly, in principle, a university is open to all in the sense that any exclusion is not arbitrary. The European mediaeval universities were international communities, accepting scholars from wheresoever they might come.[43]

This is reminiscent of, though probably, less negative than Frank Webster's view. Characterizing the contemporary situation as an embodiment of the postmodern, he says:

> The postmodern university is an oxymoronic institution, a collection of differences devoid of distinguishing characteristics and lacking in internal unity. This poses major problems for the standing and practices of the human sciences.[44]

He argues that the nature of the university, one of the oldest institutions in western culture, is undermined in a number of critical ways:

> This article considers three defining ideas of the university: the collegium dedicated to the pursuit of truth, the national institution, and the driver of research. It argues that all such are no longer sustainable and each is undermined by the postmodern university, an institution that proffers simultaneously a plethora and a dearth of ideas of the university.[45]

One might legitimately point out that the ideals of universality and openness would, at various times, have applied to very limited sections of the particular societies of which the universities were part. People have been excluded from engagement in this world of knowledge for all manner of reasons including gender, religion, poverty, social status and role. Nonetheless, in principle enquiry without pre-set limits, public and open to critique and without arbitrary exclusion, in Barnett's terms, or Webster's vision a collegial institution, dedicated to the search for truth, that serves the nation, rather than the interests of a narrow elite, offer useful parameters in which to understand the relationship between the university and knowledge.

The emergence of the corporate university, which is probably the dominant trend in the development of the university in the early part of this 21st century, challenges this ideal at every level. If the corporate university were taken to mean only the advanced educational and training functions developed by large commercial organizations, this might present some challenge to the traditional university. However, the widespread adoption of the corporate model across the higher education sector, where universities have transformed their management so that they are run on 'sound business principles' with students as customers, and the quest for funding becoming the primary role of the President, will doubtlessly magnify the impact of the challenge. Epistemological boundaries will be set in advance. The humanities, may suffer as 'knowledge claims and forms of understanding will be prized so far as they might be felt to have cash value' for a sponsoring company, or in fulfilling the economic agenda set by government. Secondly, when the corporate domain colonized the educational space, knowledge is no longer open to all and research outputs are patented and commoditized for commercial exploitation by sponsoring companies. Thirdly, corporate universities, in the narrow sense, far from being open institutions, are closed to their own employees. The corporate university – in the sense of a corporatized university - must also become more closed due to funding requirements and contracts.

However, the picture need not be entirely negative. Corporatism is only a part of the contemporary world, a world that has progressed beyond complexity to what Barnett describes as supercomplexity:

> The modern world is supercomplex in character: it can be understood as a milieu for the proliferation of frameworks by which we might understand the world, frameworks that are often competing with each other. In such an age of supercomplexity, the university has new knowledge functions: to add to supercomplexity by offering completely new frames of understanding (so compounding supercomplexity); to help us comprehend and make sense of the resulting knowledge mayhem; and to enable us to live purposefully amid supercomplexity. Knowledge, as a pure, objective reading of the world does have to be abandoned. But the university is not, thereby, delegitimised. In an age of supercomplexity, a new epistemology for the university awaits, one that is open, bold, engaging, accessible, and conscious of its own insecurity. It is an epistemology for living amid uncertainty.[46]

Supercomplexity is more than a merely complex situation in which 'the demands before one exceed the resources to meet them: consequently, one is faced with an overload'. Such a situation is manageable if one has access to the resources. Supercomplexity, on the other hand,

> arises under conditions of a conceptual overload: in short, supercomplexity is the outcome of a multiplicity of frameworks. This is precisely what we have just encountered in our reflections on the epistemological hinterland of the university. No longer are the boundaries, or the forms of right knowing clear.[47]

Stephen Rowland explains the term as follows: 'The term "supercomplexity" (Barnett 2000) has been coined to describe the fluidity of academic practices and identities amidst such uncertainty.'[48]

Barnett has examined the features of supercomplexity in his book entitled *Realizing the University in an Age of Supercomplexity*[49] and he identifies four key concepts, contestability, challengeability, uncertainty and unpredictability as central. Further describing the landscape in which the contemporary knowledge is set he says:

> These four concepts are surrounded by others such as change, turmoil, turbulence, risk and even chaos. Together, this set of concepts mark out the conceptual geography of our supercomplex age as an age of fragility (Barnett 2000a). It is an age in which nothing can be taken for granted. In short, all bets are off. It is an age of conceptual and, thereby, emotional insecurity.[50]

Barnett goes on to argue that this characterization of supercomplexity is not to be confused with the postmodern. He says:

> This supercomplexity is not to be confused, we may note, with post- modernism. On the classic definition, postmodernism is to be understood as 'an incredulity towards metanarratives' (Lyotard 1984). Nothing could be further from the situation being picked out here. For, under conditions of supercomplexity, we are faced with a surfeit, an embarrassment, of frameworks; and some pretty large frameworks at that.[51]

This is a defensible understanding of the postmodern but it is an extreme statement of the orientation. A less extreme position with respect to the postmodern would embrace Lyotard's 'incredulity towards metanarratives' with its rejection of the project of modernism, without rejecting the grounded narratives or knowledges of a multiplicity of communities. On this understanding, the surfeit of frameworks, rather than being a contra-indication is precisely characteristic of the postmodern. In arguing that 'what counts as knowledge takes on multiple formations' in the age of supercomplexity, Barnett seems very close to a postmodern sensibility.

Arguing that 'knowledge is not ended but is transformed into multiple knowledges', Barnett maintains the possibility of a meaningful relationship between knowledge and the university while acknowledging that the 'forms of knowledge . . . represented by the university, are now challenged'.[52]

Conclusion

The idea that quality constitutes a central organizing principle for higher education is, in my experience, less clear. The onslaught of a neoliberal ideology, a belief that universities can and indeed must be managed like any other business, with a narrowly defined monetary focus, is probably closer to the policy that lies behind university management today. Societal contexts variously characterized as postmodern, post-truth and super-complex are also part of the mix. Nonetheless, whether because of, or despite all of the above, teaching has developed and the ordinary decent academic generally meets students with the benefit of specific teacher education and a set of technological assets that would have been rare to impossible at the time of writing of the original article. The students whom they meet are generally much more diverse, bring with them a wide range of social and cultural assumptions and experiences than might have been the case 25 years ago, though caveats apply – and there are wide variations in student recruitment across the sector.

Practice in teaching and learning development has moved on significantly as has research in the area of enhancing teaching in higher education. And, lest practice be allowed to uncouple from theory, it is fair to say that diversified understandings of what universities are and do are available to assist us in our comprehension of the teaching task in higher education.

Notes

1 Magennis, Saranne, "Appraisal Schemes and Their Contribution to Quality in Teaching". In Ellis, Roger, *Quality Assurance for University Teaching* (Milton Keynes: SRHE and Open University Press, 1993), pp. 235–246.

2 Deem, Rosemary, '"New Managerialism" and Higher Education'. *International Studies in Sociology of Education*, 8:1, 1998.

3 Ibid.

4 Smith, Anthony, and Frank Webster, "Changing Ideas of the University". In Smith, Anthony, and Frank Webster (Eds), *The Postmodern University?: Contested Visions of Higher Education in Society* (Buckingham: Society for Research into Higher Education, 1997), p. 1.

5 Ibid.

6 Warner, David, and David Palfreyman, *The State of UK Higher Education: Managing Change and Diversity* (Buckingham: Society for Research into Higher Education & Open University Press, 2001), p. 3.

7 Pring, Richard, "The Changing Nature of Universities: economic relevance, social inclusion or personal excellence?", pp. 1–13. http://citeseerx.ist.psu.edu/viewdoc/ download? doi=10. 1.1.200.390&rep=rep1&type=pdf

8 Ibid., p.1.

9 Pelikan, Jaroslav, *The Idea of the University: A Reexamination* (New Haven: Yale University Press, 1992), p. 12.

10 Collini, Stefan, *What are Universities For?* (London: Penguin, 2012), p. 40.

11 Newman, *The Idea of a University* (http://www.gutenberg.org/files/24526/24526-pdf. pdf). Discourse 7, p. 181. Downloaded 20 August 2015.

12 Ibid., p. 206.

13 Zimmerman, Linda, "The Long Shadow of Cardinal Newman: New Ideas on the University". *Stanford Humanities Review*, 6:1 (1998); *Review of Jaroslav Pelikan* The Idea of the University*: A Reexamination* (Yale University Press, 1992); and John Henry Newman, *The Idea of a University*, (Ed.) Frank M. Turner (Yale University Press, 1996). http://web.stan ford.edu/group/SHR/6-1/html/zimmerman.html. Downloaded 15 August 2015.

14 Ibid.

15 Castro-Klarén, Sara, quoting Newman in: Newman, John Henry, Martha McMackin Garland, Sara Castro-Klarén, George P. Landow, and George M. Marsden, *The Idea of a University*, (Ed.) Frank M. Turner (Yale University Press, 1996), p. 325. http://www.jstor.org/ stable/j.ctt1npknj.

16 Ibid., p. 261.

17 Barnett, R. *The Idea of Higher Education* (Buckingham: Open University Press and SRHE, 1990), p. 155.

18 Collini, Stefan, *What are Universities For?* (London: Penguin, 2012), p. 9.

19 Adorno, Theodor W. "Resignation". In *Critical Models: Interventions and Catchwords*, trans. Henry W. Pickford (New York: Columbia University Press, 1998), p. 289.

20 Pring, op. cit., p. 1. http://citeseerx.ist.psu.edu/viewdoc/download?doi=10.1.1.200.390& rep=rep1&type=pdf

21 Ibid.

22 Barnett, "Head in the Clouds, Feet on the Ground". 1 March 2013. https://www.timeshigher education .co.uk/head-in-the-clouds-feet-on-the-ground/422221.article. Downloaded 6 August, 2015

23 Ibid.
24 Ibid.
25 Ibid.
26 Collini, *What Are Universities For?* p. 59.
27 Ibid., p.1
28 Ibid., p.18.
29 Ibid., p. 6.
30 Ibid.
31 Ibid., p. 7.
32 Kavanagh, Donnacha, "The University as Fool". In Barnett, Ronald (Ed.), *The Future University: Ideas and Possibilities* (Abingdon: Routledge, 2011), pp. 105–106.
33 Smith, Andrew and Frank Webster (eds), *The Postmodern University.*
34 Kavanagh, p. 106
35 Ibid.
36 Ibid.
37 Ibid.
38 Ibid.
39 Barnett, Ronald, "University Knowledge in an Age of Supercomplexity". *Higher Education*, 40: 409–422 (2000).
40 Ibid., p. 410.
41 Ibid,. p. 409.
42 Ibid., p. 411.
43 Ibid., p. 413.
44 Webster, Frank, "The Postmodern University, Research and Media Studies". *Journal of Biological Physics and Chemistry,* 13:3, 96–104 (September 2013). Available at http://cjms.fims.uwo.ca/issues/07-01/Frank%20Webster.pdf, p. 1. Downloaded 19 May 2016.
45 Ibid., p. 96
46 Barnett, p. 409.
47 Ibid., p. 415.
48 Rowland, Stephen, "The Integrity of Academic Enquiry: A Keynote Speech for Policies and Practices for Academic Enquiry". April 2007, p. 1. Downloaded 9 September, 2015. Available at https://www.ucl.ac.uk/jdi/research/evidence-network/docs/Stephen RowlandsColloquium07PaperFull.pdf
49 Barnett, R. *Realizing the University in an Age of Supercomplexity* (Buckingham: Open University Press, 2000).
50 Barnett, "University Knowledge in an Age of Supercomplexity", pp. 416–417.
51 Ibid., p.416.
52 Ibid.

29 Developing Teaching Standards

A Professional Development Perspective

Lynnette Matthews and Ruth Pilkington

Introduction

One of the most significant influences on higher education (HE) over the past decades has been a shift to a more consumer-orientated, market-driven environment. Alongside the accompanying trend to market institutional work and HE courses as offering something different, valuable, worth-the-money, or high quality and above average, this has predictably resulted in greater focus on teaching quality and standards, the qualifications of academic faculty, and drivers for making visible teaching and learning excellence. These trends have prompted HE sectors across the globe to engage more with the professional development of academic faculty with respect to their teaching alongside the sustained requirement to research. It has created a tense context for academic practitioners and challenged the work of academic developers.

There has also been a growth in initiatives, policies and national strategies to address this. These are framing teaching quality in HE. Nationally, the UK has emerged, alongside Australia, as a leader in the field, we would argue, purely on the basis of how they have each developed and applied a national professional standards framework. This chapter explores how these drivers on quality, and in particular those constructed around professional teaching standards, are changing the way academic faculty are supported and developed within institutions.

Exploring professional development frameworks as a tool for generating quality and standards for teaching does raise concerns. For example, in preparing for this chapter it became evident that most of the evidence for impact takes the form of individual evaluative case studies. Peer-reviewed articles and meta-analyses on impact highlight the difficulty of arguing a direct causal relationship between good teaching and student learning (Hattie, 2012; Stes *et al.*, 2010; Parsons *et al.*, 2012; Bell & Brooks, 2016). On the other hand, large numbers of national and international studies have explored student learning, in particular the pedagogies and the excellent or innovative teaching practice that influence student learning (Buckley, 2012, 2015; Evans *et al.*, 2015; Pauli *et al.*, 2016; Middlehurst & Fielden, 2016). The conclusions from such studies reiterate the importance of informed, critical and skilled teaching faculty when supporting engaged, interactive, deeper approaches to learning. This argues the value of having high-quality teaching staff informed by clear standards and expectations of what comprises good teaching and effective learning. Within the HE academic developer community an appreciation of these issues and the research that informs them can be observed in the work and publications of, for example, the Staff and Educational Development Association (SEDA), the Higher Education Academy (HEA), the Society for Research in Higher Education (SRHE), and the considerable number of HE journal articles and conferences that are flourishing world-wide.

Whilst, arguably, it remains questionable to assume direct or causal relationships between teaching and learning, this chapter bears witness to mounting evidence that impact is in fact occurring, and that the combination of factors that are reframing teaching standards are also influencing quality within HE institutions. This chapter focuses on the impact of the UK Professional Standards Framework (UK PSF), which is attracting widespread global interest for its value as a mechanism for rewarding and recognising teaching quality and as a tool for shaping professional development to this end (HEA, 2011). The chapter draws on two examples: firstly, the Higher Education Academy's review of over 88 schemes to award Fellowship using the UK PSF (Pilkington, 2016a); secondly, it uses a single case study to exemplify the transformational potential of this framework at the University of Leicester, UK, and how it has reshaped teaching quality at the institution.

The international context of teaching quality

The HE sector has for a long time relied on its academic faculty as subject experts to provide a guarantee of quality learning provision within HE. In contrast, sectors with learners below 16 years of age have tended to adopt an approach of requiring a teaching qualification as a professional pre-requisite. A series of brief illustrations reveal the way HE attitudes towards teaching qualifications have shifted:

1   The NETTLE Project funded under Socrates involved academics from 23 countries. A primary aim for this was to generate a reference framework for teaching in HE (Baume, 2008; Marentic Pozarnik, 2009). The project focused on the competencies of beginning HE teaching faculty, building on the expectations of the Bologna Treaty and addressed the issue of HE teachers not needing teaching qualifications to teach in HE.

2   The Australian National Standards for HE Teaching (undated) have been drafted and trialled across a number of Australian universities. This extremely detailed framework has criteria aligned with professional level (career stage) as well as discriminating between aspects of practice (expectations). It specifically highlights increasing diversity within the student body and the need to provide high-quality teaching within a dynamic and complex sector. Its criteria closely reflect those of UK PSF as can be seen in its seven teaching criteria.

The seven teaching criteria are:

a   Design and planning of learning activities
b   Teaching and supporting student learning
c   Assessment and giving feedback to students on their learning
d   Developing effective learning environments, student support and guidance
e   Integration of scholarship, research and professional activities with teaching and in support of student learning
f   Evaluation of practice and continuing professional development
g   Professional and personal effectiveness

(Australian National Standards for HE Teaching, p. 1)

3   New Zealand's Ako Aronui Professional Standards Framework (2015) provides a culturally situated framework that bridges the UK Professional Standards Framework offering a culturally relevant adaptation so HE providers can support the recognition and development of their teaching. Whilst aligned to UK PSF, it articulates strongly the community-based, active approach of sharing and development characteristic of the Maori.

4   Ireland launched its own consultation on professional standards for HE teaching in February 2016 led by the National Forum for the Enhancement of Teaching and Learning (2015), again reflecting national concerns to shape professional status and standards of teaching in HE.

Finally, in a review of literature on teaching excellence and global frameworks in HE, Courtney's (2014) discussion of global approaches to teaching excellence expands on the above, providing examples of how HE sectors worldwide are attempting to raise standards of teaching and learning. He concludes largely that this drive is still in its infancy, and there remain huge challenges around how teaching quality is being conceptualised and measured. It appears that in many respects the UK PSF stands out as being in advance of other national trends in terms of its influence and formal accreditation of teaching. This makes it an appropriate and significant area to discuss within the context of this text.

Within the UK, the issue of teaching qualifications for HE academics was originally addressed by various bodies, which in 1993 merged to form the Staff and Educational Development Association (SEDA, 2013), whose Professional Development Framework still informs and guides educational development across further and higher education through the SEDA community. After the advent of the White Paper on Education (Dearing, 1997), the responsibility for recognising teaching standards was assumed by the Institute of Learning and Teaching, and in 2006, the UK PSF was launched by its successor, the Higher Education Academy (HEA). The requirement by Dearing (1997) for high-quality teaching resulted in a proliferation across the UK HE sector of postgraduate taught programmes for in-service teacher training of academic faculty. The UK PSF provided a set of standards for accrediting the quality of such programmes and awarded national professional status to graduates from such programmes. This framework was the culmination of a range of funded interventions throughout the 1990s that aimed to develop teaching and learning in HE, e.g. FDTL, CETLs, JISC,[1] and Scottish Enhancement Projects. Whilst these initiatives had varied impact, they changed the landscape for HE teaching and learning in the UK by developing the capacity and expertise of personnel within HE providers to lead and support the professional learning of academic faculty, and they supported scholarship and research in the new field of academic and HE teaching and learning development.

The revised UK Professional Standards Framework (PSF)

UK PSF articulates standards and expectations for those in academic, teaching and learning support roles, and recognises the dual professional expertise of staff: the application of both subject and pedagogic expertise within HE student learning. In 2011, UK PSF was reviewed and relaunched providing four Descriptors for Fellowship based on refined Dimensions of Practice (Areas of Activity, Core Knowledge and Values). This framework could award and recognise the contribution made by faculty to student teaching and learning across an even wider range of roles and levels within HE institutions. A new direction was also established for the HEA in 2011: to act as gatekeeper for standards and nominated guardian of the PSF, assuming the role of accreditor. Between 2011 and 2016, the HEA has developed, piloted and enhanced systems whereby institutions can gain accreditation for institutional schemes to award Fellowships internally for all Descriptors. This parallels the HEA's own national process of individual Fellowship recognition, which involves submission of a written claim that is assessed by a panel of trained peers. Through these developments, over 65,000 academics (Summer 2016) gained recognition as Fellows of the HEA using the UK PSF. The outcome is a twofold approach to recognising and visibly awarding teaching and learning staff for institutions developing accredited schemes: on the one hand, there is the established approach of having taught provision that primarily targets the needs of early teaching academics, and on the other, there are accredited schemes so experienced staff across learning and teaching roles – including those at strategic levels – can gain recognition for their teaching practice contributions, hence raising the standards and profile for teaching across HE providers. Experiential Fellowship schemes are diverse, institutionally and contextually relevant, employing written, oral, online and face-to-face mechanisms. However, they all have to meet standards of quality in judgement and parity aligned to UK PSF and evidence quality assurance in their provision.

Accreditation of HE providers is also being offered by the HEA with institutions emerging globally, e.g. in Australia, the Middle East, and the Americas. The PSF is valued as an internationally recognised, rigorous set of standards that can attest teaching standards, and direct professional development of faculty.

So how has the impact of PSF influenced teaching quality?

The literature suggests teaching and other professional faculty gain significant benefits from engaging in a critical, systematic reflection and examination of practice, especially when informed by scholarship (Evans *et al.*, 2015). Furthermore, research suggests good teaching faculty will benefit student learning (Hattie, 2012). Therefore, the introduction of both professional recognition and an accredited scheme for awarding Fellowship into higher education providers should have a positive influence on teaching, and cumulatively, on student learning. In her analysis of Continuing Professional Development (CPD) models, Kennedy (2005) characterises standards-based models of CPD, coaching and communities of practice models as 'transitional', however the evidence here argues that together they can in fact transform institutional environments for teaching and CPD. For example, the few evaluations of the impact of Fellowships and Accreditation undertaken so far suggest that these can be transformative personally (Eccles & Bradley, 2014), and transformative for an institution in terms of their impact on the learning and teaching culture (Beckman, 2016; Pilkington, 2016a) and their systems and processes (ibid.). This transformational impact is attributed to the process of professional reflection and review of practice by an individual, and how it is informed and developed, that underpins a Fellowship application.

The HEA has also sought to explore impact from accredited schemes and the introduction of Fellowship to reinforce its work. Several studies have been undertaken by academics as a result enquiring into this and, alongside case studies suggesting significant effects from introducing an accredited scheme, claim that the quality, status and practice of teaching are being affected.

Zaitseva (2015), for example, investigated the relationship between HEA Fellowships and student engagement. She based her study in research-intensive HE providers in the UK (Russell Group) using UKES[2] data. Her findings suggested a positive relationship between the percentage of teaching faculty holding Fellowship and student engagement. A follow-on study into rewarding educational leadership in Russell Group institutions (Fung & Gordon, 2016) concluded that Fellowship impacts on student learning because faculty have to think about how their actions impact on students, and how they enhance their practice. This reinforces research from Hattie for the HE sector. Beckmann (2016), working from an Australian perspective, identified significant positive changes in institutional cultures and teaching excellence from the introduction of accreditation into her institution. Drawing on the growing number of Senior and Principal Fellows, who are notable for acting in a leadership and strategic capacity in relation to institutional teaching and learning, Bradley and Eccles (2014) conducted an online survey and qualitative investigation into the impact of gaining Fellowship. Fellowship processes, it appears, strengthen self-awareness and effectiveness as a leader, encouraging excellent practice. Fellowship also appears to develop individuals' appreciation of factors such as institutional policies and culture, and offers a purposeful means of undertaking reflection on leadership.

In those case studies on the subject, for example, Thornton (2014), who evaluated the impact at Huddersfield University, one of the first HE providers to achieve 100 per cent Fellowship, and Crookes (2015), who examined the impact of Fellowship on personal worth for individual practitioners, their attitudes to practice and to the value of a more critical approach to teaching is particularly prevalent and strongly expressed.

A national evidence base for impact of standards

In view of the leadership being offered by the HEA in providing accreditation for HE teaching activity aligned to the UK Professional Standards Framework, it was natural for that organisation to seek further data on impact from the introduction of teaching standards through accreditation. This was possible because institutions with accredited schemes were asked to report on the activity of the accredited programmes for the first time in 2015. Annual Monitoring Reports from 2014–15 were required to summarise strengths and weaknesses, impacts and challenges emerging from the introduction of an accredited scheme for awarding Fellowship into a HE institution. In the first review of such reports (Pilkington, 2016a), 88 accredited institutions across the UK were reviewed and themes identified across reports. In the most recent iteration of this review, 124 institutions submitted reports on internal schemes for awarding Fellowship showing an increase of 50 per cent since 2014. It was immediately apparent from the qualitative analysis of reports that UK PSF is having significant impact through such schemes, especially as national policies introducing reporting measures and student quality measures force institutions to invest in the quality and visible standards of academic faculty.

The review of annual monitoring reports in the UK suggests that the introduction of UK PSF and institutional Accreditation is enacted at three levels:

1 Sector level through raising the profile and status of teaching, and offering a recognised benchmark for quality – this was noted across reports, and was visible in how institutions were using Fellowship to benchmark themselves against competitors and prepare for the forthcoming Teaching Excellence Framework (TEF).

2 Institutional level by promoting learning and teaching conversations, influencing strategies and policies, and raising and recognising the profile of learning and teaching, changing the culture of an institution. This was particularly strong in how reports described the impact of processes introduced for supporting Fellowship such as mentoring, training workshops and retreats. They also describe how communities of practice emerge around Fellowship activities, and through engaging faculty in wider exchanges and sharing of practice. Senior manager recognition and support for Fellowship provides visible, top-down reinforcement of the raised profile and status of teaching. Almost universally, reports link Fellowships and accredited schemes with changes in strategic goals with respect to learning and teaching. Many reports announce HR changes because UK PSF is being incorporated into HR systems and job specifications.

3   Individual level by enhancing feelings of self-efficacy, recognition, reflection on teaching and career, and informing practice. This impact is universal and backed by numerous anecdotes, informal and formal feedback mechanisms, and examples of how faculty showed greater willingness to engage with teaching and learning initiatives.

The above three examples reflect approaches adopted by institutions within similar and related contexts such as the use of Teaching Commons across US and Canadian institutions to encourage teaching conversations; the adoption of Fellowship as a model for promoting excellence through, for example, the innovative 'decamod' approach by Australian National University, which is accredited through the HEA; and reflective approaches to enhancing teaching through course teaching portfolios at Indiana University in the USA (all reported in Pilkington, 2016b). In the next section, we use a detailed case study to show how the University of Leicester as a relatively recent adopter of an accredited scheme, has experienced significant impact and engagement of staff over the first year of implementation.

Introducing an accredited scheme at the University of Leicester

The University of Leicester is one of the UK's older universities (founded in 1921 and gaining its Royal Charter in 1957) and is known for the invention of genetic fingerprinting, its space research and for discovering the remains of King Richard III. Ranked in the top 2 per cent of universities in the world by the QS World University Rankings, the University elected to build on this reputation by establishing a Continuing Professional Development (CPD) scheme aligned to the UK PSF to support the development of teaching practice and, importantly, to demonstrate the professionalism of its teaching staff to students and other stakeholders in the sector. Prior to the University's CPD scheme, the University actively encouraged staff to submit experienced-based applications to the HEA for the award of Fellowship. The University also provided a postgraduate teaching qualification for new and inexperienced early-career academics, which was HEA-accredited to Descriptor 2 of the UK PSF. The decision to implement an internal CPD scheme was taken in July 2014 when it was agreed that having such a CPD scheme would enable the University to take a more holistic approach in providing progression pathways for all teaching and learning support staff. It was envisioned that this scheme would align with national requirements, standards and sector-wide developments and be tailored in ways which reflected the University's strategic priorities, not least, increasing the proportion of teaching staff with a recognised teaching award. This was identified as a key performance indicator in the University's Learning Strategy.

The Scheme: PEERS

The resulting CPD scheme – the Professional Educational Excellence Recognition Scheme (PEERS) – was accredited by the HEA in August 2015 for all the Descriptors of the UK PSF. It provides a Programme and Experiential Route. The Programme Route includes a suite of training that extends previous provision to include part-time tutors as well as early-career academics and professional services staff. This provision was aligned to Descriptors 1 and 2 of the UK PSF and HEA-accredited for the awards of Associate Fellow and Fellow. In addition, the non-credit- bearing introductory course for teaching aimed at Graduate Teaching Assistants (GTAs) became mandatory and was developed to offer clear progression for these part-time tutors to embark on the credit-bearing programme for Descriptor 1. The

Experiential Route replaced the need for experienced faculty to apply directly to the HEA. Similar to the HEA process, applicants submit a written application with references from colleagues. These are assessed by panels of HEA Fellowship holders from across the University. In addition, and a distinctive feature of the process, is the requirement of a two-year CPD plan to promote meaningful engagement in developing practice beyond the Fellowship awarded. The CPD plan is required for both the Experiential and Programme Routes so that staff can demonstrate their intentions to remain in good standing.

Assuring the quality of the Scheme

PEERS is co-ordinated by a team of three academic developers. They deliver the provision for the Programme Route, provide writing retreats for the Experiential Route, offer mentoring support to applicants and assessors as well as internally moderating judgements through chairing the assessment panels. The team members do not judge individual applications but ensure rigour and consistency in the decision-making process. Besides the external examiner for the Programme Route, an external examiner has been appointed for the Experiential Route. This examiner oversees the appropriateness of Fellowship judgements and takes part in some of the panels. Assessors meet face to face after individually reviewing their panel's allocated applications. At the panel meetings, assessors discuss each application against the criteria for the Descriptors of the UK PSF. Such discussions promote a shared understanding and are particularly important for on-going training of new assessors to the scheme.

Assessors for the first submission deadline were recruited from the University's pool of HEA Fellowship holders that had mentored colleagues applying directly to the HEA. Twenty volunteers, primarily Senior Fellows, came forward and training was undertaken by the HEA. These assessors have since become leaders for the newer recruits, which include successful applicants and PG Cert programme alumni. The newer assessors' confidence has grown through shadowing and discussing applications during the panel meetings with the lead assessors and the academic developers chairing the panels. In total, 58 assessors are currently involved in the assessment process. This number is high and is comparable to the total of HEA assessors. In order to assure consistency of judgements, the University is maintaining this number rather than recruiting further.

Levels of activity

At the time of writing, PEERS has been in operation for just over a year. Part-time tutors, who support learning, have welcomed the opportunity to undertake a credit-bearing programme to gain recognition for their practice. This interest is predicted to double the number of participants studying part of, or the full, postgraduate teaching qualification compared to previous years. However, it is the level of activity through the Experiential Route that has been the most impressive. Whilst the number of applications submitted to the HEA has steadily increased since from 19 in 2012 to 49 in 2014, the number of applications submitted through the Experiential Route from October 2015 to September 2016 was 205. Clearly, this is a significant increase in activity across the University.

The University completed its first HEA Annual Monitoring Report in April 2016 and whilst there have been three submission dates during PEERS' first year, only successful applications from the January deadline were counted in the report. This first call had the least number of applications with 34 Fellowships awarded in total and yet, figures presented by the HEA to each participating HE provider would suggest that: the number of successful applications for Senior Fellowship for this one PEERS submission exceeded the average for similar pre-92 institutions for the year and was just slightly below the sector average; the number of successful Fellow applications were only three short of the sector average. There was, however, a smaller number of Associate Fellowships awarded through the PEERS Experiential Route. This is because many part-time tutors pursue the Programme Route, and experienced staff are encouraged to apply for the category of Fellowship which accurately describes their teaching role, rather than the more easily achievable Associate Fellowship.

Whilst the University is still working towards its key performance indicator, engagement has been considerable in such a short time. Encouraging staff to engage with the process to meet the target has not just been top-down by senior management: PEERS assessors and successful applicants champion the scheme in their departments by highlighting the benefits of embarking on the process, both for recognition and for developing teaching practice. Following each submission round, the University holds a special event to celebrate achievements, acknowledge the work of the assessors, and provide networking opportunities to share good and innovative practice across the University.

Impact on practice

Throughout the year applicants and the assessors were asked to evaluate their experiences of PEERS. Applicants commented on the process of preparing their application and the impact it had on their teaching, and assessors reflected on how considering applications has helped them to develop their practice.

Many of the applicants that submitted for the first round were early adopters and recognised the value of reflective practice. As the scheme gained momentum, however, some of the later applicants were expecting a 'tick box' exercise and consequently, were surprised at the usefulness of the process:

> To be quite honest I thought it would be a monstrous waste of my time but actually it made me think quite deeply about the way I teach and has prompted me to make changes to my own teaching, as well as prompting me to address this at a department-wide level.
>
> (Senior Lecturer, Chemistry)

For some very experienced staff, the PEERS process was the first structured opportunity to engage in professional development because, either taught provision had not been available during their early career, or was not deemed necessary for their role:

> I have never undertaken any formal scheme for teacher training in Higher Education, so my teaching practice has evolved over the years through a process of trial and error. Preparing the application has given me a deeper understanding as well as the language for articulating why things worked and didn't work. Applying for Senior Fellowship has made me enjoy teaching again, and given me a renewed sense of the broader purpose and value of Higher Education teaching, which has enthused me to improve my own practice and continue helping others in my department and the wider discipline to achieve excellence.
>
> (Lecturer, Geography)

Without a doubt, preparing my application has been incredibly helpful for my teaching. The opportunity to step back, reflect, pause for thought and plan the next steps is something I am unlikely to have done without this opportunity to apply for Senior Fellowship via PEERS. Furthermore, the support structures and resources put in place, along with the thorough nature of the application process ensured this was an extremely worthwhile experience.

(Manager, Professional Services)

These experiences would concur with the findings of Crookes (2015), outlined above, that academics have appreciated the opportunity to take a critical approach to their teaching. It is also worth noting that the reflective process motivated applicants to 'enjoy' teaching again. These experiences were not unique to applicants; being involved in the assessment process also encouraged assessors to consider their impact on student learning and how they might enhance their practice:

I've been forced to think about what represents good learning and teaching, about how it can be evaluated, and about how that evaluation can – and should – be used to improve practice. I've benefited from discussing these things with colleagues as part of the PEERS panels, and by reading about new approaches in a range of disciplines in the applications.

(Senior Fellow, Genetics)

Other reported benefits of being an assessor included meeting other Fellowship holders from across the University and using the scheme to maintain their own good standing as Fellowship holders by continuing to engage with the UK PSF:

On a personal level, I've made some very useful internal connections, undertaken some excellent CPD, learned more about this aspect of the HEA, and been able to encourage a number of staff here to consider accreditation.

(Senior Fellow, Professional Services)

There is a strong ethos behind PEERS of peers supporting other peers, and either through the feedback process or during the celebration event, applicants are invited to join networks or working groups as interests or notable projects outlined in applications have surfaced. Additionally, many of the assessors have also become involved in mentoring early-career academics following the Programme Route of PEERS to maintain their good standing or to collect evidence for a future Senior Fellowship application. It has been reported that there are also discussions in departments about methods for assessing the effectiveness of learning and teaching practice as staff have been through the PEERS process. As noted by Pilkington (2016a), communities of practice appear to be emerging across the institution.

To date, only 60 per cent of successful applicants have counted in the drive to increase the percentage of teaching staff with a teaching award aligned to the UK PSF. Whilst this has meant slower progress in meeting the University's target, the fact that the remaining 40 per cent did not need to acquire Fellowship – either because they already held a different category of Fellowship, or have contracts which are not counted in the data – is testimony to how the status of teaching has been raised across the sector and individuals are embracing and valuing recognition, reiterating findings by Pilkington (2016a).

Conclusion

The chapter shows how within one nation the introduction of teaching standards can have a profound effect on teaching and how it is profiled within the sector. The multi-pronged drive to quality of teaching in the UK HE sector described here has in fact cumulatively influenced the reshaping of HE learning and teaching: no one intervention could have achieved so much. The mixture of being required to visibly and publicly account for teaching quality, accompanied by market changes and the introduction of a framework to award teaching status, have together resulted in this massive shift in HE.

Accompanied by wider national recognition of teaching excellence (National Teaching Fellowship programmes) and the recently introduced Teaching Excellence Framework for the UK (2016), the introduction of a national professional standards framework has prompted institutions to re-evaluate and re-profile teaching within HE practice, changing the landscape and environment for how academic developers are supporting and developing staff. These activities acquire institutional momentum and value where profiled as professional development of teaching standards.

Recommendations

The chapter recommends that:

- In the first instance, organisations should adopt responses to teaching standards that are cultural as well as systematised from the outset when considering how to approach teaching standards from a professional developmental perspective.
- Learning from the example of how the UK HE sector has responded to the introduction of professional teaching standards, the importance of having a strong, nationally and internationally recognised framework to recognise and promote teaching quality cannot be underestimated.
- Formal opportunities for learning at national level should be facilitated, for example, schemes in the UK have to be re-accredited by the Higher Education Academy every three years (normally) which presents an opportunity for evaluation and revision, and annual monitoring provides a tool for exchange of ideas and experience.

The case study adds detail and evidence as to how such change is realised in the implementation and makes the following recommendations to academic developers, who might be planning such a scheme, which include:

- Having discussions with other academic developers already operating a scheme provides valuable insights drawing on their experiences. Insights may embrace additional elements for evaluating teaching standards besides the written claim, such as accommodating the role played by dialogue and reflection for professional learning, and how the judgement process is operationalised. This reinforces the value of national professional bodies and networks too.
- Considering how assessors will be recruited, trained and supported. They become a resource for encouraging quality and exchange. Ideally, assessors should have prior experience of mentoring colleagues.
- Ensure that the judgement process is robust. In the UK, the HEA requires the appointment of an external examiner to moderate decisions and report on the quality assurance

and enhancement processes. In addition, academic developers should consider processes for maintaining consistency and quality of internally moderated decisions of their assessment panels.

- Developers could highlight to colleagues how mentoring and assessing Fellowship activity indicate professional good standing and also provide opportunities to learn from other disciplines in teaching development – especially if assessors meet face to face when making judgements.
- Articulating reflective practice may be a new skill for many individuals so a strong and extensive system of mentoring is crucial for supporting and enhancing teaching quality and dialogue. Providing a nurturing system is invaluable for fostering champions to encourage more faculty engagement within departments.
- And last but not least, the work of assessors and the achievements of applicants should be celebrated. One way that is widely adopted and exemplified at the University of Leicester is a series of celebration events to which assessors and successful applicants are invited. At these events applicants, evidencing innovative practice in their applications, are awarded certificates of merit and asked to share their practice. Some institutions present pins/badges to successful applicants.

Notes

1 FDTL – fund for developing teaching and learning; CETLs – Centres for Excellence in Teaching and Learning; JISC – Joint Information Systems Committee.
2 UKES – UK Engagement Survey. This surveys student engagement in HE.

References

Australian National Standards for HE Teaching (undated) *Australian University Teaching and Criteria and Standards*. Available at: http://uniteachingcriteria.edu.au/framework/about/ [accessed 24–11–16].

AUT, Pokapu Ako Centre for Learning and Teaching (2015) *Ako Aronui: Learning about Teaching Study Guide*. Available at: http://akoaronui.org/wp-content/uploads/2015/07/Study-Guide.pdf [accessed 25–11–16].

Baume, D. (2008) *A Reference Framework for Teaching in HE*. NETTLE Project Publications Series 1.

Beckmann, E.A. (2016) Teaching excellence: recognising the many as well as the few, in M. Davis & A. Goody (Eds.), *Research and Development in Higher Education: The Shape of Higher Education*, 39 (pp. 13–22). Fremantle, Australia, 4–7 July 2016, available at: http://herdsa2016.org/images/188_Beckmann__RefPaper.pdf [accessed 23–11–16].

Bell, A. & Brooks, C. (2016) Is there a magic link between research activity, professional teaching qualifications, and student satisfaction? Available at: http://recognisingexcellentteaching. wp.st-andrews.ac.uk/files/2016/01/Paper-by-Bell-Brooks.pdf [accessed 6–10–16].

Bradley, S. & Eccles, S. (2015) (Internally circulated paper) *Impact of UKPSF: personal and professional benefits of SFHEA and PFHEA*. Higher Education Academy.

Buckley, A. (2012) *Making it Count: reflecting on NSS in the process of enhancement*. Higher Education Academy. Available at: https://www.heacademy.ac.uk/making-it-count-reflections-national-student-survey-nss-process-enhancement [accessed 28–11–16].

Buckley, A. (2015) *Students' Perceptions of Skills Development*. Higher Education Academy. Available at: https://www.heacademy.ac.uk/system/files/ukes_2015.pdf [accessed 6–12–16].

Courtney, S. (2014) *Global Approaches to Developing Teaching Excellence Frameworks: A review of the literature.*, Commissioned report, no publisher name.

Crookes, P.A. (2015) *The Transforming Practice Programme: some lessons learned*. Paper presented to CELT, MMU 10-3-15.

Dearing, R. (1997) The White Paper 'HE in the Learning Society'. HMO.

Eccles, S. & Bradley, S. (2015) Reflecting on leadership: higher education academy recognition and academics as effective leaders. In: Society for Research in Higher Education, 9–11 December 2015, Newport, Wales. Available at http://eprints.bournemouth.ac.uk/22765/ (internally circulated full paper).

Evans, C., Muijs D. & Tomlinson, M. (2015) *Engaged Student Learning: high impact strategies to enhance student achievement.* Higher Education Academy, Available at: https://www.heacademy.ac.uk/resource/engaged-student-learning-high-impact-strategies-enhance-student-achievement [accessed 5–12–16].

Fung, D. & Gordon, C. (2016) *Rewarding Educators and Educational Leaders in Research Intensive Universities.* Higher Education Academy. Available at: https://www.heacademy.ac.uk/system/files/rewarding_educators_and_education_leaders.pdf [accessed 5–12–16].

Hattie, J. (2012) *Visible Learning for Teachers: Maximizing impact on learning.* Routledge.

Higher Education Academy (2011) *The UK Professional Standards Framework.* Available at: https://www.heacademy.ac.uk/system/files/downloads/ukpsf_2011_english.pdf [accessed 28–11–16].

Kennedy, A. (2005) Models of Continuing Professional Development: a framework for analysis, *Journal of In-Service Education*, 31(2), 235–250.

Marentic Pozarnik, B. (2009) Improving the quality of teaching and learning in HE through supporting professional development of teaching staff, *napredak* 150(3–4), 341–359. Available at: https://www.researchgate.net/profile/Barica_Pozarnik/publications [accessed 5–12–16].

Middlehurst, R. & Fielden, J. (2016) *Learning Excellence: a summary analysis of 26 international case studies.* Higher Education Academy. Available at: https://www.heacademy.ac.uk/system/files/learning_excellence_summary.pdf [accessed 5–12–16].

National Forum for the Enhancement of Teaching and Learning in HE (2015) *Mapping Professional Development Pathways for Those who Teach in Irish HE: where are we now and where do we want to go?* February 2015. Available at: http://www.teachingandlearning.ie/wp-content/uploads/2015/03/Mapping-PD-SUMMARY.pdf [accessed 24–11–16].

Parsons, D., Hill, I., Holland, J. & Willis, D. (2012) *Impact of Teaching Development Programmes in HE.* Higher Education Academy. Available at: https://www.heacademy.ac.uk/system/files/resources/hea_impact_teaching_development_prog.pdf [accessed 6–12–16].

Pauli, R. Barker, R. & Worrell, M. (2016) The impact of pedagogies of partnership on the student learning experience in UK HE. Higher Education Academy. Available at: https://www.heacademy.ac.uk/resource/impact-pedagogies-partnership-student-learning-experience-uk-higher-education [accessed 5–12–16].

Pilkington, R. (2016a) *Review of Annual Monitoring Reports for Accredited CPD Schemes 2014–15.* Higher Education Authority. Available at: https://www.heacademy.ac.uk/sites/default/files/downloads/annual_cpd_review_report_2014-15.pdf [accessed 28–11–16].

Pilkington, R. (2016b) Supporting continuing professional development (CPD) for lecturers, in Baume, D. and Popovic, C. (Eds) *Advancing Practice in Academic Development.* Routledge, pp. 52–68 (Chapter 4).

SEDA (2013) *A History of SEDA.* Available at: http://www.seda.ac.uk/history-of-seda [accessed 28–11–16].

Stes, A., Min-Leliveld, M., Gijbels, D. & Van Petegem, P. (2010a) The impact of instructional development in higher education: The state-of-the-art of the research, *Educational Research Review* 5(1), 25–49.

Thornton, T. (2014) Professional recognition: promoting recognition through the HEA in a UK HEI. *Tertiary Education & Management* 20(3), 225–238.

Zaitseva, E. (2015) Relationship between HEA Fellowship and student engagement. Higher Education Academy. Available at: https://www.heacademy.ac.uk/about/news/new-research-finds-link-between-high-levels-hea-fellowship-and-strong-ukes-teaching (gives link to research paper at bottom of page [accessed 6–12–16]).

30 Private Coaching for University Teachers

External Help to Find the Right Balance of Power and Responsibility

Georgina Kirk

Introduction

In theory, at least, quality assurance for university teaching serves a useful function. Even before tuition fees, it was reasonable to expect a decent standard of teaching: if students turn up to a lecture, seminar or tutorial in good faith, they ought to be able to rely on the fact that the person at the front is well prepared and able to do an effective job. However, in the light of all the other changes in higher education over the past 25 years or so, it's difficult not to see this quality assurance as yet another instance of upholding students' rights while demanding that university teachers take more and more responsibility. The mounting pressure on lecturers is a danger not only to their own health and wellbeing but also, ironically, to the success of the teaching and learning process.

My perspective on this is external: I'm not employed by any university, I'm a freelance communication coach. I teach public speaking; I train trainers; I prepare candidates for interviews, panellists for discussions, experts to share their knowledge on the lecture circuit. My clients are mainly businesspeople but also a wide variety of other individuals, including doctors, dentists, charity volunteers, authors, lawyers and politicians. I work with them over a few hours, usually one to one, equipping them with the practical skills and the confidence to put themselves across effectively.

Since the recent lurch in the balance of power towards students, lecturers from various English universities have started approaching me for help with their teaching. I'm glad to be able to assist them, for their sake and their students', but I'm concerned about the system that renders this necessary.

For lecturers to be so motivated to improve their teaching that they are prepared to seek out and pay for coaching on their own initiative is, in many ways, a positive development. With the greatest respect to my clients, some of their teaching was dire – and if consumer power is what it takes to raise standards, we should surely welcome it. Yet that power is a double-edged sword: yes, it may be driving lecturers to develop their teaching skills, but it's also reducing the quality of students' learning. Anyway, it may not, in fact, have the effect of improving teaching; often it simply makes the lecturers stressed and insecure, wanting to do better but not knowing how.

Others will write about what universities are doing to promote the quality of teaching we are all seeking to assure (and I look forward to reading their chapters!) but from where I'm standing, lecturers appear to be in an uncomfortable position, being squeezed by their employers on one side and by their students on the other. Despite constant clamouring for lecturers to teach better, the infrastructure around them does little or nothing to support that, which is why some turn to an outside consultant for guidance.

Criticising lecturers for being suboptimal teachers does not in itself make them better. As Roger Ellis points out in the first edition of this book (1993), we have to be careful not to confuse quality assurance with quality control. Quality control indicates any lecturer whose teaching is judged not good enough should be sacked, whereas quality assurance involves designing and implementing a process that guarantees, as far as possible, there are no rejects at the quality control stage (Ellis 1993). It seems to me far too much 'control' is going on and nothing like enough assurance. I put control in inverted commas because what I see is lecturers not actually losing their jobs but living under the constant threat of it, while suffering other, less terminal but still distressing, sanctions.

This punitive environment is hardly conducive to progress and is one of the reasons some lecturers approach me, rather than their employers, for help. If someone is doing a bad job, there is no point in attacking them – most obviously because if they knew how to do it better they would already be doing that, but also because human beings do not flourish under fire. Heaping opprobrium on struggling lecturers is precisely the wrong way to attempt to bring about the required change. Furthermore, the continual carping diminishes them in the eyes of their students, which undermines their effectiveness as teachers.

Attributing poor teaching to individual inadequacy is misleading and unproductive and the fact that the vast majority of my clients go on to become successful teachers proves it. Contrary to what some in authority seem to think, teaching is a skill that needs to be learnt. Of course there are those with more aptitude for it than others, but nobody is innately brilliant at it: we all have to learn how it's done. Someone who is floundering can, through a few hours' coaching, be set firmly on the path to success – provided that coaching is offered and received in a positive spirit. If it's viewed as a punishment, it's unlikely to work.

It may be a caricature but the picture as I see it is of lecturers carrying the full weight of responsibility for providing good-quality teaching, while their employers have all the power in that relationship. And, on the other side of the coin, lecturers are shouldering the burden of trying to keep the customers satisfied, while the students hold the whip hand in that relationship. If teaching quality is to be assured, both of these relationships need to be recalibrated.

What is the purpose of university teaching?

This deceptively simple question is fundamental to quality assurance. If teachers aren't sure exactly what their objectives are, how can they hope to meet them? If the teacher's objectives don't correspond with those of the students, the university, potential graduate employers or any of the other stakeholders in the process, whose definition of success should prevail?

One reason it's so complicated to address these issues is the anomalous position of universities: part school, part business, part public good, part private good. The changes to tertiary education imposed by successive governments over the past quarter of a century have highlighted and put pressure on the fissures, leading to uncertainty, insecurity and stress as lecturers' workloads have increased exponentially, while what is actually required of them as teachers has become less and less clear.

The abolition of polytechnics and the subsequent drive to widen participation in higher education called for a reappraisal of the objectives of university teaching, with education for its own sake giving way to more utilitarian outcomes. This caused a major upheaval for teaching staff, who found themselves having to adapt their courses and methods to meet the needs of ever-expanding numbers of diverse students, with a view to equipping those students for rewarding careers.

The introduction of tuition fees has created a slightly different tension, between universities' desire to set and maintain high academic standards and the necessity to provide a service that will attract and satisfy customers. University teachers now have to consider not only how vocational to make their courses but also to what extent it may be expedient to give students' ostensible success priority over their underlying learning – in other words, to give the students what they think they want, rather than what they need.

All this is particularly hard on staff who would never have elected to be teachers. There is an inherent flaw in a system that piles such responsibility on to people who applied for the post, and were appointed, on the basis of their interest and expertise in an area unrelated to teaching. With the right support, these individuals can flourish as teachers, but bringing this about takes care and diplomacy.

In the midst of all these conflicting priorities and confusion, the risk is that the value of a university education is falling, even as its price is rising. Teachers and students must share responsibility for turning this around, though it's teachers who must lead the way and show students how to assume responsibility for their own learning. With the balance of power hanging so heavily on the students' side, it can take quite a bit of courage and grit on the part of teachers to stand firm against the tide, but it's in everyone's interest that they do so.

What I tell my clients is to look at the big picture. Work out clearly what the purpose of your teaching is and keep that as your guiding light.

The big picture

Although it may feel as if commercial and pedagogic demands are pulling in different directions, this needn't – and shouldn't – be the case. Where there is tension, it's because of the mismatch between what is being advertised and what is being delivered. If a degree is portrayed as a passport to a high-paid job, this is not only a hostage to fortune, it reduces the perceived value of the education being provided. This leads to a drop in its actual value, as teachers strive to supply the results promised in the brochure, instead of the knowledge and skills a university course is supposed to be about acquiring.

Equally, there need – and should – be no contradiction between the public and the private good. If education is no more than a commodity, a ticket into employment, then the benefit is restricted to the individual students buying it. If, on the other hand, education is the development of an enquiring mind, an ability to think outside the box and a way of understanding the world that comes with deep specialist knowledge, then society as a whole benefits from students gaining it. Since the introduction of tuition fees, the emphasis has naturally shifted away from consideration of the public good, putting universities in danger of throwing the baby out with the bathwater.

In his obituary of Sir Michael Dummett, Professor John Haldane (2011) laments the decline of erudition:

> Dummett was outstanding but also . . . an example of a type that was once familiar but has become rare, and may even be disappearing. This "type", believe in knowledge and learning, in reading, writing and understanding; in excellence in art, in scholarship, and in science; in the importance of breadth and depth of achievement across more than one field of endeavour; in the value of experience under testing conditions; in holding oneself and others to high standards; in aiming for decency, integrity and justice in public life, and making a direct contribution to achieving these.

He goes on, 'Standards of attainment are in doubt, but triviality and mere celebrity are daily announced and applauded . . . "Dumbing down" is certainly part of the problem, but so is "Bigging up" by which I mean making a lot of not very much.' In Haldane's judgement, 'If blame is to be assigned, most of it should be laid at the doors of the educators not of the uneducated.'

Putting aside the fact that Michael Dummett was my great-uncle, I find this an inspiring pep talk. As far as blame is concerned, I would reframe this as responsibility, which is a more positive spin because it implies the power to bring about change. When lecturers are down-hearted and overstretched, raising their eyes to contemplate the good they can do, not only for the students in front of them but, as the effects ripple out, to the country – nay, the world! – at large, will, I hope, fill them with renewed enthusiasm.

Let's look at the other end of the spectrum. In his 2007 book *The 4-Hour Work Week*, Timothy Ferriss describes winning the gold medal at the USA Chinese Kickboxing National Championships. He entered the contest for a dare and had four weeks to prepare for it, so the normal route of training, work and practice was not open to him. Instead, he identified and exploited two loopholes in the rules. Firstly, weigh-ins were the day before the competition, so he dehydrated himself for that and then hydrated back up to fight three weight classes below where he should have been. Secondly, the small print stated: 'If one combatant fell off the elevated platform three times in a single round, his opponent won by default.' 'I decided,' says Ferriss, 'to use this technicality as my single technique and just push people off.' As a result, he went home national champion.

Ferriss was acting on a dare and, within that narrow definition, he triumphed, though by wider standards it's a hollow achievement. The title is a façade: if he ever found himself needing to kickbox to survive or to save someone else, he would be struggling. That is not the point here, it was a bit of fun – but if British higher education carries on in its current direction, this is where it's going to end up. A degree is not about the certificate; it's about the substance behind it. Teachers who do nothing but facilitate passing exams are letting their students down. They are also letting down everyone who has a stake in students' learning, including the public.

In any case, the suggestion a degree guarantees a job at all, let alone a desirable one, is difficult to justify. As Erica Buist (2014) puts it on the *Guardian* blog, 'We were told that education was a ticket to employment, when really it's more like vague directions to the station.' This could be characterised as universities mis-selling their service to unsuspecting young people, many of whom end up in serious debt to finance something they might not have bought if they had known the truth. The whole charade seems somewhat futile: the political and sociological commitment to widen participation, along with universities' commercial imperative to find customers, means more and more students are coming into the system, obtaining the qualification and then struggling to secure employment. The net result is not a better educated society – or even workforce – but increasing numbers of graduates who either fall into depression at the hopelessness of the jobs market or feel obliged to buy more 'education' in order to set themselves apart.

That participation is being widened at the same time as a degree is being reduced to job-ticket status is at best a wasted opportunity. What really overturns poverty of aspiration is not so much landing a fat job (even when this actually happens) as being educated. In my role as a communication coach, I've worked with many clients who came from deprived backgrounds and have gone on to achieve great things but, however successful they are, they remain inwardly insecure, because they feel like frauds. This is a lot about upbringing and parental messages but it's also about lacking the firm foundation of a solid education.

This is the pivotal factor: education changes a person's view of the world, so the next generation will receive more confident parental messages, nurturing aspiration as opposed to trying to stifle it. In *To Kill a Mockingbird* (Lee 1960), Jem Finch defines 'background' as 'how long your family's been readin' and writin''. He goes on to scoff at the idea of his aunt 'being proud her great-grandaddy could read an' write' and, of course, at one level he is right: coming from an educated family doesn't make someone a superior human being – but it is undeniably an advantage in life. Although this clearly needs to be addressed in primary and secondary education too, university teachers can play a big part in transforming the outlook of underprivileged students.

What about assuring the quality of learning?

Like a magic trick, teaching cannot be assessed in a vacuum. In the following exchange between two magicians in the novel *Carter Beats the Devil* (Gold 2001), Ledocq illustrates his argument using a silver dollar:

> He held the coin by its edge, and then placed it in his palm. He squeezed his palm shut, made a pass over it, and opened his hand again. Carter stared. In Ledocq's palm was a silver dollar.
> 'Have I missed something?'
> 'Yes.' Ledocq did it again. And a third time. Finally, Carter noticed: the date on the coin changed from 1921 to 1923.
> 'That's a tedious sort of trick,' Carter sighed.
> 'That is true. But why?'
> 'If you do a trick that the audience doesn't notice–'
> 'Ah! Yes! I've got you! An audience. You need an audience.'

If magic has no effect on the audience, it is pointless – and the same goes for teaching. The way the trick is performed or the teaching delivered must be excellent: if you are offering this as a professional service, your customers are entitled to expect you to be good at your job. Essential though they are, however, the techniques practised by both magician and teacher are only half the story. Success is measured by what takes place in the mind of the beholder.

This being the case, let's have a look at the issue through the other end of the tube: what can be done to enhance the quality of learning at universities? Before we consider what goes on in the classroom, we need to contemplate the wider context, both because undergraduate years should involve learning at a more macro level than study, and because what happens at the macro level strongly influences what is accomplished at the micro level.

Since the introduction of tuition fees, the relationship between university teachers and their students has taken a significant turn for the worse, though this is only partly a matter of cause and effect. Where it has been a direct consequence, this is because of the shift in universities' priorities as they morphed from seats of learning into purveyors of a service, so that lecturers have come under pressure from their employers to keep the customers satisfied.

On the student side, however, tuition fees are more like a lightning conductor. Fees provide a convenient shorthand for the overall outlook ('I'm paying for this, so you owe me the result I want'), as well as a convenient banner to obscure the blurred boundaries of rights and responsibilities. What is impeding students' learning is not the so-called marketisation of higher education but their attitude (Williams 2013). The fact that students are paying for their courses is coincidental to their thinking of themselves as customers: their view is a reflection of the Zeitgeist, not the financial transaction. 'Put simply,' says Joanna Williams (2013), 'if university tuition fees were ended tomorrow, the assumptions that educational success is a right irrespective of intellectual endeavour, and that the purpose of a degree is to make people employable, would remain.'

The real problem is the culture, the infantilisation and the sense of entitlement that lead students to demand their teachers present the answers – and, ultimately, their degree certificates – on a silver platter. It is a contradictory and stultifying culture, combining lack of respect for authority with dependence on that same authority, and unless and until it changes, the quality of learning is never going to improve.

British society as a whole has become almost obsessively risk-averse, forever on the look-out for anything that could go wrong, in order to ban or avoid it. This concentration on the negative increases stress and fails to prepare us to cope with the misfortunes that inevitably happen anyway. It is a mistaken strategy but one adopted in earnest across university campuses up and down the land. As Frank Furedi (2016) points out, 'When youngsters are constantly discouraged from engaging with the risks of everyday life, they miss out on important opportunities to learn sound judgments and build up their confidence and resilience.'

Wrapping young people in cotton wool, rather than helping them learn how to handle adversity, is as much to do with their mothers and fathers as it is the universities. The phenomenon of 'helicopter parents', always hovering, ready to swoop down at a moment's notice to sort out any situation for their offspring, has created a new dimension to student life. This is partly because '[p]reventing the exposure of children to the risks of everyday life now is perceived as the hallmark of responsible parenting' (Furedi 2016) and partly an extension of the proverbial 'sharp elbows' parents use to gain as much advantage as possible for their sons and daughters – entry to the best available schools, work placements, help with extracting maximum utility from time spent at university.

In line with social expectations (and mindful of the commercial implications), universities vie to provide the most extensive facilities, the most modern conveniences, the highest-specification accommodation, the widest-ranging welfare services; in short, the most attractive 'student experience'. While of course amenities, equipment and support are good things to offer, there are two major drawbacks to this ethos. The first is that the experience is too prescribed, imposed top-down. Peter Scott (2015) sums it up thus:

> [U]niversities are meant to be places for exploration and experimentation. The whole point is that students do it by, to and for themselves. The danger with universities' new enthusiasm for managing the student experience is that it may restrict the potential for exploration and experimentation.

With their freedom to fend for themselves so curtailed, and with them never having known it otherwise, it's little wonder students insist on being spoon-fed and insulated. At the macro level, this leads to no-platforming controversial speakers and retreating into 'safe spaces', avoiding conflict as opposed to developing mature and productive ways to deal with it. At the micro level, it means demanding the answers be laid out for them, as opposed to grappling with the questions themselves. At every level, this is inhibiting students' learning.

The other downside to higher education institutions competing for customers in this way is that is places the power squarely in the hands of the buyer, exacerbating students' sense of entitlement to success. Their side of the bargain is to pay the fees and enrol on the course: the rest is up to the university. Where results go awry, it's because the exam was unfairly difficult and/or their teachers didn't prepare them properly. 'If they fail, it must be someone else's fault. As customers, they must have been let down' (Scott 2015). Whether or not lecturers end up awarding inflated marks, the quality of students' learning is clearly suffering.

Although obviously it's beneficial to all concerned if university teaching improves, giving students to understand that any obstacles they encounter are down to inadequate teaching is bound to reinforce not only their belief that it's their teachers who should be doing all the work but also their infantilisation. Casting students as passive recipients of their education, rather than active participants in it, stunts their intellectual and emotional growth. That raising standards should be seen to be all about the teaching serves both parties badly. It puts undue pressure on lecturers and it compounds students' misconceptions, creating false expectations. However much he or she might occasionally want to, no teacher can wave a magic wand and have the student absorb information with no effort on the latter's part. Yes, the quality of university teaching needs to be enhanced and assured, but students will not thrive unless they take responsibility for their learning.

Quality teaching for university customers

What, then, does quality teaching actually look like? The following section is my attempt to sketch it, an overview of the advice I give my clients.

On most courses at UK universities, teaching is conducted in roughly two categories: lectures for large numbers of students, which consist almost exclusively of input from the teacher, and seminars/tutorials/workshops for smaller numbers, where the students take a more active role.

Lectures

In the same way as magically changing a silver dollar into a different one is a waste of time if the audience doesn't notice what has happened, rattling off a load of information in the general direction of the students does nothing but destroy the souls of all present. It is the lecturer's responsibility not merely to enumerate facts and ideas but to lift them off the page (or screen) and bring the topic to life.

One of the most useful skills a teacher can develop is empathy. Like a successful entertainer or salesperson, a good teacher knows his or her audience, what their points of reference are, what makes them tick, and packages the material accordingly. This does not mean dumbing down, it means making the subject accessible and interesting: there is a world of difference.

When my clients ask me how to make their delivery more engaging, they are often surprised when I start talking about content, yet this has to be the starting point. If the content is not organised so as to support strong delivery, no amount of finesse can overcome that handicap – it's like trying to run with one's knees tied together.

In most cases, the bind around my clients' legs is PowerPoint. Courses are prepared within the framework of this software, with lecturers producing sets of slides mid-way between a script and a textbook, intended to serve triple duty as notes for them, visual aids and a handout for the students. This rigid system dooms delivery to stilted monotony and kills the energy in the room, yet few seem to question that this is how it must be done. Lecturers are not alone in this; they took their cue from the business sector and it's a mistake replicated everywhere presentations are made. Nevertheless, university teachers need to rethink this method radically if they are going to get beyond reciting into the space and actually connect and communicate with the students.

The principal purpose of a slide is to illustrate something it's difficult, or would take too long, to explain in words. For instance, in a lecture about a medical condition, showing a photograph or diagram makes sure everyone understands exactly what is being discussed; to compare and contrast statistics, it makes sense to display a chart or a graph. The visual nature of a slide can also reinforce the message, helping the students to interpret and retain the information – though this does not apply if the slide is cluttered with text.

The assumption that the slides should tell the story by themselves is self-defeating, since it renders the speaker redundant. Going through the motions of trying to present the material makes for a dull (at best!) experience for both teacher and students, perpetuating the vicious circle: lectures are boring, so students don't attend them. Having not gone to the lecture, students want to know what was covered, so they ask for a copy of the slides. Students who do attend find it more convenient to be given a copy of the slides than to make their own notes.

As an interim step, I recommend creating a separate set of documents to supply as handouts, either in printed or electronic form, so any slides used can be designed to enhance the lecture rather than to reproduce or replace it. In the longer run, as lectures become more interesting and worthwhile, and as students become more motivated and independent, handouts may cease to be required but, until that day dawns, the extra work involved in distinguishing them from slides will pay enormous dividends.

One of the problems with conflating slides and handouts is the level of detail. The aim in university teaching is not to air as much information as possible in the time available, it is to impart a few key points that will enlarge the students' understanding of the subject, give them some insight and, with luck, pique their curiosity so that they want to know more. Until students are self-sufficient enough to be able to dig deeper by and for themselves, teachers may feel it necessary to furnish them with all the relevant little facts, figures and footnotes, but there is no need to get bogged down in detail during the lecture: all that can go in the handout.

Even when PowerPoint is not used, inexperienced teachers are often so afraid of boring or patronising the students that instead they overwhelm them. Overdoing the input, either by exploring unnecessary minutiae or by galloping across too much ground, is counterproductive. This is where empathy comes in: as the teacher, you know all this; to the audience, it's new information that takes time and energy to process. There is a limit to how much even the most sponge-like student can absorb in one sitting and most will simply let a relentless flow of words wash over them without penetrating the surface.

The fundamental difference between lectures and the other teaching formats is the scope for interactivity. In the slightly artificial environment of a lecture, with one person typically doing all the talking, it can be particularly difficult to hold the students' attention. In everyday discourse, if someone hasn't heard or grasped what is being said, or wants to check her understanding, she can interrupt and ask. While I suggest lecturers encourage students to do this, in large theatres it may not be viable or individuals may feel intimidated by the size of the group. It is therefore imperative that the lecturer makes himself clearly heard and understood and puts the information across in a way the students will take in and remember.

It may sound obvious but the audience is not going to listen to a lecture they can't hear. One might hope students would have the gumption to move nearer the front or to let the lecturer know if they're unable to follow what's being said, but the teacher has at least equal responsibility for pre-empting any problems of this sort. The solution may be a microphone, though it's worth considering other possibilities first, since often the real issue is not volume but clarity.

As with all public speaking, the secret to a successful lecture is thorough planning, preparation and practice. The first step, as indicated above, is to organise the content so as to promote clear and stimulating delivery. This involves identifying the key ideas to be conveyed – and, crucially, how best to express them: being an expert in the subject is a completely separate matter from being able to talk about it fluently, coherently and with impact. I usually recommend my clients begin by thinking how they would describe the concept in question to their friends over coffee, then polish it up. A lecture delivered in anything other than the lecturer's natural speech patterns, intonations and vocabulary will be difficult to listen to, though with increasing numbers of non-native English speakers in the audience, allowance must be made for that. By saying it out loud and experimenting, the teacher can work out in advance how to express each idea succinctly, in straightforward, unambiguous language, without too many idioms or cultural references. Because teaching is not regarded as a performance, it generally doesn't occur to those doing it to rehearse, but it's amazing what a difference it makes: not only does the lecture become more focused and effective, the lecturer no longer has to spend so much brain power on finding the right words, and thus has more energy for connecting with the students.

Returning for a moment to slides, the time to create visual aids is after the content has been organised. If a point needs illustration, that's what slides are for – but designing the course as a set of slides is, as discussed, the wrong way round. For those concerned that, without PowerPoint to guide them through the material, they will forget what they wanted to say, I suggest using bullet-point notes on paper or card. In fact, I recommend every teacher to have a few bullet points to refer to, to keep them on track and to free them from having to remember what's up next.

Language barrier or no, delivery is enhanced by a reduction in speed. Nervous teachers, especially, tend to talk much too fast, but virtually everyone's performance is improved by slowing down. It takes practice to speak more slowly while maintaining the colour and texture of one's natural speech, but it can be done and the students will benefit.

A powerful yet woefully under-used tool in the teacher's kit is the pause. Pausing between points gives the students a chance to process what they've just heard. It's the didactic equivalent of a computer's Save button.

If students are finding lectures difficult to follow, this is usually remedied by the lecturer rethinking the structure and presentation of the content, working out in advance how to express the ideas, slowing down and pausing. This makes for technically better teaching and also increases the lecturer's confidence, which helps with clarity and projection.

A successful lecture is delivered with conviction and enthusiasm and resembles a conversation, even though only one party is actually speaking. To achieve this, the lecturer must address the audience directly, rather than talking generally into the space. If the auditorium is of a size and shape to allow eye contact, that is a huge boon; otherwise, this needs to be simulated as much as possible. Looking at the students draws them in, because they feel the lecturer is talking to them, and it also lets the lecturer see whether they are listening and understanding. The latter aspect can take courage but connecting with the students in this way makes it much more likely they will be paying attention.

Although it may not be feasible to ask the type of question that involves students answering out loud, effective use of semi-rhetorical questions can get the students thinking. For example, before announcing a statistic, the lecturer can ask everyone to ponder what it might be. Anything like this that makes the lecture more interactive will make it more stimulating and the content more memorable.

All this adds up to an enormous amount of work for already overstretched lecturers. However, the rewards are infinite and the alternative dismal. It's positive work, more satisfying – and more dignified – than the endless struggle to pacify students who are flinging their weight about because they are not, in fact, getting what they need.

Lecturers will know when they're doing it right, because it will feel right. At first, it will just feel much easier (because it is: trying to make densely packed slides sound interesting is exhausting and demoralising). As time goes by and they really start connecting and communicating with the students, the students will respond to this and synergy will ensue.

Seminars, tutorials and workshops

Enervating as a bad lecture is, a session that's supposed to be interactive but where the students don't actually participate is an even more painful experience. Again, it is the teacher's responsibility to make these sessions work and a change in approach will yield more fruitful outcomes.

Broadly speaking, students don't get involved either because they're anxious about doing so or because they can't be bothered. In both cases, the carrot is more effective than the stick. Using empathy, modelling and guidance – and with one eye on the higher purpose – the tutor must create an environment that is both safe and stimulating. Seminars, tutorials and workshops are a wonderful opportunity to teach and develop skills and attitudes that will stand the students in excellent stead in every area of university life and far beyond.

It can be instructive for teachers to reflect on the parallel between them-and-their-students and them-and-their-employers. Management putting pressure on lecturers to do a better job, without showing them how, does nothing but generate stress. Why should it be any different for insecure students in a seminar?

Once students feel comfortable with the format of these sessions and what is expected of them, the tutor will be able to take a seat further and further back in the bus, while the students do most of the driving. Until that stage is reached, however, there is no point in sitting in a stationary vehicle and continually asking whether someone would like to get us moving – and commanding an individual to take the wheel can do more harm than good.

In terms of preparation, students are more likely to do a task if it is active and specific. Reading is notorious for not being done, and being asked to think about X or come up with some ideas about Y is too vague. Some sort of worksheet, available in advance either on paper or electronically, usually makes a reasonably firm foundation for a session. The questions help the students to focus their thoughts and, on the day, those who have prepared their answers will have something to say, while those who haven't even looked at the sheet beforehand can be encouraged to make a stab at a response. The hope here is that students will come to realise that if they put in some work prior to the session, they will enjoy the discussion more and get much more out of it.

For this to pan out successfully, the teacher needs to bear in mind that the skills required to participate in an academic debate are not innate but have to be learnt. Mis-steps will be made along the road and it is essential no-one be ridiculed or criticised for them; nothing will be achieved if the students don't feel safe to take risks. If someone is paying attention but doesn't understand, that is the teacher's fault, not the student's, and it's up to the teacher to find better ways to explain. Equally, if people have differing views, that is to be embraced: it's through adroit handling of this that the teacher can help timid students to have the courage of their convictions, while instilling in all of them respect for others.

Throwing beginners in at the deep end is not a teaching strategy I usually recommend anyway but university students in the current era are exceptionally unsuited to benefiting from it; no good will come of expecting them to accomplish something they haven't first been carefully taught how to do. The increasingly widespread practice of requiring students to give presentations is a prime example of this, with tutors being apparently unaware of the trauma it causes in many cases. (I know this because it's not only teachers who contact me for help but students too.)

Through patient guidance and relaxed good humour, the teacher can gradually build up the students' skills and confidence. This is not about having low expectations or giving students prizes just for turning up, it's about meeting their needs as learners and equipping them properly for the tasks ahead. As the sessions begin to flow and become more invigorating, students will be more motivated to get involved, which will become a virtuous circle.

Striking the right balance of power and responsibility

It's an accepted truth – even a cliché – that psychotherapy doesn't work unless the client wants to change: the desired outcome is achieved by therapist and client working in partnership. The same principle applies in teaching. Instead of striving for self-improvement, however, students are in denial about the need for that and are making strident demands for 'happy pills'. University teachers are in an invidious position. If they supply the pills, they are selling themselves out and their students down the river. If they refuse, they face the wrath not only of the students but of their employers as well.

Young people are being failed by a system that on one hand controls and directs their 'student experience' in a way that infantilises them, while on the other hand gives them far too much responsibility for deciding how their courses should be organised and delivered. How can they know? Somehow, teachers have to find the strength and confidence to withhold the happy pills and get students working on the substantive issues.

For inexperienced teachers or those who have never really taken to it, this is more easily said than done. What these people need is coaching in the techniques of effective teaching and also support in working out and establishing the right balance of power and responsibility between them and their students. The latter aspect is crucial: without the right attitude behind it, even technically good teaching will lack impact. This is partly because the right attitude conveys authority and partly because it will help the teachers to define their boundaries. Teachers are not there to be the students' friends and courting popularity is likely to backfire. Still less are they the students' servants.

Continuing the therapy theme, Claude Steiner (1974) makes it clear that if the therapist is putting in more than 50 per cent of the effort, this is destined to end badly.

> Most therapists have worked enthusiastically in behalf of persons who eventually proved to have been not only disinterested in their help but actually disdainful of it. Most of us have had the experience of becoming more and more concerned and active with someone who subtly became more and more passive until it seemed that his welfare concerned us more than it did him. Most of us have, at one time or another, been lured into a false sense of accomplishment as therapists only to suddenly fall from our pedestals as our star 'patient' got drunk, attempted suicide, or got arrested for shoplifting.

That resonates with me as a teacher, as I'm sure it will with many a modern university lecturer. By taking too much responsibility, we are doing our customers a grave disservice; we cannot do the work for them and it's wrong to try. 'For good therapy to take place,' Steiner

(1974) goes on, 'it is essential . . . that the persons seeking help be seen as complete human beings capable of taking power over their lives'.

Success will be achieved through teachers owning their power and responsibility and encouraging the students to take theirs. Once this is entrenched, lecturers will be in a much stronger position vis-à-vis their employers and that relationship will become more harmonious.

It is university teachers who must take the initiative in this revolution and the aim of quality assurance must be to smooth the path for them. The paradox is that assuring the quality of teaching may be seen as expecting more from the lecturers than the students, thus interfering with the balance of power and responsibility. Perhaps the process should be carried out under cover.

Summary of advice for university teachers

- Let your love for the subject shine. Be enthusiastic, bring energy to your teaching and enjoy it. As the teacher, you set the tone, so make it an upbeat one.
- If you're using slides, remember they are there to support you, not the other way round. First work out what you want to say. Then, if it needs illustration, create slides to illuminate your meaning. Keep text to a minimum.
- If you feel you've got to supply your students with handouts, make these separate from your slides. They serve a different purpose and conflating the two casts a pall over your teaching.
- Have notes to prompt you, to keep you on track and prevent you having to waste brain power on remembering what you wanted to cover.
- Know your audience and put yourself in their position. How much can they realistically absorb in one session? Are you expressing yourself in a way they can understand?
- Speak slowly and pause between your points, to allow your listeners to take in and reflect on what you've said. Yes, you can speak slowly and convey enthusiasm; it just takes some practice.
- A lecture is a performance: rehearse it.
- Make eye contact with your students and talk to them, rather than simply speaking into the space. As far as possible, include everyone, not only the ones who brought you an apple.
- For tutorials, seminars and workshops, consider what it would be useful to ask the students to prepare in advance, to facilitate participation on the day.
- If your system is not working, don't ignore the fact, blame the students or force yourself to push harder. Change it.
- Give a man a fish and you feed him for a day; teach a man to fish and you feed him for a lifetime. Resist the pressure to provide fillets on demand and keep your eyes on the big picture.

References

Buist, Erica (2014) 'Telling a young person to "Just get a job" is like going to the Sahara and yelling "Just rain!"' *Guardian* blog, 17 March 2014.

Ellis, Roger (1993) 'A British standard for university teaching?' In Ellis, Roger (ed.) *Quality Assurance for University Teaching*. Open University Press.

Ferriss, Timothy (2007) *The 4-Hour Work Week*. Vermilion.

Furedi, Frank (2016) 'Paranoid parenting means university students are treated as kids', *The Australian*, 2 April 2016.

Gold, Glen David (2001) *Carter Beats the Devil*. Sceptre.

Haldane, John (2011) 'Philosopher's death is great loss to UK culture', *The Scotsman*, 31 December 2011.

Lee, Harper (1960) *To Kill a Mockingbird*. Arrow Books.

Scott, Peter (2015) 'Once students went to university for education. Now it's an "experience"', *Guardian*, 6 October 2015.

Steiner, Claude (1974) *Scripts People Live*. Grove Press.

Williams, Joanna (2013) *Consuming Higher Education: Why Learning Can't be Bought*. Bloomsbury Academic.

Part IV

Case Studies of Quality Assurance in a Selection of Subjects

31 Quality Assurance in North American Medical Schools

Implications of Standards and Processes on Institutional Practices

Marie C. Matte and Joel H. Lanphear

Section I: Introduction and definition

The concept of quality assurance in medical education is linked historically to the process of accreditation of medical schools in North America. In this section we discuss the impact of changing accreditation standards on medical school practices and provide recommendations for successful accreditation outcomes. A full discussion of the political, economic, social-cultural, and historical impacts on the milieu in which the North American model operates is not within the purview of this paper. Nevertheless, the authors acknowledge the importance of understanding the contextual milieu in which an institution functions is critically important to successful processes.

The US Council for Higher Education defines accreditation as both a process and a status. As a process, it is designed as a means of quality assurance that helps to ensure continuous improvement in the quality of education as measured against a set of standards developed by peers. A school's accreditation status is a result of the outcomes of the process. (1) The process of medical school accreditation in North America is a voluntary, peer review process. In keeping with our definition of quality assurance, the process is designed to insure that standards are specified and met consistently for a product or service. (2)

Section II: The genesis of current medical school accreditation processes in the United States and Canada

The current model for LCME accreditation of North American medical schools grew from the World War II demand for more physicians to treat the injuries of US servicemen and women.

In February of 1942 an historic meeting was held between representatives of the American Medical Association, the Council of Medical Education and Teaching Hospitals (CMTH) and the Executive Committee of the Association of American Medical Colleges (AAMC). (3)

This meeting set the basis and formed the ideas and underpinnings of the Liaison Committee on Medical Education (LCME), initially with three members from the AMA's CMTH and three members from the AAMC Executive Council. This became a joint board and quickly had the now familiar title of liaison committee. Subsequently, school surveys were conducted jointly and recommendations for the school to implement were sent jointly to the CMTH and the AAMC. Currently, the LCME is a 19-member committee including two student members, two community members and 15 medical educators. Seven of the medical educators are nominate by the AAMC and seven are nominated by the AAMC. One member is appointed by the Committee on Accreditation of Canadian Medical Schools (CACMS). (4)

Since 1979, the LCME in partnership with the Committee on Accreditation of Canadian Medical Schools (CACMS) have shared responsibility for the accreditation of complete and independent medical education programs delivered in Canada and the United States. The LCME is sponsored by the American Medical Association and the American Association of Medical Colleges and CACMS is sponsored by the Canadian Medical Association and the Association of Canadian Medical Colleges, later the Association of Faculties of Medicine in Canada (AFMC). (5)

Section III: The impact of changing accreditation standards on medical schools' practices

Perhaps the most influential publication to impact the initial process of identifying "quality medical education" was the titled "Medical Education in the United States and Canada" commonly referred to as the Flexner Report. Published in 1910 the report based on Abraham Flexner's visits to 155 Canadian and US medical schools, provided the framework for identifying "quality" medical education in the next 60 years, much of which is still with us today. Essentially, the report called for high admission standards, university-based medical schools, two years of science followed by two years of physician supervised hospital training, laboratory experiences and instruction by physician-scientists. (6)

Over one hundred years after the Flexner Report we continue to consider, with a renewed focus, the interests of society in the design, development, implementation, management and quality assurance of our medical school. As Flexner stated "the public interest is then paramount, and when public interest, professional ideals, and sound educational procedure concur in the recommendation of the same policy, the time is surely ripe for decisive action." (7) Prior to this report, the American Medical Association (AMA) and the Association of American Medical Colleges (AAMC) had been inspecting medical schools, and by 1910, the AMA Council on Medical Education published the *Essentials of an Acceptable Medical College* based on existing standards and recommendations already in use by the AMA and the AAMC. These standards related to the essentials of medical education – i.e. the length, administration, and requirements of the curriculum, the types of faculty required, the requirement that the medical college own or control a teaching facility, and the adequacy of resources for both clinical and didactic teaching. (8)

It is important to note that LMCE standards have, since their inception, been "non-prescriptive" in nature. That is in contrast to much of the US and Canadian postgraduate education, which until recently has used checklists specifying the number of items faculty required for compliance for an individual standard. In addition, LCME accreditation standards have focused on outcomes and procedures not the specifics of the curricular approach nor the specific evaluation of faculty endeavor. This has been a subject of debate for many years in US and Canadian schools where the question of "how many biochemists are sufficient" has never been answered with a numeric response.

Over the next 40 years, these standards were revised eight times (1913, 1927, 1933, 1934, 1936, 1938, 1945, 1951), with the last major revision conducted in 1951. It was also during this 40-year period that the Liaison Committee on Medical Education (LCME) was established as the joint AMA and AAMC committee for the accreditation of medical schools in North America.

With input from the AAMC, and an examination of the leading American medical schools, the AMA Council on Medical Education revisions to the standards still closely followed the original and accepted intent and principles outlined in the 1910 report. The benefit of these revisions was the clarification of medical education concepts, and the recognition of the changing face of medical education with respect to technology, curricular content, simulation, and teaching strategies and philosophies. For example, the 1951 revisions made it explicit that any school that does not conduct a continuous review of the curriculum "must be regarded as deficient." (9) Additionally, admission requirements for medical college were reviewed and it was agreed that the minimum requirement for admission to medical college would be three years of training for the average student, as opposed to the established practice of admitting students with a prior two years of training. Further clarification on the types of faculty members required was articulated as the standards now included clinical faculty requirements for the disciplines of medicine, surgery, obstetrics, and psychiatry, while noting requirements for dedicated faculty to conduct research and supervise the medical education program.

> IMPACT: In specifying the implementation of continuous curricular review, many medical schools needed to develop new policies and procedures or risk being cited by the LCME. The change in requiring three years of undergraduate training impacted several schools who had been admitting to six-year MD programs. Finally, by adding reference to specific clinical specialties as well as dedicated research faculty, financial implications and recruitment burdens were placed on a number of smaller medical schools.

In 1958, a document titled "The Structure and Functions of a Medical School" was approved with narrative descriptions of medical school requirements and intent falling into the general categories of organization and administration, faculty, students, facilities, and educational program. Narrative further defining the sufficiency of full-time basic science and clinical faculty to oversee the didactic and clinical components of the program, the research endeavors of the medical school, and the integration of the basic sciences and clinical areas was added "so that the latter occurs to a significant degree in the first two years of the curriculum." In addition, narrative was added to the educational program requirements, highlighting the need for the "case method" approach to clinical education. (10)

> IMPACT: While not specifying numbers of faculty by discipline, the inclusion of integration of basic and clinical sciences in years 1 and 2 of the curriculum and mentioning the case method approach to learning caused many schools to revise curriculum. These were concepts to be include but the schools were left to decide how.

In 1969, at a meeting of the AAMC Executive Committee of the Council of Deans, recommendations for further definition of the 1958 report were discussed. The standards/criteria of main interest at this meeting were the objectives of the medical school program in light of the 1953 review of the standards. (11) Based on their findings, the authors recommended that the LCME consider providing clearer definition of standards, and conduct a review of each standard to confirm the validity and relevance of each standard.

By 1997, the LCME accreditation standards were once again revised. Remaining in the narrative format, the eight pages of standards included approximately 156 "must or should" standards relating to the function and structure of the medical school. While many of these standards remained prescriptive, it was perceived by schools that many standards could not clearly be aligned with measurable outcomes of structure, function, and/or performance of the medical school. The use of the term "should" contributed in many ways to the lack of clarity of the standard, resulting in schools simply ignoring the standard. What remained after years of scrutiny and review by the AMA and the AAMC was a narrative/prose description of the function and structure of a medical school in North America. The actual sentences written in the document served as the standards. This was all medical schools and their accreditation survey teams had to use in order to assess a medical schools achievement of accreditation. (12)

> IMPACT: The use of "must" or "should" as noted above resulted in many schools focusing on must and ignoring should. The terms compliant or non-compliant were still used to comment on accreditation standards and the narrative format continued to cause confusion for schools.

Hunt *et al.* state that lack of a clear definition of the standards attributed at times to the inability of site survey teams to "find relevant standards to link to their concerns about a medical education program." (13) In a 1997 study the authors examined the meaning and application of the existing 48 standards linked to medical school performance between 1984 and 1986 and 1994 and 1996, in the areas of teaching, learning and evaluation. The term application was used in this context to indicate that the school offered evidence of compliance for each standard. Application was assessed by a review of the schools' medical education databases and the institutional self-study reports. The authors found that schools provided evidence of compliance for 42 of the 48 standards. In the authors' view, schools were provided with clearer guidelines on how to respond based on instruction provided to each school by the LCME on how best to complete both documents. Standards that schools paid less attention to appeared to be those with "ambiguities in the construction and meaning of the standards." (14)

The accreditation standards remained in the narrative/prose format until 2002. Using the existing standards as the foundation for revision, the LCME, in an effort to reduce the subjectivity and increase the objectivity of each standard, introduced a numerical format to the document. Each standard was assigned a number, and was linked to a specific identified domain for further clarity. There were a total of 132 standards. The domains were Institutional Setting (IS), Educational Program (ED), Faculty Affairs (FA), Medical Students (MS), and Educational Resources (ER). This numbering of the standards, served in large part to decrease the redundancies in content areas that had occurred during the continuous revisions of the narrative standards. (15)

> IMPACT: The creation of five domains numbering each of the 132 standards and assigning them to each domain increased clarity and reduced some ambiguity. This did result in a more evidence-based approach but also led to a substantial increase in non-compliance findings as noted above.

To further increase clarity of the meaning and intent of each standard, a series of questions relating to each standard were introduced. Medical schools now had specific guidelines on information schools were required to provide in the medical education databases in order to achieve compliance. The result was a much more evidence-based document and an easier means for the LCME to track school compliance/non-compliance with specific standards over time. The LCME now also had the ability to examine each standard and assess for the critical nature of each, and the associated accreditation decision by the LCME committee.

In a 2012 study severe LCME Accreditation action decisions for two cohorts of medical schools were examined. The authors defined a severe action decision as one that is critical in nature and required follow-up such as an interim visit, the shortening of the accreditation period (< 8 years), the decision of probation, or withdrawal of accreditation. These decisions were examined against the standards as they appeared in the narrative format (Study Period 1–108 medical schools), and against the newly formatted standards (Study Period 2–107 medical schools). The authors noted an increase in severe action decisions during Study Period 2 with a notable increase in the LCME recommendation for probation. There was a substantial increase in noncompliance during this period for standards relating to the Education Program (ED) section of the document. The authors attributed these increases in part to the greater clarity of each standard provided by the numerical reformatting of the standards, and the identification of specific requirements for compliance for each, thus allowing survey teams to better link their findings to a specific standard. (16)

In March 2014, the LCME published a revised version of the *Functions and Structure of a Medical School* for use by medical schools beginning July 2015. While the fundamental content remained the same, the 132 previous standards were reformatted into 12 standards, each including a specific set of elements associated with each. The elements numbered 95. The elements identified for each standard essentially describe each component part of the standard for which the school must supply evidence of compliance. In this way, LCME decisions about compliance vs non-compliance for each standard were based on an examination of the school's response to each individual element associated with each standard. The intent of this change in formatting was to further define and clarify for the schools and for the LCME survey teams exactly what is expected of schools along each stage of the accreditation process. Subsequent to the 2014 publication, the standards and elements have been regularly reviewed for validity and clarity by the AMA, the AAMC, and members of the medical education community. This reformatting included a large reduction in the total number of questions to be answered by reducing redundancies. (17)

IMPACT: With this recent change, the number of standards was reduced from 132 to 12, and the original 132 reduced in number to 95 elements of the 12 standards. This had the impact of providing a "big picture" view of the 12 major categories and reducing the potential that a school would be placed on probation for minor issues associated with one or more of the 132 original standards. Compliance or non-compliance is assigned against the entire standard, not the individual elements. However, the question still remains how many non-compliant elements equate to non-compliance with the entire standard.

Section IV: Application of the LCME accreditation standards today – issues and process

As noted earlier the accreditation of a medical school is a voluntary, peer-review process. In keeping with our definition of quality assurance, the process is designed to ensure "that standards are specified and met consistently for a product or service." (18) The product we refer to are the students we graduate, and the service is the provision of quality health care by our graduates who exhibit the general professional and clinical competencies required to meet the needs of the populations they serve. The standards for the accreditation of a medical school have evolved over time, to a point where the clarity and validity of each standard and element has improved with each iteration.

The process of accreditation of a medical school is rigorous and comprehensive, and one that requires the dedication of all faculty, staff, administration, and students. Typically, the preparation of an LCME full site visit begins 18–20 months prior to the visit. Schools benefit from the identification of an accreditation lead who is responsible to coordinate all matters relating to the site visit, and the writing of all accreditation-related documents required for submission to the LCME.

In order to apply each standard and element, schools are required to complete the Data Collection Instrument (DCI) approximately nine months prior to the site visit. The writing of this document requires vast input from faculty, staff, administration, and students. The DCI is organized by standard and associated elements. The school is required to provide responses to all questions associated with each standard and element, and as part of the DCI, the schools must supply evidence of compliance for each in the form of a narrative response, and appended documents. With the reformatting of the standards in 2012, the LCME added further clarity to this process by providing the school with a list of required appendices associated with each standard.

Once the DCI is completed, work begins on the schools Institutional Self-Study (ISS) report. This report is a summary document, compiled by the school, outlining the perceived strengths and weaknesses of the program, and strategies for sustainability and continuous quality improvement. This document is prepared by an Institutional Self-Study Task Force through which a number of subcommittees report. Each subcommittee, as defined by the school, is tasked with a thorough review of specific sections of the DCI and the formulation of responses to LCME questions relating to standards and elements. The writing of this report requires a careful honest look at the school as a whole, and should align with findings in the DCI. The ISS report is sent to the survey team along with the DCI, three months prior to the site visit.

RECOMMENDED PRACTICES:

1   It is recommended that schools hire a dedicated expert in accreditation – one who has experience as an LCME survey team member in a school's preparation and implementation of an accreditation process, and who holds a senior academic leadership position in the school, and at best, who has been an LCME Team Secretary of a site visit team.

2   The accreditation expert be given the authority by the Dean to oversee all matters relating to the preparation and implementation of the school site visit.

3   The accreditation expert be given the responsibility of managing the school's processes for the ongoing monitoring of compliance with accreditation standards.

4   The ongoing monitoring of compliance with accreditation standards occurs in a timely and comprehensive fashion in an effort to avoid "wet paint" immediately prior to an LCME site visit. The notion of "wet paint" is often associated with a school who begins preparation for an LCME site visit less than 18 months prior to the visit, thus requiring schools to modify policies and processes in time for the visit. This however often results in the lack of evidence of compliance with these new initiatives, requiring the LCME to seek this evidence on an ongoing basis following the visit in order to ensure compliance.

5   The process of accreditation and ongoing monitoring compliance with LCME standards must be a priority for each school as evidenced by clear and ongoing communication about the process with all faculty, staff, administration, community stakeholders, and students.

6   It is recommended that each school assign one writer for the documents submitted to the LCME in order to ensure consistency of language, tone, and style. It is recommended that the accreditation lead fulfill these roles.

Medical students play a critical role in the accreditation process. In addition to providing input into the development of both the DCI and the ISS, students are required to conduct an independent review of the program as a whole to include areas such as the learning environment, adequacy of resources, support services, and the educational program. Their findings are presented in the Independent Student Analysis (ISA) report. To accomplish this, the students, usually members of the student government, develop a survey for dissemination to all classes. Students have the ability to add specific questions addressing their own local medical school experience. The LCME provides students with guidelines pertaining to the development of the survey, reporting of survey results, and specific questions to ask of the student body. (19)

RECOMMENDED PRACTICES:

1   The school make every effort to engage busy year 3 and year 4 students involved in their clinical experiences, to stay involved in the process.

2   Schools select a balanced representation of students for the LCME site visit. It is important that students are educated in the value of the accreditation process, and that they understand their voice is paramount for the site visitors to hear, therefore written and oral comments must be evidenced-based, balanced, and constructive for the school.

3   The students understand that the school has the opportunity to address student concerns noted in the Independent Student Analysis (ISA) in their response to the ISA document that is submitted to the LCME team alongside all other required documents.

The process is entirely student driven, although the school does provide administrative and technical support. The school must not participate in the development of the survey, the analysis of data, or the writing of the IA report. This a particular strength of the LCME process. Once written, the ISA is reviewed by the school, and results of the survey incorporated into both the DCI and the ISS report. The school is required to prepare a written response to the program strengths, weaknesses, and issues requiring monitoring as outlined in the ISA for review by the survey team prior to the site visit.

The DCI, ISS, ISA, and the school's response to the ISA are sent to the survey team three months in advance of the site visit. Members of the survey team are appointed by the LCME from a pool of experienced medical school faculty and administrators. There are typically five to six team members.

The survey team, under the leadership of the Team Secretary, reviews all documents. Team members conduct an initial assessment of the program based on findings in the documents, and then begin to draft the Team Report (Appendix) in advance of the site visit. Areas where the team cannot make a judgment on the compliance of certain standards due to lack of evidence or conflicting evidence, are noted for the Team Secretary. The school may be asked to provide further evidence of compliance for these standards prior to the site visit, or at the time of the visit. All communications with the school are conducted between the Team Secretary and the faculty accreditation lead for the school. Scheduling of the activities for the two-and-a-half-day visit are also arranged by these parties.

At the time of the site visit, the survey team meets with predetermined groups of faculty, staff, administration, and students. During the meetings, the team has the opportunity to gather additional information if needed, verify information, and clarify any outstanding issues, in order to make an assessment of how well the school complies with each standard and element. A tour of the educational facilities and student facilities is usually included as a component of the site visit. In cases where there are distributed campuses, this could mean a visit to another community. At the end of the survey visit, the team presents a summary of its findings to the Dean and the Chief Executive of the university. Over the next two months, the team finalizes the draft report. This report includes narrative information relating to the school's compliance with each standard and each element. This report is sent to the Dean of the school for a review of errors of fact and tone of the report. After any adjustments are made, the Team Secretary forwards the final report to the LCME Secretariat for their review and determination of the school's accreditation status. (20)

The entire accreditation process is rigorous and laborious. It requires an ongoing commitment to the process by the school's faculty, administration, and staff. The evolution of the LCME standards has served as a means of clarifying meaning of each standard in order for schools to more easily provide evidence of compliance.

The process and content of accreditation of North American medical schools has evolved and changed in response to ever-increasing requirements to assure quality in the outcome of medical education. As societal needs and demands impact the nature of medical education, quality assurance methods must evolve to meet these changes.

Section V: Challenges in implementation of the accreditation standards

The process for institutional implementation of the LCME accreditation standards can best be described as comprehensive, intensive, and time-consuming, and at the same time rewarding. The provision of high-quality medical education to the country's future physicians is the mandate we as medical schools are obliged to fulfill.

As outlined in Section IV, the process to apply the standards is multi-faceted. Each component of the process however requires committed leadership, dedicated experts in accreditation, and sufficient resources. Each of these components are described in more detail below.

Committed leadership: The full accreditation cycle is eight years in length. As such, there is a tendency for medical schools to push the demands of accreditation to the side following a successful full accreditation site visit. Such a "lull" in the accreditation process is evidence that an institution has not implemented continuous quality improvement processes. Institutions trapped by a false sense of accreditation security have often found themselves on probation or warning of probation status in the next site visit.

In order to address this potential problem, the Canadian medical schools have adopted an interim accreditation process conducted at the mid-point of the eight-year cycle. This internal, comprehensive process requires the school to examine ongoing compliance with each standard. The reports generated at the end of the process are not shared with the accrediting bodies, rather schools may disseminate the results to the key stakeholders of their choosing. This change in the "culture of accreditation" required commitment from not only the leadership of the medial school, but the leadership of the University and affiliated clinical teaching sites.

Medical school leadership must play an active role in bringing about this culture change. It requires that issues of LCME accreditation are communicated regularly and effectively to all stakeholders. In many cases, these communications are delivered during faculty, staff, student, and curriculum committee meetings. In addition, regular updates on the compliance and a process for the monitoring of the achievement of each accreditation standard is now clearly articulated in LCME Standard 1.1 which states "a medical school engages in ongoing planning and continuous quality improvement processes that establish short and long-term programmatic goals, result in the achievement of measurable outcomes that are used to improve programmatic quality, and ensure effective monitoring of the medical education program's compliance with accreditation standards." Compliance with this standard is facilitated when schools frame all activities in the context of the LCME accreditation standards.

Leadership also plays a key role in the drafting of the Institutional Self-study Report as describe in Section IV. Here, the school has the opportunity to honestly examine their perceptions of the progress made in achieving each accreditation standard. Honest institutional self-reflection is not an easy process when new accreditation issues arise or old ones remain unresolved. Leadership can help to positively identify the issues, and provide assistance to faculty, staff, students, and administration in developing realistic and sustainable solutions.

Dedicated experts in accreditation: In keeping with the true intent of the accreditation process – i.e. continuous quality improvements, a school is well served by placing a dedicated expert or experts in administrative positions in order to help ensure a successful accreditation process. The LCME asks that one of these positions, the faculty Accreditation Lead, be assigned to a senior school administrator, one with expertise and experience with LCME accreditation. This person is responsible for working with the LCME site survey team prior to each site visit, and to oversee the design, development, and writing of the DCI and the ISS. Excellent written and oral communication skills are considered a great asset to this position as adherence to the LCME "language" is imperative as well as maintaining the proper "tone" of all written documentation.

The Faculty Accreditation Lead must pay continued attention to the evolving LCME standards, and to monitor those standards that are commonly cited for North American medical schools, and those the school has been previously cited as non-compliant or compliant with a need for monitoring. The LCME provides all medial schools with ongoing updates on common issues through their website, webinars, and through annual national and international meetings of medical educators.

Dedicated resources: To maintain compliance with the accreditation standards, medical schools must plan and budget dedicated resources that include the Faculty Accreditation Lead position, administrative support for this position, clerical support for meetings of al LCME working groups and task force groups. Dedicated time for staff, administration, students, and faculty to participate in the accreditation process in a meaningful way must also be included. Additionally, as a component of continuous quality improvement, schools should, as best they can, have a plan for succession of those in accreditation leadership positions. In this way, sound accreditation practices and processes can be learned, sustained, and maintained.

As part of the entire continuous quality improvement strategy, resources should also be allocated to ensure that best practices in program and faculty performance evaluation are developed, implemented, and monitored. This will provide evidence not only to the LCME, but to the faculty and students that feedback is gathered, analyzed, and acted on in cases the school deems appropriate. This is especially important as graduating classes prepare to complete the annual American Association of Medical Colleges Graduate questionnaire. Annually, students in their final year of medical school are asked to provide feedback to the school on the performance of the curriculum, student support services, financial aid services, and overall program performance. These data collected for each school, are then compared again national averages in order for schools to assess their individual performance. Students completing these questionnaires need to be assured that their feedback on program performance was heard, and in cases, acted upon. This feedback to students is essential as students are asked to indicate their perception of the quality of their medical education program. Dedicated faculty, staff, and administrative resources are often required to maintain an appropriate and compliant level of performance.

RECOMMENDED PRACTICES:

1   The school articulates its Continuous Quality Improvement activities relating to the ongoing monitoring of compliance with LCME standards in formalized policy/procedure form. This would include the strategic planning for succession and ongoing leadership for accreditation at the school.
2   Medical school leadership continues to improve the culture of accreditation by modeling best communication practices concerning the process, supporting the accreditation lead in all matters relating to the process, and supporting those educational and school activities that align with the vision and mission of the school and with the LCME accreditation standards.
3   Ensure all medical students are well educated in matters concerning the accreditation process, and their important role. Consistent and ongoing communication from senior leadership is highly valuable.

Summary and conclusions

The process of medical school accreditation in North America is certainly not perfect, but the fact that it has evolved with input from the constituent institutions and members is testimony to the democratic process and the honest desire to improve the quality of education and ultimately the output of our schools and colleges. It is a process and a product of a complicated cultural milieu that in itself changes and evolves in response to the external and internal forces acting upon it. In the end success will be obtained with strong organizational leadership that values the process of accreditation as a tool for quality improvement; identified expertise for leadership in the process and staff to support them; buy-in from faculty and staff throughout the institution; and a student body willing to provide honest, balanced comment and evaluation of their experiences.

References

1. Council for Higher Education and Accreditation Specialized/National Panel: Council for Regional Accrediting Commissions: The Value of Accreditation.
2. Ellis, Roger, Storey,S.,Whittington,D and EllisRoger, Gibson, Norman, Stringer, Maurice and Finlay, Catherine Woodward, RogerEllis, Roger (ed). *Quality Assurance for University Teaching* (Buckingham, UK: Open University Press, 1993).
3. Kassenbaum, Donald G., *Academic Medicine*, Volume 67, Number 2, February 1992, pp. 85–87.
4. Retrieved from https://lcme.org/about/meetings-members/ 2017.
5. Retrieved from https://lcme.org/about/meetings-members/2016.
6. Pritchett, Henry S., and Abraham Flexner, *Medical Education in the United States and Canada: A Report to the Carnegie Foundation for the Advancement of Teaching* (New York: Carnegie Foundation, 1910).
7. Ibid., p. 19.
8. AMA Council on Medical Education and Hospitals, 1910. Retrieved from https://babel.hathitrust.org/cgi/pt?id-mdp, November 2016.
9. American Medical Association. Essentials of an Acceptable Medical School. (revised). *Journal of the American Medical Association*, 1952, pp. 374–378.
10. Council on Medical Education and Hospitals and the Association of American Medical Colleges. *Functions and Structure of a Modern Medical School*, 1957.
11. Association of American Medical Colleges, Executive Committee of the Council of Deans. Meeting Minutes, April 9–10, 1969.
12. Liaison Committee on Medical Education. *Standards for Accreditation of Medical Education Programs Leading to the MD Degree* (LCME, Washington D.C., 1997).
13. Hunt, Dan, Migdal, Michael, Eaglen, Robert, and Barzansky, Barbara. The Unintended Consequences of Clarity: Reviewing the Actions of the Liaison Committee on Medical Education Before and After the Reforming of Accreditation Standards. *Academic Medicine* 2012: 87; 560–566.
14. Kassenbaum, Donald G., Eaglen, Robert, and Ellen R. Cutler. The Meaning and Application of Medical Accreditation Standards. *Academic Medicine* 1997: 72; 807–818.
15. Hunt *et al.*, 2012.
16. Ibid
17. LCME. *LCME Guide to the Institutional Self-Study* (Washington D.C., 2016).
18. Ellis, 1993.
19. LCME. *The Role of Students in the Accreditation of Medical Programs in the United States.* (Washington D.C. June, 2016) 20 p.
20. Liaison Committee on Medical Education. *Rules of Procedure* (Washington D.C., 2016) 37 p.

32 Quality Assurance in Nurse Education

Professional and Academic Perspectives

Marian Traynor

Introduction

Quality assurance is a key element within a Higher Education Institution's strategic approach to developing and delivering academic courses. Its aim is to offer students the highest possible quality of learning so that they can deliver their professional knowledge and skills to a world-class standard and thus enhance the industry in which they work. A high level of quality assurance also contributes significantly to the reputation and profile of the institution. Thus quality assurance is pivotal to the success of the HEI in attracting students who wish to be associated with courses that have been quality assured and benchmarked against recognised quality standards. It also means that employers can recruit the HEI's graduates, confident in the knowledge of their expertise.

This chapter aims to provide information on how quality assurance is developed and managed for professionally accredited courses, such as nursing, and it will also attempt to discuss some of the challenges that can be associated with a joint validation and quality assurance process.

Quality assurance and nurse education

Quality assurance of all nurse education in the UK is governed by both the professional accreditation body for nursing, the Nursing and Midwifery Council, (NMC), and the quality assurance processes that exist within the particular HEI. This approach is designed to provide for a robust process for programme review and revalidation to ensure nurse and midwifery education programmes remain current and fit for purpose. This integrated approach to quality assurance allows a system in which modules are reviewed after they are taught, programmes are monitored every year and programmes revalidated on a five–six yearly basis, and is designed to ensure that nurses and midwives at the point of graduation are fit for practice, purpose and award.

Nurse education is however not only subject to the quality processes within HEIs and the NMC but also the demands of the NHS to produce graduates who are 'fit for practice'. Other stakeholders such as government bodies who fund nurse education (though in some parts of the UK this is subject to change), self-funding students, patients and the learners themselves also have a legitimate interest in the outcomes of nurse education. With today's financial constraints there is also an onus on educators to demonstrate cost-effective education provision.

Over the last decade the Nursing and Midwifery Council (NMC) has taken important steps in an effort to further improve quality in nurse and midwifery education. This will culminate in the publication of new standards for nursing education in 2018. The new standards will embed and be reflective of the NMC Professional Code of Conduct and, in addition, will place more accountability on HEIs to ensure that programmes are evidence-based and fully compliant with NMC standards for nurse and midwifery education. To meet the requirements of the NMC all HEIs that deliver nurse and midwifery education programmes will have to demonstrate effective engagement and involvement of the public, service users and HSC staff at all levels of programme development.

The context of nurse education

In the UK the study of undergraduate nursing and midwifery is a subject taught within Higher Education Institutes by Schools of Nursing and Midwifery. These schools are subject to the HEI quality assurance mechanisms (Quality Assurance Agency 2010). However the attainment of a degree in nursing is not only recognition of academic achievement but also an entitlement to register as a nurse with the Nursing and Midwifery Council, part of whose function as the regulatory body for nursing, is to maintain a register of appropriately qualified nurses. Therefore the award of a nursing degree is equated to the granting of a licence to practice and an associated level of clinical competence. Consequently any HEI that offers nurse education is therefore subject to inspection and monitoring by the NMC in its statutory capacity to oversee the provision and standards of nurse education in the UK (NMC 2016)

Academic and professional standards and nurse education

HEIs need to assure themselves and the professional accrediting body for nurse education, the NMC, that the quality and standards for its educational provision are being maintained. To do this most HEIs have a dedicated quality assurance department whose job it is to review the quality of educational provision, to monitor that academic standards are maintained and to ensure that steps are taken to enhance the quality of it education provision. The quality assurance body within any HEI refers to the UK Quality Code for Higher Education and defines quality as follows:

> Academic Quality is concerned with how well the learning opportunities made available to students enable them to achieve their award. It is about making sure that appropriate and effective teaching, support, assessment and learning resources are provided for them. In order to achieve a higher education award students participate in the learning opportunities made available to them by their provider.

The NMC's courses that have a professional accreditation such as nursing must meet the standards as set by the NMC for education and training of nurses and midwives which included the 'outcomes to be achieved by that education and training'. The Nursing and Midwifery Order 2001 (the Order) defines the NMC role in the education and training of nurses and midwives. The NMC set standards of education and training, maintain a register of those who meet these standards and take action when a nurse's or midwife's fitness to practise is called into question.

Approval and monitoring of nurse education programmes within an educational institution

The first stage in the approval process is twofold; the school makes a formal application to the NMC to indicate that they wish to seek approval/re-approval at least six months prior to the date for which approval is required and they also inform the Head of Academic Affairs within their institution of their intention to seek approval for a new programme. To oversee the process and to demonstrate the positive partnership relationship between education and service providers, and to embrace the concept of a shared responsibility for the preparation of nurses, the school will establish a curriculum steering group and a curriculum working group.

The curriculum steering group is chaired by the Head of School and will have representation from senior clinical colleagues (normally Director of Education and Workforce Planning or equivalent), representation from the quality assurance department in the HEI (normally a senior administrator from courses and regulations committee or equivalent), service user, student representation, Director of Education from the school, and the school manager. The remit of this group is to give direction to the curriculum working group on issues such as NMC standards and local policies and health care directives that might impact on nurse education programmes. The curriculum working group is normally chaired by the Director of Education from the school and will have representation from the school programme leads, senior clinical colleagues (normally Practice Education Coordinator or equivalent), service user and student representation and a senior school administrator. The remit of this group is to agree particular modules; to agree the CATS per module; to agree the learning outcomes and the methods of assessment for each module.

The NMC, upon receipt of the request for approval of a new programme, will establish a timeline for the approval event and appoint a major reviewer for the school to liaise with. The programme approval event is then scheduled in conjunction with the HEI's Department of Academic Affairs and normally takes place on one full day. The event is referred to as a joint validation and is therefore subject to the HEI quality assurance procedures as well as the NMC quality assurance procedures.

The joint validation panel is established by the HEI and the NMC in line with agreements between the two parties on constitution and procedure. The joint validation panel consider the NMC report on the proposed new programme and the details of the course are discussed with the representatives of the HEI proposing the new programme including senior management, representatives from the curriculum planning group, programme leaders and prospective teachers. Feedback to the school is provided by the joint panel at the end of the validation event. The joint validation panel then prepares a report including its conclusions and recommendations for submission to the HEI Academic Affairs Department and the NMC. The NMC report will include confirmation (or otherwise) of approval of the programme, any conditions which apply and an indication of the duration of approval. The confirmation of approval from the NMC is made on the basis that the HEI will also confirm final approval.

Curriculum validation from the programme provider's perspective

Although the formal process for seeking approval for nurse education programmes is clear, adherence to quality control mechanisms for those programmes can be challenging. This is primarily because to meet HEI quality control criteria there is the assumption that all learning outcomes for professional courses such as nursing are measurable and that within the programme tests can be applied to verify that students have achieved the learning outcomes. Programme developers therefore have to balance what will meet the quality control matrix with what is possible to measure. Boursicot and Roberts (2006) argue that this is particularly challenging when it comes to the measurement of the professional attributes associated with being a professional such as attitudinal and ethical aspects, prejudice reduction, or the reflective and critical appraisal characteristics that cannot be easily taught or measured. The challenge is to devise measurement techniques for what is required to be tested.

This can be frustrating from the programme developers' perspective, particularly when coupled with a sometimes inexperienced review panel, which does not necessarily appreciate that the difficult questions have to be asked in order for the review to be meaningful. For example prior to the joint validation event there will have been several meetings with both clinical and academic staff to agree curriculum content and how it should be taught and assessed. This normally generates significant discussion and variation of opinion and the resulting material presented to the review panel may not necessarily reflect current best evidence but rather the opinion of one or two. As a result the material presented may not necessarily be reflective of the evidence that supports the numerous diverse educational approaches available to support student growth and development. In these instances the programme developers are dependent on the review panel to scrutinise the programme specifications and module templates thoroughly so that they can make evidence-based recommendations on programme approval.

One area that always seems to cause particular problems for programme developers and therefore validation committees relates to the assessment of clinical competence. Clinical competence is a key part of any professional course and for nursing it counts for 50 per cent of the programme. It does not help that currently the NMC does not offer explicit guidance on how clinical competence should be assessed and therefore leaves it up to each HEI to decide on the most appropriate assessment method. This has resulted in a variety of approaches to the assessment of clinical competence across HEIs and a resulting reliance by the programme development teams on the validation panels to ask the programme developers to defend the assessment methods selected and to justify why other evidence-based approaches have been omitted. Experience to date would indicate that review panels are hesitant to ask these questions and are therefore more likely to accept what has been presented. This may be in part due to the fact that validation panels do not always have a subject expert in the area of clinical assessment and is something that review panels may need to consider in the future.

Competency-based assessment is an accepted part of most nursing curricula, however, we must also accept that within competency statements there exists qualities that do not lend themselves to being additive. Within nursing curriculum there are numerous qualities for which measurement is attempted: caring, empathy, communication etc. If we accept that measurement is always the same and can be read from an instrument, learned or memorised, without being altered by the differences of perception (Jarvis and Gibson 1997), we must also consider that subjective, value-laden statements regarding an individual's kindness, integrity and motivation add a dimension to assessment which is beyond the scope of competency measures (Jarvis and Gibson 1997). The question then arises as to how something that cannot be measured can be quality assured.

Another key area that can be challenging to a validation committee looking at professional courses such as nursing is the whole area of professionalism and how they can be assured that it is adequately taught and assessed. Again, the programme developers are dependent on the review panel having sufficient expertise in the area of assessment of professionalism so that they can robustly review the tools selected by the programme developers and comment on the feasibility and validity of these tools. Much like in the assessment of clinical competence, the guidance from the NMC does not extend to providing evidence-based examples of how assessment of this important area might be managed and, once again, programme developers are at the behest of a review panel to challenge appropriately.

Can we measure all learning outcomes?

Robust quality assurance mechanisms require all learning outcomes to be measureable. In terms of competence, knowledge and understanding, this normally presents few problems. However, quality assurance in nursing also relies on certain values and attributes which go beyond competence and the measurement techniques used to measure it. These include, for example, attitudinal characteristics which tend towards personal qualities rather than professional competencies. The development of a nurse with the values and attributes for nursing is dependent on the existence of a measurement technique against which critical judgements can be made and that does not trivialise professional skill. Criterion-based assessment which measures how well the student performs in relation to predetermined criteria, is used within the competency model. Important decisions are made about individuals depending on whether they meet the standard as specified within the competency. There is a need to design a tool that can measure values and attributes such as empathy and communication and the discrete elements intrinsic to professional competence, which together contribute to the role of the nurse.

For example the use of Multiple Mini Interviews as a values-based recruitment tool is a recognised valid and reliable tool to select individuals suitable for nursing. The Multiple Mini Interview (MMI) was devised by Eva and his colleagues at McMaster University in Canada and is designed to test candidates from the cognitive and non-cognitive skills perspective (Eva *et al.* 2004). The MMI consists of a number of stations each with a different examiner. The stations are designed to test specific values and attributes such as communication, empathy, knowledge of course, critical thinking and ethical decision making. They give admission officers flexibility in blueprinting the qualities they would like to select and can be adapted by individual institutions to reflect their own values and curriculum (O'Brien *et al.* 2011) The MMI as reported by Traynor *et al.* (2016) was in response to the fact that it is good practice for HEIs to review selection methods against the best available evidence and to demonstrate the application of robust quality assurance procedures to the selection methods used for entry to university. The MMI does not necessarily indicate academic success, however, it is capable of discriminating between candidates and it shows little evidence of bias. This raises the question as to whether a similar technique, or a process based on a similar theoretical foundation, might be adapted for use in assessing what has hitherto been regarded as too nebulous to measure. It may not be possible to do so, but it may be a first step in stimulating a new avenue of research, which is an essential requirement to maintain the integrity of the quality assurance system. In the absence of alternative proposals, the only other option would appear to be not to attempt to measure these characteristics. While this may offer intellectual safety, it will do little to ensure that quality assurance in nursing programmes is sufficiently robust to guarantee that objectives are being met. If certain attributes can be measured at the recruitment stage of a nursing course, if those attributes could also be measured both during and on completion of the course, the quality of the course could be robustly assured. It is a goal worth pursuing.

Conclusion

HEIs must ensure that there is a robust process to review programmes to ensure that programmes remain current and fit for purpose and provide assurance to external agencies such as the NMC that the quality and standards of its educational provision are being maintained In the absence of direction from professional bodies such as the NMC on how certain characteristics should be measured, the HEI could take a decision to go beyond the minimum standards which degree-awarding bodies must use to make the award of qualifications at a particular level of the UK frameworks for higher education qualification and introduce a requirement for courses that have professional accreditation to develop a set of standards or values on which critical judgements can be met. The use of the MMI is one way of ensuring a standards-based approach to selection and provides the clarity needed to make a judgement about the values a candidate holds that might make them suitable for a career in nursing. No such standards-based approach exists however for the assessment of a student in the clinical context which accounts for 50 per cent of the nursing programme. There is no doubt that the development of such an instrument would be expensive and time consuming. However if the NMC and HEIs are committed to maintaining standards then it would seem imperative that time is set aside to develop assessment procedures which are fit for purpose and will detect unsatisfactory students. This is the challenge facing the NMC as it prepares to develop a new set of standards for nurse education.

References

Boursicot, K. and Roberts, T. (2006) Setting standards in a professional higher education course: defining the concept of the minimally competent student in performance-based assessment at the level of graduation from medical school. *Higher Education Quarterly* 60(1): 74–90.

Eva, K.W., Rosenfeld, J., Reiter, H.I. and Norman, G.R. (2004) An admissions OSCE: The multiple mini interview. *Medical Education* 2004c(38): 314–326.

Jarvis, P. and Gibson, S. (1997) *The Teacher Practitioner and Mentor in Nursing, Midwifery, Health Visiting and the Social Services* (2nd Ed). Cornwall: Stanley Thornes Ltd.

NMC (2016) *Quality Assurance (QA) Framework for Nursing and Midwifery Education and Local Supervising Authorities.* London: NMC. https://www.nmc.org.uk/news/news-and-updates/first-universities-and-local-supervising-authorities-to-be-visited-using-new-quality-assurance-framework/

O'Brien, A., Harvey, J., Shannon, M., Lewis, K. and Valencia, O. (2011) A comparison of multiple mini interviews and structured interviews in a UK setting. *Medical Teacher* 33(5); 397–402.

Quality Assurance Agency for Higher Education (2010) www.qaa.ac.uk

Traynor, M., Galanouli, D., Roberts, M., Leonard, L. and Gale, T. (2016) Identifying applicants suitable to a career in nursing: a value-based approach to undergraduate selection. *Journal of Advanced Nursing*, doi:10,1111/jan.13227

UK Quality Code for Higher Education (2015) *Safeguarding Standards and Improving the Quality of UK Higher Education.* http://www.qaa.ac.uk/publications/information-and-guidance/publication/?PubID=2968#.Wk4Dbk1LGUk

33 Experience of an OfSTED Inspection of an Initial Teacher Education Partnership

Liz Fleet

Introduction

During 2016, my university, as the accredited body for our Initial Teacher Education (ITE) Partnership, was subject to an inspection carried out by the Office for Standards in Education, Children's Services and Skills more commonly referred to as 'OfSTED'. The inspection came in two parts: the first visit took place in the summer during the 2015–16 academic year (May) and, as was the case under the inspection framework of the time, the second visit took place in autumn of the subsequent academic year 2016–17 (October). This chapter is presented as a case study of an ITE Partnership undergoing an OfSTED inspection, and is written as a personal account, drawing on my experience at the time as Deputy Dean within the faculty with responsibility for Quality Assurance and OfSTED inspection, and as the Initial Teacher Education Partnership's OfSTED link person, otherwise termed by OfSTED as the 'provider's representative'.

The material thus presented is a first-hand account of what it means to anticipate, to prepare for and to undergo an OfSTED inspection. In the account there are details of the processes, the documentation, the meetings and the organisational structure – all of which have to be 'fit for purpose' to respond to the requirements of OfSTED. The chapter refers in more depth to the build-up and preparation prior to the inspectors' visits than the actual visits themselves as this is where the significant effort of any ITE Partnership is focused. By the time the inspectors call there will be limited activity aside from organisational, though not none, which can be undertaken to significantly influence the outcomes.

The 'story' of an OfSTED inspection goes far beyond re-telling what happened during the inspection visits. Wilkins, in his chapter in this book (Chapter 11), refers to the notion of 'OfSTED readiness'. For those of us engaged in Initial Teacher Education (ITE), especially with significant OfSTED responsibility and accountability, I would say that being 'OfSTED ready' becomes 'a way of life' and is never far from one's thoughts. As time moves on the anticipation of the next inspection grows. This notion is explored within the chapter in regard to what this meant in practice for our ITE Partnership.

Background

The university is situated in the north-west of England and, having started out as a Church of England training college for male student teachers over 175 years ago, has its roots firmly embedded in teacher education. Whilst education programmes remain significant today, a wide variety of other courses, including a range of professional courses, are now on offer at the university. Student numbers, from the United Kingdom and overseas, have also expanded significantly over this time.

In ITE, primary and secondary student numbers increased overall by approximately 12 per cent during the period 2009 to 2016. Numbers fluctuated during this period with a dip between inspections when a four-year Bachelor of Education became a three-year Bachelor of Arts (Education) programme and core[1] numbers in Secondary were reduced before rising again when School Direct[1] was introduced and PGCE Primary core* provision was expanded.

The ITE provision was inspected in 2010, this being the most recent inspection prior to the one discussed in this chapter. It resulted in Primary being graded as 'outstanding' whilst Secondary had been graded 'good' in terms of 'Overall Effectiveness' and 'outstanding' in relation to 'Capacity to Improve'. The Further Education provision was graded as 'good' and the Early Years (0 to 5 years) programme did not at that time exist.

The inspection framework for ITE has undergone several changes over the years. At the time of the 2010 inspection one single visit of a week's duration to conduct inspections of all phases and routes across the Partnership was the norm. Prior to this framework, two visits in the same academic year had been the norm, usually taking the form of a fact-finding short visit in the autumn combined with a summer visit to confirm or otherwise the grades being awarded trainees during school placement. In 2015 a significantly different format for inspection was introduced with two visits to the Partnership effectively spanning two academic years. The first visit would be scheduled to take place in the summer term with a focus on training, and the assessment and attainment of the trainees. The second visit would be to assess the trainees (from the same cohort of 'leavers') during their first teaching posts as NQTs comparing grades given by the Partnership with their inspection findings. This new format for inspection was the one against which we were inspected in 2016, the framework only undergoing some relatively minor revisions applicable to any inspections commencing after September 2015. The other key difference to the framework was the heightened expectation in regard to the key outcomes of attainment, completion and employment rates and the relative position of these when compared to the sector.

At our university, we prefer to refer to the trainees as Associate Teachers or ATs; Newly Qualified Teachers are commonly referred to across the sector as NQTs. These acronyms are used within the subsequent text.

Learning from previous inspection findings and other considerations

The story of an inspection unfolds almost from the moment the inspectors complete their previous inspection which, as noted above for our ITE Partnership, was in 2010. There is no intention here to provide a step-by-step account of events which transpired in the five and a half years between inspections, but simply to indicate that effectively once one inspection is complete, managers will be concerned to ensure areas for development, as identified through the inspection process, are addressed and that the ITE Partnership continues to make improvements across its provision. This was no different for our Partnership. Subsequent changes in staffing including vacancies arising due to retirement or natural role changes, were also considered, to some degree at least, in the light of the OfSTED results. Successes as overall lead for the Primary phase in 2010 led, in part, for example, to my subsequent appointments as Head of Department (ITE), Associate and then Deputy Dean with overall OfSTED and QA responsibility.

Two key areas had contributed significantly to our success in Primary during the 2010 inspection. The first was the strength of the Partnership with schools and the second was the proven effectiveness of our use of data to inform decision-making and drive improvements. There were lessons we could learn from both of these areas as we moved towards the next inspection. There had also been significant changes since the 2010 inspection in regard to our student numbers and the range of programmes we offered, which needed to be taken into account. The introduction of School Direct and also as an increased allocation of student numbers to our 'core' Primary PGCE provision, itself as a result of positive OfSTED grades, were important considerations. With growth comes opportunities to work with an increased number of schools and of course, alongside this, the necessity to ensure that high-quality provision is maintained across a potentially much more complex context. This too can create its own tension; success at managing a smaller Partnership built on mutual understanding and trust can lead directly to an increase in size, which means new and 'untested' partners, who maybe do not initially share your understandings. The complexities of scaling up operations should not be underestimated and requires significant resource and investment. Success can therefore bring with it new and more challenging opportunities.

Partnership and the role of schools

Having partner (school) colleagues play a significant role is clearly crucial to any successful Partnership. This too does not come without some tensions.

At the time of the inspection there was no formal requirement on schools to engage in Initial Teacher Education, a matter which in my experience has been voiced widely as a concern within the sector. Whilst many schools generously fulfil a significant role in the development of successive generations of teachers there are other schools in which this is not seen currently as a professional responsibility, and accommodating trainee teachers is seen as 'doing the university a favour'.

No-one could argue that a school's primary function is anything other than to provide the best education possible for its pupils. However that should include, I would strongly argue, a full commitment to supporting the education and training of the next generation of teachers – for if the best schools do not fully participate in this process, sharing their expertise with future teachers, then future populations of pupils of those and other schools cannot receive the best possible education. I believe that 'paying it forward' must be an essential principle in education at all levels. It is our responsibility, and our duty, not just to educate the pupils in our care, but to train educators for future generations, to share with them what we have learnt, to contribute our expertise, our knowledge and our understandings so that future generations are educated to ever higher levels.

Even as far back as 2003, those involved in Initial Teacher Education were pointing out that although Ofsted sees involvement in ITE as part of good practice for schools, this aspect of their work is not routinely scrutinised:

> OfSTED inspectors see the provision of ITT as a positive aspect of a school's activity and, where it is done well, as indicative of good practice as well as high quality management and leadership. Only a minority of inspection teams saw fit to comment on this aspect. It is likely that were the Inspection Handbooks to consider ITT provision as a core activity of most schools, and not just Training Schools or those Beacon and Specialists with special responsibility, this would encourage schools to become, and to stay,

involved. Those schools that have considerable experience of being involved with ITT identified many benefits and very few drawbacks.

(Coldron *et al.*, 2003, p. 13)

Under the current system schools are now expected to engage more in the process of Initial Teacher Education but unless they are part of a SCITT provider (School-Centred Initial Teacher Training) the schools are not directly accountable for this element of provision. For example, under the inspection process described here, there was no requirement that any of the partner schools should participate in teacher education: a school could have been rated as 'outstanding' by Ofsted even though they had never trained a single teacher. Within the current inspection framework for schools there are nine occurrences of the word 'trainee'. There is no suggestion that accommodating trainees is expected and it does state that, 'Inspectors should not take trainees' performance into account when assessing the quality of teaching, learning and assessment across the school.' (OfSTED, 2016, pp. 22–23). This statement does not however prevent some schools from suggesting they cannot accommodate trainees because they are anticipating an inspection. The nearest suggestion of any accountability appears on page 22 of the Framework and clearly relates to the salaried route:

> Inspectors should meet any trainees who are training on the School Direct (salaried) route and are employed by the school in order to assess the support, mentoring and induction given to these new teachers.
>
> (OfSTED, 2016, p. 22)

Thus one of the many paradoxes here is that while it has been recognised that schools are important repositories of expertise, and that schools should, in principle, play a greater role in training, the onus and responsibility for ensuring that this occurs has remained with universities, and not the schools themselves. It is true that within what are termed 'university-led' and 'School Direct' Partnerships much responsibility for the actual training is owned by the schools, but the responsibility for ensuring quality, and the accountability for the quality of training, continues to lie solely with the university.

In the future, this might change; there are moves elsewhere, for example in Wales, to have a system of accountability which more greatly acknowledges the significance of the role of schools. In the Furlong Report on the future of Initial Teacher Education in Wales, it has been proposed that the inspection process by Estyn (the Welsh equivalent of Ofsted) should 'explicitly values schools' contribution to initial teacher education' (Furlong, 2015a). Indeed, Recommendation 5 from this report states that: 'Estyn's "Guidance for Inspection" for schools be revised to include specific recognition of the contribution of a school to Initial Teacher Education'. In a further comment, Furlong (2015b) spells out how this is to be done. He envisages that from 2017 Estyn should adopt 'more flexible inspection procedures', which would examine the contribution of schools to ITE, including: how schools collaborate 'with other providers to raise quality', and how their professional development impacts 'on staff effectiveness and provision'.

Envisioning the Partnership

In assessing the effectiveness of the leadership and management of ITE Partnerships, the first point OfSTED seeks to evaluate is 'how relentlessly leaders and managers pursue a vision for excellence, focused on improving or sustaining high-quality provision and outcomes for trainees' (OfSTED, 2015). A key activity for our Partnership, and this would be the same for others, was to agree and articulate our vision and share it with all partners. Over time together we generated a set of statements to clarify what it was we considered to be the underlying principles and values, and the vision for our Partnership. These included key references, for example, to: our drive for self-improvement through critical reflection; our care to promote and foster the well-being of all learners; and crucially our pursuit to have a positive impact on outcomes for learners. Our strapline, 'Partnership with the learner at its heart' came to me in the middle of the night on one of the many occasions when I would find myself lying awake with too many things to think about. I remember 'googling it' the next morning and being relieved that it had not already been claimed.

In lots of ways the phrase does have a familiar ring; many educational organisations claim to focus on the learner, or take the learner's interest to heart. However, the focus for us was that the learner is actually at the heart of what we are about. The emotive use of the word 'heart' refers to the fact that we care a great deal about doing the best we can for the learners. Additional to this is the interpretation of the reference to the learner; for us we were promoting the view that in various senses we are all learners. The 'learner' was clearly identifiable as the child and young person but moreover was also used to represent the teacher, the mentor, the leader, the teacher educator as all are encouraged to continue to learn throughout their careers. As a Partnership we felt that this was something we both aspired to and could play a significant role in developing. Seeking ways in which to put the vision into practice was very helpful both in consolidating our beliefs and also in our development and improvement as a Partnership.

Operationalising the Partnership

Clearly, ensuring that a vision is shared and implemented requires strategy and hard work. It was crucial that discussion of the vision and its implications began with ITE candidates at the interview stage, and progressed with ATs on programmes, and Mentors and Leaders in school as well as colleagues at the university. A dedicated Director of Partnerships for School Direct played a valuable role in effectively sharing this vision in his negotiations and discussions with Alliance partners. Similarly, the Director of Partnerships for core provision and the Mentor Development Team were key to the success of sharing the vision.

It was also important to have structures in place to both drive forward our vision and monitor our impact and effectiveness. Creating an over-arching Quality Assurance and Enhancement committee which I joint chaired with a leading partner head teacher complemented the separate management groups we had in place for all phases: Primary/Early Years; Secondary and Post-compulsory. We held yearly 'verification' meetings with each Lead School Direct partner to consider and review the plans for the subsequent year's programmes. This gave an opportunity for professional dialogue in which good practice was shared but matters of compliance were also specifically addressed. All of these groups were able to fulfil demonstrably useful and distinctive key roles in our Partnership development and improvement. They enabled us, for example, to make effective decisions based on analysis of an extensive range of data sets from outcomes data on attainment, completion and employment rates as well as evaluations from all stakeholders including ATs, school and university colleagues. We were able to examine current issues in schools and consider the impact of these on our provision and to consider a range of areas, for example, disability matters in the context of school-based learning.

In addition, a number of other partner groups (termed Fixed Focus Groups) were created to enable us to focus on key developmental areas, sometimes for a fixed period of time, other times for lengthier periods or ongoing dependent upon the nature of the task. For example, separate short-term School-based learning groups were set up to address expectations of ATs during specific periods in school, whereas other groups were created and developed over a longer time period as the area of focus continued to require attention in new and innovative ways. These longer-term groups have included 'Behaviour and Engagement', 'Alumni/Newly Qualified Teacher (NQT)', 'Mentor Development' and numerous 'Subject' groups. The newest one prior to the inspection visit was the 'Well-being' group which had sparked from the particular interest of colleagues in the faculty in response to a national and local recognition that both teacher and pupil well-being was becoming of increasing concern. It was very important that these groups became much more than simply opportunities to discuss ideas (though that is clearly crucial), but that they had an impact on the Partnership through improving the provision for the ATs and enhancing learner experience within school.

Planning for the inspection

Considering the next inspection we clearly wanted to aim for 'outstanding' across the whole provision and to build on the 2010 successes. However we recognised that the brand new Early Years Teacher Status (EYTS/0–5 years) course and the Further Education (FE/post compulsory) were more closely aligned with a 'good' grade rather than 'outstanding'. This was nothing to do with the actual quality of the programmes and in FE a very robust quality assurance process was in place and managed by the university-employed post-compulsory Lead. Rather, the issue was the challenge of providing an inspection team with a significant evidence base demonstrating a sustained partnership, and a record of high-quality outcomes. For example, the EYTS provision had started out with only four ATs in its first year, and there were some deep issues surrounding FE at the time with one college graded inadequate in its FE-specific inspection and suffering from significant staff turnover. These matters, which required responses and support from the university, were ongoing.

A key element to planning effectively for the inspection was to ensure a thorough understanding of the OfSTED Inspection Framework of the moment and to constantly re-evaluate the work of the ITE Partnership with direct reference to it (OfSTED, 2015). A second crucial element was to monitor regularly and carefully the 'ITT Criteria' (DfE, 2017) which outlines what it is for an ITE Partnership to be 'compliant'. These criteria can change regularly, so it was essential to check the website regularly. OfSTED Partnership letters, sent electronically to the Provider's Representative (i.e. me, in this instance) would normally alert us to changes so checking the detail of these was helpful. It is not enough however to simply digest the contents of these key documents; every element needs to be embedded within the programmes and matters such as compliance and roles and responsibilities need to be understood and appreciated by all within the ITE Partnership. Cognisance of the requirements is an ongoing necessity, and rapid responses and pro-active decision-making are essential. Newsletters to partner schools and updating of staff responsible for quality assurance visits to schools were key considerations. I found reading other providers' inspection reports and sharing highlights of these with the ITE team was a helpful activity and kept colleagues alert to the priorities.

Clearly, while an inspection is there to examine your day-to-day activities as well as to scrutinise the data collated as the cumulative record of past work, and all of these are an essential part of any educational undertaking, an inspection itself is not normally part of an institution's day-to-day activities, and therefore needs to be planned for, and staff prepared in advance both for what might occur, and how they should act and respond. It is important that although an inspection has the potential to disrupt normal activity that it does not actually do so. An organisation which cannot take an inspection in its stride is never going to be considered 'outstanding'. A set of procedures in the form of a flow chart was created so that in the event of receiving the call colleagues would understand their operational roles and be able to action these swiftly. Being sure to carry one's personal mobile was also essential so that contact could be made easily should the call come when away from the office.

In any Partnership there are going to be times when things do not go to plan or exactly as one might hope or envisage. There may be a natural tendency within an organisation to want to hide potentially problematic issues from an inspection team, however this would be both naïve and potentially irresponsible. The inspection team will expect there to have been issues, and they will wish to see how these have been addressed. The presentation of these issues and the way they have been dealt with is crucial here. If issues are seen as not being viewed with their full significance, this can count negatively. On the other hand, if too much emphasis is placed on the issue rather than the way it has been dealt with, this too can be a negative. The balance can be quite difficult to achieve. The mark of excellence is to minimise such occurrences, to know how to handle them when they occur, and to ensure that lessons are learnt and procedures put in place to obviate any recurrence. This can best be achieved in an atmosphere of trust where colleagues feel able to openly express any concerns or anxieties and know that they will be supported to find appropriate solutions.

It was particularly important for all colleagues to be able to discuss with confidence our Partnership's strengths and areas for development, after all our outcomes were very good; on the other hand any display of over-confidence would have been inappropriate and unhelpful. Engaging in a professional dialogue was what we aimed to achieve with the inspectors. As part of our preparation, we employed a consultant, with the credentials of being a well-regarded former Her Majesty's Inspector (HMI). This person was engaged to act as a critical friend, to engage with colleagues and to visit a sample of schools, particularly those engaged in the newer School Direct route. In engaging colleagues in high-quality professional dialogue, she was able to nurture confidence and ability, and for me also to have engagement with such a highly knowledgeable and experienced former HMI was invaluable.

Maintaining 'OfSTED readiness'

I mentioned the term 'OfSTED readiness' earlier in this chapter. My approach to 'OfSTED readiness' was mainly derived from my own approach to leadership: one of providing direction along with guidance and mentorship. An OfSTED inspection effectively involves the sampling of the distillation of many years of work; that work needs to be shared, understood and owned by all members of the Partnership. No one person can be present at every meeting of the inspection team with every mentor, every tutor and every AT to guide them through the process. In the search for excellence, every single person has to understand the shared vision, and be motivated to express it, and to interpret their work in terms of that vision for the inspectors.

Some of the key initiatives which were further developed during the period between inspections included monitoring and review. Regular reporting by the Programme Leaders (PLs), on matters relating to recruitment, retention and attainment in particular was undertaken in formal meetings. Clear records of ATs were maintained so that we were always aware of the progress of each individual and any cases where one might be identified as 'at risk' either through health and well-being matters or by not achieving the anticipated progress in their teaching. We moved quickly to provide support and intervention both in school and in university wherever this was thought necessary. There are some ATs who can overcome the most difficult circumstances to go on to become very successful teachers and my colleagues and I have always done our utmost to enable this to happen. As well as having an open door policy for ATs, some of the practical support offered included very small group and one-to-one sessions on developing presence and confidence in classroom situations, and bespoke support on planning and assessment. A problem-based learning approach was adopted in some aspects of the programme to enable tricky issues and case studies to be shared and discussed.

Being 'OfSTED ready' meant that key data sets were regularly updated and the self-evaluation and improvement planning were never static, although there are of course key data capture points which enable year-on-year comparisons to be made. Sharing key data and information with all partners formed another strand of OfSTED readiness. It is important to note that all of these activities had been ongoing for some years prior to notification of the initial inspection visit in May 2016.

Notification of the inspection

For a significant number of mornings (mostly Thursdays in term time) over the five years and, in common with many Providers' Representatives, we knew we could expect a morning phone call from OfSTED. In the last change to the Framework this changed so that providers would only be contacted in the summer term if they were to be inspected in that year. Follow-up calls were then known to be coming in the following autumn term. The arrangement however meant that we needed to be 'ready to go' whenever the phone call arrived.

Ours came in May 2016. During the initial call, the OfSTED administrator explained clearly that our Partnership was to be inspected the following week, and arranged for a further call with the Lead Inspector, which followed almost immediately. In one sense, after years of anticipation, the immediate atmosphere was one of an overwhelming sense of calm – and a relief that the agonising wait was over, as this would now enable us to operationalise the very detailed processes that we had rehearsed to ourselves on multiple occasions.

The Lead Inspector described precisely what would happen next and what was required. The detail of this was much as anticipated and it was reassuring that there were no 'surprises', or changes to the inspection process, or requirements to present previously unexpected types of data, which can often happen. Key documents, such as the Self-Evaluation Document (SED), were given a final tweak and review and contact details for phase leads were shared.

As overall lead, I needed to assign phase leaders for the four phases: Primary, Secondary, Further Education and Early Years. In doing this, I retained phase lead role for Primary, as this was the largest and most complex area of our provision covering effectively six programmes (3–7 and 5–11 years, BA and PGCE plus both core and School Direct routes). One of the motivations for this decision was that the overall Lead Inspector was acting in the capacity of Primary phase lead, and it was useful to mirror the inspection structure so as to monitor what was happening on a daily basis during the inspection.

This decision on my part in no way represented a lack of confidence in the Primary programme leaders but was taken more as a result of us having always worked together very closely and the fact that I possess a detailed overview across the complexity of routes. I also took the decision to assign members of the Faculty Management Group to each of the other three phase groups to support and monitor protocols during the phase meetings with the inspectors. This included allocating my fellow Deputy Dean to support the FE provision, the Head of Department (ITE) to support the Secondary leaders and a second departmental head in the faculty to support the Early Years team. Each phase group also was responsible for agreeing with the Lead Inspector for their phase the timetable of activities for the following week.

Many of the housekeeping tasks, such as allocating parking places and timetabling for both base and meeting rooms for inspectors, were undertaken by the Faculty Administrator. These tasks might sound fairly straightforward, but with a team of around 15 inspectors due on site at different times, this inevitably causes some disruption to normal timetabling.

By Friday evening, less than 36 hours after the initial phone call, the details of inspector activity for the following week were complete: the inspectors had selected the schools they wished to visit, the ATs they wished to observe teaching and the groups they wanted to meet. Activity was to be intensive as in addition to visiting schools the inspectors were keen to meet with school colleagues, our partner groups, teams of 'trainers' from university and school, and additional groups of ATs at the university. During this planning period the faculty and ITE administrative offices resembled a war cabinet engaged in manoeuvres with new and important information flowing in and instructions flying out fast, in response to the reports of telephone discussions with phase groups which were being held simultaneously. Large and complex charts were constructed to document the inspectors' ongoing activities. These included details of what documentation and personnel would be required in each location at each time.

Despite being 'OfSTED ready' there were a number of tasks which required completion during the weekend prior to the phase one visit, and which could not have been completed beforehand. This included the preparation of the compulsory 'pen portraits' of the ATs who were to be observed in school and, through our choice, the QA records for each of the selected schools, giving details of mentor development and school visits; all of these needed to be sourced from our electronic folders. We were asked for paper copies of materials given some issues with the OfSTED portal so a number of documents, including our programme and subject-level self-evaluation documents and improvement plans, were also printed out in preparation for Monday's arrival of inspectors.

The week of the inspection

Monday morning was relatively quiet save for a few further documents being taken to the inspectors' base rooms and, aside from one early arrival at 9 am, most inspectors arrived closer to lunchtime after their first visits to schools. Telephone calls were made to partner schools by allocated team members to check that visits had gone to plan. Feedback from both schools and ATs was generally very positive. One somewhat alarming issue however had occurred, in which on the very first inspection visit, a pupil in one of the schools had been quite disrespectful to an inspector. Such events are completely out of our control and, as stated earlier, it is the way we respond to such events that is important, not the events themselves. Fortunately, the inspector had taken this completely in her stride and made sure that in the autumn return visit she followed the same AT into her employing school to check on behaviour management, and undertook a return visit to the original school where the incident had occurred. In this particular case, these checks demonstrated that whilst such behaviour is relatively rare that ATs are able to cope with challenging behaviour.

Under the (then) fairly new inspection framework, we were invited to send representatives to observe the 'end of day' mutual feedback meeting of inspectors within each phase. This was extremely useful for two of the phases (Primary and Secondary) in particular where there were several inspectors contributing to the discussion. Following these 'end-of-day' phase meetings, there was then a meeting of all phase leads which I was also able to observe.

Colleagues and I found this to be a fascinating experience. In determining grades for the ITE Partnership, the methodology the inspectors were required to employ was a 'bottom-up' strategy of evaluation. The inspectors had to be convinced that the Partnership had met all the requirements at the lower level before considering any criteria for the level above. In practical terms, this means that an inspection team starts off by checking the ITE Partnership's performance against each of the criteria describing 'inadequate' provision. Inspectors must be convinced that all compliance criteria have been met, in order to even be considered for the next grade up, 'requires improvement'. Even though this was expected, it was, at first, quite an unnerving experience to observe. We knew we had been absolutely meticulous in arranging and confirming that ATs had received all entitlements, such as teaching across the required age-phases but it was absolutely clear that a provider could be deemed 'non-compliant' if a single anomaly was evident even if the trainee concerned might be performing brilliantly in wonderful schools.

In many ways, the inspection progressed as envisaged. At the end of the first visit, interim feedback was provided for the team. Whilst it was intended to keep the feedback recipient group to quite a small gathering, the large teaching room filled as all of the Faculty Management Group and the Vice Chancellor, a staunch supporter of teacher education at the university, appeared in addition to those of us who had been engaging with the inspectors on a daily basis. Feedback at that point was extremely encouraging. Very positive comments were made in regard to the ATs themselves, the involvement and support from school colleagues and leadership across the Partnership. We were given what we perceived to be appropriate areas for development from the inspectors and most reassuring of all was that each of these had already been, in some measure, identified by the team in our self-evaluations and improvement plans as 'enhancements to current practice' or 'areas for development', and that actions against these improvements were currently in hand. Because the suggestions for improvement were very clear and they matched our own, this enabled us to feel very confident around where we would need to focus our efforts.

Across Primary we needed, for example, to examine and address reasons for withdrawal from programmes, particularly focusing on key groups such as mature female students on the PGCE School Direct route. We were also to seek to improve attainment of male ATs at the very highest levels. We had already put in place across all Primary programmes bespoke interventions which not only built on the usual practice of supporting ATs to move from grade 3 to grade 2 (good) but also good to outstanding (grade 1) by the end of final placement. Whilst not able to fully evidence the impact of this activity there was certainly very sound evidence to support us in demonstrating effective practices to ensure male ATs made very good progress. In regard to withdrawals, with reference to individual ATs we were able to demonstrate how periods of interrupted studies to support, for example, family and personal circumstances, had enabled many ATs to go on to successfully complete their programmes albeit slightly out of sync with their peers.

In Secondary, the focus was on ensuring School Direct ATs based in relatively non-diverse school alliances were all given ample opportunities for a diverse range of placements. This had already most definitely been on our radar. Placement swaps across alliances were noted to be valuable in some instances. We also had plans in place for the end of the programme in any case because enrichment activity had been specifically programmed in June to account for the small number of instances where this might otherwise have been an issue.

Between the first visit and the second, which occurred in October, business continued more or less as normal. Summer was busy as usual. My task was the preparation of the end-of-year data for all programme and subject leaders and undertaking some broad analysis to support them prior to programme- and subject-specific analysis by the relevant leaders. Programme Leaders were inevitably getting ready for the new intake of students.

The second inspection visit

From around the second week in September anticipation grew for the telephone call notifying us of the second visit. Our usual activity with NQTs and their schools was underway. Programme and Subject Leaders had completed their analysis of outcome data and were implementing their new improvement plans. By the time the call came in mid-October the team was ready. A strength for us, in addition to the provision of individual support offered to NQTs, was the programme of NQT development offered through collaboration between the university, the local authority and several School Direct alliances.

Effectively a sample of the same cohort of 'trainees', as they made the transition into their first posts as teachers, and normally within the first three months of doing this, were to be observed. The process of arranging this was very similar to the one followed for the first visit. The phone call occurred on the Thursday prior to the Monday when the inspection was due to recommence. Detailed spreadsheets, containing attainment grades and names of employing schools, of those who had exited the programmes in the summer were provided. The inspectors selected a range of NQTs and schools to visit and as soon as we were informed of the selection we notified all concerned using OfSTED's pre-prepared letters and our own preamble.

Whilst a significant focus of this second visit of the inspectors was to visit NQTs and to confirm, or otherwise, the accuracy of our grading of them there were several other areas of consideration. The new self-evaluation documents and focused improvement plans with evidence of impact against our actions were well received. We also presented many case studies demonstrating the impact of our faculty activity within the Partnership. In keeping with our vision we were able to showcase many activities which had been undertaken for the benefit of children and other learners across the Partnership. These were very diverse including, for example, broadening of children's intercultural awareness by arranging for our partners from Nippon Engineering College, Katayanagi Institute, Japan to engage children and staff in a number of our partner schools through our long-term intercultural applied drama project, which included taiko drumming. Something else that we were proud of was the partnership with Manchester Camerata who supported us in celebrating 175 years in teacher education. For this celebration, colleagues worked with children from six partner schools to put on an evening's performance of drama, dance and music (much of which the children had composed) in the city's cathedral.

The inspectors spent some time confirming that the strengths identified during the first visit were apparent still. We received high praise in relation to leadership of the Partnership. This I felt was particularly pleasing. As lead for the OfSTED preparation I had been keen to ensure continued close contact, throughout the five-year build-up, at both strategic and operational levels with the head of department (Initial Teacher Education), Directors of Partnership and the Programme and Subject Leaders. This had entailed fortnightly meetings with them and meant that we really shared a thorough understanding of what was important. It also enabled colleagues to learn from each other, to provide mutual support and to share best practices. With the Head of Department, I also led meetings of the full ITE team and this ensured that we were quickly able to address any concerns being voiced by colleagues. Leadership extended to those school colleagues involved in our Partnership groups as it was within these that many innovative ideas to enhance practice were conceived. It was important that the fulfilling of OfSTED expectations became part of our normal activity rather than being something which could potentially be viewed as an 'add-on' by the team.

The inspection result and afterwards

At the end of the inspection, there was a further formal gathering in which the phase Lead Inspectors delivered their judgements. The Vice Chancellor, this time unable to attend in person due to being in China, was nonetheless at the end of the telephone keen to hear the final results. Our Partnership was graded 'outstanding' across the vast proportion of the provision (i.e. all Primary 3–7 and 5–11 programmes and Secondary programmes). The much smaller FE provision was graded 'good' and the Early Years (0–5) programme also was graded 'good'. Watching my colleagues' faces as the feedback was given I could see a mix of great delight and huge relief. Whilst an inspector's comment made at some point during the inspection had been a reminder that working hard alone was not necessarily enough, I was very pleased that the significant effort of the teams had in fact been recognised as being highly effective. The audience was reminded of the confidential nature of the results until such time as their publication and the feedback session concluded. The full report can be accessed online at https://reports.ofsted.gov.uk/inspection-reports/find-inspection-report/provider/ELS/70132.

In conclusion

While it is not possible in this piece to capture all the thoughts and activities undertaken during the interim period between the 2010 and the 2016 inspections and then at the time of the inspection itself, I hope to have given a flavour of what happened within our ITE Partnership.

The chapter explores some of the tensions faced by those involved in Initial Teacher Education. Whilst many schools willingly play a significant role in supporting ITE there are others for whom this is far from a priority. There are strong arguments for schools viewing contribution to ITE as one of their responsibilities, and whilst there may be legitimate reasons from time to time for non-engagement with ITE, a permanent state of non-engagement cannot be seen as an acceptable status quo for any school. Such an increased responsibility for schools would normally be expected to carry with it an increased accountability via OfSTED. However, under the current OfSTED Framework it is the university that continues to be held accountable for the training in schools.

When a Partnership is judged outstanding by OfSTED, its allocation of 'trainees' can increase quite suddenly and dramatically. The point is made that the quality of provision can suffer if insufficient attention is paid to the issues which arise through sudden growth. Where new partner schools are sought there will be a need to ensure all mentors understand their roles and responsibilities and that sufficient resources are provided to enable crucial relationships to be forged between partners.

On a personal note at this point, I firmly believe that a Faculty of Education (ours being the 'Faculty of Education and Children's Services') can offer so much more to its community, the wider university and the surrounding local and regional area than is reflected in any inspection grade. However in the current climate an inspection grade has become a crucial indicator of quality, carrying with it specific consequences and potential repercussions. The grade is significant, not only because it establishes the faculty's reputation across schools and other ITE Partnerships, but also because the future well-being and even the existence of a faculty can be dependent on securing a positive OfSTED outcome. Although recently there have been changes to the system which allocates students to providers (NCTL, 2017), for many years the National College for Teaching and Leadership (NCTL) and its predecessors considered the OfSTED grading to be a significant criterion in determining the allocation of future student numbers. In an open market situation, OfSTED grades may prove to be an important factor when potential student are choosing their training locations. Under either one of these systems, an OfSTED grade can influence a faculty's ability to secure student numbers, and this in turn will affect its financial viability as a provider. All in all, reputations not-withstanding, when OfSTED calls there is a lot at stake for all concerned, and tensions and anxiety levels can understandably be raised, even where a provider is confident in the quality of its provision, with indicators consistently showing it to be of a very high standard.

On a final note it should be recognised that the team involved in providing excellence in ITE extends well beyond teachers and academics to administrative and technical staff, student support and guidance colleagues and also to domestic and security staff, some of whom were concerned and dedicated enough to escort me safely to my car in the early hours of the mornings during the busiest inspection periods. I am very grateful to all my wonderful colleagues in university and school who every day work tirelessly to provide an excellent service to our Associate Teachers and contribute through this, in a significant manner, to the betterment of children's and young people's lives across our region and beyond.

Note

1 'School Direct' is the phrase used to identify provision whereby candidates apply directly to the school or alliance for a place on the programme as opposed to 'core' provision whereby candidates apply directly to the university.

References

Coldron, J., Williams, J., Fathallah-Caillau, I. and Stephenson, K. (2003) 'An investigation of what Ofsted reports, and a sample of Beacon, Training and Specialist schools say about schools' involvement with ITT in the Yorkshire and Humberside region. Project conducted by members of Sheffield Hallam University School of Education for the Teacher Training Agency.' Available at: http://www4.shu.ac.uk/_assets/pdf/ceir-schools20itt.pdf

DfE (2017) "Initial teacher training criteria and supporting advice Information for accredited initial teacher training providers", Department for Education. Reference: [NCTL-20077-2017]. Available at: https://www.gov.uk/government/uploads/system/uploads/attachment_data/file/594123/Initial_teacher_training_criteria_and_supporting_advice.pdf

Furlong, J. (2015a) 'Teaching Tomorrow's Teachers: A Report to Huw Lewis, AM, Minister for Education and Skills', University of Oxford. Available at: http://gov.wales/docs/dcells/publications/150309-teaching-tomorrows-teachers-final.pdf

Furlong, J. (2015b) 'Teaching Tomorrow's Teachers: Re-forming Initial Teacher Education Together'. Available at: http://learning.gov.wales/docs/learningwales/publications/161118-prof-john-furlong-en.pdf

NCTL (2017) 'The Allocation of Initial Teacher Training Places: Methodology for the 2018 to 2019 academic year'. Available at: https://www.gov.uk/government/uploads/system/

uploads/attachment_data/file/644642/FINAL_The_allocation_of_initial_teacher_training_
places_methodology_for_.._.pdf

OfSTED (2015) 'School Inspection Handbook. Handbook for inspecting schools in England
under section 5 of the Education Act 2005.' Reference No. 150066. Available at: https://
www.gov.uk/government/publications/school-inspection-handbook-from-september-2015

OfSTED (2016) 'Initial Teacher Education Inspection Handbook. For use from September
2015.' Reference No. 150033. Available at: https://www.gov.uk/government/publications/
initial-teacher-education-inspection-handbook

34 Teaching Quality in Art, Design and Media

Tacit Knowledge and Experience

Roni Brown

Introduction

The practice of art and design is a creative endeavour that speculates upon and challenges its own nature and purpose and which demands high levels of self-motivation, intellectual curiosity, speculative enquiry, imagination, and divergent thinking skills. Students learn to recognise the interactive relationship between materials, media and processes, between ideas and issues, and between producer, mediator and audience. Similarly, art and design practice demands the ability to position the individual's practice within an appropriate contextual framework.

This paragraph is taken from the *Subject Benchmark for Art and Design* (2016: 11) in the section describing the nature and extent of Art and Design. It provides a useful setting to begin a discussion of the complexities of *quality* in Art and Design that must first identify some of the essential problems with creative disciplines and modern environments for teaching and learning. Using the Subject Benchmark also helps to define the group of disciplines that form the context of this discussion. It embraces art, design, craft and media production disciplines, but excludes performing arts and architecture that are covered by different Subject Benchmarks. However, given these disciplines are also concerned with conceptual and material practice, this discussion may also be relevant to teaching practitioners of these disciplines.

Capturing the entire system of learning means developing an understanding of the non-material, tactic elements of learning in addition to the well-conceived and tested objects that exist by way of graduate knowledge, understanding and skills.

The first section of the chapter isolates key concepts associated with creativity, not to rehearse the history of this literature but to set up the problems for institutions, quality assurance and learners of creative disciplines that appear particular to these fields. This section will explore the nature of creative practice, the creative practitioner and the notion of discipline as a starting point for exploring in the second section the institutional settings for teaching and learning. In this section I wish to discuss the idea of specialisation of, and within, institutions as a response to the need to tailor the environment, policy and practice in ways that nurture disciplinary characteristics. In the third section the chapter will open out a discussion of curriculum, teaching and learning addressing paradigmatic issues of the creative curriculum within the Academy. This section will reflect on the Coldstream reports of the 1960s and 1970 to provide an historical context for the nuanced relationship between technical and vocational skills and the academic and intellectual purpose of creative education that still has implications for curriculum today. The following section focusses on assessment and feedback through the lens of the student experience. In this area there is a great deal of scholarly work as it represents one of the most complex and arguably distinctive areas of HE practice, residing at the intersection of educational process and professional practice. The final section will discuss perhaps the most challenging area for quality in Art, Design and Media: resources. This is not addressed as a problem of quantity or currency (though these are highly connected to discussions about quality) but the ability of institutions via explicit pedagogy, to allow students to negotiate and navigate their own resource requirements and the expertise they require to inform the direction of their work. In so doing, this section will also address the wider resource implications for institutions including the tailoring of the management of resources for different learning objectives. The chapter conclusion summarises the pivotal issues for quality in Art and Design and attempts to offer an answer to the question of how quality can be recognised in these disciplines.

Creativity and implications for quality assurance

> Any act of artistic and scientific creation is an act of symbolic subversion, involving a literal or metaphorical transgression not only of the (unwritten) rules of the arts and sciences themselves but also of the inhibiting confines of culture, gender, and society. Re-thinking creativity means challenging established borderlines and conceptual categories while re-defining the spaces of artistic, scientific and political action.
>
> (Pope, 2005: 33)

Although creativity is not limited to Art, Design and Media, it is fundamental to what characterises and problematises them as disciplines and therefore frames a discussion of quality. I have set out some of these propositions in *Art, Design and Media* (Brown, 2015: 360–361) that I will briefly summarise here. Understanding creativity as a philosophical, spiritual, material, political and economic activity is a necessary starting place in debates about pedagogy and quality assurance. Pope's comprehensive overview of creativity (*Creativity: Theory, History, Practice,* 2005) demonstrates the range of philosophical approaches to the topic of creativity and the divergence of views produced, for instance, by the discourses of Humanism, Romanticism and Materialism. Despite its complexity as a subject there is some distillation of what is at stake in the creative process, accepting creativity as essentially dialogic (at once solved and not solved, neither divinely 'creative' nor entirely the realm of production, but something beyond (Pope, 2005: 9)). Csikszentmihalyi's thesis on flow develops a Western conception of creativity that is based on the production of outcomes that 'have not been seen before and that make a difference in the context in which they appear' – making them significant (1996: 47). For Csikszentmihalyi, producing significant creative outcomes is underpinned by knowing the culture (internalising its values) and is reliant on the judgement of experts (for instance teachers, curators, critics). We can therefore add to the already complex debate about creativity that it is facilitated by 'schooling' and a state of mind that is habitually disruptive. Teachers of disciplines that foster creative development will be continually observing and nurturing the innate creative quality of the individual, gauging the maturity of the individual to manage the external judgemental (assessment) processes, and overseeing the successive development of highly complex thinking, making and application skills – moving between, for instance, playfulness and discipline, objectivity and subjectivity, self and other, fantasy and reality, risk, experimentation and pragmatism.

There are three particular facets to creative practice that arise from these brief observations that are pertinent to a discussion of quality: those that pertain to the social context of creative practice meaning it is a mediated practice; the context of the individual's creative practice (the process of drawing-out and developing the unique *personality* of practice); and the development of high-level material skills that enables the *exposition* of creative work.

While the individual's unique approach is critical to creative practice, little professional practice exists in isolation. A variety of professional mediators (for instance, gallerists, curators, agents, producers, critics, commissioners, design managers) judge, select and connect the work of artists and designers with clients, audiences and the public. Mediation occurs at all points along the creative process – from posing a problem to the judgement of quality (for instance, originality, execution, presentation) and appropriateness (fitness to problem, purpose, client, audience). Divergent perspectives will be commonplace to professional practice and will be experienced by students as a fundamental aspect of learning. This introduces a number of challenges for learners and institutions. For instance, the variety of practitioners that are implicated in guiding the development (and judgement) of work including professionals, technical experts and academic staff, and therefore the need for students to develop skills to navigate the *disruptive* characteristics of learning. In addition to multiplicity of opinion is the necessary absence of certainty about outcomes given that what is produced is individual in each case. As such there is an essential *vulnerability* to learning as teachers and students contend with the unknowable in creative practice. This will pose challenges to the sense of security of learners, the way they perceive fairness in assessment and their feelings about feedback. Further, there is the need to ensure this social aspect of learning is embedded within institutional culture: through collaborations and external briefs; the regular practice of exhibition; and peer-to-peer critique of work.

The second area to draw into the discussion is the requirement for Art and Design education to nurture individuality – to observe innate capability and to fully acquire and extend this into a unique capacity for creative practice. The emphasis on learning environments that observe difference, plurality and independence of mind will require specialist teaching and learning strategies to support the transition to independent learning (for instance Orr *et al.*, 2010) and resource strategies that reflect substantial early individual contact time and an environment that allows students to explore a variety of materials and technologies. This requires learner-focussed approaches that are inevitably challenging given the constraints and operational complexities of institutions.

The third theme to draw out from this introduction is the range of skills that creative practitioners develop (perceptual, conceptual, disciplinary, theoretical, visual, analytical, material and technical). For detailed discussion of each of these capabilities it is worth reviewing Koestler's extensive exposition of them in *The Act of Creation* (1964), Sternberg's *Handbook of Creativity* (2007) and Pope's *Creativity: Theory, History, Practice* (2005). In later sections on 'Curriculum, teaching and learning' and 'Resources' consideration is given to the particular problems of the integration of skills (focussing on the *project*) and specialisation of skills (focussing on *repetitive* and *sequential* learning). Curriculum design is a political arena and is too often polarised to the detriment of learners around vocational and technical and creative and academic skills. Ideas about quality will be implicated in the way institutions respond to these problems and bring about a holistic conceptualisation of graduate skills.

Institutions and specialisation

While the many elements of creativity will be implicated in pedagogy, it is the social, economic and cultural aspects of creativity that institutions will seek to address through curriculum development. Inevitably scale and demand for creative subjects is relevant as this impacts on the range and types of provision in UK higher education. Undergraduate enrolments for disciplines under the Higher Education Statistics Agency (HESA) category 'Creative Arts and Design' accounts for 7.45 per cent of enrolments, accounting for 169,825 full-time equivalent students. This is a sizable sector, with only Science disciplines and Business and Administration being substantially larger (HESA data, 2015/16). Creative Arts and Design has also seen significant growth (and diversification of discipline). Since 2002/3, HESA data shows a growth of 28 per cent of students studying Creative Arts and Design compared with far more modest growth for the sector as a whole. The growth in provision and diversification of discipline reflects changes in the creative economy. For instance, between 1997 and 2014 the Gross Value Added (GVA) of the creative industries increased by 6 per cent each year compared with 4.3 per cent for the UK economy as a whole and the value of services exported by the UK creative industries in 2013 was £17.9 billion, a 3.5 per cent increase compared with 2012 (DCMS, Jan 2016). The Department of Culture, Media and Sport statistics also show the changing scale of different parts of the creative sector – for instance, the scale of growth in computer games (GVA of £156 million in 2008 compared with £426 million in 2014); the boost to 'Film, TV, video, radio and photography group' as a result of recent developments in on-line distribution and the sustained strength of the 'Design: product, graphic and fashion design' group that had the largest increase in GVA between 2013 and 2014 (16.6 per cent).

The obvious point to make in relation to the size and shape of the creative industries is the dynamic impact on higher education provision, including the creation of new disciplines and pedagogies. The first report on Art and Design Education by the National Advisory Council on Art Education (Coldstream, 1970) that introduced the degree-equivalent Diploma in Art and Design, offered only four programmes: Fine Art, Graphic Design, Three-Dimensional Design and Fashion/Textiles. Lens Media was considered a subset of Fine Art or Graphic Design rather than a distinctive discipline. Today HESA provides over 100 different course codes for degree provision in Creative Arts and Design, which are further amplified by courses in the groups Architecture and Planning and Computer Science. More recent additions to the Academy include for instance Creative and Imaginative Writing; Lens and Digital media; and Sound, Performance and Interactive Media.

The 1970 Coldstream report (1970: 4) that signalled the integration of creative disciplines into the UK system of higher education, suggests the sector at the time comprised 142 units or 'art establishments' or which 68 were Colleges of Art, the remainder being provision with further education providers or proposed for inclusion within polytechnics. Although the volume of independent Colleges of Art has significantly reduced since this time (there are 20 specialist institutions listed as HE providers by HESA) there is considerable specialist HE provision within the independent and private sector. Of 122 'alternative providers' with course-specific designation in 2015/16, 16 per cent offer HE provision in Creative Arts and Design, bringing many more specialist institutions into the UK system of higher education[1]. With the exception of the University of the Arts London, specialist providers are small institutions with less than 5,000 HE students and the majority of alternative providers having less than 100 HE students.

The landscape and history of UK creative arts education, stemming back to founder art schools of the 19th century, is retained in the character of these institutions (and in the organisation of provision within multi-faculty universities that share this history).

Professor Simon Ofield-Kerr, Vice-Chancellor of the University for the Creative Arts (UCA), says of the character of UCA:

> UCA is special because it's specialist – a community that is entirely focussed on learning, teaching and researching creativity. Crucially, however, it is our breadth within this

specialism that really provides our creative project with the vitality so characteristic of the British art school. At UCA, film, acting and creative writing students study alongside one another, as do architects and fine artists, fashion designers, photographers and journalists. They work together on projects in shared workshops, and it is in creating together, this meeting of minds and hands, that most fundamentally exemplifies the creative specialist's uniquely successful form of education.

(Ofield-Kerr quoted in Henley, 2016: 66)

Ofield-Kerr raises a particular concern that will be developed later in the chapter regarding quality in Art and Design education: that of discipline distinctiveness and proximity to other disciplines and material processes that extend knowledge and is generative of opportunity. It is also a feature of specialist environments that niche disciplines are retained and promoted as central or integral to institutional missions, for example in the highly specialised techniques in hand embroidery at the Royal School of Needlework.

The purpose of this section is not to promote one kind of institutional model over another but to indicate that the strength of UK Art and Design is related to a distinctive history of specialised education and this has implications for a discussion about quality[2]. These can be summarised as follows:

- Creative disciplines are understood to have distinctive pedagogical approaches, for instance, self-direction and reflective practice, sequential, project-based learning, visual and material research practices. Further, each discipline, evolving from and informing a particular creative field of practice, will have different approaches to teaching and learning. Various and specialist approaches will need supporting through particularised teaching and learning strategies, credit and assessment frameworks; The development of specialised digital and material skills and the ability to experiment across a wide range of media, often as a consequence of self-directed study, will require supportive, flexible, cross-departmental approaches to resource leadership and management.
- Particularised teaching and learning strategies will need to reach into, and inform other institutional strategies such as the approach to resource management, including for instance contact hours, arrangements for technical support, academic selection and promotion criteria, support for practice as research and leadership development.
- Understanding creative education as an individual, social, cultural and economic practice has implications for the way curriculum is developed and delivered. For instance, the kinds of spaces and opportunities that institutions provide for the internal and external dissemination of student work; opportunities for students to collaborate with their peers within and between disciplines; the way curriculum balances opportunities for intellectual exploration, risk and experimentation and vocational and industry-specific skills, including the role of industry and Professional, Statutory and Regulatory Bodies (PRSBs) in course design and delivery.

Although this list is by no means exhaustive it proposes that ideas about quality are connected to ideas about discipline and that *problems with quality* can be linked to the degree to which the needs of disciplines are understood within the provider setting (i.e. that disciplinary knowledge is strongest at a local, departmental or course level). In this section I also hope to have alluded to other *problems with quality* in Art and Design education in that delivering an experience at discipline level often requires a different kind of relationship between students and their institution. For instance, the specialist institution is defined by scale and the focus of resources towards disciplines (i.e. the student experience will be impacted by institutional character as well as course design and quality).

Curriculum, teaching and learning

> What prevailed before the 1950s was a system devoted to conformity, to a misconceived sense of belonging to a classical tradition, to a belief that art was essentially technical skill.
>
> (Thistlewood 1992a: 152)

Thistlewood's essays, *A Continuing Process: the New Creativity in British Art Education* (1992a) and *The Formation of the NSEAD: A Dialectical Advance for British Art and Design Education* (1992b), provide useful contextualisation of the polarised views of the curriculum at the moment it was poised for significant reform. Prior to the 1960s, opinions about the purpose of Art and Design education were considered on the one hand to protect the professional standards of disciplines (National Society of Art Masters), and on the other, the educationalists' agenda, to support individual creativity and imagination (Society for Education in Art (SEA)). Herbert Read was the chair of the SEA for 23 years and his work *Education through Art* (1943) was highly influential in the changes to occur in art school education during the 50s and 60s. Influenced by the methods of teaching at the Bauhaus[3], this involved three core areas of study: the activity of self-expression; the activity of observation; and the activity of appreciation (Thistlewood 1992: 157). These remain recognisable elements of Art and Design education today: open-ended, reflective, individually led approaches; pragmatic, programmatic, disciplinary knowledge and skills; history, theory and critique. Thistlewood's examples of the early adopters of Read's curriculum show how readily the challenges of curriculum design presented themselves. Thistlewood paraphrases the experience of Tom Hudson who worked at Leicester and Cardiff College of Art as follows:

> He maintained that if he were to teach students accepted practices of, for example, joining materials (jointing wood, riveting sheet metal . . .) they would then tend to design only those things they could realise by the 'proper' means. If, however, they were asked simply to analyse for themselves the problems of joining it was probable that many of their discoveries would later be confirmed in existing craft practices, and also probable that as a result of exploiting materials beyond normal limitations, new techniques might be invented.
>
> (Thistlewood 1992a: 166)

Hudson demonstrates the importance of training in process, material and technique where the beginning is defined and programmatic, and the equal importance of open-ended, self-directed research and experimentation that leads to innovation. Rather than being discrete curriculum 'activities' Hudson's curriculum integrates vocational knowledge and skills with intellectual and creative processes, leading to an independent way of thinking about problems. This approach was also reflected in the development of visual literacy for courses in basic design through the building up of knowledge through repeated actions, trial and error to create *fluency* (by this I mean the level of skill that allows for experimentation, deviation from established techniques and creation of new meaning). The importance of balancing the technical and vocational with individual development was echoed in the recommendations of the Coldstream reviews of the 1960s and 1970 that made clear the distinction between training for technicians and the goals of the Diploma in Art and Design (awarded as a three-year-degree equivalent from 1961), warning of the danger of an overemphasis on pure training that may result in obsolete skills. 'It will be for the Colleges to devise courses which will meet industrial requirements but which at the same time will fully extend the students and provide an educational stimulus of a more general kind' (Coldstream 1970: 29). More recently Daniel Ashton revisits these tensions in his exploration of the Games Design curriculum concluding that:

> Asking students to attune their critical faculties to the distinctive and novel possibilities of games is an enterprise vital to games design and students seeking to enter industry, but one that absolutely must be integrated with an account of that industry. Tensions around being a 'potential employee' cannot be pushed to the side or seen as 'external' in favour of ensuring the formation and development of that employee.
>
> (Ashton 2010: 49)

In offering this short illustration of early curriculum development, a number of important observations can be made that remain relevant:

- Early phases of the curriculum will require significant investment in material skills and technique – to enable the skilled *exposition* of ideas and solutions.
- Curriculum will need to be designed in a way that allows for repeated and sequential performing of the creative process allowing for build-up and eventual fluency of thinking and skills.
- Project-based learning is more often than not the vehicle for integrating the different activities associated with creative development (continuum between programmatic and independent learning and the different weighting placed on these at each phase of learning).
- The techniques of reflective-critical-independent learning are essential to creative practice in stimulating original thinking and application.

For discussion on the centrality of skills for reflection and meta-cognition to educators and learners of Art and Design, articles by Orr *et al.* (2010), Winters (2011) and Webster (2004) show how these skills are linked to professional practice and therefore to teaching methods. Further, the example given by Orr *et al.* critiques the claim that reflective practice leads to deep learning without more rigorous enquiry into the kinds of activities that generate insight and lead to informed and refined work (i.e. the right kinds of reflection, 2010: 205). Webster (2004) discusses the different approaches to tutoring in architectural education as part of a wider account of reflective practice, but is equally concerned that the tutor's role be examined and constructed for the purpose of enabling high-quality student-centred learning. Winter's article on meta-learning in Art and Design (2011) also reinforces the idea that learning/teaching is strengthened when its very characteristics are the subject of analysis, and that conceptions of the particular characteristics of learning in the discipline are essential for bridging prior and new educational experiences[4].

  There is a significant focus in educational research in Art and Design on project-based learning in that it simulates 'the actual processes of professional action by requiring students to apply previously learnt knowledge and skills in an integrated way towards producing a novel solution to a design problem' (Webster 2004: 102). As such, project-based learning offers a rich environment to examine the unique methods and problems of Art and Design education, an area that is explored by Orr *et al.* (2014) in their examination of the responses of students to the National Student Survey. A key purpose of project-based learning is to allow for a diversity of student outcomes, enabling students to demonstrate a disciplined understanding of the brief and the kind of initiative that tests the boundaries of those limitations. This produces a number of problems: one of these is the idea of a fixed curriculum and its delivery. Beyond the foundational knowledge and skills that underpin the project, content will be generated from individual responses and as such the student experience 'will vary dependent on the nature of the work they pursue' (Orr *et al.* 2014: 35). The method of teaching and learning is one based on discovery (rather than testing knowledge) and is reliant on teacher–student collaboration in proposing the direction of learning. This will often require open-ended resources (within and beyond the institution) as students discover the kinds of materials and processes that support the realisation of their ideas and, further, the ability of students to navigate the multiplicity of advice of both technical, academic and professional staff in perusing their work. The work of Orr *et al.* (2014) points to the various forms of instability for teachers and students that arise from this method of working, not least among these is how students understand the way meaning and value is ascribed to their work, which is open to multiple and different interpretations as the work progresses. This lack of prescription that requires students to gain sufficient independence of thinking to begin to resolve the dilemmas of the discipline is a particularly nuanced *contract* between learners, teachers and their establishments. The degree to which students express satisfaction with learning will depend on the mutual success of teachers and learners in navigating their individual and co-responsibilities in this approach.

Assessment and feedback

> [A]t school when the teacher told you something it was all about what you had to do to get a better grade, here it's more about getting something to help you improve and develop . . . It's also about learning to take feedback as guidance and opinion that you can take on board but the final decision is up to you.
>
> (Second year student in Alden *et al.*, 2015: 42)

This quotation from a student in the research by Alden *et al.* on the Open Studios initiative at Newcastle University highlights the implicit challenges of assessment and feedback in Art and Design, and the educational benefits when students develop insights into *what is going on* with assessment. This includes how perplexing it must feel, particularly in the early stages of an undergraduate degree, not to be *instructed*; the confusion (and uncertainty) that arises from different perspectives being offered at different points of project development; a feeling that assessment decisions (made by experts as well as educators) are based on intuition rather than objective criteria; and further, the meaning of feedback can appear obscure on at least two related counts: because the basis of judgement appears to flow from tacit knowledge, and secondly, the difficulty of translating tacit knowledge about visual text into words and numbers. In Elliot Eisner's work *What Do the Arts Teach?* (2009), he explains this problem by analysing the cognitive processes of creating work (concept formation, imagination, realisation) and the necessary role of dialogue and the judgement of experts to ascertain the importance of the work as art. Eisner emphasises the limitations of language to express what we know, and more so when knowing is sensory or tacit. In earlier work for the Higher Education Academy (Brown, 2015: 366–370), I summarise key points from educational research on assessment and provide a number of provocations for improving quality. For instance, in addition to the research by Alden *et al.* (2015) I point readers to the work of Drew and Shreeve (2005), Blair (2007), Orr (2010) and Cowdroy and Williams (2006) for a focus on the disciplinary issues associated with studio and project-based learning and how this can be used to build the confidence of learners.

In the work of Cowdroy and Williams (2006) on assessing Design, and Orr (2010) on assessing Fine Art, their research acknowledges what is authentic to creative practice and at the same time formulates ways to make assessment accessible and meaningful to students.

> Despite the alignment of curriculum, learning outcomes and what was required for assessment we had to acknowledge our reliance on our own intuitive understanding of what creative ability is, our assumption that our students understood what we understood by creative ability and our tendency to assess students' creative ability on the basis of what teachers like.
>
> (Cowdroy and Williams, 2006: 98)

> A respondent in Orr's research comments on being utterly and profoundly moved by a piece of student work and comments '. . . how do you measure that kind of intellectual[ism]? You have to make part of that judgment with your heart if you like, which is what art and stuff is about so there clearly is a role for that and maybe you can't write criteria.
>
> (Orr, 2010: 12)

Educators are encouraged to draw on the forms of dialogue relevant to professional practice, but re-construct them as explicit learning processes. Educators are encouraged to use methods of assessment and feedback as ways to develop the pedagogic literacy of students – to share and develop the language and criteria by which judgement is made and dwell on the difficulties of language in assessing sensory, experiential phenomena. Drew and Shreeve (2005) refer to this as 'assessment as participation in practice' – creating a community of practice where informal, continuous and divergent forms of assessment are conceptualised and decoded in ways that support learning and professional development. Improving the student experience of assessment might include the following:

- Does assessment language (for instance, learning outcomes) help students to understand expectation (this is complex and varies according to creative discipline, but for instance could unpick *conceptualisation* and the intellectual work of creativity; *schematisation* and idea development; and *realisation*, for instance making skills, editing, refining and giving point to)?
- Have assessment teams discussed and unpicked the language of assessment and do they share a common interpretation of it and agree how it is applied to level and phase of learning?
- Is the language and practice of assessment shared with students as part of their understanding of pedagogy and professional practice – is meta-cognition of assessment process an implicit element of curriculum, teaching and learning?
- Do feedback mechanisms consistently reinforce and embed the language of assessment?
- The basics: does feedback support development as well as offer judgement? Is it timely? Are there opportunities for students to discuss the feedback (and unpick the language)? Does assessment and feedback build confidence and support a growing sense of learner independence? Are students adopting the language of assessment in their critiques of their own and others' work?

Resources for learners

Earlier sections have indicated that notions of quality in Art and Design education are insep-
arable from consideration of creative practice: that this is essentially social and material, and
resource requirements will reflect the need of disciplines for individualised practice and public forums for dissemination. As such spaces for learning in Art and Design need to be adaptive (the studio remains an important spatial concept for teaching Art and Design in that it
can be adapted to the needs of the project) and receptive to the direction and development
of individual projects (Fortnum and Pybus, 2014: 5) points to the range of spaces for the
production of student work including classroom, workshop, studio, library and canteen. At
my own institution student work is often produced off-site, in corridors, courtyards, galler-
ies and other private/public spaces. In this regard, institutions should expect the pedagogy
of Art and Design to challenge ideas about the ownership of space and the challenges that
are posed by the location of student work in the public spaces of institutions.

Defending the importance of specialised and dedicated space (studio/gallery) when
costs in higher education are increasingly pressurised is brave and particularly so when the
production of work will take place under highly individualised circumstances. However, as
we have seen in previous sections, the studio/workshop/gallery is not only where production occurs but also where professional practice is encountered. Learning spaces will be
extended further and perhaps beyond the 'taught' curriculum to include, for instance, the
idea of the 'final show' (the dissemination of the work of finalists), gallery show, catwalk
show, screening and so forth. Not simply a celebration of achievement, final shows are the
moment when interpretation of the work and ultimately judgement by different audiences
occur. Learning happens steeply in these contexts – thinking about *how to disseminate* constitutes a significant and further element of learning. So the frequency and quality of curatorial opportunity is important to creative education (the Open Studios initiative discussed
by Alden *et al.* occurs during all years of the undergraduate programme but is 'scaffolded'
in response to increasingly challenging assessment criteria' (2015: 50)). These opportunities often constitute an unwritten curriculum yet are significant to learning and graduate
outcomes.

Arrangements for staff resource will also need to be tailored to discipline. In addition to
academic staff, technical, professional and curatorial staff will play different roles in supporting learners. Those familiar to Art and Design education will know that the composition and organisation of this expertise is crucial for learning and is implicated in the quality
of the student experience. Yorke's analysis of NSS data across a number of subjects draws
him to conclude that 'NSS ratings in the broad area of Art and Design are in many respects
weaker than those from some other subject areas, and there does seem to be an association
between weaker ratings and higher levels of PT staff' (Yorke, 2014: 565). The effect of
higher proportions (than many other subjects) of part-time staff (including many hourly
paid staff with mainly professional expertise) to those on full-time contracts significantly
adds to the complexity of course organisation and management; communication between
staff; the ability for students to gain regular access to staff; and for teams to develop and
share their understanding of educational practice. However, Yorke's research clearly points
to the possibility of overcoming these challenges through the number of instances of institutions scoring highly in the NSS and having high instances of part-time staff (Yorke, 2014:
566) and I would suggest that overcoming the challenges, rather than importing models
from other disciplines, is the imperative for the reasons given in previous sections of this
chapter.

The following questions about the resource environment in Art and Design stem from empirical evidence of the kinds of approaches that appear beneficial, for instance:

- the extent to which the selection, appointment and promotion of staff recognises disciplinary (professional and practice-based research) as well as educational expertise and traditional academic qualifications, accepting the need for translation of policy if creative practice is to be properly recognised within the Academy;
- ensuring that 'practice' is at the heart of teaching and learning and research strategies – this will support the idea of a whole team ethos (for instance, the professional development of technical staff might also incorporate practice-based research as one model of development, alongside other forms of technical training);
- whether there are supported and regular reviews of the philosophical basis for the organisation of technical provision to ensure it reflects both traditional specialisation of process (that can be regularised and anticipated) and experimental and project-led processes (that require responsive and open approaches). This is perhaps one of the most difficult areas of resource management to accomplish but ensures that organisation and expenditure on technical provision is adaptive and accessible and at least questions the historical footprint of technical resource within and across departments;
- the extent to which the institutional culture encourages the enterprise of Art and Design beyond the studio and into public and tertiary spaces of the institution;
- that staff development in teaching and learning is tailored to discipline and to the different inputs of staff, including those with a small number of teaching hours and with mainly professional expertise;
- the extent to which the structure of leadership and management enables and support cross-disciplinary engagement of staff and students (for instance in the co-location of disciplines, staff and student spaces; systems for sharing practice and stimulating innovation);
- that senior leadership support recognises the particular challenges of course leadership in Art and Design (as they have been discussed here).

Conclusion – conceptualising quality in Art and Design

The chapter began by suggesting that conceptualising quality in higher education Art and Design lies in capturing the entire system of learning, which extends beyond the adequacy of the various objects of the system to an understanding of the way they are interpreted and received by staff and students, including the way creativity is performed within the institution.

The chapter urges those with a responsibility for the wider systems of learning (including Staff Development, Quality, Registry, Estates, IT) alongside teaching colleagues and students, to consider disciplinary distinctiveness for the obvious benefits that arise from a shared understanding of the nature of the learning project. This demands that quality assurance is understood to be a much wider set of inter-relationships and dependencies, understandings and discourses than the delivery of stated standards. At UCA creative learning is the project of the institution as well as schools and courses and we see this increasingly in the systems we employ to enhance learning. Recent reviews of the credit framework, annual course monitoring and retention strategy, for instance, have been undertaken through the lens of UCA's Creative Education Strategy to ensure alignment with the principles we believe are fundamental to student success in our disciplines.

As said previously, I am not advocating one institutional model over another, only stressing that discussion of quality in higher education Art and Design pervades the wider systems, beliefs and activities of institutions.

Notes

1 HEFCE's notes about the scale and distribution of alternative providers (those with QAA Course Designation) is available: http://www.hefce.ac.uk/analysis/HEinEngland/providers/aps/ (accessed 25/08/16).
2 Significant recent interest in the history-culture-value of the Art School is exemplified in recent conferences discussions (What's the Point of Art School? Central Saint Martins, UAL 14 May 2013; Art School Educated Tate Britain 11–12 Sept 2014; Art School – Location – Agency, CHEAD 16–19 March 2016).
3 Walter Gropius explains the curriculum of the Bauhaus in Gropius, W. (1923) 'The theory and organisation of the Bauhaus', in Bayer, H. Gropius, W. Gropius, I. (eds) (1959) *Bauhaus 1919–1928* (3rd edition). Boston: Charles T Branford Company.
4 For further reading about the barriers to successful progression into higher education Art and Design, and the various issues connected to entry to higher education Art and Design, see Vaughan, D. and Yorke, M. (2012) *Deal or No Deal: Expectations and Experience of First Year Students in Art and Design*, Higher Education Academy and HEAD Trust. Available at https://www.heacademy.ac.uk/resource/deal-or-no-deal-expectations-and-experiences-first-year-students-art-and-design (accessed 25/08/16).

References

Alden, S. Jones, C. Pollock, V. L. and Wilkinson, B. (2015) 'Open Studios is the beginning of a conversation: Creating critical and reflective learners through innovative feedback and assessment in Fine Art' in *Art, Design & Communication in Higher Education*, 14 (1), pp. 39–45.

Ashton, D. (2010) 'Productive passions and everyday pedagogies: Exploring the industry-ready agenda in higher education' in *Art, Design & Communication in Higher Education* 9 (1), pp. 41–56.

Blair, B. (2007) 'At the end of a huge crit in the summer, it was "crap" – I'd worked really hard but all she said was "fine" and I was gutted' in *Art, Design and Communication in Higher Education*, 5 (2), pp. 83–95.

Brown, R. (2015) 'Art, Design and Media' in Fry, H., Ketteridge, S. and Marshall, S. (Eds) (2015) *A Handbook for Teaching and Learning in Higher Education: Enhancing Academic Practice*. Oxon: Routledge, pp. 360–375.

Coldstream, W. (1970) *The Structure of Art and Design Education in the Further Education Sector*. National Advisory Council and the National Council for Diplomas in Art and Design. HMSO.

Cowdroy, R. and Williams, A. (2006) 'Assessing creativity in the creative arts' in *Art, Design and Communication in Higher Education*, 5 (2), pp. 97–117.

Csikszentmihalyi, M. (1996) *Creativity: Flow and the Psychology of Discovery and Invention*. New York: Harper Collins.

DCMS (2016) *Creative Industries Economic Estimates*, January 2016 https://www.gov.uk/government/uploads/system/uploads/attachment_data/file/523024/Creative_Industries_Economic_Estimates_January_2016_Updated_201605.pdf (accessed 25/08/16).

Drew, L. and Shreeve, A. (2005) 'Assessment as participation in practice' in Rust, C. (Ed.) *12th ISL Symposium Improving Student Learning through Assessment*, Oxford: OCSLD, pp. 635–654.

Eisner, E. W. (2009) *What do the Arts Teach?* Lecture at Vanderbilt University, November. Available at: https://ww.youtube.coKm/watch?v=h12MGuhQH9E&noredirect=1 (accessed 24/08/16).

Fortnum, R. and Pybus, C. (2014) 'Challenging fine art pedagogies' in *Art, Design & Communication* 13 (1), pp. 3–6.

HESA data '2015/16 Table 1' and 'subject 0203', https://www.hesa.ac.uk/stats (accessed 08/08/17).

Koestler, A. (1964) *The Act of Creation*. London: Hutchinson of London.

Henley, D. (2016) *The Arts Dividend: Why Investment in Culture Pays*. London: Elliott & Thompson.

Orr, S. (2010) 'We kind of try to merge our own experience with the objectivity of the criteria: The role of connoisseurship and tacit practice in undergraduate fine art assessment', in *Art, Design and Communication in Higher Education* 9 9 (1), 5–19.

Orr, S., Richmond, J. D. and Richmond, D. (2010) 'Reflect on this!' in *Journal of Writing in Creative Practice* 3 (3), pp. 197–210.

Orr, S. Yorke, M. and Blair, B. (2014) 'The answer is brought about from within you: A student-centred perspective on pedagogy in Art and Design' in *International Journal of Art and Design Education* 33 (1), pp. 32–45.

Pope, R. (2005) From 'Transgressing Culture: Rethinking Creativity in Arts, Science and Politics' conference, September 2002, in Pope, R. (2005) *Creativity: Theory, History, Practice*. London: Routledge.

Read, H. (1943) *Education through Art*. London: Faber and Faber.

Sternberg, R. J. (2007) *Handbook of Creativity*. New York: Cambridge University Press.

Subject Benchmark for Art and Design (2016) Quality Assurance Agency for Higher Education. http://www.qaa.ac.uk/en/Publications/Documents/SBS-Art-and-Design-consultation-16.pdf (accessed 25/08/16).

Thistlewood, D. (Ed.) (1992a) 'A continuing process: The new creativity in British art education 1955–1965', in *Histories of Art and Design Education: Cole to Coldstream*. Essex: Longman, pp. 152–168.

Thistlewood, D. (Ed.) (1992b) 'The formation of the NSEAD: A dialectical advance for British Art and Design education', in *Histories of Art and Design Education: Cole to Coldstream*. Essex: Longman, pp. 180–189.

Webster, H. (2004) 'Facilitating critically reflective learning: excavating the role of the design tutor in architectural education' in *Art, Design & Communication in Higher Education* 2 (3), pp. 101–111.

Winters, T. (2011) 'Facilitating meta-learning in Art and Design education' in *International Journal of Art and Design Education* 30 (1), pp. 90–101.

Yorke, M. (2014) 'The impact of part-time staff on Art and Design students' ratings of their programmes' in *Journal of Higher Education Policy and Management* 36 (5), pp. 557–567.

35 Performing, Composing, Reflecting and Researching

Recognising and Managing Quality in Undergraduate Music Programmes

Michael Russ

Introduction

This chapter is a personal reflection on quality assurance and quality enhancement in undergraduate programmes in university music departments (as distinct from conservatoires). For the most part the focus is on mainstream largely 'classical' music programmes, although some reference is made to the teaching of music technology and popular music. Whatever their repertoire, music provision will engage to a greater or lesser extent with four core activities: (i) performing; (ii) composing (whether free or pastiche); (iii) discussing musical repertoires and their cultural significance; and (iv) developing supporting technical skills in analysis, notation, harmony, musical computing and so on. Students will of course specialise, but area (iii) will generally be at the heart of attaining a graduate status in music that meets the description of level 6 (undergraduate degree) in the UK Quality Code for Higher Education and the QAA Benchmark Statement for Music.[1]

The teaching of music in British universities has changed significantly over my professional lifetime. Perhaps the biggest changes in recent years have been the move away from an almost exclusive focus on classical music and the greater emphasis on performance. As a student at Sheffield University in the early 1970s performance was a kind of bolt-on to the curriculum. If you wanted to offer instrumental performance as part of your final examination, you found your own tutor and paid for your own lessons. At that time too, 'free' rather than 'pastiche' composition had only just become an accepted part of the curriculum.

The balance of theory to practice in modern universities has undoubtedly shifted towards the latter, not least because that is what students have increasingly demanded. For academics planning quality music provision, this has led to debates on how practice should be undertaken in an academic context. Terms such as 'practice as research' together with 'informed', 'historically aware' and 'thinking performers' have found their way into descriptions of practice teaching, suggesting that while many performers at university will not quite attain the performance levels of their peers at conservatoires, they will be well equipped to discuss the issues surrounding the performance of the works they include in their assessed and unassessed recitals. In composition, an additional factor has been the impact of the REF and its predecessor (the RAE). In order to gain funding, composers have had to demonstrate that their works constitute a form of research, and this has led, in many departments, to an emphasis on the more radical forms of contemporary music (except that is in courses devoted, for example, to popular music, commercial music and jazz).

Quality assurance of music programmes

How quality is assured has also changed dramatically, both internally and externally. University music courses are not accredited by any external body, so for many years the quality of teaching and learning in undergraduate music programmes was left largely to the relevant academics and their institutions to manage. While the Associated Board of the Royal Schools of Music (ABRSM) and similar bodies offer a series of graded performance examinations familiar to many school children and to those seeking performance diplomas, they have not generally had a role in the universities.

As music courses were introduced in the then polytechnics from the 1970s onwards, a more heavy-handed kind of validation process regulated and administered by the Council for National Academic Awards (CNAA) was introduced. The visits of CNAA to the polytechnics was somewhat feared by the academics on the receiving end, and if not well managed there was always a danger that the supplicant department could be talked down to by academics from long-established university departments. However, the CNAA validation process did require staff to reflect in detail on the construction of the curriculum and how it would be taught. At this time, the idea that programmes should be broken down into modules, each of which represented a certain proportion of the course as a whole and each of which has its own sets of aims and objectives (now more fashionably 'learning outcomes') and assessment requirements was establishing the grip on course design that it has maintained ever since. Packaging music programmes into a modular framework has never been easy, particularly when it comes to the teaching of performance.

The polytechnics became universities in 1992, by which time the benefits of regular validation and review were now embedded across higher education. In order to assess the effectiveness of these processes and to encourage a focus on the quality of teaching, a 'Teaching Quality Assessment' (TQA) was conducted of every subject by the Higher Education Funding Council for England in England and Northern Ireland and by its sister organisations in Wales and Scotland.[2] In 1994–5 music came under scrutiny. This was, to date, the only nationwide assessment of the health of the subject to include observation of teaching and scrutiny of student work (academic and practical). While to some extent feared by staff (and perhaps even resented) because the evaluating panels included practicing music professionals and academics, it provided a rare opportunity for real and often useful dialogue between assessors and staff and often generated useful feedback. The starting point for the exercise was a self-evaluation document and, compared with more recent quality assessments, the use of metrics was quite limited. The outcomes of this process for music were encouraging, in that a very high proportion of claims for excellence made in the self-evaluation reports were confirmed by the visiting assessors, and only one department was rated as unsatisfactory. The overview report paints a rosy picture of music provision with a good supply of well-qualified students enjoying a close relationship with staff and producing work of good quality and the subject was generally well resourced. The financial pressures described in the Dearing Report (1997) were beginning to bite but were not at the level where they were, in the students' minds at least, impacting on quality and their levels of satisfaction (not that this was measured formally at the time). At the heart of quality provision in any subject is a close relationship between students and staff. Music departments as predominantly (but not exclusively) small, relatively close-knit, groups of well-qualified and highly motivated staff and committed students, were at a considerable advantage in this respect. Generally speaking, deficits in resources have a more marginal effect on student performance and satisfaction than poor relationships between students and staff. Small departments that know their students and address their problems are likely to do better in assessments of teaching quality and student satisfaction. As the report concluded:

> Music provision is notable for the excellent quality of working relations between and amongst students and staff, ensuring a high level of academic and pastoral support for

students. In many music colleges and departments there is a strong sense of academic community and a shared commitment between students and staff to the study and making of music.[3]

To examine every subject in every institution of higher education using the TQA model was a huge undertaking and the process was not repeated. Instead, with the establishment of the Quality Assurance Agency (QAA) in 1997 the focus shifted, over time, to establishing an academic infrastructure comprised of a Framework for Higher Education Qualifications, Codes of Practice, Benchmark Statements and a requirement for all programmes to have publicly available Programme Specifications. Whole institutions have subsequently been audited for their compliance with this framework and for the effectiveness of their internal procedures for managing quality. As a result, there has been no particular focus on music teaching except where music was one of the small number of subjects in any particular institution selected for a 'discipline audit trail', the purpose of which was less to examine the quality of teaching in that subject (the trail was not necessarily conducted by subject experts) and more to test the robustness of the university's systems. Such trails were subsequently dropped from the audit process and the focus in more recent audits has been almost entirely upon examining and testing compliance with mechanisms and procedures and with garnering the views of students across an institution. For music the impact of such processes is no different to many other subjects. Success at these events tends to depend on being able to produce evidence that you do what you say you do and that you do so consistently.

In recent years, more significant than occasional institutional audits for those managing quality in music as in so many other subjects, has been performance in the National Student Survey (NSS) introduced in 2005. More recently, key data from this and a range of other sources (including employability and salary statistics, class sizes and teaching hours) has been made publicly available through the website 'Unistats' and form part of the increasingly sophisticated and influential league tables published by the national press. To some extent, the need to ensure consistently high ratings (and inter-institutional rankings) has driven at least part of the quality agenda. The concept and design of this survey has been subject to frequent criticism, and in a sense universities have learned to 'play the game' rendering the survey less useful than it was in its earlier years.[4] The survey was introduced in part to allow students to have a 'voice', particularly as the levels of fees increased. Listening to that voice and ensuring that the concerns of students are responded to (and, for the purposes of audit, ensuring there is evidence of this response) has become increasingly important in managing quality. Music NSS scores (like those for many other subjects) have often revealed assessment and feedback to be an area of relative dissatisfaction. Probing this further, music students are often quite sensitive about the 'fairness' of assessment, particularly when it comes to the marks they receive for (musical) performances. This is not only a problem in music; courses in art and design and drama both suffer from lower levels of satisfaction with the assessment of creative and performing work since this area of assessment is so close to their heart. For the most part, the work of staff managing and developing quality in music programmes will comprise close examination of information from a number of sources. These will include feedback from students (for example, student panel minutes and module evaluation remarks), and statistics relating to student performance at both course and individual module level (for example, numbers attaining each grade band). A close eye too will be kept on attrition, both at module and course level. Monitoring attendance data is often a useful starting point for spotting students who are beginning to disengage. In music, students work closely with others in rehearsals and performances and there is a close link between students not feeling they fit in, or perhaps that their skills as performers have not been recognised (they have not been selected for a particular ensemble for example), and the onset of disengagement. Students who have been star performers at school may find their abilities are less remarkable at university. Trying to ensure that all students are engaged in some way in the activities of the department and that their contributions are recognised and appreciated is difficult but important. Ensuring that all first-year students who are not otherwise placed in ensembles contribute to the choir is a way often used to ensure a contribution and develop musicality. But this does need the choir to be taken by someone with a degree of enthusiasm and charisma, sensitive to the needs of students, who is also prepared to chase the non-attenders! Sadly, the increased pressure on staff to conduct research has meant that they have less time available to conduct and participate in ensembles and performances; ensembles are now routinely directed by part-time staff or postgraduates. The result has been a loss of a valuable source of feedback on the progress and contentedness of students.[5]

As with any subject, in addition to annual course evaluations, music courses will be subject to periodic reviews in which staff from outside the department will be joined by external subject experts to examine the performance of the subject. Typically at the heart of such an event is a self-assessment document summarising the performance of the course and the issues that have arisen. The panel usually has access to all documentation relating to the course to help them audit its performance. Inevitably there will be a focus on the performance of the students and their eventual destinations, including masters courses in universities and at conservatoires using metrics such as employability, attrition, number of firsts/2.1s, performance in NSS and so on. Meetings will be held with staff and students. There is likely to be an input from the university's central management in setting the agenda – they may, for example, have set institutional targets to improve employment figures, increase levels of student satisfaction or to make progress in reducing attrition figures. In these revalidation/review events student panel minutes are often revealing and the discussions with students helpful. In my experience students will generally try to support the staff and it is necessary to read between the lines – what isn't said may be as important as what is! In discussing feedback with students for example they may not wish to reveal that they haven't always got their work back within the set time frame or if they are satisfied with feedback (yet they may then complain anonymously in the NSS). Recurrent themes in music programmes are often concerned with resources – the availability of practice spaces, lack of IT resources with specialist software and even, more trivially, the lack of music stands! Historically lack of books, scores and recordings was always an issue, but with more material online this kind of problem has tended to abate. Other issues will be largely the same as in many other courses, not least issues with the timing of assessments to avoid overload, lack of clarity with briefs for tasks and so on.

The administration of music courses can be complex because it involves the programming of rehearsals and practical sessions of various types, organising concerts, liaising with a large body of part-time instrumental tutors, arranging for the examination of a wide range of instruments at several different levels, the timetabling of practice rooms, recording and music technology studios in addition to timetabling the normal diet of lectures, seminars and tutorials. All this must operate seamlessly if levels of student satisfaction are to be maintained, and a dedicated, well-trained administrative team is essential to successful function of a music department. Making the arrangements clear to students is always problematic: assuming that students will find out things for themselves from course and module handouts without further explanation and reinforcement rarely works. The remainder of this chapter will explore a number of aspects of music programmes that in my experience have an ability to impact significantly on quality.

Understanding transition

Understanding the process of transition from school to university is crucial to ensuring quality music provision.[6] Undergraduates coming straight from school may have expectations of the university curriculum and life in a university music department, but find the actual experience very different. In some cases they may become disaffected and drop out. Furthermore, with the payment of substantial fees, students' expectations are higher and if a course does not match their expectations they may well express strong dissatisfaction.

The growth in the numbers attending UK universities has meant that students, particularly those attending the post-1992 institutions, come from a wide range of backgrounds. The typical student enrolling a few decades ago may well have been educated at a grammar school, had the benefit of fairly lavish provision of free instrumental lessons in school and participated in a youth orchestra or band. As a group these students tended to be quite highly motivated and enthusiastic about 'classical' music. Furthermore, prior to 2000 they would have undertaken an A level curriculum that was fairly standard across the UK and included a number of skills that were seen as essential prerequisites for a BMus degree; performance was often optional, but skills in harmony and counterpoint and analysis and writing essays about the classical repertoire were core. Now music curricula in schools take many forms with the consequence that there may be a mismatch between what is taught at university and what the students have come to expect from their experience at school or college. In particular, the repertoires studied in AS/A2 units of study will vary sharply, with some students, for example, having specialised in film and/or popular music. The extent to which students have studied traditional techniques of harmony and counterpoint will also vary markedly and students may have gained only limited experience of researching musical topics and presenting their research in essay form. In this respect, students who have taken other humanities subjects, history or English for example, at A level may be better prepared for the academic aspects of a music programme than those who have mixed music with, say, science subjects at A level.

Furthermore, the manner in which students engage with music may differ sharply. Many students who work with popular music styles for example will learn through improvisation and imitation whereas those working with 'classical' styles will have learnt more through performing from scores (working their way through the graded examinations of the ABRSM) and learning theory and some harmony using, for the most part, paper-based exercises.

So, it can no longer be assumed that students have undertaken a preparation for university in sixth form or at college. Rather the qualifications gained at school must be regarded as ends in themselves and a more successful approach to university teaching in the first year is likely to come from regarding it as a new start, as an opportunity to do something fresh. But this must be handled sensitively. Students are very open to new things and are willing to be challenged but some find this daunting. One particular experience I had of this was that a number of students coming to study a music technology course became disengaged because of the focus on electro-acoustic music rather than the more popular repertoires they were familiar with and had worked with at school/college. As a consequence, the course had a poor retention rate for first-year students. By shifting the balance of the course towards popular music, while still providing opportunities to work in the electro-acoustic genre, student retention improved dramatically. Similarly, a student who has done well at school, but whose experience of music is primarily tonal and whose experience of free composition has largely been song writing, may react negatively to composition teaching that is primarily focused on cutting-edge contemporary music, while another might find this a refreshingly new challenge.

Music provision of quality will have the ability to draw the best from students from a wide variety of backgrounds. Weaknesses that students have in their knowledge of the Western Canon may be more than compensated by their knowledge of other repertoire and an ability to improvise and make use of music technology. A successful music programme must strike a balance between, on the one hand, what is easily perceived as an elitist insistence on the traditional curriculum and, on the other, adapting programmes to the market, to the desires and strengths of the students (which might be regarded as 'dumbing down'). A strong programme will connect with the students and exploit their strengths and desires while challenging them with exposure to the new, the unfamiliar and with music of the highest quality whatever its genre.

Teaching performance

The one-to-one tutorial and the part-time instrumental tutor

The team of part-time instrumental tutors is at the heart of any music department. The quality of their one-to-one performance tuition has a strong impact on student satisfaction. Students may in some cases have been attracted to the programme because of the reputation of the individual tutors. For example, in my time as head of department at a university in the north of England, we had a cornet teacher (and director of our brass band) of legendary reputation who was a major factor in attracting students. Appointing the best instrumental tutors is of paramount importance, as is being able to provide as many hours of one-to-one tuition as possible. Given the high costs of this type of tuition, a lesson of one hour per teaching week (usually about 22 hours per year) is generally as much as most universities can afford and tuition is usually restricted to one instrument. In the past some programmes may have offered a 'second study' but now this is not usually available unless the student is particularly talented and splits their allocation of lessons between two instruments. While it is sometimes possible for students to be paired or taught in small groups, students will generally wish to have the benefit of tailored individual tuition.

Integrating the work of instrumental tutors into the quality assurance systems of a university is often challenging because the tutors are not academics; they are typically drawn from regional and national orchestras or from the ranks of prominent regional freelance performers and instrumental or vocal teachers. Many of the older tutors will often not be graduates, but will have come through conservatoires (or other forms of training such as military bands) before those institutions offered degrees, when the focus was overwhelmingly on the acquisition of a high level of technical and interpretive skills on a particular instrument or voice. Understandably therefore, they may find the university context a little at odds with their own backgrounds, and may not always understand the relevance of quality assurance frameworks and enhancement initiatives to them. On the other hand, many tutors are genuinely conscientious and keen to find out how their contribution relates to the larger whole, particularly as they often have little opportunity to discuss issues with other staff.

A particular weakness in the system is that part-time instrumental tutors are rarely given any specific training to undertake their work. A great deal of the training offered by postgraduate certificates in university teaching would not be relevant to this category of staff, nor could they in most cases find time to fit it in to their professional schedules. Initiatives have occasionally been taken to provide bespoke training and this can prove beneficial, but needs considerable and sustained funding to support both teaching and attendance and this is generally not available.[7] In consequence, these initiatives tend not to survive, nor are they easily disseminated to other departments. Universities that insist on their teaching staff having postgraduate degrees and teaching qualifications are likely to find that they have to make exceptions for instrumental tutors.[8] Possibly the best and most efficient way for part-time staff to receive training and feedback on what they are doing is through some form of peer observation. This can be challenging to organise since tutors often attend at different times and the observing tutor may wish to be paid (and would also need to be given some training). However, peer observation can be undertaken by full-time staff who are enthusiastic about performance and sensitive to the needs and abilities of the students (a full-time member of staff with some experience as a professional performer is likely to be the best choice here). The follow-up session after an observation can also be a useful place to discuss how the tutor's work fits in with that of the department as a whole and with the quality management framework of the department.

Instrumental or vocal tutors who work with a student specialising in performance throughout their course will deliver a high proportion of the teaching received by that student (for example, a final-year 40-credit module in performance may be largely delivered by a part-time tutor). Performance teaching is a very private affair and a close, or at least respectful, relationship between tutor and student is all-important. At times this can break down, and it is important that channels exist for the student to express their feelings and that departments allow students to move from one tutor to another.[9] Although universities often establish personal tutoring systems, students often bypass this in favour of speaking to other members of staff they prefer to discuss performance issues with. This may well be the full-time staff member overseeing the performance modules. It is important that this module leader not only has a strong relationship with the individual tutors, but also is able to monitor student progress through, for example, bringing students together in seminars to perform informally and discuss performance issues, and listening to them perform in lunch-time concerts and elsewhere. Mid- and end-of-year feedback forms are important and can sometimes suggest areas of performance teaching where all is not well; problems can usually be dealt with through sensitive discussion with the individual tutor or tutors concerned. Sometimes evidence of poor instrumental/vocal teaching only comes to light in examinations, possibly in connection with post-performance discussion with the student. For example, it may be apparent that the tutor has failed to help the student correct a technical problem, or has not encouraged them to engage with a sufficiently wide repertoire (there is sometimes a tendency for tutors to bequeath the repertoire they were taught and play themselves rather than encouraging the student to explore). It may also be evident that the tutor has poorly advised the student on their choice of examination repertoire.

Students entering university will have a wide range of performing levels and there may be a tension between the standard of performance of a student admitted to university on the basis of a suitable A-level score and an ability to gain grade 8, and the tutor's perception of what someone undertaking a musical training should be. Furthermore, the increasing numbers undertaking music degrees has coincided with a reduction in the availability of free instrumental tuition at school and there can be little doubt that this has resulted in a fall in the standards of instrumental playing in universities. Anecdotal reports from tutors suggest that there are fewer 'stars' and a general weakening in standards of instrumental and vocal performing; but this is not to say that students cannot make enormous progress during the three years of their undergraduate programme.

On the one hand, performance teaching might be perceived to be straightforward: adhering to time-honoured principles you just try to develop the student's technique and get them to think about the interpretive principles involved in the music they are studying.

It is as much a form of coaching as teaching. On the other hand, the best teachers will be performers who have thought deeply about what they are doing and can bring that depth of knowledge and experience to the student; as such they are often held in high regard by their students.

Assessing 'classical' performance

Because they often come to music through performance and because performance is at the core of what they do, students care deeply about excelling in this area. They are often very sensitive not only about the marks and the feedback they receive but also about the other performance opportunities that are open to them (for example, there may be too many flutes for everyone to have an opportunity to play in the university orchestra). Students often over-estimate their own capabilities as performers. To reach the end of their first or second year only to find that they have received what for them are relatively poor marks is often quite distressing, particularly if under the university's degree structure the mark is too low for them to be admitted to a 'major performance' module in their final year.[10] Counselling students that they may well do better taking a more academic module diet instead is often necessary and has to be handled carefully, stressing the positive benefits rather than the dwelling on the deficits in performance.

Performance tends to favour end-assessment, product over process. The end result – the ability to stand up and perform in front of examiners or, preferably, with an audience – is what counts. Part-time staff can, through regular reports, give valuable information on student progress. However, inputting this feedback more formally into the assessment process can be problematic as part-time tutors tend to have relatively poor judgement as to where their students sit relative to grade boundaries and in relation to other students on other instruments. This is unsurprising as they have few opportunities to listen to students other than their own. Ideally, they should listen and give input into formative and summative assessed recitals, but both time and money make this largely impracticable. The provision of comprehensive handbooks with very clear statements of what is expected can of course help to inform the tutor, but assessment criteria for this kind of activity are difficult to formulate and there is no real substitute for participation in the process.

The teaching of performance does not sit easily in a semester-long modularised framework. Development as a musical performer is continuous and uneven; it doesn't easily divide into six neat phases each with distinct outcomes, level descriptors and assessment criteria. The crafting of the documentation for such a sequence of modules is more an exercise in verbal creativity than a reflection of reality. In practice, instrumental tutors will take the student that enters their teaching studio and work with them to improve. The role of the tutor is to give advice and guidance reacting to what the student has achieved since the previous lesson; by and large it cannot be pre-packaged into weekly lessons with pre-determined outcomes, although there will be broad plan in the student's and tutor's mind about when to undertake new repertoire and to move on to new technical challenges.

Nevertheless, it is necessary to articulate in some way what is expected at the end of each year. The specifications of outcomes for modules of this kind are often rather vague. Words and phrases such as 'fluency', 'control', 'imagination', 'convincing', 'projection', 'stylistic awareness', 'technically secure', 'demonstrates technical skill', which are ultimately not easily, if at all, measurable tend to appear in documentation. How, precisely, do you distinguish between foundation, intermediate and honours levels of fluency for example? Yet this word appears as an outcome at each level of one university's set of module documents for

performance. Furthermore, outcomes and assessment criteria have to fit a range of repertoire from the Renaissance to the present day with markedly different challenges, and for
many different instruments and voices. Outcomes and assessment criteria may also need to
embrace popular music, jazz and improvisation. Inevitably, however cleverly the documentation is worded, there is always an element of informed subjectivity in the assessment of
performance.

In the past, examinations of other bodies such as the ABRSM might have been used as a
benchmark, e.g. 'comparable with teaching/performance diploma of Associated Board of
the Royal Schools of Music'. This kind of benchmarking is now largely superseded by the
need to produce module documentation detailing outcomes, assessment strategies and so
forth to the satisfaction of auditors internal and external. The range of repertoire available
to students and the desire to encourage them to explore makes it both inappropriate and
impractical to specify repertoire in the way that the Associated Board of the Royal Schools
of Music does for its graded examinations which students will be familiar with from school.
As the student progresses from year to year more demanding repertoire and longer performances are generally expected. Selection of appropriate and varied repertoire may be part
of the examination requirements and often repertoire forms are submitted in advance for
approval. Module documentation will usually give broad guidance on repertoire ('three
contrasting pieces from different periods'; 'at honours level the recital should usually include
a concerto movement or the performance of a complete sonata'). It will also indicate the
required length of the assessed recitals and their setting: final recitals are often public and
concerto movements may well be performed with the university orchestra; popular music
and jazz performances may take place in a club or pub!

It is important that examiners document the reasons for their decisions carefully and that
these are conveyed to the student in a way that is constructive and helpful for their future
development. Most universities will use two internal examiners together with an external
examiner for summative assessments at intermediate and honours level. An expectation that
a single external examiner can reliably examine across the full range of instruments places
an onerous burden on the individual concerned. Some universities will use specialist wood-
wind, string, piano, brass and vocal external examiners rather than expecting the chief examiner for the programme to attend all the recitals. The examining of performance is therefore
expensive and a considerable administrative challenge. In some universities recordings may
be kept of the performances (and in some cases the externals may work from these) but even
with very high-quality recordings this is always an unsatisfactory way to judge performance,
which is best experienced live.

Concerns about fairness were mentioned above and students may mistrust a particular
examiner who they feel assessed them harshly in the past. Where the panel is judging a range
of instruments the student may feel that the panel does not understand his or hers – this can
particularly be the case with less common instruments (accordion for example). Furthermore, the student may feel that the panel is not sufficiently open to the way they perform.
The panel may be perceived for example, to have a particular view on the way early music
should be performed and may not be sufficiently open to arrangements and transcriptions
(Bach played on the piano rather than harpsichord). Students from the brass band tradition playing instruments which lack the mainstream classical repertoire of, say, the violin or
piano, may sometimes feel the repertoire they play in concerts and tests (often variations
on popular themes) is not fully appreciated by examiners thought to be a little elitist in
taste! Generally, however, these perceptions are more in the minds of the students than the
panels themselves. The way to mitigate such concerns is to make sure the feedback gives

precise reasons for the decision made, reasons which are evident in the way the performance communicated with the panel and the way the performer coped with technical challenges as would be the case with any musical instrument or repertoire. A mark with some bland comments is not enough!

Ensuring the decisions of the panels are fair and equitable is not straightforward. The make-up of panels may vary from session to session (in a large department, performance examining may take two weeks to get through). Following a recital, disagreements between examiners can be quite sharp and the decision on a final mark is not always easy (for one examiner a minor lapse in intonation or technique may not mar the overall performance whereas for another it spoils the whole thing). There is always an element of subjectivity in examining performance; gut feeling about how convincing a performance is may over-rule more inaccuracies for one examiner than another. Talking differences through rather than splitting the difference is always the best approach and where the external is a specialist more familiar with both repertoire and instrument, their expert input can usually help the panel to agree by pinpointing key issues in the recital.[11] As it is not generally realistic to moderate marks following the conclusion of the practical examinations (they are generated by too many different sets of people and diverse performances) moderators who 'drop in' to sessions across the exam can prove invaluable. The range of marks awarded in performance exams was often, in my experience, wider than in academic work. An outstanding performer who really grabs the audience and the examiners can gain marks in the high 80s and 90s in a way that a more academic student submitting essays and projects may find more difficult. The way to deal with this is not in my view to curtail the performer, but to encourage the use of a wider mark range for academic work.

A viva voce is sometimes required as part of performance examinations; often this is seen as a way to encourage students to think about the nature of their performances (as part of fostering a distinctive university-trained kind of 'thinking' musician) and to be able to articulate their views. However, many students do not fare particularly well when placed on the spot in this way and the conversation may be desultory. It is now generally conceded that such parts of the examination should only be used to enhance, not detract, from the overall performance mark. In fairness, students are often ill-prepared for such vivas and arguably, if one is to form part of the assessment process then students should be given some training and practice. Another way in which students are encouraged to reflect on the music they are to perform is through the production of programme notes which may be given a small element of the performance mark.

Peer learning/assessment and music performance

One of the most positive outcomes from TQA during my time at Ulster was the way it led on to the 'Peer Learning in Music' FDTL project.[12] This was a powerful project because it channelled and capitalised upon student experience. Its catalyst was an element of student dissatisfaction with the assessment of performance; it sought to address this by involving students in the assessment process and giving them a voice.

This project began from the observation that students attending lunch-time concerts that might well be assessed by staff panels had strong views on how well their peers had performed and were quite vocal about what they heard, discussing performances at length in their common room. Many students shared their mark and feedback with their peers and there was often a lively discussion as to whether the staff mark was fair or not. These lunch-time concerts were 'low-stakes' assessments relative to the final examination in front of the external. The project was an experiment in integrating these informal and lively discussions into the learning process thus helping students to understand how performance is best examined and helping them to learn what makes a good performance (a number of other 'transferable' skills around group working were also developed).

While it is impossible to give a full description of all the activities of the project here, in short, students worked in groups with staff to consider the nature of performance. They then went on to develop their own criteria for performance examining which they then used to act as examiners for second-year lunch-time concerts. The examining groups had to agree their marks and produce reports, they then had to negotiate a final mark with the staff moderators who had also been at the performances. Often the students proved remarkably perceptive; they often suggested marks that were close to what the staff would have come up with and provided appropriate comments and advice to the student under examination, suggesting that reaching an informed view about a performance does not always require expert knowledge of the particular instrument or voice. This is not to say that the 'expert' is not needed, indeed in the provision of feedback identifying the precise reasons why a student should gain a particular mark and suggestions for improvement, expert input remains invaluable.

This project was a win–win for all involved and helped greatly with improving student understanding of performance and performance examining. As many students would subsequently go on to become teachers, this training was perceived to be of benefit to their future careers as well as to their education. The work of this project was widely disseminated and a number of universities (not just as a result of the project) now use elements of peer assessment in the teaching of performance, often in performance seminars or platforms where students are able to feedback on each other's performances.

Academic aspects

The ability to research musical topics and to write about music is a key characteristic of undergraduate programmes in music. Most undergraduate courses will include a compulsory musicology (or whatever term is used) module in their final assessment.

The QAA Benchmark Statement for Music encapsulates this in the following way:[13]

Threshold level	*Typical level*
Demonstrate a broad-based body of knowledge in one or more of the sub-disciplines of music, including a detailed grasp of appropriate repertoires, texts and technologies, and familiarity with relevant concepts and issues.	In addition, show knowledge of less familiar areas of the discipline(s) and the ability to refer to, evaluate, apply or challenge relevant scholarly literature and current research.
Demonstrate the ability to develop ideas and construct arguments in both verbal and written form and to evaluate such ideas and arguments critically.	Demonstrate more developed skills in these areas, including the ability to defend viewpoints, postulate hypotheses, identify problems and propose solutions.

What constitutes these 'sub-disciplines' and 'appropriate repertoires' is for the universities themselves to decide. The best teaching of musicology will encourage students to complement up-to-date authoritative course materials and readings, with working from primary sources including scores, recordings, sketches, manuscripts, letters and historical documents. Students should be required to develop their analytical skills and to demonstrate the ability to describe and discuss musical languages, accurately recognising formal and stylistic features. They may also be introduced to critical theory exploring, for example, feminist, positivist, modernist and post-modernist narratives.

Key research in the discipline should be at the heart of the curriculum and the starting point may well be the research, enthusiasms and creative strengths of staff. The curriculum must allow a degree of flexibility, both to give students choice and to allow for staff undertaking sabbaticals and funded research projects.[14] In recent years the range of possible areas for study has widened as the interests of staff have become increasingly diverse. Universities may still make an appointment in eighteenth-century musicology, but they are equally inclined to appoint an electro-acoustic composer, a film music specialist, an authority on music and gender, a music theorist, a popular music musicologist or a representative of many other strands of music research. Often the appointment process is governed not so much by a desire to fill a gap as to appoint a person with strong research who can communicate well with the students and offer something new to the curriculum. While staff are often able to teach beyond their particular field of research expertise, wherever possible students should always have the opportunity to engage with staff in their areas of expertise as that is precisely where students are likely to encounter the most stimulating and new views on musical repertoires.

In the first year, musicology modules comprising a series of short topics or projects in which a variety of staff (including the most senior and the most research focused) introduce a series of stimulating topics is a good way to motivate students and demonstrate something of the breadth and depth of the subject. Such modules must also be supported with appropriate library inductions and introductions to music research and should provide opportunities for students to assess their progress in formative or low-stakes assessment early on in the programme.[15] So, for example, a four-week project at the beginning of the module that concludes with an assessed group presentation, allows students to immediately engage with their peers and to make at least a preliminary judgement of how they are getting on. Topic-based strategies tend to work well with students because they expect to listen, read and subsequently be assessed within quite constrained and well-defined bodies of knowledge. As students develop through the programme, the topics and approaches will become more extended and sophisticated, and should be complemented, especially for students who intend to specialise in musicology (perhaps undertaking a project in their final year), with research methods seminars or supporting studies modules.

The Canon

A fundamental problem in designing music courses is to determine the expectations the course team have with regard to repertoire. The issue is similar to the one encountered in the teaching of literature in schools where, at the highest levels, there has been a constant debate as to exposure of school children to the 'great classics' of English literature, whatever they might be. On the face of it, it seems fair to assume that no music graduate would leave university without some knowledge, say, of Beethoven's symphonies or Mozart's sonatas. In practice, the repertoire that might be considered 'essential' is vast, and the issues surrounding each composer are complex. Understanding the music of Schoenberg for example, requires not only knowledge of his musical forebears, but also knowledge of Viennese society at the turn of the twentieth century, expressionism and modernism in art and literature as well as needing a quite sophisticated ability to analyse complex atonal and twelve-note music. In recent years it has been accepted that it is more important for students to learn a series of skills necessary to research musical topics and to discuss repertoire accurately, clearly and succinctly. Students tend now to study a few areas in depth rather than assimilating vast amounts of repertoire and writing somewhat superficial essays on the works of the great composers. There has been a shift away from discussing the canon of great works, not least because the very nature of that canon is highly debatable, as is the very nature of what constitutes a musical work! In the 1970s a music undergraduate who could demonstrate that they knew and could place in historical and cultural perspective (usually through several three-hour examinations and a viva voce) a great range of classical pieces (mostly composed before 1900) would be likely to do well. Today, students are more likely to present more focused academic work, often employing quite sophisticated critical perspectives or analytical methodologies, but drawn from repertories including, for example electro-acoustic music, popular music, world music and film music. Comprehensiveness is no longer an issue, rather it is the depth of understanding, the rigour and the powers of written and spoken communication that students demonstrate with regard to their particular set of academic music modules that has become more significant, not least because these skills are ultimately more 'transferable' than, say simply gaining a superficial overview of the masterpieces of maybe five centuries.

Reflecting on practice

Students whose interests are mainly in practice may have the opportunity to take complementary modules which might, for example, evaluate and contextualise their contribution to the university ensembles, document their participation in a chamber group, or reflect on their taking their music-making into the community. Often such modules have a written component in the form of a learning journal or log and possibly some kind of final reflective assessment. The most capable students can of course always find interesting and worthwhile things to write in journals and logs, but in general the standard of reflection in them is often disappointing, overly subjective and repetitive in nature. It may be the case that students who are only themselves honing their practical skills need considerably more experience before they are able to reflect properly on putting them into action in particular contexts. The heavy emphasis on project-type work will always tend to lead to a very heavy workload at the end when the final projects, performances and so on take place. Too much end-assessment can leave some students very vulnerable. Such modules should not, in my view, be used as a substitute for a core musicology module. They succeed best when led by an enthusiastic member of staff with a specialism for example, in music in the community, and a body of research and resources for the student to draw upon.

Essay writing

The writing of essays is often used almost unthinkingly as a means to develop and assess students' capacity to respond to musical repertoires in written words (typically complemented by a written examination and the presentation of a seminar paper). An assessment strategy that comprises two or three assessed essays and an examination, possibly with a seminar paper or some kind of presentation (possibly as a form of formative assessment) is, in my experience, all too common. However, given the nature of the music curriculum at school, first-year students will have little prior experience of writing essays on musical topics and may be ill at ease with this area of their course. The requirement to write substantial academic essays can be daunting, particularly when their knowledge of repertoire is often quite restricted and their musical experiences have often come principally through their instrument, perhaps in participating in a youth orchestra or brass band. Furthermore, at school students use written answers to convey 'facts and comments rather than analysis and interpretation'.[16] Students may also have a limited grasp of the analytical skills needed to describe and discuss music or of historical context: few students have anything more than a rudimentary grasp of European and American history; even fewer have a grasp of any foreign languages. For these reasons, it is essential that students are able to get feedback on short written exercises and drafts early in their programme and are provided with clear guidance on basic research methods, referencing and essay-writing skills.[17] If this does not happen and the first task on which the student gets feedback is a substantial essay, given the time to introduce the topic, the time to write the essay and for it to be assessed the student may go for a term without getting any substantive feedback on their progress.[18]

The research on transition mentioned earlier found that university music staff tend to bemoan students' lack of real familiarity with the music they are discussing. Yet essays, which together with examinations are the mainstay of assessment for academic modules, are a poor means of testing this. Academics, almost unthinkingly, tend to use essays to:

> assess students' knowledge of writing about music, not their knowledge of music. Music staff should question whether essays are there to assess students' capabilities in terms of humanities skills rather than their music skills. Unlike, say, History degree students who are in a constant iterative process of essay writing and have been since school, Music students write relatively few essays, and these often come at critical moments, e.g. end-of-year formative assessments.[19]

What essays assess is the ability to develop an argument in a substantial piece of prose and how well students employ the secondary literature online or print. In contrast, aural assessments that require students to answer questions on recorded or performed music are rare, even though they are often a better way to test students' knowledge of the music itself.[20] Analytical skills are best built and tested using short concise exercises.[21] As a consequence a student may be penalised for poor essay writing while any compensatory knowledge and/or enthusiasm for music that might be displayed is less valued. Not employing the house referencing skills consistently may play an overly large part in determining a mark as may other factors of structure and length. To some extent these skills are easier to test and measure than any sense one has of how well the student can engage with the music under discussion. The usefulness of essay writing is often taken at face value during validation events, but there is a need to interrogate its purpose and suitability at each stage of the student's development.

Composition and analysis

The teaching of free composition is an important part of any music programme. The best teaching will seek to encourage students' creativity and will be open to a great range of styles. Many teachers of composition in universities are submitting their own work as part of the REF and this tends to encourage their own work towards experimental 'research-led' types of composition which might be regarded as less audience-friendly and more distant from the students' own experience. Occasionally students complain that they are forced in this direction, but for the most part they appreciate a new approach that may contrast sharply with the rather limited explorations of styles that they have encountered in school.

Being in a context that values and encourages contemporary music of all kinds is a great motivation for composers; the Huddersfield Contemporary Music Festival for example, can provide a huge stimulus for students who really listen and are engaged. Interestingly students coming from popular music backgrounds where they have not been systematically taught an instrument and immersed in classical music from earlier centuries, and where they have learnt in a less structured and more intuitive way through improvisation, are sometimes more open to cutting-edge contemporary music.

There is an argument that composition as a creative skill needs to be nurtured in individual tutorials, despite the expense of so doing. However, while there may be a small number of keen, gifted student composers arriving from school who could benefit from individual tuition, for the most part students in the early stages of a degree programme will benefit most from a mixture of class and small group teaching in which there is a systematic exploration of recent styles and students can be introduced to the practicalities of composition, exploring the capabilities of instruments and voices, notational issues and the parameters of music in structured analyses and exercises. Models can be put in front of the student, but good composition teaching will allow them to begin to explore for themselves rather than to pastiche in the end of year assessment. An excellent practice is to encourage students to write their final assessed work for a particular professional performer or performers; knowing it will be played well is a strong motivation and hearing the performance an excellent learning experience. In later stages of the degree, students specialising in composition will benefit from more individual tutorials in which the tutor must try to develop the student's own style and 'voice' while continuing to challenge them to try new things and widen their experience of the contemporary repertoire. Again, opportunities to have their work performed will help shape development.

Harmony, counterpoint and analysis remain essential skills for the music student to develop. However, as with the teaching of musicology, the way in which this is taught has needed to change to match the more diverse backgrounds of students. As this is such a crucial, but often neglected, part of the music curriculum, I will offer a few details that come from my own teaching in this area.[22] Whatever their backgrounds, it remains of crucial importance for students to learn the basic structural principles of tonal music through engaging with techniques such as figured bass, recognising formal structures and so on. Few students come to university with a secure understanding of matters such as score reading and their knowledge of transposition and clefs other than treble and bass is often very shaky. Often the study of these basics will be complemented by a course of what is often called harmony and counterpoint, although the very traditional study of Bach chorales and Renaissance ('species') counterpoint may profitably be replaced by exercises in other genres. I found for example, that working on completing exercises based on English madrigals was useful as the style in the simplest madrigals was quite straightforward; students from more popular backgrounds can learn harmony through song writing and working with jazz forms. Whatever the repertoire, the best teaching will involve short weekly exercises which can be self- or peer-marked when the solution is worked through the following week; with the tutor regularly reviewing what is going on. Problem-solving approaches such as completing 'skeletons' where a passage is presented to the student with crucial elements in the contrapuntal or harmonic structure removed, are useful. Helping the student by playing the missing element(s) enables them to make connections between the paper exercise and its sound. When working in class students are often reluctant to proffer answers to questions, or the answers come from a few keen contributors. One simple and useful way of getting whole-class feedback to a problem is to ask them all to provide their suggested answer to a problem anonymously on a sticky note. This can be as simple as asking to provide a figuring for a harmonic progression or identifying the type of suspension in a Renaissance cadence. One perennial problem with students' understanding of tonal harmony is to understand its relationship with rhythm, form and texture. A useful exercise with more advanced students, possibly in their second year, is to get them to write the exposition of a classical quartet, piano sonata or even a symphony in early classical style, using relatively simple chordal progressions but varying the harmonic rhythm according to the point in the structure. So the first part of this task might simply consist of providing an assertive opening statement built entirely on the tonic, or perhaps tonic and dominant, which is then followed by a passage built on a recurring motive over a simple but more mobile harmonic progression.

Clearly these skills need to be taught in classes rather than large lectures and streaming the students according to their ability on intake is usually necessary if one is to help those for whom these skills are unfamiliar, while challenging those to whom it is old hat. Assessment of this kind of work is usually straightforward. Students will present folios of their worked exercises while also undertaking exercises under examination conditions (some possibly involving an element of listening).

In the second and third years of their programme a few students may wish to continue formal studies in theory and analysis, possibly exploring, for example, Schenkerian analysis. But whether or not they specialise it remains important to continue to develop analytical skills in whatever repertoire context they are working in their various academic modules. The first-year skills training needs to be embedded in work in the second and final years. Difficulties with score reading and transposition, and with properly describing modulation, not to mention the problems of describing music which uses non-tonal, improvisatory or aleatoric languages are never eradicated by a first-year course but need reinforcement in subsequent years. I have often found final-year students writing dissertations struggling to properly analyse and describe music since the skills they learnt in their first year have already become rusty!

Assessment and feedback

I end this chapter with what I consider to be the aspect of university teaching that is most critical to the quality of provision: assessment and feedback. The National Student Survey has consistently indicated poorer levels of satisfaction in this area across a wide range of subjects. Leading a university-wide project[23] involving staff, students and senior managers, charged with improving the quality of assessment and feedback, emphasised to me the importance of the following: (i) timeliness; (ii) marking according to criteria that are clear and evident to students in advance; (iii) the provision of feedback that is sufficiently detailed to allow students to learn from it ('feed forward') and is written in language that is supportive rather than overly-critical; (iv) the ability to contact staff easily if clarification of what is meant by the feedback is needed. It was also apparent that students were not clear on the distinction between formative and summative assessment and that staff were not themselves making distinctions between assessments that were for learning and feedback as opposed to end-assessments which are primarily for establishing final awards. A tendency towards over-assessment was also identified.

Students are key to the process and have a responsibility to act upon and interrogate the feedback they receive. At the end of the project just mentioned, they agreed to in their student charter to 'Take responsibility to submit work by stated deadlines and actively participate in feedback'.[24] In music programmes students need to be more alert to the feedback they are receiving. They perceive the term 'feedback' as relating to the comments received on major assessed pieces of work and performances, not to the regular formative feedback they receive in instrumental lessons, composition tutorials and techniques seminars or comments they receive on drafts and other formative work. There is a strong case for spending more time actively introducing students to how feedback is given in universities and the importance of acting upon it – a paragraph in the student handbook and a mention during induction is not generally enough. During the delivery of teaching, feedback and suggestions on how to respond needs to be highlighted by staff.

The timing and nature of assessment and feedback also needs more thought in course design. It is worth remembering that at school students receive constant feedback; on arriving at university, it is quite possible for them to receive little substantive feedback until they are well into the first semester of their courses. Students need lots of low-stakes assessment early in their course to see how they are getting on. In music, this can be addressed by first-year modules being organised in short blocks with low-stakes assessment, a presentation or group presentation for example, at the end, and through the use of regular weekly technical exercises which are peer- or self-marked and the solutions discussed in class. Assessment timelines are also a useful way to ensure that not too many summative assessments are being required at the same time.

For summative assessments it is reasonable to expect that students will have their assessed work with feedback returned in three working weeks, with staff encouraged to give earlier informal feedback on broad issues emerging during the marking process to the class if they can. Again, designing and managing programmes so that a huge volume of marking does not arrive in one person's inbox at a point when it cannot be dealt with is key to this. Electronic submission and marking is now widely established and this enables not only plagiarism checking, but also allows for a more rigorous monitoring both of hand-in and return times. Auditing the quality of feedback is also a useful exercise. Feedback should always indicate not simply that the criteria have been met or not (tick box feedback) but should indicate why and how to improve. In such audits I have found many instances of students receiving similar comments, or apparently meeting the criteria, but receiving radically different marks and comments that leave the student perplexed as to how they should go forward. Such audits can take place anonymously, avoiding any need to name and shame staff. A properly thought-through assessment and feedback strategy plays an important part in any high-quality music programme.

Conclusion

It is hoped that this short overview of quality assurance in music programmes will inform course leaders, heads of subject and heads of department and others charged with ensuring these courses perform both to the satisfaction of students and to university authorities. I hope it might also be of interest to anyone designing a music programme. As will have been apparent, in my view excellent music provision is characterised by its ability to enthuse students, arouse their curiosity and allow them to follow their own interests and strengths rather than being shoehorned into a particular view of the subject. The best programmes will build on an awareness of where students are coming from and be open to a wide range of repertoires, styles and approaches; they should be able to develop their own strengths in performance, composition or musicology. Whatever their background students should be challenged to discuss music with precision, rigour and awareness of current research and the programme should ensure they develop the core values and competencies (as set out in the

Benchmark Statement) that enable them to make sound judgements and good creative or performative use of musical materials. There are many ways in which this can be achieved and the particular research and creative interests of the staff should be harnessed to make available new perspectives to students. Students need a flexible curriculum that allows them to thrive, to have opportunities for creative practice and performance and they also need a supportive, well-managed environment. Get these things right and the metrics for student satisfaction, attrition and level of achievement will, if not look after themselves, at least head in the right direction!

Notes

1 *Benchmark Statement for Music* (Quality Assurance Agency for Higher Education, 2008).
2 The overview report for music may be found at http://webarchive.nationalarchives.gov. uk/20100202100434/http://www.hefce.ac.uk/pubs/hefce/1995/qo_15_95.htm (accessed 27 June 2016).
3 Ibid.
4 See for example Joanna Williams, 'The National Student Survey should be abolished before it does any more harm', *Guardian,* 14 August 2015. https://www.theguardian.com/ higher-education-network/2015/aug/13/the-national-student-survey-should-be-abol ished-before-it-does-any-more-harm (accessed 15 July 2016). The operation of the survey is currently under review. See Claire Callender, Paul Ramsden and Julia Griggs, *Report to the UK Higher Education Funding Bodies by NatCen Social Research, the Institute of Education, University of London and the Institute for Employment Studies* (HEFCE, 2014).
5 I was saddened a few years ago to attend an end-of-year concert at one of our top-ranked universities. No members of staff were in evidence. It may not be unconnected that the closure of the department was announced not long after.
6 For a much more comprehensive study of these issues see Julia Winterson and Michael Russ, *Understanding the Transition from School to University in Music and Related Subjects* (University of Huddersfield, 2008). The contents of this report were summarised in Julia Winterson and Michael Russ (2009) 'Understanding the Transition from School to University in Music and Music Technology', *Arts and Humanities in Higher Education*, 8 (3), pp. 339–354.
7 A 'Performance Teachers' Development Project' which sought to train and accredit part-time performance teachers in universities was run by the University of Southampton (with University of Surrey and Royal Holloway) in the late 1990s. It was funded under the HEFCE Fund for the Development of Teaching and Learning initiative. However, like many such one-off initiatives, it does not appear to have lived on beyond the length of the project except in so far as it has impacted on the culture in the institutions concerned.
8 Upskilling all staff to doctoral level was an institutional goal during my time at Huddersfield, but this could not be applied to part-time tutors. Insistence that they gain professional accreditation (for example, Fellowship of the Higher Education Academy) is likely to be difficult to implement, not least because their experience of teaching is limited to a very specific activity and they may have little role in the final assessment.
9 Occasionally, the behind closed doors one-to-one tutorial can also be a relationship that is open to abuse. Although such instances are extremely rare, some recent well-publicised experiences in a specialist music school and a conservatoire have served to lead managers to think whether this kind of teaching can continue. Some simple protocols such as ensuring that all teaching rooms have a window in the door and making sure that students have pro-active personal tutors to whom they can report difficulties may be safeguards in this respect.
10 Some universities will impose hurdles for progress to major performance, usually 40 credit modules, e.g. attaining 60 per cent in the linked second-year module, not least to limit large amounts of expensive individual tuition required).
11 Care has to be taken that the externals are aware of the context in which they are working – universities are not conservatoires. Furthermore, internal examiners may not wish to challenge the view of a distinguished practitioner when they perceive them to be expecting too much!

12 Russ, M. and Hunter, D. (eds), *Peer Learning in Music* (Coleraine: University of Ulster, 2000). Hunter, D. and Russ, M., 'Peer Assessment in Performance Studies', *British Journal of Music Education*, 13 (March 1996), pp. 67–78.

13 *Benchmark Statement for Music* (Quality Assurance Agency for Higher Education, 2008), p. 25.

14 In this respect it is often useful to validate 'shell' modules which can be filled with different content so long as the broad outcomes and assessment requirements are fulfilled.

15 Matters such as plagiarism and referencing will also need to be introduced. In my view these topics should be explained in class (and emphasised on several occasions) and not just left to the student to glean from the student handbook.

16 Winterson and Russ (2009), p. 350.

17 Although sometimes derided as a symptom of 'dumbing down', the availability of academic skills tutors who can assist students with essay-writing skills can be invaluable. See for example Pat Hill, Amanda Tinker and Stephen Catterall, 'From Deficiency to Development: The Evolution of Academic Skills Provision at One UK University', *Journal of Learning Development in Higher Education* 2 (February 2010).

18 It is a common practice to give students seven weeks' notice of essay topics and deadlines. Given that three working weeks are allowed for marking, ten weeks can elapse before the student gets feedback. Shorter tasks with more immediate feedback can be much more helpful developmentally and problems can be identified more quickly.

19 Winterson and Russ, p.350.

20 This is kind of assessment that students, albeit often in a rather low-level way, will be familiar with from A level.

21 Short tabular analyses of formal structure or requirements to figure and detect modulations in particular passages for example.

22 This was an area of the curriculum that I continued to teach with a degree of enthusiasm even when my administrative responsibilities would have allowed me to delegate the work!

23 At Huddersfield in 2009–10, supported by the Higher Education Academy 'Change Academy' programme.

24 University of Huddersfield Student Charter. http://www.hud.ac.uk/ce/welcome/induction info/studentcharter/ (accessed 28 July 2016).

36 Professional Regulation, Research Training and the Development of Peer Mentorship in UK Psychology Programmes

Ronnie Wilson

Psychology is the scientific study of the nature and causes of the mind, mental processes and behaviour. Through advances in knowledge produced by psychological science, it has also become a major international applied and professional discipline, in which psychologists analyse, assess, and endeavour to influence and change behaviour at individual and group levels. Psychology has grown enormously as a university taught subject throughout the world, for example in the UK it has been in the top three of applications per subject for several years. Its growth as a profession, and the wide range of interactions of psychologists with people, has also brought extensive regulation of both the training and conduct of psychologists by professional bodies. Prior to the 1990s these functions were organised by the British Psychological Society (BPS). However since 1998, dramatic changes have taken place, which have made the education and training of psychology students somewhat more complex. These changes, and their impact, will be discussed in the present chapter, along with some innovations in programme delivery, particularly regarding research methods teaching and peer tutoring, which have taken place in parallel with modifications in the professional status of degrees.

Changes in the governance of UK psychology degrees

The major professional organisation for psychology in the UK is the British Psychological Society (BPS), which provides a wealth of information, support material and a large number of scientific/professional journals for its members. Non-members can also access much of this valuable material through university libraries and the BPS website. Suitably qualified graduates of psychology degree programmes are able to use the term 'psychologist' as a self-description, and can gain employment as a psychologist in a wide range of settings. However, in the professional accreditation of psychologists, difficulties have recently emerged – while the BPS was the main arbiter of the professional recognition of psychologists until recently, this is no longer the case. Before discussing recent changes in this important aspect of the profession, however, it is worth briefly reviewing the history and role of the BPS before the changes took place.

The BPS began as a learned society in 1902, was incorporated in 1941, and acquired a Royal Charter in 1965. Since this date, the Society took the leading role in standardising the recognition, education and training of psychologists in the early 1970s by introducing the Register of Chartered Psychologists and a process through which undergraduate and postgraduate degrees in universities were evaluated at regular intervals for two levels of accreditation. Graduates of accredited undergraduate programmes were eligible for the *Graduate Basis of Registration*, whilst full membership of the Charter was possible on successful completion of one of a number of accredited postgraduate degrees, each of which included extensive training in professional settings. The major accredited professional areas were designated as Clinical Psychology, Counselling Psychology, Forensic Psychology, Educational Psychology, Health Psychology, Occupational Psychology, and Sport and Exercise Psychology. Thus, through the Charter, the BPS controlled the progression of psychologists from entry to university undergraduate courses until the completion of the postgraduate programme upon which professional recognition was based.

Major changes in the way psychologists and psychology programmes in the UK are awarded professional accreditation began to emerge just after the turn of the century. During the 1990s a number of events gave rise to adverse publicity regarding psychotherapy, which persuaded the UK government to seek statutory regulation of professions related to mental health, including psychology. In response, the BPS proposed the creation of a Psychological Professions Council, but this proposal was declined, as argued by Health Service authorities. In 2009, the decision was taken to bring the major psychology professions, along with a number of other professional areas, under the newly formed Health and Care Professions Council (HCPC). An important change for the BPS was the replacement of the Register of Chartered Psychologists by the Directory of Chartered Psychologists, membership of which permits use of the letters C. Psychol. after a graduate's name. Official accreditation of postgraduate programmes is now undertaken by the HCPC rather than the BPS, and is normally undertaken by a selected accreditation team which visits the university developing the programme, to assess the syllabus, staffing and physical resources (HCPC, 2016). However BPS representatives have played a major role in the development of HCPC syllabuses, procedures and standards of proficiency, such that the graduate outcomes, published most recently in 2015, are broadly similar. The HCPC have also retained the seven areas set up for professional registration by the BPS, and have added *Practitioner Psychologist* and *Registered Psychologist* to the protected titles. Universities are accredited for the delivery of their programmes and for accreditation of graduates on the basis of two-day visits by HCPC panels every four years. The BPS still retains the authority to organise the education and training of individuals toward accreditation, but application to the HCPC is still required before accreditation is granted.

Modifications in the status and accreditation of undergraduate programmes in psychology have also taken place, but these have not been as pronounced as in the postgraduate training qualifications. Most if not all HCPC accredited programmes require applicants to be eligible for the GBC of the Society, so that the BPS has retained a key role in the governance of the undergraduate syllabus and the resources universities need to provide to support undergraduate psychology. Importantly, members of the BPS and its committees met with members of the Higher Education Psychology Network and the Association of Heads of Psychology in 2011 to discuss and agree proposals to meet the main challenges to undergraduate teaching in psychology during the five years until 2015 (Trapp *et al.*, 2011). The conclusions of the meeting undoubtedly had a major influence on BPS policies. Later, BPS members who are strongly involved with teaching and learning in a variety of universities also played a key role in the QAA review leading to the Subject Benchmark Statement of October 2016. In turn, the BPS has adjusted the criteria for reviews of undergraduate psychology programmes taking into account the recommendations of the QAA decisions.

Following these professional interactions, a key BPS policy document and guidelines to assist universities in the accreditation of undergraduate programmes was published in 2016. The seven core areas for which in-depth coverage is required were still designated as *biological psychology, cognitive psychology, individual differences, developmental psychology, social psychology and research methods,* including an independent final-year *research project,* and *conceptual and historical issues* (which can be covered across modules). Thus, although there have been some attempts to modify the core elements of the syllabus, it is gratifying that psychology graduates will still have the broad knowledge and skills provided by the biological, behavioural and social sciences, with extensive experience in research methods. This enhances their employability as well as giving them access to the range of professional HCPC programmes. In addition to the syllabus reviews, the BPS also evaluates the resources which underpin degrees, including the number and backgrounds of teaching staff, additional human resources such as support and technical staff, the number and range of laboratories, and the library. It is also worth noting that the BPS accredits two other types of course for graduates of programmes other than psychology. One type of course is a 'conversion programme', which is available for students who have passed some psychology modules as part of their degree, but do not have enough psychology credits for the GBC. A second type of course is an MSc programme, which covers the core areas of psychology and requires the completion of a research dissertation.

So to summarise, in the main route to becoming a professional psychologist, most students must first take, and pass with at least second-class honours, an undergraduate degree that is accredited by the BPS for the Graduate Basis of Chartership (GBC). Having achieved this, they are eligible to be considered for a postgraduate degree in one of the seven areas recognised by the HCPC. Alternatively, graduates who decide to enter the psychology profession but who did not take a psychology degree may acquire the GBC by taking a top-up programme that contains the elements they missed, or a Masters that covers the curriculum designated by the BPS. These alternative routes must be accredited by the BPS for graduates to be eligible to apply for HCPC programmes. For students, the route to professional status has changed little, although it is somewhat stronger with HCPC membership. However for the BPS and universities the changes have been challenging, and there is some uncertainty about the future given the control the HCPC has over professional status and the postgraduate curriculum and resources.

The Psychological Wellbeing Practitioner Programme

An important initiative in the NHS took place during the early 2000s, following the recognition that many people with mild psychological disorders, such as mild depression or anxiety, were not receiving adequate advice or treatment, and that around 70 per cent were simply given medication by their GP. Some with more serious depression were referred to clinical psychology services, but these were much fewer in number than those treated with medication. Thus a major initiative termed *Improving Access to Psychological Therapies* (IAPT) began in 2008, and within this the approach to mental health treatment within primary care in the UK was reviewed. A new post termed *Psychological Wellbeing Practitioner* (PWP) was created and training guidelines for the posts were released. In a key development for psychology, the BPS had a central role in producing the syllabus for training courses, and currently has the sole agency which accredits such courses. However, since community psychiatric nurses and social workers have had an important role in dealing with mild psychiatric disorders already, access to Psychological Wellbeing Practitioner courses was made available to a range of graduates, as well as psychologists. The clients, who include adults, young people and children, are counselled in the self-management of their recovery. The Practitioner provides low-intensity, evidence-based interventions, based on cognitive behavioral principles. Practitioners administer the least intrusive treatment in the first instance, although the client may be referred to a clinical psychologist if deemed necessary. Rather than administering therapy, practitioners are more like coaches, working with the client to choose the direction of how they will deal with their condition. Psychology graduates have been successful in being appointed to these posts, with obvious possibilities for future training as clinical psychologists or in other professional areas. For universities, it is worth considering including the training package in undergraduate psychology programmes, or as a separate award with the course.

Research training and SoTL in psychology

Although there has been considerable debate about the role of the BPS in prescribing the subject content of psychology programmes in relation to the GBC, there has been widespread agreement on the emphasis on research methods, practical training, and maintaining the importance of the independent final-year project (Trapp *et al.*, 2011). The emphasis on practical work across five core areas, and the preference for a diversity of optional topics for the final-year project, supports the need for departments to maintain a staff group with diverse research interests and backgrounds. In some ways this conflicts with the increasing trend, in response to pressures from the Research Excellence Framework, for departments to appoint staff in a small number of largish research groups, but it emphasises the importance of maintaining an overall staff group with variable expertise in promoting the student experience in the high-pressure environment of modern universities. Of course, this also means the development and maintenance of a set of laboratories and other research facilities, which would promote the scientific standing of departments.

Research training, viewed as being so important in psychology programmes, has been strongly influenced by scholarship on the development of teaching methods. As well as having a diverse staff group, Wilson-Doenges, Troisi and Bartsch (2016) have argued for evaluating different elements of teaching schemes through measures of student performance and feedback from students, and for altering approaches and assessing the effectiveness of innovations in the same way. Their work is part of the SoTL (Scholarship of Teaching and Learning) movement in psychology, which is developing strongly through publications in several journals which focus on the effectiveness of teaching and learning initiatives. The role of SoTL in psychology has been twofold: firstly, it encompasses and promotes the sharing of novel initiatives in teaching and learning, many of which have been in the area of research methods; secondly it has led to the publication of critical analyses and evaluation research in relation to the effectiveness of new initiatives and methods. By publishing the results of changing approaches in peer-reviewed journals or other forms of communication such as conferences, teachers of research methods have been able to share and innovate methods of teaching this difficult area.

Wilson-Doenges and Gurung (2013) argued for the adoption of a formal framework for research on SoTL in psychology, based on the use of benchmarks by researchers, moving toward what they termed a 'gold standard'. They argued for eight elements in 'gold standard' research – guidance by hypotheses based on well-regarded theory; longitudinal evaluations of teaching effectiveness; the use of experimental methods where possible; large sample sizes from a number of sources with adequate statistical power; the use of multivariate methods of data analysis; the use of different methods to approach a topic, including qualitative methods if possible; prior assessment by independent ethical committees. In their more recent paper, Wilson-Doenges *et al.* (2016) reviewed a number of studies that have achieved many aspects of the 'gold standard', showing that collaborative studies across institutions with good statistical power, most based on measures of student performance and student experience, have begun to make important contributions to the effectiveness of Year 1 research methods and statistics teaching. However, whilst this work is a laudable attempt to promote the highest standard of research methodology, it is important that journals and academic conferences continue to publish smaller-scale evaluations of innovative methods, which later could be evaluated by more extensive studies.

There is no doubt that the development of large class sizes in psychology courses has had an impact on research methods teaching, and many who teach courses in introductory psychology where the majority of students are not taking a psychology major have simply abandoned methods on the introductory course. Consequently, it is left to dedicated research methods modules elsewhere in the programme. This is problematic for both psychology and non-psychology students because it does not foreground the scientific basis of the subject in the main introductory module. However a number of recent studies have demonstrated that simple methods can be strikingly effective in teaching the scientific basis of the subject as well as giving students some basic knowledge of research design and the interpretation of data. For example, Stevens, Witkow and Smelt (2016), in two studies on students taking introductory psychology classes in community and liberal arts colleges, found that groups of students who took a small number of structured seminars on real-world research projects acquired a significantly higher level of knowledge of research methods than groups who took different types of seminars. Students who took the research-based seminars performed significantly better than students in control groups on problems concerned with research concepts, basic features of research design, interpretation of data in graphs and tables, and drawing conclusions from data. In a further recent study, LaCosse and her colleagues (LaCosse, Ainsworth and Shepherd, 2017) demonstrated the effectiveness of using an online method to run a small-scale practical in a large introductory psychology class of 851 students. The project included an experimental group of 174 students who took an 11-week practical based on a carefully structured one-hour session per week, with each involving feedback by an instructor. At the end of the project students prepared a PowerPoint presentation on their study and a poster in a session involving the class. The control groups went through the semester carrying out different tasks but were not involved in the practical. At the end of the module, in a separate test on research methods, it was found that the intervention group performed significantly better than the control groups, showing that it is possible to teach research methods effectively and to give students in a large introductory class experience in conducting research and in preparing presentations on research, using an online communication method.

Peer Assisted Study Sessions (PASS)

The idea of formally organising peer-assisted tutorials for students entering degree programmes was first developed by Dr Deanna Martin, who was concerned about high attrition rates among minority students on health care courses at the University of Missouri, Kansas City. She developed a peer mentoring initiative, which was first termed *supplemental instruction*, which was highly successful in maintaining students, and which rapidly developed an international reputation. Similar schemes began to be adopted in a large number of universities. In the UK, it was first introduced by Jenni Wallace at Kingston University, who also adopted the term *peer assisted study sessions* (PASS) as a name for the scheme. This is now the main term used for peer support in learning. The first formal system was introduced by the

University of Manchester, at which the PASS National Centre is now located. According to its website, PASS systems have now been adopted in 50 UK and Irish institutions.

In most cases, the system involves mentoring sessions for Year 1 students led by students in a later year. The system is organised by staff but is relatively informal, and is used to help first-year students adapt to university life as well as to assist in the development of learning skills. The students who take the sessions, termed 'PASS tutors', are mentored by staff in the development of group communication and leadership skills. According to Wallace, the PASS tutor is someone 'who serves as a catalyst bringing about a cognitively important reaction between (students) and events in their experience'.

A number of evaluations of the scheme have found that for Year 1 students it is associated with a significantly lower likelihood of withdrawal from the programme, relatively higher levels of adjustment to university, and in some cases, an enhancement of academic performance (Rodger and Tremblay, 2003; Collings, Swanson and Watkins 2014, Pugliese *et al.*, 2015; Giles, Zacharapoulou, and Condell, 2016). It has also been found that the PASS scheme facilitates communication between students and staff, is linked to a relatively higher level of enthusiasm for the subject, and in the crucial early months enhances the student learning experience (for a review see Giles *et al.*, 2016).

However there has been less substantial research on the experiences of and changes in PASS leaders, and most of that work has been carried out in Australia and the USA. Giles *et al.* (2016) have noted that PASS leaders in their UK university often experience difficulties related to behaviours such as note-taking and attendance at lectures, so have had to develop activities that engage the group with learning material, thereby enhancing their own creative experience and independent learning. There is additional evidence that PASS leaders develop strongly in their self-confidence, communication skills and leadership ability, as well as developing their experience of building relationships with management and being able to understand how an organisation works. However, as Giles *et al.* (2016) point out, most of the research evidence on PASS leadership has been based in Australia and North America, where it has been included in work primarily on students in PASS groups. More work is needed on the experiedsnces and development of PASS leaders in the UK, as a topic in itself, and also to provide evidence on changes necessary in training or in the organisation of PASS systems.

References

British Psychological Society (2016) *Standards for the Accreditation of Undergraduate, Conversion and Integrated Masters Courses in Psychology*. Partnership and Accreditation Team, www.bps.org.uk/partnership

Collings, R., Swanson, V. and Watkins, R. (2014) 'The impact of peer mentoring on levels of student wellbeing, integration and retention: a controlled comparative evaluation of residential students in UK higher education', *Higher Education: The International Journal of Higher Education Research*, 68(6), 927–942. DOI: http://dx.doi.org/10.1007/s10734-014-9752-y

Giles, M., Zacharopoulou, A. and Condell, J. (2016) 'An overview of the benefits of peer mentoring for PASS leaders', *Centre for Higher Education Practice –Perspectives on Pedagogy and Practice*, 3, 67–80.

Health and Care Professions Council (HCPC) (2016) *Practitioner Psychologists: Standards of Proficiency*. http://www.hpc-uk.org/publications/standards/index.asp/Publicationcode 2010 1001

LaCosse, J., Ainsworth, S. and Shepherd, M. (2017) 'An active learning approach to fostering understanding of research methods in large classes', *Teaching of Psychology*, 44(2), 117–123.

Pugliese, T., Bolton, T., Jones, G., Roma, G., Cipkar, S. and Rabie, R. (2015) *Evaluating the Effects of the Faculty of Arts and Social Sciences Mentor Program*. Toronto: The Higher Education Quality Council of Ontario. http://www.heqco.ca/en-ca/Research/ResPub/Pages/Evaluating-the-Effects-of-the-Faculty-of-Arts-and-Social-Sciences-Mentor-Program-.aspx

Rodger, S. and Tremblay, P. (2003) 'The effects of a peer mentoring program on academic success among first year university students', *Canadian Journal of Higher Education*, 33(3), 1–17.

Stevens, C., Witkow, M. R., & Smelt, B. (2016) 'Strengthening scientific reasoning skills in introductory psychology: Evidence from community college and liberal arts classrooms', *Scholarship of Teaching and Learning in Psychology*, 2(4), 245–260. http://dx.doi.org/10.1037/stl0000070

Trapp, A., Banister, P, Ellis, J., Latto, R., Miell, D. and Upton, D. (2011) *The Future of Undergraduate Psychology in the United Kingdom*. The Higher Education Psychology Network, University of York.

Wilson-Doenges, G. and Guring, R.A.R. (2013) 'Benchmarks for scholarly investigation of teaching and learning', *Australian Journal of Psychology*, 65, 63–70.

Wilson-Doenges, G., Troisi, J.D., and Bartsch, R.A. (2016) 'Exemplars of the Gold Standard in SoTL for psychology', *Scholarship of Teaching and Learning in Psychology*, 2(1), 1–12.

Index

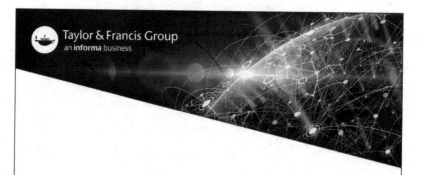